Using PC DOS, 2nd Edition

Chris DeVoney

Que™ Corporation
Carmel, Indiana

Dedication

To Frank, my little brother,
who is not so little any more

Product Director
David Paul Ewing

Editorial Director
David F. Noble, Ph.D.

Acquisitions Editor
Pegg Kennedy

Editors
Lois Sherman
Lloyd Smart
Terrie Solomon
Rebecca Whitney
Jeannine Freudenberger
Barbara Potter
Steven Wiggins

Technical Editors
Timothy S. Stanley
Estel Hines
David Gobel
Philip Sabotin
Kirk Demaree

Book Design and Production
Dan Armstrong
Jennifer Matthews
Joe Ramon
Dennis Sheehan
Peter Tocco
Carrie Torres

*Composed in Garamond
and American Typewriter
by Que Corporation*

About the Author

Chris DeVoney received his B.S. degree from the University of Gloucester and has been employed in the microcomputer industry since 1975. Mr. DeVoney has written and edited numerous books and articles about microcomputers. He is the author of *IBM's Personal Computer* (first and second editions), *MS-DOS User's Guide*, and contributing author of the best-selling *Managing Your Hard Disk*, all published by Que Corporation.

Contents at a Glance

Table of Contents

Part I   A Short Course on DOS for New Users

1   Using DOS the First Time 7

15 Making DOS Go International

Part V   Managing Your System

16   Managing Your Files

17   Gaining Control of Drives, Devices, and the Printer

Part VI   DOS Command Reference

Appendix A

Appendix B

Appendix C

Appendix D

Appendix E

Appendix F

Appendix G

Preface

In August of 1981, IBM announced its Personal Computer; IBM and Microsoft announced the IBM Personal Computer Disk Operating System; and the world of microcomputing changed again. Evolution is nothing but change, and revolution is simply fast evolution. On that fateful August day, IBM revolutionized the microcomputer industry to the same degree that Apple Computer revolutionized microcomputing in 1977.

At the madding fast-track pace this industry sets, the Personal Computer has come and gone. The Personal Computer XT has begun its final journey to obscurity. The astonishing Personal Computer AT is now a commodity machine. And the Personal System/2 family threatens retirement of the entire PC family.

With each new machine comes a new evolution of the operating system. PC DOS V2.0 came because of the need to address fixed disks. DOS V2.1 came because of the uniqueness of half-height floppy disk drives on the PC*jr*. DOS V3.0 arose when the 1.2-megabyte floppy disk drives and 20- and 30-megabyte fixed disk drives of the Personal Computer AT became commonplace. DOS V3.1 was DOS V3.0 with working facilities for the IBM PC and Token Ring Networks, the only version of PC DOS released for a peripheral rather than for a computer. DOS V3.2 came out when the first truly portable IBM computer, the IBM Convertible, was announced. The current version of DOS, V3.3, coincides with the release of the Personal System/2 family.

New possibilities emerge from each new machine and operating system; yet old problems remain. The chief problem is getting work from your computer. An important part of the solution is learning to use the new operating system.

When PC DOS V2.0 emerged, I used my standard learning method— understanding by trying. The task was difficult, but rewarding. The only problem is that my technique has two inherent flaws. One, it's the hard way to learn. And two, if there is a problem, I'm bound to find it. Both flaws surfaced when I tackled V2.0.

Unfortunately, I have not found a better way to learn an operating system. I used the same approach to DOS Versions 2.1, 3.0, 3.1, 3.2, and 3.3. Each time, I encountered new surprises—some pleasurable, some frustrating. I also encountered several undocumented features, the computer industry's euphemism for *lurking bug*. Overall, I'm pleased with my discoveries and am happy to share them with you.

My first DOS book, *PC DOS User's Guide*, was written because I thought that no one should have to learn an operating system the way I must, the hard way. The first edition of this book, *Using PC DOS*, was written for the same reason plus one other. Computer experience is directly related to the amount of data ruined. I am very *experienced* with all versions of DOS and hope you can gain experience without repeating my mistakes.

This second edition of *Using PC DOS* incorporates the knowledge I have gained since I wrote the first edition. New commands added to DOS have solved certain problems, and new features of DOS have added some new wrinkles. I will attempt to guide you through both. Throughout the book, I intersperse hints, suggestions, and occasional warnings. I report what DOS finds acceptable and what DOS finds objectionable. I test DOS to its limits and sometimes show when to expect the unexpected. Actually, DOS never does the unexpected. DOS faithfully executes your commands. The problem arises when the commands you give do not correspond to what you want to do. These "failures of communication" are usually the most frustrating of all for users of computers.

I'd like to share a personal story to those who are newcomers to DOS. I learned to ride a bicycle at the ripe old age of twelve. Before then, I was scared, terrified, of bicycles. One cold autumn afternoon, I went into the backyard with an old Sears three-speed bike. I kept trying until I got the knack of balancing on two very thin tires. Yes, I fell a few times. When I discovered that falling off a bike was unpleasant but not fatal, I gained the courage to master that two-wheel demon.

My advice to newcomers is simple: Don't be intimated by DOS V3.3. I did not learn to ride a bicycle simply by reading a book. I had to physically try. You won't learn just by reading the examples; you'll learn by trying the examples and doing more.

When you make a mistake, look at what you typed. Most frequently, a word will simply be misspelled. Find what is wrong with the line and try the command again. The *DOS Command Reference* is helpful for this task. Then experiment! Be daring occasionally (but use practice diskettes that do not hold vital information). Become acquainted with DOS. DOS is friendly once you become accustomed to it.

For those of you who have read the previous books, don't stop now. DOS V3.2 and V3.3 have some powerful features that are worth exploiting. The sections on batch files (Chapter 12), customizing DOS (Chapter 14), and using your fixed disk (Chapter 19) are enlarged with fresh ideas and new DOS commands. The *DOS Command Reference* discusses the old and new DOS commands in detail.

By the way, if you are ever on the north side of Indianapolis, look for someone in a white bicycle helmet and gloves on a ten-speed racer. Pass him carefully, but do wave hello. I normally ride for an hour in the late afternoon. Just as I have faced and conquered my fears of the bicycle, may you conquer DOS with equal confidence and esteem.

Trademark Acknowledgments

Introduction

Using PC DOS, 2nd Edition, is for anyone who wants to be proficient in
using the disk operating system for the IBM PS/2 and Personal Computer
family of microcomputers. If you have never used a personal computer,
you can use Part I of this book to learn the basic commands you need to
know to get started. This part includes hands-on exercises that should give
you confidence quickly even though you are a beginner. If you are an
intermediate or advanced user, this book will help you understand and use
with ease some of DOS's more sophisticated commands, especially those
introduced or extended in Version 3.

What You Should Know

Before you read this book, you should familiarize yourself with the
following: the control and editing keys, the FDISK program (if you have a
fixed disk system), and the EDLIN line-editing program. If you are using a
PS/2, you should know the configuration program on the Reference
diskette provided with your computer. If you use a Personal Computer AT,
you should be familiar with the SETUP program also.

The *Quick Reference* or *Guide to Operations* manual provided with your
computer is the best source of information on the editing and control
keys. Additionally, each computer comes with an excellent tutorial for
becoming familiar with the keyboard and layout of the computer. Run the
programs; they are helpful and congenial. Before proceeding, you should
know the cursor control keys. The DOS editing keys can be learned at
your leisure. Appendix F of this book contains some information on the
DOS editing and control keys.

The FDISK program configures your fixed disk for use. Most dealers run
FDISK on your fixed disk system before you receive the computer. If
FDISK has not yet been run, follow the instructions in Appendix E of this
book.

The EDLIN program is a *text editor.* EDLIN allows you to record text into
a disk file and alter text in the file. EDLIN is half of a word-processing

1

program. (The other half is the printing process.) As a simple, limited, line-oriented text editor, EDLIN is acceptable. When compared to other programs such as Brief™, WordStar®, MultiMate Advantage™, or WordPerfect®, EDLIN is rather pale.

You need a text editor later in this book, starting with Chapter 12. If you want to use EDLIN, the tutorial is located in Chapter 8 of the DOS V3 manual. You may decide to use a different text editor or word-processing program. If you use a word-processing program, use the ASCII text, nondocument, or programmer mode. The exact term will vary between word-processing programs. Some text editors, such as WordStar or WordPerfect, store and manipulate the characters differently in document and nondocument modes. The text to be used by DOS should always be written in nondocument mode.

What You Should Have

To use this book most effectively, you will need the following:

1. Your computer system, connected and working

2. The diskettes provided with your copy of DOS

3. Several blank diskettes, labels, and, if you are using 5 1/4-inch diskettes, the accompanying protective envelopes

What Versions of DOS Are Covered

All versions of DOS V3 (V3.0 through V3.3) are covered in this book. When DOS commands work differently between DOS V2 and DOS V3, the differences are mentioned in the chapters. Significant differences in commands between the various versions of DOS V3 are also mentioned.

Most screen illustrations in the book are derived from DOS V3.3 programs, using a PS/2 Model 60. If you are using a different version of DOS V3, you may see slight variations in the wording and capitalization of messages on the screen. Also, because of the difference in the diskettes used on the PS/2s and Personal Computers, what you see on your screen may occasionally be different from what the book shows. Significant differences are explained. Other differences are cosmetic; the meaning of the messages is the same.

What Is Covered in the Book

Chapter 1 provides hands-on practice at the computer. You'll make working copies of the DOS diskettes. You'll also learn how to start DOS and stop running programs.

Preparing diskettes and copying files are discussed in Chapter 2. Chapter 3 explains some basic DOS concepts and operations, such as getting a list of files, freezing the video screen, naming files, and running DOS commands.

Chapter 4 covers four common operations: copying files, erasing files, changing file names, and copying complete diskettes. Chapter 5 explores the different parts of DOS and discusses how DOS devices work. Chapter 6 examines floppy disk drives and diskettes. Chapter 7 examines fixed disks and discusses how DOS subdivides and uses all types of disks. Chapter 8 covers naming disk drives and files.

Chapters 9 through 11 cover the DOS features borrowed from the UNIX operating system. Chapter 9 demonstrates the concepts of I/O redirection and piping. Chapter 10 introduces the use of hierarchical directories to organize your disks. Chapter 11 expands the concepts of hierarchical directories and shows how to use various DOS commands with subdirectories.

Chapter 12 introduces batch files, a way for DOS to run itself. Chapter 13 examines special commands that can be used with batch files.

Chapter 14 is a detailed discussion of the CONFIG.SYS file and shows how to configure the system automatically each time your computer starts. Chapter 15 discusses the procedures for using DOS in languages other than English.

Chapter 16 presents more information on the COPY command and information on the new XCOPY command. Chapter 17 discusses how to recover a flawed file and presents ways to control your equipment and printer with MODE and PRINT.

The vital subjects of backing up and restoring the fixed disk are examined in Chapter 18. Chapter 19 details four DOS commands that make the fixed disk more convenient and faster to use. Chapter 20 presents guidelines on moving information between systems that use different types of diskettes. Chapter 21 reviews some of my favorite programs and offers some thoughts on using your computer.

The final section of the book is the *DOS Command Reference*, which lists all DOS commands in alphabetical order. The reference shows the correct phrasing and rules for using the command and often gives examples and notes about the command. The *Command Reference* is a valuable tool for quickly locating and correctly using any DOS command.

What Is Not Covered

No book can cover DOS completely. This operating system has so many aspects that no book can be a tutorial on learning DOS, a DOS reference guide, and a system programmer's guide, all at the same time. For this reason, several subjects are omitted from this book:

1. EDLIN (a line editor), DEBUG (an assembly language debugger), and LINK (a program linker)

2. The Configuration and SETUP programs for the PS/2 and Personal Computer AT computers

3. An explanation of the ANSI control codes. (The codes are listed in Appendix D.)

4. The DOS function calls and other technical information about DOS

5. The writing of device drivers

Most of this information is important to programmers. If you do not program, or if you program only in BASIC, the absence of this information will not matter to you. If you would like more information on the programing aspects of DOS, you can refer to the *DOS Technical Reference* manual from IBM.

Part I

A Short Course on DOS for New Users

1

Using DOS the First Time

DOS is the acronym for *disk operating system*. An operating system is a collection of programs that gives control of a computer's resources to the computer's user. These resources are all elements that make up the computer system, including the keyboard, display, printer, and modem. A disk operating system is the software that controls these elements as well as the computer's disk drives for storing and retrieving programs and data.

Introducing DOS

Anyone who uses a personal computer should have some working knowledge of DOS. What you need to know depends on what you want to do with the computer. You may want to know only how to start DOS and issue one or two commands. Or you may use your computer so much that you need some understanding of all the commands and how they work. Most people fall somewhere in between.

What should you know about DOS? This question has no exact answer. The amount of knowledge you need depends on the use of your computer. All computer users need some fundamental knowledge: how to prepare diskettes for use, get a list of files on a disk, copy and erase files, and perform other common computer operations.

If, however, you use your computer extensively, or if others depend on your knowledge of computers, you need to know more. Knowing how files are stored on a disk, finding the amount of free space on a disk, establishing and using hierarchical directories, redirecting input and output, and setting up configuration and batch files will be important to you. If you fall into this "frequent user" or "frequent helper" category, you should read about all the features and commands of DOS.

DOS has many commands and functions. Fortunately, you are not obligated to use all of them; nor do you need to learn every aspect of each command you use. The first time you encounter a new command, just try to remember its basic function. Later, you can return to this book and learn more about the command. The *DOS Command Reference*, Part VI of this book, will be especially helpful as you gain more experience with your computer.

Learning DOS is a circular process. Often, before you can learn one thing, you need to learn something else. But don't be alarmed. DOS is not complicated. As you progress, each piece of DOS falls into place, and you will begin to master the commands you use.

I am a firm believer in learning by doing. I am also an eager person. If you are a newcomer to DOS and are like me, you may want to leapfrog the first few sections of this chapter and immediately try the hands-on exercises. As you do the exercises, be certain to read carefully each step as you work along with the computer—not only in this chapter, but in the next three chapters as well. If you don't, you may miss some small detail, and things may not work the way they should.

This chapter and the next three have hands-on sessions. If you have just started using your computer, go through each chapter step-by-step. If you have already used your computer and are comfortable with it, move on to Chapter 5 for a discussion of how DOS works.

In this chapter, you'll start the computer and make a copy of your DOS Startup diskette. Before starting out, we'll take a brief tour of your computer and become acquainted with the disk drives. We'll also take a brief look at the diskettes you use.

Knowing Your Disk Drives

Depending on the type of computer you own, you may have one or more floppy disk drives, and none, one, or two fixed disk drives. You'll need to know what kind of disk drives you have before you can do the exercises in this chapter and in the next several chapters. The discussion in the next section is limited to floppy disk drives. We'll talk about fixed disk drives in Chapter 2.

Kinds of Floppy Disk Drives

The IBM PS/2 computers and IBM Personal Computers and compatibles use two basic types of floppy disk drives: microfloppy and minifloppy. Both types of disk drives use different kinds of diskettes, come in different capacities, and are used on different computers.

Microfloppy disk drives use 3 1/2-inch diskettes. These diskettes come in a hard plastic shell that measures about 3 3/4 inches on each side.

Microfloppy disk drives come in two capacities: either 720 kilobytes (K) or 1.44 megabytes (M). (A *kilobyte* is roughly a thousand characters, and a *megabyte* is roughly a million characters. These terms are described further in Chapter 2.) The PS/2 Models 25 and 30, the PC Convertible, and many compatible computers have 720K disk drives. The other PS/2 models have 1.44M disk drives. Figure 1.1 shows a typical microfloppy disk drive.

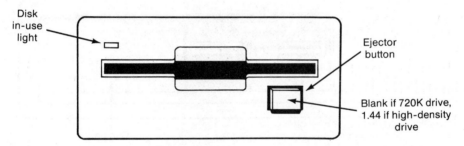

Fig. 1.1. *Front view of a microfloppy disk drive. The label on the ejector button indicates the type of drive.*

To verify the capacity of the disk drive on your PS/2 computer or PC Convertible, look at the blue button on the disk drive. If the button is blank, the disk drive is a 720K disk drive. If you see *1.44*, the drive is a 1.44M disk drive.

Minifloppy disk drives use 5 1/4-inch diskettes that come in a soft plastic envelope about 5 1/2 inches square.

Minifloppy disk drives come in two forms: *full height* and *half-height*. The Personal Computer and older PC XT machines use full-height disk drives with a black faceplate. Unless you have a very old Personal Computer, the capacity of the drive is 360K. Figures 1.2 and 1.3 show full-height minifloppy disk drives.

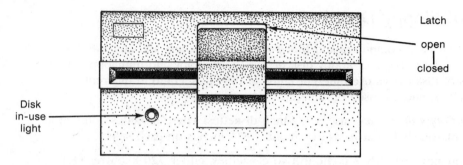

Fig. 1.2. *A full-height, minifloppy disk drive for the Personal Computer or PC XT. The latch securing the diskette flips up and down.*

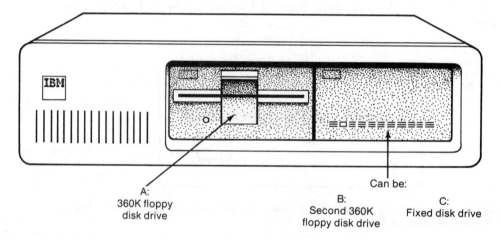

Fig. 1.3. *A disk drive layout for a Personal Computer or PC XT. The name of the left drive is A:. If the right disk drive is a floppy disk drive (not shown), the drive is named B:. If the right disk drive is a fixed disk (shown), the drive is named C:.*

Other Personal Computers and compatibles use half-height disk drives—so named because the disk drive is one-half the height of a full-height disk drive. The PC*jr*, PC XT, and PC 286-XT have half-height drives with a black faceplate. You'll see a tan faceplate on Personal Computer ATs, on external half-height minifloppy disk drives used with the PC Convertible, and on PS/2 computers (see fig. 1.4).

Half-height disk drives come in two capacities: 360K and 1.2M HC (high capacity). The PC*jr* and PC XT half-height drives have a capacity of 360K.

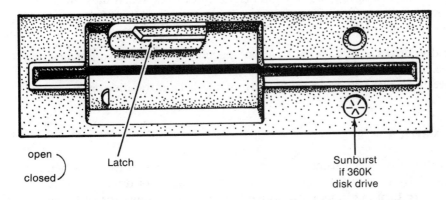

open
closed
Latch
Sunburst
if 360K
disk drive

Fig. 1.4. *A half-height minifloppy disk drive for the Personal Computer family. A drive with the sunburst symbol on the lower right side is a 360K disk drive. A drive without the sunburst symbol is a 1.2M high-capacity (HC) disk drive.*

The PC 286-XT, some later models of the PC XT, and the Personal Computer AT use both 360K disk drives and 1.2M high-capacity disk drives. To determine the disk-drive capacity on these machines, look for a sunburst symbol on the bottom right of the faceplate. If you see one, the half-height drive is a 360K disk drive. If you do not see the symbol, the drive is a 1.2M HC disk drive.

There are a couple of slight differences in the way you insert and remove diskettes from microfloppy and minifloppy disk drives. To insert a diskette in a microfloppy disk drive, slide the diskette into the slot on the front of the disk drive and push gently on the diskette with one finger. To remove the diskette, push the blue or red button on the front of the disk drive. This button ejects the microfloppy diskette.

When you insert the diskette into a minifloppy disk drive, gently slide the diskette into the slot and push the diskette with one finger until you hear a slight click. Full-height minifloppy disk drives have a latch located on the top side of the drive. You gently push the latch down to secure a diskette. To remove the diskette, place your finger under the latch and gently flip the latch up.

Half-height disk drives use a handle rather than a latch to secure the diskette in the drive. To close the drive, gently turn the handle down. Turn the handle up to release the diskette.

Most half-height disk drives use a spring that pops the diskette about half an inch out of the disk drive when you turn the handle up. To remove diskettes from this kind of drive, you can simply pull gently. For half-height drives without a spring and for full-height disk drives, reach into the recessed front plate, grasp the diskette between your thumb and forefinger, and pull.

The disk drives with a spring have one peculiarity. If you have just inserted a diskette, you can remove it only by closing and opening the handle. There is no place to grasp the diskette while it is in the disk drive.

Drive Names

Each disk drive has a name. The name is a single letter of the alphabet, followed by a colon (:)—for example, *A:* is the name of drive A. If you have more than one floppy disk drive housed in the computer and your floppy disk drives are placed side by side, the left disk drive is drive A. If the disk drives are stacked, the top disk drive is drive A (see fig. 1.5). The single disk drive housed inside a PC*jr* is drive A.

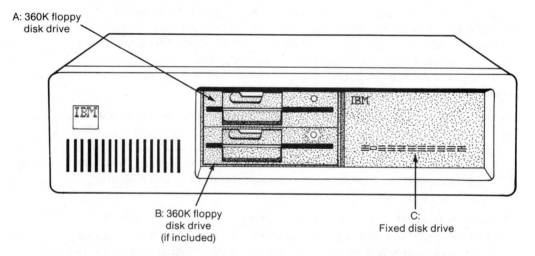

A: 360K floppy
disk drive

B: 360K floppy
disk drive
(if included)

C:
Fixed disk drive

Fig. 1.5. *A disk drive layout for newer Personal Computers, PC XTs, and 286-XTs. The top drive on the left is drive A. The bottom floppy disk drive, if included, is drive B. The disk drive on the right side is the fixed disk drive, drive C.*

The next disk drive is usually drive B. On Personal Computers, PC XTs, PC 286-XTs, or PS/2 Model 25, 30, or 50 machines that have two floppy disk drives, drive B will be the rightmost floppy disk drive. On the Personal Computer AT and on PS/2 Model 60 or 80 machines that have two floppy disk drives, drive B is the lower disk drive. Figures 1.6, 1.7 and 1.8 show disk drive layouts on PS/2 Models 30, 50, and 60/80, respectively.

An external floppy disk drive on the PC family is usually called drive E, regardless of how many internal disk drives are used. The external disk drive on the PS/2 family is drive B if one internal floppy disk drive is used. If the computer has two internal floppy disk drives, the external drive is drive E.

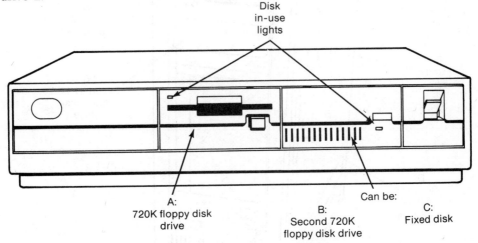

Fig. 1.6. *The PS/2 Model 30. Drive A has a capacity of 720K. The second drive may be another 720K floppy disk drive or a hard disk drive.*

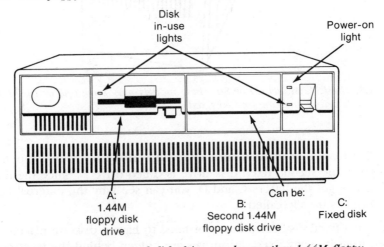

Fig. 1.7. *The PS/2 Model 50. The second disk drive can be another 1.44M floppy disk drive or a fixed disk drive.*

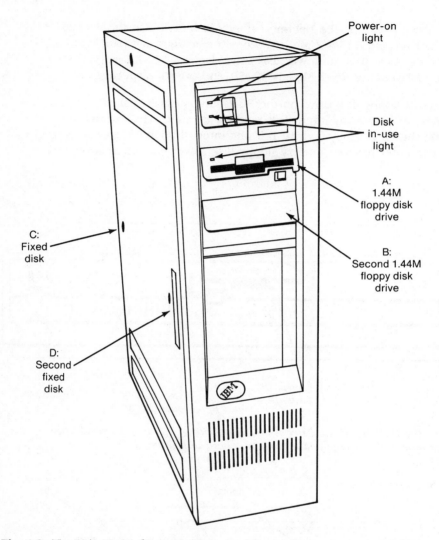

Fig. 1.8. *The PS/2 Model 60 or 80. These models may have one or two 1.44M floppy disk drives and one or two fixed disk drives.*

The first fixed disk drive is normally called drive C. If your computer is so equipped, the second fixed disk drive is called drive D. Since the fixed disk drives get the letters C and D, you can see why the external floppy disk drive is usually called E.

Because a fixed disk drive does not need to have a diskette placed in or taken from it, many fixed disk drives are hidden behind the front cover.

This is so on the Personal Computer AT and PS/2 computers. On the PC XT and 286-XT, the fixed disk is the visible, rightmost disk drive.

Remember the number and type of floppy and fixed disk drives your computer has. Some exercises in this book have different instructions based on the various disk-drive setups.

Knowing Your Diskettes

Basically, there are two kinds of microfloppy diskettes and two kinds of minifloppy diskettes. Microfloppy diskettes hold either 720K or 1.44M of data. Minifloppy diskettes hold either 360K or 1.2M of data. There is no visible difference between 360K and 1.2M diskettes. To tell the difference, you must look at the label on the box or the diskette. Figure 1.9 shows microfloppy and minifloppy diskettes.

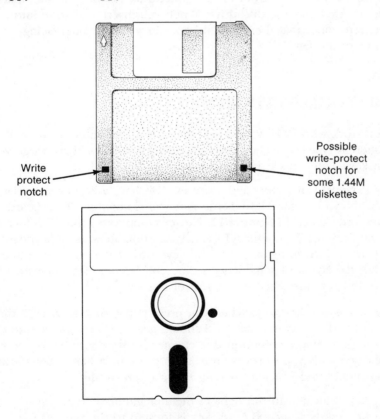

Write
protect
notch

Possible
write-protect
notch for
some 1.44M
diskettes

Fig. 1.9. *A 3 1/2-inch microfloppy and 5 1/4-inch minifloppy diskette.*

All diskettes, mini- or microfloppy, are used on both sides. Hence, you'll normally see the letters *2S* (two sided) or *DS* (double sided) on the box or on the diskettes themselves. If you see *2D* or *DD* (double sided, double density), the diskette is a 360K diskette. If the minifloppy diskette has the letters HC (high capacity) or HD (high density) on the label, the diskette is a 1.2M diskette. For microfloppy diskettes, *2D* or *DD* indicates a 720K diskette. HC or HD means a 1.44M diskette. The only visible difference between 720K and 1.44M microfloppy diskettes is that a second write-protect hole may be present on some 1.44M diskettes.

For all diskettes, the side of the diskette with the label is "up." When you insert the diskette into the disk drive, the label should face up. Or, if the disk drives are mounted on their sides, the label should face left. For microfloppy diskettes, the end that holds the sliding metal bar is the front of the diskette. For minifloppy diskettes, the oblong opening where the diskette itself is visible is the front of the diskette. Some manufacturers place a small arrow on the front of the diskette to indicate the side that should be inserted into the disk drive. When you insert a diskette into a disk drive, remember that the front end goes in with the label facing either up or to the left.

Knowing Your Keyboard

Before you work with DOS, you should know that computers come with several different types of keyboards. You should also know these three very important keys: Enter, Backspace, and Escape (Esc).

The early Personal Computers and some PC XTs have a keyboard similar to the one shown in figure 1.10. Some Personal Computer AT keyboards are like the one shown in figure 1.11. Newer computers (the PC XT, 286-XT, and the Personal Computer AT) and PS/2 computers use a keyboard similar to that shown in figure 1.12. The keyboards function in the same manner, but the layout of some keys is different. Become familiar with the position of the keys discussed in the rest of this section.

The Enter key is the "go" key. When you press Enter, you signal DOS that you have finished typing and that DOS should act on your command or answer. The first sample session in this chapter shows the Enter key as ↵. This symbol reminds you to press Enter after you type a line. After a few times, you should find yourself pressing Enter automatically.

The Enter key is located to the right of the alphanumeric keys. On Enhanced Keyboards, a second Enter key is located to the right of the

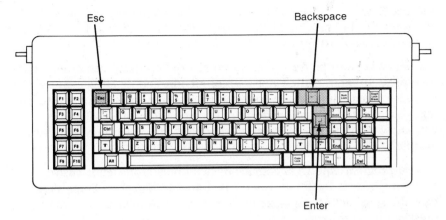

Fig. 1.10. *The Enter, Backspace, and Esc keys on a Personal Computer keyboard.*

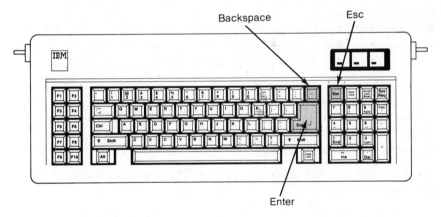

Fig. 1.11. *The Enter, Backspace, and Esc keys on a Personal Computer AT keyboard.*

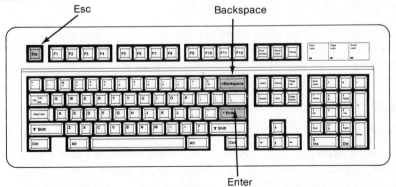

Fig. 1.12. *The Enter, Backspace, and Esc keys on the Enhanced Keyboard.*

numeric keypad. The two Enter keys function identically, although the Enter key on the numeric pad does not have the ↵ symbol. Either key can be used to signal DOS that you have finished answering.

The Enter key can be the "point of no return." In many cases, once you have pressed Enter, you cannot reenter a command or change an answer you have given. Therefore, before you press Enter, take a moment to check that your typing is correct. After you become acquainted with DOS, you will know when typing mistakes are harmless and when they can cause trouble.

Several programs and DOS commands need only a one-letter answer, such as Y for yes or N for no. In some cases, you do not press Enter after you type the single-letter response. But for now, always finish what you type by pressing the Enter key.

You can use the Backspace key (←) when you make a mistake. Each time you press the Backspace key, the cursor backs up one character and erases the character. The *cursor* is the flashing underscore that shows where the next character will be placed on the screen. After you move the cursor backward and erase a mistake, you can retype the rest of the line.

If you make a major typing mistake, you can use the Esc key. When you tap the Esc key before you press enter, DOS puts a backslash (\) on the screen and drops to the next line. DOS ignores what you typed on the previous line and lets you retype the entire line. If you hit the Esc key by accident, just retype your line.

The keyboard also has other special keys. These will be discussed later in the book.

Knowing What You Type

Take a moment to become familiar with the conventions used throughout this book to distinguish what you type from what the computer displays. What you should type is shown like this. What the computer displays is shown like this. For example, in this line

A>DIR

DOS provided the A>, and you would type DIR.

The one symbol you don't see is ↵, the symbol for the Enter key. After you type DIR, you must press Enter. As mentioned, only the first sample session in this chapter shows the symbol for the Enter key. Remember to press Enter when you finish typing a line.

Getting Ready for Hands-on Practice

To practice using DOS V3, you will need the following:

1. Your PS/2 computer or Personal Computer, plugged in and ready to go.

2. The single microfloppy diskette or the two minifloppy diskettes that come with DOS V3.

   The single microfloppy diskette is labeled "Startup/Operating" and is the diskette you'll use. The minifloppy diskettes for DOS V3.3 are labeled "Startup" and "Operating"; the diskette labeled "Startup" is the diskette you'll use. If you are using a version of DOS before V3.3, your two diskettes are titled "DOS" and "Supplemental Programs." The startup diskette is the one that does not read "Supplemental Programs." The DOS diskettes are shown in figure 1.13.

3. One blank microfloppy diskette or two blank minifloppy diskettes plus labels. If you are using minifloppy diskettes, you also need two write-protect tabs. On microfloppy diskettes, the tab is built into the diskette (see figs. 1.14 and 1.15). Labels and write-protect tabs normally come in the box with the blank diskettes.

PS/2 owners may need one 720K diskette to complete this exercise. Personal Computer AT users may need two 360K diskettes (the type that typical personal computers use) to complete this exercise.

If you have a PS/2 computer or a Personal Computer AT, you must run the CONFIGURATION (PS/2) or SETUP (Personal Computer AT) program before you start the exercise. (See your documentation for directions.) If you have a fixed disk drive and have not yet set it up, don't worry. You don't need your fixed disk set up properly until the next chapter. When you finish this chapter, follow the instructions in Appendix E. Then proceed to the next chapter.

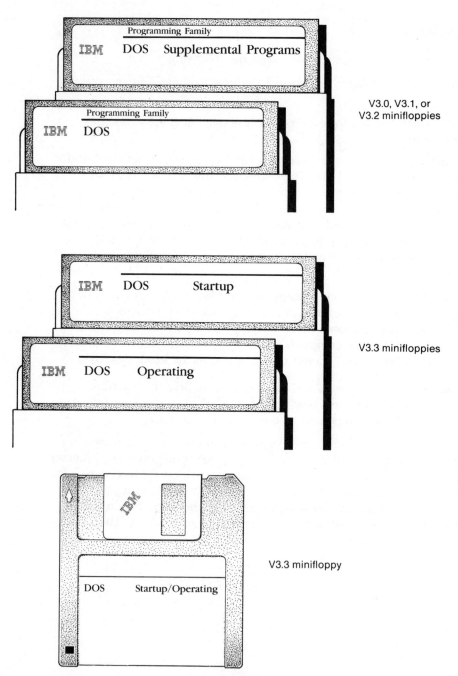

Fig. 1.13. *DOS V3 comes on a single microfloppy diskette or on two minifloppy diskettes.*

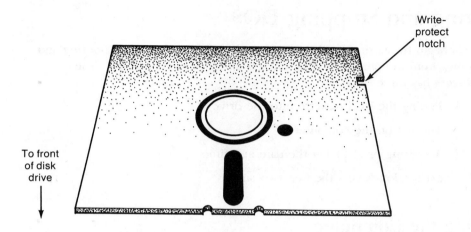

Fig. 1.14. *Covering the notch on a minifloppy diskette protects the information from accidental erasure or alteration. Leaving the notch uncovered allows information to be written to the diskette.*

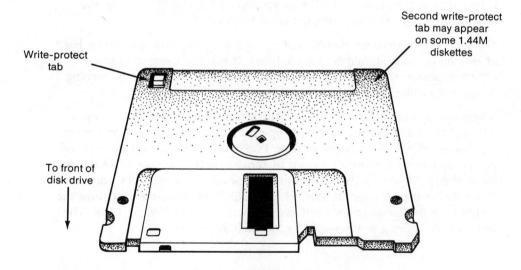

Fig. 1.15. *Microfloppy diskette showing built-in write-protect tab.*

Starting and Stopping DOS

Let's begin by starting up the computer. This process is called *booting* and comes from the phrase "pulling oneself up by one's bootstraps." The process has three steps:

1. Putting the DOS diskette into the drive

2. Turning on the computer

3. Accepting or changing the date and time

The next section covers the first two steps.

Starting the Computer

Place in the first floppy disk drive, drive A, the Startup diskette provided with your copy of DOS. (Use the diskette labeled "Startup" if you are using minifloppy diskettes and DOS V3.3. Use the single microfloppy diskette labeled "Startup/Operating" if you are using microfloppy diskettes. If you are using a version of DOS earlier than V3.3, you should use the diskette that does not say "Supplemental Programs.")

The label of the diskette should face up, and the side with the sliding bar or oblong opening should be inserted first. If you are using minifloppy diskettes, secure the diskette in the drive. Start your computer by turning the power switch on.

When you power-up your computer, the system does a self-test to check whether the computer is working properly. This test is called a *Power-On Self-Test* or *POST*. The amount of time POST takes depends on the type of computer you have and the amount of *random-access memory* (RAM) in the computer. Users of PS/2 computers, Personal Computer ATs, and 286-XTs will see the message Ø64KB OK or 128KB OK while the test runs; the numbers in the message are displayed in increments of 64K or 128K. The test can take from a few seconds to as much as two minutes.

Resetting the Computer (Ctrl-Alt-Del)

If your computer is already on, you can use the key combination Ctrl-Alt-Del to reboot or reset the computer. Simply hold down the Ctrl and Alt keys while you press and release the Del key. It makes no difference whether you press the Ctrl key before the Alt key, but you must hold them down together before you press and release Del.

On older Personal Computer keyboards and on the Personal Computer AT keyboard, the Ctrl key is located just to the left of the A key (see figs. 1.16 and 1.17). The Alt key is just to the left of the space bar, which is the longest key on the keyboard. The Del key is on the lower right part of the numeric keypad, on the right side of the keyboard. Del shares a key with the period (.).

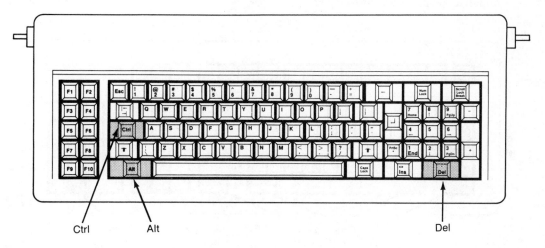

Fig. 1.16. *The Ctrl, Alt, and Del keys on a Personal Computer keyboard.*

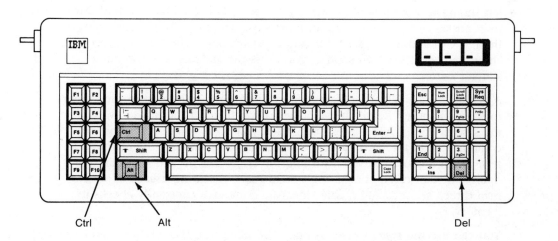

Fig. 1.17. *The Ctrl, Alt, and Del keys on a Personal Computer AT keyboard.*

For the new Enhanced Keyboards (the ones that have the special-function keys at the top), there are two sets of Ctrl and Alt keys, one set on either side of the space bar. The Ctrl keys are farther from the space bar and have black letters. The Alt keys are located next to the space bar and have green letters. There are two Del keys. The first Del key is located on the six-key editing pad between the alphanumeric keys and the numeric keypad. The second Del key also shares a key with the period on the numeric keypad (see fig. 1.18).

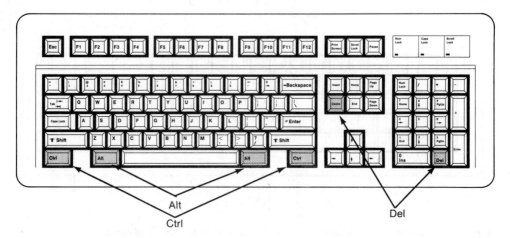

Fig. 1.18. *The Ctrl, Alt, and Del keys on the Enhanced Keyboard.*

The easiest way to press the Ctrl-Alt-Del key combination is to use your left thumb to hold down the Alt key and your left forefinger to hold down the Ctrl key. (If you have an Enhanced keyboard, you'll be holding down the left Ctrl and Alt keys.) With your right hand, tap the Del key; then release all three keys. As soon as you press the Del key, the computer starts a system reset.

A *system reset* is slightly different from turning off and on again the power to your computer. Remember that when you turn on the power switch, the system does a full self-test. But when you do a system reset, the computer skips the parts of the self-test, including the lengthy memory test. Given a choice between turning the computer off and on again or doing a system reset, choose the system reset. Resetting usually takes less than fifteen seconds and is safe since the computer constantly checks its memory.

You can use the system reset as one of three "panic buttons" on your computer. If something is drastically wrong with the computer, you can do a system reset. Note that when you do a system reset, what you are working on is lost, for you are restarting the computer from scratch. But what you have saved on the computer's disks is safe.

Another panic button is jokingly named by my friends the "master reset" key. This is the computer's on/off switch, and it is the last resort. You'll learn about the third panic button (which is actually the first in order of preference) later in this chapter.

Entering the Date and Time

After you have started or reset your system, the red light on the first floppy disk drive should come on. DOS then asks for the current date and time. If your computer has a built-in clock (the Personal Computer AT and PS/2 computers do), DOS will give the date and time automatically. If there is no clock, you will need to supply the date and time manually.

I finished this chapter at 9:04 p.m. on June 16, 1987. My system has a built-in clock, and it gave this information. If, instead, I had had to give the date and time manually, I would have answered DOS's request in the following manner:

```
Current date is Tue 1-Ø1-198Ø
Enter new date (mm-dd-yy): 6-16-87 ↵
Current time is Ø:ØØ:13.47
Enter new time: 21:04:42 ↵
```

Notice how the current date and time are entered. The date is entered as numbers in the form *mm-dd-yy*, where

  mm is the month, 1 to 12

  dd is the day, 1 to 31

  yy is the last two digits of the year

Note that I indicated the month of June with the single digit 6. I also could have used 06. I used hyphens between the numbers, but I could have used slashes instead.

DOS is a little fussier about how you enter the time. You enter the time as *hh:mm:ss.xx*, where *hh* is the hour, 0 to 23

mm is the minutes, 0 to 59

ss is the seconds, 0 to 59

xx is the hundredths of a second, 0 to 99

You must use either a colon (:) or a period (.) between the hours, minutes, and seconds; but you can use only a period (.) between the seconds and hundredths of a second. DOS gets annoyed if you use any other punctuation.

DOS uses a 24-hour clock, which is similar to military or universal clocks. To indicate the afternoon hours to DOS, you add 12 to the 12-hour clock time. For example, 2:00 p.m. becomes 14:00.

If you do not have a Personal Computer AT or a PS/2 computer, enter the current date and time now. Don't bother entering the hundredths of a second (*xx*), and don't forget to press the Enter key after you finish typing.

If you have a built-in clock, the date and time should be correct. If they are correct, just tap Enter after each is displayed. If the date and time are incorrect, enter the correct information. With DOS V3.3, entering the date and time resets the system clock.

This is not true of versions of DOS before V3.3. With earlier versions, setting the date and time does not reset the system clock. The entered date and time values are lost at power-off time. This is a DOS bug. If you use a version of DOS before V3.3, you need to use a custom assembler program or the SETUP program on the IBM-provided diagnostic diskette to set the clock.

Your screen should now look something like this one:

```
Current date is Tue   6-16-1987
Enter new date: ↵
Current time is 21:Ø4:43.47
Enter new time: ↵


The IBM Personal Computer DOS
Version 3.3Ø (C)Copyright International Business Machines Corp 1981, 1987
             (C)Copyright Microsoft Corp 1981, 1986
A>
```

If your screen shows something else or nothing at all, you have a problem. If you have the message Invalid Date or Invalid Time on your screen, you did not enter the numbers correctly. You may have typed a nonsense date or time or incorrectly punctuated the date or time. You may also have used the numeric keypad instead of the number keys.

When you reboot a Personal Computer, the keypad is set in the "cursor control/editing" mode. To use the keypad to enter numbers for the date and time, you must either hold down the shift key as you type the numbers or press the Num Lock key once. (PS/2 computers intelligently start with the numeric keypad in the numeric, not the editing, mode.)

If your video screen looks similar to the one just shown, DOS has successfully started and is in control of your computer system. You have completed the booting process. Now everything you type will be handled by DOS.

Don't worry if the numbers after the decimal point are different from those in the example, or if the copyright message is slightly different. You have a different revision of DOS, which does not matter for now. The first digit, however, should be 3 or higher. If the first digit is something else, this book does not match your program.

Stopping DOS with Ctrl-Break (or Ctrl-C)

Before you continue, you should learn about the third "panic button" on your computer, which, as mentioned earlier, is the first in order of preference. In this section, you will use the Ctrl-Break or Ctrl-C panic button to interrupt the execution of a DOS command.

If you are using minifloppy diskettes and DOS V3.3, take the Startup Diskette out of the disk drive and place the diskette labeled "Operating" into the disk drive. Close the disk drive door. Otherwise, make sure that the diskette you used to boot the computer is still in drive A and that the door is closed. At the A> prompt, type

A>DISKCOPY A: A:

Then press Enter. Always press Enter after you finish typing a command. For now, type your commands in capital letters. In most cases, DOS does not care whether you use upper- or lowercase letters.

The red light on the left drive should come on briefly. Then the following message will appear:

```
Insert SOURCE diskette in drive A:
Press any key when ready . . .
```

Press either Ctrl-Break or Ctrl-C. (On older keyboards, the Break key is the same key as the Scroll Lock key, which is on the upper right side of the keypad. On the new keyboards, the Break key is the same as the Pause key, which is also on the upper right side of the keyboard.) You implement these key sequences by holding down the Ctrl key and then tapping either the Break key or the C key.

Your screen should now look like this:

```
Insert SOURCE diskette in drive A:
Press any key when ready . . .
^C

A>
```

Pressing Ctrl-Break or Ctrl-C initiates the "stop what you are doing" command. Whether you press Ctrl-Break or Ctrl-C does not matter. Either key sequence works the same way. When you press this sequence, you are telling DOS to stop immediately the program that is running, exit the program, and take control again. That's what the ^C on the screen shows.

Ctrl-Break is the first panic button to use if you get into a situation where things are drastically wrong, such as having the wrong diskette in the drive, invoking the wrong command, or giving the wrong file name. You should be able to stop the program by pressing Ctrl-Break or Ctrl-C. Note that this panic button does not always work, and later in the book, you will learn why. If all else fails, you can use the system reset sequence or turn off the power. Avoid these last two panic buttons whenever possible, however.

Here is one other item to keep in mind: when DOS says to

```
Press any key when ready...
```

DOS really means that you should press *almost* any key when ready. If you press the Shift, Alt, Caps Lock, Num Lock, Scroll Lock, Pause, Sys Req, or—on the new keyboards—the Print Screen key, DOS will continue to wait. The system-reset sequence, however, is guaranteed to reset your system. Don't use this sequence unless you want to reset your computer. Generally, the Enter key and the space bar are two good, large targets to use when DOS says that it wants any key pressed.

Copying the DOS Startup Diskette (DISKCOPY)

You may have heard from your friends that making copies of diskettes is important. The statement is true. You should make copies of any important program diskettes before you use the program. In this section, you'll make a copy of the diskette or diskettes that hold DOS. If you have microfloppy disk drives, you'll make a copy of the single microfloppy diskette that comes with DOS. If you use minifloppy disk drives, you'll copy the two minifloppy diskettes that come with DOS.

This exercise has two sets of instructions. The first set is for users who have computers with two floppy disk drives. The second set is for users whose computers have one floppy disk drive.

The Personal Computer AT can fit into both groups, however. This computer can have one floppy disk drive, two identical, or two different floppy disk drives. If you have an AT with different floppy disk drives, use the instructions for a single disk drive.

Within each set of directions are separate instructions for microfloppy- and minifloppy-diskette users. The separate instructions are given at the end of each section.

During this exercise, you may see an unusual message on the screen. Owners of systems that have either high-capacity disk drives (the PC 286-XT and Personal Computer AT) or 1.44M diskette drives (PS/2 computers) are most likely to see such a message. If you see something quite different from the screen display, go to the section "Did Something Go Wrong?" for additional instructions.

You may want to skim the directions that do not apply to your computer. Then you'll be familiar with the proper procedure whenever you use a computer with floppy disk drives that are different from your computer's disk drives.

Copying with Two Floppy Disk Drives

The instructions in this section are for users of computers with two identical floppy disk drives. These instructions are for most Personal Computer users and for any PC XT, 286-XT, AT, or PS/2 owners whose computers have two identical floppy disk drives.

For the copying process, be sure that the DOS Startup/Operating diskette (or the Operating diskette if you are using minifloppy diskettes) is still in drive A and that the door is closed. Place a new, blank diskette in drive B and close the door. Then type

```
A>DISKCOPY A: B:
```

You should see the following message:

```
A>DISKCOPY A: B:
Insert SOURCE diskette in drive A:
Insert TARGET diskette in drive B:
Press any key when ready...
```

The *source* diskette is the diskette to be copied, which in this case is the DOS Startup diskette. The *target* diskette is the blank diskette in drive B. This diskette will become an exact copy of your DOS Startup diskette.

If you are using microfloppy diskettes, you already have the right diskettes in the correct disk drives, and you can press any key to begin copying. For minifloppy diskettes, you must first remove the Operating diskette from drive A and place the Startup diskette in drive A, and then press any key to begin copying. The light on drive A will go on. If you are using microfloppy diskettes, you will see this message:

```
Copying 80 tracks
9 Sectors/Track, 2 Side(s)
```

If you are using minifloppy diskettes, you will see this message:

```
Copying 40 tracks
9 Sectors/Track, 2 Side(s)
```

In 10 to 50 seconds, the light on drive A will go out, and the light on drive B will go on. Afterward, you'll see the following message:

```
Formatting while copying
```

This message tells you that DOS is preparing your blank diskette in drive B to hold the information that will be transferred from the DOS Startup diskette in drive A.

You'll probably notice that the lights on the drives go on and off several times. The number of times this happens depends on the amount of random-access memory in your computer and the type of floppy disk drives you have.

After DISKCOPY has finished copying the diskette, you will see this message:

```
Copy another diskette (Y/N)? _
```

DOS is asking whether you want to copy another diskette. At this point, the directions vary for users of microfloppy and minifloppy diskettes.

Directions for Users of Microfloppy Diskettes

If you are using microfloppy diskettes, you have copied the single DOS Startup/Operating diskette. Answer **N** for no to the

```
Copy another diskette (Y/N)?
```

question. You do not need to press Enter. The A> symbol will reappear.

Find one of the diskette labels and write DOS V3.x Startup on the label. Substitute a 3 for the x if you use DOS V3.3 or a 2 if you use DOS V3.2. Take the diskette out of drive B and put the label on the diskette. Always label a diskette after you perform a DISKCOPY operation. The label reminds you that the diskette has something useful on it.

Turn the diskette over and locate the sliding tab on the upper left part of the diskette. Slide the tab up so that you can see through the hole. This action write-protects the diskette. Sliding the tab up protects the microfloppy diskette from having information erased or changed.

Keep this Startup diskette handy. You'll need it in Chapter 2. Put your original DOS Startup diskette back in its cover and store the diskette in a safe place.

Skim the instructions in the section "Copying with One Floppy Disk Drive" and do the steps at your leisure. The instructions for machines with one floppy disk drive work on your computer also, but those procedures are slightly less convenient to use.

Directions for Users of Minifloppy Diskettes

If you are using minifloppy diskettes, you have made a copy of the DOS Startup diskette. You also need to make a copy of the Operating diskette (or Supplemental Programs diskette if you are using a version of DOS before V3.3).

Before you make the copy of the second diskette, find one of the diskette labels and write DOS V3.x Startup on the label. Substitute a 3 for the x if you use DOS V3.3, a 2 if you use DOS V3.2, a 1 for DOS V3.1, or a 0 for DOS V3.0. Remove the diskette from drive B and put the label on the diskette. Always label a diskette after you perform a DISKCOPY. The label reminds you that the diskette has something useful on it.

On your screen, the following message should still be displayed:

```
Copy another diskette (Y/N)? _
```

Answer Y for yes. You do not need to press Enter. You will see this message again:

```
Insert SOURCE diskette in drive A:
Insert TARGET diskette in drive B:
Press any key when ready...
```

Do not press any key yet. Take the Startup diskette out of drive A. Place the Operating (or Supplemental Programs) diskette in drive A and place the second, blank diskette in drive B. Make sure that both disk drive doors are closed.

Press any key to start copying the second diskette. You will see messages indicating the number of tracks and sectors being copied and stating that your diskette is being formatted during the copying process.

Then the following message will appear:

```
Copy another diskette (Y/N)? _
```

Answer N for no. Again, you do not need to press Enter. The A> symbol will reappear.

You have just made a copy of your DOS Operating (or Supplemental Programs) diskette. Find another diskette label. If you are using DOS V3.3, write DOS V3.3 Operating Diskette on the label. If you are using an earlier version, write DOS V3.x Supplemental Programs Diskette on the label. Substitute a 2 if you use DOS V3.2, a 1 for DOS V3.1, or a 0 for DOS V3.0. Remove the diskette from drive B and put the label on the diskette.

Find two write-protect tabs and place one tab over the notch in the upper right side of each diskette (see fig. 1.14). This action protects the information on the diskettes from being erased or changed.

Keep both diskettes handy. You'll need them in the next chapter. Put your original DOS Startup and Operating diskettes back in their envelopes and store the diskettes in a safe place.

Now skim the instructions in the next section and do the steps at your leisure. The instructions for machines with one floppy disk drive work on your computer also, but those instructions are slightly less convenient to use.

Copying with One Floppy Disk Drive

This section is for users of computers that have one floppy disk drive, such as most Personal Computer XTs, 286-XTs, Personal Computer ATs, and PS/2s, or for owners whose computers have two different types of floppy disk drives. Only one disk drive will be used to copy the diskette(s).

At the end of this section, instructions are given first for users whose computers have microfloppy disk drives (who will make one diskette copy). Then come instructions for those users whose computers have minifloppy disk drives (who will make two diskette copies).

Make sure that your DOS Startup/Operating microfloppy or Operating minifloppy diskette is in drive A and that the door is closed. Type

```
A>DISKCOPY A: A:
```

You should see the following message:

```
A>DISKCOPY A: A:
Insert SOURCE diskette in drive A:
Press any key when ready...
```

The source diskette is the DOS Startup diskette, which is already in drive A, if you are using microfloppies; just press the space bar. If you are using minifloppies, remove the Operating diskette from drive A and place the Startup diskette in drive A, and then press the space bar. The light on your floppy disk drive will go on. If you are using microfloppy diskettes, in a few seconds, you should see this message:

```
Copying 80 tracks
9 Sectors/Track, 2 Side(s)
```

If you are using a minifloppy disk drive, you should see this message:

```
Copying 40 tracks
9 Sectors/Track, 2 Side(s)
```

After 10 to 30 seconds, the following message should appear:

```
Insert TARGET diskette in drive A:
Press any key when ready...
```

Take your DOS Startup/Operating or Startup diskette out of the floppy disk drive, put the blank diskette into the same drive, close the door, and press a key. You should then see this message:

```
Formatting while copying
```

DOS is now preparing your blank diskette to hold the information from the original DOS Startup diskette. After a brief period (anywhere from 20 seconds to about one minute), you may see the following message appear a second time:

```
Insert SOURCE diskette in drive A:
Press any key when ready...
```

Take out the second diskette and again place your DOS Startup diskette in the drive. Close the door and press a key. After another brief period, you should see the following message:

```
Insert TARGET diskette in drive A:
Press any key when ready...
```

Change diskettes again, close the door, and press a key. These messages may appear once, or they may appear several times. The number of times the messages appear (and the number of times you exchange diskettes) depends on the type of floppy disk drive you have and the amount of random-access memory in your computer. Each time the messages appear, simply exchange diskettes and press a key.

Finally, you should see this message:

```
Copy another diskette (Y/N)? _
```

This message indicates that DISKCOPY has finished making the copy of your DOS Startup diskette. DOS is now asking whether you want to copy another diskette. At this point, the directions vary for users of microfloppy and minifloppy diskettes.

Directions for Users of Microfloppy Diskettes

If you are using microfloppy diskettes, you have copied the single DOS Startup diskette. Answer **N** for no to the Copy another diskette (Y/N)? question. You do not need to press Enter. The A> symbol will reappear.

Find one of the diskette labels and write DOS V3.x Startup on the label. Substitute a 3 for the x if you use DOS V3.3, or a 2 if you use DOS V3.2. Take the diskette out of drive A and put the label on the diskette. Always label a diskette after you perform a DISKCOPY operation. The label reminds you that the diskette has something useful on it.

Turn the diskette over and locate the sliding tab on the upper left part of the diskette. Slide the tab up so that you can see through the hole. This action write-protects the diskette. Sliding the tab up protects the microfloppy diskette from having information erased or changed.

Keep this Startup diskette handy. You'll need it in the next chapter. Put your original DOS Startup/Operating Diskette back in its cover and store the diskette in a safe place.

For your information, you can perform the diskette-copying operation by typing

```
A>DISKCOPY A:
```

When you give a single disk drive name with the DISKCOPY command, DOS assumes that only one disk drive will be used to hold both the source and target diskettes.

Now skim the instructions in the next section and then skip to the chapter summary.

Directions for Users of Minifloppy Diskettes

If you are using minifloppy diskettes, you have made a copy of the DOS Startup diskette. You need to make a copy of the Operating diskette (or Supplemental Programs diskette if you are using a version of DOS before V3.3).

Before you make the copy of the other diskette, find one of the diskette labels and write DOS V3.x Startup on the label. Substitute a 3 for the x if you use DOS V3.3, a 2 if you use DOS V3.2, a 1 for DOS V3.1, or a 0 for DOS V3.0. Remove the diskette from drive A and put the label on the diskette. Always label a diskette after you perform a DISKCOPY. The label reminds you that the diskette has something useful on it.

On your screen, the following message should still be displayed:

```
Copy another diskette (Y/N)? _
```

Answer Y for yes. You do not need to press Enter. You will see this message again:

```
Insert SOURCE diskette in drive A:
Press any key when ready...
```

Do not press any key yet. Take the Startup diskette out of drive A. Place the Operating (or Supplemental Programs) diskette in drive A. Make sure the disk drive door is closed and then press any key. You'll see the message stating the number of tracks and sectors being copied. The following message will appear:

```
Insert TARGET diskette in drive A:
Press any key when ready...
```

Take the Operating diskette out of the disk drive, place your second blank diskette in the disk drive, close the door, and press a key. Within a few seconds, you'll see a message that your diskette is being formatted during the copying process. The instructions to insert the source and target diskettes may appear again. When the messages appear, exchange the Operating diskette with the second diskette and press a key.

Finally, the following message will appear:

```
Copy another diskette (Y/N)? _
```

Answer **N** for no. Again, you do not need to press Enter. The A> symbol will reappear.

You have just made a copy of your DOS Operating Diskette. Find another diskette label. If you are using DOS V3.3, write DOS V3.3 Operating Diskette on the label. If you are using an earlier version, write DOS V3.x Supplemental Program Diskette on the label. Substitute a 2 if you use DOS V3.2, a 1 for DOS V3.1, or a 0 for DOS V3.0. Remove the diskette from drive A and put the label on the diskette.

Find two write-protect tabs and place one tab over the notch in the upper right side of each diskette you have made (fig. 1.14). This action protects the information on the diskettes from being erased or changed.

Keep both diskettes handy. You'll need them in the next chapter. Put your original DOS Startup and Operating diskettes back in their envelopes and store the diskettes in a safe place.

For your information, you can perform the diskette-copying operation by typing

```
A> DISKCOPY A:
```

When you give a single disk drive name, DOS assumes that only one disk drive will be used to hold both the source and target diskettes.

Now, unless something went wrong, you can skip to the chapter summary.

Did Something Go Wrong?

If you are using high-capacity disk drives (HC disk drives) and high-capacity diskettes, this exercise may not work right for you. This exercise may also not work on PS/2 computers that use 1.44M disk drives and 1.44M diskettes. If you see any messages indicating that something is wrong (the message may say something about invalid media or about track 0 being bad), press the Ctrl-Break sequence when DOS asks you to place a new diskette in drive A. To do this exercise properly, you need to begin the copying exercise again, using 360K or 720K diskettes.

The other potential error message may be one of the following:

```
Unrecoverable read error on drive A

Unrecoverable write error on drive A

Unrecoverable write error on drive B
```

The next line of the error message will state the side and track of the error. If you see the first message, either your DOS diskette is bad, or the drive may be faulty. Stop DISKCOPY by pressing the Ctrl-Break sequence. Take the diskettes to another computer and try the exercise again. If it works, your disk drive probably has problems. If the exercise still does not work, your copy of DOS is probably faulty. Either way, see your dealer about the problem.

If you see the second or third error message (about a write error), the blank diskette you are using may be bad, or your disk drive may be faulty. Most likely, the problem is the diskette.

Press the Ctrl-Break sequence to stop the program. Repeat the DISKCOPY directions for the kind of diskette you are copying. If you are using two disk drives, before you start, remove and reinsert the diskette in drive B. Sometimes a diskette does not sit properly on the spindle. Reinserting the diskette may correct the problem.

If you get the same error message, repeat the exercise with a different blank diskette. If this tactic works, the first diskette is bad and should be replaced. If the tactic does not work, you probably have a disk-drive problem. Check with your dealer to have the drive repaired.

Summary

In this chapter, you learned some facts about disk drives, diskettes, and the keyboard, as well as how to start the computer. You booted (started) DOS and made a copy of the original DOS Startup diskette. The following are the key points to remember:

1. The Personal Computer and PS/2 families have two different types of floppy disk drives: microfloppy (3 1/2-inch) and minifloppy (5 1/4-inch). The capacities of the disk drives are different: 720K and 1.44M for microfloppy disk drives, and 360K or 1.2M for minifloppy disk drives.

2. When you start DOS from a diskette, you use the first disk drive, drive A.

3. Three important keys are the Enter key, which informs DOS that a typed line has been completed; the Backspace key, which erases a single character; and the Escape key, which ignores the current line and enables you to start over.

4. Three "panic buttons" are

   a. Ctrl-Break (Ctrl-C), which stops a running command

   b. Ctrl-Alt-Del, which resets the computer and restarts DOS

   c. The power switch, which should be turned off if all else fails

5. You use the DISKCOPY command to copy a diskette.

6. Three frequently used DOS commands are DATE, TIME, and DISKCOPY.

The next chapter introduces two more commands: FORMAT and COPY.

Table 2.1
DOS Survival Commands and Keystroke Sequences

Command Function	Name	See Chapter
Copy a diskette	DISKCOPY	1
Copy a file	COPY	2
Prepare a diskette	FORMAT	2
See the files on a disk	DIR	3
Check free space on a disk	CHKDSK	3
Change a file's name	RENAME	2
Remove a file	ERASE	2

Survival Keystrokes

Stop a program	Ctrl-Break or Ctrl-C	1
Stop a program and reset the computer	Ctrl-Alt-Del	1
Freeze the video screen	Ctrl-Num Lock, Ctrl-S, or Pause	3
Unfreeze the video screen	Any key	3
Print the contents of the video screen on the printer	Shift-PrtSc	3
Print on the printer and on the video screen at the same time	Ctrl-PrtSc	3
Change the current disk drive	*d:* (drive letter followed by a colon and Enter)	3
Run DOS programs	*programname* (the name of the program, followed by Enter)	

2

Preparing Diskettes and Copying Files

In Chapter 1, you made a copy of your DOS Startup diskette. To copy the diskette, you used the command DISKCOPY. You also learned about the Enter, Backspace, and Esc keys and about the Ctrl-Break or Ctrl-C sequence. This chapter and the next three chapters cover other "survival" commands and concepts, basic DOS commands, and operating techniques that all computer users must know.

You'll learn how to prepare a diskette for use and how to copy files. Users who own computers with a HC disk drive or a fixed disk will make a single copy of the programs that are on the two minifloppy DOS diskettes. Owners of computers with one floppy disk drive, like the PS/2 computers, will see that this kind of computer really has two disk drives. Before you do this copying exercise, we'll quickly go over the basic commands and skills you'll learn in the next few chapters.

Learning Survival Commands and Keystrokes

There are seven commands that all DOS users must know. These commands make copies of disks and files, prepare diskettes for use, change the names of files, erase files, show what files are located on a disk, and show the amount of space that has been used and is free to be used on a disk. You also will learn keystroke sequences for freezing the display and printing the contents of the video screen onto paper.

The key commands and keystrokes are listed in table 2.1. You need not memorize the function of each command or key sequence now. Just glance at the table, paying attention to what the command or key sequence does. Learning the corresponding command's name or keystroke sequence will come with time.

A trick to gaining control over your computer is learning what tasks the DOS commands and sequences can do and then remembering a key word in the command that performs the task. For example, to copy files from one diskette to the fixed disk, the key words I remember are "copy files." The command name COPY springs to mind.

Another example is getting a printed copy of the contents of my screen. The key words are "printed screen." I then remember the keystroke sequence Shift-Print Screen or Ctrl-Print Screen.

Table 2.1 is a handy command list for this part of the book. Each command listed in table 2.1 is covered in Part I. You will find an expanded list of commands in the *DOS Command Reference* in Part VI of this book.

Getting Ready for Hands-on Practice

For this session, you will need the following:

1. Your Personal Computer or PS/2 computer, plugged in and ready to go.

2. The DOS Startup and Operating diskette or diskettes (the copy or copies you made in Chapter 1).

3. One blank microfloppy diskette plus label if you are using microfloppy diskettes. If you are using minifloppy diskettes, one blank HC diskette (if you have a HC disk drive) or two 360K minifloppy diskettes, plus label(s) and write-protect tab(s).

If you have a fixed disk, it should be set up. If it is not, follow the instructions in Appendix E of this book before you continue.

Preparing Your Diskettes (FORMAT)

When you get a new, blank diskette, it is not quite ready to receive information. You must prepare the diskette by using the FORMAT command.

Formatting a Boot Diskette (All Users)

Everyone should try the following exercise. Get the diskette labeled DOS
V3.x Startup, which you created in Chapter 1. Make sure that a write-
protect tab covers the notch on the upper right edge of the minifloppy
diskette or that the write-protect tab for the microfloppy diskette is
pushed up (so you can see through the hole). Then put the diskette back
into drive A.

If you are using microfloppy diskettes for this exercise, you will need one
diskette appropriate to the type of disk drive you have. If you have a 720K
disk drive, you should have a 720K diskette. If you have a 1.44M drive, you
should have a 1.44M diskette. Users of HC disk drives will need one HC
diskette, and users of 360K disk drives will need two 360K minifloppy
diskettes. The exercise will not work if the wrong type of diskette is used
in the HC minifloppy or 1.44M microfloppy disk drive.

Your computer should still be on, with DOS running. If it is not, turn on
the computer and start DOS now from your Startup diskette.

To format the disk, make sure that the Startup diskette is in drive A and
that the door is closed. Type

```
A>FORMAT A: /S /V
```

Notice how this command line is phrased. First, you type the name of the
command (FORMAT). Then you type the name of the disk drive that will
hold the diskette to be formatted (in this case, A). Next, you enter the
two switches /S and /V. The /S tells DOS to put a copy of the operating
system onto the diskette you are formatting. The /V tells DOS you want to
put a volume label on the diskette. These switches are discussed in detail
later in the book, but here is a brief overview for now.

What is a *switch*? Most DOS commands have options that affect the way
the command works. Switches allow you to select these options. Two
options of the FORMAT command are to place a copy of the operating
system onto the newly formatted diskette and to place a volume label on
the diskette for identification. To use an option, you must indicate a
switch for the option when you use the command. That way, you tell the
command to do extra work or to handle things in a different manner.

To use a switch, you type a slash (/) and the character for the switch. A
switch is always typed on the same line as that of the DOS command and

is usually the last item typed on the line. Some switches need extra information. For now, you will use only the switch character (/) and the single character for the switch.

After you type the FORMAT command line, the red light on the disk drive goes on for a few seconds. You will then see the following message:

```
Insert the diskette for drive A:
and strike ENTER when ready_
```

Take the DOS Startup diskette out of drive A, put your blank diskette in the drive, and press the Enter key. The FORMAT command will not continue until you press Enter. FORMAT is one of the rare commands for which DOS wants you to press a specific key, not just any key.

After you press Enter, the red light on the first disk drive will go on again, and the following message will appear:

```
Head:    Ø Cylinder:      1
```

You'll see the numbers on the screen change constantly. The number after the word Head flips between 0 and 1. The number after Cylinder starts at 1 and increases to either 40 (for 360K minifloppies) or to 80 (for HC minifloppy diskettes and for microfloppy diskettes).

After 20 to 40 seconds, the line with the numbers disappears, and the following message appears in its place:

```
Format complete
```

The disk drive will continue to spin. After a few more seconds, you will see another message:

```
System transferred
```

Now DOS asks the following:

```
Volume label (11 characters, ENTER for none)? _
```

Type **My DOS Disk** and press Enter.

The diskette will spin, and DOS will tell you how much total information the diskette can hold, how much space is taken by DOS, and how much free space is on the diskette:

360K	362496 bytes total disk space 78848 bytes used by system 283648 bytes available on disk
1.2M	1213952 bytes total disk space 78336 bytes used by system 1135616 bytes available on disk
720K	730112 bytes total disk space 78848 bytes used by system 651264 bytes available on disk
1.44M	1457664 bytes total disk space 78336 bytes used by system 1379328 bytes available on disk

The top set of numbers is for a 360K diskette; the second set is for a HC diskette; the third set is for a 720K microfloppy diskette; and the final set is for a 1.44M microfloppy diskette. Remember that the numbers for different versions of DOS V3 will be slightly different.

To understand the capacity of each diskette, you should know two computer terms: byte and kilobyte (K). A *byte* is eight binary digits (bits). A byte is the smallest unit of storage on a computer, holding a single computer instruction or character. For example, the word "character" uses 9 bytes. K stands for *kilo-*, a thousand. A kilobyte is around a thousand bytes; actually, it is 1,024 bytes.

For the first minifloppy diskette, which is normally used in Personal Computers and PC XTs, the total disk space is 362,496 bytes. Dividing 362,496 by 1,024 produces 354K. For the HC diskette, the total disk space is 1,213,952 bytes. This is equivalent to 1,185.5K. The capacity of the microfloppy diskettes is 730,113 bytes—713K—and 1,457,664 bytes— 1,423.5K.

The actual storage capacity of the floppy diskettes is higher. DOS does not report on three small sections of a diskette that are used exclusively by DOS. The actual capacity of the first minifloppy diskette is 368,640 bytes, or 360K. The capacity of the high-capacity diskette is 1,228,800 bytes. This is 1,200K or 1.2M. The M stands for *megabyte*, which is 1,048,576 bytes (1,024 × 1,024). The capacity of the first type of microfloppy diskette is 737,280 bytes or 720K. The true capacity of the second microfloppy diskettes is 1,474,560 bytes or 1,440K. In Chapter 7, you'll learn about the invisible "holes" in the diskette and how DOS uses them.

You may have lines on-screen that say:

```
...bytes in bad sectors
```

or

```
Invalid media or track Ø bad - disk unusable
```

The first line means that DOS found some sectors on the diskette that are bad and cannot be used to hold information. If the line stating bytes in bad sectors appears, your disk is usable, but the total amount of free space on the diskette is reduced by the number of bytes in bad sectors. If the Invalid media message appears, the areas on the disk that hold key DOS information are bad, and the diskette cannot be used at all. If you see either message, answer **Y** to the following question:

```
Format another (Y/N)?
```

Then press Enter. You will see a repetition of the messages that instruct you to insert a diskette to be formatted. Do not press Enter yet to start formatting. First, take the diskette out of the drive, reinsert the diskette, and close the door if necessary. Press Enter again. Some diskettes that do not format correctly the first time do so the second time.

If the diskette does not format properly the second time, something may be wrong with either the disk drive or the diskette (most likely the diskette). You can either take a diskette that has some bad sectors back to the dealer for a replacement, or you can just live with the fact that you won't have all the storage space you should from the diskette.

If you got the second message (the invalid media message) again, the diskette cannot be used at all. This message can appear if you use a 360K diskette in a HC disk drive or a 720K diskette in a 1.44M disk drive. If you used the wrong type of diskette, get the right type and try this exercise again. If you used the right type of diskette and got this message, take the diskette back to your dealer for a replacement.

FORMAT should now be asking the following question:

```
Format another (Y/N)?
```

Answer **N** for no and press Enter. The A> prompt should reappear. You have now formatted one diskette that holds a copy of the disk operating system. Find a diskette label. If you are using a 360K disk diskette and using DOS V3.3 or later, write a name like "DOS V3.x Master Startup Diskette." If you are not using 360K diskettes *or* you are using a version of DOS before V3.3, write a name like "DOS V3.x Master Diskette." (Substitute the right version number for the x on the diskette.)

If you are using 360K diskettes, follow the additional directions in the next section. If you are using another type of diskette, skim the directions concerning formatting diskettes without the /S switch; then go to the section on using the DIR command.

Additional Directions for Users of 360K Disk Drives

If you are using a 360K floppy disk drive, you need to format a second diskette. You do not, however, need to place a copy of the operating system on the second diskette. Place the Startup diskette back into drive A and type

```
A>FORMAT A: /V
```

Notice that the command is phrased almost the same way as the first FORMAT command, with the exception that you omit the /S switch. When you omit the /S switch, DOS does not place the operating system on the diskette. You should see the message:

```
Insert the diskette for drive A:
and strike ENTER when ready
```

Take the DOS Startup diskette out of drive A; put your second, blank diskette in the drive, and press Enter. As before, the disk drive light will go on, and the message displaying the head and cylinder numbers will appear. This message will be followed by the Format complete message. You will then be asked for the volume label. Type

   2nd Disk

The diskette will spin, and DOS will display the statistics on how much information the diskette can hold:

```
362496 bytes total disk space
362496 bytes available on disk
```

When the message appears that asks if you want to format another diskette, answer N for no and press Enter. The A> prompt should reappear.

Find a diskette label. If you are using DOS V3.3 or later, write "DOS V3.x Master Operating Diskette," substituting the right version number for the x. If you are using a version of DOS before V3.3, write "DOS 3.x Supplemental Programs Diskette," substituting the right version number for the x. Take the diskette out of the drive and place the label on the diskette. For the next exercise, you will need the first diskette you formatted. Put the diskette labeled "DOS V3.x Master Startup Diskette" into the disk drive A and close the door.

Looking at a Directory (DIR)

With the Master or Master Startup diskette in drive A, type DIR and press Enter. If you are using DOS V3.3, you should see:

```
A> DIR

Volume in drive A is MY DOS DISK
Directory of  A:\

COMMAND   COM    25307   3-17-85   12:00P
```

One of the following statements should be on the next line:

```
1 File(s)     283648 bytes free

1 File(s)     651264 bytes free

1 File(s)    1135616 bytes free

1 File(s)    1379328 bytes free
```

The information shown on these lines applies to a 360K minifloppy diskette, to a 720K microfloppy diskette, to a 1.2M minifloppy diskette, and to a 1.44M microfloppy diskette, respectively.

When you typed **DIR**, you asked DOS to display a list of the files on the diskette in drive A. The purpose of the DIR (for *dir*ectory) command is to display the files that are on a disk.

The first line shown on the screen is the volume label for the diskette. As indicated previously, this label helps you identify the diskette. DOS uses the volume label in two ways. DOS displays the label when you use certain commands. DOS also uses the label to confirm your intention to format a fixed disk. The label has no other special uses to DOS.

Notice that the volume label was entered in upper- and lowercase letters, but that DOS converted the letters into all uppercase. When you type most names, the case of the letters does not matter. DOS usually converts the characters to uppercase.

The next line on the screen tells you what disk drive and directory path are being displayed. These concepts are discussed in later chapters.

Next, you see one line for every file on the disk. The only file now in the list is COMMAND.COM. The line shows the name of the file, the length of the file in bytes, and the date and time that the file was created or last changed. The final line tells you the number of files displayed by the DIR command and the amount of diskette space available.

You may remember from the discussion of the FORMAT command that a certain amount of space on the formatted disk was taken up by system files. When you used the DIR command, you saw that the COMMAND.COM file takes up 25K.

Is something wrong? Didn't the FORMAT command indicate that more than 78,000 bytes were used by the system? Where is the rest of DOS?

Nothing is wrong. The remaining space of approximately 53,000 bytes is taken by two files you cannot see: IBMBIO.COM and IBMDOS.COM. These files hold the remaining pieces of the operating system. The files are hidden from you and do not show in the list when you ask for a directory (using the DIR command).

Literally, there is more to DOS than meets the eye. The DIR command is covered in more detail in the next chapter. And Chapter 5 provides more information on the two hidden files and about DOS. For now, remember that the DIR command displays the files on a disk and that, when you format a disk with the /S switch, two additional files are placed on the disk.

In the next exercise, you will copy to another diskette the files from the DOS diskette you made earlier.

Copying Files with the COPY Command

For the task of copying files, separate instructions are provided for the following categories:

1. Computers that have two floppy disk drives, of which at least one disk drive must be a 720K, 1.2M, or 1.44M disk drive

2. Computers that have two 360K floppy disk drives

3. Computers that have at least one floppy disk and one fixed disk

4. Computers that have only one floppy disk

Some computers may "qualify" for more than one category. Classic examples are PC 286-XT and Personal Computer AT computers that have one 1.2M disk drive and one 360K disk drive, which qualifies those computers for both the first and third categories. If your computer has a fixed disk, use the third set of instructions. The third set of instructions also covers PS/2 computers that have a fixed disk.

There are small differences between each version of DOS V3, and small differences between using microfloppy and minifloppy diskettes. If you use a version of DOS other than V3.3, what your computer displays and what is shown in the book will be different.

Copying with Two Floppy Disk Drives

These instructions are for those using two disk drives, one of which must be a 720K, 1.2M, or 1.44M disk drive. The procedure will not work correctly if both disk drives are 360K drives. This procedure requires four steps for microfloppy disk users and six steps for HC minifloppy disk drive users.

Step 1. *Place into drive A the diskette you formatted (the one labeled "DOS V3.x Master Diskette").*

Step 2. *Place into drive B the copy you made of your DOS Startup/ Operating or Startup diskette (the one labeled "Dos V3.x Startup/ Operating" or "DOS V3.x Startup").*

There is a reason for putting the formatted diskette into drive A and the DOS Startup diskette into drive B. If your floppy disk drives are not identical, the first disk drive usually has the highest capacity. The diskette in drive A, which has the same or greater capacity than the diskette in drive B, will receive the files. For this reason, we have reversed the normal order for copying between diskettes and copied the files from the diskette in drive B to the diskette in drive A.

Step 3. *Now type*

```
A>COPY B:*.* A: /V
```

The light on drive B will go on first; then the light on drive A. The lights will alternate for a minute or so while each file is copied from the second diskette to the first. The names of each file will appear on the screen as the file is being copied.

Notice the /V switch you typed. This switch tells COPY to *verify* that the copy being made of each file is correct. Many DOS commands use the same switch, but the meaning of the switch varies among the commands. For example, /V means *volume label* to the FORMAT command, but to the COPY command, it means *verify*. Watch out for this distinction.

Shortly, microfloppy users will see the first message that follows; minifloppy users will see the second message:

```
50 File(s) copied
22 File(s) copied
```

The message on the screen tells you that DOS has copied 50 files (from the microfloppy diskette) or 22 files (from the minifloppy diskette). This message informs you that the copying was successful.

If you use microfloppy diskettes, skip to Step 6.

Steps 4 and 5 are for users of minifloppy diskettes only. In these two steps you will copy the programs from the Operating or Supplemental Programs diskette to your Master diskette.

Step 4. *Take the DOS Startup diskette out of drive B.*

Put the Operating diskette (or Supplemental Programs diskette if you're using a version of DOS before 3.3) into drive B.

Step 5. *Now type*

```
A>COPY B:*.* A: /V
```

This command copies the files from the Operating or Supplemental Programs diskette onto the diskette in drive A. As before, the lights on disk drives B and A will flash briefly, and the name of each file will appear on the screen as the file is copied. Shortly, you should see the message:

```
31 File(s) copied
```

The COPY process is complete.

Step 6. *Take the diskettes out of the disk drives.*

Minifloppy diskette users should put the diskettes back in their envelopes. The DOS 3.x Master Diskette should be kept nearby as you will use this diskette later. The other diskettes should be stored in a safe place.

You are done for now. If you like, you can skim the instructions for other computer setups before you continue.

Copying with Two 360K Floppy Disk Drives

These instructions are for users who have two 360K disk drives, such as owners of Personal Computers or PC XTs. There are seven steps to follow and you will need the two diskettes you formatted earlier.

Step 1. *Place into drive A your copy of the DOS Startup diskette.*

Step 2. *Place the diskette you formatted, the one with the label "DOS V3.x Master Startup Diskette," into drive B.*

Step 3. *Now type*

```
A>COPY A:*.* B: /V
```

The light on drive A will go on first; then the light on drive B. The lights will alternate for a minute or so while each file is copied from the diskette in drive A to the diskette in drive B. The name of each file will appear on the screen as the file is copied.

Notice the /V switch you typed. This switch tells COPY to *verify* that the copy being made of each file is correct. Many DOS commands use the same switch, but the meaning of the switch varies among the commands. For example, /V means *volume label* to the FORMAT command, but to the COPY command, it means *verify*. Watch out for this distinction.

In a few seconds, you should see the message:

```
        22 File(s) copied

A>
```

The message on the screen tells you that DOS has copied the 22 files from the Startup diskette. This message informs you that the copying was successful.

***Step* 4.** *Take the DOS Startup diskette out of drive A.*

Put the Operating diskette (or Supplemental Programs diskette if you are using a version of DOS before V3.3) into drive A.

***Step* 5.** *Take the "Master Startup" diskette out of drive B.*

Insert the formatted diskette you labeled "DOS V3.x Master Operating Diskette" into drive B.

***Step* 6.** *Now type*

```
A>COPY A:*.* B: /V
```

This command copies the files from the Operating or Supplemental Programs diskette onto the diskette in drive B. As before, the lights on disk drive A and B will flash briefly, and the name of each file will appear on the screen as the file is copied. Shortly, you should see the message:

```
    31 File(s) copied
A>
```

The COPY process is complete.

***Step* 7.** *Take the diskettes out of the disk drives.*

Put all diskettes back into their envelopes. You should store the Startup and Operating diskettes in a safe place. Keep the Master Startup and Master Operating diskette nearby. You will use these diskettes later.

You are done for now. If you like, you can skim the instructions for other computer setups before you continue.

Copying with Both Floppy and Fixed Disk Drives

This section is for users whose computers have at least one floppy disk and one fixed disk drive: most PS/2, Personal Computer AT, PC XT, and PC 286-XT users.

This section is divided into three sets of instructions: One set is for users who have a 720K, 1.2M, or 1.44M disk drive. In other words, the first set of instructions is for users who do *not* have 360K disk drives. I labeled this set of instructions "Steps for Users of Higher-Capacity (not high-capacity) Disk Drives. You will need the single floppy diskette you formatted earlier.

The second set of instructions is for users who have 360K disk drives. You will need both of the floppy diskettes formatted earlier.

The third set of instructions is for everyone. These final instructions are presented after the instructions for users of 360K disk drives.

Steps for Users of Higher-Capacity Disk Drives

There are four steps for those using 720K and 1.44M disk drives and five steps for those using 1.2M disk drives. The additional step for 1.2M disk drives is necessary because DOS comes on two minifloppy diskettes, but one microfloppy diskette. To transfer the files, you have to copy data twice from the minifloppy diskette, but only once from the microfloppy diskette.

Step 1. Place your copy of the DOS Startup diskette into drive A.

Before you do Step 2, make sure your fixed disk is set up properly. If it is not, see Appendix E for instructions.

Step 2. Type

```
A>MKDIR C:\BIN
```

This command creates a new BIN directory on your fixed disk.

If you see a message that DOS is unable to create the directory, the directory already exists. You may have created the directory earlier (which happened if you followed the instructions in Appendix E). Since you need a "fresh" directory for this exercise, we will change the command. Type

```
A>MKDIR C:\DOS
```

This command creates a directory named DOS. If you make a DOS directory, remember to substitute DOS for BIN in the following instructions. If you forget, the exercise will not work properly.

Step 3. Copy the files from your Startup diskette to the BIN directory by typing

```
A>COPY A:*.* C:\BIN /V
```

You will see a light go on, first on the floppy disk drive. Then the light for the fixed disk will go on. The disk drive lights will alternate, and file names will appear on the screen as the files are copied.

Notice the /V switch you typed. This switch tells COPY to *verify* that the copy being made of each file is correct. Many DOS commands use the same switch, but the meaning of the switch varies among the commands. For example, /V means *volume label* to the FORMAT command, but *verify* to the COPY command. Watch out for this distinction.

Shortly, users of microfloppy diskettes will see the first message that follows, and users of minifloppy diskettes will see the second message:

```
50 File(s) copied
22 File(s) copied
```

The messages inform you that the copying was successful: DOS has copied 50 files (from the microfloppy diskette) or 22 files (from the minifloppy diskette).

If you use microfloppy disk drives, skip to Step 5.

Step 4 is only for those using 1.2M disk drives.

Step 4. Take the copy of the Startup diskette out of drive A.

Put the copy of the DOS V3.x Master Operating diskette (or DOS V3.x Supplemental Programs diskette, if you are using a version of DOS before V3.3) into drive A. Type

```
A>COPY A:*.* C:\BIN /V
```

This command copies the files from the Master Operating (or Supplemental Programs) diskette in drive A to the fixed disk. As before, the disk drive lights will alternate, and file names will appear on the screen as the files are copied. Shortly, this message will appear:

```
        31 File(s) copied
A>
```

The message informs you that DOS has successfully copied the 31 files from the Master Operating diskette.

Step 5. Remove the Startup diskette (or the Master Operating diskette, if you followed Step 4) from drive A.

Place the formatted diskette you labeled "DOS V3.x Master Diskette" into drive A. Type

```
A>COPY C:\BIN A: /V
```

The disk drive lights will alternate, file names will appear on the screen, and within a minute or so you should see the following message:

```
        5Ø File(s) copied
A>
```

The message indicates that the copying of the DOS files was successful.

If you wish, you can skim the directions in the section for 360K disk drive users and join us at "Steps 6/7 for All Others."

Steps for Users of 360K Floppy Disk Drives

If you have a fixed disk and a 360K disk drive, this section is for you. You will need the two formatted diskettes you made earlier.

Step 1. Place your copy of the DOS Startup diskette into drive A.

Before you do Step 2, make sure your fixed disk is set up. If it is not, see Appendix E for instructions.

Step 2. Type

```
A>MKDIR C:\BIN
```

This command creates a new BIN directory on your fixed disk.

If you see a message that DOS is unable to create the subdirectory, the subdirectory already exists. You may have created the directory earlier (which happened if you followed the instructions in Appendix E). Since you need a "fresh" directory for this exercise, let's change the command. Type

```
A>MKDIR C:\DOS
```

This command creates a directory named DOS. If you make a DOS directory, remember to substitute DOS for BIN in the following instructions. If you forget, the exercise will not work properly.

Step 3. Copy the files from your Startup diskette to the BIN directory by typing

```
A>COPY A:*.* C:\BIN /V
```

You will see a light go on, first on the floppy disk drive. Then the light for the fixed disk drive will go on. The disk drive lights will alternate and file names will appear on the screen as the files are copied.

Notice the /V switch you typed. This switch tells COPY to *verify* that the copy being made of each file is correct. Many DOS commands use the same switch, but the meaning of the switch varies among the commands. For example, the /V means *volume label* to the FORMAT command, but *verify* to the COPY command. Watch out for this distinction.

Shortly, you'll see the following message:

```
      22 File(s) copied
```

The message on the screen tells you that the copying was successful.

Step 4. *Remove the Startup diskette from drive A.*

Place the formatted diskette you labeled "DOS V3.x Master Startup Diskette" into drive A. Type

```
A>COPY C:\BIN A: /V
```

The disk drive lights will alternate, file names will appear on the screen, and within a minute or so you should see the message:

```
      22 File(s) copied

A>
```

The message indicates that the copying of the DOS files was successful.

Step 5. *Remove the Master Startup diskette from drive A. Put the diskette in its envelope.*

Step 6. *Create a directory on your fixed disk to temporarily hold the files on the Operating or Supplemental Programs diskette.*

Type

```
A>MKDIR  C:\TMP
```

Step 7. *Place your copy of the Operating diskette (or the Supplemental Programs diskette if you are using a version of DOS before V3.3) into drive A.*

Copy the files to the temporary directory on the fixed disk by typing

```
A>COPY A:*.*  C:\TMP  /V
```

The disk drive lights will go on alternately, and file names will appear on the screen. You'll soon see the following message:

```
        31 File(s) copied

A>
```

The files from the Operating (or Supplemental Programs) diskette have been copied successfully.

Step 8. *Take the Operating diskette from drive A and place the diskette in its envelope.*

Take the diskette you formatted and labeled "DOS V3.x Master Operating Diskette" and place it in drive A. Copy the files from the fixed disk to the floppy diskette by typing

```
A>COPY  C:\TMP  A:  /V
```

After the copy is complete, you'll see a message that 31 files were copied.

Step 9. Take the DOS Master Operating diskette out of drive A and put the diskette into its envelope.

Keep this and the Master Startup diskette handy. You'll need them in later chapters.

Step 10. Copy the Operating or Supplemental Programs files from the TMP directory to the BIN directory by typing

```
A>COPY C:\TMP C:\BIN /V
```

Step 11. Erase the files in the TMP subdirectory by typing

```
A>ERASE C:\TMP
```

DOS will respond with the message:

```
Are you sure (Y/N)?_
```

Because you have copied the files from the TMP directory to the BIN directory, your fixed disk now has two copies of the files, one in \TMP and one in \BIN. You need only one copy, so you may safely remove the files in TMP. Answer Y for yes; then DOS removes the files in TMP.

I suggest that you do not remove the TMP subdirectory after the files are erased. You will have uses for this subdirectory later when you need to copy files between diskettes and do not want to use the DISKCOPY command.

Steps 12/13 for 360K Users; Steps 6/7 for All Others

Step 6/12 is only for those who have followed the procedures in Appendix E. Step 7/13 is only for those who have *not* followed the procedures in Appendix E.

In Step 6/12, which should be performed if and only if you have followed the procedures in Appendix E, you will erase the files in the DOS directory and remove the directory.

Step 6/12. To erase the files in the DOS subdirectory, type

```
A>ERASE C:\DOS
```

DOS will respond with the message:

```
Are you sure (Y/N)?_
```

Because the files in the DOS subdirectory are already in BIN, and you need only one copy of these files, you may safely remove the files in DOS. Answer **Y** for yes and DOS removes the files in the DOS directory.

Now remove the DOS subdirectory by typing

```
A>RMDIR C:\DOS
```

The fixed disk drive light will flash briefly and the A> prompt will reappear. You have removed the DOS subdirectory.

You're done for now (Step 7/13 is only for those who have not followed the procedures in Appendix E). If you like, you can skim the directions for other computer setups before you continue.

Step 7/13 is for those who have *not* followed the procedures in Appendix E. If you have followed those procedures, skip to the next section.

Step 7/13. Type

```
A>PATH C:\BIN;C:\
```

Do not put any spaces in the line except between the word PATH and the
first C. Be careful that you do not confuse the semicolons with colons.
(For now, don't worry about what this command does. The PATH
command will be explained in detail in Chapter 10.)

Remember to type this line whenever you start your computer, after you
either turn on the computer or reset the system. After you read Chapter
12, you'll be able to execute this command automatically.

You're done for now. If you like, you can skim the directions for other
computer setups before continuing.

Copying with a Single Floppy Disk Drive

Everyone should read all the following instructions. This section shows
how a single disk drive is actually two different disk drives.

If you have a computer with a single floppy disk drive, you can do the
steps if you like after you read the instructions. Reading the instructions is
strongly suggested, because the actual copying process requires that you
exchange diskettes from a minimum of 44 times (if you are copying the
360K minifloppy Startup diskette) to 100 times (if you are copying the
720K Startup/Operating diskette). Labeling the single disk copying process
"laborious" vastly understates the issue. If you have a single floppy disk
drive and no other type of disk drive, I strongly encourage you to use the
DISKCOPY command (which takes about one-tenth the time this
procedure takes). Otherwise, try to borrow a friend's computer that has
two floppy disk drives.

Directions are provided for copying the DOS Startup diskette, which has
22 files for the minifloppy version. The same basic directions apply to
copying the minifloppy DOS Operating diskette (31 files) or the Startup/
Operating diskette (50 files). If you are dedicated to trying the procedure,
be aware that the process takes from 10 to 25 minutes per diskette to
complete. You'll need one formatted diskette for each diskette to be
copied.

Step 1. *Place the DOS Startup diskette into drive A.*

Step 2. *Start the copying process by typing*

```
A>COPY A:*.* B: /V
```

Two items on the command line may seem unusual to you. If you have read the other sections of this chapter, you already know the /V switch, which means that the COPY command should *verify* that the copy being made is correct. You also know that some DOS commands use the same switch, but that the switch has different meanings to each command. The COPY command uses the /V switch to *verify*, but the FORMAT command uses the same switch for a *volume label*. The distinction is important.

The second unusual item is the B:, the disk drive where the command will place a copy of your files. Where is drive B? Follow the remaining steps to see. In the section that follows Step 6, I'll explain how one disk drive can become two.

After you have entered the command, the disk drive light will come on, and the name of the first file that will be copied will appear on the screen. Then this message will appear:

```
Insert diskette for drive B: and strike
any key when ready
```

Step 3. *Take the Startup diskette out of drive A. Insert the diskette you formatted and labeled previously.*

The label should be DOS V3.x Master Startup if you are copying the minifloppy Startup diskette, DOS V3.x Master Operating if you are copying the minifloppy Operating diskette, or DOS V3.x Master Diskette if you are copying the microfloppy diskette or a master diskette for a version of DOS before V3.3.

Press a key. The disk drive light will go on, and another file name will appear on the screen. Then this message will appear:

```
Insert diskette for drive A: and strike
any key when ready
```

Step 4. *Take the formatted diskette out of the disk drive.*

Insert the diskette you are copying, such as the DOS Startup diskette, into the disk drive. Press any key.

Step 5. *Each time one of the* insert diskette *messages appears, exchange diskettes and press any key.*

Continue this process until the following message appears:

```
    22 File(s) copied
```

This message indicates that the COPY command has successfully copied 22 files and has completed its work. If you are copying a different diskette, the number of files displayed and the number displayed in this message will be different.

Step 6. *Remove the diskette from the disk drive.*

If you are using a minifloppy diskette, place the diskette back into its envelope. Store the original diskettes in a safe place.

You're done.

How One Disk Drive Can Be Two

In the last exercise, you used the command

COPY A:*.* B: /V

to copy files on a computer with a single floppy disk drive. Where was drive B? A clue came when DOS prompted you to insert a diskette for drive B and you inserted the diskette into the same disk drive you had been using. Drive A is the same disk drive as drive B.

When you have only one floppy disk drive, DOS makes two "logical" disk drives out of the single physical disk drive. In computerese, *logical* means apparent. Although you may have only one physical disk drive, DOS treats the real disk drive as if it were two different disk drives.

DOS keeps track of which logical disk drive you are using. When you request a different logical disk drive, DOS stops the program you are using and instructs you to insert the proper diskette and to tap a key. If the correct diskette is already in the disk drive, just tap a key. Otherwise, insert the proper diskette and tap a key. DOS then permits the program to continue running.

The best use of the second logical disk drive is to copy a couple of files between diskettes. You simply give the COPY command as if you have two disk drives. DOS then uses the single disk as if it were two physically different disk drives. The only difference is that you must exchange diskettes and press a key each time. Copying more than a few files this way, however, becomes boring—real fast.

If you have a fixed disk drive and need to copy files between diskettes, use the technique shown in the exercise for copying between floppy and fixed disks. Copy the files from the floppy diskette into the subdirectory TMP. The command would be

A>COPY A:filename.ext C:\TMP /V

where **filename.ext** is the name of the file or files you want to copy. Then place in the disk drive the target diskette you want to copy, and type

A>COPY C:\TMP A: /V

This command copies the file from the TMP subdirectory to the second floppy diskette. After the copying is completed, remove the files from the fixed disk by typing

A>ERASE C:\TMP

DOS will then display the Are you sure (Y/N)? message. Answer **Y** for yes, and the files you have copied to the floppy diskette will be erased from the TMP subdirectory on the fixed disk. This technique is faster and simpler than using the "two-in-one" copying approach.

Summary

In this chapter, you used the FORMAT and COPY commands of DOS. The key points to remember are the following:

1. FORMAT prepares new diskettes for use.

2. COPY copies individual files.

3. Many DOS commands have switches that affect the way each command works.

4. To give a switch, you type a slash (/) and then the character for the switch (for example, /V or /S).

5. Some switches have different meanings to different DOS commands. For example, the /V switch means *volume label* to the FORMAT command but *verify* to the COPY command.

6. On a computer with one floppy disk drive (or an external disk drive), DOS enables you to use that floppy disk drive as if it were two disk drives.

The next chapter reviews most of the commands you have used and provides information about file names.

3

Learning Basic DOS Commands

In the first two chapters, you used several DOS commands to prepare diskettes and to copy files and diskettes. In this chapter and in Chapter 4, we'll discuss further the commands you used and introduce additional DOS commands. You'll also learn some more key DOS concepts and some basics about file names. This chapter and the next are the most important chapters of this survival course on DOS—a quick start if you are beginning to use a computer. Additional information about the commands that are presented in these chapters is included later in the book.

This chapter contains additional hands-on exercises for which you will need DOS running on your computer. If your computer is off, place the copy of the DOS Startup diskette you made in Chapter 1 into the disk drive and turn on the computer. If your computer is already on, have the DOS Startup diskette ready. If you use 360K minifloppy disk drives, have the copy of the Operating diskette handy as well. You'll use it for some exercises in this chapter. Also have on hand the DOS Master diskette (or the Master Startup and Master Operating diskettes) you created in Chapter 2.

Getting a List of Files (DIR)

You will recall that you use the DIR command to see a list of the files you have on your disk. The *directory* is the area of the disk where the list of files is kept. DIR is the second most frequently used DOS command. (The most frequently used DOS command is COPY, which is discussed in more detail in Chapter 4.)

With the copy of the DOS Startup diskette in drive A, type

```
A>DIR
```

You should see a list of files appear on your screen. The top part of the list will move off the top of the screen. Don't worry about that now. You'll soon learn how to stop the screen's movement.

The following list of files is a full directory of the microfloppy DOS Master diskette for V3.3. (The minifloppy version of DOS V3.3 will show fewer files and number of bytes free.)

```
A>DIR A:

Volume in drive A has no label
Directory of  A:\

COMMAND   COM     25307    3-17-87    12:00p
ANSI      SYS      1678    3-17-87    12:00p
APPEND    EXE      5825    3-17-87    12:00p
ASSIGN    COM      1561    3-17-87    12:00p
ATTRIB    EXE      9529    3-17-87    12:00p
BACKUP    COM     31913    3-18-87    12:00p
BASIC     COM      1063    3-17-87    12:00p
BASICA    COM     36403    3-17-87    12:00p
CHKDSK    COM      9850    3-18-87    12:00p
COMP      COM      4214    3-17-87    12:00p
COUNTRY   SYS     11285    3-17-87    12:00p
DEBUG     COM     15897    3-17-87    12:00p
DISKCOMP  COM      5879    3-17-87    12:00p
DISKCOPY  COM      6295    3-17-87    12:00p
DISPLAY   SYS     11290    3-17-87    12:00p
DRIVER    SYS      1196    3-17-87    12:00p
EDLIN     COM      7526    3-17-87    12:00p
FASTOPEN  EXE      3919    3-17-87    12:00p
FDISK     COM     48216    3-18-87    12:00p
FIND      EXE      6434    3-17-87    12:00p
FORMAT    COM     11616    3-18-87    12:00p
```

```
GRAFTABL COM      6128     3-17-87    12:00p
GRAPHICS COM      3300     3-17-87    12:00p
JOIN     EXE      8969     3-17-87    12:00p
KEYB     COM      9056     3-17-87    12:00p
KEYBOARD SYS     19766     3-17-87    12:00p
LABEL    COM      2377     3-17-87    12:00p
MODE     COM     15487     3-17-87    12:00p
MORE     COM       313     3-17-87    12:00p
NLSFUNC  EXE      3060     3-17-87    12:00p
PRINT    COM      9026     3-17-87    12:00p
PRINTER  SYS     13590     3-17-87    12:00p
RECOVER  COM      4299     3-18-87    12:00p
REPLACE  EXE     11775     3-17-87    12:00p
RESTORE  COM     34643     3-17-87    12:00p
SELECT   COM      4163     3-17-87    12:00p
SHARE    EXE      8608     3-17-87    12:00p
SORT     EXE      1977     3-17-87    12:00p
SUBST    EXE      9909     3-17-87    12:00p
SYS      COM      4766     3-17-87    12:00p
TREE     COM      3571     3-17-87    12:00p
VDISK    SYS      3455     3-17-87    12:00p
XCOPY    EXE     11247     3-17-87    12:00p
EGA      CPI     49065     3-18-87    12:00p
LCD      CPI     10752     3-17-87    12:00p
4201     CPI     17089     3-18-87    12:00p
5202     CPI       459     3-17-87    12:00p
BASIC    PIF       369     3-17-87    12:00p
BASICA   PIF       369     3-17-87    12:00p
MORTGAGE BAS      6251     3-17-87    12:00p
        50 File(s)      128512 bytes free

A>_
```

Take a look at the first two lines of the directory listing. The first line shows the disk drive whose directory is displayed and the electronic volume label for the disk. This diskette has no volume label. Because the original DOS Startup/Operating diskette did not have a volume label, its copy does not have a label either.

The next line shows the disk drive and directory you are viewing. The directory is A:\. This means that you are viewing the main directory of the diskette in drive A. DOS V3 disk directories will be explained in greater detail in Chapter 10.

Now look at the line that begins with COMMAND COM. (For DOS V3.1, the listing is on the tenth line; for other versions of DOS, the listing is on the fourth line.) The directory listing for COMMAND.COM is repeated in figure 3.1.

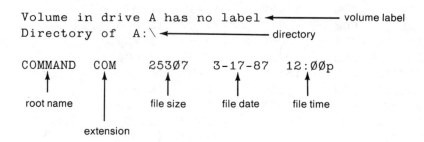

Fig. 3.1. *The elements of a directory listing.*

COMMAND.COM is one of the three files of DOS itself. The listing consists of the *root name* of the file, one or more spaces, and the suffix, or *extension*. The next number is the size of the file, followed by the file's date and time of creation. When an established file is changed, the file's date and time reflect when the file was altered. The date and time of the computer is the basis for the file's date and time "stamp" in the directory.

Now look at the last line of the directory listing. If you are using microfloppy diskettes, the line is

```
    5Ø File(s)      128512 bytes free

A>
```

If you are using the minifloppy Startup diskette, the line is

```
    22 File(s)       9216 bytes free

A>
```

The first number on each line shows how many files were displayed, and the second number shows how much free space is on the disk. The second figure is usually the most important. It tells you how much room is left on the diskette for adding new files or expanding older files.

Freezing the Screen
(Ctrl-S, Ctrl-Num Lock, Pause)

In the preceding exercise, you noticed that some of the lines of the directory list scrolled off the top of the screen before you could read them. The problem of missing information in this manner is not uncommon. Fortunately, DOS provides several keystroke controls to stop, or freeze, the scrolling of the screen.

To try these keystrokes, type

A>DIR

As the list begins to scroll by, hold down the Ctrl key and press the S key. The screen should freeze. If the directory has already gone by, type DIR again and try pressing Ctrl-S again. To start the screen moving again, press any key. To freeze the screen again, press Ctrl-S again.

A second way to freeze the screen is using Ctrl-Num Lock (holding down the Ctrl key and pressing the Num Lock key at the top of the numeric keypad). I find, however, that Ctrl-S is easier to use on the older keyboards because it takes only my left hand to press the key sequence. To press Ctrl-Num Lock, I must use my left hand to hold the Ctrl key while tapping Num Lock with my right hand.

The easiest key sequence that freezes the screen is available on the enhanced keyboards. The Pause key is located on the same key with Break, to the immediate left of the green Num Lock indicator light. Pressing this key accomplishes the same freezing action as the Ctrl-S or Ctrl-Num Lock sequence. To restart the screen, press any key.

Making the DIR Command More Convenient (DIR /W, DIR /P)

Ctrl-S, Ctrl-Num Lock, and Pause are helpful in freezing the screen so you can read the display produced by the DIR command. The DIR command also has two switches that can make the command more convenient to use. The switches are /P for *pause* and /W for *wide*.

The /P switch pauses the listing of the files after 23 lines of files are displayed. When you press a key, the next set of file names is displayed. You use this switch when a directory is long, you don't want the listing to scroll off the screen, and you don't want to use the freeze-screen keys to hold the screen. The disadvantage of using the /P switch is that the top few lines that contain the volume label, disk drive name, and path leave the screen before DIR pauses. You must use the freeze-screen keys to see these lines on long displays.

The /W switch gives a wide display of the directory listing. Five file names are displayed per line. This switch is useful when you are looking for one or a few specific file names in long directories. The disadvantage is that the file size, the DIR symbol for directories, and the file date and time are not displayed.

Try using these switches by first typing

> **A>DIR /P**

Then type

> **A>DIR /W**

The following screens show what I saw when I used the /P and /W switches with the DIR command on my copy of the microfloppy DOS Startup/Operating diskette. Remember that the first few lines of the directory roll off the top of the screen before DIR pauses.

```
A>DIR A: /P

 Volume in drive A has no label
 Directory of  A:\

 COMMAND   COM    25307    3-17-87   12:00p
 ANSI      SYS     1678    3-17-87   12:00p
 APPEND    EXE     5825    3-17-87   12:00p
 ASSIGN    COM     1561    3-17-87   12:00p
 ATTRIB    EXE     9529    3-17-87   12:00p
 BACKUP    COM    31913    3-18-87   12:00p
 BASIC     COM     1063    3-17-87   12:00p
 BASICA    COM    36403    3-17-87   12:00p
 CHKDSK    COM     9850    3-18-87   12:00p
 COMP      COM     4214    3-17-87   12:00p
 COUNTRY   SYS    11285    3-17-87   12:00p
 DEBUG     COM    15897    3-17-87   12:00p
 DISKCOMP  COM     5879    3-17-87   12:00p
 DISKCOPY  COM     6295    3-17-87   12:00p
 DISPLAY   SYS    11290    3-17-87   12:00p
 DRIVER    SYS     1196    3-17-87   12:00p
 EDLIN     COM     7526    3-17-87   12:00p
 FASTOPEN  EXE     3919    3-17-87   12:00p
 FDISK     COM    48216    3-18-87   12:00p
 FIND      EXE     6434    3-17-87   12:00p
 FORMAT    COM    11616    3-18-87   12:00p
 GRAFTABL  COM     6128    3-17-87   12:00p
 GRAPHICS  COM     3300    3-17-87   12:00p
 Strike a key when ready...
```

```
Strike a key when ready...
JOIN       EXE       8969    3-17-87    12:00p
KEYB       COM       9056    3-17-87    12:00p
KEYBOARD   SYS      19766    3-17-87    12:00p
LABEL      COM       2377    3-17-87    12:00p
MODE       COM      15487    3-17-87    12:00p
MORE       COM        313    3-17-87    12:00p
NLSFUNC    EXE       3060    3-17-87    12:00p
PRINT      COM       9026    3-17-87    12:00p
PRINTER    SYS      13590    3-17-87    12:00p
RECOVER    COM       4299    3-18-87    12:00p
REPLACE    EXE      11775    3-17-87    12:00p
RESTORE    COM      34643    3-17-87    12:00p
SELECT     COM       4163    3-17-87    12:00p
SHARE      EXE       8608    3-17-87    12:00p
SORT       EXE       1977    3-17-87    12:00p
SUBST      EXE       9909    3-17-87    12:00p
SYS        COM       4766    3-17-87    12:00p
TREE       COM       3571    3-17-87    12:00p
VDISK      SYS       3455    3-17-87    12:00p
XCOPY      EXE      11247    3-17-87    12:00p
EGA        CPI      49065    3-18-87    12:00p
LCD        CPI      10752    3-17-87    12:00p
4201       CPI      17089    3-18-87    12:00p
Strike a key when ready...
```

```
NLSFUNC    EXE       3060    3-17-87    12:00p
PRINT      COM       9026    3-17-87    12:00p
PRINTER    SYS      13590    3-17-87    12:00p
RECOVER    COM       4299    3-18-87    12:00p
REPLACE    EXE      11775    3-17-87    12:00p
RESTORE    COM      34643    3-17-87    12:00p
SELECT     COM       4163    3-17-87    12:00p
SHARE      EXE       8608    3-17-87    12:00p
SORT       EXE       1977    3-17-87    12:00p
SUBST      EXE       9909    3-17-87    12:00p
SYS        COM       4766    3-17-87    12:00p
```

```
TREE      COM      3571    3-17-87   12:00p
VDISK     SYS      3455    3-17-87   12:00p
XCOPY     EXE     11247    3-17-87   12:00p
EGA       CPI     49065    3-18-87   12:00p
LCD       CPI     10752    3-17-87   12:00p
4201      CPI     17089    3-18-87   12:00p
Strike a key when ready...
5202      CPI       459    3-17-87   12:00p
BASIC     PIF       369    3-17-87   12:00p
BASICA    PIF       369    3-17-87   12:00p
MORTGAGE  BAS      6251    3-17-87   12:00p
        50 File(s)     128512 bytes free

C>
```

```
A> DIR A: /W

Volume in drive A has no label
Directory of   A:\

    COMMAND   COM   ANSI      SYS   APPEND    EXE   ASSIGN    COM   ATTRIB    EXE
    BACKUP    COM   BASIC     COM   BASICA    COM   CHKDSK    COM   COMP      COM
    COUNTRY   SYS   DEBUG     COM   DISKCOMP  COM   DISKCOPY  COM   DISPLAY   SYS
    DRIVER    SYS   EDLIN     COM   FASTOPEN  EXE   FDISK     COM   FIND      EXE
    FORMAT    COM   GRAFTABL  COM   GRAPHICS  COM   JOIN      EXE   KEYB      COM
    KEYBOARD  SYS   LABEL     COM   MODE      COM   MORE      COM   NLSFUNC   EXE
    PRINT     COM   PRINTER   SYS   RECOVER   COM   REPLACE   EXE   RESTORE   COM
    SELECT    COM   SHARE     EXE   SORT      EXE   SUBST     EXE   SYS       COM
    TREE      COM   VDISK     SYS   XCOPY     EXE   EGA       CPI   LCD       CPI
    4201      CPI   5202      CPI   BASIC     PIF   BASICA    PIF   MORTGAGE  BAS
        50 File(s)     128512 bytes free
```

Printing What Appears on the Screen

Often you will need a printed copy of what you see on the video screen.
The next two DOS controls allow you to print the screen display. Before
you move on, try the exercises in this section only if you have a printer
attached to your computer.

Printing What You Send to the Screen (Ctrl-PrtSc, Ctrl-P)

You can print what you send to the screen with the PrtSc key (Print Screen on newer keyboards). The PrtSc key on older keyboards is a tan key that is also an asterisk [*] key (see figs. 3.2 and 3.3). On the newer keyboards, the Print Screen key is a tan key between the F12 key and the Scroll Lock key on the upper right side of the keyboard (see figure 3.4).

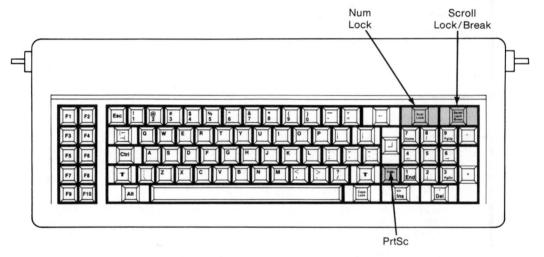

Fig. 3.2. *The PrtSc (Print Screen), Num Lock, and Scroll Lock/Break keys on a Personal Computer keyboard.*

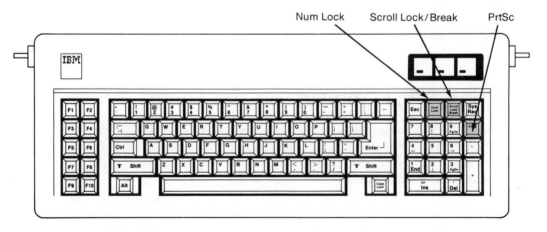

Fig. 3.3. *The PrtSc (Print Screen), Num Lock, and Scroll Lock/Break keys on a Personal Computer AT keyboard.*

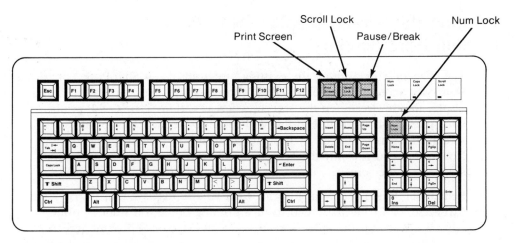

Fig. 3.4. *The Print Screen, Num Lock, Scroll Lock, and Pause/Break keys on an Enhanced Keyboard.*

Make sure that the printer is on and ready to print. Hold down the Ctrl key and press either the PrtSc or Print Screen key. Then type

A>DIR

Notice that whatever appears on the screen is also printed. To turn off the printing, press the Ctrl-PrtSc or Ctrl-Print Screen sequence again.

Ctrl-P works the same way as Ctrl-PrtSc and Ctrl-Print Screen. Any one of the key sequences sends whatever is written to the video display to the printer as well.

To print a long directory listing, turn on the printing with either Ctrl-P (which I prefer), Ctrl-PrtSc (old keyboards), or Ctrl-Print Screen (enhanced keyboards) and then do the DIR command. Again press Ctrl-P, Ctrl-PrtSc, or Control-Print Screen to turn off the printing.

Printing the Screen Display (Shift-PrtSc or Shift-Print Screen)

The sequence for printing the existing screen display is Shift-PrtSc (or Shift-Print Screen on the enhanced keyboards). Shift-PrtSc prints the display that is already on the screen, whereas Ctrl-PrtSc or Ctrl-P prints what goes to the screen. Use the Shift-PrtSc key sequence to print the screen that was produced by the DIR command in the preceding section. Notice that you get only the last part of the directory list. The first part scrolled off the screen.

Remember, when you want to print what will be displayed, use Ctrl-P, Ctrl-PrtSc, or Ctrl-Print Screen to turn printing on. If you want to print what is already on the video screen, use Shift-PrtSc or Shift-Print Screen.

Naming Your Files

A *file* is simply related information stored by DOS under a single name. Chapter 8 presents more information about files, but this definition will do for now.

As mentioned previously, a file has one or two parts to its name: the root name and the extension. The file name consists of the root name (1 to 8 characters), a period if you are using an extension, and the extension (1 to 3 characters). Look at the following file name:

```
COMMAND.COM
```

This file's root name is COMMAND. The root name can be from one to eight characters long. COM is the file's extension, which can be from one to three characters long. Every file must have a root name, but the extension is optional. If you use an extension, you separate the root name from the extension with a period (.).

Many computerists verbalize file names by giving the file's root name, using the word "dot" for the period, and then pronouncing the extension, if possible, or spelling the extension. For example, I call this file "command dot com."

Although the DIR command lists each file name with one or more spaces between the root name and the extension, you cannot insert a space into a file name. Certain other characters are also not allowed in a file name. For now, use alphabetic characters and Arabic numerals. Chapter 8 contains some examples of legal and illegal file-name characters.

Using Wildcard Characters
for Speed and Ease (? *)

You can use two special characters with file names. These are called
wildcard characters. The power of wildcard characters is that you can use
them to make one file name match a number of files. Wildcards are used
most frequently with the DIR command.

The two characters are

?   Matches any one character in the file name

*   Matches any number of characters in the file name

Naturally, when you name a disk file, you cannot use either ? or * in the
file name. These characters are reserved for the many DOS commands that
accept wildcard characters in a file name that is part of the command line.

When you use a file name that contains one of these characters, your file
name becomes *ambiguous*. In other words, the file name you give can
match more than one file on the disk. Wildcards are allowed in some
programs and DOS commands but not in others.

Both ? and * can even match places in file names where no characters
appear. For example, the file name

   WORDS?

matches the files

   WORDS1   WORDST
   WORDSA   WORDS

In the case of the file name WORDS, the ? matches the nonexistent
character after the S in the file's root name.

These wildcard characters work with many DOS commands. Try using
some wildcard characters with the DIR command. Don't worry about
mistakes in typing here. You cannot harm any files by giving the DIR
command.

Begin by inserting into drive A the DOS Startup diskette you made. Make
sure that the door is closed. Now type the following commands:

   1. A>DIR *.COM

      This command shows a directory listing of any file whose
      extension is COM.

2. A>DIR D*.COM

This command shows a directory listing of any file whose root name begins with the letter D and whose extension is COM.

3. A>DIR KEY*.*

This command shows a directory listing of any file whose root name begins with the three letters KEY. The file name can have any extension.

4. A>DIR MO?E.COM

This command shows a directory listing for any file whose root name begins with the letters MO, whose fourth character in the root name is E, and whose extension is COM. The ? matches any character in the third position of the root name.

Wildcard characters make many DOS commands easy to use. But wildcards can make a file name match more files than you want. The most common ambiguous file name is *.*, which matches every file in the directory. This file name is most potentially dangerous when it is used with the ERASE command, which is discussed in Chapter 4. You'll learn more in Chapter 4 about wildcard characters and when to be especially cautious with them.

Changing the Current Disk Drive

You can run any DOS command while you are at the system prompt. The system prompt is the A> or C> symbol that appears on the screen. When you see this symbol, you know that DOS is ready to accept a command.

The system prompt indicates the current disk drive. The *current disk drive* is the drive where DOS searches for commands. If the command you want to use is not on the current disk drive, you must specify the disk drive to be searched. In some cases, if you don't supply additional information for a command, the command operates on the current disk drive.

The letter in the system prompt tells you the current disk drive. When you see A>, the current disk drive is drive A. Because A is the most frequently used disk drive on non-hard-disk systems, the system prompt is sometimes called the "A prompt." A B> system prompt tells you that drive B is the current drive. And C> indicates that drive C, the fixed disk, is the current disk drive.

To change the current disk drive, you simply type the letter of the disk drive followed by a colon and press Enter. For example, to change the current disk drive to C, you type C: and press Enter. The system prompt changes to C>, showing that drive C is the current disk drive (see fig. 3.5). To make drive A the current disk drive again, type A: and press Enter.

To make drive C the current disk drive

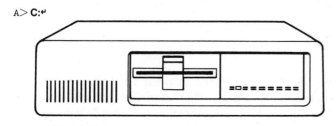

To make drive A the current disk drive

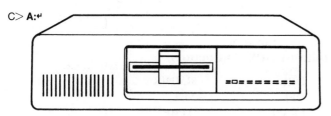

Fig. 3.5. *Changing current disk drives.*

In the hands-on practice session at the end of this chapter, you'll practice changing disk drives.

Running DOS Commands

To run any DOS command, you type its root name and press Enter. The only complication in running commands is knowing whether the command is always available, or whether you must load the command from the disk before the command can be run.

DOS has both internal and external commands. *Internal* commands are built into DOS and can be executed at any time. You do not need a diskette in the disk drive in order to start these commands. You can run them whenever the DOS system prompt appears, without having to load a program from a disk.

External commands are disk-based commands that reside on the DOS disk. To execute such a command, the disk that holds the command must be in the disk drive, and you must load the command from the disk. An example is the DISKCOPY command, which you used in Chapter 1.

Internal Commands

DOS has 21 built-in commands. These are listed in table 3.1. For now, don't worry about what each command does. Their functions are discussed in detail later in the book. To use a built-in command, you simply type its name at the DOS system prompt. Some commands need more information than the command name. That, too, is explained later.

Table 3.1
Built-In DOS Commands

BREAK	DIR	RMDIR
CHCP	DEL	SET
CHDIR	ERASE	TIME
CLS	MKDIR	TYPE
COPY	PATH	VER
CTTY	PROMPT	VERIFY
DATE	RENAME	VOL

External Commands

To use an external command (a DOS command that is not listed in table 3.1), you must type its root name. Use the form

   *d:*dos_command

The *d:* is the name of the disk drive that holds the DOS command. dos_command is the root name of the DOS command. Typing the name of the disk drive is optional. If the command is on the current disk drive, you can omit the disk drive name. If the command is on a different disk drive, you must give the disk drive followed immediately by the command's root name. Do not put a space between the name of the disk drive and the root name of the command.

Hands-on Practice: Using an External Command To Check Disk Capacity (CHKDSK)

In the following exercise, separate directions are provided for users whose computers have two floppy disk drives (identical or different) and for users whose computers have one floppy disk drive and one fixed disk. If you fit both categories, try both examples.

If your system has two floppy disk drives, put a diskette into drive A. The diskette should be the one that holds some files. Put a diskette that holds the CHKDSK program into drive B. (You can use the DOS Master Diskette you made in Chapter 2. If, however, drive B is a 360K disk drive, put in drive B the copy of the DOS Operating diskette you made in Chapter 1 or the Master Operating diskette you made in Chapter 2.)

If you are using a fixed disk, CHKDSK should be on the fixed disk. Put a diskette that holds some files into drive A. If drive A is not the current drive (that is, if the system prompt doesn't say A>), make drive A the current drive. (Type A: and press Enter.)

To run the CHKDSK command on a two floppy disk drive system, type

```
A>B:CHKDSK
```

Users who have a fixed disk system will type

```
A>C:CHKDSK
```

Notice how the command is phrased. The disk drive name and the root name of the program are given, but the extension COM is not needed.

What happened when you typed the command? Did you see what you expected?

Because you used a disk drive name in front of the command name, DOS was directed to get the CHKDSK program from drive B or from drive C. DOS got the program from one of these disk drives. This is exactly what you told DOS to do.

However, CHKDSK analyzed the diskette in drive A. Why? You didn't tell CHKDSK which disk to analyze. The explanation is that CHKDSK did not find a disk drive name after the word CHKDSK. Therefore, the current disk drive, drive A, was analyzed.

Unless you tell DOS otherwise, DOS always uses the current disk drive to run a program and to be the object of an action. In this case, the action (CHKDSK) was to analyze the disk. Drive A, the current disk drive, was automatically the object of the action. Understanding this concept is important.

To analyze the disk in drive B or the fixed disk (C), you have the following two options:

1. Make the drive that holds CHKDSK the current disk drive and then run CHKDSK.

2. Tell CHKDSK which disk drive to check.

To use the first option, enter the following:

(For diskette users)   (For fixed-disk users)

```
A>B:
B>CHKDSK
```

```
A>C:
C>CHKDSK
```

To use the second option, enter

(For diskette users)   (For fixed-disk users)

```
A>B:CHKDSK B:
```

```
A>C:CHKDSK C:
```

Try both options.

Most DOS commands expect some additional information when you type command lines. The additional information required is called a *parameter* or an *argument*. The two terms have identical meanings and can be freely interchanged. For the line

A>**CHKDSK B:**

the **B:** is a parameter. It directs CHKDSK to check the diskette in drive B. Notice the space between the command CHKDSK and the **B.** You must put a space between a command name and a parameter. You must also use spaces between any two parameters. If you omit the space, DOS becomes confused, and commands do not work the way they should.

Summary

In this chapter, you learned the following key points:

1. The DIR command gives you a list of files.

2. Ctrl-S, Ctrl-Num Lock, or Pause freezes a screen as it scrolls.

3. Either Ctrl-P, Ctrl-PrtSc, or Control-Print Screen immediately sends to the printer the same characters that are printed on the screen. You turn off the function by again pressing Ctrl-P, Ctrl-PrtSc, or Control-Print Screen.

4. Shift-PrtSc prints what is already on the screen.

5. The DIR command has two switches: /P for pausing the screen display and /W for showing a wide display.

6. A file name has two parts: the root name, which is one to eight characters long, and the optional extension, which is one to three characters long. If you have an extension, you separate the root name from the extension with a period.

7. The wildcard character ? matches a single character in a file name. The wildcard character * matches all remaining characters in a root name or extension.

8. Typing the appropriate letter followed by a colon and pressing Enter changes the current disk drive.

9. To run an internal command, you type the name of the command when the DOS system prompt (such as A>) appears.

10. For DOS to run an external command, the disk that holds the command must be in a disk drive. If the current disk drive holds the command, you simply type the root name of the command (such as CHKDSK). If the current disk drive does not hold the command, you precede the command name with the name of the disk drive that holds the command (such as A:CHKDSK or C:CHKDSK).

11. Some commands accept additional information, called *parameters* or *arguments*. If you do not provide this additional information, most DOS commands work on the current disk drive.

Chapter 4 introduces the command RENAME and provides more discussion of the commands COPY, DISKCOPY, and ERASE.

4

Gaining More Control over Your Files

This chapter completes your survival training and covers the remaining frequently used DOS commands. The new commands discussed are RENAME, the command that changes a file name, and ERASE, the command that removes files from disks. You'll also learn more about using the COPY and DISKCOPY commands.

For the hands-on exercises in the chapter, you'll need your computer ready to go with DOS running, and you'll need a formatted diskette. Follow the directions for the FORMAT command in Chapter 2 if you need to prepare a diskette. If you like, use the /V switch to make a volume label, such as "Practice." If you don't have a fixed disk, you'll also need the DOS Master diskette (or diskettes if you are using the 360K floppy diskettes) you made in Chapter 2.

More on Copying Files (COPY, /V)

The COPY command copies files. You were introduced to this most frequently used DOS command in Chapter 2. This section presents more information about the COPY command and shows you how to make the command work the way you want it to.

Understanding the Syntax of the COPY Command

A command's syntax is simply the way the command is phrased. The easiest way to remember the syntax of the COPY command is to think of it in this manner:

COPY *where and what it is now* to
    where it is going and what it will be

The *where it is now* is the name of the disk drive that holds the files you want to copy. The *what it is now* is the name of the file you want to copy. The *where it is going* is the name of the disk drive where the copy of the file will be placed. And the *what it will be* is the new name of the file to be copied.

A more formal way of expressing the command is

COPY *source disk drive and file name* → *destination disk
    drive and new file name*

The COPY command accepts two file names. The first file name, the *source* file, tells DOS which file to copy. The source file name may be preceded by an optional disk drive name. The source file name can include the wildcard characters ? and *. By using wildcards with a single file name, you can match and copy several files at the same time.

The formal notation for source disk drive and source file name(s)—the file or files to be copied—is

*ds:*filenames.*exts*

ds: is the name of the disk drive that holds the file(s). If the source files are on the current disk drive, you may omit the disk drive name. Remember that if you use a disk drive name, you must place the colon between the disk drive letter and the file name, but you must not put a space before or after the colon.

filenames (the final *s* signifies *source*) is the name of the file or files to copy. You must give the root name, which can contain wildcards. The optional extension is *.exts*. If the file or files you will copy have an extension, you should give this extension. With the COPY command, you may also use wildcards in the extension. Don't forget to use the period between the root name and the extension and not to use a space between the root name and the extension.

Notice that *ds:* and *.exts* are in italic. As mentioned previously, when parts of a command appear in italic in this book, they are optional. If the source file is on the current disk drive, you can omit the disk drive name *ds:*. If the file does not have an extension, you omit the extension *.exts*.

Although letters or numbers may be added to file names in our notation, the limits on filename length discussed in Chapter 3 remain. Eight characters in the root name and three in the extension are the maximums.

To copy a file, you must provide at the very least the command name, **COPY**, and the source file name, **filenames**. Both parts of the command appear in boldface to indicate that you must give these parts.

The second file name, the destination file, tells DOS where to place the file or files that are to be copied. The destination can be just a disk drive name, or a new name for the file or files to be copied, or both. The notation for the destination is

   dd:filenamed.extd

dd: is the name of the disk drive to receive the copy of the file or files. If the destination is the current disk drive and the source is another drive, you can omit the disk drive name *dd:*.

filenamed.extd (the final *d* signifies *destination*) is the new name for the file or files copied. *filenamed* is the new root name, and *.extd* is the new extension. You may use wildcards in either part of the destination file name. If you give only the *filenamed*, that in itself will be the new name. To give an extension, you must give *filenamed* and specify that the new extension will be *.extd*.

The formal syntax for the COPY command is

   COPY *ds:***filenames.***exts dd:filenamed.extd* /V

All elements that contain an s are part of the source file name. All elements with a d are part of the destination file name. COPY also has several switches that affect how files are copied. The most frequently used switch, /V, verifies that the copy of the file is correct. The verify switch is given last.

Only the words **COPY** and **filenames**, which appear in boldface, are mandatory. All other information (disk drive names, destination file name, and the verify switch) may be optional.

Note that you cannot copy a file when the source and destination drives are the same drive unless the *filenames* and *filenamed* are different. In other words, you cannot copy a file onto itself. DOS gives you an error message if you try. Either the source and destination drives must be different, or the source and destination filenames must be different.

You give the destination disk drive name when you want to copy files between disk drives. You give a new destination file name when you want the copy of the file to have a different file name.

Now that you have more basic information on how the COPY command works, try using the command several different ways.

Hands-on Practice: Copying Files

For this practice session, make sure that DOS is running on your computer. You'll need two disk drives. If your computer has two floppy disk drives, you should put the DOS Master Diskette or Master Operating Diskette into drive A and a formatted diskette into drive B. Make sure that the current disk drive is drive A. (If necessary, type A: and then press Enter.)

Owners of fixed disks should place a formatted diskette into drive A. The current disk drive should be drive C. (If necessary, type C: and then press Enter.) The current directory should be the one that holds the DOS programs. If you set up your fixed disk as shown in Appendix E, issue a CHDIR \BIN command to change to the directory that holds the DOS programs. If you have not set up your fixed disk by using the instructions in Appendix E, change the BIN to the appropriate name for the directory holding DOS.

If you have two floppy disk drives, type

> A>COPY CHKDSK.COM B: /V

If you have a fixed disk, type

> C>COPY CHKDSK.COM A: /V

This command copies the file CHKDSK.COM to the diskette in drive B
(for users of floppy disk drives) or to the diskette in drive A (for users of
fixed disk drives). You should see the following message:

```
1 File(s) copied
```

If you see any other message, you have the wrong diskette in drive A, or
you are using the wrong directory on drive C. Either get the right diskette
or change to the correct directory.

Look at the screen for a few seconds. Do you remember using the COPY
command in Chapter 2? When you copied files in that chapter, you used
wildcard characters in the file name. When you copied CHKDSK, however,
you used a file name without a wildcard character. Do you remember any
difference between the video screen now and the video screen as it
appeared when you copied with wildcard file names?

The difference is that the COPY command does not display file names
when you use an unambiguous file name. If you use a file name that
contains wildcard characters, COPY displays the name of each file it
copies. If you do not use wildcard characters in the file name, COPY
displays the File(s) copied message, but does not display the name of
the file.

Now copy the Disk BASIC (BASIC.COM) and Advanced BASIC
(BASICA.COM) files. First, you'll want to ensure that the files you want to
copy are on the diskette or directory you are about to copy from. Use the
directory command, DIR, to look. Type

```
C>DIR BASIC*.*
```

If you are using floppy disk drives, you will see an A> in place of the C>.
In this example, I'll show the result from a computer with a fixed disk.

To look at the files, you used the name **BASIC*.***. You recall from Chapter
3 that the asterisk wildcard matches any characters in a file name. The
name **BASIC*** matches all names that start with BASIC and have any other

characters in the root name. The asterisk for the extension matches a file with any extension or none. The result is the display of any file name that starts with BASIC.

Your screen should display something like this:

```
C>DIR BASIC*.*

 Volume in drive C is
 Directory of C:\BIN

BASIC     COM     1Ø63    3-17-87   12:ØØp
BASICA    COM    364Ø3    3-17-87   12:ØØp
BASIC     PIF      369    3-17-87   12:ØØp
BASICA    PIF      369    3-17-87   12:ØØp
          4 File(s)    xxxxxx bytes free

C>
```

The display lists the two files you wish to copy, BASIC.COM and BASICA.COM. However, two other file names appear in the list: BASIC.PIF and BASICA.PIF. These files are *program information file*s that are used by IBM's windowing system software, TopView™, and Microsoft's windowing system software, Microsoft Windows®.

You have a problem. You wish to copy the files BASIC.COM and BASICA.COM, but not the two files that have the extension PIF. COPY is an all-or-nothing command. You can only use a single source file name. If you use the same name you gave to the directory command, you'll copy too many files. What should you do?

The obvious solution is to use different file names. You could give the COPY command twice, once for each file name. But why give the command twice when one command will do? Look again at the file names shown in the preceding screen. What source file name could we give to COPY that would match the two BASIC program files but omit the two program information files?

Actually, two different names could be used. The possible source file names are

BASIC?.COM

and

BASIC*.COM

Each file name starts with BASIC. BASICA.COM contains one more letter in the root file name than BASIC.COM. Hence, you can use the ? wildcard character in the sixth position of the root name to match the A in BASICA or the non-existent character after the C in BASIC. You can also use the asterisk to match all characters in the sixth through eighth position in the root file name. Hence, the file names BASIC?.COM and BASIC*.COM work equally well.

The key to making these names work is that you specify a particular extension, .COM. If you use the * for the extension, you will get all four files. By specifying .COM, you only get files with the extension .COM.

The file names BASIC?.COM and BASIC*.COM match any file whose first five characters are BASIC and whose extension is .COM. The name BASIC?.COM restricts the match to those files that have no character or any character in the sixth position, but do not have any characters in the seventh and eighth position. BASIC*.COM matches files that have any or no characters in the sixth through the eighth position in the root file name.

Although I can locate the * on my keyboard easier than I can the ?, the preferred file name and the one I use is BASIC?.COM. The reason for this choice is that using the asterisk wildcard rather than the question-mark character might lead to surprises, because the * matches more files than the ?.

In the case of copying the BASIC files, you know that you want to copy both files that match the name BASIC*.COM. There might be times, however, when you do not check the directory beforehand. When you are not absolutely sure of what files will be copied with a wildcard file name, use as restrictive a file name as possible—in this case BASIC?.COM. When you know what files will be copied, you may use the * wildcard with impunity. We'll discuss this subject again later in this chapter.

Now that you know the correct file name to use, copy the files. If you use a floppy disk computer, type

```
A>COPY BASIC?.COM B: /V
```

If you have a fixed disk, type

```
C>COPY BASIC?.COM A: /V
```

You'll notice that two file names appear on the screen. Because you just used an ambiguous file name, DOS shows the names of the files that match the wildcard name. Your screen should look something like this:

```
C>COPY BASIC?.COM A: /V
BASIC.COM
BASICA.COM

        2 File(s) copied
C>
```

Next, copy the DISKCOPY program to the diskette, but change the name of the copied file.

If you have two floppy disk drives, type

```
A>COPY DISKCOPY.COM B:COPYDISK.COM /V
```

If you have a fixed disk, type

```
C>COPY DISKCOPY.COM A:COPYDISK.COM /V
```

Now verify that you have copied your files. Look at the directory of the disk you have been copying from and the directory of the diskette you have copied to. If you have a computer with a floppy disk, type the commands:

```
A>DIR A: /P

A>DIR B: /P
```

If you have a computer with a fixed disk, type the commands:

```
C>DIR C: /P

C>DIR A: /P
```

Look for the names DISKCOPY.COM and COPYDISK.COM in the directory listings. Notice the date and time for each file. The dates are the same, and so are the times. When you copy a file, DOS gives the copy the date and time of the original file. The file sizes should also be the same.

The next exercise shows what happens when you omit a disk drive name or make a similar mistake. Change the current disk drive to drive B (if you have two floppy disk drives) or to drive A (if you have a fixed disk).

If you have two floppy disk drives, type

```
B>COPY COPYDISK.COM B: /V
```

If you have a fixed disk, type

```
A>COPY COPYDISK.COM A: /V
```

You should see the following message:

```
File cannot be copied onto itself

     Ø File(s) copied
```

What you attempted to do was to copy COPYDISK.COM on the current disk drive (either drive B or A) back onto drive B or A. DOS correctly informed you that you are really trying to copy the file back to the same diskette under the same name. DOS simply gives an error message and does not perform the copying.

Don't remove diskettes or turn off your computer yet. You'll need this setup for the following hands-on exercises.

Mistakes You Can Make When You Copy Files

As previously suggested, omitting a disk drive name or using the wrong name can be a problem. The problem occurs when the COPY command overwrites a good file with a totally different file. The trap is in the file names.

Using Duplicate File Names

The COPY command can be dangerous if you are not careful about file names. For example, suppose that you have a diskette in drive A that holds a file called MYFILE.DAT. This file holds the names and addresses of your clients. You have a diskette in drive B that also has a file called MYFILE.DAT, but this file holds the names and addresses of your personal friends. Even though the names of the two files are identical, there is no problem, because each file is on a separate diskette.

If, however, you copy MYFILE.DAT from drive A to drive B, DOS first deletes from drive B the file with your friends' names and then copies the file that holds your clients' names to the diskette in drive B. You lose the file that holds the information on your friends.

DOS deletes the MYFILE.DAT on drive B as a self-defense move. No two files listed in the same directory can have the same name. When you tell DOS to copy files, it checks the names. If a file in the destination directory has a name identical to the name of the file you are copying, DOS deletes the file in the destination directory. No warning is given. The contents of that file are lost. Then DOS executes the COPY command.

This DOS practice is not a problem when you're replacing an outdated version of a file with a new version. The practice *is* a problem when the name of the copied file inadvertently matches another file name, even though the two files are fundamentally different, as in the example of MYFILE.DAT. Mistakes occur most frequently when you use wildcards in a file name. You often "select" more files than you intend. Once the file has been copied over, it's too late. The file is lost.

When in doubt about file-name clashes, check both directories for duplicate file names before you copy. Use the DIR command on both disks. If file names match, the matching file on the destination diskette will be deleted. If you don't want to remove the matching file on the destination disk, you must change the file name. You have two options:

1. You can change the name of the file on one of the two disks by using the RENAME command, which is discussed in the next section.

2. You can give a unique destination file name so that the names do not match.

Reversing Disk Drive Names

Another "popular" mistake is reversing the disk drive names when attempting to copy files. My fixed disk is drive C, and my floppy disk drives are drive A and B. Suppose that I want to replace all the outdated files on my fixed disk with the files on a diskette I have in drive A. The correct command is

```
C>COPY A:*.* C: /V
```

This command copies all files from the diskette in drive A to the fixed disk. If you type the following command, an unpleasant surprise awaits:

```
C> COPY  C:*.*  A:  /V
```

I call giving this command an "asleep at the switch" error. The command is dead wrong! It replaces the new files on drive A with the old files from drive C. When you copy files, take a second to check your typing. The results are seldom pleasant when you confuse disk-drive names.

Changing File Names

A frequent task of managing disk files is to change the name of a file. You can change the name of a file's copy by using the COPY command. You may, however, sometimes wish to change the name of a file without making a copy of the file. The command you use to change a file's name is RENAME. RENAME also has a shorthand name, REN. Either form is acceptable to DOS, and both forms work the same.

Using the RENAME Command (RENAME/REN)

The use of RENAME is fairly straightforward:

RENAME *old file name* → *new file name*

The syntax for RENAME is

RENAME *d:* oldfilename*.oldext* newfilename*.newext*

d: is the optional disk drive that holds the file you want to rename. The disk drive name must be given when the file whose name will be changed is not on the current disk drive.

The oldfilename is the root name of the file whose name will be changed. If the file has an extension (*.oldext*), you must give it.

The *newfilename* is the new root name for the file. When you change the file's name, you can keep the same file extension by giving the current extension for *.newext*; you can change the extension by giving a different name for *.newext*; or you can drop the extension by giving no name for *.newext*.

Wildcard characters are allowed in the root file names and extensions for the old and new name. Obviously, wildcards are not allowed for disk drive names. (No DOS command uses wildcards for names of disk drives.)

Notice that you don't give a disk drive name with the new file name. You only give a disk drive name with the original file. DOS remembers where the file is located (from the original file name) and changes the name but does not move the file. That's why you don't need to (nor should you) give a disk drive designation with the new name.

DOS protects itself from having two files with the same name. If you try to rename a file and use the same name for two files, DOS issues an error message. For example, if you use wildcards in a file name, and these wildcards could produce two files with the same name, DOS will give the following error message:

```
Duplicate file name or File not found
```

Any files that are renamed before the error message appears will have new names, but remaining files are left unchanged. You must use the RENAME command again to change the names of the remaining files.

Remember that the RENAME command does not touch the contents of the file. RENAME changes only the file's name in the appropriate directory. But just as your friends may not immediately recognize you when you wear a different outfit or shave a beard or mustache, DOS does not recognize a new file by its old file name. DOS "sees" the file that has a different file name as a different file. You can't use the old file name with the new file unless you change the name back to the original name.

Hands-on Practice: Renaming Files

Make sure that the practice diskette you are using is in the appropriate disk drive (drive B for two floppy disk drives and drive A for a fixed disk). The current disk drive should be the one that holds the diskette (drives B and drive A, respectively). In this section, the instructions are the same for users of computers with floppy disk drives and computers with fixed disk drives.

Type the following command:

```
A>RENAME COPYDISK.COM DISKCOPY.COM
```

This command changes the name of the copy you made of DISKCOPY.COM back to its original name. Notice that when you are successful in changing a file's name, DOS does not give you any message. For some DOS commands, no news is good news. You see a message only when an error occurs.

Now type

```
A>REN CHKDSK.COM CHECKDSK.COM
```

This renames the check-disk program, CHKDSK.COM, to CHECKDSK.COM. The shorthand form REN is used here. Remember that DOS accepts either REN or RENAME. Because most people prefer to type as few characters as possible, REN is the more popular form.

Next, type these two commands:

```
A>CHKDSK
A>CHECKDSK
```

When you type CHKDSK, you will see this message:

```
Bad command or file name
```

This DOS catch-all message states that DOS could not find the command or program you requested. The reason you see the error message when you give the command CHKDSK is that the check-disk program is no

longer called CHKDSK.COM on the diskette. It is now called
CHECKDSK.COM. When you type the second line, DOS runs the check-
disk program under its new name. Renaming the program does not change
what the program does; it only changes the name by which the program is
invoked.

Now type the following commands:

```
A>REN *.COM *.XXX

A>DIR
```

Notice that all files that had an extension of .COM now have an extension
of .XXX. The first wildcard in the old file name says, "Match any
characters in the root name." The corresponding wildcard in the new file
name says, "Don't change the root name." A wildcard character is
frequently used in the same position in an old and new file name to tell
DOS not to change that part of the name.

Now try to run the check-disk command by typing **CHECKDSK**. What
happened?

DOS is selective about the files it considers to be directly runable
programs. Unless a program ends with a .COM or an .EXE extension, DOS
does not attempt to execute the file. (A third type of executable file, a
batch file, must end in the extension .BAT.)

In this example, the files that had the .COM extension now have the
extension .XXX. DOS looks for a file by the name of CHECKDSK.COM,
CHECKDSK.EXE, or CHECKDSK.BAT and finds a file CHECKDSK.XXX.
Because DOS does not know how to handle a file with an .XXX
extension, it keeps looking. Finding no qualifying file, DOS gives up and
displays an error message.

You know, of course, that the file CHECKDSK.XXX holds a good version of
the check-disk program, but DOS doesn't know that. Be careful when you
change the extension of a program file. DOS may not be able to run the
program.

To run the check-disk program, you must change the file back to its original name. To do so, type

```
A>RENAME *.XXX *.COM
```

This command changes the name of your program files so that they have their original extension. Now type the following command:

```
A>CHECKDSK
```

The check-disk program executes normally.

The last thing you should do is change the check-disk program's name back to its original name. Type

```
A>REN CHECKDSK.COM CHKDSK.COM
```

Don't remove the diskettes or turn off your computer yet. You'll need this setup for the next several exercises.

Removing Unwanted Files (ERASE/DEL)

It takes work to put a file on a disk. You must either copy the file using a command like COPY or build the file using a program. Although it seems a waste to destroy work we have done, there are occasions when you will want to remove from a disk a file that is no longer needed. To delete a file, you use the ERASE command.

Like RENAME, ERASE has a short form, DEL, which is short for delete. The syntax for the ERASE command is

ERASE *d:*filename.*ext*

The *d:* is the optional disk drive that holds the file or files to be removed. If the file is on the current disk drive, you omit the disk drive name.

filename is the root name of the file to be removed. Giving the root name is mandatory. The .ext is the extension. You give the extension if the file has one.

When a file is erased, its name is removed from the list of files on the disk. The disk space used by the file is freed and can be used to store more files or to extend the information in current files.

DOS offers no facility to retrieve files that have been removed. Once a file has been removed, you cannot unerase it with a DOS command. The information in the file is lost. Therefore, the ERASE command is considered a dangerous command, one you should use cautiously. Giving the wrong file name or disk drive name or omitting a necessary disk drive name can result in the wrong file being removed. Check your typing when you give the ERASE command.

Wildcards are allowed in the root name and the extension when you use the ERASE command. But wildcards make ERASE even more dangerous. When you give the ERASE command an ambiguous file name (a name with wildcards), you may remove more files than you want to.

Erased files can sometimes, but not always, be recovered with the help of programs that you purchase separately. If you erase a file by accident, the three important steps are: don't panic; don't record any additional information on the disk; and have a program like the Norton Utilities™ on hand. (The utilities are discussed in Chapter 21.)

Hands-on Practice: Erasing Files

For this session, you can use your practice diskette. The instructions are the same for users of computers with floppy disk drives and computers with fixed disk drives.

Because files you erase are not retrievable, you must be certain that the current disk drive is the correct disk drive for the exercise. The current disk drive is drive B for systems with two floppy disk drives and drive A for fixed disk systems. If you inadvertently erase the wrong file, you can copy the erased files from your DOS Master or Master Operating diskette. But making sure that you are removing the correct file is always important.

After you give each ERASE command, perform a DIR command to see the results of the erase operation. Notice that the bytes available increase each time you remove a file.

Now type the following command:

```
A> ERASE DISKCOPY.COM
```

This command removes the DISKCOPY program from your practice diskette.

Then type

```
A> DEL BASIC*.*
```

This command deletes all the BASIC language program files from the diskette. Note that DEL is interchangeable with ERASE.

Finally, type

```
A> ERASE *.*
```

DOS responds with this message:

```
Are you sure (Y/N)?
```

You are about to erase all the remaining files on the diskette. When you give the file name *.* to ERASE, DOS confirms your intentions. If you answer Y for yes and then press Enter, DOS removes all the files on the diskette. If you answer N for no and press Enter, DOS does not delete any of the files.

In this example, answer Y for yes and press Enter. Issue the DIR command to see that all files are removed from the directory.

Remember the caution about the ERASE command. If you are in doubt about which files will be erased, use the file name first with the DIR command. If a file you don't want erased shows up in the list of files, use a different file name with ERASE.

More on Copying Complete Disks (DISKCOPY)

In Chapter 1, you used the DISKCOPY command to make a "carbon copy" of your original DOS diskette. DISKCOPY copies the entire contents of one diskette to another.

DISKCOPY is an external command that is not built into DOS. You must load DISKCOPY from a diskette. The correct notation is

*dc:*DISKCOPY *ds: dd:*

The notation *dc:* represents the name of the disk drive that holds the DISKCOPY command. If the command is on the current disk drive, you can omit the disk drive name. If DISKCOPY is on a different disk drive, you must give the disk drive name.

ds: is the name of the disk drive that holds the diskette to be copied. This is the source diskette, indicated by the *s* in the name. *dd:* is the disk drive that holds the diskette to receive the information. This is the target (or destination) diskette.

Unlike the other commands in this chapter, with the DISKCOPY command, the filename and extension are missing. Some DOS commands use file names; some do not. DISKCOPY is one command that does not accept a file name.

Notice that the source and destination disk drive names are optional. If you do not give a source disk drive name, and the current disk drive is a floppy disk drive, the current disk drive will be used for the copying.

If, however, the current disk drive is the fixed disk drive, you must specify at least the source disk drive name. You cannot use the DISKCOPY command to copy a fixed disk. If the current disk is the fixed disk, and you type the DISKCOPY command, DOS responds with this error message:

```
Invalid drive specification
Specified drive does not exist,
or is non-removable
```

If you specify only a source disk drive, the same disk drive will be used to make the target diskette. DISKCOPY prompts you to change diskettes at the appropriate time.

If the diskette you are copying to, the target, is not formatted or is formatted differently, DISKCOPY formats the target diskette. The message Formatting while copying indicates that the DISKCOPY command is formatting the diskette.

A good practice is to format your diskettes ahead of time, before you need to use them. Then, if the FORMAT command reports any bad sectors on a diskette, you know you cannot use that diskette as the target diskette with the DISKCOPY command. The DISKCOPY command would attempt to write to the bad sectors of the target diskette and would not produce a good copy.

Like the ERASE command, DISKCOPY is another dangerous command. DISKCOPY destroys whatever information is on the target diskette. Obviously, you should never use as the target diskette a diskette that contains files you want to keep! When in doubt, use the DIR command on the potential target diskette to check the files. If the DIR command shows that files you want are on the diskette, use a different target diskette.

Because DISKCOPY is a dangerous command, use the write-protect tab to protect your source diskette. Move the write-protect tab up (for microfloppy diskettes) or put a write-protect tab over the notch (for minifloppy diskettes). This precaution is particularly important when you make a copy of a diskette by using only one floppy disk drive. If the source diskette is write-protected, you cannot damage it if you accidentally reverse the source and target disk drive names or put the wrong diskette into the drive.

Summary

In this chapter, the following key points were covered:

1. When you use the COPY command, you can change a file's name or leave it unchanged.

2. To change a file's name, you use the RENAME (REN) command.

3. The ERASE (DEL) command removes files.

4. DISKCOPY makes a "carbon copy" of a diskette.

5. DISKCOPY, COPY, and ERASE can be dangerous commands if you give the wrong disk drive or file name.

You're done with your computer for now. You can put the diskettes away and relax. In the next few chapters, you'll look inside DOS to see how the operating system works.

Part II

Expanding Your Knowledge of DOS and Disks

INCLUDES

Understanding DOS and Devices

Understanding Floppy Diskettes and Their Drives

Understanding Fixed Disks and How DOS Uses Disks

Naming Disk Drives and Files

Using Redirection and Piping

5

Understanding DOS and Devices

This chapter provides some background about DOS and about how DOS works with *devices*. The chapter will discuss devices: what they are and how to use DOS to control devices. The chapter also covers DOS's major parts and explains how these parts work together.

Although this chapter's first sections are somewhat technical, the chapter does lay the foundation for understanding how DOS really works. The section on the Command Processor tells you about COMMAND.COM, and this information is the most important technical information about DOS that you'll need to know. Sections on devices and device names are also important. In addition, you will learn how to use a device name with the COPY command to create text files quickly.

The Three Parts of DOS

Although DOS may appear to be one large, nebulous "program," DOS actually consists of a multitude of programs. You can classify these programs by function into three major parts: the I/O system, the Command Processor, and the utilities. You may be surprised to learn that you've already used all three parts of DOS in the hands-on practice exercises in Chapters 1 through 4.

To use DOS effectively, you do not need to understand exactly which DOS part performs what function. But an acquaintance with what each part does will help you understand DOS's overall operation.

DOS's first major part is the *input/output* system, which is abbreviated I/O. The I/O system handles every character that is typed on the keyboard, displayed on-screen, printed on the printer, and received or sent through communications adapters. The I/O system also contains DOS's disk filing system, a management system that stores and retrieves information from the disk drives.

DOS's second major part, the Command Processor, has several built-in functions, or subprograms, that handle most of DOS's common tasks—copying files, displaying file lists on-screen, and running programs.

DOS's third major part, its utilities, are not discussed specifically in this chapter, but they are described throughout the book and in Part VI, the *DOS Command Reference*. DOS's utilities are used primarily for housekeeping tasks such as formatting diskettes, comparing files, finding the amount of free space on a disk, and printing in background mode.

In the next two sections, we'll take a look at both the I/O system and the Command Processor.

The I/O (Input/Output) System

The I/O system comprises all activities related to the computer's *central processing unit* (CPU—the computer's "brain") and to the computer's memory. When you enter a character from the keyboard, the signal for that character moves from the keyboard to the CPU and to the computer's memory. This activity is *input*. When the computer prints a line on the screen or printer, the signals for the line move out from the CPU and the computer's memory to the screen or printer. This activity is *output*.

Input and output take place between the computer and the computer's *peripherals* such as the screen, keyboard, printer, and disk drives (see fig. 5.1). Peripherals are used by the computer's CPU and memory, but they are not themselves part of the CPU and memory. Peripherals are important to the computer because, without them, the CPU and memory would have no way to communicate to the outside world.

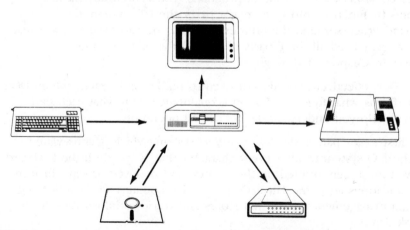

Fig. 5.1. *Input and output between the computer's peripherals.*

DOS's System for Controlling Peripherals (BIOS)

The part of DOS that communicates with the computer's peripherals is called the *BIOS*, which stands for Basic Input/Output System. The BIOS consists of routines that provide some control for the keyboard, video display, disk drives, and other peripherals. The BIOS gives programs a standard way to communicate with these peripherals and to control them. BIOS includes the *RIOS* and the *IBMBIO.COM*, each of which is discussed in this section.

The RIOS. The computer's BIOS is actually located in two places. The first is on the computer's system board (or mother board). On this board, the BIOS is contained in a read-only memory chip called a *ROM*. The nickname for the routines contained in this chip is ROM BIOS, or RIOS (pronounced RYE-ose). The ROM holds the basic routines for communicating with most of the devices used by personal computers.

The IBMBIO.COM. The disk file IBMBIO.COM (called IO.SYS for MS-DOS machines) is the second location for these routines. The file holds the next level of software routines for controlling and communicating with peripherals. The routines build on the routines in the ROM BIOS.

The IBMBIO.COM file is one of the two "system" files on the diskette(s) you created in Chapter 1. You will recall that these files are hidden from you to prevent accidental alteration or erasure. If you unintentionally erase or alter IBMBIO.COM, you cannot properly use the operating system on the altered diskette.

The Filing System (IBMDOS.COM)

The final part of the I/O system is the file called IBMDOS.COM, or MSDOS.SYS on MS-DOS computers. Like IBMBIO.COM, IBMDOS.COM is a system file that cannot be altered or erased. The file contains the major part of the operating system and holds the routines for controlling the information passed between the computer and its peripherals. IBMDOS.COM has two separate filing systems: one for disk drives and one for all nondisk peripherals.

As the control center, IBMDOS communicates its directions to the BIOS. The BIOS, in turn, does the actual "talking" to the devices and transmits the filing system's directions.

The Command Processor (COMMAND.COM)

The Command Processor, COMMAND.COM, is the second major part of DOS. COMMAND.COM is the program with which you communicate, and it, in turn, tells the rest of DOS what to do.

COMMAND.COM displays the A> system prompt on the video screen when you start DOS. This prompt indicates that you are talking to COMMAND.COM. When you type a command, COMMAND.COM interprets the command and takes the appropriate action.

One of the most important tasks that the Command Processor handles is managing critical interrupts. A critical interrupt occurs when a hardware device (peripheral) demands attention. At this point, COMMAND.COM diverts the computer's attention to the device. The Command Processor also handles critical errors, usually disk problems or divide-by-zero errors. If you have ever tried to perform the directory command (DIR) on a floppy disk drive that contains no floppy diskette, COMMAND.COM is the program that gave the message:

```
Not ready error reading drive A
Abort, Retry, Fail? _
```

(If this situation should happen to you, you can remedy it by placing a diskette into the disk drive and typing R for Retry. You can also simply type A for Abort to stop the DIR command, and COMMAND.COM will redisplay the system prompt.)

The COMMAND.COM program is operationally organized into two parts. One part is resident. After you load DOS, the resident part of COMMAND.COM remains in memory until you restart DOS or turn off your computer. Most of the COMMAND.COM functions you have just read about are in the resident part of the program.

The second part of COMMAND.COM is transient. This part usually stays in RAM. But the transient part can be discarded, and the RAM space formerly occupied by this portion can be used by other programs. When a program attempts to allocate memory used by the transient portion of COMMAND.COM, the transient portion is freed.

If one of your programs uses this RAM that was occupied by COMMAND.COM, then COMMAND.COM must reload itself from the disk when you have finished with the program. You will know that you must reload COMMAND.COM into RAM if you see the following message:

```
Insert disk with \COMMAND.COM in drive A
and strike any key when ready
```

You'll encounter this message when you start DOS from a diskette and the diskette currently in the disk drive does not hold a copy of COMMAND.COM. If you see this message, simply insert a diskette that has a copy of COMMAND.COM, such as your DOS Startup diskette, and press any key. DOS will reload COMMAND.COM, and the system prompt will reappear.

COMMAND.COM's transient part has built into it several commonly used DOS commands. These built-in commands are listed in table 3.1 in Chapter 3. When you see the system prompt, you can use any of the commands listed in table 3.1. You don't need to remember which commands are part of the resident or transient part of COMMAND.COM.

Other functions that COMMAND.COM handles include processing batch files, executing batch-file subcommands, and redirecting input/output. Each of these activities is discussed in later chapters. For now, just remember that you can execute any batch-file or I/O-redirection command when you see the system prompt. You don't have to load a program into memory to use these DOS functions.

The last function of COMMAND.COM that will be mentioned in this section is the most frequently used: loading external DOS commands and applications programs into memory and giving them control of the computer.

This book is about DOS, but you spend less than 1/20th of your computing time interacting directly with DOS. You spend most of your time working with applications programs such as spreadsheets, word-processing programs, accounting programs, and the like. These programs are the real reason you choose to use a microcomputer. Therefore, loading and executing your applications programs are the most important functions of COMMAND.COM.

Learning about Devices

As previously mentioned, a device is a peripheral you connect to your computer. The keyboard, the video screen, and the printer are devices. Each device uses some connection, or *interface*, to talk to the computer. An interface represents both the physical connection (the cable, plugs, and wires) and the electronics that handle communications between the computer and the device.

Some interfaces, such as the one that operates the keyboard unit, are built into the computer. To use a device for which the computer does not have a built-in interface, you have to place a special card or adapter in the computer. (A big difference between Personal Computers and PS/2 computers is that more interfaces are built into PS/2 computers.)

Devices for computers fall into two classes: character-oriented and block-oriented devices. Both types of devices may use either parallel or serial interfaces. The next few paragraphs describe parallel and serial interfaces. Then character-oriented and block-oriented devices are discussed.

The computer and its devices usually communicate with each other one byte at a time. A byte can be transmitted and received in one of two ways. *Parallel* connections transmit the entire byte at one time. A parallel connection uses eight separate wires or lines for the eight bits in a byte, as well as other wires to coordinate the movement of the character. IBM printers use parallel connections.

The other type of connection is a *serial* connection in which the byte is sent one bit at a time. The hardware also sends some additional bits to coordinate the movement of information between the devices. Most modems, the keyboard unit, and the mouse (a menu-selecting and pointing device) use serial connections.

Video screens are exceptions. Video interfaces, either by the adapters or the PS/2 family's Video Graphics Array (VGA), use memory-mapped video. The interfaces project a video image based on the adapter's memory or the array. For video displays, the terms *parallel* and *serial* have no real meaning.

Character-oriented devices are peripherals that communicate to the computer one character at a time. Almost all devices that attach to the computer system are character-oriented, including printers, modems, the keyboard, the video display, and selection devices such as a mouse.

Block-oriented devices are peripherals that move information that consists of a group of characters. By this definition, disk drives fit into this category and are the main block devices.

In fact, however, disk drives are serial, character-oriented devices. Bytes are stored on the disk, or platter, one bit at a time. The adapter's electronics collect and combine the bits into characters, and then the characters into blocks. But this action occurs so fast that you never see the extra work the adapters and disk drives do. It is in this sense that disk drives may be considered block-oriented devices.

Magnetic tape cartridges used for backing up fixed disks can be either character- or block-oriented devices. If your tape drive is a streaming tape drive, it is technically a character-oriented device. Otherwise, the tape drive is considered to be a block-oriented device. Whether a tape cartridge is character- or block oriented does not really matter; that the tape drive works is what's important.

The software used to control these devices (except magnetic tape drives) is in the computer system's BIOS. Higher-level routines are located in DOS's nondisk filing system.

Using Device Names

Every device has a name. PC DOS "knows" several device names. In most cases, the name is based not on the device itself but on the type of adapter the device uses to communicate with the computer.

Device names are three to four characters long. All device names end with a colon. Note, however, that the colon is optional with most commands. When you use a device name in a command, DOS attempts to use the specified adapter or device.

Because of the way DOS is constructed, you can use a device name wherever you can use a file name, meaning that you can direct DOS to get information from a device (such as a modem) or send information to a device (such as a printer).

Each device name is reserved within DOS. You cannot use a device name as the root name of a disk file.

Table 5.1 lists the character-oriented device names that DOS recognizes. This list also includes two additional device names that Disk BASIC and Advanced BASIC (BASICA) use, but DOS does not recognize them. The colon is shown after each device name, but the colon is optional.

Beginning in this chapter, you will learn "rules" for using DOS functions and commands. These rules indicate how to phrase a name or command, what happens when you give or don't give correct command information, and what you can and cannot do with these commands. The first set of rules summarizes the information that was presented in these sections on using devices.

The rules in the list following table 5.1 show how you should use device names. Note that if you try to use the root name of a file that is identical to a device name, DOS will use the device instead of the file.

Table 5.1
Character-Oriented Device Names

Name	Device
CON:	The video display and keyboard. Input from CON: comes from the keyboard; output to CON: goes to the video display.
AUX:	The first asynchronous communications port, or COM1:
COM2: COM3: COM4:	The second, third, and fourth asynchronous communications ports, respectively.
LPT1: or PRN	The first line or parallel printer. On PCs, this device is used only for output. On PS/2s, LPT1:, LPT2:, and LPT3: are used for input and output.
LPT2: LPT3:	The second and third parallel printers.
NUL:	A nonexistent (dummy) device.

Disk and Advanced BASIC

Name	Device
KYBD:	The keyboard of the system (an input-only device).
SCRN:	The video display (an output-only device).

The following are the rules for character-oriented device names:

1. Valid names for character-oriented devices are CON:, AUX:, COMx:, LPTx:, PRN, and NUL:.

2. The colon after the device name is usually optional.

3. You may use a character-oriented device name wherever you can use file names.

4. If you give an extension with a device name, DOS ignores the extension. For example, DOS treats CON.TXT the same as it does CON:.

5. Do not use a device name for a device that does not exist. For example, if your computer has only one printer, do not use the device name LPT2:. You may, however, use NUL:. It is the exception to this rule.

6. When you use NUL: for input, you immediately get an end-of-file condition. When you use NUL: for output, DOS acts as though it is writing information, but it does not record any information (the data goes into the "bit-bucket").

Rule 5 is especially important. Don't try to use a device you don't have. At best, DOS will give you an error message. At worst, DOS may act erratically.

Using the COPY Command with a Device (COPY CON)

Later in this book, you will be asked several times to create files that hold just a few lines of text. The technique in this section shows you a "quick and dirty" way to transfer information from the keyboard directly into a file. You will find this technique useful, and faster than using a text editor for creating short files.

Try the following exercise:

Step 1. Put a formatted practice diskette into a disk drive and type

COPY CON SHOWFILE.TXT

When you type this line and press Enter, the cursor will move to the beginning of the next line.

Step 2. Next, type the following line:

This is a file copied quickly between a device and a disk.

Step 3. Press Enter at the end of the line.

Step 4. After you press Enter, press the F6 function key.

DOS will display a ^Z on the screen.

Step 5. *Press Enter again.*

You'll see a message indicating that DOS has copied one file.

Step 6. *Now use the TYPE command to see the file you copied. Type the following command:*

TYPE SHOWFILE.TXT

The line that began "This is a file . . ." should appear on your screen.

You have just copied a "file" from the keyboard to a disk file. The letters CON represent a DOS abbreviation for *console*, which is the keyboard and the video screen. In the steps you have just followed, you used the COPY command to take what was typed on the keyboard and put the characters into the disk file called SHOWFILE.TXT.

Can this process work the other way? To find out, type this command:

COPY SHOWFILE.TXT CON

Yes, the process does work the other way. This process is identical to using DOS's TYPE command to display the file. You can copy files between the console, serial adapters, printers, or other devices as though you were copying disk files. You cannot, however, use COPY as a general-purpose communications program like Crosstalk® or Procomm®. But the process illustrates the versatility of both DOS and the COPY command.

To use the COPY command to create text files, follow these three steps:

Step 1. *To start the process, use the following command syntax:*

COPY CON *d:*filename.*ext*

The COPY CON part of the command copies from the keyboard (CON) to a file. The *d:* is the disk drive name (optional). filename is the root name of the file you want to create, and *.ext* is the extension for the file (optional).

Be aware that if a file already exists by the same name you use in the COPY process, DOS will erase that file before it creates the new file. Therefore, you should not use a name that is used for another file in the directory unless you want to erase the previously existing file.

Step 2. *Type the information you want to place in the file and press Enter at the end of each line.*

Be careful as you type lines into the file. Once you have pressed Enter, you cannot correct mistakes you may have made while you entered the line. If you make a mistake and have already pressed Enter, omit Step 3, which saves the file, press Ctrl-Break (or Ctrl-C) to stop the COPY process, and start again at Step 1.

Step 3. *After you have entered all the lines, press the F6 function key.*

DOS will display a ^Z on-screen. Press Enter and the disk drive light will come on.

Soon DOS will display a message saying that it has copied one file. You have created a text file with the COPY command.

Summary

In this chapter, you have learned some important facts about DOS:

1. DOS has three major sections: the input/output system (I/O system), COMMAND.COM, and housekeeping utilities that are stored on disk.

2. The I/O system contains the ROM BIOS, plus IBMBIO.COM and IBMDOS.COM.

3. When you boot the computer, IBMBIO.COM and IBMDOS.COM load into the computer. COMMAND.COM (the Command Processor) also loads into the computer.

4. COMMAND.COM has several built-in functions and DOS commands.

5. DOS has several names that are reserved as device names. You may use these names whenever you would use a file name.

6. You can use the command **COPY CON filename** to create text files quickly.

6

Understanding Floppy Diskettes and Their Drives

Disk drives are your computer system's most important peripherals. It is true that keyboards and video screens are useful input/output devices. And printers, plotters, and modems extend the capabilities of your system. But with disk drives, the computer can store and retrieve large amounts of information. The first word in "disk operating system" says it all.

A computer uses random-access memory (RAM) to temporarily hold your programs and data, including DOS itself. RAM is volatile, however. When you turn off the computer's power, whatever is in RAM disappears. Disk storage, however, is not volatile. When you turn off the power, whatever is on the disk stays. That is why diskettes are important.

The next part of this chapter is a tour of the floppy diskette.

Understanding Floppy Diskettes

If you use minifloppy diskettes, get one of the two diskettes that came with your copy of DOS V3.3. If you use microfloppy diskettes, get the single microfloppy diskette that came with your copy of DOS. We'll start with a look at the minifloppy diskette. Then we'll examine the microfloppy diskette.

Looking at Minifloppy (5 1/4-inch) Diskettes

The floppy diskette got its name because the diskette and the black, flexible jacket it comes in will "flop" if you flip them back and forth. The diskettes and their jackets come in protective envelopes. Because the jacket does not provide much protection for your diskette, you should handle minifloppy diskettes with care.

Take your diskette out of its envelope. The diskette should slide right out. If it looks as if you need to cut something open to get at the diskette, you have probably confused the protective envelope with the diskette's jacket.

The inside of a diskette's jacket often has a gauzelike, plastic material glued to it. This material traps small particles of dust and keeps them from contacting the diskette as it spins. The material is usually lubricated with silicone so that the diskette does not rub as it spins.

Inside the jacket is the diskette itself, which is usually made of polyurethane coated with metal oxide. Most diskettes are dark brown and shiny, but some diskettes are red, gold, or even green. The diskette itself is circular. Its diameter is 5 1/4 inches.

Technically, an 8-inch diskette, which is used on larger computers, is called a *floppy diskette*. The 5 1/4-inch version is a *minifloppy diskette*. And the 3 1/2-inch version is a *microfloppy diskette*. Because of sloppy usage, the distinction between these terms has been blurred. The term floppy is often used to refer to 5 1/4-inch or 3 1/2-inch diskettes, but technically these should be called minifloppy and microfloppy diskettes, respectively.

(To my chagrin, I, too, sometimes interchange the terms floppy, minifloppy, and microfloppy. In this book, however, if the difference between the types of diskettes is important, I specifically use the terms minifloppy and microfloppy. Otherwise, the term floppy applies to either minifloppy or microfloppy diskettes.)

Now, to continue the tour, make sure that the side with the printed label is facing you (fig. 6.1). This side is the front of the diskette. In the middle of the diskette is a large *centering hole*. The disk drive grasps the diskette by this hole. Sometimes a plastic ring is placed on the centering hole to provide extra strength and to help center the diskette when it is in the disk drive.

On both front and back of the diskette jacket, at the bottom, are oblong openings through which the diskette can be seen. These openings are the *access holes*, where the disk drive recording heads make contact with the diskette.

Now, hold the diskette by the edge of the jacket. The top side of the diskette has the printed label and should face you. Hold the diskette so that the access holes are at the bottom, in the six o'clock position.

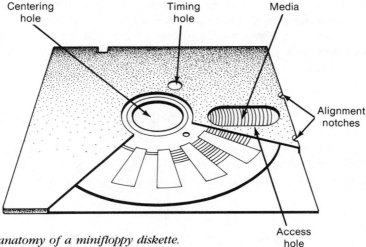

Fig. 6.1. *The anatomy of a minifloppy diskette.*

You'll notice to the right of the access hole a small hole in the jacket. This is the *index* or *timing hole*. Put two fingers in the centering hole and grasp the edge of the diskette. Gently rotate the diskette until you see a smaller hole, the index hole, in the diskette itself. The disk drive shines a light through this index hole to help determine where data is stored on the diskette. Diskettes with single index holes are called *soft-sectored* diskettes. Most personal computers use soft-sectored diskettes.

The other type of diskette is *hard-sectored* diskettes, which can have 11 to 17 index holes. These diskettes and disk drives are no longer popular and have fallen from use. Because you cannot use hard-sectored diskettes in your disk drives or soft-sectored diskettes in hard-sectored disk drives, you now have one less diskette type from which to choose. You also have one less chance of getting the wrong type of diskette for your disk drive.

Hold the diskette vertically and look at the right edge of the jacket near the top. You should see a small notch in the jacket, called the *write-protect* notch. When you leave the notch uncovered, the computer can write information on the diskette. When you cover the notch, the computer cannot write, change, or erase information on the diskette. When you cover the notch, the diskette is *write-protected*. Technically, we should refer to the notch on the 5 1/4-inch diskette as the *write-enable* notch, but, again, our sloppy use blurs the terms write-protect and write-enable.

Using the write-protect notch is an easy way to protect your diskettes. If you cover a diskette's write-protect notch, no information can be put on the diskette, and no files can be erased from that diskette. If you look at the diskettes provided with DOS V3.3, you'll notice that the IBM DOS diskettes do not have write-protect notches. The information on these diskettes is permanently write-protected from alteration or erasure by the computer.

Looking at Microfloppy (3 1/2-inch) Diskettes

As you look at a microfloppy diskette, you'll notice that it is covered by a buff, blue, or black plastic shell (fig. 6.2). The rigid shell protects the diskette better than the flimsy plastic cover protects a 5 1/4-inch diskette.

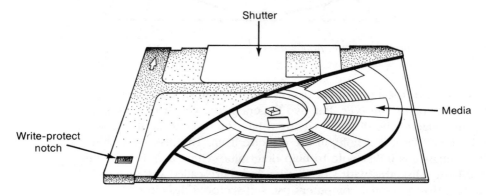

Fig. 6.2. *The anatomy of a microfloppy diskette, top side.*

Hold the diskette with the label facing you. A sliding metal cover should be at the top. The metal slide, called a *shutter*, covers both the front and the back sides of the diskette. Hold the diskette in your right hand. With your thumb and forefinger, grasp the leftmost part of the metal slide on both sides of the diskette. Pull the shutter to the left.

The shutter has rectangular holes on both sides of the diskette. When you move the shutter to the left, you expose the microfloppy shell's access hole. By turning the diskette over without releasing the shutter, you should see both sides of the microfloppy diskette that is inside. The shutter is attached to the shell by a spring. When you release the pressure, the shutter returns to its normal position to cover the access holes.

When you insert the diskette into the microfloppy disk drive, the disk drive slides the shutter so that the disk drive heads can make contact with the diskette. When the diskette is not in the disk drive, the shutter should be closed to protect the diskette.

By the way, the microfloppy's hard shell might seem to antiquate the term floppy. However, the diskette inside the shell is flexible and "flops" when shaken, so the term floppy is still appropriate.

Now flip the microfloppy diskette over. In the center of the diskette is the metal spindle, which has two holes (fig. 6.3). The centering hole is the smaller hole in the center. The *sector one* hole is the larger rectangular hole near the edge of the spindle.

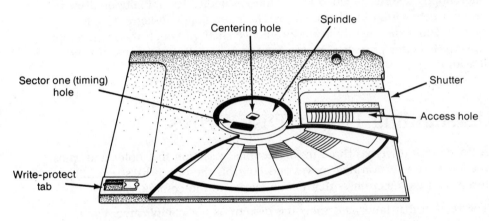

Fig. 6.3. *The anatomy of a microfloppy diskette, bottom side.*

The microfloppy disk drive does not use a light shining through the index hole to determine where the first sector is located on the diskette. The timing is done by the disk drive's spindle, which seats itself into the two holes on the diskette's spindle. When the diskette is placed into the disk drive, the disk drive's spindle turns until the spindle properly seats itself. After the spindle is settled, the hardware of the microfloppy disk drive determines where the first sector is located.

On the upper left side of the microfloppy diskette is the write-protect notch and a small sliding tab. Some disk drives use an infrared light to sense where the tab is, and others have a mechanical feeler.

To write-protect a diskette, you move the bar up and uncover the hole so you can see through it from the front. To write to the diskette, you move the bar down and cover the hole. If you want to "permanently" write-protect a diskette, gently pry the tab out of the slot. (If you subsequently want to write information on the write-protected diskette, cover the write-protect hole with black electrical tape or with a write-protect tab that you would use with a minifloppy diskette.)

Some diskettes have a second notch on the upper right side. These diskettes follow an impending standard for 1.44M disk drives. Some drives use the second notch to determine if the diskette is a 720K or 1.44M diskette. However, IBM disk drives do not sense or care about this notch on the right side.

A major difference between floppy and microfloppy diskettes is that the microfloppy diskette is glued to the metal spindle. The minifloppy diskette moves freely within its plastic cover. The microfloppy diskette, too, is flexible and slides slightly in the protective shell. Although the microfloppy diskette is better protected by the hard plastic shell, you must still handle it with care.

Understanding Floppy Disk Drives

A floppy disk drive has three major sections: a section that holds and spins the diskette, a section that moves and controls the disk drive's recording heads, and the electronics that communicate to the computer.

The section that holds and spins the diskette is not complicated. On a minifloppy disk drive, when you close the door, two clutches, one on either side of the diskette, grasp the diskette's centering hole. The bottom clutch is connected by a belt to a motor. The motor, connected to the disk drive's electronics, spins the diskette inside its plastic jacket at 300 rpm.

On a microfloppy disk drive, a metal panel pushes the diskette onto the spindle. The disk drive's spindle has two nubs to anchor it to the centering hole and to the first sector hole. The microfloppy disk drive's spindle, like the minifloppy disk drive's spindle, is connected to the motor by a belt.

The second section of both types of disk drive includes two connected, mobile arms that hold the recording heads. A disk drive recording head is smaller than a tape recorder head and is made mainly of ceramic material.

PCs and PS/2s use double-sided disk drives. These drives have a recording head at the end of each arm. The two recording heads face each other. On most minifloppy disk drives, the arms are connected to the disk drive's door or to the knob used to close the disk drive door. In that way, the recording heads clamp onto the diskette when you close the disk drive door. Some drives use a magnetic relay to clamp the arms onto the diskette. All Personal Computer minifloppy disk drives use the first method. Some microfloppy disk drives use the relay method. The remaining microfloppy disk drives simply use levering systems that clamp the recording heads into position when you insert a diskette into the disk drive.

As the arms clamp onto a diskette, the diskette is held between the recording heads. This positioning keeps the diskette from bouncing away from the recording heads and allows the drive to write or read information reliably.

The coordinated mobile arms move back and forth down the center of the drive. A small "stepper" motor connected to a cam or gear moves the arm. Look at the diskette's access holes and think about how you insert the diskette into the disk drive. From this, you can imagine how the recording heads move.

The recording heads, the stepper motor, and the magnetic relay (if used) are also connected to the disk drive's electronic components. This last section of the disk drive is the part that "talks" to the computer. The write-protect switch is also connected to these circuits. If the switch senses that the diskette is write-protected, the disk drive's electronics stop the drive from recording information on the disk's surfaces.

The small light on the front of the disk drive comes on whenever the computer is using the disk drive. This light tells you that the disk drive is in use. Generally, you should not open a minifloppy disk drive door or eject a microfloppy diskette until the light goes out.

Other electronic components of the disk drive receive signals from the computer to start the motor that spins the diskette, to clamp the recording arm on the diskette, to move the recording arm, and to get information from or put information on the diskette.

Another piece of electronics on some drives is a *change line*, whose purpose is to inform the computer when the diskette may have been changed. Disk drives with change lines have a switch connected to the minifloppy disk drive door or to the microfloppy eject button. When the disk drive door is opened or the eject button is pushed, the disk drive signals the computer that the diskette has been changed. It does not matter whether the diskette is changed; only that the door has been opened or the button pushed. This change line mechanism is on some 360K disk drives, on all 1.2M drives, and on all microfloppy disk drives.

A floppy disk drive is a fairly "dumb" peripheral. Most of the "intelligence" needed to control the disk drive is on a board or is part of integrated circuits within the computer itself. This intelligence is located mainly on a diskette controller adapter or on a diskette controller board. The operating system's BIOS coordinates and governs the floppy disk drive's actions.

The floppy disk drive is more reliable today than it was several years ago. More information (1.2 or 1.44 million bytes) can be packed into a 5 1/4-inch or 3 1/2-inch diskette than could be held in an 8-inch floppy diskette only five years ago (241,000 bytes).

Maintaining Your Diskettes and Drives

The following sections cover the care of your floppy diskettes and floppy disk drives. Some suggestions are offered for maintaining your diskettes and protecting your disk drives from damage.

Taking Care of Your Floppy Diskettes

Floppy diskettes are fragile. The plastic jacket provides protection from about 80 percent of the dust, fingerprints, smoke, and other contaminants that can come into contact with the diskette. That protection plus a little common sense will ensure a long life for your diskettes. Treat the diskettes as you would your personal or business records. In some cases, the diskettes *are* your records.

Some diskette manufacturers put instructions on the back of the envelope about caring for your diskettes. You may want to read these instructions after you read this section. Some of these instructions are less critical for microfloppy diskettes than for minifloppy diskettes because of the greater protection the hard shell gives the microfloppy diskette. Note, however, that microfloppies are not immune to damage. Exercising common sense prolongs the life of any diskette.

Some Do's for Diskettes

Put diskettes into the disk drive carefully. "Easy does it" is the best advice. Microfloppy diskettes need a slight push when you finish the move that inserts the diskette. When the diskette is almost completely inserted, pushing the diskette forces the retaining panel to secure the diskette into the drive. This securing push takes just slightly more force than you would use when you insert a minifloppy diskette.

You should be able to slide a minifloppy diskette into the disk drive with little resistance. You may even hear a soft click as the metal bar or write-protect switch slides into place. Minifloppy disk drive doors should close with little resistance.

In a short time, you will know by touch whether you've properly inserted a diskette. If you insert a diskette or close a disk drive door and sense a problem, remove the diskette and put it back in again. You can damage both diskette and disk drive if you try to force a diskette into a disk drive. The possibility of damaging a minifloppy diskette by forcing the drive door closed is especially likely.

When you have finished using a minifloppy diskette, put it back in its envelope. The envelope prevents dust and most other contaminants from getting to the surface of the diskette.

Putting microfloppy diskettes back into the clear envelope is not so important. However, the envelope can protect the diskette from liquids, a major danger to microfloppy diskettes.

Label every diskette. Diskettes seem to multiply like rabbits. Nothing is more frustrating and time-consuming than trying to find one particular diskette in a group of 50 diskettes that appear to be identical. Many computer users buy diskettes in bulk packaging, so the diskettes without labels all look alike. Save yourself time by not wading through scores of unlabeled diskettes to find the one you need.

After you format a diskette, put a label on it. You might also include the date you formatted the diskette and the version of the program you used or other pertinent information. When you label a diskette, use meaningful names and abbreviations so that they will make sense to you at some later date. A diskette without a label is "fair game" for accidental reformatting or erasing and, therefore, less useful to you. Give each diskette the care and protection that it deserves: give each diskette a label.

Once you have placed a label on a minifloppy diskette, use a felt-tipped pen to write on the label. Don't press hard or use a ball-point pen or pencil. Undue pressure can damage the diskette under the jacket. For labels attached to a microfloppy diskette's hard shell, you can use any type of pen or pencil, short of an engraver. (Using an engraver probably would not actually damage the diskette, but why take chances when you don't have to?)

If a label comes loose, remove it and put on a new one. I learned the importance of this lesson the hard way while I was writing the previous version of this book, the *PC DOS User's Guide*.

I took home the diskette that held several chapters of the book. When I got home, I stuck the diskette into the disk drive and began to work. I noticed that the label was beginning to peel away from the diskette, but I didn't think that this fact was important. Later, when I removed the diskette from the disk drive, the label came off inside the drive and became lodged on the bottom of the drive. I did not notice that the label was missing.

That evening, I searched for a diskette to format and grabbed one from the top of a pile of unlabeled diskettes. Several hours later, I came back to work on my book again. For 20 minutes, I looked for the diskette that held part of the book. A sickening thought struck. I carefully reached inside the disk drive and found the diskette label on the bottom of the drive. I had formatted the wrong diskette and lost my chapters! Fortunately, I had a day-old backup copy of the diskette. All I had lost was one day's work. As I said before, "I am an experienced computer user."

Another piece of good advice comes from this lesson. *To avoid costly loss of information, always check a diskette you are about to format.* Make sure that it is blank or has no useful information on it. Make the DIR command your friend.

Back up diskettes frequently. What saved me from having to reenter several weeks of work was my backup diskette. You should back up vital information daily or at least every two days if you are changing information such as accounting records. You should back up less vital, but still important, information every couple days, or at least once a week. Backing up diskettes is an extremely cheap form of insurance.

Another reason to make backup copies of files is that diskettes have a finite life. In the past (1978-81), diskettes had spin lives (the amount of time that a disk drive actually reads or writes information on the diskette) of 40 to 80 hours. The newer diskettes can be used much longer, even several years, before they wear out. Diskettes do wear out, but computer malfunctions or inadvertent operations (such as erasing the wrong file) cause more losses than wear.

Keep infrequently used diskettes and backup copies of diskettes away from your computer. Why clutter the place where you work? Why have to dig through diskettes to find the one you need? Have at hand just the ones you constantly need. When you need a different diskette, get it, use it, and put it back. You'll find managing diskettes to be much easier this way.

Keep your diskettes "comfortable." Like phonograph records, minifloppy diskettes can bend or warp if they are not stored perfectly flat or vertical. Warping a diskette takes several weeks, but why risk this kind of damage? A number of holders on the market do a good job of storing diskettes. Although microfloppy diskettes do not warp, diskette holders keep the diskettes organized and readily accessible.

Keeping diskettes comfortable also means watching the temperature. Maintain the temperature between 50 and 125 degrees Fahrenheit (10 and 52 degrees Celsius).

If your diskettes get cold, let them warm up before you use them. This precaution is critical for high-capacity and microfloppy diskettes. Cold diskettes become rigid and shrink slightly. Disk drives record information at a slightly different position on shrunken diskettes. The disk drive does not change its position for recording, but the diskette itself is different. As the diskette warms up and expands, the disk drive cannot locate the recorded information. This problem is especially true of high-capacity (1.2M) and microfloppy diskettes and disk drives, where the "width" of the recording is very narrow.

Be especially careful about excessive heat. On bright, warm days, keep diskettes you leave in your car out of direct sunlight. The hot summer sun has made roller coaster rides out of minifloppy diskettes I left on the back seat of my car. Your car's trunk can also get hot. Microfloppy diskettes are almost as vulnerable to heat as their minifloppy counterparts. Needless to say, when diskettes turn into hot Frisbees, the information stored on them is lost.

Buy the right type of diskette for your disk drive. If you have a double-sided disk drive, buy double-sided diskettes. For high-capacity minifloppy and microfloppy disk drives, buy high-capacity diskettes that undergo a strenuous certification procedure. A bad high-capacity diskette can turn up to 1.44 million bytes of information into instant trash.

Disk prices are extremely competitive, and you can buy high-quality diskettes at good prices. Also, diskette manufacturers recently have restored my faith in inexpensive, no-name diskettes. In the past two years, I have found only four unusable diskettes out of more than two thousand diskettes.

You can tell whether you have a usable diskette when you format it. One way to tell is that DOS will report a large amount of diskette space lost to bad sectors on unusable disks. You should always format diskettes before you first use them, even if you use them with the DISKCOPY command.

(DISKCOPY will format a diskette "on the fly.") Formatting diskettes individually will immediately expose problem diskettes.

You don't trust important personal or business records to scrap paper. Why trust your important computer information to "scrap" diskettes?

When you move your computer, take the diskettes out of the drive. When the disk drive door is closed, the recording heads are in contact with the diskette's surface. If the disk drive gets bounced around severely, the heads can scrape the diskette and damage it. When you move your computer, particularly if it is a portable, take the diskettes out of the disk drives. To protect the drives, insert into the drives some unusable diskettes or the cardboard protectors that came with your computer.

Some Don'ts for Diskettes

Don't touch the diskette's magnetic surface, particularly the area under the access holes. The oil from your fingers can interfere with the recording heads' ability to read and write information on the diskette. Hold minifloppy diskettes by the jacket. If you need to spin the diskette, put your fingers in the centering hole and turn your hand.

For microfloppy diskettes, leave the shutter closed. If you need to look at the diskette, open the shutter and use a pencil or pen in the sector one hole to rotate the diskette.

Keep your diskettes away from magnetic fields. Following this instruction can be tricky. You may not keep a magnet by your diskettes, but what about a video monitor, a fan, a microwave oven, or even your telephone? Each of these appliances generates a magnetic field that has the potential to "clean" your diskettes and ruin precious information.

Generally, most appliances will not affect your diskettes unless you keep them near the appliance for a long time. As a rule, keep your diskettes one foot away from any possible offender. Increase the distance for appliances that have very strong electric motors, including everything from pencil sharpeners to heating and air conditioning motors. The heavier the motor, the farther away you should keep your diskettes. Plastic holders do not stop magnetic fields. Metal boxes do a better job.

Airport security systems are a problem for the traveling diskette in the 1980s. Generally, the X-ray machines used at airports do not generate a strong enough field to erase diskettes. In addition, the distance between the X-ray source and your luggage is more than a foot. In the dozens of flights that I have taken, I have yet to lose a diskette to the X-ray machine.

If, however, you trigger the metal detector and are carrying diskettes, ask the security people to hand-inspect the carry-on diskettes. Don't allow your diskettes to be placed on top of the X-ray machine and don't permit examination with a hand scanner. The diskettes might be too close to damaging magnetic fields. Airport security people, who are now accustomed to travelling diskettes and computers, are usually happy to cooperate with such requests.

If you are mailing diskettes or carrying them and want extra protection, wrap them in aluminum foil. This extra measure of caution will reduce the possibility of magnetic fields reaching your diskettes.

Don't let your diskettes take the "Pepsi Challenge" or the "Sanka Break." Be careful with any liquids near diskettes. That also goes for cigarette, cigar, or pipe smoke and ashes, food, and similar contaminants. If any of these materials gets on your diskette and leaves a residue, the recording heads may not be able to retrieve information from the diskette. This residue can also lodge on the recording head, making it a menace to other diskettes.

A friend of mine once spilled some sweet, dessert wine on a diskette. That diskette gummed up the disk drive's recording head and ruined several other diskettes. But the cost to repair the disk drive (several hundred dollars) was minor compared to the pain of losing the information on the diskettes.

Although the shell protects microfloppy diskettes from most hazards, spilling liquids on the diskette will cause problems. The microfloppy shell is not waterproof; liquids can reach the diskette inside the shell. Also be cautious when you transport microfloppy diskettes in a shirt pocket. If you perspire, the moisture can reach the diskette.

Don't bend diskettes. Information is tightly packed on a diskette. If you put a crease in the diskette, the recording head will "jump" over the crease, and you will lose information. Remember the saying for the old punch cards: "Do not fold, spindle, or mutilate."

Don't let your diskettes get too full. Some programs generate temporary files for your data. If a diskette gets too full, you might lose the material on which you are working. For example, WordStar®, the word processing program I use, is not gracious about full diskettes. If you can't free up some room on the diskette, you will lose the last revision of your work. I don't blame Wordstar; I curse myself when I let this happen.

Periodically, use the commands CHKDSK or DIR to see how much room is left on a floppy diskette or fixed disk. To make room, erase files, or copy and then erase them.

Taking Care of Your Floppy Disk Drives

Floppy disk drives are fairly rugged pieces of equipment, but they can be damaged. The following general rules about disk drives will help you minimize damage.

When you insert a diskette, close the minifloppy drive door carefully. As I previously mentioned, if you jam a diskette into the disk drive and try to close the door, you may damage the clutches that clamp down on the diskette, the diskette itself, or both. With some practice, you will be able to tell when you have jammed a diskette.

Clean the recording heads infrequently. Disk recording heads are ceramic and require only infrequent cleaning, perhaps once every three months, or even once a year. Overcleaning disk drive heads can cause problems. Cleaning diskettes and solutions can be abrasive. Alcohol-based cleaning solutions, if overused, can erode the glue that holds the recording head on the arm. If that happens, the recording head will fall off. Generally, the gauzelike material inside the diskette jacket will catch and hold most dust and dirt that come along, so frequent cleaning is not necessary.

Many suppliers of diskette-cleaning kits insist that cleaning diskettes and solutions are less abrasive than floppy diskettes. Forgive my opinion from the "old school," but I stand by what I have said.

If you get diskette errors, run the diagnostics program that came with your computer. First, format some blank diskettes on a disk drive you know is good. Then run the diagnostics on the suspect system. If you still get diskette errors, use the cleaning diskette and rerun the diagnostics. If you still have errors, the disk drive may have other problems, or the diskette with the errors may be an unusable diskette.

Don't shock your disk drives. In other words, don't give them a strong bump or jar. The arms with the recording head can get out of place. The belt that makes the diskette spin can fall off. The disk drive door or ejector button can break. A floppy disk drive is made of metal and plastic. The plastic can break if you drop the disk drive or slam something into it.

When you move or ship your disk drives long distances, put the cardboard protectors in the drives and close the drive doors. The disk drive recording heads face each other. When the door is closed, the recording-head faces touch each other. If the disk drives receive many bumps or jolts, the recording heads can clap against each other and become damaged. If you put the cardboard protectors in the disk drives and close the doors, the cardboard pieces protect the recording heads. If you have lost your cardboard protectors, you can use unusable diskettes in place of the cardboard.

Have your disk drives serviced periodically. Disk drives need a little preventive maintenance every one or two years. For example, the belt that spins the diskette may stretch. The diskette recording heads may move a little out of the track, or the arm mechanism may wear. On minifloppy disk drives, the write-protect switch may also wear. The timing on the disk drives' motors may be off. Usually, a good service technician can test and shape up your disk drives at a reasonable cost. Such maintenance will prevent a small problem from getting bigger.

At the first sign that something is wrong with your disk drives, run your diagnostics. If the disk drive is malfunctioning, get it repaired before you ruin information on good diskettes.

Summary

In this chapter, you learned the following key points:

1. Several types of floppy diskettes are available. The PS/2 family uses microfloppy (3 1/2-inch) diskettes. The IBM Personal Computer family mainly uses minifloppy (5 1/4-inch) diskettes.

2. Diskettes are fragile and should be handled with care.

3. Disk drives are fairly rugged, but you can break them if you mishandle them. Disk drives also require occasional maintenance.

4. You should frequently back up diskettes that contain important information.

Chapter 7 focuses on fixed disk drives and how DOS uses diskettes.

7

Understanding Fixed Disks and How DOS Uses Disks

This chapter provides a description of fixed disks for Personal Computers and for PS/2 computers. The discussion also includes tips for the care of fixed disk drives. If you don't have a fixed disk yet, skip to the second part of the chapter, and read about how DOS uses disks. If you have a fixed disk or will be purchasing one soon, read on.

Understanding Fixed Disks (Winchesters)

The Winchester disk is the most commonly used fixed disk for personal computers. This fixed-disk technology was developed at IBM in 1973 under the code name Winchester. The disks have since become a practical addition to personal computers.

The Main Parts of a Fixed Disk Drive

Unlike a floppy disk drive, the recording surface, and recording heads of a Winchester disk drive are part of a sealed unit (see fig. 7.1).

Instead of floppy diskettes, a hard disk drive uses rigid, circular platters coated with metal oxide. From these platters the fixed disk drive gets the name *hard* disk drive.

The platters are fixed on a spindle (hence, the name fixed disk) that rotates at approximately 3,600 rpm. This speed is much faster than that of a floppy disk drive. Some Winchester drives use a motor directly connected to the spindle to rotate the platters. Others use a belt-and-spindle arrangement like that of the floppy disk drive.

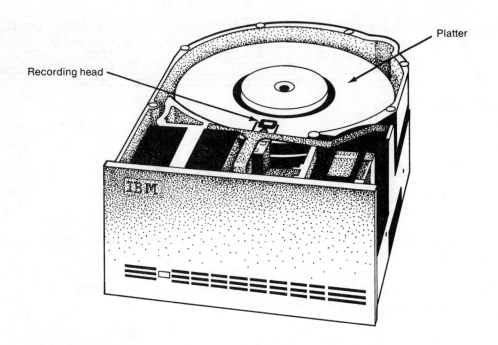

Fig. 7.1. *An exposed view of a Winchester (fixed) disk showing the fixed disk platters and recording heads.*

Because the fixed "disk" is sealed, fixed onto the spindle, and cannot be removed, the Winchester disk drive and similar drives are called nonremovable disk drives. *Fixed disk drive* and *hard file* are the terms IBM usually uses. (By the way, the term nonremovable disk also applies to RAM disks, which are discussed in Chapter 14.)

A mobile arm within the fixed disk holds the recording heads: one at the top and one at the bottom of each platter. The entire arm moves back and forth like the floppy disk drive's recording heads, but the mobile arm moves in smaller, more precise increments. The Winchester's mobile arm moves faster than the arm of a floppy disk drive, and the recording heads of the fixed disk drive are also smaller than those of a floppy disk drive. With more controlled movement and smaller recording heads, the surface of a fixed disk drive platter can receive more information.

Winchester disks for personal computers usually have platters whose diameters range from 3 1/2 to 8 inches. The most common size is the 5 1/4-inch platter, but the 3 1/2-inch platter is gaining popularity. The

5 1/4-inch platter usually holds between 2 1/2 and 10 megabytes of data per side. Fixed disk drives with the combination of two sides per platter and two platters have capacities of between 10 and 40M.

The Winchester is an "intelligent" peripheral. Most units have built-in electronics with which you can automatically verify the information you have written to the fixed disk. The units use sophisticated error-correcting techniques. Because of these capabilities, little additional time is needed to verify the writing of information to a Winchester disk.

The Hazards of Fixed Disks

Some potential problems are unique to fixed disk drives. The air pressure generated by the spinning disk lifts the recording heads just thousandths of an inch off the platter's surface. Should the heads hit any contamination (such as a hair, a particle of cigarette smoke, or even a fingerprint), they will bounce over it and crash into the platters. The physical shock of the heads crashing into the moving platters will scrape off the disk's metal coating where information is stored or will damage the recording heads. Fortunately, the Winchester's sealed environment prevents contamination from getting to the platters.

Another potential danger to most Winchester disks is damage from severe physical shock. Because the recording heads hover close to the platter's surface, a strong blow to an operating disk drive can cause the recording heads to crash into the disk surface. For this reason, you should not indiscriminately bump a Winchester disk; nor should you strongly jar the table or desk that holds the disk. And obviously, you should not drop a Winchester disk.

Winchester disks can take some punishment, however, especially when the disk drives are at rest. When a drive is not in use, it can withstand a shock of 20 to 30 times the force of gravity. When the drives are in use, some can survive shocks of only 10 times the force of gravity.

Newer Winchester disk drives use platters that have a hardened coating called *plated media*. This coating prevents the loss of information due to physical shock. The coating, often used on Winchester drives that are mounted into portable computers, forms an additional layer of protection. While plated-media drives are operating, they can withstand shock levels between 15 and 20 times the force of gravity. If you don't know how much punishment your Winchester can take, for safety's sake don't exceed 10G shocks.

Another problem with Winchester disks is disk failure. A hard disk will fail eventually, but that failure is difficult to predict. It can happen at any time during a broad time span, usually between 8,000 and 20,000 hours of use.

Because failure of a hard disk is unpredictable, you should make a habit of frequently backing up the information on the fixed disk. You cannot remove hard disk platters. Therefore, you must transfer information to separate media for backup. Most personal computer users use floppy diskettes to back up their fixed disks. If you have a fixed disk, be sure to read about the BACKUP and RESTORE commands in Chapter 18.

You can reduce the danger of damage if you prepare your Winchester disk before you move or ship it. The manufacturer of your disk drive will have included instructions for moving or shipping the fixed disk drive. The preparation procedure is usually the reverse of the procedure for installing the disk drive. Note that, as a rule, Winchester drives are more fragile than floppy disk drives.

Most disk operating systems for Winchester drives include a program you must run before you can move or ship the disk. The programs move the recording heads to the edge of the disk where no information is stored. This process of moving the recording heads into the "safety" zone is called *parking* the heads.

The parking program provided with IBM Personal Computers is called SHIPDISK.EXE and is located on the Diagnostics Disk. Run the program whenever you move the fixed disk more than a few feet.

The program for PS/2 computers is called PARKHEAD.COM and is located on the Reference Disk. You do not need to run this program as religiously as you do the program for the standard Personal Computer family. Most of the PS/2 computers use fixed disk drives that automatically park their recording heads when you turn off the computer. Still, for safety's sake, you should run PARKHEAD.COM whenever you move the hard disk.

Understanding How DOS Divides Disks

To simplify and speed the handling of a disk, DOS divides the disk into smaller pieces. Then, DOS can move rapidly to the smaller pieces and use them. Notice the use of the word disk. This term can apply to a diskette or to a fixed disk. In this book, the terms *floppy diskette*, *disk drive*, and *floppy disk drive* are used to clarify any differences.

DOS divides the disk into a series of concentric circles called *tracks* (see fig. 7.2). The number of tracks your disk uses depends on the disk drive. The motor that *steps* or moves the recording heads determines the number of tracks. The smaller the step, the more tracks a disk will have.

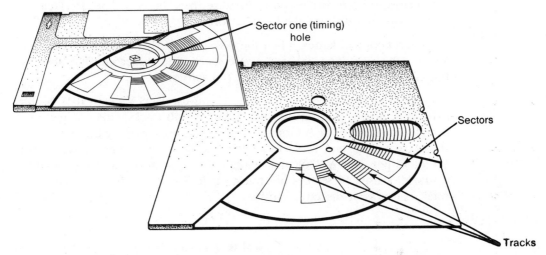

Fig. 7.2. *Layout of tracks and sectors on floppy diskettes. The number of tracks and sectors varies between types of diskette.*

Minifloppy disk drives record 48 or 96 tracks per inch. (The standard abbreviation for tracks per inch is *tpi.*) 360K disk drives record 48 tpi, and high-capacity disk drives record 96 tpi. Microfloppy disk drives record 96 tpi.

How DOS Divides Floppy Diskettes

The entire surface of a floppy diskette cannot be used for recording. Minifloppy and microfloppy disk drives record within a circular band in the middle of the diskette. The band is five-sixths of an inch wide. Thus, 48-tpi drives can create only 40 tracks. 96-tpi disk drives can create 80 tracks.

The tracks are sliced into *sectors*. DOS V1 uses 8 sectors per track. DOS V2 and V3 use 9 sectors on the same disk drive. The 720K microfloppy diskette also uses 9 sectors per track. The HC disk drives use 15 sectors per track. The 1.44M microfloppy diskette uses 18 sectors per track.

The single index hole on a minifloppy diskette signals when sector one passes under the recording head. DOS determines when the other sectors pass beneath the recording head. Because these other sectors are located by software, the disk is called soft-sectored.

For microfloppy diskettes, when the disk is properly centered on the spindle, the disk drive "knows" where sector one is located. DOS also tracks the remaining sectors through the software.

How many sectors are on your disks? If you use DOS V3 with IBM double-sided disk drives, you can use disks that have 40 tracks, either single- or double-sided, and 8 or 9 formatted sectors. A high-capacity disk has 80 tracks, two sides, and 15 sectors per track. Both microfloppy diskettes use 80 tracks per side. A 720K microfloppy uses 9 sectors per track, and the 1.44M disk uses 18 sectors per track. Table 7.1 shows the calculations of total sectors your diskettes can have.

Table 7.1
Calculating the Number of Sectors on a Diskette

Tracks	Sectors	Sides		Total Sectors
40 ×	8 ×	1	=	320
40 ×	8 ×	2	=	640
40 ×	9 ×	1	=	360
40 ×	9 ×	2	=	720
80 ×	9 ×	2	=	1,440
80 ×	15 ×	2	=	2,400
80 ×	18 ×	2	=	2,880

These figures can also indicate how much information is stored on a disk. Each sector on any disk (and on a fixed disk) holds 512 bytes. Table 7.2 shows the total bytes each disk can store.

Table 7.2
Calculating the Number of Bytes on a Diskette

Total Sectors		Bytes per Sector		Total Disk Space
320	×	512 bytes	=	163,840 bytes
640	×	512 bytes	=	327,680 bytes
360	×	512 bytes	=	184,320 bytes
720	×	512 bytes	=	368,640 bytes
1,440	×	512 bytes	=	737,280 bytes
2,400	×	512 bytes	=	1,228,800 bytes
2,880	×	512 bytes	=	1,474,560 bytes

You determine the number of kilobytes (K) on a disk by dividing the disk space by 1,024, as shown in table 7.3.

Table 7.3
Determining the Number of Kilobytes on a Diskette

Tracks	Sectors	Sides	Space in Bytes	Space in K
40	8	1	163,840	160K
40	8	2	327,680	320K
40	9	1	184,320	180K
40	9	2	368,640	360K
80	9	2	737,280	720K
80	15	2	1,228,800	1,200K
80	18	2	1,474,560	1,440K

If you format a minifloppy diskette on a regular double-sided IBM disk drive, the diskette will have 40 tracks, with 9 sectors per track. DOS uses both sides of the diskette. The maximum capacity of the diskette is 360K; thus these disk drives are called *360K disk drives*.

HC minifloppy diskettes have 80 tracks, 15 sectors per track, and 512 bytes per sector. DOS uses both sides of the diskette. The capacity of such diskettes is 1,200K and therefore, the capacity of the disk drive is 1,200K or 1.2M.

Microfloppy diskettes have 80 tracks, 9 or 18 sectors per track, and DOS uses both sides of the diskette. The 9-sector diskette holds 720K. The 18-sector diskette holds 1.440M. And, as with minifloppy diskettes, the disk drives are called 720K and 1.44M disk drives, respectively.

As a side note, high-capacity disk drives, and both types of microfloppy disk drives, are double-sided. DOS's FORMAT command from V3.0 through V3.2 does not allow you to format a single-sided HC diskette. The FORMAT command in DOS V3.3 formats a single-sided diskette at a 160K or 180K capacity, not at a 720K capacity.

How DOS Divides Fixed Disks

Fixed disks are divided in a manner similar to that of floppy diskettes. The major difference is that the fixed disk uses the concept of cylinders.

First, let's reconsider floppy diskettes. Each side has 40 or 80 tracks. The first track on the top side is directly above the first track on the bottom side; the second track on the top is above the second track on the bottom, and so on, for each of the other 38 or 78 tracks. If you were to draw a three-dimensional figure that passed through both sides of the disk at any track, you would have a *cylinder* (see fig. 7.3).

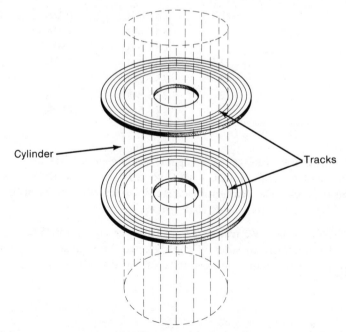

Cylinder

Tracks

Fig. 7.3. *Cylinders of a fixed disk drive are created by connecting the corresponding tracks on each side of the platters.*

For the fixed disk, think of two platters stacked on top of each other on the spindle. The tracks for each side of each platter are aligned. If you were to connect any one track through all four surfaces, you would again have a cylinder.

The PS/2's typical 40M fixed-disk drive has 731 cylinders, meaning that each surface of the eight platters has 731 tracks. The typical PC 286-XT or AT fixed disk (20M) has 615 cylinders, which means that each surface of the four platters has 615 tracks. (Each of these computers uses one cylinder for internal purposes. This single cylinder is not available for storing information.)

Fixed disk drives use 17 sectors per track. And, as with floppy diskettes, fixed disk sectors have 512 bytes per sector.

DOS places information on a diskette in the following manner. The process starts with the first side and the first track. The first side is side 0. The first track is the outermost track, track 0. Computers use 0 as a real number, not just as a placeholder. Side and track numbers start with 0.

The first sector is sector 1 (contradictory, but true). DOS starts with sector 1 and fills sectors in ascending order. The last sector filled is 9, 15, or 18, depending on the type of diskette. Then DOS flips to the second side (side 1) and uses track 0, sectors 1 through 9 (or 15 or 18). DOS goes back to side 0 and uses track 1, sectors 1 through the highest sector per track and then goes back to side 1, track 1. This process continues until the entire diskette is full. The process works the same way for the fixed disk, except that DOS uses each side of the platter (a cylinder) before moving to the next track. (The platter numbering also starts at 0.)

Why does DOS work this way? The answer is speed. Switching between the drive's recording heads is faster than moving the recording heads to a new location. This is true for both floppy and fixed disk drives.

Understanding How DOS Uses Disks

When you get a new diskette or fixed disk, it is not ready to be used. DOS must first record some "dummy" information on the disk. This process is called formatting, which you learned to do in Chapter 2.

When you format a diskette or a fixed drive, DOS records dummy data in each sector. (Additional housekeeping information is also recorded, but this information does not concern us now.) Then DOS sets up three important areas on the diskette. The first area is on the first side of the diskette in the first sector of the first track (side 0, track 0, sector 1). This area is called the *boot record*. It contains the bootstrap routine DOS uses to load itself.

After the boot record is recorded, the FORMAT command sets up two copies of the file allocation table, or FAT, which will be discussed shortly. The size of each FAT depends upon the capacity of the diskette, as shown in table 7.4.

Table 7.4
Size of the FAT for Diskettes of Various Sizes

Diskette Capacity	Size of each FAT (in sectors)
160K	1
180K	2
320K	1
360K	2
720K	3
1.2M	7
1.44M	9

Each copy of the FAT ranges from a size of 1 sector (for DOS V1, 8-sector diskettes) to 9 sectors (for 1.44M 18-sector microfloppy diskettes). The larger-capacity diskettes use larger-sized FATs. One FAT function is to indicate what type of diskette you are using: 8-, 9-, 15-, or 18-sector; 40- or 80-track; and single- or double-sided.

After the FAT is set up, DOS lays out the directory. DOS holds six pieces of information about each file in the directory:

1. The file's name

2. The file's creation date or the date the file was last changed

3. The file's creation time or the time the file was last changed

4. The file's attributes (characteristics)

5. The file's starting cluster entry in the FAT

6. The file's size in bytes

The file's attributes tell DOS whether the file needs special handling or protection. The file's attributes can be any combination of the characteristics shown in table 7.5.

Table 7.5
File Attributes Held in the Directory

Attribute	Description
Read-only	A file that may not be altered or erased.
System	A file used by the operating system. This file is normally hidden from view during regular DOS operations.
Hidden	A file hidden from view during normal DOS operations.
Volume label	An 11-character label that helps you identify the diskette. You'll see the volume label when you execute DOS commands such as DIR, CHKDSK, or TREE.
Subdirectory	A directory, instead of a file, that holds similar information about other files.
Archive	An attribute that tells DOS a file has not been backed up. This attribute is turned on when DOS creates a file or when you change a file.

Every file you use or create has one directory entry. The entry is 32 bytes long. The directory, which spans several sectors, can hold a fixed number of entries. Table 7.6 indicates how many directory entries various diskettes can have.

As you can see, single-sided diskettes (160K or 180K) use 4 sectors (2,048 bytes) and hold 64 entries in their directories. Double-sided (minifloppy 320K or 360K, or 720K microfloppy) diskettes use 7 sectors (3,584 bytes) and can hold 112 file entries. 1.2M minifloppy or 1.44M microfloppy diskettes have 14 sectors (7,168 bytes) for their directories and can each list up to 224 files.

Table 7.6
Maximum Number of Directory Entries for Diskettes

Diskette Type	Directory Sectors	Maximum # of Directory Entries
160K 180K	4	64
320K 360K 720K	7	112
1.2M 1.44M	14	224

Unlike some other operating-system directories, a DOS directory does not tell you where a particular file is stored on the disk. Instead, each file's entry in the disk directory points to an entry in the FAT. The FAT tells DOS which sectors on the diskette actually hold the file. In other words, the FAT guides DOS in finding information stored on the diskette. The FAT also indicates the sectors that are not being used.

The FAT is an important item to DOS. In fact, the FAT is so important that DOS keeps two copies of the FAT for every disk. DOS uses the directory entry to go to the correct part of the FAT for the file you use. DOS then locates your file on the disk by using the entries in the FAT.

When a file grows, DOS checks the FAT to see what sectors are not being used. When the FAT finds a free sector, DOS uses the sector.

In filling free sectors, DOS uses a first-found, first-used routine. In other words, DOS takes the first free sector it finds and puts as much of the file as possible in that sector. DOS then looks for the next free sector and places more of the file in the second sector. After a while, a file can be contained in sectors all over the disk.

Actually, when DOS looks for free sectors, it looks for a cluster. A *cluster* is the smallest unit of disk space that DOS will work with in the FAT. For a single-sided diskette, a cluster is the same as a sector. When DOS searches for a free cluster on a single-sided diskette, DOS is looking for a free sector. Double-sided minifloppy diskettes and 720K microfloppy diskettes use two sectors for each cluster. When DOS looks for a free cluster on a double-sided diskette, DOS is looking for a free pair of adjacent sectors. For the higher-capacity diskettes (1.2M or 1.44M), DOS again returns to searching for one sector.

When you instruct DOS to format a diskette with system files (you use the /S switch), the FORMAT command also places the files IBMBIO.COM, IBMDOS.COM, and COMMAND.COM on your disk. If you use the /V switch, DOS also creates a volume label. DOS places this label into the directory, thus reducing by one the number of files a disk can hold. The volume label has no entry in the FAT, however, and therefore does not take up any disk space.

All DOS programs and utilities automatically deduct the disk space used by the boot record, the FAT, and the directory. Because you cannot use these areas to record your own information, DOS does not count these areas for your total disk space. Thus, when you calculate what a disk's capacity should be, the capacities will be larger than those shown by the DIR, FORMAT, and CHKDSK programs.

In Chapter 2, you learned that the disk space that DOS lists is different from what the disk can actually hold. A double-sided disk with 40 tracks per inch and 9 sectors per track has a capacity of 360K—not the 354K that DOS shows. The calculations indicate that HC disks have a capacity of 1.2M, and not DOS's calculation of 1.1M. A microfloppy diskette's calculations are 720K and 1.44M, not DOS's 707.5K and 1.443M.

The figures that DOS gives you indicate total *user* space, not total disk space. This discrepancy presents no real problem. Just think in terms of 360K or 1.2M for disks, and remember that DOS gives you the actual number of bytes you can use on your disks.

There is one more discrepancy between the calculated capacity figures and the "true" capacity of disks. This difference is most apparent with microfloppy diskettes. You might note that the diskettes IBM provides with DOS are marked "1.0 MB capacity" for the 720K drive and "2.0 MB capacity" for the 1.44M drive. (Both MB and M stand for megabyte.) Does this mean the microfloppy diskettes can hold more information? The answer to this question is yes, the diskettes do hold more information, but you cannot directly use that additional storage space.

The 720K diskettes actually hold 1M, and the 1.44M drives hold 2M. The space "reduction" comes from the need to format the disk. When you format a disk, either floppy or fixed, additional "dummy" information is recorded that permits the disk-drive electronics and DOS to find information on the disk. Some information consists of electronic markings that identify each track and sector. DOS uses this information to ensure that the drive is reading or writing information at the correct disk location. Additional information, called a *cyclic redundancy check* (CRC), is used to verify that the disk information has been recorded correctly.

This additional, but vital, overhead information is recorded on all disks and occupies approximately thirty percent of the potential storage area. Because of this need for auxiliary information, manufacturers of disk drives quote two capacities: an unformatted capacity (without subtracting the space used by this overhead information), and a formatted (or usable) capacity.

As I mentioned earlier, DOS retains some space from a disk's usable storage area to hold data-tracking information. For this reason, a 1M formatted microfloppy diskette has a usable data-storage area of 720K. A 2M formatted diskette has 1.44M of usable data-storage areas. After DOS dedicates some space for its use, a 2M floppy diskette has a usable storage area of only 1.42M and the 1M microfloppy has a usable storage area of 703K.

When you buy diskettes for microfloppy drives, you can buy diskettes marked *DS/DD, 2S/2D,* (both designating double-sided, double-density diskettes), or diskettes marked *1M* or *1MB* for 720K disk drives. If you have a 1.44M disk drive, you should buy microfloppy diskettes marked *HC* or *HD* (high-capacity or high-density) or diskettes marked as having a *2M* or *2MB* capacity.

Summary

In this chapter, you were introduced to the following important points:

1. Fixed disks are high-speed, high-capacity storage devices that are more resistant to problems than other types of disks.

2. DOS uses certain sections of each disk or fixed disk. DOS uses concentric rings, which are called tracks. Each track is divided into sectors. The number of tracks, sectors, sides of a disk or fixed-disk platter, and platters determines a disk's capacity.

3. DOS records a directory and a file allocation table (FAT) on each disk when you format the disk. The number of files that a disk's directory can hold is based on the size of the directory.

4. DOS maintains a list of attributes you can assign to every file. The attributes indicate whether you can alter the file, whether you can list the file in the directory, whether you can back up the file, and whether the file is actually another directory.

5. Disk drives have two rated capacities: formatted and unformatted. When you format a disk, DOS places on each disk necessary file-tracking, internal information. Storing this information reduces the disk's usable capacity.

Chapter 8 discusses names for disk drives and other devices. You'll also use the LABEL command to assign a volume label to a disk, and you'll learn another use for the COPY command.

8

Naming Disk Drives and Files

Part I of this book discussed disks and disk files and how to use them, but said little about what files are. In this chapter, you'll learn more about files, particularly how DOS uses them and how to name them. You'll also see how to use the TYPE command to display a file's contents.

Before you learn about disk files, you will be introduced to a list of rules for disk drive names, and you will learn how to use the LABEL command to create or change a disk's volume label.

Naming Disk Drives

As you already know, a disk drive name consists of two characters—a letter followed by a colon. With DOS V3, a computer can have up to 26 disk drives. Most computer systems, however, use between two and six disk drives, which are given the names A, B, C, D, E, and F. (You may recall that DOS V3 also automatically translates lowercase letters into uppercase, so when you type drive names, you can use either upper- or lowercase characters.)

Chapter 5 outlined the rules for naming devices, but did not discuss naming disk drives. The following rules govern the use of disk drive names:

Rules for Naming Disk Drives

1. A disk drive must have a two-character name. The second character must be a colon (:).

2. The first disk drive is A; the second disk drive is B; and so on.

3. The character for each additional disk drive is one character higher in the ASCII character set. The final usable letter is Z.

4. You may use either upper- or lowercase letters for disk drive names.

5. When you tell DOS to run a program from a disk, you may precede the program name with the disk drive name.

6. Almost any time you give a file name, you may precede the file name with the disk drive name.

7. Don't try to use a nonexistent disk drive. If you do, DOS usually will display an error message.

Notice rules 5 and 6. These rules govern how you tell DOS where to find your programs and other files. These rules are a more formal statement of the discussion of the current disk drive you encountered in Chapter 3.

Having given the rules for disk drive names, we'll cover the LABEL command next.

Labeling a Disk Electronically

DOS V3 allows a disk to have a volume name, which is an electronic disk label. Volume names have two purposes. First, the volume name helps you to identify the disk. The FORMAT command uses the disk's volume label to confirm your intent to reformat a fixed disk. Second, volume names are a convenient way to group disks. The volume name appears when you ask for a directory of a disk, perform a CHKDSK (check disk), display the directory path (using the TREE command), or use a variety of other commands.

When you format a disk with the FORMAT command and use the /V switch, DOS asks you for an 11-character volume name. The request appears after DOS has physically formatted the disk. FORMAT is one of two DOS commands that make a volume label. The other command, LABEL, is discussed here and in the next section.

The following list summarizes the rules for volume labels. These rules are almost identical to those for file names, which are discussed later in this chapter.

Rules for Volume Labels

1. A volume label can be from 1 to 11 characters long.

2. Valid characters for volume labels are the following:

   a. The letters A through Z or a through z

   b. The numbers 0 through 9

   c. The special characters and punctuation symbols

   $ # & @ ! & ( ) - { } ' _ ~

d. The space (the use of which is illegal for file names)

3. The following characters cannot be used in a volume label:

a. Any control character, including Esc (27d or 1Bh)
   and Del (127d or 7Fh)

b. The characters

   + = / [] " : ; , ? * \ <;>| .

4. If you type a name that is too long or use an illegal character, DOS V3.3 will use the first eleven characters. For versions of DOS before V3.3, DOS asks you to enter the volume label again.

5. A disk drive name cannot precede the volume label when you use the FORMAT command. A disk drive name may precede the volume label when you use the LABEL command.

6. FORMAT and LABEL are the only DOS-supplied programs that make disk labels. To make a disk label with FORMAT, you must use the /V switch.

Remember the three most important rules for volume names. First, each floppy diskette or fixed disk drive can have only one volume name. Second, a volume name is the only name that can have a space in it. Third, a volume label, unlike a file name, cannot contain a period (.). For the most part, the rules for volume names are a little less restrictive than the rules for file names.

With DOS V2, you had only one opportunity to give a volume label: when you formatted the disk. The LABEL command gives you the flexibility to add, change, or delete volume labels at any time.

The syntax for the LABEL command is

   *dc:*LABEL *d:volume_label*

dc: is the disk drive that holds the LABEL command. LABEL is an external command. You may recall from Chapter 4 that an external command must be loaded from a disk before you use the command.

d: is the name of the drive that holds the disk to be labeled. If you don't give a disk drive name, the disk in the current drive will be labeled. If the specified or current disk drive is a floppy disk drive, the diskette will be labeled. If the drive is a fixed disk, the fixed disk will be labeled.

The volume label can contain 1 to 11 characters. For versions of DOS prior to V3.3, if you give the volume label on the command line, you cannot use a space in the name. You can use a space with LABEL V3.3.

With LABEL pre-V3.3, the reason for not allowing a space is that DOS interprets the command as having two volume labels (one before the space and another after the space). When that happens, you will get the following message:

```
Illegal characters in volume label
```

When you include a space on the command line, DOS sees the space as a *delimiter* (an item separator), not as a "legal" character. LABEL pre-V3.3 simply becomes confused. You'll get the `Illegal characters in volume label` message if you enter an improper volume label on the command line when the LABEL command requests a volume name. LABEL V3.3 knows that spaces are legal in a volume label and does not become confused.

If you omit the volume label on the command line, DOS responds with:

```
Volume in drive A is current_label
Volume label (11 characters, ENTER for none)?_
```

Here, `current_label` is the existing volume label of the disk. If the disk has no label, DOS displays the message `no label`.

To add a label to a disk or to replace a current label, type a valid volume label and press Enter. For any version of DOS V3, you may use a space in the label. When you press Enter, DOS replaces the nonexistent or old label with the volume label you entered.

You can use the LABEL command to remove a label from a disk. To delete a volume label, type:

   dc:LABEL *d*:

Don't give a volume label. When DOS asks for the volume label, just press Enter. DOS will respond:

```
Delete current volume label (Y/N)?_
```

To delete the label, type a Y for yes, and press Enter. If you don't want to delete the label, enter N for no, which stops the LABEL command, leaving the current label intact.

The LABEL command does not harm existing files on a disk. You may use the LABEL command as often as you want. Remember that volume labels are available for your convenience in identifying disks. When you use LABEL, try to select names that are meaningful to you.

Understanding Files

Disk storage is often compared to a filing cabinet that has several drawers (fig. 8.1). Inside each drawer are file folders. Each folder is used for a particular subject (fig. 8.2). The folder contains facts about the subject, such as personnel records, charge-card receipts, bank statements, invoices, appliance warranties, automobile repair records, and so on.

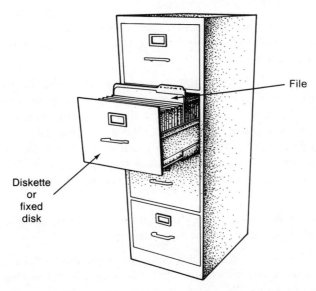

File

Diskette
or
fixed
disk

Fig. 8.1. *Electronic files are like a traditional file cabinet. The drawers are diskettes or fixed disk platters. The file folders are files.*

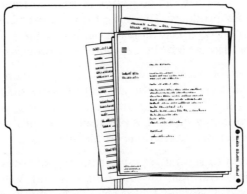

Fig. 8.2. *Inside an electronic file, a record is like a sheet of paper. The physical size of the record, like the sheet of paper, has little bearing on what information is held in the record or how the information is used.*

A file folder can be empty, or it can hold one or more papers relating to the subject. For example, a folder for a checking account may hold monthly bank statements and the canceled checks returned from the bank.

The person controlling the filing cabinet decides how the files should be arranged. The file folders may be sorted alphabetically or by some other coding system. For example, the folders can also be organized by time with newer folders placed after older folders as new topics are filed. The arrangement helps the person find a particular file. Of course, the folders can also be left completely disorganized.

Inside each file folder, the information can be organized in some similar manner. Again, the person in control of the filing cabinet decides how the records should be arranged.

There's something to be said for filing systems. When a system is used properly, it works well. But when you don't file new items in their proper order, either in the cabinet or in the file folders, a lot of work is required to straighten up the cabinet. The same is true if a drawer falls out of the cabinet, and the file folders fall out. The worst disaster is a fire or theft, which permanently removes the information from the cabinet. The information is lost unless another copy of the records is stored somewhere else.

This analogy fits disk storage. The filing cabinet is the disk drive. The drawers are the floppy diskettes or fixed disk platters.

A file is a set of related items. A disk file is the equivalent of the file folder. You can store any information in a file folder. You can also place any related data in a disk file.

For example, you can place in a disk file any of the following: the programs you use, the names and addresses of your customers or friends, or the orders for your products. The text of this chapter is in a disk file. The only restriction on what can be placed in a disk file is that the information must be data which the computer can process electronically.

A file's smallest allowable size is 0, which is no information at all. The size of the largest disk file depends on the amount of disk storage available. You cannot create a file that is larger than the capacity of your disk. If a file is stored on two floppy disks, it is physically two files, not one. Some programs may place further restrictions on file size.

DOS allows files of up to several *gigabytes* (billions of bytes). At present, no magnetic disk drive can hold this much information. Video disks, the emerging frontier of disk storage, will eventually be able to hold gigabytes of information. However, the current generation of video disks, called *compact disk ROMs* or *CD ROMs*, can hold just 550 megabytes of information. IBM's optical disk holds 200 megabytes. For the next year, DOS's multigigabyte limit will be appreciated but not approached.

Just as with a filing cabinet, you determine the information you put in a disk file. You also determine the way information is organized in the file. In other words, you have full control of the filing system and your programs.

Let's carry the analogy further. Each item inside the file folder is called a record. There are two types of records: physical and logical.

A DOS *physical record* is comparable to a sheet of paper. Each sheet is a certain size, 8 1/2 by 11 inches, for instance. Each DOS physical record is 512 bytes. Both records are fixed in size.

A logical record is a set of related items. Each record in the file is organized according to some basic information, such as a person's name, address, city, state, and ZIP Code. Each person occupies one record in the file. Most programs use this definition of a logical record. (For more information on both types of records, look at books on assembly language programming, other programming languages, and data management.)

Viewing a File's Contents

If a file can hold anything, how do you know what is in any one disk file? There are several ways to find out. First, every disk file has a name listed in the directory. Each file name must be unique, or DOS gets confused. Ideally, if you can remember the file name, you can remember what is in the file.

When you look at the file names in a directory, you may spot a familiar file name. You know that the file holds the names and addresses of your friends. How do you display this information? That will depend on what is really in the disk file. If the file is stored on disk as ASCII text—which I'll explain in a moment— you can use DOS's TYPE command to display the file's contents on-screen.

ASCII is the acronym for American Standard Code for Information Interchange, the standard way your computer translates its binary ones and zeros into letters, numbers, punctuation, symbols, and special computer characters. Appendix C contains the ASCII chart for characters.

"As ASCII text" means that the program you used took each character as you typed it and put it into the disk file with no changes to the code. The TYPE command tells DOS to display on the video screen the information from a file. The TYPE command "types" on the screen the information from the file. Thus, TYPE provides a quick way to display the contents of an ASCII file without your having to use another program.

If your program transforms information and then stores it on disk, you will need a program that can undo this transformation. For example, if your program crunches or encrypts information so that a file takes less disk space, the information is not stored character by character as ASCII text. Should you try to use the TYPE command on the file, the information will look like gibberish. Generally, the program that crunched the stored information can reverse any encoding.

Remember that DOS stores arbitrary bytes on the disk. In computer terms, arbitrary means "any possible." The bytes can be humanly readable text, manipulated data, or program instructions. DOS does not care. It stores the bytes it was told to store. What these bytes represent is not DOS's concern. DOS is a mindless file clerk that follows your instructions. You and your programs tell DOS what to store.

When you want to use a file, you give DOS the name of the file. DOS goes to the drawer (the floppy or fixed disk), searches for a file with the appropriate name, grabs the file, and "opens" it. If there is no file by the name you gave, DOS reports that fact.

You can also tell DOS to create a new file. If a file folder (disk file) with the name you provide already exists, DOS empties the file folder before putting any new information into it. Otherwise, DOS prepares a new file folder (puts the file name into the directory).

On your command, DOS pulls (reads) information from the file or places (writes) information into the file. DOS can be told to start at the beginning of the file or to go to a specific location (record) in the file. In each case, DOS does the hard part of the work. The operating system handles the mundane problems of creating a file, expanding a file, and retrieving information from or placing information into the file. You and your programs just tell DOS what to do.

Viewing a File's Contents with the TYPE Command

To view a disk file's contents, you can use the TYPE command that is built into COMMAND.COM. The TYPE command's syntax is

TYPE *d:*filename*.ext*

The *d:* is the optional name of the disk drive that holds the file you want to view. **filename** is the file's mandatory root name. *.ext* is the file's optional extension. If the file has an extension, you must type the extension because it is part of the file's exact name. If the file does not have an extension, don't include one.

TYPE is one DOS command that does not allow you to use a wildcard (* or ?) in the file name. To use TYPE, you must enter an exact, unambiguous file name.

To try the command, first list a file's directory with the DIR command. If you have a file that ends in .BAT or .TXT, try to use the TYPE command to display one of the files. At the DOS system prompt (A>), type the command TYPE followed by a space and the name and extension of the file. When you press Enter, you should see the contents of the file on the video screen.

A file's contents will frequently exceed the 24-line limit of the video screen. To pause the display to read the lines, use the Ctrl-S, Ctrl-Num Lock, or Pause keys. When you have read the screen, press any key to unfreeze the screen.

Now try to type a program file. Ask for a directory of a disk again. Do you see any files that end with COM or EXE? At the DOS system prompt (A>), type TYPE followed by a space and the complete file name, including the file's extension if it has one. Don't be alarmed by what you see on the screen. The information should look like nonsense. You may recognize a few words or phrases, but the screen looks mostly incomprehensible. This type of display results when you use the TYPE command to type a program file.

Although TYPE displays any file's contents, you will be able to read only the files that contain ASCII text. Files that are not stored as ASCII text will be unintelligible.

To view a program file's contents, you must use another program. If the program is written in interpretive BASIC (Disk or Advanced BASIC), use BASIC to load and list the program. If the program is in machine language (the native language of the computer's CPU), you'll need a disassembler, a program that transforms the binary language of the computer into humanly readable instructions. (DEBUG, a program provided with DOS, handles this function and many others. A discussion of DEBUG, however, is beyond the scope of this book.)

Facts about Files

The following list outlines some basic information about files:

1. A file holds a set of related information.

2. Information in a file is arbitrary. This information can be in a form you can read (ASCII text), can be readable only by programs, or can be a program itself.

3. You can use the TYPE command to display a file's contents. If the file holds only ASCII text, the display will be meaningful. If the file holds something else, the display will look like nonsense.

4. Every file has a name. The name must be unique in the directory for the disk that holds the file.

5. DOS acts as a file clerk, handling the storage and retrieval of files. You are responsible for what the file contains and how its contents are organized.

Understanding File Names

We usually think in terms of names. A name is a word or phrase we associate with a person, object, or action. When a name is understood and accepted, two or more people can use it to identify someone or something.

To converse with computers, we also use names. You've already seen how DOS knows a disk file by its name. This name becomes the handle, the common phrase you, your programs, and DOS use to work with a file.

Recognizing Legal File Names

As you'll recall from Chapter 3, a file name has two parts, a root name and a suffix. The root name can have from 1 to 8 characters. The suffix, or extension, can have from 1 to 3 characters. If a suffix is used, it is separated from the root name by a period (.). The suffix is optional.

There are restrictions on the characters you can use in a file name. Some programs may even demand certain names. Some files don't need extensions. Other files need specific root names or extensions. The need for an extension, and the extension's name depends on what is in the file and how the file will be used.

Why use an extension? In some cases, DOS or your programs force you to use a certain extension. In other cases, your applications programs assume that you will use a certain extension unless you indicate otherwise.

Each program file requires a certain extension. Whenever you want DOS to run a program stored on the disk, the program must have an extension of .COM or .EXE. The abbreviation .COM stands for a machine language *command* file. The extension .EXE stands for a DOS-*executable* file. The program file's extension informs DOS that the file is a program and tells DOS how to execute the file.

A batch file must have the extension .BAT, or DOS will not recognize the file as a batch file. Batch files are discussed in Chapters 12 and 13.

If you look at the directory of the DOS V3 Operating Disk, you'll see a file called MORTGAGE.BAS. This file, a sample program that is written in the BASIC computer language, calculates mortgage payments. Notice that the file's extension is .BAS. Unless you otherwise instruct BASIC, BASIC automatically stores BASIC programs with the .BAS extension. That BASIC automatically assigns this default extension is extremely convenient. If you wanted to load and run the mortgage program from BASIC, you would type:

   RUN "MORTGAGE"

instead of

   RUN "MORTGAGE.BAS"

In this case, BASIC allows some shorthand by automatically adding the .BAS extension to the file name. Whenever you load or save the program, BASIC adds the .BAS for you.

Table 8.1 lists some standard extensions. Included are file-name extensions that programs use automatically, extensions that files must have, and some common-sense extensions that will help you identify files. Usually the programs you use will determine the extensions you'll need.

Of the extensions listed, four are the most common: .COM, .EXE, .TXT, and .DAT. Beware of the .TMP, .BAK, and .$xx extensions. (This last extension can have any two characters in the place of xx.) Don't use these extensions for your files. If you do, and your programs create files that use these extensions, you will wipe out files you want to keep.

Table 8.1
Common File Name Extensions

Extension	What It Is
.ASM	Assembler source file
.BAK	Backup file
.BAS	BASIC program file
.BAT	Batch file
.BIN	Binary program file
.C	C source file
.COM	Command (program) file
.CPI	Code page information file (DOS)
.DAT	Data file
.DBF	dBASE III® database file
.DOC	Document (text) file
.DTA	Data file
.EXE	Executable program file
.IDX	Index file (Q&A™)
.HLP	Help file
.KEY	Keyboard macro file (ProKey™)
.LET	Letter
.LST	Listing of a program (in a file)
.LIB	Program library file
.MAC	Keyboard macro file (Superkey®)
.MAP	Linker map file
.MSG	Program message file
.NDX	An index file (dBASE III)
.OBJ	Intermediate object code (program) file
.OVL	Program overlay file
.OVR	Program overlay file
.PAS	Pascal source file
.PIF	Program Information File (TopView/Windows)
.PRN	Listing of a program (in a file)
.SYS	System file or device driver file
.TMP	Temporary file
.TXT	Text file
.$xx	Temporary or incorrectly stored file
.WK1	Lotus 1-2-3®, Release 2 worksheet file

The following list summarizes the rules for file names.

Rules for Naming Files

1. A file name must have

   a. A root name of 1 to 8 characters

   b. An optional extension of 1 to 3 characters

   c. A period between the root name and the extension name
   if an extension is used

2. The characters permitted in a file name are

   a. The letters A through Z. (Lowercase letters are
   transformed automatically into uppercase.)

   b. The numbers 0 through 9

   c. The special characters and punctuation symbols
   $ # & @ ! ^ ( ) - { } ' _ ~

3. The following characters cannot be used in a file name:

   a. Control characters, including Esc and Del

   b. The space character

   c. The characters
   + = / [] " : ; , ? * \ <> |

4. If DOS finds an illegal character in a file name, DOS stops at the
   character preceding the illegal one and uses the legal part of the
   name.

5. A device name can be part of a root name but cannot be the
   entire root name. For example, CONT.DAT or AUXI.TXT are okay,
   but CON.DAT or AUX.TXT are not.

6. Each file name in a directory must be unique.

7. A drive name and a path name usually precede a file name. (Path
   names are discussed in Chapter 10.)

Note: Previous versions of Microsoft® BASIC are notorious for not
translating lowercase letters for file names into uppercase letters. Be wary
of this problem.

You might notice what seems to be a slight contradiction in the rules for
file names. A file name cannot use the wildcard characters ? and *. With
some DOS commands, however, you can use file names that contain
wildcard characters. The contradiction is simple to explain: No file can use

a wildcard character in its name, but file names in DOS commands can contain wildcards when DOS searches for file names.

Table 8.2 lists two sets of file names. Each file name in the first set is correctly phrased and has no illegal characters. The file names in the second list are illegal. An explanation of why the name is illegal follows each name.

Table 8.2
Legal and Illegal File Names

Legal Names	Illegal Names	Explanation
ABCDEFGH.IJK	ABCDEFGHIJ.KLM	Too many characters in the root name
MYLETTER.TXT	.TXT	No root name
TOGO.COM	TO:GO	Cannot use a colon
MYFILE	MY FILE	Cannot have a space in the name
PRINT.EXE	PRN.TXT	PRN is a device name
12-4PM	THIS,WAY	Cannot use a comma
CINDY2	ABCD.EFGH	Too many letters in the extension
(CARL)	?ISIT.CAL	Cannot use ?

Table 8.2 lists valid and invalid file names. A valid file name is correctly phrased; an invalid name has an illegal character. (The next section explains what happens when you use an illegal file name.)

But what about good and bad file names?

A good file name has two characteristics. The first characteristic is that the file name is meaningful to you and to others who use your files. The file name %$!12.XYZ is perfectly valid, but how can you tell what is in the file? Will you remember its contents when you come back to use it in several days or weeks?

Give each file a name that identifies how the file is used or what it contains. Using an easily remembered file name helps you quickly locate the file you want. For example, the file FRIENDS.DAT is easy to remember as a data file that holds your friends' names and addresses.

The second characteristic is that a group of related files should have similar names. Use names with some common element such as, for example, the extension .LET for all files that are letters. Using common elements makes copying and deleting files easier. The first part of the root name should be common to command files. The latter part of the root name should be changed to reflect the contents of the specific file. The extension, which should reflect the file type, can be the same or different for all files.

Two examples of how to use good file names can be seen in the way I named files that contain chapters of this book and files that contain letters to an associate. Every chapter of this book is in a file whose name begins with the letters CHAP, followed by two numbers to indicate the chapter, and the extension .PCD (for *PC DOS*). For example, this chapter has the name CHAP08.PCD. My letter to William Smith is in a file whose name consists of the name SMITH, followed by a letter that indicates order, and the extension .LET for letter. The file names are SMITHA.LET, SMITHB.LET, SMITHC.LET, and so on.

You will see greater advantages to naming files in this fashion when you become familiar with your computer. You will quickly be able to locate and remember the contents of the many files you create, and you will be able to quickly perform DOS commands on these files by using wildcard file names.

Avoiding Illegal File Names

When you use an illegal file name, one of two things can happen. DOS will give you an error message and will not perform the operation, or DOS will perform the operation and create a strange file name, based on what you typed. If you know how DOS will react to illegal file names, you will be able to avoid some problems and quickly correct others if they occur.

How DOS reacts to illegal characters depends on what illegal characters are used and where they are located in the file name. Generally, DOS stops forming the root name or extension when it finds the first illegal character. The following list shows what DOS does when it encounters file names whose lengths are illegal:

Illegal File Name	*What DOS Does*
ABCDEFGHIJ.KLM	Uses the file called ABCDEFGH.KLM
ABCD.EFGH	Uses the file called ABCD.EFG

If you use too many characters, DOS ignores the additional ones. This applies separately to the root name and to the extension. In this first example, DOS ignores the characters IJ. In the second example, DOS ignores the fourth character (H) in the extension.

If you try to use just an extension (such as .TXT) as a file name, DOS displays an error message. DOS reacts this way because a file must always have a root name.

DOS treats punctuated or separated file names as follows:

Illegal File Name	*What DOS Does*
TO:GO	Uses two names, TO and GO
THIS,WAY	Uses two names, THIS and WAY
MY FILE	Uses two names, MY and FILE

DOS separates file names that contain a colon, semicolon, comma, quotation mark, equal sign, or space. These punctuation marks and the space act as separators, or delimiters, in file names. In each example, DOS sees two names: one name before the delimiter and another after it. The delimiter itself is discarded and does not become part of the file name. What happens next depends on the program you are using. Suppose that you are using the COPY command and you type

A>**COPY TO;GO MYFILE**

The COPY command will display an error message indicating that you have given too many parameters—three file names (TO, GO, and MYFILE) when you should have given two. (Parameters are discussed in Chapter 12.)

Other programs can react differently. A program expecting only one name may not check for additional file names. In the example just given, such a program would use only the file name TO. GO and MYFILE would simply be ignored.

DOS handles the file name PRN.TXT in the following manner:

Illegal File Name	*What DOS Does*
PRN.TXT	Uses the printer for input or output

PRN is a reserved device name that represents the printer. A *reserved* name has special meanings to DOS. If you use the name PRN.TXT as a file name, one of three things may happen:

1. DOS attempts to get information from the "file" (that is, tries to get input from the printer) and quickly returns without getting anything. What happens next depends on the program used. In most cases, the result is not what you want.

2. If you are putting information into this file and the printer is turned off or not selected, DOS waits for 20 to 30 seconds and then gives an error message telling you that PRN (the printer) is not ready.

3. If the printer is on and selected, DOS writes the information to the printer and does not save the information to a disk file.

These possibilities apply whenever you use a device name as a root name. DOS uses the device instead of the disk file. If you use such names as AUX.TXT, LPT2.MAC, or NUL.COM as file names, the results will not be what you want.

A word of caution about unique file names is necessary. Two files in the same directory cannot have the same name. A file name can be considered the "identity property" of a disk file. You must make sure that each file name is different by adding, subtracting, or changing characters in either the root name or the extension of similarly named files. If you try to use file names that are not different, DOS will be confused and won't know which file you are designating.

If you try to change a file name to match a name already in the directory, DOS gives you the message:

```
Duplicate file name or File not found
```

and will not rename the file. DOS protects you and itself from having two files with the same name in the same directory.

Remember the caveat from Chapter 4 about the COPY command. When duplicate file names exist on the source and destination disks, the destination file is deleted, and then the source file is copied. In other words, the existing destination file is lost, and DOS gives no warning. When in doubt, you should check both directories for duplicate file names before you copy. Use the DIR command on both disks. This check can keep you from inadvertently losing a good file.

Summary

In this chapter, you learned the following key points:

1. Certain rules apply when you use disk drive names, create volume labels, or use files.

2. The LABEL command adds, changes, or deletes volume labels.

3. A file is a set of related information stored under a common file name.

4. A file can hold any information.

5. A valid file name contains legal characters. A good file name is a valid file name that is meaningful to you. Use part of a common name for files that are related.

6. If you use an invalid file name, the results may vary, but they will seldom be what you want.

In Chapter 9, you'll learn about I/O redirection, and I'll also show you some tricks that make the computer easier to use.

9

Using Redirection and Piping

Understanding redirection and piping is not vital to your use of the computer. But if you know how to use these techniques, you can make several computer-related tasks easier. In this chapter, you'll learn how to use redirection and piping. One of the tips you'll learn is how to "read" a directory of a disk into a document created by a word-processing program.

If your system has a printer, turn it on, and make sure that it is ready to print. Now press Ctrl-PrtSc (or Ctrl-Print Screen). You learned to use Ctrl-PrtSc in Chapter 3. This sequence prints what you send to the screen.

Now type DIR, and press Enter. The directory of the disk prints on your screen and on the printer. Press Ctrl-PrtSc again to turn off the printing.

Now type

   DIR >PRN

What happened? DOS printed on the printer a directory of the disk. DOS did not print the directory on the screen. You have just used an interesting DOS feature: I/O redirection.

The Meaning of Redirection

What is I/O redirection? You know that I/O stands for input and output. In *redirection*, you tell DOS to change the source or destination that is normally used for input and output. Let's look at three new terms that help explain the concept of redirection.

DOS has three standard places from which it usually receives or to which it sends characters (see fig. 9.1). *Standard input* is the keyboard, where your programs and DOS normally expect characters to be typed. Typed characters usually come from standard input. *Standard output* is the video screen, where programs and DOS usually display information. Displayed characters normally go to standard output. *Standard error* is also the video screen, where your programs and DOS report any errors that occur. Error messages go to standard error.

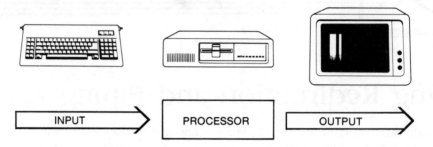

Fig. 9.1. *The standards for input and output. The keyboard is used for input, and the video display for output. The video display is also used for reporting errors.*

When you redirect I/O, you tell DOS to use a device other than the keyboard or video screen to receive characters or to send the characters somewhere other than where they are normally sent (see fig. 9.2). Instead of letting DOS get characters from the keyboard, you can have DOS get characters from a disk file or from any other device. You also can tell DOS to display characters in a disk file, on a printer, or on another device.

Redirection occurred when you typed DIR >PRN. When you issued that command, DOS tricked the program into thinking that it was putting information on the standard device: standard output (that is, the screen).

The most frequent use of input redirection is to create a "canned" set of answers to a frequently used program. Programmers often use this trick: They create a disk file that contains a set of standard "answers" for the program with which they are working. When users run the program, DOS is directed to "trick" the program into getting its answers from the file, rather than from a person typing responses at the keyboard. The user runs the program by using input redirection, rather than by remembering the answers that the program requires.

Output redirection is most commonly used to print on the printer data that is normally displayed on the video screen. The other common use for output redirection is to "capture" into a disk file data that is displayed on the video screen. You can then edit the file or print copies of it.

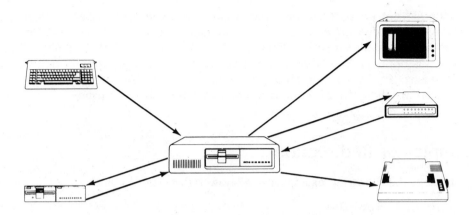

Fig. 9.2. *A "carousel" of devices can be used to redirect input and output. Notice that some devices (such as disk drives and modems) can be used to send input and receive output. Other devices can be used for input only (the keyboard) or output only (the video display or printer).*

The Symbols for Redirection ($<$, $>$, $>>$)

Redirection uses three reserved symbols:

$<$ Redirects a program's input

$>$ Redirects a program's output

$>>$ Redirects a program's output but adds the text to an established file

You can use these symbols only at the DOS system level when you want them to have their reserved meanings. You add the symbol(s) and the file or device name to the command you type. The syntax is

   symbol devicename

or

   symbol *d:***filename.***ext*

For the first syntax form, you use the appropriate redirection symbol followed by the name of the device, for example, $>$**PRN**. In the second syntax form, you use the appropriate redirection symbol followed by a file name. You may *not* use wildcards (* or ?) in the file name. (Although this book has not yet covered the topic of paths, you can place a path name between the disk drive name and the file name. This subject is covered in Chapter 10.) Using a space between the symbol and the device or file name is optional. You *cannot*, however, have a space within the device or file name. The redirection (the symbol and device and/or filename) can appear anywhere on the command line *after* the command name.

Examples of Redirection

Look at the following examples that show redirection:

1. **DIR** >**DISKDIR**

   This sequence redirects the output of the directory command (DIR) to a disk file called DISKDIR.

2. **CHKDSK** >**COM1**

   This command redirects the CHKDSK program's output to the serial port.

3. **MYPROG** <**B:ANSWERS**

   This command redirects the input of MYPROG from the file ANSWERS on drive B.

In the third example, MYPROG is not expecting you to type anything from the keyboard. Instead, MYPROG will get its input from the disk file called ANSWERS.

Be cautious in using the > symbol. Don't use an existing file name if you want to keep that file. When you use > to redirect output to a disk file, DOS erases any disk file in the directory that has the name you used. DOS then creates a new file to hold the output. In example 1, if a file in the current directory has the name DISKDIR, that file will be erased.

To add redirected output to an established file, use the symbol >>. This symbol *appends* the output to the end of an existing file but does not erase the file's original contents. To change example 1 and add the additional copy of the directory to DISKDIR, you type

   DIR >>**DISKDIR**

If you look at the way each symbol points, you will remember how redirection works. The < points away from the device or file and says, "Take the input from here." The > and >> point toward the device or file and say, "Put output there."

If you are thinking about what can happen to error messages when you redirect the output to a printer or a disk file, for example, you are one step ahead. The result depends on the program. If your program uses standard error to display error messages, the message appears on your video screen, not in the redirected file output or in the output redirected to a device. If the program does not use standard error, the error message is also redirected.

Fortunately, all DOS commands and programs use standard error. (Disk and Advanced BASIC also have provisions for standard input, output, and error.)

Hands-on Practice: Using I/O Redirection with SORT

One of the programs provided on your Operating diskette is SORT.EXE. SORT sorts lines, items, or characters in ASCII order. You'll read more about SORT later in this book, but for now you'll use SORT to practice I/O redirection. You'll first use SORT without I/O redirection to see how the program works. Then you'll try SORT again, first redirecting the input, next redirecting the output, and finally redirecting SORT's input and output.

SORT is an external DOS program, and you must have your master Operating diskette in drive A. Or if you have a fixed disk, you must use the PATH command to do this exercise. In this example, I'll use the fixed disk, drive C, which must be the current disk drive. If you use the floppy disk, make sure that the A drive is the current disk drive.

Using SORT and Redirection

In this first example, you'll enter lines from the keyboard that SORT will use. SORT will display the lines in an ASCII-sorted order on the video display. Type

    SORT

The cursor will drop to the next line. Because you did not direct SORT to get its lines from another location, SORT is waiting for you to input lines from the keyboard. Type these lines:

This is the last line.
This is the intermediate line.
This is the first line.

After you have typed the end line, press Enter. Then you must tell DOS you have completed entering lines by pressing F6, the special-function key. Press Enter again.

SORT sorts the lines and displays the lines on the video screen. Because you did not redirect SORT's output, SORT will display the results on the video screen. Your screen should look something like this:

```
C>SORT
This is the last line.
This is the intermediate line.
This is the first line.
^Z
This is the first line.
This is the intermediate line.
This is the last line.

C>_
```

The lines are sorted in ASCII order (similar to alphabetical order).

Using SORT and Redirection on a Disk File

In the next practice session, you'll redirect input to the SORT command from a disk file. You'll first create a file of lines by using the COPY CON command. Type

COPY CON MARY

This line directs the COPY command to take input from the keyboard and place it in the file called MARY. The prompt will disappear, and the cursor will appear on the following line. Now type these lines:

Mary had a little lamb
whose fleece was white as snow
and everywhere that Mary went
the lamb was sure to go

After you have entered the last line, press the F6 key, and then press the Enter key. You should see the message 1 File(s) copied. The DOS prompt will reappear. Now you can use the TYPE command to look at the lines you entered. Type

TYPE MARY

The lines you entered will appear on the video screen.

You can sort the lines by entering the command:

SORT <MARY

This command instructs DOS to "trick" SORT into getting its input from the file called MARY, rather than getting the input from the keyboard. Instantly, the poem's sorted lines should appear on the display. Here is what you should see:

```
C>TYPE MARY
Mary had a little lamb
whose fleece was white as snow
and everywhere that Mary went
the lamb was sure to go

C>SORT <MARY
and everywhere that Mary went
Mary had a little lamb
the lamb was sure to go
whose fleece was white as snow

C>
```

Again, the lines from the file are sorted in ASCII order.

In the last exercise, you'll sort the file MARY that you created, and send the result to another file and then to the printer. This technique involves redirecting the SORT output to a disk file. Type the line:

SORT <MARY >MARYSORT

The disk drive light will blink once or twice, and then the DOS system prompt will appear. To see the sorted lines, display the file by using the TYPE command. Type

TYPE MARYSORT

The lines from the file that appear on your screen should be in the same ASCII order you saw when you earlier used SORT. To make a print of the file with its sorted lines, make sure your printer is turned on and ready to print. Then type

SORT <MARY >PRN

This command directs SORT to sort the lines from the file called MARY and then to send the output (the sorted lines) to the printer (PRN).

As mentioned earlier in the chapter, you may use spaces between the redirection symbol and the file or device name. DOS will accept the line

SORT < MARY > PRN

Try experimenting on your own. First try to redirect the output. Use the > and >> symbols to redirect the output of the DIR and CHKDSK commands. Redirect the output to the printer and to a disk file.

Once you are comfortable redirecting output, make a text file that answers a program's questions. See what "responses" you can make come from a disk file.

Be careful when you redirect input. Most programs expect all, not some, answers to be in the file. If enough answers are not in the file, the program ends. You should experiment with programs before you try to redirect input on "live" (useful or valuable) files. See how the program reacts to redirected input when enough answers are provided.

After you have tried a few experiments, move on to the following section on piping, a form of I/O redirection that uses more than one program.

Using Filters and Piping (|)

The concept of using filters and piping goes with I/O redirection. With filters and pipes, you can combine smaller, useful programs to achieve more useful results or simply make using the computer easier.

A *pipe* is a computer-made line that connects two programs. The first program's output becomes the second program's input. A simple example to illustrate piping is a program called MORE. MORE first displays one full screen of information obtained from the standard input; then it displays the message --More--. When you press a key, MORE displays the next full screen of information. MORE repeats this process until the entire input has been displayed on-screen.

MORE is a *filter*: a program that manipulates the stream of standard-input characters, one character after another, as they go to the standard output. A filter gets data from the standard input, modifies the data, and then writes the modified data to the standard output (screen). This modification is called *filtering* the data. After MORE filters and displays a full screen of data, the program waits for you to press a key.

Now try the following exercise. If you are wondering how a filter like MORE can be useful, this example will show you.

You can begin this exercise in one of two ways. You can make your BIN subdirectory your current directory by typing **CD C:\BIN**, or you can place a diskette that contains many files, such as the DOS Master Operating diskette, in drive A. Now type

C>**DIR** | **MORE**

You will see 23 lines displayed on-screen and then the prompt --More--. When you see the --More-- message, press the space bar. Another set of 23 lines appears on-screen. Keep pressing the space bar each time you see the prompt --More-- until the system prompt reappears.

Now let's examine the syntax of the example. You remember that DIR displays a listing (directory) of files. MORE presents one screen's worth of information at a time. The vertical bar between the words DIR and MORE is the pipe symbol. If you combine the functions of DIR and MORE through piping, you can view long directory listings, one screen at a time.

Piping has more powerful uses, including the use of I/O redirection. You'll try more examples later in the chapter, but you must first read a few details about piping. In this material, you'll learn more about the DOS filters MORE and SORT and be introduced to the FIND filter.

Some Details About Piping

Piping's most important aspect is that, like I/O redirection, it works only at the DOS command level. You cannot use piping after you have run a program. You must pipe things when you type the line to run the program.

You are not restricted to using just one pipe at a time. If you desire, you can pipe information between three, four, or even more programs. However, only one program name may be on each side of the pipe: You must give the pipe symbol once between program names. You can also redirect the first program's input and the final program's output in the pipe.

Piping and I/O redirection are features borrowed from AT&T's UNIX™ operating system. Although DOS resembles UNIX in these respects, DOS does not perform these functions in the way that UNIX does. DOS uses temporary disk files. UNIX does not.

Technically, piping is the chaining together of two or more programs with automatic redirection. DOS creates temporary files in the disk's root directory for this redirection. (Don't worry now about root directories; they are discussed in the next chapter.) Each temporary file's name is eight characters long and is based on the current date and time. Because the name is formulated on date and time expressed in the hexadecimal numbering system (base 16), which uses the digits 0 through 9 and the letters A through F, the names of these temporary files have little chance of conflicting with file or program names you create.

When you use piping, make sure your disk has enough room to hold the temporary file(s) that DOS will create. If your disk doesn't have enough room to hold the temporary files, piping will not work. Take a look at the size of the file on which the piping operation will be working. If you are piping information between two programs, you'll generally need at least as much free space as the file's current size. You'll need twice as much free space if you are piping between three or more programs. If your program removes information from the file, you'll need less free space. If the program adds more information to the file, you'll need more free space.

The Filters

DOS has three standard filters, two of which have already been mentioned:

FIND	Finds a string
MORE	Displays a screen's worth of information and then waits for a keystroke
SORT	Sorts information in ASCII order

This section again discusses MORE and SORT and presents a brief overview of FIND. You'll find a more detailed discussion of the filters in Part VI, the *DOS Command Reference*.

The MORE Filter

As mentioned in the earlier discussion, MORE displays one screen's worth of information at a time. If the display has more than 23 lines, MORE displays the prompt --More-- and waits for you to press a key. If the display is less than 23 lines, MORE displays all the lines in one screen's worth and returns to the system prompt. In the latter case, MORE does not display the message --More--. Computer users often call the full video screen of information that MORE displays a *page* and call what MORE produces a *paged output*.

MORE and the other two DOS filters, FIND and SORT, expect their input from the keyboard (standard input) and place their output on the video screen (standard output). You must use I/O redirection or piping for the filters to work with a disk file or other DOS command.

MORE, FIND, and SORT are external DOS commands, which means you must load these programs from a disk. The syntax to use MORE is simply

   *dc:***MORE**

where *dc:* is the name of the disk drive that holds the MORE program. (Technically, you can place a path name between the disk drive name and the filter's name. All DOS filters allow the use of path names. This subject is covered in detail in Chapter 10.)

MORE is commonly used to type a file's output one page at a time. For this use, the syntax is

   *dc:*MORE <*d:*filename.*ext*

where *d:***filename**.*ext* is the name of the file you want MORE to display. If you want to display the contents of a file called ACCEPT.LET, the command is

   MORE <ACCEPT.LET

MORE will display the contents of the file, one screen's worth at a time. To stop MORE's output on the screen, simply press the Ctrl-Break or Ctrl-C sequence.

The SORT Filter

If you need to sort a file's lines, SORT is the DOS-provided filter to handle the task. SORT's syntax is

*dc:*SORT /R /+c

where *dc:* is the name of the disk drive that holds the SORT program. SORT has two switches that affect the command's operation. The switches are

/R   *Reverse* the sort (sort in reverse order)

/+c   Start the sorting at the *c*th character (or column) in
        each line. *c* is a number ranging from 1 to the length
        of the longest line.

You'll most often want to sort the lines in ascending ASCII order. Look at the ASCII table in Appendix C. You'll notice the following order: control characters, characters and punctuation symbols, numbers, more symbols, uppercase letters, more symbols, lowercase letters, and another set of characters and punctuation symbols. SORT follows this order for sorting characters, with two exceptions:

1. Lowercase letters are treated as if they are uppercase letters.

2. Characters with an ASCII value above 127 are sorted by the
   specific value based on the current country code. (Country codes
   are discussed in Chapter 15, which explains how DOS is used
   internationally.)

Exception 1 is beneficial if you want to sort alphabetically rather than by ASCII order. Note that in the ASCII chart, the uppercase A is the first letter, followed by the uppercase letters through Z. Several positions down in the chart come the lowercase letters a through z. If SORT distinguished upper- and lowercase letters, the first two lines in the sorted poem would have been

```
Mary had a little lamb
and everywhere that Mary went
```

because the uppercase M in Mary comes before the lowercase a in the ASCII chart. By ignoring the difference between upper- and lowercase letters, SORT sorts letters in true alphabetical order. Most people will prefer true alphabetical order to the computerized ASCII order.

Exception 2 is important if you use PC DOS with a foreign language character set. The proper sorting order for each foreign language is different. For example, the single German character ß sorts as if it were a two-character SS. The Spanish æ sorts as if it were an a or an e, depending on its use in the word. Many foreign languages do not have a one-to-one sorting sequence for their characters. As discussed later in the book, SORT uses the collating information appropriate to the language used, based on the COUNTRY command in the CONFIG.SYS file.

Of the two exceptions to ascending ASCII order, the upper- and lowercase exception is the more important to North American computer users.

The /R switch reverses the normal sorting order so that Z comes before A. This switch is useful when you need to sort something in reverse order.

The second switch, /+c, tells SORT to start the sorting with the character in column c. This switch is most useful when the information on which you are working is aligned in columns, and the column by which you want to sort the file is not the first column. You use /+ followed by the number of the column where sorting should start. SORT skips the front of the lines and sorts on the latter part of the lines.

To see how the /+c switch works, try this example:

    SORT /+8 <MARY

This command will sort the MARY poem based on the characters in the eighth column of each line. The result you'll see on your screen is

```
the lamb was sure to go.
Mary had a little lamb
whose fleece was white as snow
and everywhere that Mary went
```

SORT sorted the lines of the poem based on the d, l, r, and b in each line's eighth position. You'll try more exercises with the SORT filter later in this chapter.

The FIND Filter

FIND is the DOS filter that automates searching for specific lines in a file. FIND locates in a file lines that match a set of characters you specify, or it locates lines that do not match the specified characters. FIND's syntax is

    dc:FIND /V/C/N "string" d:filename.ext

dc: is the disk drive that holds the FIND program. *d:filename.ext* is the optional name of the file to search. If you do not give a file name, FIND will look for its information from the keyboard.

The set of characters for which you are searching is the **"string"**. In computer terms, a *string* is any set of ASCII characters, including symbols, numbers, and letters. A string can consist of any number of characters, including no characters at all (an *empty string*). To specify a string for FIND, you must surround the string with double quotation marks. FIND searches only for the characters within the double quotation marks.

Unlike the SORT filter, FIND distinguishes between upper- and lowercase characters. With FIND, "THE" is not the same as "the" or "The". To use FIND correctly, you must specify either upper- or lowercase characters.

FIND has three switches:

/V   Displays the lines that do *not* contain the specific string.

/C   *Counts* the lines that have the string, but does not display the lines.

/N   *Numbers* the lines that FIND displays. The numbers appear before the line and are based on the line's position in the file.

If you want to use any of the switches, you have to place them after the command **FIND** but before the **"string"**. FIND is one of the few DOS commands that requires switches to appear directly after the command instead of at the end of the command line.

FIND's most important switch (and the only switch we'll cover in detail in this chapter) is /V. This switch directs FIND to search for lines that do not match the string, as opposed to FIND's normal string-matching operation. With the /V switch, FIND locates the strings that do not match the specified string.

Let's use our sample file MARY, which contains the poem "Mary Had a Little Lamb," to test FIND's operation. To find the lines that contain the word "Mary," use the command:

FIND "Mary" MARY

Notice that the letters "ary" in the string "Mary" are lowercase. When you run the command, you should see two lines on the screen:

```
Mary had a little lamb
and everywhere that Mary went
```

Now try searching for lines that do not contain the string "Mary". Type

FIND /V "Mary" MARY

The two lines that do not contain "Mary" should appear on your screen.

To see how specifying the wrong case affects FIND's operation, try these two commands:

FIND "MARY" MARY
FIND /V "MARY" MARY

In the first exercise, no lines should appear. In the second exercise, all the lines will appear. Remember that FIND considers uppercase letters to be different from lowercase letters.

Using I/O Redirection, Piping, and the DOS Filters

The fullest power of redirection, piping, and filters occurs when you are challenged to perform some housekeeping task that seems to take longer than the task is worth. I believe that the moment you suddenly realize that using redirection, piping, and the DOS filters can make a task easier, you have an "inspirational" operation.

The most frequent housekeeping task is manipulating the output of the DIR command. DOS's capabilities are ideal for demonstrating these operations. Try the exercises in this section on your BIN subdirectory or on the DOS Master Operating diskette.

First, try sorting DIR's list of files. Although the IBM-provided DOS V3.3 Operating diskette is almost sorted, you'll quickly find that most other disks or directories are not sorted. To sort file listings, use the command:

DIR | SORT

This command directs DIR's output through the SORT program. The SORT program begins sorting with the first character of the line—the root file name. The DIR | SORT command results in an alphabetized list of files.

Using SORT with the /+c Switch

You can use SORT with the /+c switch to sort the output by other categories of information that the DIR command displays. You can sort the DIR listing by file extension, file size, file date, or any combination of these options. To sort a DIR listing in these ways, you'll need the information in table 9.1, which lists the column in which DIR begins the display of file extensions, file size, file date, and so on.

Table 9.1
DIR Information by Column
(to be used with SORT)

Information	Columns	Switch	
Root file name	1 – 8	/+1	
File extension	10 – 12	/+10	
File size	14 – 21	/+14	
File date	24 – 31	/+24	
File time	34 – 39	/+34	(24-hour time only)

To sort the DIR command's output by file size, use the command:

DIR | SORT /+14

To sort the output by date, use the command:

DIR | SORT /+24

You can sort the output by more than one column by simply adding another SORT command to the pipe. For example, to sort the DIR command's listing first by extension and then by root file name, use the command:

DIR | SORT | SORT /+10

The first time SORT is used, the files are sorted by root name. The second time SORT is used, the output of the first SORT command is sorted by extension.

Here's a tip for running SORT more than once in a pipe: You must sort in *inverse* order, sorting first on the least important item and then on the most important item. If you sort the list first by file extension and then by file name, you'll have a file list sorted first by file name and next by extension, which is not what you want. If you need to sort the list by root name and then by file extension, the first example of DIR | SORT sorts the list in this order.

I do not advocate using SORT on file times that are represented by a 12-hour clock. The technique works correctly only if the directory time is displayed in 24-hour clock style. SORT is "dumb" when it sorts numbers. SORT collates numbers based on the ASCII values of their characters and not on their real numeric values. To us, 12 is the number 12, but the computer sees 12 as the character 1 followed by the character 2. To illustrate this problem, take a look at the following numbers:

```
1
2
11
15
21
35
112
241
367
```

If you use SORT to sort these numbers, it will produce this output:

```
1
11
112
15
2
21
241
35
367
```

To see how SORT sorts times, look at this example:

```
12:00a
 2:25a
10:57a
12:00p
 1:45p
 5:00 p
```

The resulting SORT is

```
 1:45p
 2:25a
 5:00p
10:57a
12:00p
12:00a
```

This time the sort is not quite in proper time order. (Because a space has an ASCII value less than the character *0*, times from 1:00 to 9:59, whether a.m. or p.m., come before 10:00, a.m. or p.m.) With the 24-hour format, the times are sorted correctly because afternoon and evening times are greater than morning times.

Using SORT with a MORE Filter

An annoying aspect of using SORT on the output of the DIR command is that long directory listings scroll off the top of the screen before you can read them. You cannot solve this problem by using the /P (pause) switch with DIR, because DIR's output is fed to SORT. You don't want *this* output delayed. You want, instead, to delay the output of SORT, which is displaying the information you want. If you did use a /P switch with DIR, this addition would force you to press a key each time DIR presented a (nondisplayed) screenful of information to SORT. Needless to say, that solution is less than ideal.

The ideal solution to this problem is to force SORT's output through the MORE filter, which you'll recall is the one-page-at-a-time filter. To do so, use this set of commands:

DIR | SORT | MORE

With this set of commands, the sorted directory listing is displayed one screen's worth at a time.

Another problem with the DIR | SORT | MORE sorting technique is that the lines listing the volume label, the name of the directory being displayed, the statistics on the number of files being displayed, and the amount of free disk space are listed out of order. Because the DIR command includes displaying the volume label, directory name, and disk statistics, and these displays cannot be suppressed, you must use a different means to remove these lines. FIND offers you the capability of displaying lines that contain certain strings or that do not contain certain strings.

To remove the volume label, displayed directory, and disk statistics lines, you have to use an intuitive approach. You must find some information contained in lines for each displayed file that does or does not appear in the other three lines. This information will be a string you feed to the FIND command.

If you look at the output of DIR, you'll notice that one character is unique to the lines concerning files. This character doesn't appear in the other columns. The date separator (-) appears in the date column but does not appear in the other lines. If you add the FIND command to your sorted directory command, the command becomes

> DIR | FIND "-" | SORT

This pipeline first invokes DIR to feed its output to FIND. FIND then looks for lines that contain the hyphen (-). FIND's output is filtered by SORT, which sorts the remaining directory information. If you wanted to page a long directory listing, you can add MORE to the end of the pipeline, as in the command:

> DIR | FIND "-" | SORT | MORE

If you want to place the sorted directory listing in a disk file, such as a file named DIRS, the command is

> DIR | FIND "-" | SORT > DIRS

Using Redirection within a Program

You may recall from Chapter 5 that COMMAND.COM, the Command Processor, runs your programs and DOS's built-in functions. Did you know that many programs make the capabilities of COMMAND.COM available to you while you are using an applications program? I'll use WordStar in this example, but many other applications programs have the ability to run DOS's "shell" (COMMAND.COM).

With WordStar Release 4.0, for example, you can run a program while you are working with WordStar's main menu, or while you are editing a file. To run another program from within WordStar, you type R if you are at the Main Menu, and Ctrl-KF if you are editing a document.

Computer users frequently use WordStar to merge print several files as one lengthy document. To merge print, you must construct a file to hold the individual names of the files you want to merge-print. Rather than remembering the file names, I use I/O redirection to trick the DIR command into placing its results into a disk file. Then I read that file into my WordStar document and edit the document to produce the merge-print commands.

Here's the technique:

Step 1. *Begin by typing* R *from WordStar's Main Menu or* Ctrl-KF *from within a document.*

Step 2. *When WordStar asks you to enter the name of the DOS command you want to run, type*

    DIR filename.ext >TDIR

Substitute the appropriate file name for **filename.ext**. To get the list of all files that end with .PCD, for example, I use the command:

    DIR *.PCD >TDIR

This command produces a list of the files that end with .PCD and places the output of DIR in a disk file called *TDIR* (for temporary directory) on the current disk drive.

Step 2 is the important step. In this step, you asked DOS to run the DIR command and place its output in a disk file. Even though you are using an applications program (in this case, WordStar), the applications program allows you to talk to DOS directly. When you talk to DOS, you can run any command, including a built-in DOS command. You can also use I/O redirection and piping.

Step 3. *If you are working from WordStar's Main Menu, open the file (WordStar's* D *option) that will hold the names of the files to be printed.*

If you are working within that file, read in the temporary file by using WordStar's *Ctrl-KR* command. When WordStar asks you the name of the document to be inserted into the file being edited, answer *TDIR*.

Step 4. *If the file-name list is short, retype the names and add WordStar's file-include directive (.FI) before each file name; delete the original lines of the directory using WordStar's line-delete command (Ctrl-Y).*

If the file-name list is long, first delete the lines that do not contain file names: the ones that show the volume label, directory name, and free-space statistics. Then delete the file size, date, and time information from each line, leaving only the file names and extensions.

Replace the blank spaces between the root name and extension with a single period. Insert a **.FI** before each file name. (You might try using a search-and-replace operation, searching for a carriage return and replacing it with a carriage return and .FI. You may need to delete an extra .FI from the bottom of the file.)

You now have a file that holds the merge-print commands for printing the documents. You "printed" the directory to a file, read the list into your document, and cleaned up the line. Once you have used the technique a few times, you'll find it fast and easy.

Remember that, with many applications programs, you can use any DOS command with or without I/O redirection and piping. Running programs from within other programs has many possibilities. The only limitation is the available RAM to run the second program.

Summary

This chapter introduced redirection, piping, and the DOS filter programs. The best way to learn about redirection, piping, and filters is to try the commands. You can read more about FIND, SORT, and MORE in the *DOS Command Reference* at the back of this book. Experiment with these filters and with piping.

Don't forget the caution about redirection. If you use the > symbol to redirect a program's output to a disk file, make sure that the disk file's name is unique. If you use a disk file name of a file that already exists, DOS will erase the contents of that file and write the new information into the file. You will have lost the original information. Be careful about the file names you use.

In this chapter, you learned the following important points:

1. DOS has three standard places to receive and send information: standard input, standard output, and standard error.

2. By using redirection and piping, you can change where DOS and your programs receive and send information.

      <   Receives information from a device or disk file
      >   Sends information to a device or disk file
      >> Appends information to a device or disk file

| Takes the output of the program on the left side (of the symbol) and makes it the input of the program on the right side

3. The MORE filter displays one screen's worth of information at a time.

4. The SORT filter sorts information from the keyboard or from a file.

5. The FIND filter finds lines from the keyboard or in a file that match or do not match a given string.

Chapter 10 introduces the hierarchical directory system.

Part III

Expanding Your Use of DOS

10

Using Hierarchical Directories To Manage Files

You know that every disk has its own directory. Each disk has one, and only one, directory. This arrangement works well for floppy diskettes. If, for example, you store 112 or 224 files on a diskette (the maximum number of files for 360K diskettes and HC diskettes, respectively), you can still wade through the directory to find a file.

Fixed disks, on the other hand, are capable of storing hundreds or thousands of files. Storing these file names in a single directory would be inefficient, and working with the files would be awkward. Such storage would be inefficient because when you look for a file, DOS wades internally through the directory to find the file you want. From the standpoint of performance, a one-directory solution does not work very well. From the standpoint of usability, locating a perhaps long-forgotten file name from a list of hundreds of files is time-consuming at best. A single directory is an ineffective method of organizing your files.

Fortunately, DOS offers a solution that still allows you to store many files on a disk, but in smaller, more organized, and distinct compartments. Microsoft, the author of DOS, borrowed the concept for the solution from the UNIX operating system: *hierarchical directories*.

Understanding Hierarchical Directories

With hierarchical directories, you can group files on a fixed disk the way that most people physically organize diskettes. (Users generally categorize diskettes by purpose. They arrange each diskette so that it contains all the programs and data files they need for a certain task.) For example, I have one diskette for my word-processing programs, another diskette for infrequently used DOS utilities, and some other diskettes for programming in C and in assembly language. I have other diskettes for my spreadsheets and still other diskettes for creating models. This arrangement, which logically groups programs and data files, works well.

How about the fixed disk? How can files be organized on the fixed disk in the same way that files are organized on diskettes? The "secret" is the use of subdirectories. For an understanding of this concept, let's look at the directory system as a whole.

Every formatted disk has one directory. The directory is stored on the disk and holds the names of your files, along with other information. The directory itself is really a file in which DOS stores its own data. You may not have considered this before, but if you can think of the directory as a file, the rest is easy.

The Root Directory and Subdirectories

The starting directory of every disk is the main or *root directory*. The root directory holds information about programs or data files. More significantly, the root directory holds information about other directories. In fact, the unique feature of the directory system is that each directory can also hold information about other directories. These additional directories are called *subdirectories*.

Think of the root directory as a large box. In this box, you can store file folders. You can also store additional boxes within the larger box. These additional boxes (the subdirectories) can hold file folders and even more boxes (more subdirectories). Each box—the main box (root directory) and smaller boxes (subdirectories)—can hold files and other boxes.

Like the main directory, each subdirectory is a file. The root directory and subdirectories are set up in the same manner and can hold the names of files and other information *and the names of other subdirectories*.

The only fault with comparing the root directory to a box is that no box can hold more than the main box, and the number of boxes is limited by the size of the main box. With subdirectories, no such fault exists. DOS endows subdirectories with a "magic" property that allows the size of subdirectories to grow larger than the root directory. The number of subdirectories is limited only by the capacity of your disk.

There is one major difference between a root directory and its subdirectories you should know about: restrictions on the root directory. The root directory is fixed in both its size and in the number of files the directory can hold. The maximum number of files a root directory can hold is 112. You cannot store more files than the number listed for the various sizes of diskettes and fixed disks. DOS cannot make the root directory larger.

Unlike the root directory, a subdirectory can be extended as needed. Its expansion is limited only by the availability of disk space. As you add more files or subdirectories to a subdirectory, DOS automatically makes the subdirectory larger. As long as free disk space exists, you may create additional subdirectories, and your existing subdirectories can grow larger.

The Tree Analogy

The terms "parent" and "child" are often used in discussing the directory system. To understand the relationship between directories in a system, imagine a family tree with the founding parents as the base of the tree. Their children are branches on the tree. When the children grow up, marry, and have children of their own, the tree grows more branches. The process continues for each generation, as children marry and have children.

The root directory is like the founding parents. Just as parents have children, the root directory can have subdirectories. Each subdirectory (child) of the root (parent) directory can in turn become a parent to another generation of subdirectories. As you create each new subdirectory, you create a new branch on the tree.

The parent directory "owns" its child subdirectories. Although a parent directory can have many child subdirectories, each child subdirectory is owned by only one parent directory. You can, therefore, trace any subdirectory back to the root directory of the disk.

The terms "up" and "down" describe movement in the directory system. Let's flip the tree upside down. When you move up, you move from the child subdirectory to its parent directory. When you move down, you move from a parent directory to a child subdirectory. The root directory is the "highest" directory. The subdirectories farthest from the root are the "lowest" branches of the directory tree.

A Sample Hierarchical Directory

Appendix B contains a sample hierarchical directory. The directory is also illustrated in figure 10.1. The sample directory is used only to demonstrate how the directory system works; it is not intended to show the best way to organize your files.

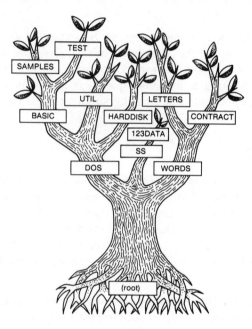

Fig. 10.1. *This tree illustrates the sample hierarchical directory that is included in Appendix B.*

In the directory in Appendix B, the root directory is at the top. It contains several nondirectory files: IBMBIO.COM, IBMDOS.COM, AUTOEXEC.BAT, CONFIG.SYS, VDISK.SYS, COUNTRY.SYS, and KEYBOARD.SYS. You may recognize some of these file names. The root directory also has two subdirectories: DOS and WORDS. The DOS side of the directory contains DOS programs and other program files. The WORDS side has word-processing files. In this case, the parent directory owns two children: the DOS and WORDS subdirectories.

Note that there is no directory named ROOT. The root directory uses a special symbol for its name: the backslash (\). If you see only a backslash as the directory name, that backslash signifies the root directory. If you call for the directory of any DOS disk in drive A, you will see the following line:

```
Directory of A:\
```

The single backslash tells you that you are getting a directory listing of that disk's root directory.

Let's descend one level on the word-processing side of the directory, down to the WORDS subdirectory. If you are familiar with WordStar, you will recognize the names of three WordStar program files. In addition to these files, WORDS owns two children: the LETTERS and CONTRACTS subdirectories. The LETTERS subdirectory holds letters I have written—letters to IBM, Jack, and Doug. LETTERS also holds the previous revisions of the letters to IBM and JACK (the files that end in .BAK). The CONTRACTS subdirectory holds the drafts of my contracts with Meyer and Anderson. I have used the hierarchical directories to organize word-processing files by purpose: letters and contracts.

Now follow the WORDS subdirectory back to the root directory. Move down one level to the DOS directory. This directory holds several files: the CHKDSK (check disk) program and three other DOS programs, FIND, SORT, and MORE. A copy of the Microsoft Macro Assembler® (MASM.EXE) is also in this subdirectory.

DOS owns two children: BASIC, and HARDDISK. Two versions of the BASIC language are in the BASIC directory, and programs for the fixed disk are in the HARDDISK directory.

Did you notice that the term directory was used for subdirectory in the preceding paragraph? The two terms are interchangeable when you are referring to any directory other than the disk's root directory. The root directory can be only a directory, but a subdirectory can be thought of as a directory in its own right. From this point on, I'll use the term subdirectory only when it is needed for clarity.

Follow the BASIC directory down one step further. BASIC owns two directories: a SAMPLES directory, which contains a mortgage program provided with IBM DOS V3.3, and a TEST directory, which contains some BASIC programs I created to test the disk speed (DSKSPED.BAS) and the screen (SCRNTST.BAS).

Before you start using hierarchical directories, take some time to learn about an important disk-directory term, *path*. A *path* is a chain of directory names. It tells DOS how to maneuver through the directories to find the directory or the file you want. Each directory name is separated by the path character, the backslash (\ ).

Don't let this dual use of the backslash confuse you. Remember that whenever the backslash is the first character of the path, the path starts at disk's root directory. Used otherwise, the backslash just separates directory names. Remember also that whenever you need to use a file name with a path, a path character (\ ) is also required before the file name.

In Chapter 4, you learned that no two files listed in the same directory can have the same file name. Note that the word "directory" in this rule does not mean "disk." A fixed disk or diskette can have several directories. The same file name can exist in each directory on the same diskette or fixed disk. This duplication does not confuse DOS at all. You just can't use a duplicate file name in the same directory.

A word of warning: For a program or a batch file, avoid using a file name that duplicates the name of a subdirectory in the same directory. For example, in a directory that has a subdirectory called DOIT, don't have a program named DOIT.COM or a batch file called DOIT.BAT.

Here's the reason for the warning: When you execute a program or batch file, you use only the file's root name. If the root name of a program or batch file in a parent directory is identical to a subdirectory name in that same directory, DOS may not know whether you are talking about the program, the batch file, or the subdirectory.

Rules for Directory and Path Names

The following list summarizes rules for directory names. You may notice some similarities among the rules for directory names and rules for file names. They are closely related.

Rules for Directory Names

1. A directory name has the following:

    a. A root name that contains from 1 to 8 characters.

    b. An optional extension that contains from 1 to 3 characters.

    c. A period separating the root name from the extension.

2. Valid characters for a directory name are the following:

    a. The letters A through Z. (Lowercase a to z are changed to uppercase A to Z.)

    b. The numbers 0 through 9.

    c. The following special characters and punctuation symbols:

    $ # & @ ! ^ ( ) - { } ' _ ~

3. The following characters cannot be used in a directory name:

    a. Any control character, including Esc and Del

b. A space

c. The characters

+ = / [ ] " : ; , ? * \ < > | .

4. You cannot create a directory called . (single period) or ..
   (double period). The single period is DOS's shorthand designation
   for the current directory, and the double period (..) is the
   shorthand designation for the parent directory.

5. A device name may be part of a directory name but not the entire
   directory name. Remember that CON is the device name for
   console. Therefore, CONT as a directory name is allowable, but
   CON is not.

6. You cannot create a subdirectory called DEV in the root
   directory.

The following list summarizes the rules for path names.

Rules for Path Names

1. A path name can contain from 1 to 63 characters.

2. The path is composed of directory names separated by the
   backslash character (\ ).

3. A drive name may precede a path.

4. Generally, a file name may follow a path. When this happens, use
   a backslash to separate the path name from the file name.

5. DOS keeps track of the current path for each drive.

6. The characters . (single period for the current directory) and ..
   (double period for the parent directory) are valid in a path name.

7. To start with the root (uppermost) directory, you begin the path
   name with a backslash. (A drive name before the path character
   does not contradict this rule.)

8. If you don't start with the root directory, DOS starts with the
   current directory of the disk.

You will recall the notation used earlier in this book for a disk drive and a
file name. The new notation that includes the path designation is

d:path\filename.*ext*

This notation is a *full file specification* or a *full file name*. It starts with the optional disk drive name, followed by an optional path name, the mandatory root file name, and finally the optional extension. In the DOS manual, this file specification is called a *filespec*. Almost all DOS commands accept this type of file name: a file name preceded by a drive and path name.

Navigating through Subdirectories

To use DOS effectively, users of fixed disks and high-capacity disks need to know how to navigate through subdirectories. Knowing how to navigate depends principally on understanding path names.

To understand path names, consider the analogy of a major airline's routing system. The airline uses a major city as the central hub for its flights. When the airline cannot offer travelers direct flights between cities, passengers going to different cities go first to the hub city of the routing system. At the hub, the travelers change planes and fly to their final destinations. If a traveler's plane has a stopover at his destination on the way to the hub, the traveler need not go to the central hub. He simply departs the plane at the stopover city. If the airline is large, several cities may serve as minor hubs to other cities. There is, however, a central hub to which these minor hubs connect.

Navigating through subdirectories is like traveling through an airline's routing system. The root directory is the "central hub." The subdirectories are the outlying "cities" on the hub's rim. Subdirectories that contain other subdirectories are minor hubs. DOS is the air-traffic controller. And just as the tower that controls departures and arrivals must be informed about aircraft movements, you must inform DOS when you want to travel to another subdirectory.

The tower (DOS) is always aware of your current position (current directory). If you are located at one city and want to go to another city, you must inform the tower how you will reach that city. If the city is not on the path to the hub, you can restart your journey at the main hub and travel outward to your final destination. If the city is on the way to the hub, you can go directly to the desired destination.

If your destination is on the path to the main hub or is serviced by a minor hub (the current subdirectory), you can use shorthand notations to speed the communication process (the typing of the path). Depending on the location, you may move away from the main hub or toward the main hub and back again. If your destination is the current directory, you can omit almost all the path directions.

The next section includes instructions on giving DOS directions for moving through the subdirectory system.

Moving through Directories (CHDIR/CD, TYPE)

The following exercises are based on the sample disk directory in Appendix B.

Let's start at the root directory. The objective is to get to the LETTERS directory to see what was written to Doug (DOUG.LET), and then run CHKDSK to see how much space is left on the disk.

You can accomplish this task in two ways: the hard way and the easy way.

The hard way is to move down to the WORDS directory and then to the LETTERS directory. At that point, you could use the TYPE command to display the DOUG.LET file. (Remember that TYPE displays a file's contents on-screen.) Then you could return to the root directory of the disk. This procedure involves typing several commands.

The following screen shows the commands you would have to issue to reach DOUG.LET by the first method. These commands begin at the disk's root directory.

```
A>CHDIR WORDS

A>CHDIR LETTERS

A>TYPE DOUG.LET

A>CHDIR \

A>
```

Here is the explanation of the commands. To move to the WORDS directory, you use the DOS command CHDIR (change directories). The command is

```
A>CHDIR WORDS
```

DOS checks the root directory to find a subdirectory called WORDS. DOS finds the subdirectory and "moves" there. (You move down one level.) WORDS becomes the disk's current directory. Had DOS not found a subdirectory called WORDS, it would have displayed the following message:

```
Invalid directory
```

This error message indicates that DOS could not find the subdirectory you specified.

CHDIR is a "no news is good news" command. When DOS successfully executes the CHDIR command, no message is given. Only a blank line is printed. Most of DOS's hierarchical directory commands do not return messages when they work properly.

The next command line moves you down one level to the LETTERS directory. The command is

A>CHDIR LETTERS

LETTERS, which holds DOUG.LET, now becomes the current subdirectory. To finish the objective, you would use the TYPE command to display DOUG.LET. Because your word processor may do funny things to a file, the file's display may contain some strange characters when the file is displayed on-screen with TYPE. If, for example, you display a document file created with WordStar (the word processor I use), you will see strange characters.

The last command returns you to the root directory. The command is

A>CHDIR \

The CHDIR command contains a backslash (\). This command is a complete path name that returns you to the root directory. Remember that when you start the path with a backslash, you are instructing DOS to start with the root directory. In the case of CHDIR LETTERS, DOS assumes that you want to start with the directory you were in, because you did not start the path with a backslash character.

The second, and easier, way to move through the directories and display this file is to use the single command line:

```
A>TYPE WORDS\LETTERS\DOUG.LET
```

The TYPE command accepts a path name before the file name. DOS interprets this command in the following way:

1. Look in the current directory for the subdirectory called WORDS. Move into this directory.

2. In the WORDS directory, find a subdirectory called LETTERS. Move to the LETTERS subdirectory.

3. In the subdirectory LETTERS, find a file called DOUG.LET. Type the file's contents on-screen.

4. Move back to the beginning directory.

Notice that this command line used a path character between each directory name. A path character was used also between the last directory name and the name of the file to be typed. You must phrase your command to DOS this way when you use a path name and a file name. If you omit the final path character, DOS becomes confused and sees a large directory name (such as LETTERSDOUG.LET) or two names (WORDS\LETTERS DOUG.LET). The usual result will be an Invalid path or file name message from DOS, not the result you want.

Notice also what DOS did after executing the TYPE command. DOS returned to the directory where the TYPE command was issued. DOS remembers the current directory for every disk you use. If you give DOS a command to go into a different directory to get a file, DOS bounces back to the starting directory after getting the file. The only way you can change the current directory on a disk is to use the CHDIR command.

The second objective in this exercise is to run the CHKDSK (check disk) program on the disk. As before, you have a hard way and an easy way to accomplish this task.

The hard way is to move to the DOS subdirectory, execute the CHKDSK command, and return to the root directory:

```
A>CD  DOS

A>CHKDSK

(DOS displays information about the disk here.)

A>CD  \

A>
```

CD is another abbreviation for the change directory command. Like
RENAME and ERASE, DOS recognizes the shorthand form of CD as CHDIR.
This command instructed DOS to move from the root directory to the
DOS subdirectory. When the DOS directory became the current directory,
DOS ran the CHKDSK program. Then DOS returned you to the root
directory after CHDIR was complete.

The easy way to accomplish the same thing is to type the following:

```
A>DOS\CHKDSK
```

DOS displays information about the disk here and returns to the root
directory:

```
A>
```

Notice you can give a path in front of an external command, too. Both a
drive name and a path can precede a command name.

You have just seen one of the important differences between DOS V2 and
V3. In DOS V2, you can execute commands in your current directory only.
(The PATH command is an exception; PATH is discussed later in this
chapter.) DOS V3 allows you to execute commands in any directory from
any directory. This capability is a major benefit. Many of the tips you'll see
later in this book are based on this capability.

CHDIR (or CD) has one additional capability. CHDIR can indicate the
current directory. If you type CHDIR or CD without a path name, you will

see the name of the directory for your current disk drive. You can, for example, switch to the LETTERS subdirectory and indicate the current subdirectory and then move back to the root directory and indicate the current directory again. The following commands carry out this activity:

```
A>CD WORDS\LETTERS

A>CD
A:\WORDS\LETTERS

A>CD \

A>CD
A:\
```

You can also use CHDIR to display the current directories of other disk drives. Give the command (CHDIR or CD), followed by a space and a disk drive name. You'll see the current directory for the specified disk drive.

Now that you know the basics of using CHDIR and hierarchical directories, you can try a hands-on practice that will expand your understanding of the CHDIR command and introduce two other hierarchical directory commands.

Hands-on Practice: Using CHDIR/CD, MKDIR/MD, and RMDIR/RD

In this session, you will use the three hierarchical directory commands CHDIR (change directory), MKDIR (make a new directory), and RMDIR (remove a directory). These commands are also abbreviated CD for CHDIR, MD for MKDIR, and RD for RMDIR. Because DOS recognizes both forms in each case, the shorter abbreviations are used here. For the session, you'll need the following:

1. A computer with two disk drives. One drive must be a floppy disk drive (any type); the other drive can be either a floppy disk drive or a fixed disk drive.

2. The DOS 3.x Master Diskette (or Master Operating diskette for users of 360K disk drives).

Users with fixed disk drives need the DOS diskette(s) just mentioned, but these users will need to copy the files from the fixed disk to the diskette. The files to copy are in BIN on the fixed disk.

3. If you are using two floppy disk drives, you will also need one formatted diskette. Do not put DOS on this diskette. (In other words, don't use the /S switch when you format the diskette.) Write something like Practice Directory Diskette on the label of the formatted diskette. If you give a volume label (FORMAT /V), call the diskette PRACTICE. Owners of fixed disk drives do not need an additional diskette.

As in earlier chapters, I'll provide separate instructions for users whose computers have two floppy disk drives and for users whose computers have one floppy disk drive and one fixed disk. For the demonstration, I'll use 720K floppy diskettes. If you own a fixed disk, use the second set of directions only, regardless of how many floppy drives you have.

Instructions for Two Floppy Disk Drives

Step 1. *Put your copy of the DOS V3.x Master or Master Operating diskette into drive A.*

Step 2. *Put the practice diskette into drive B.*

Step 3. *Type*

```
MD B:COMS
```

MKDIR, or its short form MD, makes a new subdirectory called COMS on the disk in drive B.

Step 4. *Type*

```
MD B:COMS\SAMPLES
```

This command makes a new subdirectory called SAMPLES in the subdirectory COMS.

At this point, the root directory owns a directory called COMS, which, in turn, owns a directory called SAMPLES. Notice that you have used a path in this command. DOS moves down through the path. When DOS reaches the last name in the path (SAMPLES), it knows to make a new subdirectory called SAMPLES, instead of trying to move farther in the directory structure.

Many beginning users are confused by path sequences. To keep the path's order and structure clear in your mind, separate the path from the final destination at the last backslash. The part before the final backslash (B:COMS) tells DOS where the action should take place (make a subdirectory called SAMPLES). The part after the final backslash (SAMPLES) is the object of your action (the subdirectory that DOS is to create).

Step 5. *Type*

```
DIR B:
```

When you ask DOS for a directory of drive B, what you see on-screen is a listing of the disk's root directory files. Your screen will look something like the following screen:

```
Volume in drive B is PRACTICE
Directory of  B:\

COMS            <DIR>      7-24-87  1Ø:43p
        1 File(s)    728Ø64 bytes free
```

The appearance of the <DIR> symbol in the second column after a name indicates that the entry is a subdirectory, not a normal file. Because COMS is a subdirectory, COMS has this <DIR> designation following it.

The third column shows the date and time you created the subdirectory or file. Make a note of the time you see on the screen.

Look at the rest of the screen. Notice that the directory listing's first line tells you what disk drive you are using and what directory you are viewing. Study the screen for a few seconds and then move to the next step.

Step 6. Type

```
DIR B:COMS
```

Now you will see a listing of the COMS subdirectory. The listing will look something like the the following listing:

```
Volume in drive B is PRACTICE
Directory of B:COMS

.              <DIR>        7-24-87   10:43p
..             <DIR>        7-24-87   10:43p
SAMPLES        <DIR>        7-24-87   10:43p
        3 File(s)     728064 bytes freeb
```

The SAMPLES directory should hold no surprises, but what are the period and double-period directories? Both are special shorthand symbols used for maneuvering in the directory system. The period represents the subdirectory you are viewing, or the current directory. You can think of it as the subdirectory's "I exist to myself" symbol. The double period represents the parent directory of the COMS subdirectory. In this case, the double period represents the root directory.

Compare the first directory to the second. Notice that the root directory does not contain these period- and double-period-directory symbols. Only subdirectories have the period (.) and double-period (..) symbols. Because the root directory is the base directory, the root directory has no parent.

If you want to tell DOS explicitly to start with the directory you are using, you use the period as the first character in the path. This method is infrequently used because, unless the path begins with a \, DOS starts movement with the current directory. To tell DOS to move up one level of subdirectories, use the double period. This method is used more frequently. We'll cover this shorthand symbol again in Chapter 11.

Take a look at the dates and times on the lines with the period and double-period symbols. These dates and times should be the same as those for the COMS entry in the root directory. When DOS creates subdirectories, it not only makes an entry in the parent directory; it also establishes the . and .. files, giving all three items the same date and time.

Step 7. Type

```
COPY A:*.COM B:\COMS /V
```

This command copies to the subdirectory COMS on drive B all the files
from drive A that have the extension .COM. As you learned earlier, the /V
switch tells DOS to verify that it has copied the files correctly.

When you specify a disk drive name in a path, the drive name must appear
first. You then specify the path and then the file name. You do not need
to specify a path for the diskette in drive A because you are currently
using the root directory of the diskette; that directory contains all the DOS
programs you want. For the diskette in drive B, you specified a disk drive
(**B:**) and a path (**\COMS**). Because you didn't want to give the files new
names as they were copied, you didn't use file names.

The usual order of elements is a drive name, followed by a path, and
finally, a file name. If you don't need one part, such as the path or the
drive name, leave it out.

Step 8. Type

```
CD B:COMS
```

This command makes COMS the current directory on drive B.

*Step 9. Display the list of files for the root, COMS, and SAMPLES directories.
Briefly look at each directory before you display the next one. The
required commands are*

DIR B:..

DIR B:

DIR B:SAMPLES

The first command tells DOS to step up one level of directories and show
the list of files. The second command tells DOS to list the files in the
current directory. And the final command tells DOS to list the files in the
SAMPLES subdirectory.

For these three commands, I'll show you what I saw on-screen on my computer. If you are using DOS V3.3 and 720K disk drives, you'll see screens identical to mine. If you are using DOS V3.3 with 1.2M or 1.44M diskettes, you will notice that only the line listing the number of bytes free in the directories will be different. You'll notice more differences in the screens if you are using 360K diskettes or a different version of DOS.

```
A>DIR B:..

 Volume in drive B is PRACTICE
 Directory of  B:\

COMS            <DIR>       7-24-87  1Ø:43p
        1 File(s)      41Ø624 bytes free


A>DIR B:

 Volume in drive B is PRACTICE
 Directory of  B:\COMS

.               <DIR>       7-24-87  1Ø:43p
..              <DIR>       7-24-87  1Ø:43p
SAMPLES         <DIR>       7-24-87  1Ø:43p
COMMAND   COM   253Ø7       3-17-87  12:ØØp
ASSIGN    COM    1561       3-17-87  12:ØØp
BACKUP    COM   31913       3-18-87  12:ØØp
BASIC     COM    1Ø63       3-17-87  12:ØØp
BASICA    COM   364Ø3       3-17-87  12:ØØp
CHKDSK    COM    985Ø       3-18-87  12:ØØp
COMP      COM    4214       3-17-87  12:ØØp
DEBUG     COM   15897       3-17-87  12:ØØp
DISKCOMP  COM    5879       3-17-87  12:ØØp
DISKCOPY  COM    6295       3-17-87  12:ØØp
EDLIN     COM    7526       3-17-87  12:ØØp
FDISK     COM   48216       3-18-87  12:ØØp
FORMAT    COM   11616       3-18-87  12:ØØp
GRAFTABL  COM    6128       3-17-87  12:ØØp
GRAPHICS  COM    33ØØ       3-17-87  12:ØØp
KEYB      COM    9Ø56       3-17-87  12:ØØp
LABEL     COM    2377       3-17-87  12:ØØp
MODE      COM   15487       3-17-87  12:ØØp
```

```
MORE      COM      313    3-17-87   12:ØØp
PRINT     COM     9Ø26    3-17-87   12:ØØp
RECOVER   COM     4299    3-18-87   12:ØØp
RESTORE   COM    34643    3-17-87   12:ØØp
SELECT    COM     4163    3-17-87   12:ØØp
SYS       COM     4766    3-17-87   12:ØØp
TREE      COM     3571    3-17-87   12:ØØp
          28 File(s)    41Ø624 bytes free

A>DIR B:SAMPLES

  Volume in drive B is PRACTICE
  Directory of  B:\COMS\SAMPLES

.              <DIR>      7-24-87   1Ø:43p
..             <DIR>      7-24-87   1Ø:43p

      2 File(s)    41Ø624 bytes free
```

Step 10. *Copy the BASIC program(s) to the SAMPLES directory.*

If you use 360K diskettes or a version of DOS before V3.3, the BASIC programs are on a different diskette. Take the DOS Master diskette out of drive A. Put the Operating Diskette or the DOS Supplemental Programs diskette into drive A. Don't change the diskette in drive B.

If you don't use 360K diskettes, you should have the BASIC program(s) on the diskette you are using.

DOS V3.3 has only one BASIC program, MORTGAGE.BAS, a mortgage calculator. Versions of DOS prior to V3.3 have many BASIC programs. To copy the BASIC programs, you will use a command that will copy simultaneously one or many BASIC programs. To copy the BASIC program files from drive A to the SAMPLES directory, type

COPY A:*.BAS B:SAMPLES /V

You'll see the name of each file as DOS copies it from drive A to drive B.

Step 11. *Move to the SAMPLES directory by typing*

```
CD B:SAMPLES
```

Step 12. *Type*

```
DIR B:
```

DOS shows the list of files in the SAMPLES directory. Look briefly at the directory, and then go to the next step.

Step 13. *Exchange the diskette in drive A with the diskette in drive B. Use the DIR command to list the directory of drive A; then do the same for drive B.*

What happened? In both cases, you got a listing of the files in the root directory. If you change diskettes and the current directory does not exist on the changed diskette, DOS resets the current directory to the root directory. This way, DOS does not get confused when you change diskettes.

Step 14. *Move back to the SAMPLES directory in drive A by typing*

```
CD COMS\SAMPLES
```

Step 15. *Create a new directory called TEST in SAMPLES. Use the following command*

```
MD TEST
```

Now call for a directory of TEST. (Use the command **DIR TEST**.) You should see only the **.** and **..** entries.

Step 16. *Copy BASIC into the TEST directory by typing*

```
COPY ..\BASICA.COM TEST /V
```

This command tells DOS to step up one directory to COMS, get
BASICA.COM (Advanced BASIC), and copy it into the TEST subdirectory.

Step 17. *Type*

```
RD TEST
```

Now you should see the following error message:

```
Invalid path, not directory,
or directory not empty
```

RD is the remove directory command. You just told DOS to erase the
TEST directory. The message you see on your screen tells you that you
cannot remove a directory that is not empty. A subdirectory is empty if
the only files in the subdirectory are the . and .. directory symbols. If you
want to remove the directory, that directory cannot contain any other files
or subdirectories. This precaution is for the safety of the files. DOS
assumes that if you want to remove a subdirectory, you will empty it first.

You cannot use RD on the current directory, nor can you remove the root
directory of the disk. You will also get an error message if you try. On
your own, move to the TEST directory and try to remove it. Move back to
the SAMPLES directory before going to the next step.

Step 18. *Remove the TEST directory by deleting all files in TEST and using
the RD command. Make certain you type the following command
correctly before you press Enter*

```
ERASE TEST\*.*
```

DOS will ask:

```
Are you sure (Y/N)?
```

As discussed earlier in the book, this message is another safety precaution. You have just told DOS to erase all files in the TEST subdirectory. Whenever you tell DOS to erase all files, DOS will ask you to confirm your request.

Because you do want to erase all the files, answer Y. If you did not want to erase all of the files, you would answer N. The system prompt will reappear.

Next, call for a directory of TEST (using **DIR TEST**). You will see that BASICA.COM was erased but the . and .. entries remain. You cannot erase a subdirectory with the ERASE command. The only way to remove a subdirectory is to use the RMDIR (or RD) command.

Remove the directory by typing

```
RD TEST
```

Now call for a listing of the SAMPLES directory. You will see that the TEST directory has been removed.

Step 19. *Run the MORTGAGE program. First, try to invoke Advanced BASIC, which is in the COMS directory with the mortgage program. Type*

```
..\BASICA MORTGAGE
```

Advanced BASIC loads into the computer, executes, and then loads and runs the mortgage calculator program. If you haven't tried the program, try it now.

To exit the program, press the Esc key when you see the menu. You will see an Ok. Then type the word **SYSTEM**, and press Enter. The DOS prompt reappears.

The command ..\BASICA told DOS to move up one directory and get Advanced BASIC. Now try the same command a different way. Type

```
\COMS\BASICA MORTGAGE
```

This command also loads and runs Advanced BASIC and the mortgage calculator. At the menu, press the Esc key. Then type SYSTEM to get back to DOS.

Now try to load Advanced BASIC without a path name in front of the word BASICA. Type

```
BASICA MORTGAGE
```

You'll see the message:

```
Bad command or file name
```

Because you received a DOS error message, you can presume that DOS could not find BASICA.COM. DOS looked in the current directory, but it could not find the command name you wanted in the directory you specified. Because you did not correctly tell DOS where to find the program, DOS could not find the program. The file is not in the SAMPLES directory; it is in the COMS directory.

You could give a path name whenever you wanted to load Advanced BASIC. However, there is another way: using the PATH command. The PATH command enables you to tell DOS to search in other subdirectories for a program you want to run. If DOS does not find the program in the current directory, DOS will search the directories you named in the PATH command.

Type the following command:

```
PATH A:\COMS
```

This command tells DOS to look in the COMS subdirectory if DOS cannot find in the current directory the program you want to run. The last directory named in the path (COMS) is searched, but no other directory is searched (in this case, the root directory of the disk). If you want DOS to search both these directories, you must use the PATH command and type the names of all the directories to be searched, separating the names with semicolons. To have DOS search both the root directory and the COMS subdirectory, you would type

```
PATH A:\;A:\COMS
```

Now that the PATH command has been properly set, type

```
BASICA MORTGAGE
```

This command will load Advanced BASIC from the COMS directory. BASIC will then load and execute MORTGAGE. Now get out of the menu and back to DOS.

This step was the last instruction for users with two floppy disk drives. You can skim the next section for fixed disk users, and then skip to the discussion of the PATH command.

Instructions for Floppy and Fixed Disk Drives

Step 1. Put the practice diskette into drive A.

Step 2. Type CD C:\ to make sure you are at the root directory of the fixed disk. If your fixed disk is not drive C, substitute the appropriate letter of the fixed disk drive for the letter C. Also, disconnect the PATH command by typing PATH=;. You will need to disconnect the PATH command to see how to run programs from different directories.

Step 3. Type

```
MD A:COMS
```

This command makes a new subdirectory called COMS on the disk in drive A. MKDIR, or its short form MD, creates a new subdirectory.

Step 4. Type

```
MD A:COMS\SAMPLES
```

This command makes a new subdirectory called SAMPLES in the subdirectory COMS.

At this point, the root directory owns a directory called COMS, which, in turn, owns a directory called SAMPLES. Notice that you have used a path name in this command. DOS moves down through the path. When DOS reaches the last name in the path (SAMPLES), DOS knows to make a new subdirectory called SAMPLES instead of trying to move again.

Many beginning hard disk users are confused by path sequences. To keep the path's order and structure clear in your mind, separate the path from the final destination at the last backslash. The part before the final backslash (A:COMS) tells DOS where to do what you've asked (make a subdirectory called SAMPLES). The part after the final backslash (SAMPLES) is the object of your instruction (the subdirectory that DOS is to create).

Step 5. Type

```
DIR A:
```

What you see is the listing of files in the root directory on the disk. Your screen will look something like this:

```
Volume in drive A is PRACTICE
Directory of  A:\

COMS          <DIR>      7-24-87  10:43p
        1 File(s)    728064 bytes free
```

The <DIR> symbol after a name means that the listed "file" is a directory, not a normal file. The COMS directory has this <DIR> designation following it.

The date and time when you created the directory should also appear on the line with the name. Make a note of the time you see on the screen.

Look at the rest of the screen. Notice the line that tells you what disk drive you are using and what directory you are viewing. Study the screen for a few seconds, and then move to the next step.

Step 6. *Type*

```
DIR A:COMS
```

Now you will see a directory of the COMS directory. The listing will look something like the following:

```
Volume in drive A is PRACTICE
Directory of A:\COMS

.               <DIR>        7-24-87    10:43p
..              <DIR>        7-24-87    10:43p
SAMPLES         <DIR>        7-24-87    10:43p
        3 File(s)       728064 bytes  free
```

The SAMPLES directory should hold no surprises, but what are the period and double-period directories? Both are special shorthand symbols used for maneuvering in the directory system. The period represents the subdirectory you are viewing, or the current directory. You can think of it as the subdirectory's "I exist to myself" symbol. The double period represents the parent directory of the COMS subdirectory. In this case, the double period represents the root directory, the parent of the COMS subdirectory.

Compare the first directory to the second. Notice that the root directory does not contain these period (.) and double-period (..) directory symbols. Only subdirectories have these symbols. The root directory has no parent; hence, you will not find the . and .. entries in the root directory.

If you want to tell DOS explicitly to start with the directory you are using, you use the period as the first character in the path. This method is infrequently used because, unless the path begins with a \, DOS starts movement with the current directory. To tell DOS to move up one level of subdirectories, use the double period. This method is used more frequently. We'll cover this shorthand symbol again in Chapter 11.

Take a look at the dates and times on the lines with the period and double-period symbols. These dates and times should be the same as those for the COMS entry in the root directory. When DOS creates subdirectories, it not only makes an entry in the parent directory; it also establishes the . and .. files, giving all three items the same date and time.

Step 7. *Type*

```
COPY BIN\*.COM A:\COMS /V
```

This command copies to the subdirectory COMS on drive A (A:\COMS) all the files from the subdirectory BIN that have the extension .COM (BIN*.COM). The /V switch tells DOS to verify that it has copied the files correctly.

When you specify a disk drive name in a path, that drive name must appear first. You then specify the path and, finally, the file name. For the BIN*.COM portion of the command, you needed to specify a path because the directory that contains all the DOS programs you want is BIN, which is not the current directory. For the diskette in drive A, you specified a disk drive (A:) and a path (\COMS). Because you didn't want to give the files new names as they were copied, you didn't use file names.

The usual order of elements is a drive name, followed by a path, and finally, a file name. If you don't need one part, such as the path or the drive name, leave it out.

Step 8. *Type*

```
CD A:\COMS
```

This command makes COMS the current directory on drive A.

Step 9. *Display the list of files for the root, COMS, and SAMPLES directories. Briefly look at each directory before you display the next one. The required commands are*

DIR A:..

DIR A:

DIR A:SAMPLES

The first command tells DOS to step up one level of directories and show the list of files. The second command tells DOS to list the files in the current directory. And the final command tells DOS to list the files in the SAMPLES subdirectory.

For these three commands, I'll show what I saw on-screen on my computer. If you are using DOS V3.3 and 720K disk drives, you'll see screens identical to mine. If you are using DOS V3.3 with 1.2M or 1.44M diskettes, you will see that only the line listing the number of bytes free in the directories is different. You'll notice more differences in the screens if you are using a different version of DOS.

```
C>DIR A:..

 Volume in drive A is PRACTICE
 Directory of  A:\

COMS            <DIR>       7-24-87  10:43p
        1 File(s)     401624 bytes free


C>DIR A:

 Volume in drive A is PRACTICE
 Directory of  A:\COMS

 .              <DIR>       7-24-87  10:43p
 ..             <DIR>       7-24-87  10:43p
SAMPLES         <DIR>       7-24-87  10:43p
COMMAND   COM    25307      3-17-87  12:00p
ASSIGN    COM     1561      3-17-87  12:00p
BACKUP    COM    31913      3-18-87  12:00p
BASIC     COM     1063      3-17-87  12:00p
BASICA    COM    36403      3-17-87  12:00p
CHKDSK    COM     9850      3-18-87  12:00p
```

```
    COMP     COM      4214    3-17-87   12:00p
    DEBUG    COM     15897    3-17-87   12:00p
    DISKCOMP COM      5879    3-17-87   12:00p
    DISKCOPY COM      6295    3-17-87   12:00p
    EDLIN    COM      7526    3-17-87   12:00p
    FDISK    COM     48216    3-18-87   12:00p
    FORMAT   COM     11616    3-18-87   12:00p
    GRAFTABL COM      6128    3-17-87   12:00p
    GRAPHICS COM      3300    3-17-87   12:00p
    KEYB     COM      9056    3-17-87   12:00p
    LABEL    COM      2377    3-17-87   12:00p
    MODE     COM     15487    3-17-87   12:00p
    MORE     COM       313    3-17-87   12:00p
    PRINT    COM      9026    3-17-87   12:00p
    RECOVER  COM      4299    3-18-87   12:00p
    RESTORE  COM     34643    3-17-87   12:00p
    SELECT   COM      4163    3-17-87   12:00p
    SYS      COM      4766    3-17-87   12:00p
    TREE     COM      3571    3-17-87   12:00p
        28 File(s)     410624 bytes free
```

C>**DIR A:SAMPLES**

```
  Volume in drive A is PRACTICE
  Directory of  A:\COMS\SAMPLES

  .              <DIR>      7-24-87   10:43p
  ..             <DIR>      7-24-87   10:43p

      2 File(s)     410624 bytes free
```

Step 10. *Copy the BASIC program(s) to the SAMPLES directory.*

DOS V3.3 has only one BASIC program, MORTGAGE.BAS, a mortgage calculator. Versions of DOS prior to V3.3 come with many BASIC programs. These files are located in the BIN subdirectory. To copy the programs, you will use a command that will copy simultaneously one or many BASIC programs. To copy the BASIC program file(s) from drive A to the SAMPLES directory, type

```
COPY \BIN\*.BAS A:SAMPLES /V
```

You'll see the name of each file as it is copied from drive C to drive A.

Step 11. *Move to the SAMPLES directory by typing*

```
CD A:SAMPLES
```

Step 12. *Type*

```
DIR A:
```

DOS shows the list of files in the SAMPLES directory. Look briefly at the directory, and then go to the next step.

Step 13. *Remove the practice diskette in drive A, and insert the DOS Master Startup/Operating or Master Startup diskette into the drive. Use the DIR command to list the directory of drive A.*

What happened? You got a listing of the files in the root directory. If you change diskettes and the current directory does not exist on the changed diskette, DOS resets the current directory to the root directory. This way, DOS does not get confused when you change diskettes.

Step 14. *Remove the DOS diskette from drive A, and put the practice diskette back into the drive. Make the floppy disk drive the current disk drive, and then make the SAMPLES directory the current directory. The commands are*

```
A:
CD COMS\SAMPLES
```

***Step 15**. Create a new directory called TEST in SAMPLES. Use the following command:*

```
MD TEST
```

Now call for a directory of TEST. (Use the command **DIR TEST**.) You should see only the **.** and **..** entries.

***Step 16.** Copy BASIC into the TEST directory by typing:*

```
COPY ..\BASICA.COM TEST /V
```

This command tells DOS to step up one directory to COMS, get BASICA.COM (Advanced BASIC), and copy it into the TEST subdirectory.

***Step 17.** Type*

```
RD TEST
```

Now you should see the following error message:

```
Invalid path, not directory,
or directory not empty
```

RD is the remove directory command. You just told DOS to erase the TEST directory. The message you see on your screen tells you that you cannot remove a directory that is not empty. A subdirectory is empty if the only files in the subdirectory are the **.** and **..** directory symbols. If you want to remove the directory, that directory cannot contain any other files or subdirectories. This precaution is for the safety of files. DOS assumes that if you want to remove a subdirectory, you will empty it first.

You cannot use RD on the current directory, nor can you remove the root directory of the disk. You will get an error message if you try. On your own, move to the TEST directory, and try to remove it. Move back to the SAMPLES directory before going to the next step.

Step 18. *Remove the TEST directory by deleting all files in TEST and using the RD command. Make certain you type the following command correctly before you press Enter:*

```
ERASE TEST\*.*
```

DOS will ask

```
Are you sure (Y/N)?_
```

This message is another safety precaution. You have just told DOS to erase all files in the TEST subdirectory. Whenever you tell DOS to erase all files, DOS will ask you to confirm your request.

Because you do want to erase all the files, answer Y. If you did not want to erase all of the files, you would answer N. The system prompt will reappear.

Next, call for a directory of TEST (using DIR TEST). You will see that BASIC.COM was erased but that the . and .. entries remain. You cannot erase a subdirectory with the ERASE command. The only way to remove a subdirectory is to use the RD command.

Remove the directory by typing

```
RD TEST
```

Now call for a listing of the SAMPLES directory. You will see that the TEST directory has been removed.

Step 19. *You are ready to run the MORTGAGE program. First, try to invoke Advanced BASIC, which is in the COMS directory with the mortgage program. Type*

```
..\BASICA MORTGAGE
```

Advanced BASIC loads into the computer, executes, and then loads and runs the mortgage calculator program. If you haven't tried the program, try it now.

To exit the program, press the Esc key when you see the menu. You will see an Ok. Then type the word **SYSTEM**, and press Enter. The DOS prompt reappears.

The command **..\BASICA** tells DOS to move up one directory and get Advanced BASIC. Now try the same command a different way. Type:

```
\COMS\BASICA MORTGAGE
```

This command also loads and runs Advanced BASIC and the mortgage calculator. At the menu, press the Esc key. Then type **SYSTEM** to get back to DOS.

Now try to load Advanced BASIC without a path name in front of the word BASICA. Type

```
BASICA MORTGAGE
```

You'll see the message:

```
Bad command or file name
```

Because you received a DOS error message, you can presume that DOS could not find BASICA.COM. DOS looked in the current directory, but it could not find the command name you wanted in the directory you specified. Because you did not correctly tell DOS where to find the program, DOS could not find the program. The file is not in the SAMPLES directory; it is in the COMS directory.

You could give a path name whenever you wanted to use Advanced BASIC. Another alternative is to put your files "together" in one directory, move to that directory, and run the programs from there. However, there is another way: using the PATH command. The PATH command enables you to tell DOS to search in other subdirectories for the program you want to run. If DOS does not find the program in the current directory, DOS will search the directories you named in the PATH command.

Type the following command:

```
PATH C:\BIN
```

This command tells DOS to look in the BIN subdirectory on drive C if DOS cannot find in the current directory the program you want to run. The last directory named in the path (BIN) is searched, but no other directory is searched (in this case, the root directory of the disk). If you want DOS to search both these directories, you must use the PATH command and type the names of the directories to be searched, separating the names with semicolons. If you want DOS to search both the root directory and the BIN subdirectory, you type:

```
PATH C:\;C:\BIN
```

Now that the PATH command has been properly set, type

```
BASICA MORTGAGE
```

This command should load Advanced BASIC from the C:\BIN directory. BASIC will then load and execute MORTGAGE. Now get out of the menu and back to DOS.

This step is the last instruction for this exercise. The next section discusses the PATH command.

Understanding the PATH Command

Two facts make the PATH command important. The first is that the PATH command allows you to use programs that are not stored in the current directory. That is, you can run a program command file (a file with a .COM extension), an executable file (a file with an .EXE extension), or a batch file (a file with a .BAT extension) when the file is not in the current directory. The second fact is that when you use a disk with many subdirectories, you may frequently be in a directory other than the one with the .COM, .EXE, or .BAT file you want to use.

You could solve the problem by leaving whatever subdirectory you are in, going to the directory that contains the desired program file, and using the file there. Or, preferably, you could invoke the PATH command to name explicitly the path to the program or batch file you want to use. The convenience of the PATH command is that it lets you automatically use a .COM, .EXE, or .BAT file anywhere from any directory.

The PATH command is thus an important command for users of hierarchical directories, particularly those who have created complex arrangements of multiple subdirectories. Because owners of fixed disks and high-capacity disks will most likely use hierarchical directories, these persons especially should know how to use the PATH command.

The syntax of the PATH command is

   PATH = *d1:path1;d2:path2;d3:path3* . . .

PATH is an internal DOS command and does not need a disk drive name or path name to run the command.

The next part of the command line is an equal sign. A space can precede the equal sign.

Next you specify the disk drives and directories that DOS should search to find a program. Each combination is called a path set and consists of an optional disk drive name (*d:*), followed by a path name. The path name (*path*) is the full name of the chain of directories that lead to the directory to be searched. Only the last directory named in the *path* is searched.

The disk drive names are optional. If you do not include drive names, PATH will cause DOS to search for the directories on the current disk drive.

You can give one path set or many path sets. The additional path sets are designated by the . . . in the syntax. When you give more than one path set, separate each path set with a semicolon. Do not use a space in any path set or between path sets. Only the semicolon is allowed between path sets.

If you wish to change the PATH, simply issue the PATH command again using the new list of path sets DOS should use. To display the current PATH, type

PATH

DOS displays the list of current paths or the message No path if the PATH command has not been used. To clear and disconnect the PATH command, give the command

PATH=;

The command is the word PATH, followed by an equal sign and a semicolon. This clears the directory paths, and instructs DOS to look only in the current directory for programs.

As you have noticed, the PATH command accepts a disk drive name in front of the path name. Use drive names in the path sets. DOS will automatically go to the named floppy disk drive or fixed disk drive to find a program in the specified path, regardless of your current disk or directory.

When you use the PATH command, always start paths with the root directory. This way, you can be in any subdirectory on the disk, and DOS will always start at the root directory. If you don't specify the root directory as the beginning of these paths, DOS will try to move down your specified path, starting with the current directory. You will have to give a new PATH command whenever you change subdirectories. The easier way is to start your paths for the PATH command at the root directory with a disk drive name and a backslash. For more information about the PATH command, check the *DOS Command Reference* in Part VI.

The PATH command has one limitation. The PATH command works only when you are running programs or batch files from the DOS system prompt. Your programs must know where to get any additional programs or data files that might be needed. The PATH command does not help your programs locate additional programs or data files. Fortunately, however, DOS V3.3 features an additional PATH command for data files—APPEND. APPEND is discussed in Chapter 11.

Summary

In this chapter, you learned the following key points about the hierarchical directory system:

1. Each diskette or fixed disk starts with a single root (system) directory.

2. Each subdirectory (a child) is owned by exactly one directory (a parent). Each child subdirectory (as well as the root directory) can be a parent to many child subdirectories.

3. The three directory commands are

   a. CHDIR, or CD, which changes a current directory

   b. MKDIR, or MD, which creates a new subdirectory

   c. RMDIR, or RD, which removes a subdirectory

4. Each disk has a current directory. If you change diskettes, and the current directory does not exist on the changed diskette, the root directory becomes the current directory.

5. The path character is the backslash (\ ).

6. A path is a series of subdirectory names separated by the path character.

7. When the path character begins the path name, the directory movement starts at the root directory of the disk. If the path character does not start the path, the directory movement starts with the current directory of the disk.

8. When you place a path name in front of a file name, you must separate the two names with a path character.

9. When you run a program, you can precede the program name with a drive name followed by a path.

10. The PATH command enables DOS to execute programs and batch files that are not in the current directory of the current disk drive. However, PATH does not help your programs find additional program or data files.

Chapter 11 expands your knowledge about the hierarchical directory system. In that chapter, you'll learn more about the APPEND command, and I'll show you shortcuts you can use with many DOS commands.

11

Gaining Better Control with Hierarchical Directories

In Chapter 10, you were introduced to hierarchical directories. In this chapter, you will extend your knowledge of how to use multiple directories. Specifically, you will learn some shortcuts for path names. You will also learn how to list the entire directory system with the CHKDSK and TREE commands. And you will read more about the APPEND command, the PATH command for data files. This information will be of interest to all personal computer users, and especially to those who own fixed disk computers.

Shortcuts for Specifying Paths

Recall the comparison of a hierarchical directory to an airline's routing system. The airline has a major hub, minor hubs, and planes going to outlying cities. Analogous to the airline, a hierarchical directory has a root directory, subdirectories, and files. When you instruct DOS, you are giving instructions to the system's "control tower." You communicate how you will reach your destination.

Of the directions that you give DOS, some parts can be viewed as optional; but other parts are essential. The mandatory directions are the minimum information you must give so that DOS will know where to find the files it needs. The optional directions make your instructions more clear, but DOS doesn't absolutely need them. As you learned in Chapter 4, these mandatory and optional instructions are called the command *syntax*.

Using the airline analogy, if the airline's main hub were in Chicago (your current location), and you wanted to go to New York, you would take a "Chicago to New York" plane. Because the tower (DOS) knows the current location (the disk drive and current directory), indicating

"Chicago" is optional. The inclusion of "Chicago" in the instructions helps to clarify the planned travel, but it is not essential. Stating the destination (New York), however, is mandatory so that the tower (DOS) will know where the plane is to go.

This analogy especially fits the use of DOS's COPY command—a command frequently used with hierarchical directories. The COPY command's syntax is similar to that of many DOS commands. Table 11.1 shows different ways to use directions (paths) with the COPY command to copy files to other locations.

The examples in table 11.1 assume that you are using a personal computer with at least one floppy disk drive and a fixed disk. The floppy disk drive is the A drive, and the fixed disk drive is the C drive. When you use table 11.1, assume that the fixed disk has the subdirectory layout shown in Appendix B.

In the table, the *Current Location* is the current disk drive and directory. (Recall Chapter 2's discussion of the current disk drive and Chapter 10's discussion of *current directory*.) The *Current Location* is the directory in which you are working when you give DOS instructions.

The *Source* column in the table shows the drive and subdirectory from which you want to copy a file. *Destination* is the drive and subdirectory where you want the copy of the file to go. If the name of the file is changed when the file is copied, you will see a *Y* (for Yes) in the *Name Change* column. An N (for no) in the column indicates that the name is to remain unchanged.

Look carefully at the *Syntax To Use* column. Notice that entries appear in blue and black characters. The black characters are optional: You can leave them out of the syntax, and you will still be able to accomplish the desired operation. The blue characters are mandatory: You must use them to accomplish the operation. The blue- and black-character combination represents the full, formal syntax, which best shows you how the path works. After you understand how each operation works, you can use just the mandatory syntax to perform the task.

To use table 11.1, assume that the root directory of drive C (C:\) has a file named SAMPLE1.TXT. The subdirectory called C:\WORDS\LETTERS has a file named SAMPLE2.TXT. Notice that only the numbers before the extension (.TXT) are different. The directories C:\DOS\BASIC\TEST, C:\DOS\HARDDISK, and the disk in drive A have files named SAMPLE3.TXT, SAMPLE4.TXT, and SAMPLE5.TXT, respectively.

Table 11.1
Examples of Full and Mandatory Syntax

Current Position	Source	Destination	Name Change	Syntax To Use
C:\	C:\	C:\WORDS\LETTERS	N	COPY C:\SAMPLE1.TXT C:\WORDS\LETTERS\SAMPLE1.TXT
C:\	C:\	C:\WORDS\LETTERS	Y	COPY C:\SAMPLE1.TXT C:\WORDS\LETTERS\NEW1.TXT
C:\	C:\	C:\DOS\BASIC\TEST	N	COPY C:\SAMPLE1.TXT C:\DOS\BASIC\TEST
C:\	C:\	C:\DOS\BASIC\TEST	Y	COPY C:\SAMPLE1.TXT C:\DOS\BASIC\TEST\NEW1.TXT
C:\DOS	C:\	C:\DOS\HARDDISK	N	COPY C:\SAMPLE1.TXT C:\DOS\HARDDISK
C:\DOS\HARDDISK	C:\DOS\HARDDISK	C:\DOS	N*	COPY C:\DOS\HARDDISK\SAMPLE4.TXT C:\DOS
C:\DOS\HARDDISK	C:\WORDS\LETTERS	C:\SS\123DATA	N	COPY C:\WORDS\LETTERS\SAMPLE2.TXT C:\SS\123DATA
C:\DOS\BASIC	C:\WORDS\LETTERS	C:\DOS\HARDDISK	N*	COPY C:\WORDS\LETTERS\SAMPLE2.TXT C:\DOS\HARDDISK
C:\WORDS	C:\DOS\BASIC\TEST	C:\WORDS\LETTERS	N	COPY C:\DOS\BASIC\TEST\SAMPLE3.TXT C:\WORDS\LETTERS
C:\DOS	C:\WORDS\LETTERS	A:\	N	COPY C:\WORDS\LETTERS\SAMPLE2.TXT A:\
A:\	A:\	C:\SS\123DATA	N	COPY A:\SAMPLE5.TXT C:\SS\123DATA
C:\	C:\	C:\DOS	N	COPY C:\SAMPLE1.TXT C:\DOS
C:\WORDS\LETTERS	C:\DOS\BASIC\TEST	C:\WORDS\LETTERS	N	COPY C:\DOS\BASIC\TEST\SAMPLE3.TXT C:\WORDS\LETTERS

Each of the following explanations shows the syntax for each line in table 11.1. As you study the examples, note the places where you must enter spaces. One place is after the command name (COPY, in this set of examples). Another place is after the source file's extension (.TXT), between the source specification and the destination specification.

1. The first command line shown in the *Syntax To Use* column copies the file SAMPLE1.TXT from the root directory of C (**C:**) to the drive C subdirectory named \WORDS\LETTERS. When, as the table indicates, the current directory is the root directory, you do not need to enter the characters that appear in italic typeface (the source and destination disk drive name and root directory indicator) to accomplish the operation.

   If you are not changing the file name, you do not have to give the file name in the destination. If you do not give a name in the destination, DOS will keep the file name the same when it copies the file. Hence, the file name in the destination is also optional.

2. The second command line performs the same operation as the first line, except that the file name is changed from SAMPLE1.TXT to NEW1.TXT. Because you give a file name in the destination name, DOS will copy the file and give it the new name.

3. The third command line copies the file named SAMPLE1.TXT from the root directory to the drive C subdirectory named \DOS\BASIC\TEST.

4. The fourth command line performs the same operation as the third line, except that the file name is again changed as it was in the second line. After the fourth example, no file name changes are illustrated, because the process is as simple as tacking the new file name, preceded by a backslash, onto the destination directory's path name. Each of the preceding examples is useful if you copy a file immediately after you start DOS from the fixed disk, because your current directory will normally be the root directory after DOS starts.

5. The fifth command line copies the SAMPLE1.TXT file from the root directory to the \DOS\HARDDISK subdirectory on drive C. Notice that you don't need to type the "\DOS" (pronounced "backslash DOS") shown in italic characters to get the file into the \DOS\HARDDISK subdirectory. Your current directory is \DOS, and HARDDISK is a subdirectory of \DOS.

6. The sixth command line copies SAMPLE4.TXT from C:\DOS\HARDDISK to C:\DOS. This example is significant because it shows that you need to put a backslash before DOS in order to copy a file to a higher level in this branch (from \DOS\HARDDISK to \DOS). At first glance, this requirement may seem inconsistent with the preceding example, but the backslash is necessary.

7. In the seventh command line, the paths of all three subdirectories are different; therefore, you must specify the full name of the source and destination paths. This form of the syntax is the fullest for copy operations on one drive (unless, of course, other subdirectories are at lower levels in the hierarchical directory). If you know the full syntax, you won't have to use the CHDIR (or CD) command to change directories. You can be positioned in any subdirectory and use the full syntax to copy a file from any subdirectory to any other subdirectory.

8. Line 8 shows you how to copy a file from a subdirectory of one path (\WORDS\LETTERS) to a subdirectory of another path (\DOS\HARDDISK) when you are positioned in a different subdirectory (BASIC) of the \DOS path. Only the drive designation is optional (italic).

9. Line 9 shows the syntax for copying a file from a level-three subdirectory (\DOS\BASIC\TEST) to a subdirectory (LETTERS) of the path where you are positioned (\WORDS).

10. Line 10 shows how to copy a file from a drive C subdirectory (\WORDS\LETTERS) to another drive (A:) when you are positioned in another drive C subdirectory (\DOS).

    This example illustrates two common situations. It shows that the phrasing of path names is identical on all disk drives: floppy, fixed, or semireal. When you use path names for another drive, such as drive A in this example, you use a syntax similar to that used for drive C in the preceding examples. This line also illustrates the syntax for copying files to a floppy diskette. The only changes are that the source path name and file name will be different for different files.

11. The eleventh line presents the syntax for receiving a file from another computer or for installing onto a fixed disk a program that has no installation routine. In this example, SAMPLE5.TXT is copied from the root directory in drive A to a drive C

subdirectory (\SS\123DATA) when you are positioned in a drive C subdirectory (\DOS).

12. Line 12 shows you how to copy between subdirectories on drive C if you are positioned in drive A.

13. Line 13 shows how to copy a file from a totally different path of subdirectories into the current directory. Note that, except for the drive designation, you must give the entire source. But because the destination is the same as the current position, you don't need to specify the destination at all.

Let me repeat something you know already, which I call the *rule of currents*: If you don't give the complete position portion of the command syntax to DOS, DOS uses the current position.

If you do not give a disk drive name to a DOS command, the current disk drive is used. If you do not give a path name, the current directory is used. If you do not give a file name, either all files are used or the file name used in the preceding part of the command is used. The *rule of currents* yields several guidelines for table 11.1, which are discussed in the rest of this section.

One guideline is that if the current drive is neither the source nor the destination, you must enter the drive name of the source and destination. Another guideline is that if the current directory (the current path) is neither the source nor the destination, you must enter the path name of the source and destination. An important variant is that if the source or the destination is in a subdirectory of your current directory, you need to start the path name with that subdirectory. Example 5 in the table demonstrates this point.

On the other hand, if you can omit part of the full syntax, you have created a shortcut. You need only type the necessary parts of the command. After you have learned what syntax parts you can omit, you will become faster at typing commands and more proficient at using DOS.

One shortcut is to use shorter path names where possible. Notice in table 11.1 the two lines that contain asterisks (see the *Name Change* column). For both of these lines, you can learn even easier ways to tell DOS how to copy the files you want. You have already learned that the current directory is represented by one period, and the parent directory is represented by two periods. To simplify the two command lines, you can use the double-period symbol. Here are the two command lines:

COPY SAMPLE4.TXT ..

COPY \WORDS\LETTERS\SAMPLE2.TXT ..\HARDDISK

In these two examples, the current directory is *owned* by \DOS. In the first case, you are copying to the DOS directory. The destination is the parent directory (DOS), represented by the **..** symbol. In the second example, you are copying to another subdirectory owned by DOS. Instead of typing **\DOS\HARDDISK**, you can substitute the double-period symbol. The destination becomes **..\HARDDISK** (moving up to DOS and down to HARDDISK).

If you know the layout of your fixed disk, type the shortest route for a path. DOS will navigate the directory system using the long path starting at the root directory or the shorter path starting at the current directory. It makes little difference to DOS. If you are like me, you will want to type the shortest command line you can use. If you take some time to look for shortcuts, you will find that using the computer is more fun.

Listing a Disk's Directories (TREE, CHKDSK /V)

The files in your hierarchical directories are probably organized in a manner similar to the way you would physically organize floppy diskettes. But as the number of directories and files grows, your ability to remember which directory holds what file decreases. Instead of asking yourself the question "Which diskette holds my file?" your question becomes "Which directory holds my file?"

DOS thoughtfully provides a command that will list all the directories of a disk: the TREE command. TREE will also list the files in the directories. In addition to using TREE, you can also use the CHKDSK command with the /V switch to list all the subdirectories and files on a disk. If you have a fixed disk computer, you will find these two commands useful.

TREE's command syntax is

dc:pathc\TREE *d: /F*

TREE is an external command. The *d:path* is the optional disk drive and path name for the TREE command. *d:* is the name of the disk drive that holds the directories you want to list. If you omit *d:*, TREE lists the directories on the current disk drive.

TREE accepts the single switch */F*, which directs TREE to list the *files* in the directories. Use this switch if you are trying to locate a file. If you do not give the switch, you will get only a list of the disk's directories—not the disk's files.

Notice that you do not give a path or file name with the drive name. TREE is not the same as the DIR command. TREE automatically starts its listing with the root directory of the specified or current disk drive, so you don't give TREE the choice of where it starts. Also, you cannot specify a file for which you want to search. With TREE, you get an all-or-nothing listing of the disk's directory.

The following example shows the TREE command used on the practice diskette you made in Chapter 10:

```
C>TREE A:
DIRECTORY PATH LISTING FOR VOLUME PRACTICE

Path: \COMS

Sub-directories:  SAMPLES


Path: \COMS\SAMPLES

Sub-directories:  TEST


Path: \COMS\SAMPLES\TEST

Sub-directories:  None
```

```
C>TREE A: /F

DIRECTORY PATH LISTING FOR VOLUME PRACTICE

Files:          None

Path: \COMS
```

```
Sub-directories:   SAMPLES

Files:             COMMAND  .COM
                   ASSIGN   .COM
                   BACKUP   .COM
                   BASIC    .COM
                   BASICA   .COM
                   CHKDSK   .COM
                   COMP     .COM
                   DEBUG    .COM
                   DISKCOMP.COM
                   DISKCOPY.COM
                   EDLIN    .COM
                   FDISK    .COM
                   FORMAT   .COM
                   GRAFTABL.COM
                   GRAPHICS.COM
                   KEYB     .COM
                   LABEL    .COM
                   MODE     .COM
                   MORE     .COM
                   PRINT    .COM
                   RECOVER  .COM
                   RESTORE  .COM
                   SELECT   .COM
                   SYS      .COM
                   TREE     .COM


Path: \COMS\SAMPLES

Sub-directories:   TEST

Files:             MORTGAGE.BAS


Path: \COMS\SAMPLES\TEST

Sub-directories:   None

Files:             BASICA   .COM
```

The CHDSK command accepts the /V switch, which, in this case, means give a *verbose* listing of the disk's directories and files. CHDSK's command syntax is

> *dc:pathc*CHKDSK *d: /V*

CHKDSK /V is like the TREE command. The *dc:pathc* specifies the command's disk drive and path. The *d:* is the optional name of the disk drive to be checked. The /V switch lists the directories as well as the files. The following sample output shows the results when the CHDSK command was used on Chapter 10's practice diskette:

```
C>CHKDSK A: /V

Volume PRACTICE     created Jul 12, 1987 10:52p
Directory A:\
     A:\PRACTICE
Directory A:\COMS
Directory A:\COMS\SAMPLES
     A:\COMS\SAMPLES\MORTGAGE.BAS
Directory A:\COMS\SAMPLES\TEST
     A:\COMS\SAMPLES\TEST\BASICA.COM
     A:\COMS\COMMAND.COM
     A:\COMS\ASSIGN.COM
     A:\COMS\BACKUP.COM
     A:\COMS\BASIC.COM
     A:\COMS\BASICA.COM
     A:\COMS\CHKDSK.COM
     A:\COMS\COMP.COM
     A:\COMS\DEBUG.COM
     A:\COMS\DISKCOMP.COM
     A:\COMS\DISKCOPY.COM
     A:\COMS\EDLIN.COM
     A:\COMS\FDISK.COM
     A:\COMS\FORMAT.COM
     A:\COMS\GRAFTABL.COM
     A:\COMS\GRAPHICS.COM
     A:\COMS\KEYB.COM
     A:\COMS\LABEL.COM
     A:\COMS\MODE.COM
     A:\COMS\MORE.COM
```

```
A:\COMS\PRINT.COM
A:\COMS\RECOVER.COM
A:\COMS\RESTORE.COM
A:\COMS\SELECT.COM
A:\COMS\SYS.COM
A:\COMS\TREE.COM


730112 bytes total disk space
     0 bytes in 1 hidden files
  3072 bytes in 3 directories
361472 bytes in 27 user files
365568 bytes available on disk


654336 bytes total memory
522368 bytes free
```

Notice that CHKDSK performs its normal disk analysis in addition to listing the files and directories.

With CHKDSK /V and TREE, the resulting output can be lengthy. This type of output is ideally suited for redirection. For example, you could use the MORE filter to display one screen's worth of information at a time. To use MORE for output redirection with CHKDSK or TREE, the command syntaxes are

CHKDSK /V | MORE
TREE | MORE

You can also redirect the output of either TREE or CHKDSK to the printer with these commands:

TREE >PRN
CHKDSK /V >PRN

You can place TREE's or CHKDSK's output into a disk file with these commands:

TREE >treelist
CHKDSK /V >dsklist

If you store the output in a disk file, you can print the output at any time. I recommend that you occasionally run TREE or CHKDSK /V on your fixed disk to get a printed copy of your disk's entire contents, which you can keep near your computer. This type of output is a good roadmap of your fixed disk's structure and can help coworkers or friends when they must use your computer.

Helping Programs Find Their Data Files (APPEND)

In Chapter 10, you learned that the PATH command allows you to run any command (.COM), executable (.EXE), or batch (.BAT) file from any directory. When you type a command that is not preceded by a path name, DOS searches the current directory for the program or batch file. If the file does not appear in the current directory, DOS then searches the directories listed in the PATH command. If the file appears in any of these directories, DOS automatically loads and executes the file.

But PATH only works for files with .COM, .EXE, or .BAT extensions. PATH solves the problem of running program files located in different directories. PATH does not solve another problem: using programs that know nothing about hierarchical directories.

Most software publishers write programs that take advantage of hierarchical directories, making larger-capacity diskettes and fixed disks easier to use. But some older, "brain-damaged" packages do not use hierarchical directories, and they need special help. If you are using a program that does not take advantage of hierarchical directories, you must keep your programs and data files together in a single directory. You cannot place your programs in one directory and your data files in a subdirectory—an organizational pattern that most fixed disk users follow.

You will find that the most problematic software is the type that requires additional program files while the main program is running. WordStar Release 3 is an example of this type of software. This version of WordStar uses two overlay files, WSOVLY1.OVR and WSMSGS.OVR while WordStar is running. Although you can put the main WordStar program file in the subdirectory that the PATH command uses, you must also keep copies of the two overlay files in each subdirectory you use with WordStar Release 3. (Fortunately, WordStar Release 4 knows and uses hierarchical directories well.)

New with DOS V3.3, APPEND is the PATH command for use with data files. If you need to trick main programs into finding other needed files, you can now use APPEND. APPEND is a more complex command than

PATH, and its syntax requirements are somewhat more complicated. APPEND's syntax is more complex because the phrasing changes, depending on whether you are using it for the first time or at some later time.

When you use APPEND for the first time, the syntax is one of the following:

>*dc:pathc*APPEND *d1:path1;d2:path2; . . .*

>*dc:pathc*APPEND */X /E*

For both commands, the *dc:pathc* names the disk drive and path that hold the APPEND command. Both drive name and path are optional.

For the next part of the command line, you specify the disk drive and directories that APPEND should search when a main program is looking for a data file. Each path set is in the form:

>*d:path*

where *d:* is the drive that holds the directory to search. *path* is the full name of the directory path that leads to the directory to search. Only the last directory specified in each *path* is searched.

You can specify more than one drive-directory simply by separating each set with a semicolon. As with the PATH command, do not use a space between the paths. For example, to have APPEND search the directory C:\WORDS\LETTERS, the command is

>**APPEND C:\WORDS\LETTERS**

To search both \WORDS\LETTERS and \WORDS\CONTRACTS, the command is

>**APPEND C:\WORDS\LETTERS;C:\WORDS\CONTRACTS**

Notice the semicolon that separates the two paths. No spaces appear except between the D in APPEND and the first path.

With APPEND's second form, you can use two optional switches, but you cannot specify a directory path for APPEND to use. You can use none, one, or both switches, but, if used, they must appear only the first time you use APPEND during a working session. APPEND's switches are

>/X   process *extended* searches using the DOS SEARCH FIRST, FIND FIRST, and EXEC functions

>/E   place the paths given to APPEND in the *environment*

The /X switch handles directory searches. Some programs search the directory for files to use rather than simply loading the files into memory. For example, DIR, BACKUP, and TREE search directories for files. To have APPEND intercept these programs, you must use the /X switch. Also, using the /X switch will cause APPEND to trick the DOS EXEC function, which allows a program to run another program. Many application programs commonly use the EXEC function.

If you use the /E switch, the paths you specify to APPEND are placed in the environment. The *environment* is an area of RAM in which information can be placed. Chapter 12, which discusses batch files, provides a complete description of the environment. For now, you need only to know that if you give the /E switch, the paths are placed in the environment. If you do not give the /E switch, APPEND stores the paths internally.

Once you have used APPEND, APPEND becomes part of DOS; it becomes an internal command and remains an internal command until you restart DOS. Therefore, you can use APPEND without designating a path to the command. APPEND's internal form is

APPEND   *d1:path1;d2:path2;* . . .

If you compare this form to the first form for APPEND, you will see that this command is almost identical to the first. Here, you simply indicate the command and the disk drive names and paths you want APPEND to use. If you have specified APPEND once with the /E or /X switch, use this form of the command to specify the directories that APPEND should search.

To clear the APPEND command, you simply type

APPEND;

If you use the APPEND command with a semicolon, the command deactivates itself until you issue APPEND again.

To see the current directories that APPEND is using, type

APPEND

without any additional information. APPEND displays the current set of directories it is using, such as:

APPEND=C:\WORDS\LETTERS;C:\WORDS\CONTRACTS

Each path set will be separated by a semicolon.

APPEND has some caveats about its use. First, APPEND cannot trick all programs. Some programs do absolute reading or writing to the disk. APPEND cannot trick these programs.

If your program writes information to files, be cautious in using APPEND. Programs always write information to files in the current directory, regardless of where the original files may be. For example, if the current directory is \WORDS and APPEND has tricked a program into finding the file MEYER.TXT in the directory \WORDS\CONTRACTS, the program will save the file in \WORDS. However, the original file in \WORDS\CONTRACT remains unchanged. You can be astonished when a program saves files in the current directory and you are not aware of it. Be cautious when you use programs that write information back to files.

If you use the APPEND and the ASSIGN commands, which are discussed in Chapter 19's section on pretender commands, use the APPEND command first. APPEND and ASSIGN will have allergic reactions to each other if you use ASSIGN before APPEND.

If you misspell a path that you use with APPEND or delete the directory, APPEND does not notice any error until DOS attempts to use the paths. You will not see any error messages if you specify invalid paths. DOS simply skips any missing or misspelled path names and proceeds to the next path. If you use an invalid path name, APPEND may skip the directory you intended APPEND to use.

To see how APPEND /X can fool you and your programs, I'll show a sample session demonstrating how I was tricked. I placed a blank, formatted disk in drive A:. I invoked APPEND /X and then set APPEND to use a directory. I then tried to get a directory of the diskette. The result was astonishing.

```
C>DIR A:

Volume in drive A is TEST DISK
 Directory of  A:\

File not found

C>DIR C:\BIN\DRIVERS

Volume in drive C is CHRIS'S DSK
Directory of  C:\BIN\DRIVERS
```

```
     .           <DIR>      1Ø-Ø1-87    2:14p
     ..          <DIR>      1Ø-Ø1-87    2:14p
ANSI      SYS     1678      3-17-87   12:ØØp
COUNTRY   SYS    11285      3-17-87   12:ØØp
DISPLAY   SYS    1129Ø      3-17-87   12:ØØp
DRIVER    SYS     1196      3-17-87   12:ØØp
KEYBOARD  SYS    19766      3-17-87   12:ØØp
PRINTER   SYS    1359Ø      3-17-87   12:ØØp
VDISK     SYS     3455      3-17-87   12:ØØp
         9 file(s)   5256794 bytes free

C>APPEND /X

C>APPEND C:\BIN\DRIVERS

C>DIR A:

Volume in drive A is TEST DISK
 Directory of  A:\

     .           <DIR>      1Ø-Ø1-87    2:14p
     ..          <DIR>      1Ø-Ø1-87    2:14p
ANSI      SYS     1678      3-17-87   12:ØØp
COUNTRY   SYS    11285      3-17-87   12:ØØp
DISPLAY   SYS    1129Ø      3-17-87   12:ØØp
DRIVER    SYS     1196      3-17-87   12:ØØp
KEYBOARD  SYS    19766      3-17-87   12:ØØp
PRINTER   SYS    1359Ø      3-17-87   12:ØØp
VDISK     SYS     3455      3-17-87   12:ØØp
         9 file(s)   5256794 bytes free

C>
```

Instead of DOS's reporting that there were no files to be found on the diskette in drive A, the DIR command shows the C:\BIN\DRIVERS directory! When there are no files on the diskette, APPEND tricks DOS into searching the first directory specified to APPEND. You get a false answer from the DIR command. It took several minutes for me to understand why a blank diskette suddenly held several files. After I disconnected APPEND, everything worked correctly.

If you use APPEND with the /X switch, some programs may react allergically. The result will be that a perfectly working program will mysteriously not perform correctly. If you encounter this problem, restart DOS and use the APPEND command without the /X switch. If the program then works correctly, remember not to use the APPEND with the /X switch with that program. Or restart the computer just before you need to use that program.

If the program continues to work incorrectly, try using the APPEND; command to deactivate APPEND. If the program still doesn't work correctly, your mixing of the program with APPEND is not the problem. Although I have not yet had a problem using APPEND with my applications programs, I suspect that some applications programs that I do not use will not work correctly with APPEND.

Finally, do not mix DOS V3.3's APPEND with another version of APPEND, such as the ones provided with the IBM PC Network or IBM PC LAN software. The programs are incompatible, and you will have unsatisfactory results.

Despite these caveats, APPEND is a very useful command. With APPEND, you can place your programs in one directory and organize your data files in a subdirectory. Remember that what PATH does for command files, APPEND does for data files. Both PATH and APPEND are useful commands.

Summary

In this chapter, you learned the following:

1. The *rule of currents* means that if you omit a disk drive or path name, DOS uses the current disk drive and the current path.

2. Giving disk drive and path names to a command is optional when the current disk drive and path are involved. If the current disk drive or path is not involved, the drive-path name is mandatory and must be given.

3. You can use the CHKDSK /V and TREE commands to list all the subdirectories and files of a disk.

4. You can use the APPEND command to trick programs into using files that are not in the current directory.

In Chapter 12, you will learn how to create and use batch files.

12

Understanding Batch Files

Up to now, you've learned how you can use DOS. But have you ever thought of making DOS use itself? Batch files enable you to make DOS work for you. This convenient and time-saving feature is useful to all PC DOS users. At first, the concept may seem elusive to you, but understanding and using batch files can speed up and ease many tedious computer tasks.

A batch file is a series of DOS commands placed in a disk file. When instructed, DOS executes the commands in the file, one line at a time. DOS treats these commands as though they were individually typed from the keyboard.

Batch files have several advantages. Once you have placed the correctly phrased commands in a batch file, you can, by typing the batch file's root name, direct DOS to execute the commands. You can direct DOS to perform one or hundreds of commands in a batch file.

Another advantage is that once a batch file has been invoked, DOS does not need your attention until it has finished running the batch file. This capability comes in handy for programs that may take a long time to run. For example, if you need to run several long programs back-to-back, you ordinarily start each program and wait until it has finished running before you start the next one. But why should you wait for the computer if you don't have to? A batch file will execute commands to run the programs without your intervention. You can do other tasks or just relax while the computer does the hard work.

If a program needs your input—to change diskettes, for example—the batch file cannot do this task for you. Your attention is still required. You can use a batch file, though, to execute programs or commands without having to type the program or command name each time. By redirecting the input of the program to a file, you can avoid having to answer manually a program's questions.

Batch files are available for your convenience. After a few experiments, you will probably find this DOS facility quite handy.

Rules for Creating and Running Batch Files

To create batch files, you must follow certain rules, which are summarized in the following list. After you read these rules, look over the rules for running batch files. You need not understand all the rules yet. They will be explained as you read through the chapter.

Rules for Creating Batch Files

1. A batch file contains ASCII text. You use the DOS COPY CON command, the DOS line editor EDLIN, or another text editor to create a batch file. If you use a word-processing program, make sure that it is in programming, or nondocument, mode.

2. The root name of a batch file can be one to eight characters long and must conform to the rules for file names.

3. The batch file name must have the extension .BAT.

4. A batch file's root name should be different from the root name of program files in the current directory (files that end with the extension .COM or .EXE). The root name should also not be the same as that of an internal DOS command—COPY or DATE, for example. If you use one of these root names, DOS will not know whether you want to execute the batch file, the program, or the command.

5. You may include in a batch file any valid DOS command you might type at the keyboard. You may also use the *parameter markers* (%0 to %9) and batch subcommands.

6. To use the percent sign (%) in a batch-file command, such as in a file name, you enter the percent symbol twice. For example, to use a file called A100%.TXT, you would enter A100%%.TXT. This rule does not apply to the parameter markers (%0 to %9).

The syntax for running a batch file is

d:path\filename *parameters*

in which *d:* is the optional name of the disk drive that holds the batch file, and *path*\ is the optional directory path to the batch file. filename is the root name of the batch file, and *parameters* is any additional information to be used by the batch file.

The following list summarizes the rules for running batch files.

Rules for Running Batch Files

1. If you do not give a disk drive name, the current disk drive will be used.

2. If you do not give a path, the current directory will be used.

3. To invoke a batch file, simply type its root name and press Enter. For example, to invoke a batch file called OFTEN.BAT, you type **OFTEN** and press Enter.

4. If the batch file is not in the current directory of the disk drive and a path name did not precede the batch file name, DOS will search the directory(ies) specified by the PATH command to find the batch file.

5. DOS will execute each command, one line at a time. The specified parameters will be substituted for the markers when the command is used.

6. DOS recognizes a maximum of ten parameters. You may use the SHIFT subcommand to get around this limitation.

7. If DOS encounters an incorrectly phrased batch subcommand when running a batch file, the message `Syntax error` is displayed. DOS ignores the rest of the commands in the batch file, and the system prompt reappears.

8. You can stop a running batch file by pressing Ctrl-Break. DOS will display the message

   ```
   Terminate batch job (Y/N)?_
   ```

   If you answer `Y` for yes, the rest of the commands will be ignored, and the system prompt will appear. If you answer `N` for no, DOS skips the current command but continues processing the other commands in the file.

9. DOS remembers which directory holds the batch file. Your batch file may change directories at any time.

10. Because DOS remembers the disk drive that holds the batch file, you may change current disk drives freely. DOS V3.0 does not remember which diskette holds the batch file, however. If you remove the diskette that holds the batch file, DOS V3.0 will give you an error message. DOS V3.1-V3.3 requests that you reinsert the same diskette into the disk drive and press a key to continue.

11. You can instruct a batch file to run another batch file after the first batch file has run. When you enter the name of a second batch file as the last command in the first batch file, control of the computer passes to the second batch file unless the COMMAND technique or the CALL subcommand is used. If the CALL subcommand or COMMAND technique is used, the second batch file is executed and control returns to the first batch file. Both commands are discussed in Chapter 13.

Rules for AUTOEXEC.BAT Files

You must follow certain rules when you use the file AUTOEXEC.BAT. The following list is a summary of these rules.

Rules for the AUTOEXEC.BAT File

1. The file must be called AUTOEXEC.BAT and must reside in the boot disk's root directory.

2. The contents of the AUTOEXEC.BAT file must conform to the rules for creating batch files.

3. When DOS is booted, it automatically executes the AUTOEXEC.BAT file.

4. When AUTOEXEC.BAT is executed after DOS is booted, the date and time are not requested automatically. To get the current date and time, you must put the DATE and TIME commands into the AUTOEXEC.BAT file. (This is important only for PCs and for PC XTs because other IBM computers "remember" the time.)

To better understand batch files, take a look at the following example of an AUTOEXEC.BAT file. The file comes on the Lotus 1-2-3® Release 1 diskette (Release 2 omits these files). When you use the TYPE command to display this file, you will see the following:

```
A>TYPE AUTOEXEC.BAT
date
time
lotus

A>
```

When you boot the computer, DOS loads itself into the computer's memory. Next, DOS scans the disk's root directory for the AUTOEXEC.BAT file. After finding the file, DOS starts executing the commands in the file. First, DOS executes the DATE command to get the current date; then it executes the TIME command to get the current time. These steps set DOS's internal clock and calendar. The AUTOEXEC.BAT file then loads and executes the 1-2-3 menu program, LOTUS.COM.

The AUTOEXEC.BAT file is a useful feature. This sample AUTOEXEC.BAT file allows the computer operator to insert a diskette into drive A, turn on the computer, and have the computer automatically load 1-2-3. This is called *turnkey* capability—you just turn on the computer's "key" (switch), and the computer automatically starts and runs its programs without additional instructions.

This batch file has one slight disadvantage on some computers. Some PCs, like the standard IBM PC and XT, do not remember dates or time, so you must manually enter them. If you do not set the date and time, DOS date-stamps each 1-2-3 data file 1-1-80, the default DOS date. When you do a directory of diskettes used on these machines, you won't be able to tell when a 1-2-3 data file was created or changed. That's why the DATE and TIME commands are included in this batch file. You don't need to change 1-2-3; just change the batch file. However, the DATE and TIME commands are unnecessary if you are using a PC AT or PS/2.

You can easily modify this AUTOEXEC.BAT file to perform different or additional functions. For example, if you use a Personal Computer AT, you could edit this batch file and delete the DATE and TIME commands, because these computers know the current date and time on startup.

When you have become familiar with 1-2-3, you might want to bypass the Lotus menu and invoke the 1-2-3 program itself when you start your computer. To do that, simply change the line LOTUS to 123, which is the name of the file that holds the 1-2-3 program. When the computer starts, the 1-2-3 program boots instead of the Lotus menu.

The concept of a batch file is simple. When you invoke such a file, the computer executes the commands from the file as if you were typing them at the keyboard.

The AUTOEXEC.BAT file is different in only one way from any other batch file. DOS automatically executes AUTOEXEC.BAT when you start the computer. You can also execute this batch file at any time by typing \AUTOEXEC while the disk that holds the file is in the current disk drive. The only "magic" to this file occurs when DOS starts up. After DOS is up and running, AUTOEXEC.BAT is just another batch file.

You can make your own AUTOEXEC.BAT file by creating a file that contains all the commands required to start your program. A line that fixed disk users should include is one concerning the PATH command. I suggest that you add this line

PATH C:\BIN;C:

to your current AUTOEXEC.BAT file or create another AUTOEXEC.BAT file with this line. If you are using a computer that doesn't have a clock, add the DATE and TIME commands to your AUTOEXEC.BAT file. Otherwise DOS will not ask for this information, and your files will never have the correct date and time.

If you have frequently used programs and batch files, you might copy these to a RAM disk. If you do, you might also add the RAM disk to your path, as in this command line

PATH E:\;C:\BIN;C:

where E is the name of the RAM disk. The reason for adding E:\ first is that PATH searches the specified directories in the order given. Therefore, DOS will search E:\ first before searching C:\BIN. You can also include in the AUTOEXEC.BAT file the commands to copy files to the RAM disk. For example, I use the commands

COPY C:\LIGHT\DISK.DIC E:\LIGHT
COPY C:\LIGHT\THES.DIC E:\LIGHT

to copy my Turbo Lightning files to the RAM disk. You can use this basic concept to copy any frequently used program or batch file to the RAM disk.

A batch file is especially convenient for executing a long series of commands you would normally have to type. Let's look at INSTALLH.BAT, the fixed disk installation batch file that comes with Borland's Turbo Lightning™. The instructions for using this file are to make the fixed disk the current disk drive and to make the current directory the directory where the Turbo Lightning files should be placed. The following screen shows the contents of the INSTALLH.BAT file.

```
ECHO OFF
CLS
ECHO This batch file will Install Turbo Lightning onto your hard disk.
ECHO Have all three  of  your  Turbo  Lightning  disks  ready.   Turbo
ECHO Lightning will be installed onto the "Default Directory" of  your
ECHO hard disk.  This means that the Dos Prompt  should  be  "C".   If
ECHO you use tree structured directories on your hard disk please make
```

```
ECHO sure that you are logged in to the directory where you want Turbo
ECHO Lightning files to reside.  For more information  on  this:  Hold
ECHO down the [CTRL] key and press [C] and  refer  to  page 9  in  the
ECHO Owner's Handbook.
PAUSE
COPY A:*.COM
COPY A:*.DIC
COPY A:LIHARD.BAC LIHARD.BAT
LIHARD
```

The first two lines of the file turn off the display of lines from the batch file (ECHO OFF) and clear the screen with the Clear Screen command (CLS). The next nine lines give instructions. The ECHO subcommand is a batch command that displays on-screen whatever follows it. The message tells you to make sure that the fixed disk drive is the current drive and that the current directory is where you want the Turbo Lightning files to be placed.

Another batch file subcommand, PAUSE, writes the message Strike any key when ready . . . on the screen and then waits. When a key is pressed, the batch file continues. The PAUSE subcommand is included so that the operator can read a long message or change diskettes. After the operator has taken the appropriate action, DOS will continue with the batch file.

The next two lines of the file (COPY A:*.COM and COPY A:*.DIC) copy the program and dictionary files to the fixed disk. The following two lines are a bit of trickery. The file LIHARD.BAC is copied to the fixed disk and the name is changed to LIHARD.BAT. The final command invokes the LIHARD batch file.

This batch file shows a second batch file being run from a first batch file. That topic will be discussed in Chapter 13.

If you have Turbo Lightning, you can separately execute the last four lines of the batch file by typing each line at the keyboard. Just typing A:INSTALLH is much simpler, however.

Making Batch Files Versatile with Parameters

Batch files can perform different operations on different files, even though the commands in the file are fixed. You can use the same batch file with different files by taking advantage of *batch file parameters*.

What is a batch file parameter? In DOS, many commands accept information you type when you run the program. COPY is an example of such a command. The name of the file you want to copy, the destination to copy the file to, and the additional switches you enter are all parameters. A *parameter* is the additional information you type after you type the program name on the command line. Programs, in turn, can use whatever information is in the parameters.

For example, in the command line

COPY FORMAT.COM B: /V

every word or set of characters that is separated by a space, comma, semicolon, or other valid *delimiter* is a parameter.

FORMAT.COM, B:, and /V are parameters. Each parameter tells the COPY command what to do. In this case, the parameters tell COPY to copy the program FORMAT.COM from the default disk to the disk in drive B and to verify that DOS has correctly made the copy.

The term *argument* is a synonym for parameter. Both terms refer to the delimiter information on the command line. (Delimiters were discussed in Chapter 8.)

Batch files also use parameters, but in a different manner than do commands. To use parameters in your batch file, you insert *markers* to tell DOS where to use the batch file's parameters. A marker is a percent sign (%) followed by a number from 0 to 9. These ten markers tell DOS to substitute for the markers whatever you type on the command line.

The first parameter on the command line is the program or batch file name. This is parameter 0. (Computers usually start numbering with 0, which is a true number, not a placeholder, as you were taught in arithmetic.)

The second word on the command line is parameter 1; the third word is parameter 2; and so forth. This arrangement works well because we often ignore the name of the program or batch file when counting parameters. We are usually concerned with the items placed after the program or batch file name. The first item placed on the command line after the program or batch file name is usually considered the first parameter. The second item after the program or batch file name is the second parameter, with each additional item on the command line one higher than the previous item.

To practice including parameters in a batch file, type the following line into a file called TEST.BAT using a text editor or the COPY CON technique:

ECHO Hello, %1

Now type TEST, press the space bar, type your first name, and press Enter. When I tried this exercise on my screen, I saw:

```
A>TEST CHRIS

A>ECHO Hello, CHRIS
Hello, CHRIS

A>
```

The ECHO subcommand is a batch subcommand. This command shows on the video display the text on the line following the word ECHO. The %1 however, is the real object of this discussion. Why didn't DOS print Hello, %1?

In this example, DOS substituted my name—the second word on the command line—for the %1 in the batch file. That is, my name became the first parameter. The %1 was replaced with my name.

When DOS executes a batch file, markers are replaced by the appropriate parameters from the command line. For this reason, the markers are sometimes called *replaceable parameters*. Let's see how DOS replaces the parameters.

Create another batch file called TEST1.BAT, which is also a one-line file:

ECHO %0 %1 %2 %3 %4

After you have created this file, type TEST1, followed by your name and street address, separated by spaces. Here's how my file looked:

```
A>TEST1 CHRIS 1234 THUNDERBIRD AVENUE

A>ECHO TEST1 CHRIS 1234 THUNDERBIRD AVENUE
TEST1 CHRIS 1234 THUNDERBIRD AVENUE

A>
```

You can see from the batch file command line that DOS was instructed to display on the video screen the parameters 0 through 4. These parameters worked out to be

Word:	TEST1	CHRIS	1234	THUNDERBIRD	AVENUE
Parameter:	%0	%1	%2	%3	%4

What happens if you don't give enough information on the command line to fill each parameter? Run TEST1 again, but this time give only your first name. In my case, I saw the following:

```
A>ECHO TEST1 CHRIS
TEST1 CHRIS

A>
```

DOS displayed the batch file name and my name. No other information "echoed" on the video display. I did not give enough parameters on the command line, and DOS replaced the unfilled markers with nothing. In other words, DOS ignores unfilled markers.

One last comment should be made about parameter 0. If you give a drive name with the name of the batch command, the drive name appears with the batch file name. If I had typed **A:TEST1 CHRIS**, the last lines on my screen would have been

```
A>ECHO A:TEST1 CHRIS
A:TEST1 CHRIS

A>
```

Constructing a Batch File Using Parameters

Let's construct a batch file that takes advantage of parameters. I use several computers, but one of my fixed disk systems is my "workhorse" where I store the files I want to keep.

I use diskettes to move information between computers. Sometimes I edit a file on one computer and then move the information to the fixed disk of another computer. Many times, I remove the file from the diskette after it has been copied back to the workhorse. Because I don't need the copy of the file on the diskette after the file has been copied to the fixed disk, I remove the file from the diskette.

The steps required are these:

1. Copy the file from the diskette to the fixed disk.

2. Erase the file from the diskette.

My batch file is called C&E.BAT (copy and erase) and consists of these commands:

COPY A:%1 C:%2 /V
ERASE A:%1

To use this file, I type

C&E oldfilename newfilename

oldfilename is the name of the file I want to copy to the fixed disk, and **newfilename** is the new name for the copied file (if I want to change the file name as it is being copied).

Now suppose that I put a diskette that contains the file NOTES.TXT into drive A and want to copy the file to the fixed disk. Here's what the screen looks like:

```
C>C&E NOTES.TXT

C>COPY A:NOTES.TXT C: /V
 1 file(s) copied

C>ERASE A:NOTES.TXT

C>
```

In this example, DOS ignores the empty markers. Because I don't want to change the file name, I didn't give a second parameter. DOS copies NOTES.TXT from drive A to drive C and then deletes the file on the diskette in drive A. The %2 parameter is "dropped," and the batch file does not get a new name when it is copied.

One of the benefits of constructing a batch file this way is that I can use a path name as the second parameter and copy the file from the diskette into a different directory on the fixed disk. For instance, to copy NOTES.TXT to the second-level directory called WORDS, I type:

```
C>C&E NOTES.TXT \WORDS

C>COPY A:NOTES.TXT C:\WORDS /V
 1 file(s) copied

C>ERASE A:NOTES.TXT

c>
```

Because WORDS is a directory name, DOS knows that it should copy the file NOTES.TXT into the directory WORDS. DOS will not give the new file the name WORDS.

Understanding Your Environment (SET)

The *environment* is a safe area of RAM memory established by DOS to hold strings. The strings are typically names of directories or frequently-used switches for programs, although any information can be used. DOS makes the information placed in the environment available to your programs.

Don't be discouraged if you do not understand the preceding paragraph yet. The use of the environment is a classic example of needing to know something before you can learn something else. In this section, we discuss the environment: how you use the environment, how your programs use the environment, and what the environment can do for you.

The reasons for discussing the environment in this chapter are two. Most information is placed in the environment by including commands in the AUTOEXEC.BAT file. The second reason is that DOS provides a mechanism that you use in your batch files to retrieve the information that has been placed into the environment.

To explain what is placed in the environment, we'll look at an example:

```
COMSPEC=C:\COMMAND.COM
```

The object on the left is called an *environmental variable*. It is a name of any length, but one to eight characters is preferred. The object on the right is a string, a group of arbitrary characters. An equal sign separates the variable name from the information.

The two ways information is placed in the environment are (1) by DOS and (2) by ourselves. DOS places information in the environment when you use the PATH, APPEND, or PROMPT commands. To place our own information in the environment, we use the SET command. SET stores strings in the environment. SET is an internal command and is always available at the system prompt or within batch files. The syntax for SET is

SET *name=information*

name is the environmental variable's name. *information* is any information that can be placed in a string, such as a path name, a file name, optional switches to programs, or anything else. When your programs search the environment for *name*, the programs find the *information*.

For example, this line

SET EXAMPLE=C:\WORDS\EXAMPLE

sets the environmental variable EXAMPLE. When programs find and examine EXAMPLE, they find the string C:\WORDS\EXAMPLE. The environment provides a non-interactive method to give your programs information. You place a string in the environment using SET. Later, your programs can locate the variable and use the string associated with the variable.

SET also displays the current environmental variables. If you type SET with no arguments, you should see at least one line something like this:

```
COMSPEC=C:\COMMAND.COM
```

COMSPEC is the environmental variable for the *command* interpreter. You see the environmental variable, COMSPEC, followed by the equal sign, followed by the disk drive, path name, and file name for the command interpreter, COMMAND.COM. This line is inserted into the environment by DOS when the system starts.

What is the significance of COMSPEC? This environmental variable tells DOS where to find the command interpreter.

COMMAND.COM does not always remain in RAM. Your programs can free part of the memory COMMAND uses so that the programs can use this memory instead. Then, when the program exits, DOS must reload COMMAND.COM from the disk.

Did you know that COMMAND.COM does not need to be in the root directory of the boot disk? If you use the SHELL directive in your CONFIG.SYS file, COMMAND.COM can be located anywhere on your disk. (SHELL and its other uses will be discussed in Chapter 14.) But if COMMAND.COM is not in the root directory, how would DOS know where to find COMMAND.COM?

DOS stores the location in its safe harbor, the environment. Until DOS is restarted (or a program writes into RAM memory that it should not use), the environment is memory sheltered by DOS for the exclusive use of storing these variables.

To find the command interpreter, DOS searches the environment for COMSPEC. When DOS locates COMSPEC, it uses the full file name stored with COMSPEC (the information on the right side of the equal sign) to reload COMMAND.COM.

When you issue the SET command, you may see other environmental variables. If you see variables, other than those created by the PATH, APPEND, or PROMPT commands, these were established by commands included in the AUTOEXEC.BAT file.

The most popular use for environmental variables is to give programs certain options or information only once. Instead of typing these options or information on the command line each time the program is run, the SET command is used to place the information into the environment. When the program runs, the program finds the environmental variables and adapts.

For example, Brief, my favorite text editor, uses several environmental variables. The variables are BFLAGS (which sets certain options), BHELP (the path to the help files), and BPATH (the path to parts of the editor program). In my AUTOEXEC.BAT file, I have these commands:

```
set bflags=-pr -mCDV
set bhelp=c:\brief\help
set bpath=c:\brief\macros
```

The first line sets up information on my display (-pr) and tells Brief which customized "macro" file to use (-mCDV). The next line sets up the location of the help file. The third line sets where the additional program pieces should be found.

When I invoke Brief, Brief immediately reads the environment looking for BFLAGS, BHELP, and BPATH variables. Upon finding the variables, Brief takes the information associated with the variables and knows which options to use and where the Brief files are located. Once the information is SET in the AUTOEXEC.BAT file, I never give it again. Brief automatically adjusts itself. If I change the AUTOEXEC.BAT, Brief will read the new environmental variables when it starts and adjust itself again.

Another example is Microspell, my favorite spelling checker-corrector. I use the line

    SET LEX=C:\WORDS\SPELL\LEX

in my AUTOEXEC.BAT file and Microspell automatically knows where to find its LEX (dictionary) files.

A further example is the environmental variable TEMP or TMP, which I usually define to be E:\, my RAM disk. Many programs use the TEMP or TMP variable as the location where they will place temporary files. By designating my fast RAM disk rather than the slower fixed disk as the place for temporary files, my programs' throughput can dramatically increase.

Many programs today use environmental variables. You should check your program's documentation to determine whether some environment variables are appropriate for your use.

Unfortunately, the environment is not unlimited. Each character stored in the environment takes one byte of RAM and each environmental variable takes one additional byte. Remember the environment is located in the same memory space your programs could use. For this reason, DOS starts with an environment size of 128 for DOS pre-V3.3 or 160 bytes for DOS V3.3. You can expand the size of the environment up to 32,767 bytes. Environment size is discussed in the SHELL directive in Chapter 14.

Since the environment is not unlimited, there are times you might want to eliminate a variable. To do so, use the form

    SET name=

giving the name of the variable you wish to eliminate, followed by an equal sign. DOS removes the variable from the environment.

Although the major use of environmental variables is to leave information for your programs, you can use environmental variables in batch files also. This technique, which works with DOS V3.1 and later versions, requires that you surround the name of the variable with percent signs. For example, this one-liner prints the contents of the COMSPEC variable

```
echo COMSPEC is set to %COMSPEC%
```

Type this example into a batch file and run it. Just place a percent sign directly before and after the environmental variable name and DOS will replace the %name% with the appropriate information from the environment. This means you have two types of replaceable batch file markers: parameters from the command line (%1, %2, etc.) and environmental variables (%name%).

SET's main use is to place information into the environment. This is usually done through AUTOEXEC.BAT. However, SET can be used at any time. Environmental variables make programs easier to use, but you rarely use the variables directly. Unfortunately, environmental variables do not make your batch files truly interactive. The missing feature is an ASK subcommand which would ask the user for some information from the keyboard and place it in an environmental variable. With this function missing, the %name% function is not fully usable.

Summary

Batch files can make your computer do the hard work for you. For example, they can replace repetitive typing with commands that execute automatically. As you work with batch files, you should remember the following key points:

1. Batch files must have a .BAT extension.

2. You invoke batch files by typing the root name of the batch file. You may also use an optional disk drive name and path name before the batch file name.

3. You can use in a batch file any command you can type at the DOS prompt.

4. The AUTOEXEC.BAT file automatically executes when DOS starts. Rather than your having to issue a command after DOS starts, you can use an AUTOEXEC.BAT file to run startup programs.

5. On a command line, each word (or set of characters) separated by a delimiter is a parameter. When you use a batch file, DOS substitutes for the file markers (%0 to %9) the appropriate parameters.

6. The SET command can place strings into the environment. You can use environmental variables in batch files by using the form *%name%*.

In Chapter 13, you'll learn about using batch subcommands and how to run batch files from other batch files.

13

Using Batch Subcommands

Chapter 12 discussed how batch files work and showed you some examples of how you might put them to work for you. This chapter focuses on special batch-file subcommands and suggests ways to construct more powerful batch files.

Table 13.1 lists batch subcommands for DOS V3. You used two of the subcommands, ECHO and PAUSE, in Chapter 12.

Table 13.1
Batch Subcommands for DOS V3

@	Suppresses the display of a line on the screen (DOS V3.3 and later).
CALL	Runs another batch file and then returns to the original batch file (DOS V3.3 and later).
ECHO	Turns on or off the display of batch commands as they execute. Also can display a message on the screen.
FOR..IN..DO	Allows the use of the same batch command for several files.
GOTO	Jumps to the line after a label in a batch file.
IF	Allows conditional execution of a command.
SHIFT	Shifts the command-line parameters one parameter to the left.
PAUSE	Halts processing until a key is pressed. Can optionally display a message.
REM	Displays a message on the screen or allows for batch comments.

You can use any of the subcommands from the preceding list in a batch file. Most cannot be used at the DOS system level. But you will see, as we discuss these commands, that you would have no reason to use most of the subcommands at the system level. In this chapter, we'll look at examples that show how each command can be used.

Controlling the Display with ECHO and REM

The ECHO command does two things. First, ECHO controls the display of lines from the batch file as the command lines are executed. Turning ECHO off is useful when you don't want to display the commands from the batch file.

Second, ECHO can be used to display messages. In this sense, ECHO is like the REM (remark) command, which also displays messages on the screen. Either subcommand can display a message with a maximum length of 123 characters.

However, setting ECHO affects REM. If ECHO is off, no REM statement appears on the video screen. If ECHO is on, it unconditionally displays the message. The echoed message *always* appears on the video display, regardless of whether ECHO is on or off. If you always want to display a message in your batch file, use ECHO rather than REM.

You can put both ECHO and REM to good use in a batch file. Often by the time you re-edit a batch file, you may have forgotten why you used certain commands or why you constructed the batch file a particular way. You can leave reminders in your batch file by using REM statements. These comments allow the batch file to be self-documenting, which you and other PC users will appreciate later. If you want to incorporate messages that you always want displayed, use the ECHO subcommand. The echoed message appears on the video display whether ECHO is on or off.

Controlling the Display with @ and CLS

A feature new to DOS V3.3 is controlling the display with the @ sign. Placed at the beginning of a batch-file line, this character suppresses the display of the line on-screen. DOS absorbs the character and executes the remainder of the batch-file line. You can use the @ to selectively hide batch-file lines as they execute, whereas ECHO controls the display of all the lines in a batch file.

The customary first two lines of a *quiet batch file* (one that issues an ECHO off command) are

```
ECHO OFF
CLS
```

The first line turns off the display of commands that are executing. The second line invokes the clear-screen command, CLS, which is built into DOS and can be used anytime at the system prompt.

The reason CLS follows the ECHO off command is that the ECHO OFF command itself appears on the screen. To keep the screen clear, you need to issue the CLS command. If you have DOS V3.3, you can replace the two lines with this line:

```
@ECHO OFF
```

By using the @ as the first character of the line, the ECHO OFF does not appear on the screen, and the ECHO off command stays in effect until the end of the batch file. The screen is not cleared, however. If you desire a clean screen when you start a batch file, you must use the CLS command in the file.

Using PAUSE to Interrupt Processing

The PAUSE subcommand performs a series of activities. It stops the batch file's processing and displays on-screen any message on the rest of the line (just as the REM subcommand does). PAUSE then displays the message Strike a key when ready... and waits for you to press a key. When you press a key, DOS continues to process the batch file. The PAUSE command allows you to change disks while you are processing a batch file. PAUSE also has another use, which is discussed in the section on the GOTO subcommand.

As just mentioned, PAUSE, like REM, can also display a message. And, as with REM, if ECHO is off, the message is not displayed. The message Strike a key when ready is always displayed, however, whether ECHO is on or off.

Leaping and Looping with GOTO

The GOTO subcommand is similar to the BASIC language's GOTO command. With DOS's GOTO command, you can jump to another part of your batch file. DOS's GOTO command uses a label, not a line number, to specify where to jump. A *label* is a batch file line that starts with a colon (:) and is followed by a one- to eight-character name. The name can be longer than eight characters, but only the first eight are significant.

When DOS encounters a GOTO label command in the batch file, DOS jumps to the line in your batch file *that follows* the line holding the label. The batch file TEST2.BAT is shown in the following screen. This file is similar to the TEST.BAT batch file you created in Chapter 12, with the addition of the GOTO and PAUSE subcommands.

```
:START
ECHO Hello, %1
PAUSE
GOTO START
```

When I invoked the batch file by typing TEST2 CHRIS, my screen showed this message:

```
A>TEST2 CHRIS
A>ECHO Hello, CHRIS
Hello, CHRIS
A>PAUSE
Strike a key when ready . . . <space>
A>GOTO START
A>ECHO Hello, CHRIS
Hello, CHRIS
A>PAUSE
Strike a key when ready . . . <Ctrl-C>

Terminate batch job (Y/N)? Y
A>
```

The batch file began by echoing the message with my name in it. The file then paused for me to press a key before it continued. After I pressed a key, DOS executed the GOTO START command. DOS then jumped to the line after :START and continued processing. When DOS paused a second time, I typed a Ctrl-C to stop the batch file. DOS then asked whether I wanted to stop the batch file. I answered Y for yes, and DOS stopped processing the batch file and returned to the system prompt. This type of batch file causes DOS to loop continuously until you type the Ctrl-Break sequence.

You can use this batch file's endless looping to repeat the batch file's contents several times, but you can also repeat the batch file a different number of times each time you invoke the file.

For example, suppose that I want to copy the files CHKDSK.COM, FORMAT.COM, DISKCOMP.COM, and DISKCOPY.COM to several diskettes. I may want to copy these programs onto one, two, or a hundred disks. With a batch file, I can make DOS do the hard work.

For this example, assume that the computer has two disk drives. The disk that contains the files CHKDSK.COM, FORMAT.COM, DISKCOMP.COM, DISKCOPY.COM, and the new batch file will be in drive A. The disk to receive the programs will go into drive B.

First, I'll create a batch file called FLOPPY.BAT (remember that the @ symbol in line 1 can be used only for DOS V3.3):

```
 (1)  @ECHO OFF
 (2)  :START
 (3)  ECHO Place the diskette to receive CHKDSK.COM, FORMAT.COM,
 (4)  ECHO DISK COMP.COM, and DISKCOPY.COM in drive B
 (5)  ECHO.
 (6)  ECHO To quit, type Ctrl-C, then press Y, or
 (7)  PAUSE
 (8)  COPY A:CHKDSK.COM B: /V
 (9)  COPY A:FORMAT.COM B: /V
(10)  COPY A:DISKCOMP.COM B: /V
(11)  COPY A:DISKCOPY.COM B: /V
(12)  ECHO Files are copied.
(13)  GOTO START
```

In this file, the GOTO subcommand causes an endless loop. The file also illustrates several batch subcommands.

Line 1 turns ECHO off so that the commands are not displayed. The @ sign at the beginning of the line stops the line from being displayed.

Lines 2 through 6 tell the operator either to put a disk into drive B or to type Ctrl-C to quit.

Line 7 has the PAUSE command that displays the message Strike a key when ready. At this point, if the operator has finished copying the files, he can type Ctrl-C and answer Y to the Terminate batch job (Y/N)? prompt.

Lines 8 through 11 transfer the four programs to the disk in drive B.

Line 12 is the "reassurance" line. It tells the operator that the files have been transferred. This line is not necessary, but it assures the operator that all has gone well.

Line 13 is the GOTO line that starts the process over again.

I've made a small change to the batch file since the DOS V2 version of this book. Notice the arrangement of lines 2 through 6. The on-screen result is

```
Place the diskette to receive CHKDSK.COM, FORMAT.COM,
DISKCOMP.COM, and DISKCOPY.COM in drive B

To quit, type Ctrl-C Y or
Strike any key when ready...
```

The Strike any key when ready line comes from PAUSE. I saw little sense in duplicating what the PAUSE command displays. That's why I depend on PAUSE's message to tell the user to just strike any key when ready.

The only batch commands that this chapter has not discussed are IF, FOR..IN..DO, SHIFT, and CALL. All four commands are simple, once you understand how they work. The following sections explain these commands.

Using IF

The IF command is a "test and do" command. When a condition is true, IF executes the command on the command line. When the condition is false, IF ignores the line. The DOS IF subcommand works like the IF statement in BASIC. The command can be used to test three conditions:

1. The ERRORLEVEL of a program

2. Whether a string is equal to another string

3. Whether a file exists

Let's look at each condition and at how the command can be used.

The first condition is ERRORLEVEL. A better name for this condition would have been "exit level." *ERRORLEVEL* is a code your program leaves for DOS when the program has finished executing. In DOS V3.3, only the BACKUP, GRAFTABL, KEYB, REPLACE, RESTORE, and XCOPY commands leave an exit code. Many other programs use exit codes, however.

A 0 exit code usually means that everything was okay. Any number greater than 0 usually indicates that something was wrong: no files were found, the program encountered an error, or the operator aborted the program. Including an IF command in a batch file lets you test ERRORLEVEL to see whether a program worked properly.

If the exit code your program leaves is equal to or greater than the number you specify in the batch file, the ERRORLEVEL condition is true. You can think of this condition as a BASIC-like statement:

IF ERRORLEVEL $\geq$ number THEN do this

Suppose, for example, that you wanted to invoke KEYB.COM, the program that changes the keyboard layout and characters to a language other than American English (see Chapter 15, "Making DOS Go International"). You could test to see whether the KEYB worked successfully by inserting the following lines:

```
KEYB US, 437
IF ERRORLEVEL 1 ECHO Could not set the keyboard!
```

These lines test KEYB's exit code. If the exit code is 1 or greater, `Could not set the keyboard!` is displayed on-screen. If the exit code equals 0, then nothing is displayed. The condition (ERRORLEVEL 1) is false, so the line is skipped.

The best way to test the ERRORLEVEL with a batch file is to use an IF statement to move around the commands that execute if the ERRORLEVEL test fails, as shown in this example:

```
KEYB
IF ERRORLEVEL 1 GOTO OOPS
    .
    .
    .
GOTO END
:OOPS
ECHO Could not set the keyboard!
:END
```

The batch file invokes KEYB. If the exit code is 1 or greater, the batch file jumps to the line after the OOPS label. If the exit code is 0, the rest of the batch file is processed. Notice the GOTO END statement placed before the OOPS label. You don't want the batch file to say Could not set the keyboard! when the KEYB *did* work. If the batch file does the rest of the work correctly, DOS jumps to the end of the file, the END label. When DOS reaches this label, it stops processing the batch file.

The **IF string1 == string2** condition is normally used with command-line parameters and markers. One simple example is the batch file ISIBM.BAT:

```
IF %1 == IBM ECHO I'm an IBM computer
```

If you type

```
ISIBM IBM
```

you will see

```
I'm an IBM computer
```

If you type anything other than IBM as the first parameter, you won't see this line on the screen.

Note two important facts about this part of the IF command. If you don't give enough parameters with the IF subcommand, DOS replaces the parameter marker with nothing. The parameter becomes a *null parameter*. Because DOS does not like to compare null parameters with anything, it displays a Syntax error message and aborts the batch file.

If you type **ISIBM** and do not give any other information, the %1 turns into nothing; the line becomes

```
IF == IBM ECHO I'm an IBM computer
```

The result is the dreaded syntax error message, and the batch file halts. The way to solve the problem is to first test if a parameter is empty before trying another test. You can see the general technique in this revised version of ISIBM.BAT:

```
IF %1. == . GOTO NOTHING
IF %1 == IBM GOTO IBM
ECHO What computer are you?
GOTO END
:IBM
ECHO I'm an IBM computer
GOTO END
:NOTHING
ECHO Pardon me, I could not hear you.
:END
```

The first line adds a period to the %1 and tests to see if this addition is the same as a single period. If %1 is null (meaning you gave no parameters), the line becomes

```
IF . == . GOTO NOTHING
```

This method succeeds in trapping the error condition of giving too few batch-file parameters. If you need to check for a nonexistent parameter, use the form as I did in line 1 of ISIBM.BAT's revised version.

If the test is false, DOS executes the next line. This line tests to see if IBM was entered at the keyboard. Notice that you use GOTO statements to jump around the batch file parts that should not be executed. If nothing was typed, the batch file displays neither the message I am an IBM computer nor pardon me. If you entered IBM from the keyboard, the batch file doesn't display the pardon me message either.

Another fact to remember about the IF subcommand is that DOS compares the strings literally. Therefore, uppercase characters are different from lowercase. If I invoke either the old or new ISIBM.BAT with the line

```
ISIBM ibm
```

DOS will compare the lowercase "ibm" to the uppercase "IBM" and decide that the two strings are not the same. The IF test will fail, and I'm an IBM computer will not appear on the display.

The IF subcommand's last part is IF EXIST filename. This IF condition tests whether the file filename is on the disk. If you are testing for a file on a drive other than the current drive, put the disk drive name in front of the file name (for example, B:CHKDSK.COM).

You can also test for the opposite of these conditions. That is, you can test whether a condition is false by adding the word NOT after IF.

IF NOT EXIST filename can be used to check whether a file is not on the disk. The file name to check is placed after IF NOT EXIST.

I'll discuss more uses of IF later in this chapter, after I explain the FOR..IN..DO command. Frequently, you can use the IF and FOR..IN..DO commands together.

Getting Creative with FOR..IN..DO

FOR..IN..DO is an unusual and extremely powerful batch command. The command's syntax is

FOR %%variable IN (set) DO command

where variable is a one-letter name. The %% in front of the variable is important. If you use a single %, DOS will confuse the symbol with the parameter markers and not work properly. The *command*, not the marker, is the action you want performed.

The set is the name of the item(s) or disk file(s) you want to use. You can use wildcard file names with this command. You can also use drive names and paths with any file names you specify. If you have more than one file name in the set, use a space or comma between the names.

An interesting example of FOR..IN..DO is a simple batch file that compares file names on a copy of the DOS master disk with those on any other disk. To see how this batch file works, find a working copy of a DOS diskette. If you have a two floppy disk drive computer, place this file, CHECKIT.BAT, on the diskette:

```
@ECHO OFF
FOR %%a IN (*.*) DO IF EXIST B:%%a ECHO %%a is on this diskette also.
```

Now put the disk with the CHECKIT.BAT file into drive A and put a copy of your DOS master disk into drive B. Type CHECKIT, and watch the results.

If you have a fixed disk computer, place this version of CHECKIT.BAT in the subdirectory that holds your DOS file (usually BIN):

@ECHO OFF
FOR %%a IN (*.*) DO IF EXIST A:%%a ECHO %%a is on this
diskette also.

Place a diskette into drive A, type CHECKIT, and watch what happens.

The first part of the FOR..IN..DO command says, "For every file specified, do the command." Here, because you gave the wildcard file name ***.***, which matches every file on the disk, every specified file corresponds to all the files on drive A. The rest of the command says, "If the file exists on drive A or B (depending on which disk drive you gave for the comparison), then display the message that the file is on the DOS disk."

I wrote a simple program in C, called PR.EXE, that produces a line-numbered printout of a text file. To print all my C text files and my macro assembler files, I wrote a simple batch file. All C text files end with a .C extension, and all macro assembler files end with an .ASM extension. The batch file that I created to print all these files contained only this line:

FOR %%a IN (*.C *.ASM) DO PR %%a

The FOR..IN..DO command finds every C and assembler text file and invokes the PR command for every matching file name. I was able to get a numbered listing of 35 C and assembler programs with one batch file command.

FOR..IN..DO also enables you to use wildcard file names with certain commands. For example, the TYPE command does not accept wildcard file names. You must use a specific file name with the command. However, you can make a batch file that uses the FOR..IN..DO command to type a series of files. The batch file TYPER.BAT consists of this command line:

```
@FOR %%d IN (%1 %2 %3 %4 %5) DO TYPE %%d
```

The command places up to five parameters in the FOR..IN..DO command. The batch file substitutes specific file names for wildcard file names and then executes the TYPE command on each file. Running the batch file on my system gave this result:

```
C>TYPER *.BAT
C>TYPE AUTOEXEC.BAT
(AUTOEXEC.BAT's contents are displayed)
C>TYPE TYPER.BAT
(TYPER.BAT contents are displayed)
C>TYPE STARTUP.BAT
(STARTUP.BAT contents are displayed)
C>
```

The next example of FOR..IN..DO developed out of necessity. I was faced with updating many diskettes to the current version of DOS. To update each disk, I had to do the following tasks:

1. Place the DOS V3 operating system on the disk if the disk held a copy of a previous DOS version.

2. Remove any old versions of the DOS utility program.

3. Put the new V3 DOS utility programs on the disk.

I made one assumption about the disks: that if a disk did not have the IBMBIO.COM file on it, the disk also did not contain a copy of DOS. (The FORMAT /S command places IBMBIO.COM, as well as IBMDOS.COM and COMMAND.COM, on the diskette. If the disk doesn't have IBMBIO.COM, the disk doesn't hold the DOS operating system.)

To complicate the matter, some disks did not have all the DOS utility programs. Some disks had FORMAT.COM, and others did not. Some disks had CHKDSK.COM, and others did not. This lack of a pattern was true for all the DOS utilities on all the old disks. Because some of the disks were almost full, I did not want to copy all the DOS utilities; I just wanted to replace the utilities that were already there.

I could have done a directory of each old disk, decided whether I should put DOS on the disk, and then replaced the old version of a DOS utility program with the new version. There is a better way, however.

I created a subdirectory on my fixed disk that held all the utility programs (all .COM and .EXE files) and DOS itself. Then I created the following batch file, called UPDATE3.BAT:

```
(1)  @ECHO OFF
(2)  :START
(3)  ECHO Type Ctrl-C to quit updating diskettes or
(4)  ECHO place the diskette to be updated in drive A
```

```
 (5)  PAUSE
 (6)  IF EXIST A:IBMBIO.COM SYS A:
 (7)  A:
 (8)  FOR %%a IN (*.*) DO IF EXIST C:%%a COPY C:%%a A: /V
 (9)  C:
(10)  ECHO Done!
(11)  GOTO START
```

This batch file is powerful, yet simple. Line 1 turns off the display of batch-file commands. I suppressed the display of line 1 by using the leading @ character. Line 2 is the label for the endless loop. Because I had to update many disks, I decided to use the GOTO command and to type a Ctrl-C when I was finished. Lines 3 and 4 tell the operator to put the disk to be updated into drive A, or to type a Ctrl-C to exit. Line 5 pauses the batch file while the operator changes diskettes or exits the batch file.

Line 6 contains the **IF EXIST filename** construction. DOS checks to see whether the file IBMBIO.COM is on the disk in drive A. If the file is there, DOS performs the SYS command that places a copy of DOS V3 on the disk. (I learned, to my surprise, that "hidden" files are not always hidden. The DOS V3 IF EXIST command always reports correctly, regardless of any hidden or system flags.)

Line 7 makes the current disk drive A. Because DOS will remember where the batch file is, I can change the current disk drive (and current directory) without confusing DOS.

Line 8, which does the majority of the work, says, "For every file on the current disk (drive A), check to see whether the file also exists on drive C. If the file exists on drive C, copy the file to drive A."

The subdirectory on drive C can contain only the DOS V3 programs and this batch file, and the subdirectory must be the current directory. DOS checks every file on the disk in drive A. Then DOS checks to see whether a file by the same name exists in the current subdirectory on drive C, where the copy of DOS V3 resides. If the file is there, DOS copies the new version of the program to the diskette in drive A. If a file on drive A is not a DOS utility, then the file doesn't exist in the subdirectory on drive C, and, in that case, no file is copied.

Line 9 switches the current disk drive back to C. Line 10 is my reassurance line. Line 11 goes back and repeats the process.

I have a good reason for switching the current drive from C to A in line 7. In the first version of this program that I tried, I used the following line 8:

FOR %%a IN (A:*.*) DO IF EXIST C:%%a COPY C:%%a A:

This first version of batch file failed miserably. Remember that the variable **%%a** becomes each matching file name that appears in parentheses, including any disk drive or path names you have added to each file name. When I tried the program the first time, the disk file on drive A was COMMAND.COM. DOS translated line 8 into the following:

IF EXIST A:COMMAND.COM COPY C:A:COMMAND.COM A:

DOS correctly added the A: in front of each file name. Because I specified C as the copy drive, DOS found this syntax objectionable. The batch-file line did not accomplish what I wanted, which was to test whether the file was on drive A, not drive C. With a little more testing, I produced the correct results.

This example works with any system that has a floppy and a fixed disk. With some changes, you can make the file work on a two floppy disk computer.

First, create a new diskette that holds DOS and all of its programs. Edit the UPDATE3 batch file by replacing the occurrences of C: with A: (lines 8 and 9). Then replace the references to A: with B: (lines 4, 6, 7, and 8). Place the new diskette in drive A. You'll use drive B to hold the diskettes you want to update.

One novel use of FOR..IN..DO is to avoid the problem of upper- and lowercase characters in DOS. The following line is a modification to the second line of the ISIBM.BAT:

FOR %%d In (IBM, ibm) DO IF %1 == %%d GOTO IBM

The new line says, "For each member of the set IBM and ibm, if the first parameter is equal to a member of the set, go to the label :IBM." This one line replaces the two lines

```
IF %1 == IBM GOTO IBM
IF %1 == ibm GOTO IBM
```

Because IF sees a difference between upper- and lowercase characters, the two tests are necessary. This FOR..IN..DO command checks both.

One final example of this technique is a little batch file that stops someone from inadvertently formatting the hard disk. In this example, you must place FORMAT.COM in a subdirectory that is not on the PATH or current directory, and you must place this batch file (FORMAT.BAT) on the PATH or in the current directory:

```
@ECHO OFF
IF %1. == . GOTO WHATDRIVE
FOR %%d IN (A:,a:,B:,b:) DO IF %1 == %%d GOTO FORMAT
GOTO BADDRIVE
:FORMAT
C:\BIN\DISK\FORMAT %1 %2 %3 %4 %5
GOTO END
:BADDRIVE
ECHO You cannot format %1!
ECHO %1 is not a floppy disk drive
:WHATDRIVE
ECHO Please try again and specify the disk drive you wish to use,
ECHO such as FORMAT A: or FORMAT B:
:END
```

FORMAT.BAT's major worker is the FOR..IN..DO command, which tests whether the first parameter (which should be the disk drive name) is A:, a:, B:, or b:. If the batch file finds a match, the batch file jumps to :FORMAT. If the batch file finds no match, the batch file jumps to :BADDRIVE. Notice the beforehand-check for a missing parameter.

If the batch file finds a matching drive name, the operator executes the FORMAT program, which is located in \BIN\DISK, a subdirectory not on the PATH. I use the additional parameters in case the operator should type some switches for FORMAT. If the operator doesn't type any switches, these parameters change to nothing and do not interfere with FORMAT.

My error messages are a little stingy. In fact, both error conditions (no parameter and the wrong drive name) use the same two lines. However, if you give an improper first parameter, my batch file does display a message that shows the proper parameter so that the operator will know what is wrong.

Before I change the subject and start explaining the SHIFT command, I want to mention one annoying aspect of the FOR..IN..DO command and I/O redirection. The FOR..IN..DO variable is *not* expanded by DOS. Like

TYPE, MORE does not accept wildcard file names. (For that matter, MORE does not accept any file name. You must redirect the input of MORE.) I thought that a batch file like TYPER would be perfect for MORE. The line I used was

@FOR %%d IN (%1 %2 %3 %4 %5) DO MORE < %%d

When I ran the file, the result was a `File not found` error message. I removed the @ to see the commands after DOS expanded the argument and got:

```
C>MORER *.BAT
C>FOR %%d IN (*.BAT   ) DO MORE < %d
File not found
C>
```

Rather than expanding %%d to the appropriate file names, DOS immediately attempts to open the file called %d so that MORE's input comes from the file. You cannot use the FOR..IN..DO variable with I/O redirection for either input or output. If you attempt to use >> %%d with some command from within a batch file, the output of the command ends up in a file called %D. If you use > %%d instead, the output from the command running ends up in the file %D. (Each time the > symbol is encountered, the earlier version of %D is destroyed.)

The FOR..IN..DO command is versatile and allows one command to handle many files. However, for I/O redirection, the command leaves something to be desired.

Moving Parameters with SHIFT

SHIFT moves the command line parameters one parameter to the left. This batch command tricks DOS into using more than ten parameters. The diagram of SHIFT is

%0 ← %1 ← %2 ← %3 ← %4 ← %5 . . .

↓

bit bucket

Parameter 0 is dropped. The old parameter 1 becomes parameter 0. The old parameter 2 becomes parameter 1; parameter 3 becomes 2; parameter 4 becomes 3; and so on.

The SHIFTIT.BAT batch file is a simple example:

```
:START
ECHO %0 %1 %2 %3 %4 %5 %6 %7 %8 %9
SHIFT
PAUSE
GOTO START
```

When you type

SHIFTIT A B C D E F G H I J K L M N O P Q R S T U V W X Y Z

the first time, ECHO shows

SHIFTIT A B C D E F G H I

After you press a key to continue, ECHO will show

A B C D E F G H I J

Press any key to keep moving down the line, or type a Ctrl-C when you want to stop.

In the DOS V2 edition of this book, I said that I had not found a good use for SHIFT. Since then, I have. A modified version of the copy-and-erase batch file, called MOVE.BAT, shows a use for SHIFT:

```
:LOOP
COPY %1 C: /V
ERASE %1
SHIFT
IF NOT %1. == . GOTO LOOP
```

This batch file copies and then erases any file. For this version, I assume nothing about the file I am copying. I can specify a disk drive, a path, and a file name. This batch file will copy the file to my current directory on drive C and then erase the file from its original disk or directory.

The extra lines shift the parameters one to the left, test whether any parameters remain, and then repeat the operation if necessary. Here are the commands' actions (with blank lines left out):

```
C>MOVE A:SYSI.EXE A:SETUP.BAT \BIN\GROUP.TXT
C>COPY A:SYSI.EXE C: /V
1 file(s) copied
C>ERASE A:SYSI.EXE
C>SHIFT
C>IF NOT SETUP.BAT. == . GOTO LOOP
C>COPY A:SETUP.BAT C: /V
1 file(s) copied
C>ERASE A:SETUP.BAT
C>SHIFT
C>IF NOT \BIN\GROUP.TXT == . GOTO LOOP
C>COPY \BIN\GROUP.TXT C: /V
1 file(s) copied
C>ERASE \BIN\GROUP.TXT
C>SHIFT
C>IF NOT . == . GOTO LOOP
C>
```

Each SHIFT brings the next parameter into action until all parameters (and files) have been processed. Note that you can give no "destination" with the SHIFT batch file. The destination—the place to copy to—would be shifted left. The destination would become the source. COPY would then object (you can't copy a file onto itself). Finally, the file would be erased! Be careful when you design batch files that can "automatically" erase files.

Running Batch Files from Other Batch Files (CALL, COMMAND /C)

On some occasions, you may need to run a batch file from another batch file. In Chapter 12, you saw how the Turbo Lightning fixed-disk-installation batch file, INSTALLH, ran LIHARD.BAT, another batch file. This section discusses three ways to run batch files from other batch files. One method is a one-way transfer of control. The other two ways show you how to run a batch file and return control to the first batch file. These techniques are useful if you want to build menus with batch files or use one batch file to set up and start another batch file.

The first method is simple. Include the root name of the second batch file as the final line of the first batch file. The first batch file runs the second batch file as if you had typed the second batch file's root name on the command line. For example, to run BATCH2.BAT, the final line of BATCH1.BAT file would be

BATCH2

DOS loads and executes the lines from the file BATCH2.BAT. The control passes one-way—from the first batch file to the second. When BATCH2.BAT finishes executing, DOS displays the system prompt. You could consider this technique an inter-batch file GOTO. Control goes to the second file but doesn't come back to the first file.

There is a technique to perform an inter-batch file GOSUB in all versions of DOS. For DOS V3.0 through V3.2, the command is accomplished by using COMMAND, the DOS command processor. In DOS V3.3, the process is simplified by the use of the CALL subcommand, which is discussed next.

The syntax of the CALL subcommand is

CALL *d:path*\filename *parameters*

where *d:path*\ is the optional disk drive and path of the second batch file you want to execute, and filename is the second batch file's root file name. You may place the line anywhere in the first batch file. DOS executes the batch file named by the CALL subcommand, and then returns and executes the remainder of the first batch file. *parameters* represents the optional command-line parameters that you want to give to the batch file on which you used the CALL command.

The following three batch files demonstrate how CALL works. If you use DOS V3.3, try typing these files into your computer. You can use upper- or lowercase characters for the lines; I have used uppercase to highlight information.

After you type the batch files, if your printer is ready, press Ctrl-PrtSc to turn on the printer. Then type BATCH1 first. Turn the printer off by pressing Ctrl-PrtSc again. If you do not have a printer, press Ctrl-S to pause the screen as needed.

(If you have a version of DOS earlier than V3.3, do not type these files yet. Later, I'll give you directions on how to change the files to make them work for you.)

BATCH1.BAT

```
@echo OFF
rem This file does the setup work for demonstrating
rem the CALL subcommand or COMMAND /C
echo This is the STARTUP batch file
echo The command line parameters are %%0-%0 %%1-%1
CALL batch2 second
echo CHKDSK from %0
chkdsk
echo Done!
```

BATCH2.BAT

```
echo This is the SECOND batch file
echo The command line parameters are %%0-%0 %%1-%1
CALL batch3 third
echo CHKDSK from %0
chkdsk
```

BATCH3.BAT

```
echo This is the THIRD batch file
echo The command line parameters are %%0-%0 %%1-%1
echo CHKDSK from %0
chkdsk
```

Look at the number of bytes of available RAM for each time CHKDSK runs. What did you see? The following screen is an abbreviated output from my PS/2 machine:

```
C>BATCH1 FIRST
This is the STARTUP batch file
The command line parameters are %0-BATCH1 %1-FIRST
This is the SECOND batch file
The command line parameters are %0-batch2 %1-second
This is the THIRD batch file
The command line parameters are %0-batch3 %1-third
CHKDSK from batch3
Volume MODEL 60    created Apr 24, 1987 5:10p
   . . .
   654336 bytes total memory
   453744 bytes free
CHKDSK from batch2
Volume MODEL 60    created Apr 24, 1987 5:10p
   . . .
   654336 bytes total memory
   453840 bytes free
CHKDSK from batch1
Volume MODEL 60    created Apr 24, 1987 5:10p
   . . .
   654336 bytes total memory
   453936 bytes free
DONE!
C>
```

So that you will understand the results, take a look at each batch file
starting with BATCH1.BAT. The first line of the first batch turns ECHO off.
Notice that with DOS V3.3, when you turn ECHO OFF, it stays off. With
DOS V2, ECHO always turns back ON each time a new batch file starts.
The next two lines are REM comments. Because ECHO is OFF, the REM
statements do not display when the batch file is run.

The following two lines are similar for all three batch files. The first of the
two lines identifies which batch file is used. The second of the two lines
shows the zero (the name by which the batch file was invoked) and first
parameters (first argument) to the batch file. Notice that to display the
strings %0 and %1 you must use two percent signs (%%0 and %%1). If you
use a single percent sign, DOS will interpret the string as a replaceable
parameter and not display the desired result.

The next line in the first and second batch files invokes another batch file.
In the first batch file, BATCH2.BAT, is invoked. In the second batch file,

BATCH3.BAT, is invoked. In each case, the batch file passes a single argument: the word second to BATCH2.BAT and third to BATCH3.BAT.

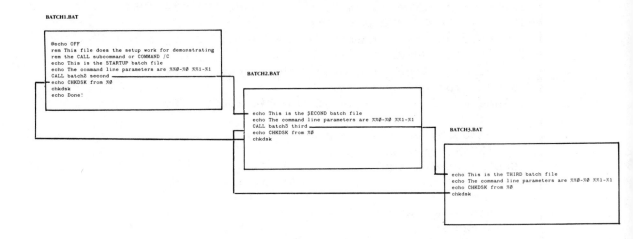

The batch file next displays the name of the file that will run CHKDSK. The CHKDSK program then runs. You use the %0 to display which batch file is running CHKDSK. When DOS encounters the end of each batch file, DOS returns to the invoking batch file.

As illustrated by the sample run, the steps that DOS takes are

1. Run BATCH1.BAT.

2. Display the two ECHO statements.

3. Within BATCH1.BAT, run BATCH2.BAT with the argument second.

4. Display the two ECHO statements.

5. Within BATCH2.BAT, run BATCH3.BAT with the argument third.

6. Display the three ECHO statements.

7. Run CHKDSK.

8. Return to BATCH2.BAT, displaying the single ECHO statement and running CHKDSK.

9. Return to BATCH1.BAT, displaying the single ECHO statement and running CHKDSK.

10. Quit processing the batch files.

These ten steps show why the batch files ran CHKDSK three times, but in "backwards" order. Because of the way the commands are ordered, the first running of CHKDSK comes from BATCH3.BAT, the second from BATCH2.BAT, and the third run from BATCH1.BAT. These batch files show what happens when you use the CALL subcommand and what happens when the batch file you CALL is completed. Control passes back to the line following the CALL subcommand, in the invoking batch file.

Also note the amount of free memory used in each CHKDSK run. The difference between the first and second, and second and third running of CHKDSK is 96 bytes. Each time you use the CALL command, DOS temporarily uses 96 bytes until the called batch file finishes running. Because of this use of free memory, you could run out of memory if you used many batch-file CALL commands (possible but not probable). Few people use so many CALL commands in a row in their batch files. This limitation affects only batch files that call other batch files. A single batch file can use the CALL command as many times as desired. The memory usage occurs only when one called batch file calls another.

As mentioned in the preceding chapter, you cannot use I/O redirection when you are invoking a batch file. This caveat includes when you use CALL on another batch file.

If you use a version of DOS prior to V3.3, you can use the command interpreter to perform this batch file GOSUB routine. The syntax is

COMMAND /C *d:path*\filename *parameters*

The only difference between the CALL and COMMAND syntax is you must use COMMAND's /C switch. The /C switch accepts a single string that can include spaces and any other information. (You still cannot use I/O redirection, however.) DOS loads another copy of the command interpreter and gives it the command line filename, as though you had typed the command line at the DOS prompt. The results are identical to the CALL batch file, except that each copy of COMMAND.COM uses more memory than if you had used the CALL subcommand.

You can use these three batch files with versions of DOS prior to V3.3 by making two changes. First, delete the @ character in BATCH1.BAT's first line. The @ feature is not available in versions of DOS prior to V3.3. Second, change BATCH1.BAT's and BATCH2.BAT's occurrences of CALL to COMMAND /C. You will then be able to run the batch files. You'll notice that this method uses slightly more memory and that the process is slightly slower. Unlike using CALL, COMMAND /C requires that COMMAND.COM be loaded again. Reloading COMMAND COM twice delays the process and makes the difference between the CALL batch-file versions and the COMMAND /C batch-file versions.

The following screen shows the abbreviated output of the batch files' COMMAND /C versions showing just the memory-available lines from CHKDSK:

```
CHKDSK from batch3
   446208 bytes free

CHKDSK from batch2
   450080 bytes free

CHKDSK from batch1
   453952 bytes free
```

You'll note that each DOS V3.3 COMMAND.COM takes slightly more than 3800 bytes. (Each of DOS's different COMMAND.COM versions uses a different amount of memory.) If you are running many batch files, you will run out of memory much faster using COMMAND /C than you will using CALL. However, you will probably never use enough batch files—20 or more—to cause such a problem.

There are two techniques for running batch files from other batch files and returning to the source batch file. DOS V3.3 users should use the CALL subcommand. Users of a version of DOS prior to V3.3 should use COMMAND /C. You'll prefer CALL to COMMAND /C because of the speed and memory used.

Summary

In this chapter you learned these major facts:

1. Several subcommands can be used within batch files.

2. The ECHO subcommand controls the display of lines on the screen and can display messages.

3. The REM subcommand displays messages. REM is affected by the setting of ECHO.

4. The PAUSE subcommand causes DOS to wait until a key is pressed. PAUSE can display an optional message, but this message is affected by the setting of ECHO.

5. The GOTO subcommand jumps to the line following a label within the batch file.

6. The IF command can test for three conditions: if two strings are the same, if a file exists, or if the exit code from a program is greater than or equal to a specified number. The IF NOT command tests for the opposite conditions.

7. The SHIFT subcommand shifts parameters one to the left.

8. The FOR..IN..DO subcommand can repeat a batch file command for one or more files or words.

9. The @ character suppress the display of a single line from a batch file.

10. The COMMAND /C command and the CALL subcommand can be used to run a second batch file and return control of the computer to the first batch file.

Part IV

Tailoring DOS
to Your Use

INCLUDES

Customizing DOS
Making DOS Go International

In this part . . .

the discussion of the CONFIG.SYS file and the use of DOS in different countries covers the inner workings of the computer, its devices, and DOS itself.

Because Chapter 14 covers the CONFIG.SYS file in considerable detail, you may want to only skim the chapter initially, and return to it at a time when you are more familiar with DOS. Or you may want simply to use the sample CONFIG.SYS file presented at the end of the chapter.

Most U.S. and non-French Canadian users do not need to internationalize their computers, and therefore do not need to follow the directions in Chapter 15. If you use English with your computer, you may want to read the first section (on code pages) and skim the remainder of the chapter. If you need to internationalize your computer, this chapter provides detailed instructions and sample files to assist you.

14

Customizing DOS

To *customize* your system means to alter it for your needs. The steps in altering your system include setting up directories, programs, and data to accommodate your tasks and to suit your style. Another necessary step is configuring your computer.

With some operating systems, establishing an operating-system configuration used to mean changing the Basic Input/Output System (BIOS)—a task that was not easy for novices.

Now, DOS V2 and V3 include a major feature that assists in the configuration process: the CONFIG.SYS file. This special text file lies in the root directory of your boot disk and contains specialized commands that can improve the performance and flexibility of your computer.

The CONFIG.SYS file is important. DOS starts with certain settings for its functions or features. But some of the settings may not be appropriate for your use of the computer. The only way to change these settings is by using a set of special commands called *directives* in the CONFIG.SYS file.

If you don't yet have this file on your disk, don't worry. By the end of this chapter, you will have made your own CONFIG.SYS file. On the way to making the file, I'll explain each directive, tell you how it works, and make some suggestions on settings that might be appropriate for your use.

What Is CONFIG.SYS?

After DOS starts, but before the AUTOEXEC.BAT file is invoked, DOS looks for the CONFIG.SYS file. This section describes CONFIG.SYS and tells you what it can do for you.

The name CONFIG.SYS stands for *system-configuration* file. CONFIG.SYS is an ASCII text file you can create with a text editor, such as EDLIN, with a word-processing program in the programmer mode, or with the command COPY CON CONFIG.SYS. You can change the file by using the text editor or a word processing program, but you can't use COPY CON to edit the file. COPY CON only creates files. In Chapter 16, you will see how you can use COPY CON+ to add new lines to an established CONFIG.SYS file, but you cannot edit the established lines.

Inside the CONFIG.SYS file are the directives that alter some of DOS's functions and features. Table 14.1 lists the directives you can use in your CONFIG.SYS file and describes the functions the directives control.

Table 14.1
CONFIG.SYS DIRECTIVES

Directive	Action
BREAK	Determines when DOS recognizes the Ctrl-Break sequence
BUFFERS	Sets the number of file buffers DOS uses
COUNTRY	Sets country-dependent information
DEVICE	Allows different devices to be used with DOS
FCBS	Controls the use of DOS V1-type file handling
FILES	Sets the number of files used at one time
LASTDRIVE	Sets the highest disk drive on the computer
SHELL	Informs DOS what command processor should be used and where the processor is located
STACKS	Sets the number of stacks that DOS uses

If you are a beginner, the directive you will be most interested in is BUFFERS. DEVICE is probably next in importance, then FILES, and FCBS. Some of these directives can be used immediately. Others are advanced features you should not use until you are experienced with DOS and comfortable with your computer.

Interestingly, when these directives are assembled alphabetically, they are almost arranged from the least to the most complex. We will generally discuss these the directives in the order they are shown in the table. Note the discussion later in the chapter of three of the five drivers that work with the DEVICE directive, including VDISK, the RAM disk provided with DOS.

The second half of this chapter also has a discussion of several files provided with DOS and some PS/2 computers to enhance the use of your video screen, keyboard, and disk drives. These files are called *device drivers*. I'll explain what each files does and how the file can be used.

Device drivers are very versatile, but with the versatility comes complexity. The discussion of the device drivers is somewhat technical. Encouragingly, you need not know all aspects of device drivers to utilize their features. Also, you will probably find that some device drivers are not suitable for your computer setup. At the start of the discussion on the device drivers, I'll mention what device drivers are appropriate for different setups.

More of the changes in DOS V3.3 concern the CONFIG.SYS file than any other single part of DOS. The largest changes involve the way the computer handles national language characters. The most affected directives are COUNTRY and DEVICE. If DOS's international features interest you, see Chapter 15, which covers the COUNTRY directive and the parts of the DEVICE directive that pertain to internationalized DOS.

Telling DOS When To Break (BREAK ON, BREAK OFF)

The BREAK directive is identical to the normal DOS BREAK command. The directive determines when DOS checks for the Ctrl-Break (or Ctrl-C) sequence to stop running a program.

If BREAK is ON, DOS checks to see whether you have pressed Ctrl-Break whenever a program requests some activity from DOS (performs a DOS function call). If BREAK is OFF, DOS checks for a Ctrl-Break only when DOS is doing work with the video display, keyboard, printer, or asynchronous serial adapters.

For long, disk-bound programs that do a lot of disk accessing but little keyboard or screen work, you may want to set BREAK ON. This setting will allow you to break out of a long program if it goes awry.

The syntax for the BREAK directive is

BREAK ON

to turn BREAK on and

BREAK OFF

to turn BREAK off.

Because DOS starts with BREAK OFF, you do not have to give the directive at all if you want to leave BREAK off.

Some older versions of word-processing programs were notorious because they poorly handled Ctrl-Break sequences when BREAK was activated. As a rule, you should generally leave BREAK off and not include the directive in CONFIG.SYS. In that case, DOS checks for a Ctrl-Break command only when it performs keyboard, screen, printer, or modem input and output. If you have a program that performs much disk activity and little screen activity, turn the BREAK directive on before you run the program, and turn BREAK off afterward.

Using BUFFERS To Increase Disk Performance

The BUFFERS directive tells DOS how many disk buffers to use. Of all the directives, BUFFERS has the greatest impact on disk performance.

A *disk buffer* is a reserved area of RAM that is set up by DOS. The purpose of disk buffers is to minimize the number of times DOS must use a slow, mechanical device—the disk drive. Although you may consider your disk drives very fast, compared to the internal workings of your computer, disk drives operate very slowly. The idea behind disk buffers is to use random-access memory more and the disk drive less.

The BUFFERS directive controls how many disk buffers you will use. The syntax is:

BUFFERS = nn

in which **nn** is the number of disk buffers you want. You can have any number of buffers, from 1 to 99. If you do not give the BUFFERS directive, DOS starts with from 2 to 15 buffers.

DOS's default starting number of buffers depends on your equipment (disk drive type and amount of memory) and the version of DOS you use. If you have 360K floppy disk drives and don't use the BUFFERS directive, DOS starts with two disk buffers. DOS starts with three if you use any other type of disk drive (including a fixed disk). If you have more RAM (256K to 512K+), DOS starts with five to fifteen disk buffers. Table 14.2 lists the different buffer configurations.

Table 14.2
Default Number of Disk BUFFERS

DOS Version	Number of BUFFERS	Hardware
DOS pre-V3.3	2	floppy disk drives
	3	fixed disk drive
DOS V3.3	2	360K disk drive
	3	any other type of disk drive
	5	more than 128K of RAM
	10	more than 256K of RAM
	15	more than 512K of RAM

You can use fewer BUFFERS than the starting numbers shown in table 14.2. You will probably find, however, that you will want more, rather than fewer, disk buffers.

Understanding How DOS Uses Disk Buffers

How do disk buffers work? Before we get to the answer to that question, remember that a disk buffer is just slightly larger than a disk sector and can hold the contents of a disk sector. A disk sector is typically 512 bytes; a disk buffer is typically 528 bytes. (The additional bytes in the buffer are used by DOS to track the information in the disk buffer.)

When DOS is asked to get information from a disk or place on a disk information that isn't the same size as a disk sector, DOS reads or writes a full sector of information. DOS cannot read or write less than a sector at a time.

Information can be moved within RAM faster than information can be moved from the disk to RAM. Hence, the object of disk buffers is to use high-speed memory-to-memory movement more often than slower disk-to-RAM movement.

When DOS gets information from the disk, DOS conserves the number of times it must access the disk. When part of the disk sector is requested by your programs, DOS reads the full sector and places it into a disk buffer. If the program requests the next group of information, the chances are strong that the needed information is in a disk buffer. Rather than wasting time rereading the sector, DOS shuffles the desired information from the disk buffer in high-speed RAM. Only when the information in the buffer is exhausted (when a different disk sector is needed) does DOS return to the disk.

Similarly, DOS conserves disk activity when it writes information to the disk. If less than a full disk sector should be written to the disk, DOS accumulates the information in a disk buffer. When the buffer fills, DOS writes the information to the disk. This writing is called *flushing* the buffer. To make sure that all information is placed into the file, DOS also flushes the buffers when a program "closes" a disk file, which signals that the file is no longer needed.

When a disk buffer becomes full or empty, DOS marks the buffer to indicate that it has been used recently. When DOS needs to recycle the disk buffers due to more disk activity, DOS goes through the list of disk buffers to find the buffer that hasn't been used for the longest time. The term for this buffer is *least recently used*. This process is repeated for any disk activity.

The net effect is that DOS reduces the number of disk accesses by reading and writing only full sectors. By discarding the least recently used buffers, DOS retains the information that is more likely to be needed next. The result is that your programs and DOS run faster.

In some ways, the system of disk buffers is similar to that used for a RAM disk, when a section of memory is used as if it were a real disk drive. The difference is that only strategic parts of the disk (rather than the entire disk) are kept in buffers. (VDISK, which is DOS's RAM disk, will be discussed later in the chapter.)

A comfort in using disk buffers is knowing that DOS handles all this activity for you. When your program reads part of a data file, DOS brings this portion of the file into RAM—the disk buffer. As your program writes information to the disk, the information goes into the disk buffer first. Disk buffers can be used with all types of files, including the additional program files used with programs such as 1-2-3 and WordStar. DOS loads these additional program files (called *overlays*) into the buffers and gives them to the main program as needed.

If your program does much *random* disk work (reading and writing information in different parts of a file), you may want a higher number of buffers. The more buffers you have, the better the chance that the information DOS wants is already hidden away in memory (the disk buffer).

However, some programs do not benefit much from using disk buffers. If your program mainly performs *sequential* reading and writing (reads and/ or writes information from the start of the file straight through to the end), using disk buffers won't give you a large advantage.

The real advantage of disk buffers is evident when your program does much random reading or writing of information in amounts that are not exactly equal to a disk's sector. This advantage applies especially to database or accounting programs. Some word-processing programs can benefit from disk buffers, but many other programs do not.

Determining the Number of Buffers

How many disk buffers should you have? The answer depends on what programs you run on your computer and how much memory you have. If your day-to-day use of the computer does not involve accounting or database work, generally the right number is from 10 to 30 disk buffers.

One reason for using more disk buffers rather than fewer is that DOS itself uses several buffers. DOS V3 achieves better performance than DOS V2 by holding a copy of the disk's file allocation table in memory. Also, the more disk buffers you have, the greater the likelihood that information you need will be in memory and the disk need not be accessed. If you use many subdirectories, using more disk buffers also increases your computer's performance.

The memory issue can be important. Each disk buffer takes 528 bytes of memory. This means that every two disk buffers you use will cost you just over 1K of RAM, which could be used by your programs instead.

If you are using a system with 256K or less, you don't have much space to devote to disk buffers. But most people use computers that have at least 512K. If you have this much RAM, you can probably use as many disk buffers as you like, simply leaving as much memory space as your programs need. Otherwise, there is little sense in robbing Peter (reducing the amount of RAM space available for your programs) to pay Paul (increasing the size of DOS's disk buffers).

DOS has a "magic" range for disk buffers. At approximately 20 disk buffers, DOS V2 bogged down and became excessively sluggish. DOS V3 also suffers from this problem, but at a higher range—40 or 60 disk buffers. The reason is that DOS spends more time searching the disk buffers for information than simply reading or writing the disk. Depending on what programs you run, you will find that more than 30 buffers cause the system to become sluggish.

The best advice is to start with 10 disk buffers for diskettes or 20 buffers for fixed disk systems. Fine-tune the number by increasing or decreasing it by 1 to 5 buffers every few hours or once a day. Reboot DOS and examine its performance. Keep doing this until you think you have the best performance. You don't need to be exact, but just get the general "feel" of the computer's performance. When you have found the number of disk buffers that is best for your system, you are done. (I run 30 disk buffers on both a 640K IBM Personal Computer AT and a 1M PS/2 Model 60 and find that this number is "just right" for what I do.)

Installing Device Drivers with DEVICE

The DEVICE directive is the "flexibility" command for DOS V3. With DEVICE and the proper software, you can make better use of your current computer hardware and use other hardware your computer could not easily use before.

The syntax for the DEVICE directive is

   DEVICE = *d:path*\ **filename**.*ext* */switches*

in which *d:* is the disk drive holding the device-driver file, *path*\ is the directory path to the device-driver file, and **filename**.*ext* is the name of the file holding the device driver. */switches* are the switches, if any, needed by the device-driver software.

What is a device driver? As you recall from Chapter 5, a device is any peripheral, such as a disk drive, keyboard, video display, terminal, or printer. A *device driver* is the software that links itself to the operating system, so that the computer can use a particular device.

DOS comes with the software that controls the peripherals provided with your computer. But what if you want to use a device that the operating system knows nothing about? The most common example is a "*mouse*," the hand-held device for moving the cursor and inputting data. Before you can use a mouse, DOS needs to know what type of device it is, how to talk to the device, and how to listen to it. Adding the appropriate DEVICE directive to the CONFIG.SYS file solves this problem.

Device-driver software, written according to the specifications in the DOS manual, may be provided by the manufacturer of the device, or you may write your own. The device driver is placed on the system boot disk. Then, to instruct DOS about the device, you include the following line in the CONFIG.SYS file:

   DEVICE = driver_filename

For **driver_filename**, you substitute the full name—including disk drive and path name if needed—of the file that holds the device-driver software. When DOS boots, it loads and installs the appropriate software. Afterward, the computer system can use the device.

One of the five device-driver files provided with DOS V3.3 is called ANSI.SYS. This software alters the way DOS handles the video screen and the keyboard. The ANSI.SYS file enables you to control the video screen's color and graphics from any program and to reprogram the entire keyboard if you like.

There are only three steps to using the ANSI.SYS device driver. These three steps illustrate how to use any device driver:

Step 1. *Copy the device driver to the appropriate startup disk.*

If you use floppy diskettes, copy the file to the root directory of a bootable diskette. If you are using a fixed disk, copy the file to either the root directory of the fixed disk or to a standard subdirectory. To keep the root directory uncluttered, I use \SYS or \DRIVERS as the subdirectory to hold my device-driver files.

Step 2. *Add the* DEVICE *= directive to the CONFIG.SYS file.*

To use the ANSI.SYS file, add this line to the CONFIG.SYS file:

   DEVICE = ANSI.SYS

If you use a fixed disk system, I suggest that you give the disk drive and path name. For example, if you copied ANSI.SYS to a subdirectory you called \SYS, the line would be

DEVICE = C:\SYS\ANSI.SYS

To use ANSI.SYS on a floppy disk-based system, the line would be

DEVICE = A:\ANSI.SYS

Step 3. *Restart the computer.*

Remember, CONFIG.SYS is read only when DOS starts. The changes are not activated until you restart DOS. When the computer restarts, DOS follows the new DEVICE directives.

You can load as many device drivers as YOU need. As each device driver is loaded, DOS extends its control to that device.

Remember that the device driver must be accessible when DOS starts. For convenience, device drivers should be placed in the root directory for floppy diskettes. Fixed disk users should make a special subdirectory called \DRIVERS or \SYS and put the device drivers into this directory, out of the way of daily files. If you put the files in a separate subdirectory, add the directory path name in front of the device-driver file name, as in DEVICE = C:\DRIVERS\ANSI.SYS or DEVICE = \SYS\ANSI.SYS.

Later in this chapter, I'll discuss three of DOS V3.3's device drivers. Chapter 15 discusses the remaining two device drivers in its explanation of how to internationalize DOS.

Accessing Files through File Control Blocks (FCBS)

Many DOS V3 users (I include myself) quickly found the FCBS directive indispensable. The FCBS directive allows useful, but antiquated, programs written for DOS V1 to be used with later versions of DOS.

FCB is an abbreviation for *file control block*. FCBs provide one way for a program to access a file. The method, which has origins in the CP/M operating system, was used in DOS V1. When DOS was directed to work with a file, the programmer asked DOS to create an FCB for each file. DOS used this FCB to communicate with the program and also kept track of each FCB.

Later versions of DOS borrow a UNIX-like method for controlling files, called *handles* (discussed in the FILES directive section). The problem is that whereas FCBs can be used with any version of DOS, handles can be used only with DOS V2 or V3.

You may have several programs that use the older-style FCB method for accessing files. The FCBS directive regulates how DOS V3 will treat the programs.

The syntax of the directive is

FCBS = maxopen, *neverclose*

in which **maxopen** is the maximum number of unique FCBs that programs can open at one time. *neverclose* is the number of FCBs that DOS is not allowed to reuse automatically.

You must specify maxopen, which can be a number from 1 to 255. The default value of maxopen is four FCBs. *neverclose*, which is optional, must be a number less than or equal to maxopen. If you don't specify neverclose, the default value is zero.

When I upgraded to DOS V3.0, my favorite spelling checker, MicroSpell™, came to a screeching halt. After some investigation, the author, Bob Lucas, and I found that the program opens 10 FCBs. Because I hadn't given an FCBS directive, I was allowing DOS to reuse FCBs behind MicroSpell's back, and MicroSpell was unable to use the files it needed.

The quick solution was to use the following line, which I placed in my CONFIG.SYS file:

FCBS = 12,12

This directive tells DOS that my programs will use up to 12 FCBs at a time and not to close any of them automatically. If one of your familiar programs worked fine under DOS V1 or V2, but doesn't work right under DOS V3, try this line.

Shortly after my experience with MicroSpell, Bob Lucas rewrote the program and now includes in his documentation a notice about this directive.

Most programs today do not use FCBs; hence this directive should have decreasing importance in the future. I mention this story to you as a caution. When you "don your coonskin cap" (become an innovator or pioneer), you should expect occasional ambushes.

The IBM documentation states that FCBs are closed only when you use the SHARE command for a local area network. I found that this isn't the case with DOS V3.0 and V3.1. If you use an older program that doesn't support UNIX-like path names, the program uses FCBs. Use the FCBS directive.

You pay a small price in RAM to use the FCBS directive. For each number above 4 that maxopen exceeds, DOS takes up about 40 bytes. Considering that most people have 256K or more in their computers, the use of this extra RAM should not be a problem.

Telling DOS How Many FILES To Handle

As the FCBS directive decreases in importance, the FILES directive gains. The FILES directive is the DOS V3 command for UNIX/XENIX®-like file handling.

DOS V2, instead of using FCBs, introduced new, UNIX-like operating system calls. The calls work in this way: Your program gives DOS the name of the file or device you want to use. DOS gives back to your program a *handle*—a two-byte number. From that point on, your programs use the handle, rather than the FCB, to manipulate the file or device.

The syntax for the FILES directive is

    FILES = nn

in which nn is the number of UNIX/XENIX-like files you want opened at any time. The maximum number is 255, and the minimum is 8. If you give a FILES directive with a number less than 8, or if you omit this directive, DOS makes the number 8. Each additional file over 8 increases the size of DOS by 39 bytes.

The name FILES is somewhat deceiving as handles are used by files and devices. In Chapter 9's discussion on I/O redirection, you learned about standard input, standard output, and standard error. DOS automatically uses two other "standard" devices: standard printer (PRN or LPT1:), and standard auxiliary (AUX or COM1:).

Each of these "standard" devices automatically receives one file handle each. If you do not specify the FILES directive, DOS starts with eight file handles and immediately takes five handles for the standard devices, leaving only three handles for your programs.

If you use BASIC or don't program at all, don't worry about the details on handles. Your concern is that the starting value of 8 may not be enough for your programs. For example, dBASE III Plus® demands at least 20 handles. Other programs may demand more. My advice is to include in your CONFIG.SYS file this directive:

```
FILES = 10
```

This directive establishes DOS with ten file handles, which should be enough for most programs. If a program gives you an error message about not having enough handles or having too many files open, edit your CONFIG.SYS file and increase the number of handles to 15 or 20 (if you are using dBASE III Plus, use 20 files). Those higher numbers are sufficient for most existing programs.

Using LASTDRIVE To Change the Number of Disk Drives

The directive LASTDRIVE informs DOS of the maximum disk drives on your system. Generally, LASTDRIVE is a directive used with networked computers or with the pretender commands, which are discussed in Chapter 19.

If you don't use the LASTDRIVE directive, DOS assumes that the last disk drive on your system is E. If you give DOS a letter that corresponds to fewer drives than are physically attached to your computer, DOS ignores the directive. The LASTDRIVE directive enables you to tell DOS how many disk drives, real or apparent, are on your system.

The syntax for LASTDRIVE is

```
LASTDRIVE = x
```

in which x is the alphabetical character for the last disk drive on your system. The letters A through Z, in upper- or lowercase, are acceptable.

Personal Computers and PS/2 computers can immediately recognize a total of four disk drives, which can be a combination of floppy disk drives and fixed disk drives. The POST (power-on self-test) checks the number of real disk drives attached to the computer.

Why would you want to use the LASTDRIVE directive? When I first read about LASTDRIVE I thought, "Why should I tell the computer something it already knows? Why should DOS assume one more disk drive than I really have?" My attitude changed rapidly.

When you add a RAM disk to your computer, you have the fifth, albeit semireal, disk drive. Because POST knows nothing about a nonphysical RAM disk, DOS assumes that you want one more disk drive. Hence, having five disk drives made sense.

The real reason my opinion changed is that LASTDRIVE must be used to establish *logical* disk drives. A logical disk drive is an apparent disk drive. A logical disk drive can be a nickname for another disk drive (see the ASSIGN command). A logical disk drive may also be the second partition of the fixed disk. And, a logical disk drive may actually be part of a disk. A logical disk drive is just a name. DOS "thinks" that the logical disk drive is real. You know that the disk drive is something else.

DOS, via the SUBST command, allows you to use subdirectories as though the subdirectory were a disk drive. This facility is important when you work with programs that know nothing about subdirectories, particularly if you use a local area network. To effectively use the SUBST command, you need to inform DOS that you have additional, albeit phantom, disk drives.

If you are unsure whether you will use SUBST, omit the LASTDRIVE directive for now. If you use a network, the network documentation should mention the proper value for LASTDRIVE.

If you want to defeat these phantom disk drives, use the directive

    LASTDRIVE = C

in your CONFIG.SYS file. This directive says that the last drive on your system is drive C, usually the fixed disk. If you add devices that act like disk drives to your computer (such as a cartridge-tape backup unit), you can bump up the last "disk drive" (as high as Z, the 26th drive).

Using the LASTDRIVE directive does not affect the size of DOS. LASTDRIVE will be mentioned again in the discussion of the SUBST command in Chapter 19.

Playing the SHELL Game

The SHELL directive was originally implemented to allow programmers to replace the DOS command processor (COMMAND.COM) with other command processors. The directive now has two additional functions: You can place the command processor in any directory—not just in the boot disk's root directory. And you can expand the size of the environment.

SHELL is a tricky directive that should be used cautiously. Giving the wrong SHELL directive can "lock up" your system. If you are unsure of the directive, omit it from your CONFIG.SYS file.

Someday you will need to use the directive, either to move COMMAND.COM from the root directory or to increase the size of the environment. When you use the directive, have handy another DOS diskette that can start up your computer. If you make a mistake, you'll need to reboot with this diskette.

The SHELL directive is slightly different for DOS V3.0, V3.1, and DOS V3.2-V3.3.

The syntax for the SHELL directive in DOS V3.0 is

SHELL = *d:path*\filename.*ext d:\path* /P

The syntax for SHELL for DOS V3.1 through V3.3 is

SHELL = *d:path*\filename.*ext d:\path* /P /E:*size*

The first item after the equal sign is the file name of the command processor you will use. *d:* is the name of the disk drive that holds the command processor. The *path*\ is the subdirectory path to the command processor. Both *d:* and *path*\ are optional, but they should be given. filename.*ext* is the name of the directive processor. The root name is required, and the extension is needed if the file does not use the suffix .COM.

The next item is the disk drive and path name to the directive processor. DOS uses this information to set the COMSPEC environmental variable. Normally, this drive and path name duplicate the first disk drive and path name. And, although this drive and path are marked as optional, they should be given.

SHELL has two switches:

/P   Stay *permanent*
/E:*size*   Set the *size* of the *environment*

The /P switch instructs DOS to load and keep resident the copy of the command processor. Without the /P switch, DOS loads COMMAND.COM, executes the AUTOEXEC.BAT file, and immediately exits. The result is a computer left "dead in the water." You must reboot the system using a different disk or diskette if you omit the /P switch.

The other switch, /E, sets the size of the environment.

If you see the message

```
Out of environment space
```

you need to use the SHELL directive.

/E:size is the optional switch which sets the amount of random-access memory that will be used for the environment. If you use the /E switch, the size of DOS increases by the amount of space you add to the normal starting value for the environment. The SHELL directive does not use any additional memory other than when it increases the size of the environment.

Note that the /E switch is not available for DOS V3.0. The size given with the switch is the same for DOS V3.2 and V3.3, but different for DOS V3.1.

DOS V3.2 and V3.3 start with an environment size of 160 bytes. *size* can be a number from 160 to 32,767. If you give a size number greater than 32,767, DOS uses 32,767. If you give a number smaller than 160 or give a nonsense size (such as using letters for *size*), DOS uses 160 bytes for the environment.

However, if *size* is not evenly divisible by 16, DOS adjusts *size* to the next multiple of 16. For example, if you use the number 322 for size, DOS adjusts up the size to 336. The adjustment is automatic and does not bother your programs or DOS.

DOS V3.1 uses a different system for *size*, which is the number of 16-byte paragraphs for the environment. DOS V3.0 and DOS V3.1 start with an environment size of 128 bytes. For DOS V3.1 only, size can be changed with the SHELL directive from 11 (11 * 16 or 176 bytes) to 62 (62 * 16 or 992 bytes). If you use a number less than 11 or greater than 62, DOS V3.1 will display an error message and ignore the /E switch.

You can reverse the order of the /P and /E switches. You can place a space can between the switches. You can also omit the /E switch. If you give the /E switch, however, do not forget to put the colon between the */E* and *size* and do not put spaces within any part of the /E switch.

The normal command processor for DOS is COMMAND.COM. You can write your own command processor if you prefer. (I am not very good at assembly language programming and would not even attempt such a task.) Why, then, use the SHELL directive?

As mentioned, the SHELL directive can expand the size of the environment. When your programs need more environment space, you'll need to give the SHELL directive. The other reason is that the command processor can be moved from the root directory of the boot disk.

Because I like to keep my root directory as uncluttered as possible, I put COMMAND.COM in a separate directory on my fixed disk. Hence, when I copy a diskette that contains another copy of COMMAND.COM, I know I am not placing an outdated version over my more current version.

The other reason I use the SHELL directive is that when I boot my computer from a floppy diskette, the SHELL directive directs DOS to look for COMMAND.COM on the fixed disk. This means that when COMMAND.COM must reload itself, DOS does not give me the annoying message to place a diskette with COMMAND.COM in the diskette drive. DOS knows to get COMMAND.COM from the fixed disk. This example may seem obscure, but it works.

By the way, the DOS manual does not mention the second item about SHELL, the drive and path name to the command processor. The DOS manual states that the SHELL directive does not affect the COMSPEC variable. If you use the second item, DOS *does* set COMSPEC.

Keeping Up with the STACKS Directive

The STACKS directive was added to DOS V3.2 and was changed slightly with DOS V3.3. If you do not have an Enhanced Keyboard, this directive may have little use for you. If you have a PS/2, Personal Computer AT, or PC 286-XT, you may find this directive necessary. To explain why the directive is necessary, you need to understand a few things about your computer's internal operation.

A *stack* is an area of RAM. The CPU (central processing unit, the "brain" of your computer) uses this area to temporarily hold information. High-speed instructions place items onto the stack and remove items from the stack. The IBM's CPU can use a stack anywhere in memory, and each program you use can have its own stack.

The second concept is the *hardware interrupt*, a signal generated by a device that is demanding attention. For example, each time you press a key, the keyboard generates a hardware interrupt. Your disk drives, modem, mouse, or other devices also generate interrupts—demands for the CPU's attention.

When a hardware interrupt occurs, the computer executes the software instructions in a fixed-memory location to satisfy the device. The first step the computer takes is to store the information that was being acted upon when the interrupt occurred. It stores this information in a stack.

The difficulty with interrupts is that they can *nest*, meaning the computer can be interrupted again, by the same or a different device, while it is handling a hardware interrupt. When additional interrupts occur, DOS must quickly store each level of information on a stack and handle the next interrupt.

Versions of DOS prior to V3.2 used the single-stack method to handle the interrupts. This system usually worked well, but when too many interrupts occurred and the stack overflowed, the system ran into problems. The computer would mysteriously lock up, and no error message would be given.

DOS V3.2 implemented a new method of using a pool of nine stacks. When a hardware interrupt occurs, DOS V3.2 draws another stack from the pool. As DOS successfully answers the interrupt, it returns the stack to the pool for use later when another interrupt occurs.

Lately, as more people use sophisticated peripherals that generate numerous interrupts, the problem of nested interrupts has become increasingly apparent. If the ninth interrupt occurs before DOS can satisfy any of the eight previous interrupts, DOS displays this error message:

```
Fatal: Internal Stack Failure, System Halted
```

When this error message appears on your screen, your computer goes catatonic: It has "blown" its stack. *You must turn the computer off and on again to restart it.* You will not be able to reboot the system with Ctrl-Alt-Del.

Most stack problems surface when you use an Enhanced Keyboard and certain programs, such as dBASE III Plus. Holding down a key can trigger stack failure.

To prevent the problem of stack overflows, DOS provides the STACKS directive. The syntax is

STACKS = number, *size*

number is the number of stacks that DOS should establish to handle the interrupts. The value of **number** should be from 8 to 64. *size* is the size in bytes of each stack. This number can be from 32 to 512.

The default value of the STACKS directive varies from machine to machine. For DOS V3.2 and V3.3 on the PS/2, Personal Computer AT, PC XT and 286-XT (with the Enhanced Keyboard), and the PC Convertible, DOS starts with 9 stacks of 128 bytes each (equivalent to giving the directive STACKS = 9, 128). DOS V3.3 on the PC, PC XT, and PC Portable has a single stack for all interrupts.

To revert to the "single-stack-fits-all" approach for handling interrupts, use the directive:

STACKS = 0, 0

Generally, you can ignore the STACKS directive. But if you get a stack error, you have a program that triggers the hardware problem. Immediately change the CONFIG.SYS file to increase the number of stacks without altering the size of the stacks. A comfortable line to use is

STACKS 12, 128

This directive establishes 12 stacks of 128 bytes each.

The preferred way to handle stack failure is to increase the number of stacks and not to increase their size. If, however, you must change the size of the stacks, increase the size. Do not not decrease it. The benefits of decreasing the size of the stacks are outweighed greatly by the chance that a program will overflow the smaller stack.

The STACKS directive does affect DOS's size. Considering that DOS starts with approximately 1200 bytes for the stack pool, increasing the number or size of the stacks correspondingly increases the size of the stack pool. Using only one DOS stack (**STACKS = 0, 0**) decreases DOS's size by approximately 1,000 bytes.

Using Device Drivers for Your Keyboard, Screen, and Disks

Six device drivers can be used on your computer with DOS V3.3 to enhance keyboard function, the display, and/or the disk drives. You can use all six drivers with the DEVICE = directive. Five of the driver files are located on the DOS Startup/Operating or Startup diskette. The sixth file is located on the Reference diskette that comes with the PS/2 Models 50, 60, or 80. The six device drivers are shown in table 14.3.

Table 14.3
Device Drivers Provided with DOS

Driver	Action
ANSI.SYS	Extends control over your keyboard and display (All versions of DOS V3)
VDISK.SYS	RAM-disk software (All versions of DOS V3)
IBMCACHE.SYS	A disk cache program (PS/2 Models 50, 60, and 80 only)
DRIVER.SYS	Extends control over your built-in or external floppy disk drives (DOS V3.2 and V3.3)
DISPLAY.SYS	Provides foreign language font support for the display (DOS V3.3 only)
PRINTER.SYS	Provides foreign language font support for the printer(s) (DOS V3.3 only)

DISPLAY.SYS and PRINTER.SYS are part of DOS V3.3 only. DRIVER.SYS made its debut with DOS V3.2. If you have earlier versions of DOS, you cannot use these features. IBMCACHE.SYS is provided only to owners of PS/2 Models 50, 60, or 80.

DISPLAY.SYS and PRINTER.SYS are device drivers that are used in DOS V3.3's non-English language functions. Chapter 15, which explains how to use DOS internationally, discusses these files.

DOS V3.3 users receive two additional .SYS files on their DOS diskettes—COUNTRY.SYS and KEYBOARD.SYS. These files are *not* device drivers. Do not attempt to use the DEVICE directive with them.

In the rest of this chapter, you'll read about the four remaining device drivers. I'll first discuss ANSI.SYS, followed by VDISK.SYS, IBMCACHE.SYS, and finally DRIVER.SYS.

Device drivers vary greatly in how difficult they are to use. The degree of difficulty is based on what the driver does. Drivers that work with very specific hardware, such as ANSI.SYS, are easy to use. You simply use the DEVICE directive to load the driver. Other device drivers, which work with a variety of hardware, have optional and mandatory parameters that increase the degree of difficulty. DRIVER.SYS is the most complex of the four device drivers in this chapter.

I rate the need for and the difficulty of the various device drivers as follows:

ANSI.SYS – required by many software packages, needed by most users, and the easiest to understand and install.

VDISK.SYS – not required by any software packages, but beneficial to most users whose computers have at least 512K of RAM or any extended memory; somewhat difficult to understand and moderately difficult to install.

IBMCACHE.SYS – not required by any software package, but useful to many users of fixed disk systems; moderately difficult to understand and easy to moderately difficult to install.

DRIVER.SYS – required for most external disk drives and optional for users who want to make additional logical disk drives out of a single physical disk drive; moderately difficult to understand and install.

Because the discussion of these device drivers is somewhat technical and detailed, I *strongly* suggest that you first skim the discussion of the device drivers and then reread the sections of interest. If you find the discussion too difficult, jump to the end of the chapter where I recommend some sample CONFIG.SYS files and simply use the sample file that most closely matches your system.

Using ANSI.SYS To Enhance Your Keyboard and Display

ANSI.SYS is a device driver. The driver replaces DOS's standard way of looking at characters that are going to the keyboard or video screen. With ANSI.SYS, your programs can do any of the following: control the video screen's colors and graphics; move the cursor anywhere on the screen; erase characters anywhere on the screen; reprogram any key, including the special function keys; and produce many characters at the press of a single key.

Many programs need the ANSI.SYS's capabilities. If any of your programs require ANSI.SYS, you must use the driver, or the program will not display properly. Check your application programs' manuals for more information.

Usually, ANSI.SYS is copied to the startup floppy's root directory. To use ANSI.SYS on a floppy disk-based system, add the following line to CONFIG.SYS:

```
DEVICE = A:\ANSI.SYS
```

For use with a fixed disk, ANSI.SYS is normally copied to the root directory or to a subdirectory dedicated to device drivers, like \BIN or \DRIVERS. Depending on the file's placement, you should add one of these lines to your CONFIG.SYS file:

```
DEVICE = C:\ANSI.SYS

DEVICE = C:\SYS\ANSI.SYS

DEVICE = C:\DRIVERS\ANSI.SYS
```

Use the first line if you have placed ANSI.SYS in your fixed disk's root directory. Use the second line if you have placed ANSI.SYS in your \SYS subdirectory. Use the third line if you have placed ANSI.SYS in your \DRIVERS subdirectory.

ANSI.SYS's name reflects its background. ANSI® is the abbreviation for the *American National Standards Institute*, the agency that formulates and publishes standards affecting items ranging from programming languages to safety shoes. ANSI is a member of the *International Standards Organization* (ISO), a multinational standards group.

Two standards, ANSI 3.64 and ISO 6429, cover terminals and display devices. The standards establish a method to control terminals by transmitting strings of characters from the computer to the terminal. The strings are called *escape sequences*, since the strings start with the ASCII Escape character (27 decimal, 1B hexadecimal). Every terminal complying with these standards understands and reacts to these escape sequences in the agreed manner.

The standard establishes escape sequences to move the cursor up, down, left, right, or to any position on the video screen. The standard also establishes sequences to erase a line or the entire video screen, and to set the mode of the screen (into alphanumeric or dot-by-dot graphics, including the color of the characters or dots and the background).

One enhancement of the ANSI.SYS standards is to reprogram your keyboard. You can define any key on the keyboard to produce a single character or many characters. This capability allows you to create keyboard *macros* where you can make a single keystroke or set of keys (such as Ctrl-1 or Alt-F6) produce a frequently typed word or complete DOS command.

ANSI.SYS has some limitations. The program is not a substitute for keyboard macro programs like RoseSoft's Prokey™ or Borland's SuperKey™ ANSI.SYS can hold about 128 characters of text for all macros, which is minuscule when compared to the 2K to 8K the other macro programs can use.

Nor does ANSI.SYS provide a method to use or control high-resolution color graphics (the 640-by-200- or 640-by-350-dot modes). Also, using ANSI.SYS to display text and graphics is much slower than using programs like WordStar or 1-2-3, which write to the screen directly or use the computer's BIOS.

Regardless of these limitations, ANSI.SYS is an essential device driver for your computer, and many programs depend on it for their video output. Because ANSI.SYS's memory burden is light, including ANSI.SYS in your CONFIG.SYS file is a worthwhile trade-off of memory resources for video screen control.

Using VDISK To Make a RAM Disk

The VDISK directive creates a *virtual disk*. "Virtual" used in this sense means *apparent*. When you install VDISK, you install what is apparently a floppy disk drive. In reality, you are using a portion of your RAM as though that RAM were a disk drive.

You can benefit greatly from using RAM disks. RAM disks can be ten to fifty times faster than using a floppy disk and five to twenty times faster than using fixed disk.

How does the RAM disk process work? The VDISK device driver tells DOS that the program wants to use some memory. DOS permanently gives the requested RAM to the program. *Permanently* means that the RAM disk has captive use of the requested memory until DOS restarts or until the computer is turned off.

The software then sets up the memory with a boot record, a file allocation table (FAT), a directory, and locations in which to store files. The memory area becomes a disk device, as accessible as any real disk drive.

VDISK.SYS is the device driver for the RAM disk. The syntax for VDISK is

DEVICE = *d:path***VDISK.SYS** *bbbb sss ddd /E:max*

d: is the disk drive that holds the VDISK.SYS file. *path*\\ is the directory path to VDISK.SYS.

The four options for VDISK are

bbbb	The size (in K) of the RAM disk
sss	The size of the RAM disk sectors
ddd	The number of directory entries (files) for the RAM disk
/E:max	The switch for extended memory use for DOS V3.0

bbbb is the size of the RAM disk in Ks and can range from 1K to the maximum amount of memory available, less 64K that DOS requires you to leave free for use by other programs. For most Personal Computers and for the PS/2 Models 25 and 30, the maximum amount of memory is 640K. Personal Computer ATs and the other PS/2 models can have up to 16 megabytes of RAM. For these computers, you can use more than one VDISK. For example, you could use three four-megabyte VDISKs and one three-megabyte VDISK. (I emphasize *could*, not *should*.)

The default value of *bbbb* is 64K. For DOS V3.2 and V3.3, VDISK adjusts the RAM disk's size disk downward if you haven't left 64K of memory free for your programs. For DOS V3.0 and V3.1, if *bbbb* is larger than the amount of your computer's RAM, VDISK uses the 64K size. If you have less than 64K of memory available, VDISK displays an error message and does not install.

When you size your RAM disk, remember that DOS treats the RAM disk as though it were a real disk drive. Because of the boot sector, FAT, and root directory on the RAM disk, the space available for storing your files will be 5K to 24K less than the size you specify. Also remember that the VDISK software itself uses 768 bytes of memory.

sss is the size of the sectors for VDISK. You can specify three sector sizes: 128, 256, or 512 bytes. The default sector size is 128 bytes. DOS disks usually use a sector size of 512 bytes. This size is best if you are storing larger files on the VDISK or if you want to maximize disk speed when you use the RAM disk. If you are storing many small files, a sector size of 256 or 128 will waste less space than a larger sector size.

ddd is the number of directory entries for the RAM disk. Each file you store on the RAM disk uses one directory entry. The volume label VDISK creates takes one of the directory entries. Thus, *ddd* actually specifies the number of files minus one that your RAM disk can hold.

The range for *ddd* is from 2 to 512 files, and the default is 64. VDISK may automatically adjust the number of directory entries in two situations: when the directory entries do not fill a complete sector and when you have insufficient space.

First, VDISK may increase the number of directory entries to fill a complete sector. Each directory entry is 32 bytes long. Sector sizes of 256 bytes will have the number of directory entries that are an integer multiple of 8. Sectors sizes of 128 will have entries that are an integer multiple of 4. If you are using a sector size of 512, the number of directory entries will be evenly divisible by 16. If you are using 512-byte sectors and you specify 72 directory entries, VDISK automatically adjusts the number of entries to 80. (72 entries requires 4.5 sectors of 512 bytes; VDISK rounds the number to the next multiple of 16.)

Second, VDISK decreases the number of directory entries by one sector's worth at a time when you have insufficient space for the FAT, the directory, and two additional sectors. If you specify a small RAM disk (64K to 128K) and have many directory entries, this problem may occur. VDISK will issue an error message and not install. The solution to the problem is to specify a smaller sector size, *sss*, or a larger RAM disk size, *bbbb*.

When you start your system, VDISK may make some size adjustments. The adjustments occur when VDISK uses the default values or when special sizes for options conflict with the RAM disk's size. The adjustments are harmless unless VDISK cannot find enough space on the RAM disk in which to fit the FAT and the directory. Harmful adjustments occur when you give improper values to VDISK, such as specifying too large a RAM disk with too small a sector size. In that case, VDISK will display an error message and refuse to install itself.

/E is the switch VDISK uses to access extended memory, that is, memory above the one million-byte point. Computers that can use extended memory—PS/2 computers (except Models 25 and 30) and Personal Computer ATs that have an add-on board which provides more than 1M of memory—can use the /E switch.

PS/2 Models 25 and 30, which use an 8086 CPU, and the PC, which uses an 8088, can use only 1M (megabyte) of memory at a time, which is the limit for the 8088/8086. PS/2 Models 50 and 60 and the Personal Computer AT use an 80286 CPU, enabling the machines to use more than 1M of RAM. The PS/2 Model 80 uses an 80386 CPU that can also use more than 1M of RAM.

If you have a different computer, including the 286-XT, don't use this switch. Although the 286-XT has a 80286 CPU, the computer cannot accommodate extended memory. VDISK will find that your computer does not have extended memory and will not install itself.

If you use the /E switch, VDISK takes up 768 bytes of regular memory, but places the RAM disk itself in extended memory. With the /E switch, the maximum size of the RAM disk is 4M. You can use multiple RAM disks, limited only by the extended memory that is available and DOS's regular memory. If the 768 bytes that each VDISK uses reduces your regular memory below 64K, the extended VDISK will not install.

DOS V3.0 uses the /E switch alone; later versions add the *max* parameter to the switch. *max* is the maximum number of sectors to transfer at one time from the RAM disk. Certain programs, primarily communications programs, may drop characters if the 80286 or 80386 CPU's attention is kept for too long on the RAM disk. If you have such a problem, set *max* to seven or less. Otherwise, omit the *max* or give eight as the value, as indicated in the next section.

If you have enough extended memory, you can have several RAM disks. Just specify additional DEVICE = VDISK lines in your CONFIG.SYS file. Each line will invoke a fresh copy of VDISK and install additional RAM disks.

If you want to use a RAM disk that mimics a single-sided DOS disk, use the command line:

```
DEVICE = VDISK.SYS 180 512 64
```

This command line sets up a 180K disk with 512-byte sectors and 64 directory entries.

To use a RAM disk that appears to be a 360K, double-sided DOS disk, use this command line:

    DEVICE = VDISK.SYS 360 512 112

If you want a RAM disk that uses all the extended memory on a 1M PS/2, use this command line:

    DEVICE = VDISK.SYS 384 512 112 /E:8

The line requests a RAM disk of 384K (1M of RAM minus 640K DOS memory = 384K of extended memory), 512-byte sectors, and 112 directory entries. The */E:8* switch tells DOS to install the RAM disk in extended memory and transfer 8 sectors to and from the RAM disk at a time. If the /E switch were omitted, DOS would install the RAM disk within the 640K DOS memory.

Determining the Size of the RAM Disk

The amount of RAM in your system, the programs you use, and the RAM disk's convenience determine the size of the RAM disk you can use. Some of the computers I work with have 640K of RAM (PCs, my Toshiba 1100+ laptop, and a PS/2 Model 30). Because DOS and many of my programs use less than 128K, I could use a 360K RAM disk on these computers.

Again, I emphasize *could*, not *should*, when I estimate the space I can devote to a RAM disk. Several programs compete with VDISK for my free memory space: SideKick®, SuperKey and Turbo Lightning™, which are from Borland; FLASH™ from Software Masters; and 1-2-3 from Lotus. Using these programs reduces rapidly the space I can devote to a RAM disk.

Depending on the system I use, DOS, my buffers, FCBs, and other CONFIG.SYS options use from 56K to 66K of RAM. In the configuration I use on all of my computers, SideKick takes about 73K of RAM. SuperKey, the keyboard macro program, uses 58K. Turbo Lightning, the on-line dictionary and thesaurus, uses 68K. FLASH, my disk caching program, uses from 40K to 200K.

In a 640K machine with all these programs active, I have an average of 360K in use, with 280K memory space left. The 1-2-3 program requires about 179K of memory space, leaving a worksheet space of 101K. That workspace accommodates many, but not all, of my 1-2-3 worksheets.

However, a 64K RAM disk (almost 65K if you include DOS's overhead) leaves only 36K. Very few of my 1-2-3 models fit into that space.

The point is you must balance your need for RAM workspace with your need for the tools you use. My DOS setup gives me the performance I need. FLASH, my disk cache program, is my most frequently used addition. I enjoy SideKick and use it almost daily. SuperKey is a valuable addition. When I write, Turbo Lightning is a vital part of my setup. When I need financial projections and sales analyses, I use 1-2-3. Given a choice between a RAM disk and 1-2-3, the RAM disk loses every time.

Actually, I have two compromises. The first compromise is to use different boot diskettes. The CONFIG.SYS file for one diskette calls for a 100K RAM disk; another diskette does not call for any RAM disk. I also use SideKick, SuperKey, Turbo Lightning, and FLASH with my first diskette. The second disk loads only SideKick and FLASH. I boot from the first diskette when I will not be using 1-2-3. I can use a RAM disk and discard it when I need 1-2-3.

The second compromise—the one I use for my other machines—is simple but slightly more expensive. The three other systems I use consistently are a Personal Computer AT with 1.6M of memory, a PS/2 Model 60 with one megabyte of memory, and my current workhouse, a Sperry IT (an AT-like computer) with 3.5M of RAM. I installed AT memory expansion boards in the AT and the AT-clone that permitted me to add the additional 1 and 2.5 megabytes of RAM. (My AT clone started with one megabyte of memory.)

I have added the /E switch to the VDISK line in my CONFIG.SYS file so that I can use the extended memory. On the AT, I have a 360K RAM disk. On the AT-clone, I have a 1.5M RAM disk. (And to think, just 10 years ago, I could not imagine what I would do with 64K of memory! Two years ago, I was wondering what to do with 1.6M of memory. Now I miss the 3.5M of memory on my AT-clone when I use another machine. I know that other PC users feel the way I do.)

Here's an explicit warning for those using RAM disks: RAM is volatile. When the power goes off or DOS is rebooted, everything on your RAM disk is lost! If you store changing files on your RAM disk, get into the habit of copying these files to a "real" disk at intervals of anywhere from every 15 minutes to two hours. If the information is critical, copy from the RAM disk to a real disk frequently. Power losses arrive at your door unannounced. When a power loss destroys information that has taken hours of work to build, the feeling in the pit of your stomach cannot be described. Copying from a RAM disk to a real disk is cheap insurance.

If you are hesitant about putting changing files in volatile memory, try my favorite use for a RAM disk: use the RAM disk just for nonchanging program files. For quick access, I copy to the RAM disk frequently used programs and files such as the dictionary files for Turbo Lightning. If the power is lost, I have lost nothing. The real copies of the programs or data files are on my diskettes or fixed disks.

By the way, here's a trick that a friend showed me that may help you. I used to use two RAM disks. One held the dictionary and thesaurus files for Turbo Lightning. I used the other for fast-access programs and copying files. I was wasting 768 bytes in regular memory by using two RAM disks and wasting about 30K in extended memory by having two boot sectors, two FATs, and two directories, one for each diskette.

I now use one RAM disk and place the Turbo Lightning files in a subdirectory of the RAM disk. I have regained the 30K of extended memory through this approach. More importantly, I have regained almost 1K of regular memory, which is much more valuable than extended memory.

RAM disks can speed computer operations manyfold. If you have the memory to support RAM disks, they are wonderful improvements. Remember, however, that a RAM disk is vulnerable to power disruptions and system resets. If you put changing data on a RAM disk, back up the data frequently. If you put only nonchanging programs and data on the RAM disk, you have little need to worry.

Making Fixed Disk Use Faster with IBMCACHE.SYS

A potential benefit of purchasing a PS/2 computer is that IBM provides a disk-cache program with the computer: IBMCACHE.SYS. IBMCACHE uses RAM to speed the performance of your disks.

A cache (pronounced *cash*) is a safe place for hiding provisions. A disk cache is a safe place for hiding and preserving disk data. Like RAM disks, disk caches operate from a section of RAM that you request from DOS. A disk cache is more similar to a DOS disk buffer than to a RAM disk, however.

Both a disk cache and a disk buffer accumulate information going to the disk or coming from the disk. When information is needed from the disk, the information is placed in a disk buffer or cache and then parceled out to the program. When information is written to the disk, the information is stored in the buffer or cache until the buffer or cache is full. Then the information is written to the disk. The performance of your programs improves because slow disk accesses are replaced by higher speed memory-to-memory transfers.

In theory, a DOS disk buffer is a form of caching. A good caching program can outperform DOS's disk buffers, however. The reason is the intelligence devoted to handling the buffer or cache.

As you recall from the discussion of the BUFFERS directive, DOS recycles disk buffers on a least-recently used basis. When another disk buffer must be used, DOS recycles the disk buffer that has not been used for the longest time. Although this information might be needed soon, DOS reuses this buffer.

A disk cache uses a different scheme to determine what information should be kept or discarded: the cache remembers what sections of the disk have been used most *frequently*. When the cache must be recycled, the program keeps the more frequently used areas and discards the least frequently used.

Given absolute random disk access (program and data files scattered uniformly across the disk), the least *frequently* used method of recycling works better than recycling the least *recently* used sector. The areas of the disk that are most heavily used tend to be kept in memory. Given the intense access of a small number of disk sectors in a short time, the least recently used method works best.

Another feature of the disk cache is *look-ahead*, a technique in which the cache reads more sectors than the program requests. Typically, a program requests DOS to read one or two sectors at a time. These sectors are held in the disk buffer. If the program needs the next sector or two, DOS will have to access the disk again to get the next sectors.

With look-ahead, the cache commands DOS to read the next one to seven sectors at one time. If the program requests information that resides in the next sectors, the cache passes the information to DOS, which gives the information to the program. By reading two to eight sectors at one time, DOS can avoid up to seven individual disk accesses. This technique greatly increases the speed of reading sequential files but decreases slightly the performance of working with completely random files.

Should you use a disk cache? I believe the answer is yes! Given a choice between a RAM disk and a disk cache, the cache is preferable—but not all the time.

A disk cache is preferable because it helps you with all disk activity. A RAM disk helps only with files that are copied to the RAM disk. The cache's activity is transparent and effortless whereas separate directives are required to place the needed files on the RAM disk. Thus, the cache is more convenient to use.

The disk cache is also preferable to a RAM disk because the danger of losing information can be less. Actually, the danger of losing files read from a RAM disk and from a disk cache is identical: nil. The original copies of the files reside on the physical disk.

But there is a greater probability of losing information when files are written to the RAM disk than when files are written to the cache. The cache, like the DOS buffers, holds the information for only a few seconds before writing it to the disk. During this brief period, the information is at risk. If power is lost to the RAM disk, however, all files on the disk are destroyed. A sudden computer power-out is more catastrophic to the RAM disk than to the disk cache.

In two situations, however, a RAM disk is preferred to a disk cache. When you need to copy files between diskettes on a computer with a single floppy disk drive, copying to and from the RAM disk is convenient. You first copy the files to the RAM disk, change diskettes, and then copy the files to the second diskette. A disk cache does not help you copy files between diskettes.

The second occasion to prefer a RAM disk is when you frequently use nonchanging files that can be completely placed on the RAM disk. The classic example is Turbo Lightning: I place its dictionary and thesaurus files on the RAM disk. Because I access these files very frequently, but seldom at the same spots in the file, having the files on the RAM disk yields better performance than using a disk cache.

I should mention two downsides to the IBM disk cache program. First, the program only works with fixed disks. IBMCACHE.SYS does not help when you read floppy diskettes. Although most personal-computer work today is done on fixed disks, having increased performance for floppy diskettes would have been pleasant. Second, the cache is not very intelligent. Many third-party, non-IBM disk cache programs offer greater features and performance benefits. My favorite is FLASH, from Software Masters (mentioned again in Chapter 21). But IBMCACHE.SYS is worth the price—free with every PS/2 Model 50, 60, and 80—and worthy of experimentation.

To install IBMCACHE.SYS the first time, you must run the program IBMCACHE from the Reference Diskette. The program, IBMCACHE.COM, and the disk cache, IBMCACHE.SYS, are hidden files on the diskette. Thus, you cannot copy the files to your computer using COPY. Running the installation program is painless, however, and does properly set up your CONFIG.SYS file for use with the cache.

The first step is to start up DOS on your PS/2 system. After DOS is running, insert the Reference Diskette that comes with your system into drive A. Then type:

C>A:IBMCACHE

Your screen should look something like figure 14.1. The highlighted bar should be over the first option, Install disk cache onto drive C:. When you press Enter to select the option, a window pops up giving information as shown in figure 14.2. Press Y to install the cache. The window will go away, the floppy and fixed disk lights will go on, and a message that the cache is installed will appear in another window (see fig. 14.3). Press Enter to continue.

Fig. 14.1. *Initial installation screen for IBMCACHE.*

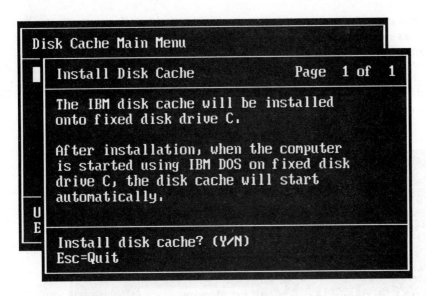

Fig. 14.2. *IBMCACHE installation information.*

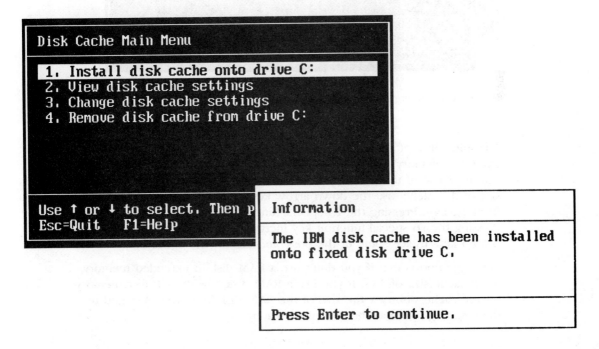

Fig. 14.3. *Successful installation of IBMCACHE.*

If you have extended memory, move the highlighted bar down to option 3, Change disk cache settings, by tapping the down-arrow key twice. Press Enter.

Change the first option, Cache Location. from Low Memory to Extended Memory by pressing either the F5 or F6 special-function key. Your screen will resemble figure 14.4. Do not press Enter yet.

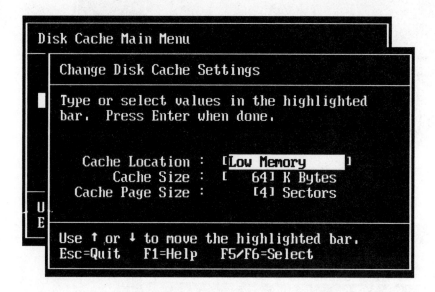

Fig. 14.4. *Changing the location of IBMCACHE to extended memory.*

The initial size of the cache is 64K. A one-megabyte computer has 384K of extended memory. You can use this entire memory for your cache or you can use some of this memory for a RAM disk. If you want to change the size of the cache, use the down arrow key to move to the next option, Cache Size. Pressing the F5 special-function key reduces the cache size. Pressing the F6 special-function key increases the size. Try pressing the F5 and F6 keys to see some of the possible sizes for the cache.

My suggestion is that if you don't use a RAM disk in extended memory, use a cache size of 384. If you use a RAM disk, use the leftover memory for the cache. Subtract the size of the RAM disk in K from 384 and use the resulting figure as the size of the cache.

You might notice that size choices offered when you press the F5 or F6 keys do not match your calculations. If the program does not have a number that matches your calculations, simply type the number you want.

In using the cache in low memory, you must balance your programs' need for RAM space against the cache's. My advice is leave the cache size at 64K or increase the size to 128K at most. If your cache size is too large, your programs will suffer.

The final option is `Cache Page Size`. This option specifies the number of sectors that should be read from the disk when DOS reads any information from the disk. Regardless of how many sectors a program may request that DOS read, DOS will always read this many sectors at a time. This strategy is excellent for programs that start at the beginning of a file and read to the end. It is not always good for programs that randomly read files.

The starting value for `Cache Page Size` is four sectors. Do not change this value initially. There is no single optimum value for this option. You and your programs must determine what is the best value. Run your system for several hours or days. If you find the performance of some of your programs declining slightly, rerun IBMCACHE and change this value to two.

Once your options are set up properly, press Enter. You will see a message stating that changes you have made have been saved (see fig. 14.5). Press Enter once more and the DOS prompt should reappear.

To start the cache program, restart DOS. Press Ctrl-Alt-Del and shortly, you should see the following message:

```
Disk Cache   Version 1.Ø
Copyright 1987 by IBM Corp.
Allocating Cache Buffers
Cache Initialization Complete
```

The cache has been successfully installed.

If you want to change the options once the cache has been installed, you can either rerun IBMCACHE or edit the IBMCACHE line in your CONFIG.SYS file. The syntax for the IBMCACHE.SYS program is:

DEVICE = *d:path***IBMCACHE.SYS** cachesize /E or /NE /Psectors

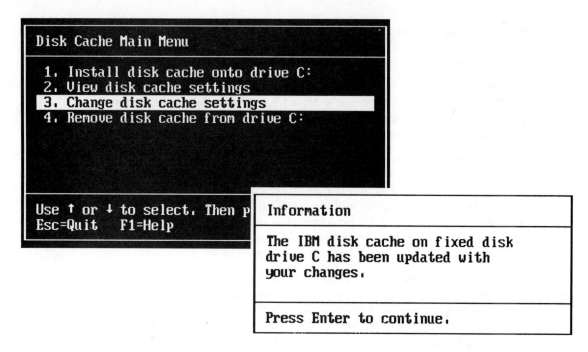

Fig. 14.5. *Changing IBMCACHE options.*

d:path is the optional disk drive and path name to the IBMCACHE.SYS program. cachesize is the size of the cache in kilobytes.

The /E and /NE switches designate where the cache will be placed: /E designates extended memory and /NE designates 640K low memory. You can use either, but not both switches.

/Psectors designates the number of disk sector that DOS should read at once. sectors should be 2, 4, or 8. Notice that, unlike many DOS switches, no colon is used to separate the P from sectors.

Should you install IBMCACHE.SYS? My opinion is an unqualified "maybe." I do believe you should experiment with the cache. You might find the cache can increase the performance of your system. However, if you use many programs that do a great deal of random accessing of files, the cache could actually be detrimental. Since the cache is easy and quick to install, alter, and remove, the effort of trying the cache is painless and may help speed your operations.

Using DRIVER.SYS To Control Additional Disk Drives

DRIVER.SYS is a device driver for disk drives. On most systems, DRIVER.SYS is an exotic extension. But for some systems that use an external floppy disk drive, DRIVER.SYS is required.

In Chapter 2, you learned that when you have only one floppy disk drive, DOS establishes two logical disk drives, A and B, from the single physical disk drive. You can perform the same kind of "trickery" on any disk drive with DRIVER.SYS.

Other occasions for using DRIVER.SYS arise when you use an external floppy disk drive or a non-IBM fixed disk drive that "looks like" (has the same physical characteristics) as the corresponding IBM fixed disk drive. You must inform DOS that the additional disk drive is attached to your system. When you invoke DRIVER.SYS for these disk drives, DOS makes the drive an integral part of the system.

You can also load an additional copy of DRIVER.SYS so that DOS will make two logical disk drives out of the single, physical disk drive. With this technique, you can copy files between two diskettes on the single external disk drive.

You must use DRIVER.SYS if you use an external disk drive with any Personal Computer. You also must use DRIVER.SYS with an external disk drive used with a PS/2 computer that has two internal floppy disk drives. But you do not have to use DRIVER.SYS for the external disk drive on a PS/2 computer that has one internal floppy disk drive.

Before you use DRIVER.SYS, read the information and explanations on the directive's switches, particularly the /D switch. If you do not provide DOS with the needed information, DRIVER.SYS will not work properly.

The syntax for DRIVER.SYS is

DEVICE = *d:path*\DRIVER.SYS /D:*ddd* /F:*f* /T:*ttt* /S:*ss* /H:*hh* /C /N

d: is the disk drive that holds DRIVER.SYS, and *path*\ is the directory path to DRIVER.SYS. Both directives are optional but should be given.

DRIVER.SYS has seven switches: **/D:ddd**, */F:f*, */T:ttt*, */S:ss*, */H:hh*, /C and /N. /D is the physical disk drive number. /F:f identifies the type of disk drive the computer uses. */T:ttt*, /S:ss and /H:hh define physical aspects of the disk drive. /C and /N refer to additional characteristics about the disk drive. DRIVER.SYS's switches are described further in the rest of this section.

/D:ddd is the mandatory physical disk drive number. The allowable numbers for ddd are 0 to 255. You use the numbers 0 to 127 for floppy diskettes. The first physical floppy disk drive, drive A, is 0, the second, drive B, is 1, and the third is 2. The values 3 to 127 for floppy disks are possible in theory, but IBM does not support these additional drives. For fixed disk drives, you use the numbers 128 to 255. The first fixed disk, drive C, is 128, the second, is 129, and so on. As with floppy disks, the values 130 to 255 can theoretically be used for additional fixed disk drives, but not in fact.

There is one potential source of confusion in giving disk drive numbers. If you have an external minifloppy disk drive for a PS/2 computer that has a single internal floppy disk, the external drive is the second physical disk drive. You use a 1 for the external disk drive.

If you give a number that corresponds to a nonexistent disk drive, DRIVER.SYS will happily install itself with no indication that anything is wrong. When you attempt to use the disk drive through its logical drive name, however, DOS will display a General Failure error. To correct the problem, you will need to edit the incorrect DRIVER.SYS entry and reboot the computer.

The /F:f switch identifies the type of disk drive used. /F:f is called the *form factor* switch. The *f* portion of the switch is a single digit from the following list:

0   160K to 360K minifloppy disk drive

1   1.2M minifloppy disk drive

2   720K microfloppy or other disk drive (any disk drive not on this list)

7   1.44M microfloppy disk drive

If you do not give the /F:f switch, a value of 2 will be used.

The T:ttt switch indicates the number of tracks per side (or cylinder) for the disk drive. The *ttt* can range from 1 to 999, and if you do not specify the switch, a value of 80 tracks is assumed. (1.2M, 720K, and 1.44M floppy disk drives use 80 tracks.)

/S:ss indicates the number of sectors per track. The range of *ss* is 1 to 99, and if you do not specify the switch, a value of 9 sectors per track is assumed. (360K and 720K floppy disk drives use 9 sectors per track.)

The /H:hh switch indicates the maximum number of recording heads per disk drive. The range of *hh* is 1 to 99, and if you do not specify the switch, two heads per disk drive are assumed. (Except for older, single-sided minifloppy disk drives, this rule is correct for all floppy disk drives.)

Never shortchange your disk drive when you give these switches. Use the correct value. For example, don't give /S:8 or /H:1 to read 8-sector, single-sided diskettes on a 360K disk drive. Don't give /S:9 to read 720K diskettes on a 1.44M disk drive. Internally, DOS usually knows how to produce a smaller capacity diskette from a higher capacity disk drive. Using settings smaller than is allowable simply shortchanges your computer capacity without adding any capabilities.

The /C switch indicates that the disk drive supports a *changeline*. This means the disk drive "knows" when the microfloppy diskette has been ejected or when the minifloppy's door has been opened. This switch is used with 1.2M, 720K, and 1.44M disk drives on PS/2, Personal Computer AT, and 286-XT computers.

The /N switch indicates that the disk drive is *nonremovable*. Basically, the /N switch refers to a fixed disk. This switch should not be used with floppy disk drives.

Table 14.4 lists the DRIVER.SYS switches for common floppy disk drives.

Table 14.4
DRIVER.SYS Switches for Common Floppy Disk Drives

Disk Drive	Switches
160K/180K	/F:0 /T:40 /S:9 /H:1
320K/360K	/F:0 /T:40 /S:9 /H:2
1.2M	/F:1 /T:80 /S:15 /H:2 /C
720K*	/F:2 /T:80 /S:9 /H:2 /C
1.2M	/F:7 /T:80 /S:18 /H:2 /C

Note: The /C switch is meaningful only with the PS/2, the Personal Computer AT, and PC 286-XTs. The switch should not be used with other PCs.

Here are some examples of using DRIVER.SYS. If you have a PS/2 computer with two internal disk drives, the syntax to use an external minifloppy disk drive is

DEVICE = DRIVER.SYS /D:2 /F:0 /T:40

/D:2 designates the third disk drive. This line is not needed if you have only one internal microfloppy disk drive. If you do not specify the /T:40 switch, DOS will assume that the disk drive uses 80 tracks per side—an error that the 360K disk cannot handle. In this case, the switch is required. The /F:0 is also required.

If you want to use the single external physical disk drive as two logical disk drives, you load the device driver twice. The syntax for this setup is

DEVICE = DRIVER.SYS /D:2 /F:0 /T:40
DEVICE = DRIVER.SYS /D:2 /F:0 /T:40

I will explain more about using DRIVER.SYS for additional logical disk drives later in this chapter.

To use an external 1.2M disk drive on a PS/2 computer, use the syntax line:

DEVICE = DRIVER.SYS /D:2 /F:1 /S:15 /C

Because the form factor and number of sectors are different from those DOS would establish if you did not specify these switches, you must provide the /F and /S switches. Notice the /C switch, the changeline support switch. PS/2s, Personal Computer ATs, and 286-XTs can recognize and use the changeline of floppy disk drives, so you specify the /C switch.

The difference in changeline support is the reason this directive would be used for an external 720K microfloppy on a Personal Computer AT or 286-XT. The syntax for this setup is

DEVICE = DRIVER.SYS /D:2 /C

Use this DRIVER.SYS syntax for an external 720K microfloppy disk drive on a PC or PC XT:

DEVICE = DRIVER.SYS /D:2

The PC and XT do not recognize disk drive changelines, so no /C switch is given. Notice that none of the other switches need be given, either. DRIVER.SYS's default settings fit the 720K disk drive.

If the 720K disk drive used in the preceding examples were an internal drive, you would use 1 for the value of the /D switch. For example, to use an internal 720K microfloppy disk drive in a Personal Computer AT, the directive is

DEVICE = DRIVER.SYS /D:1 /C

Regardless of drive type, /D:1 designates the second internal floppy disk drive.

You can also load a copy of DRIVER.SYS to use with established disk drives. The copy of DRIVER.SYS, with the appropriate switches, will establish a second logical disk drive for the physical disk.

You do not need this technique if you have a single floppy disk drive computer. But you can use the technique when you have two disk drives. For example, suppose that you have a Personal Computer AT with 1.2M and 360K internal minifloppy disk drives. To use drive A as two logical disk drives, the directive would be

    DEVICE = DRIVER.SYS /D:0 /S:15 /C /F:1

To use drive B, the 360K drive, as two logical disk drives, the directive would be

    DEVICE = DRIVER.SYS /D:1 /T:40 /F:0

You could use both directives and have four logical drives from the two physical disk drives. If you have one fixed disk drive, the "second" 1.2M drive would be D and the "second" 360K drive would be E. In this way, you could use either disk drive to copy files between diskettes.

Cautions about Logical Disk Drives

I should give you two cautions about logical disk drives. Both relate to the order of the DRIVER.SYS directives, the VDISK.SYS directive, and the disk drive names that DOS assigns to the logical disk drives.

The first caution is that the logical disk drive names that DOS assigns to DRIVER.SYS and VDISK depend on the placement of the directives in the CONFIG.SYS file. You may try to use the wrong disk drive name if you do not know how DOS assigns drive names.

Normally, CONFIG.SYS directives are *order independent*. That is, you can give the directives in any order you desire, and the computer will not change how the directive operates.

VDISK.SYS and DRIVER.SYS do not have the same independence, however. The order in which you use these directives can make a difference in how you use your computer. You can load VDISK.SYS and DRIVER.SYS in any order and the device drivers will work. But the disk drive names will change. Whenever DOS encounters a block-device driver, DOS assigns the next highest drive letter to the device. The order is first come, first served (actually, first assigned).

For example, load a copy of VDISK.SYS on a fixed disk system. DOS assigns the disk drive name D: to the RAM disk. If you load a second copy of VDISK.SYS (this works only on a machine that has extended memory), DOS assigns the drive name E: to the second RAM disk.

Instead of VDISK, load a copy of DRIVER.SYS for the external floppy disk drive on the same computer. DOS assigns the external disk drive the name D:. Load another copy of DRIVER.SYS (for example, to copy diskettes on the external disk drive) and DOS assigns the logical name E: to this disk drive.

Remember that additional fixed disks or additional logical fixed disks add to the starting letter. For example, the fixed disk drive on a 40M PS/2 system has the drive names C: and D:. Additional partitions of the fixed disk always get the next highest available disk drive letters before drives created by CONFIG.SYS directives are considered. Hence, the second partition of the fixed disk is named D:. VDISK, if used, is assigned drive E:. DRIVER.SYS, if used instead of VDISK, would be assigned E:.

The potential for further confusion comes when several block device drivers are loaded. The order of loading, which is determined by the order of the directives in the CONFIG.SYS file, determines what disk drive names will be assigned by DOS.

If you load VDISK.SYS first and DRIVER.SYS second, the RAM disk gets the next available disk drive letter (D). DRIVER.SYS will be one letter higher than the RAM disk (E). If you interchange the lines that hold the two directives, the disk drive names will be interchanged. DRIVER.SYS will be named D and VDISK.SYS will be named E.

Load two copies of DRIVER.SYS, for example, for a Personal Computer AT with a 1.2M and a 360K floppy disk drive. The lines are arranged in this order:

```
DEVICE = DRIVER.SYS /D:0 /S:15 /C /F:1
DEVICE = DRIVER.SYS /D:1 /T:40 /F:0
```

DOS assigns D to the 1.2M disk and E to the 360K disk drive. In other words, drive A and logical disk drive D will be the same physical disk drive. Drive B and logical disk drive E will be the same. Reverse the order of the lines and disk drives A and E are the same physical disk drive; drives B and D are the same disk drive.

Put the line DEVICE = VDISK.SYS in your CONFIG.SYS file before the two DRIVER.SYS lines, and the result is that the VDISK is drive D. Drives A and E would be the same; drives B and F would be the same. Put the VDISK line after the DRIVER.SYS lines and VDISK becomes drive F.

When you use DRIVER.SYS and VDISK.SYS or multiple copies of DRIVER.SYS, plan which drive names each logical disk drive should have. Also consider any logical disk drive DOS automatically adds for a partitioned fixed disk. Then add the directives in the order of the disk drive letters, lower letter driver before higher letter driver.

For example, I run an external minifloppy disk drive on a 40M PS/2, but I also use VDISK. The fixed disk is assigned drives C and D. DOS recognizes the physical minifloppy disk drive as B. To copy files between minifloppy diskettes without using the fixed disk, I invoke DRIVER.SYS once to make two logical disk drives out of the single physical disk drive. However, because I use the copy operation infrequently and I use the RAM disk more, I want VDISK to be drive E, the next letter after the two fixed disks. The lines in my CONFIG.SYS file are

```
DEVICE = VDISK.SYS 360 512 64
DEVICE = DRIVER.SYS /D:1 /T:40 /F:0
```

VDISK is drive E. The external disk drive is logical drive F (and physical disk drive B). Because VDISK appears first in the CONFIG.SYS file, DOS assigns VDISK the next available drive letter (E). The copy of DRIVER.SYS, which handles the external disk drive, is assigned the next ascending letter (F).

If I wanted the external disk drive to be E and VDISK to be F, I would reorder the lines like this:

```
DEVICE = DRIVER.SYS /D:1 /T:40 /F:0
DEVICE = VDISK.SYS 360 512 64
```

The second caution concerns using DRIVER.SYS with the external disk drive. If you have an external disk drive, the DRIVER.SYS line for this drive should appear before any additional DRIVER.SYS lines for other drives. If you reverse the order and use a copy of DRIVER.SYS for any other disk drive, you can "cover up" and lose the use of the external disk drive. This problem occurs if you do not have a system with one internal floppy and one internal fixed disk. To simplify the situation, make the first DRIVER.SYS directive the one that concerns the external disk drive.

DRIVER.SYS has two purposes. DRIVER.SYS is a required device driver when you use a non-IBM fixed disk drive, or if you use an external disk drive on the PC family of computers. DRIVER.SYS is required on PS/2 computers when two internal floppy disk drives are already in use. DRIVER.SYS can optionally make additional logical disk drives from the one physical disk drive.

I suggest that you use DRIVER.SYS only when you need to: when you use a non-IBM disk drive, when you use an external microfloppy disk drive on a PC-family computer, or when you use an external minifloppy on a PS/2 that has two internal floppy disk drives. Unless you have a compelling reason, I suggest that you avoid using DRIVER.SYS to create additional logical disk drives. If you need to copy files between floppy diskettes, first copy to the fixed disk, and then copy to the second floppy diskette. Or use DISKCOPY to make a copy of the entire diskette. These methods cause fewer problems than using DRIVER.SYS.

Making a CONFIG.SYS File

You may want to use the following major directives with DOS V3: BUFFERS, DEVICE, FCBS, and FILES. You can use any text editor, including EDLIN, or the COPY command to make the CONFIG.SYS file. Remember that the system-configuration file must be called CONFIG.SYS.

Following is my copy of CONFIG.SYS for an IBM PS/2 Model 60 and a Personal Computer AT:

```
BUFFERS = 30
FILES = 20
FCBS = 20,20
LASTDRIVE = F
DEVICE = c:\sys\ansi.sys
DEVICE = c:\sys\vdisk.sys 64 128 64 /e:8
```

This sample CONFIG.SYS file is a good one to use with any fixed disk system. The file assumes that you have a subdirectory called \SYS on your fixed disk and that device drivers are in this subdirectory. If you are using a PS/2 Model 30, or any member of the PC family except the AT, omit the /e:8 from the VDISK line.

Another line you might add for the PS/2 Models 50 through 80 concerns the IBMCACHE.SYS file. A typical line might look like this:

```
DEVICE = c:\sys\ibmcache.sys 200 /E /P:4
```

which sets the size of the cache to 200K, places the cache in extended memory, and directs the cache to read 4 sectors at a time.

The CONFIG.SYS file calls for a 64K RAM disk. If you have extended memory (RAM above the 640K point on a PS/2), you can use the following line instead:

```
DEVICE = c:\sys\vdisk.sys 360 512 112 /e:8
```

This sets up a 360K RAM disk in the extended memory of the AT. It also means you must eliminate the IBMCACHE.SYS line for the CONFIG.SYS file. Given the way the IBMCACHE.SYS works, I would opt for the RAM disk rather than the disk cache.

I use the following CONFIG.SYS file on my floppy-disk-based Toshiba 1100+®:

```
BUFFERS = 20
FILES = 20
FCBS = 20,20
LASTDRIVE = F
DEVICE = ansi.sys
DEVICE = vdisk.sys 64 128 64
```

Notice that I have assumed here that the device-driver software is in the root directory of my start-up diskette. I also have reduced the number of BUFFERS to 20.

Put the appropriate file in the root directory of your DOS boot diskette. If you are using a fixed disk system, such as the PC XT or Personal Computer AT, put the file in the root directory of the fixed disk. If you have included the fifth or sixth lines (**DEVICE** = **ansi.sys** or **DEVICE** = **vdisk.sys**), copy the ANSI.SYS file and/or the VDISK.SYS file to the disk you will use for booting.

If you use a 256K PC, you may want to omit the VDISK line and reduce the number of buffers to ten.

After you have saved the file, reboot the system, using your new disk. DOS will read the CONFIG.SYS file and alter itself to accommodate any directives in the file.

If you change the CONFIG.SYS file, the changes will be implemented the next time you boot the system from the disk. Remember that CONFIG.SYS is used only when DOS starts up.

Summary

In this chapter, you learned the following important points:

1. When DOS starts, it can alter system settings through instructions in the CONFIG.SYS file.

2. The CONFIG.SYS file must be in the root directory of the boot disk. When you alter CONFIG.SYS, the changes do not occur until DOS is restarted.

3. The CONFIG.SYS directives include:

BREAK	Determines when DOS looks for the Ctrl-Break sequence
BUFFERS	Sets the number of disk buffers
DEVICE	Assigns new or changed devices
FCBS	Sets the maximum number of FCBs
FILES	Sets the maximum number of file handles
LASTDRIVE	Sets the last logical DOS disk drive
SHELL	Sets the command processor to be used
STACKS	Sets the number of stacks used by DOS

4. VDISK, the DOS RAM-disk software, can speed disk operations if your computer has sufficient random-access memory.

5. IBMCACHE, the DOS disk cache, can speed up certain disk operations.

6. DRIVER, the device driver for disk drives, must be used for external or non-IBM fixed disk drives. DRIVER can also be used to make additional logical disk drives from one physical disk drive.

In Chapter 15, you'll learn how to make DOS operate in languages other than English.

15

Making DOS Go International

The Personal Computer, PS/2 computers, and MS-DOS, the foundation of PC DOS, are American inventions. But DOS is an international operating system. Vast changes in MS-DOS V2.11 made DOS easier to use in countries outside the United States. Additional changes have occurred in each revision of DOS V3, the most radical changes since DOS V2.11 being in DOS V3.3. If you use the computer in a country other than the United States, these changes make the computer more natural to use.

DOS V3 has several international features seldom noticed by North American users. One feature is that the date and time can be displayed in three different formats. Also, DOS can inform a program on request which characters to use for the decimal point, the thousand separator, and the currency symbol. DOS can even tell the program whether the currency symbol precedes or follows the amount and whether a space should separate the symbol from the amount.

In addition, the display and keyboard of Personal Computers and PS/2s can be changed to produce characters that are appropriate for countries other than the United States. Although non-U.S. users have had these programs since DOS V1.1, IBM now distributes the programs as part of DOS V3.

To make DOS go international, you must alter your CONFIG.SYS and AUTOEXEC.BAT files. If you "switch" countries often, you also may find that copying some files to the root directory is helpful. These changes are recommended only for those who need the international capability. If you do not need this capability, I suggest that you skip this chapter and skim it later at your leisure.

To customize DOS for international use, you may need to perform several actions:

1. Add the following items to your CONFIG.SYS file:
   a. the COUNTRY directive
   b. the DEVICE=DISPLAY.SYS directive
   c. the DEVICE=PRINTER.SYS directive

2. Add the NLSFUNC, MODE, CHCP, and/or KEYB commands to your AUTOEXEC.BAT file.

You also should be aware of the GRAFTABL program, which can affect your use of international characters.

Before you study these directives, let's look at the concept of code pages, which is new to V3.3.

Understanding Code Pages

If someone were to select the most radical change in DOS V3.3, the concept of *code pages* would be among the top choices. Code pages allow the computer to use, display, and print non-English language characters with minimal effort on the user's part.

You recall from earlier discussions that your computer speaks ASCII. ASCII is the standard manner of taking the numeric values 0 to 255 and translating the values into letters, numbers, and symbols. The dots on your screen that form the visible characters are the graphic representations of those ASCII numbers.

Think of a punchboard with holes arranged in a 16-by-16 square, for a total of 256 holes. You can move to any hole, punch it, and get the message or prize inside.

Your computer has three punchboards, one each for the keyboard, video display, and printer. Step up to the board and punch the hole marked 65. Out pops the character whose ASCII value is 65, the letter A.

When you press the A key, your computer punches the video adapter's hole for 65. The adapter, in turn, looks up the numeric value and finds the pattern of dots that corresponds to the character. The adapter turns on the appropriate dots, and the letter "A" appears on the screen.

Each video adapter displays a dot-formed representation of ASCII characters. The common name for the "shape" of characters is *font*. Depending on the adapter in use, the fonts are switchable, meaning that different character sets can be displayed.

Basically, a code page is a typeface, or font set. You may recognize names for typewriter and typesetting faces such as Courier, Elite, and Times Roman. Similarly, code pages allow for different typefaces of English and international language characters.

Five video adapters are available: the Monochrome Adapter, the Color/Graphics Display (CGA), the Enhanced Color/Graphics Adapter (EGA), the Liquid Crystal Display (LCD) of the PC Convertible laptop, and the Video Graphics Array (VGA) of the PS/2. (The LCD and VGA are not truly adapters but are integrated circuitry built into the computers and are responsible for the display of information.)

If you have compared characters on the different displays, you may have noticed that the sharpest characters are on the Monochrome and the VGA displays. These displays use characters that are 9 dots wide by 16 dots high. The next best is the EGA, which uses characters formed by a 9-dot by 14-dot matrix. The CGA and the LCD display of the PC Convertible both use an 8-dot by 8-dot matrix.

Different font "punchboards" can be used, depending on the type of video adapter in use. The layout of each punchboard is the same: 16 rows by 16 columns, for a total of 256 holes. The punchboard can change the number of dots used to display each character, or it can produce different characters at a given hole.

For example, the VGA and the EGA have two punchboards (font sets) built in. The VGA has the 9-dot by 16-dot set and an 8-by-8 set. The EGA has a 9-by-14 set and an 8-by-8 set. Both adapters can thus duplicate the results of the CGA adapter, which uses the 8-dot by 8-dot matrix for its characters. Depending on the punchboard in use, picking the 65 hole produces a 9-dot by 14- or 16-dot "A", or an 8-dot by 8-dot "A".

The VGA, the EGA, and the LCD displays can use the five international fonts sets listed below. Depending on the punchboard (code page) used, you can display various language characters as indicated in table 15.1. Monochrome and CGA adapters cannot support switchable code pages.

Table 15.1
Code Page Numbers

Font	Code Page Number
Canada-French	863
Multilingual	850
Norway and Denmark	865
Portugal	860
United States	437

To illustrate, punch the hole for ASCII character 236. Each font set except the Multilingual code page displays the infinity character. The Multilingual code page displays an accented Y. Punch position number 157 on the North American set, and you get the double-bar Y. Punch the same position on the Multilingual or Norwegian-Danish sets, and you get an O with a slash through the character. The Portuguese and French Canadian sets have a back-accented U in this position. Many characters are identical in all five sets, but some are customized for various localities.

The idea of switchable fonts is important for international use of the Personal Computer and PS/2. Although English is a worldwide language, many languages use non-English characters with diacritics: accents, umlauts, and grave (back-accent) characters. The adapters have some, but not all, of these characters.

Appendix G contains the five code pages used by PCs and PS/2 computers. You might glance at the five sets, looking especially at the characters above ASCII 127 (the columns 9 through F on the charts). The major difference between these code pages is the characters whose values are in the range of 128 through 255. There is no widely used prevailing standard for these characters. DOS sacrifices some of the scientific and graphics characters in this range and substitutes the needed language characters.

Printers also use code pages; hence, what can be displayed on the screen can be reproduced on the printed page. DOS V3.3 includes code pages for the IBM ProPrinter™ and Quietwriter® III printers. You can expect other printer manufacturers to follow Microsoft and IBM's lead and provide code pages for their printers some time in 1988.

As you now know, code pages are switchable. Although you select a starting code page, you can change code pages freely. You can start with the North American font, switch to the Multilingual font, then switch to the Danish/Norwegian font, switch back to the North American font, and so on.

To switch fonts, you must have installed two device drivers: DISPLAY.SYS for your display and PRINTER.SYS for your printer. These drivers are discussed in the section "Seeing and Printing Languages." Note, however, that DISPLAY.SYS does not work with all adapters. And PRINTER.SYS works with a limited set of printers. You may find that you cannot switch code pages because of your hardware.

Also, you may find code page switching completely unnecessary. If your video adapter starts with the "right" code page and you do not need another code page, you don't need DISPLAY.SYS. If your printer starts with the right code page and you don't need another code page, PRINTER.SYS is unneeded.

Switching code pages may be important for international users who have files that were established before the release of DOS V3.3 and for users who must process files created or used in different countries. The ability to change fonts "on the fly" is available to those who need the capability; it can be ignored by all others.

The topic of code pages produces one of two effects in computer users: excitement or complete boredom. Most North American users will find the built-in DOS code pages adequate. These users probably will never use code page switching. However, those in international corporations or those using their computers outside the United States and English-speaking Canada will find that code pages are a logical and powerful way to handle languages.

Using the COUNTRY Directive To Specify a Country

The first step in making DOS go international is issuing the COUNTRY directive to inform DOS how to customize itself for your location. We take up that topic in the next section.

COUNTRY is a CONFIG.SYS directive that allows you to specify the country the computer is configured for. When you issue COUNTRY, DOS automatically changes the date and time formats to conform to the practice in the country specified. In addition, DOS can tell inquiring programs what characters to use for lists, currency symbols, thousands, and decimal fractions.

COUNTRY for DOS V3.3 has a different syntax from COUNTRY for DOS V3.0 through V3.2. The V3.0-3.2 syntax is

COUNTRY = nnn

The syntax for V3.3 is

COUNTRY = countrycode *codepage d:path\filename.ext*

in which **countrycode** is the mandatory three-digit code for the country. *codepage* is the code page number selected from table 15.2, which lists the countries currently supported by DOS. Although the country code currently supports 19 countries, only five code pages are available.

d:path\filename.ext is the path and file name for the COUNTRY information file. The information for various countries was built into DOS itself for V2.11 through V3.2. DOS V3.3 keeps this information in a

separate file called COUNTRY.SYS, which is provided on the DOS Startup/
Operating or Startup diskette. If you use the COUNTRY directive but do
not provide this file name, DOS uses the file COUNTRY.SYS and assumes
that the file is located in the root directory of the Startup diskette.

**Table 15.2
Country Codes**

Country/Language	Country Code	Keyboard Code	Existing Code Page	New Code Page
Arabic*	785	none	none	none
Australia	061	US	437	850
Belgium	032	BE	437	850
Canada-English*	001	US	437	850
Canada-French	002	CF	863	850
Denmark	045	DK	865	850
Finland	358	SU	437	850
France	033	FR	437	850
Germany	049	GR	437	850
Israel	972	none	437	850
Italy	039	IT	437	850
Latin America*	003	LA	437	850
Netherlands	031	NL	437	850
Norway	047	NO	865	850
Portugal	351	PO	860	850
Spain	034	SP	437	850
Sweden	046	SV	437	850
Switzerland-French*	041	SF	437	850
Switzerland-German	041	SG	437	850
United Kingdom	044	UK	437	850
United States	001	US	437	850

* indicates additional to DOS V3.3

The country code for the United States is 001. If you do not set this
option in CONFIG.SYS, the country code defaults to that of the United
States. If you don't find your country listed, use the code for the most
familiar country that is listed.

For the code page, North American users of English should use the United
States code page (number 437). If you cannot find a code page number
for your country, the Multilingual code page (number 850) is probably
your best choice.

You can skip the code page or the country information file if you want. To give the COUNTRY.SYS file name but skip the code page number, use two commas between the country code and the COUNTRY.SYS file:

COUNTRY = 001,,C:\COUNTRY.SYS

The two commas instruct DOS to use the default code page. If you want to omit the file name, give either the country code or the country code and code page, such as

COUNTRY = 001

or

COUNTRY = 001 437

If you use the COUNTRY directive, however, DOS searches for the file COUNTRY.SYS in the root directory of the boot disk. If DOS cannot find the file, DOS displays the message

```
Bad or missing \COUNTRY.SYS
```

A sensible place to put the COUNTRY.SYS file is the directory that holds other SYS files. If you do so, give the full disk drive name, path name, and file name for COUNTRY.SYS. The COUNTRY.SYS file is used by several other programs. If you omit the disk drive name or path name, DOS may not be able to find the COUNTRY.SYS file later. Therefore, I strongly recommend that you always give the full file name for COUNTRY.SYS, even if the file is in the disk's root directory. This step will prevent unpleasant surprises later.

To see the effects of using various country codes, I wrote a C program that sets the country code and displays the varying information available from DOS. The output from the DATE and TIME programs is included. You can see how the information changes when different country codes are used.

```
country code is    1
country name is United States/Canada - English
code page is 437

currency information:        currency symbol is :$:
                             currency symbol precedes value,
                             with no space between symbol and
                             value.
                             digits after decimal separator in
                             currency is 2
numeric/list                 thousand separator is :,:
information:

                             decimal separator is :.:
                             data list separator is :,:
date/time information:       date separator is :-:
                             time separator is :::
                             time format is 24 hour format

Current date is Tue 7-21-1987
Current time is 16:24:39.01

country code is 44
country name is United Kingdom
code page is 437

currency information:        currency symbol is :£:
                             currency symbol precedes value,
                             with no space between symbol and
                             value.
                             digits after decimal separator in
                             currency is 2
numeric/list                 thousand separator is :,:
information:

                             decimal separator is :.:
                             data list separator is :,:
date/time information:       date separator is :-:
                             time separator is :::
                             time format is 24 hour format

Current date is Tue 21-07-1987
Current time is 16:25:13.56

country code is 46
country name is Sweden
code page is 437
```

```
currency information:        currency symbol is :SEK:
                             currency symbol precedes value,
                             with one space between symbol and
                             value.
                             digits after decimal separator in
                             currency is 2
numeric/list                 thousand separator is :.:
information:

                             decimal separator is :,:
                             data list separator is :;:
date/time information:       date separator is :-:
                             time separator is :.:
                             time format is 12 hour format

Current date is Tue 1987-07-21
Current time is 16.25.09,22
```

In addition, DOS V3.3 makes even more information about a country available to programs, including information about switching lowercase and uppercase letters and sorting characters. Although each English uppercase letter has a lowercase letter, in some languages, characters do not have direct equivalents. DOS V3.3 provides the information for programs to take any incoming character and determine if the character has an uppercase equivalent.

DOS also provides additional information about sorting characters. In sorting letters, the preferred practice in American English is to treat uppercase and lowercase characters the same. Hence, the word *SORT* is the same as the word *Sort* and the word *sort*. However, there are times when an uppercase *A* should be sorted differently than a lowercase *a*. Added to the problem are characters that don't quite fit English-language sorting sequences, such as the German ß or Latin *æ*.

The table for SORT is part of V3.3 only. Previously, SORT itself held the collation table.

Fortunately, DOS V3.3 can provide programs with the information needed to handle these problems. DOS maintains information on sorting characters based on the country code and the code page, both of which affect the sorting order. That's why both pieces of information are needed.

The COUNTRY directive is not important to most DOS users in the United States. If you do nothing, your computer adapts automatically to its local country, the United States.

COUNTRY does have some limitations. For instance, DOS does not display its prompts automatically in languages other than English. For that refinement, DOS messages must be rewritten. The COUNTRY directive does set up the fundamental information for the locale and establishes starting display, printer, and keyboard characters.

To display more than one code page or to print non-English language characters, you must use the DISPLAY.SYS and PRINTER.SYS device drivers. They are described in the next section.

Displaying and Printing Different Languages

The two device drivers that were not discussed in Chapter 14 are DISPLAY.SYS and PRINTER.SYS. Using DISPLAY.SYS in your CONFIG.SYS file allows you to switch code pages without restarting DOS. Using PRINTER.SYS allows you to download a font table to certain printers so that they can print non-English language and graphic characters. Of course, not all DOS international users need or can use these capabilities. I suggest that you read about DISPLAY.SYS and PRINTER.SYS before you make these files part of your setup.

DOS 3.3's support of different languages depends not only on these two device drivers, but also on the NLSFUNC program and on the CHCP, MODE PREPARE, MODE SELECT, MODE REFRESH, and KEYB commands. All of these will receive a complete explanation in this chapter, but table 15.3 summarizes the effect on DOS, the console (the CON: device, including both the display and the keyboard), and the printer. You may want to refer to this table as you work your way through the rest of the chapter.

Table 15.3
The Effects of Various Commands and Device Drivers
on DOS, the Console, and the Printer

		DISPLAY.SYS	PRINTER.SYS	NLSFUNC	CHCP	MODE PREPARE	MODE SELECT	MODE REFRESH	KEYB
DOS		X	–	X	X	–	–	–	–
CON:	DISPLAY	X	–	–	X	X	X	X	O
	KEYBOARD	O	–	–	X	O	O	O	X
PRINTER		–	X	–	X	X	X	X	–

KEY: X   Sets or changes
        O   Affects but does not set or change
        –   No effect

Displaying International Characters with DISPLAY.SYS

The DISPLAY driver allows the switching of code pages on most video adapters. DISPLAY.SYS is ineffective with the Monochrome or Color/Graphics adapter. The code pages of these adapters are fixed and cannot be switched. If you have a Monochrome or Color/Graphics adapter, DISPLAY.SYS is not recommended for your use.

The adapters that can be used effectively with DISPLAY.SYS are the PC Convertible LCD, the EGA, and the VGA.

The line to add to the CONFIG.SYS file is

DEVICE = *d:path*\ DISPLAY.SYS CON: = (type, *hw_codepage,*
         (added_codepages, subfonts))

After the explanation of each element in the command line, sample lines are given, showing how you can delete some elements to make the line easier to enter.

d:path\ is the drive name and path to DISPLAY.SYS. If DISPLAY.SYS is not in the root directory of your starting disk, give the disk drive and path name.

CON: is the DOS device name for the console—the keyboard and display. The colon after the device name is optional.

After the word CON comes an equal sign, followed by the parameters to DISPLAY.SYS enclosed in parentheses. The equal sign and enclosing parentheses must be given. The first parameter, the display type, can be any of the following:

MONO	Monochrome Adapter
CGA	Color/Graphics Adapter
EGA	Enhanced Color/Graphics Adapter or PS/2
LCD	Convertible LCD

The second parameter is *hw_codepage*, which stands for the *hardware* code page built into your adapter. The possible values are 437, 850, 860, 863, and 865, the five code pages that IBM provides with DOS V3.3. If you do not give the *hw_codepage*, DISPLAY.SYS uses the code page given to the COUNTRY directive.

The value for *hw_codepage* depends on two factors: the appropriate existing page for your country, and whether you are using a previous version of DOS. Look at table 15.2. Find the line in the table for your country, and look at the Existing Code Page column and New Code Page column. If you are a new DOS user or if the entry in table 15.2 in the

Existing Code Page column is *not 437*, specify 850. Otherwise, specify 437.

The reason for the different possible values is that most North American adapters have the 437 code page built in. However, some systems sold in Europe or Quebec, Canada, before March of 1987 may have a different code page built into the adapter. The Existing Code Page values in table 15.1 reflect the potential differences.

added_codepages is the maximum number of additional code pages that the adapter can use. *added_codepages* actually refers to the number of code pages you can prepare and use with the MODE command, which is discussed later in this chapter.

added_codepages can range from 0 to 12 if you are using the PC Convertible, an EGA adapter, or the PS/2. If you are using the Monochrome or CGA adapter, you must give the number 0 for *added_codepages*, because these adapters cannot support code pages. If you do not give *added_codepages*, 0 is used for the MONO and CGA display types, and 1 for EGA and LCD.

If you have an EGA or VGA display, the minimum value you should use for *added_codepages* usually depends on the value in the Existing Code Page column in table 15.2. If your existing code page is 437, specify a minimum value of 1, which allows you to use the Multilingual code page in addition to the North American code page (437). If your existing code page is not 437, specify at least a value of 2. Doing so allows you to use the code page built into your adapter plus the Multilingual code page (850) and the 437 code page.

subfonts refers to the dot resolution of the character—9 by 14, 9 by 16, or 8 by 8. This number can range from 0 to 2, depending on the adapter. For the Monochrome and CGA adapters, *subfonts* is 0, which is the value DOS assumes if you do not give *subfonts*. For the LCD display, *subfonts* is 1, which is the value used if you don't give the parameter for the LCD display. For the EGA or PS/2, *subfonts* can be 1 or 2; for the adapter type EGA, DOS defaults to 2 *subfonts* if you omit this parameter.

Note that the default values for *subfonts* usually work, which means you normally can omit this parameter. When you omit *subfonts*, you also can omit the parentheses surrounding *added_codepages* and *subfonts*. In other words, give the information in the outer parentheses as

(type*, hw_codepage, added_codepages*)

Here is a sample command for those who use an EGA or VGA and 437 as the hardware code page:

DEVICE = C:\SYS\DISPLAY.SYS CON = (EGA,437,1)

This command specifies an EGA display (EGA is used for both the EGA and VGA displays), 437 for the the starting code page, and 1 additional code page. You don't need to use additional code pages, but if you plan to, you should specify the number for *added_codepages*.

This example assumes that the DISPLAY.SYS file is placed in a subdirectory on drive C called \SYS. If DISPLAY.SYS is in the root directory, the file name to use in this example is C:\DISPLAY.SYS. The other information remains the same.

The following command assumes that an EGA display is used and that the existing code page is 863 (French Canadian):

DEVICE = C:\SYS\DISPLAY.SYS CON = (EGA,850,2)

Notice that the existing code page is 863, but that the specified code page is 850. If your existing code page is not 437, always use 850 as the new code page and 2 as the value for added code pages.

If you use ANSI.SYS and DISPLAY.SYS in your CONFIG.SYS file, the ANSI.SYS directive must appear before the DISPLAY.SYS directive. If the order is reversed, you lose the capability of ANSI.SYS. Remember that DISPLAY.SYS is not required if you will not use code page switching. If you are new to DOS and will not use a font that is different from the one built into your display, you can ignore the DISPLAY.SYS driver.

Printing International Characters with PRINTER.SYS

PRINTER.SYS is the device driver that allows the characters shown in the code page sets to be printed on certain printers. To date, DOS V3.3 supports code pages on only these two printers:

IBM ProPrinter Model 4201
IBM Quietwriter III Model 5202

To use code page switching with these printers, you must add the DEVICE=PRINTER.SYS line to your CONFIG.SYS file. The syntax for PRINTER.SYS is similar to that for DISPLAY.SYS:

>   DEVICE = *d;path*\PRINTER.SYS LPTx: = (type, *hw_codepage,*
>   *added_codepages*) . . .

or

>   DEVICE = *d;path*\PRINTER.SYS LPTx: = (type, *(hw_codepage1,*
>   *hw_codepage2), added_codepages*) . . .

After each element in this line is explained, sample lines are given, showing how the line varies for each printer.

d;path\ is the drive name and path to PRINTER.SYS. If PRINTER.SYS is not in the root directory of your starting disk, give the disk drive and path name.

LPTx: is the DOS device name for the line printer. The **x** is the number of the parallel printer: 1, 2, or 3. The colon after the device name is optional. Because you can have up to three parallel printers, you must specify which parallel port the printer is connected to. You can also have up to three DEVICE=PRINTER.SYS lines in your CONFIG.SYS file.

After the word LPTx comes an equal sign, followed by the parameters to PRINTER.SYS enclosed in parentheses. The equal sign and enclosing parentheses must be given. The printer type is the model number for the printer: 4201 for the ProPrinter and 5202 for the Quietwriter III.

The second parameter, *hw_codepage*, stands for the *hardware* code page built into your printer. As with DISPLAY.SYS, the possible values are 437, 850, 860, 863, and 865.

There is a difference between the possible *hw_codepage* values for the two printers. The ProPrinter has one font built into the printer. This font is moved to the printer's RAM. When you change the code page for this printer, DOS overwrites the font that is in memory.

The Quietwriter III, on the other hand, uses hardware font cartridges. Each cartridge holds several code pages in the same type style. To use a particular code page, you must select the correct cartridge. The Quietwriter III cannot inform DOS when a cartridge has been changed; DOS must assume that the correct cartridge is in the printer.

The result is you can specify one hardware code page for the ProPrinter and two for the Quietwriter III. However, if you specify two code pages for the Quietwriter III, you cannot prepare any code pages for the printer—DOS assumes that both code pages are fixed in hardware.

For the ProPrinter, the value for *hw_codepage* follows the same guidelines as for DISPLAY.SYS. If you are a new DOS user or if the entry in the

Existing Code Page column in table 15.1 is *not 437*, specify 850. Otherwise, specify 437.

For the Quietwriter III, follow the same guidelines with one exception. You may specify two hardware code pages, such as 437 and 850. If you specify two code pages, DOS assumes that no code pages should be prepared for the Quietwriter III.

added_codepages is the maximum number of additional code pages that the printer can use. *added_codepages* can range from 0 to 12.

For the ProPrinter, if you either specify 0 or omit *added_codepages*, you get the ProPrinter's built-in font. If you specify a number other than 0, the number is the maximum number of additional code pages the ProPrinter can use. Generally, use 1 if your hardware code page is 437; otherwise, use 2.

For the Quietwriter III, if you have specified two code pages, you must either omit *added_codepages* or specify a value of 0. The reason is that no code pages can be prepared if you have specified two *hw_codepages*.

An example of the directive to use with a ProPrinter is

DEVICE = C:\SYS\PRINTER.SYS LPT1 = (4201, 437,1)

This directive calls for a ProPrinter connected to the first parallel port (LPT1), for 437 as the starting code page, and for 1 additional code page. You don't need to use additional code pages, but if you plan to, you should specify the number for *added_codepages*.

As with DISPLAY.SYS, this example assumes that the PRINTER.SYS file is placed in a subdirectory on drive C called \SYS. If PRINTER.SYS is in a different directory, change the disk drive and path information but leave all other information the same.

The following command assumes that the ProPrinter is used and that the existing code page is 863 (Canada-French):

DEVICE = C:\SYS\PRINTER.SYS LPT1 = (4201,850,2)

Notice that the existing code page is 863, but that the specified code page is 850. If your existing code page is not 437, always use 850 as the new code page, and use 2 as the value for added code pages.

Here is an example for the Quietwriter III that uses a 437 and 850 code page cartridge:

DEVICE = C:\SYS\PRINTER.SYS LPT1 = (5202,(437,850),0)

This directive follows the general form of the ProPrinter directive, but with the model number of the Quietwriter III (5202). Notice the parentheses that enclose the two code pages. If you give two code pages, you must surround them with parentheses. Also, the number of added code pages is set to 0.

If you have more than one of these printers attached to your system, you can include that information on one directive line. Assuming that the ProPrinter is connected to LPT1 and the Quietwriter III is connected to LPT2, the command would be

```
DEVICE = C:\SYS\PRINTER.SYS LPT1 = (4201,437,2)
            LPT2 = (5202,(437,850),0)
```

You simply use a space after the information for LPT1 and before the word LPT2. DOS loads PRINTER.SYS and sets up both printers at the same time.

Remember that PRINTER.SYS is not required if you will not use code page switching. If you will not use a font that is different from the one built into your printer, or if you do not use a ProPrinter or Quietwriter III printer, you can ignore the PRINTER.SYS device driver.

Using the International Character Programs

After you have added the appropriate DEVICE directives to the CONFIG.SYS file, you use several additional commands to set up and switch code pages for your display, printer, and keyboard. The following commands accomplish the setup and switching:

NLSFUNC	Enables the CHCP command
CHCP	Activates (changes) code pages
KEYB	Loads and activates code pages for the keyboard
MODE	Loads and activates code pages for the display and printer

These four commands are closely linked. CHCP depends on NLSFUNC, and KEYB depends on MODE and CHCP. We'll look at each command and explain briefly what it does, how to use it, and what steps must be performed before and after you use the command.

Supporting National Languages with NLSFUNC

NLSFUNC, the *national language support function*, is a DOS V3.3 program that performs two tasks. First, it hooks into DOS and provides programs with extended information about the specified country. Second, the program allows you to use the CHCP (change code page) command. If you will be switching code pages for any device except the keyboard, you need this command. Fortunately, NLSFUNC is one of the easiest commands to use and is typically included in the AUTOEXEC.BAT file.

The syntax for NLSFUNC is

dc:pathc**NLSFUNC** *d:path**COUNTRY.SYS*

NLSFUNC is an external command. *dc:* is the name of the disk drive that holds the command, and *pathc*\\ is the directory path to the command. Give or omit the disk drive and path name as needed.

The single parameter to NLSFUNC is the full file name to the COUNTRY.SYS file. This information must be given in any of three cases: (1) if you did not give the COUNTRY directive in CONFIG.SYS; (2) if DOS gave you a message that it could not find the COUNTRY.SYS file while starting the system; or (3) if the COUNTRY.SYS file has been moved (for instance, if the diskette that holds the file has been changed).

To simplify the use of NLSFUNC, use the COUNTRY directive in your CONFIG.SYS file and give the full file name for COUNTRY.SYS. Also, place the NLSFUNC command in your AUTOEXEC.BAT file. Because DOS uses the AUTOEXEC.BAT commands when you start the computer, including NLSFUNC and other needed international language commands in AUTOEXEC.BAT ensures that the commands will be issued correctly each time you start the computer. Because the startup diskette has the files, you will have fewer problems changing diskettes later.

You must run NLSFUNC first if you want to use the CHCP command, which is discussed in the next section. Certain applications programs also may require you to run NLSFUNC. These programs use the new extended country information provided by DOS V3.3. Your program's documentation should state whether the program requires NLSFUNC.

Because NLSFUNC becomes part of DOS, using NLSFUNC increases DOS by almost 2700 bytes. NLSFUNC remains in memory until you turn off the machine or restart DOS. You need to run NLSFUNC only once after you have started DOS. Running NLSFUNC a second time produces an error message.

For more information about NLSFUNC, see the *DOS Command Reference*.

Changing the Code Page with CHCP

CHCP, or *change code page*, is new to DOS V3.3 and is the simplest method of changing code pages. Because CHCP can affect the keyboard also, those using the KEYB program should be familiar with CHCP. The alternative to CHCP is the MODE CODEPAGE SELECT command. Because the syntax to MODE is more complicated, however, CHCP is the preferred command.

The syntax for CHCP is

  CHCP *codepage*

where *codepage*—the new code page for DOS and all the devices to use—can be 437, 850, 860, 863, or 865.

Using CHCP sets the code page for DOS and establishes information about sorting and about switching lowercase and uppercase characters. CHCP also sets the code page for devices. If you have included DISPLAY.SYS in your CONFIG.SYS file, CHCP sets the code page for the display. If you have included PRINTER.SYS in CONFIG.SYS, CHCP sets the code page for the printer. If you have used the KEYB program, CHCP sets the keyboard's code page as well. Because of these capabilities, CHCP can be thought of as a *system-wide* program. If you have set up any device to use code page switching, CHCP will set the device.

To use CHCP, you must first issue the NLSFUNC command. Doing so loads the CHCP command into memory and hooks CHCP to DOS. CHCP then becomes an internal command. Because NLSFUNC is required, you also should have given the COUNTRY directive in your CONFIG.SYS file. You also need to issue the necessary MODE CODEPAGE PREPARE commands before using CHCP (MODE is covered later in this chapter).

When CHCP switches code pages, it may need to read the COUNTRY.SYS file. CHCP uses either the location of COUNTRY.SYS from the COUNTRY directive of CONFIG.SYS, or the optional COUNTRY.SYS file name given to the NLSFUNC. If you are using a diskette-based system, make sure that the diskette also has a copy of COUNTRY.SYS. CHCP will not change code pages if it needs to read the COUNTRY.SYS file and cannot find the file.

The command for setting the code pages for DOS and all the devices to 437 is

  CHCP 437

You can get the current code page that DOS is using by simply issuing the CHCP command without a code page number:

CHCP

You will see the message:

```
Active code page:    437
```

Interestingly, CHCP can report the current code page for DOS even if you have not yet used NLSFUNC. However, if you want to use CHCP to change the code page, you must issue the NLSFUNC command first. If you have not used NLSFUNC and you try the command

CHCP 437

CHCP reports

```
Code page    437 not prepared for system
```

The error message is bogus. The real problem is that NLSFUNC is not installed in DOS. Normally, you get this message only if you have not used the MODE command to prepare additional code pages. If you get this message and are unsure whether NLSFUNC has been run, try running NLSFUNC. If you don't get an error message from NLSFUNC, the program was not already installed. If you do get an error message, MODE has not prepared the code page that CHCP complains about. You need to run the MODE CODE PREPARE command first.

CHCP does not increase the size of DOS and can be issued as often as you want.

Selecting a Language for the Keyboard with KEYB

The KEYB command is a program (or programs) that makes the keyboard of the PS/2, Personal Computer, and compatible systems multilingual. KEYB determines which characters can be typed on the keyboard.

KEYB for DOS V3.3 has major differences from KEYB for versions of DOS prior to V3.3. DOS pre-V3.3 KEYB programs should not be used with DOS

V3.3. Instead, use the older programs with the older DOS. Each version is discussed separately in the following sections.

KEYB for DOS V3.2 and Earlier Versions

The syntax for pre-V3.3 versions of KEYB is

d:path\KEYxx

d:\path is the optional disk drive and path name to the KEYB programs. The xx, which can be any one of the keyboard codes in table 15.4, adapts the keyboard and display to the character set of a particular language.

Table 15.4
Keyboard Codes for V3.0-V3.2 SELECT and KEYBxx

Country	Code
France	FR
Germany	GR
Italy	IT
Spain	SP
United Kingdom	UK
United States	US

To use the keyboard/display changer program, load the program into memory by typing the program's name. The KEYBxx program takes about 2K of memory and becomes a resident program. KEYBxx remains in memory until you reboot DOS or turn off the computer. Once the program is loaded, the native language character set for the KEYBxx program becomes active.

KEYB for DOS V3.3

The KEYB command for V3.3 has a different syntax and a set of requirements. KEYB alters the code page of the console (CON:, the keyboard and video display). If you will use keyboard layouts that need different code pages, you must "prepare" the console; that is, you must use the MODE CON CODEPAGE PREPARE command before you use KEYB. If you don't want to switch code pages, you can omit the MODE command and use CHCP instead. You can omit both commands if you don't plan on switching the console's code page. However, KEYB complains about not knowing the code page of the console. You can avoid this warning by using either MODE or CHCP.

The syntax for KEYB V3.3 is

　　*d:path***KEYB** *keyboardcode, codepage, d:path\\filename.ext*

d:path is the optional disk drive and path name to the KEYB command. *keyboardcode* is the two-character keyboard code for your country from table 15.4. If your country isn't listed, use the keyboard code that meets your needs most closely. If you want to set the keyboard to use a different language, you must give this parameter.

codepage is the optional code page you want to use with the keyboard. If you don't specify a code page, KEYB uses the default code page.

KEYB places one further restriction on keyboard codes and code pages. The keyboard code, the code page given to KEYB, and the console code page must all be compatible. Table 15.5 shows the allowable combinations.

The reason for this requirement has to do with the way KEYB works. Basically, KEYB translates the raw on-and-off codes produced by the keyboard hardware into ASCII characters. The ASCII characters built by KEYB are determined by the keyboard code and code page used by KEYB, and by the code page used by the console. KEYB builds a table of *keystroke codes to character translations* for each prepared console code page. The different combinations substitute the correct characters for each language. With each set of substitutions some characters "disappear," and other characters appear.

However, KEYB can build these translation tables only for certain keyboard-code page combinations. Sometimes, graphics characters must be sacrificed for language characters. The characters to type for these languages appear in certain code pages but not in others. Hence, using a keyboard layout with the wrong console code page means you get the wrong characters on the video screen. You type the "right" character, but you see the wrong character. For this reason, the keyboard code and code page that KEYB uses must agree with the console code page.

Avoiding a few traps will help you use keyboard codes and code pages effectively.

- Don't give a keyboard code and code page that do not agree.

- If you are switching code pages, don't give a code page that is not in the list of code pages given to MODE CON CODEPAGE PREPARE.

- Don't give a keyboard code that does not agree with the CON (console) code page used in a CHCP command or in a MODE CON CODEPAGE PREPARE SELECT command.

- Don't use KEYB with a keyboard code or a code page that conflicts with the current console code page. In other words, use MODE CON CODEPAGE SELECT or CHCP to switch the console code page before you use KEYB for a different code page. If you don't, KEYB will mutter a warning about incompatible combinations.

Table 15.5
Compatible Code Page and Keyboard Code Combinations for KEYB

Code Page	Keyboard Codes
437	FR, GR, IT, LA, NL, SP, SU, SV, UK, US
850	All
860	PO
863	CF
865	DK, NO

The final parameter of the KEYB command is optional. *d:path\filename.ext* is the full disk drive, path, and file name for KEYBOARD.SYS, the file that holds the information that KEYB uses to build the various translation tables. If you omit the full file name, DOS searches for KEYBOARD.SYS in the root directory of the current disk. If KEYBOARD.SYS isn't there, you should specify the full file name (drive, path, and file name) for KEYBOARD.SYS.

The guide to operations manual for your computer and the DOS Reference manual have a set of templates showing the different keyboard layouts. If you would like to experiment, you can load the KEYB programs and try typing some characters.

You'll find that the extended characters, the characters with an ASCII value greater than 127, have changed. You can type these characters (and normal characters) by pressing and holding down the Alt key and then pressing the ASCII number for the character on the numeric keypad. When you release the Alt key, the character appears.

When any version of KEYB is loaded, you can switch easily between the U.S. character set and another language set. The key combination Ctrl-Alt-F1 (the F1 special function key) switches to the U.S. character set. Ctrl-Alt-F2 switches back to the other language set.

The ASCII character set is a standard adopted by the American National Standards Institute. Most non-U.S. English keyboards use a standard from the International Standards Organization (ISO). Not all ASCII characters are on ISO keyboards. A few of the missing keys are the brackets ([ ]), the braces ({ }), and the tilde (~). IBM still places these characters on non-U.S. English keyboards, but you must use the Ctrl-Alt sequence to type the characters.

Another quirk about some language sets is that certain keys are used only in combination with an accent mark. If you type the character key by itself, nothing happens. To type the character, you must first press the accent key and then the letter.

If you use any of the KEYB programs, the program stays in memory until you either reboot DOS or turn off the machine. You can use the DOS V3.3 version of KEYB as many times as you want. The first time you use KEYB, it increases the size of DOS by about 7,800 bytes. Using KEYB again does not increase the size of DOS.

If you have a DOS pre-V3.3 version of KEYB, you should load only one KEYBxx program. If you load a second KEYBxx, it assumes control, and the first KEYBxx program is deactivated. The first program, however, is trapped in memory and will continue to eat its 2K of space until you reboot DOS or turn off the computer.

Some computers are manufactured specifically for non-U.S. use. These computers have a different ROM BIOS and multilingual character set. Loading KEYB has no effect on such computers. Instead, KEYB simply loads, notices the multilingual ROM BIOS, and exits. Neither Ctrl-Alt-F1 nor Ctrl-Alt-F2 has any effect; neither combination switches between U.S. English and character sets for other languages.

KEYB is the program that makes your keyboard layout travel the world. Using KEYxx is fairly simple, but you can use it only once. KEYB, because it can be used any number of times with different code pages, is more complex but more versatile than KEYxx. If you need the versatility of entering language characters, use the KEYB command. If your keyboard layout handles your language needs, you can omit KEYB.

Changing the Code Page with MODE

When your computer starts, DOS and each device know a starting code page. Most North American computers know the 437 code page. If you want to use different code pages, you must prepare each code page for each device and then activate that code page. The MODE command prepares and selects code pages for each device.

MODE is the command that controls devices. Before DOS V3.3, MODE consisted of four subcommands. In DOS V3.3, MODE has eight subcommands. The four additional subcommands handle code-page switching. In computerese, MODE is an overloaded command. It has so many functions and different syntaxes that it can be difficult to understand. Therefore, this discussion covers only the code page parts of MODE. The remaining functions of MODE are covered in Chapter 17.

The key to learning and using MODE is simply remembering the steps for preparing code pages and paying close attention to the phrasing. MODE has many pitfalls. MODE is wordy, meaning that the commands you type are long. And the phrasing of the commands is tricky. The most common problem with the PREPARE subcommand, for example, is forgetting the set of parentheses around the code page list. Also, the order of the commands can be important; you can't use MODE SELECT before MODE PREPARE. Don't let these caveats discourage you, though. MODE can be mastered with some knowledge, some practice, and some patience.

Fortunately, you don't need to use every MODE subcommand every time you start DOS. Here are some common situations and what you should know or can ignore for each.

- If you will not be using code page switching on any device, you can ignore MODE CODEPAGE.

- If you plan to switch code pages, you need to know MODE CODEPAGE PREPARE.

- If you are using different keyboard layouts with KEYB, you may need to know MODE CODEPAGE PREP.

- If you need to know the PREPARE portion of MODE CODEPAGE, you should know about the other three subcommands of MODE CODEPAGE.

MODE will not function correctly if you do not have the correct device driver installed in the following situations:

- If you use MODE CODEPAGE PREPARE, you must use the DISPLAY.SYS or PRINTER.SYS directive in your CONFIG.SYS file.

- If you use MODE on the console, you must have the DEVICE=DISPLAY.SYS line in CONFIG.SYS.

- If you use MODE for the ProPrinter or Quietwriter III printers, you must have the correct DEVICE=PRINTER.SYS line in your file.

How MODE Affects Code Pages

To better understand MODE, remember that a code page is a printable font. Each device uses at least one such font. One possible location for the font is in read-only memory, which may be built into the video adapter, the printer, or a cartridge placed in the printer. These are the hardware code pages discussed earlier.

Another location for a code page is in a disk-based file. DOS loads the font from the disk into random-access memory, "transmits" it to the display or printer, and finally activates it for use. These disk-based fonts are *software* code pages. The code pages are replaceable and can be switched through programmed commands (software).

If you want to switch code pages, you first must load the code page for the specific device (console or printer) into the computer's RAM. Then the code page can be sent to the device and used. Transmitting the code page is called *downloading*, which means sending the information "down" from the computer to another device. After the information is downloaded, the computer signals the device to use the new code page.

To switch code pages on a device, you must assemble the code pages for use. The MODE CODEPAGE PREPARE command loads any software-based code pages into the computer's memory. The MODE CODEPAGE SELECT command downloads any needed code page to the device and tells the device which code page to use. MODE CODEPAGE SELECT can also tell the device to "forget" a software font and switch back to the font built into the device.

Because some fonts are placed in the device's RAM, you might turn the device off and lose the information. Or perhaps a stray program might wipe out the code page information. For these reasons, the MODE command has the ability to remind the device of the font in use. This reminding is the function of MODE CODEPAGE REFRESH.

The MODE CODEPAGE /STATUS command rounds out MODE, displaying the number of the available code pages for a device and which code page is active.

Tricks to Remembering MODE

The code page form of MODE has several difficult parts to its phrasing. However, remembering these four tricks will help you use the command more easily.

The first trick is the order of the words. The general form is

MODE device CODEPAGE activity

The first word is the name of the command, MODE. The second word is the device to be used. device can be the console (CON:) or any of the three parallel printers (LPT1:, LPT2:, or LPT3:). As with any DOS device name, the colon after the device name is optional. The third word is CODEPAGE. The fourth word is the activity, or subcommand, that MODE should perform: PREPARE, SELECT, REFRESH, or /STATUS. Remembering the order of the words makes the MODE command easier to use.

The next two tricks concern the MODE CODEPAGE PREPARE subcommand. The second phrasing trick is that when additional information is needed, you use an equal sign after the activity. The third phrasing trick is that although the DOS V3.3 manual shows that this information should be placed in parentheses, the parentheses are not needed. The form becomes

MODE device CODEPAGE activity = (information)

Spaces can be used before and after the equal sign. When you use parentheses, you can place spaces before or after each one. Remember, you must use the equal sign, but the outer parentheses are optional.

The final phrasing trick is that when you give the code page to PREPARE, you must place the code page numbers within parentheses. Forgetting the parentheses yields a frustrating Invalid parameter error. We'll see the phrasing for PREPARE shortly.

The final trick to MODE CODEPAGE is that DOS provides some abbreviations for parts of the command. We know that MODE is wordy, so any shortcuts are welcome. You can use the set of abbreviations in table 15.6 with MODE.

Table 15.6
MODE CODEPAGE Abbreviations

Word	Shorthand
CODEPAGE	CP
PREPARE	PREP
SELECT	SEL
REFRESH	REF
STATUS	STA

Although I show the longhand form several times in this chapter, I strongly encourage you to learn the shorthand form. You will type the commands more quickly and make fewer mistakes.

Defining Code Pages with MODE PREPARE

The first step in using switchable code pages is to use the MODE PREPARE subcommand to load the disk-based code pages into the computer's memory. The syntax of MODE PREPARE is the most complex of any MODE subcommand, but if you remember the tricks, the command is tameable. The syntax is

> *dc:pathc*MODE device CODEPAGE PREPARE = ((code_page, . . .)
>   *d:path*filename.*ext*)

dc:pathc is the optional disk drive and directory path to the MODE command. **device** is the name of the device for MODE to use. You must specify the device, which can be any of the following:

CON:	console
LPT1:	first parallel printer
LPT2:	second parallel printer
LPT3:	third parallel printer
PRN:	the current system printer, usually a synonym for LPT1:

As with all device names, the colon after the device is optional. The driver for each device specified must have been loaded via the CONFIG.SYS file. To use CON in this command, you must include DISPLAY.SYS in CONFIG.SYS; to use the remaining devices, you must include PRINTER.SYS in CONFIG.SYS.

After the word PREPARE, you type an equal sign followed by one or two opening parentheses. You can use or omit spaces between PREPARE and the equal sign and either parenthesis.

Using the parentheses is the tough part. Remember that the code pages must be enclosed within a set of parentheses. However, the entire set of information for MODE PREPARE does not need parentheses. I suggest that you enclose only the code page numbers in parentheses. One set is easier to remember.

After the opening parenthesis, give the code page or code pages that should be loaded into memory. If you want a single code page, give the number followed by a closing parenthesis. If you need more than one code page, separate the code page numbers with a comma. The ellipsis

(. . .) represents the optional additional code pages. Remember to give a closing parenthesis after the final code page.

For example, to use 850 as a code page, you would use

= (850)

To use the 437 and 850 code pages, you would use

= (437, 850)

Spaces are optional here.

Avoid giving a hardware code page number to MODE PREPARE. In other words, remember the code page you gave to DISPLAY.SYS or PRINTER.SYS. Don't give MODE PREPARE the same code page number. If you used this line in your CONFIG.SYS file:

DEVICE = C:\SYS\DISPLAY.SYS CON = (EGA, 437, 2, 2)

don't give 437 to MODE CODEPAGE PREPARE. The driver already knows that the 437 code page is built into the adapter. Giving 437 to MODE only causes MODE to reload the 437 code page, wasting memory that other fonts could use. You also force the computer to download the font each time the 437 code page is selected—a minor, but avoidable, waste of time.

The final information you must give to MODE CODEPAGE PREPARE is the drive name, path name, and file name for the file that holds the font information for the device. The general form of the file name is devicename.CPI. The CPI extension is for *code page information*, and the devicename can be any of the following:

EGA	EGA and VGA display adapters
LCD	PC Convertible LCD display
4201	IBM ProPrinter
5202	IBM Quietwriter III

The EGA.CPI and LCD.CPI files, of course, are used with the CON device. The 4201.CPI and 5202.CPI files are used with the PRN or LPT devices. Only one CPI file can be given with the command.

Unlike the NLSFUNC and KEYB programs, MODE makes no assumptions about the code page information file. If the file is not on the current disk or in the current directory, you must provide the needed information. The root name is mandatory. If the file has an extension, you must give the root name and extension. Because all DOS code page files have an extension of CPI, you'll usually give both.

You can use a space between the closing parenthesis of the code pages and the start of the file name. A space can appear after the file name and before the optional closing parenthesis. The spaces can be omitted. However, do not use a space within the full name.

If you used two opening parentheses, you must give one closing parenthesis after the code page file name. If you placed the parenthesis around the code page numbers only, don't give a closing parenthesis after the code page file name. If you use my suggestion, don't use the closing parenthesis.

Also, you cannot prepare more code pages than the number you gave to DISPLAY.SYS or PRINTER.SYS for *added_codepage*. The maximum number of code pages you can give to MODE PREPARE is *added_codepage*. If you specified a 0, you can't PREPARE any code pages. If you used a 1, you can use one additional code page. If you used 2 *added_codepages*, you can use up to two code pages to MODE. If you need more code pages, you must edit the DISPLAY.SYS or PRINTER.SYS line in your CONFIG.SYS file and then restart DOS.

Remember that if you gave two hardware code pages for the Quietwriter III, you must have given a value of 0 for *added_codepages*. DOS assumes that the two code pages are in the printer. In this case, you don't need to use MODE CODEPAGE PREPARE on the Quietwriter.

If you issue the MODE CODEPAGE PREPARE command more than once, you can skip the code pages you don't want to change. For example, you use this MODE command to load the 850, 860, and 863 code pages:

```
MODE CON CODEPAGE PREPARE = ((850, 860, 863) C:\EGA.CPI)
```

Let's say you later want to use the 850 and 863 code pages, but you want the 865 instead of the 860 page. You simply drop the number and insert a comma where you don't want to change the code page. To change the 860 code page to the 865, the command would be

```
MODE CON CODEPAGE PREPARE = ((,865,) C:\EGA.CPI)
```

Notice that the comma replaces the number. DOS knows that the missing code page should be retained. A more common example would be first using this command to load the multilingual code page into memory:

```
MODE CON CODEPAGE PREPARE = ((850) C:\EGA.CPI)
```

Later, you want to add another code page to the list. To add the 860 code page, you would use this command:

```
MODE CON CODEPAGE PREPARE = ((,860) C:\EGA.CPI)
```

The comma works as the placeholder for the previous code page. Now either the 850 or 860 code page can be used. Remember that the value for *added_codepages* given to DISPLAY.SYS must be at least 2 for this example to work, and 3 for the previous example to work.

If you make a mistake in your typing, MODE usually displays an `Invalid parameter` message. If you omit the name of the code page file, you get a similar error message. If you give the name of a nonexistent file, you get a `Failure to access Codepage Font File` message. For any of these errors, no changes take place. The previously prepared fonts are still in memory.

However, let's suppose that you give an incorrect code page number or give the name of an existing file that is not a code page information file. MODE then displays a `Font file contents invalid` message. The code page at that position is removed from the list. Using the previous example (which has the 850 and 860 code pages prepared), if you issue the command

> MODE CON CODEPAGE PREPARE = ((,836) C:\EGA.CPI)

MODE tells you that the code page file does not have the given font. 836 cannot replace the code page in the second position, which was 860. However, 860 is removed from memory. To use 860, you must issue the MODE PREPARE command again to reload 860.

Remember that the commands can be abbreviated. The way to phrase most of these commands is

> MODE CON CP PREP = (850, 863) C:\EGA.CPI

or

> MODE LPT1 CP PREP (860, 863) C:\4201.CPI

MODE CODEPAGE PREPARE defines the code pages that can be used with a device. The command loads the "soft" code pages into memory, where they can be downloaded to the device. After the code pages are prepared, they can be used. One command (but not the only one) to activate the code pages is MODE CODEPAGE SELECT.

Activating Code Pages with MODE SELECT

After you have prepared the code pages, you must activate them in one of two ways: with CHCP or with MODE SELECT. After you have started DOS and given the MODE PREPARE commands, CHCP is the preferred command to activate the code pages. You can use the CHCP command to activate the code pages for DOS and all the devices at one time. CHCP is also far easier to use than MODE SELECT. You'll usually use CHCP whenever you change code pages. However, there is one occasion when you don't want the same code page active on all devices. Then you must use MODE SELECT.

Suppose that you have edited a document using code page 437 and have started printing the document in the background. Now you want to edit another document. That document was created using the 850 code page. You need to use the 860 code page for the console (the display and keyboard).

If you use CHCP in this instance, you affect both the display and the printer. CHCP forces the printer to use the 850 code page. Either you'll get some nonsense characters on the printer, or the printer will "drop" some information from your document when the code pages are switched. Neither possibility is desirable. Your only choice is to use MODE SELECT to switch fonts on the display.

CHCP is the "all-in-one" code page switcher. Whenever the console and the printer must use different code pages, use MODE SELECT, which switches code pages on one device at a time. The syntax for MODE SELECT is

   dc:pathc\MODE device CODEPAGE SELECT = codepage

dc:pathc\ is the optional drive and directory path to the MODE command. device is the name of the device whose code page will be activated by MODE. device can be CON, LPTx, or PRN. codepage is the code page the device will use. codepage must be either the hardware code page given to the appropriate device driver or one of the code pages given to the MODE PREPARE command. Exactly one, and only one, codepage can be given.

Using the MODE SELECT command downloads the appropriate font to the device and activates the font. The device uses this font until you issue another MODE SELECT or CHCP command, or until you turn off the device or restart DOS.

The Quietwriter III is different from the ProPrinter in that it uses cartridges. Thus the computer does not know which font is in the printer. When you select a code page for the Quietwriter III, the printer beeps, warning you to check which cartridge is installed. DOS has no way of protecting itself from printing with the wrong cartridge. You are responsible for having the cartridge with the correct code page in the printer.

Normally, you cannot use MODE SELECT on a device without having first issued a MODE PREP command for the device. However, you can use MODE SELECT without giving a MODE PREP to activate the hardware code page for the device. This step has no other effect than to eliminate a warning when you use the MODE /STATUS command. If you don't switch code pages, the device automatically uses the hardware code page. Hence, giving MODE SELECT without MODE PREPARE is meaningless.

You can use MODE SELECT as often as you want to change the code page for one device. Use CHCP when you want all the devices to use the same code page.

Also remember the shorthand form. The usual way to type MODE SELECT is

        MODE CON CP SEL = codepage

or

        MODE LPT1 CP SEL = codepage

Refreshing a Device's Memory with MODE REFRESH

MODE REFRESH reminds the device which font the device should be using. Generally, the command is not needed on the video display. Unless a program has played with the video screen in an undesirable manner, the CON code page should be unaltered. The command is used more frequently on the printer. If you turn the printer off and on again, the software code page is lost. Thus, DOS can lose track of the code page that the printer is using. The printer and DOS must then be resynchronized.

Rather than issue the MODE SELECT command, you can use the MODE REFRESH command. The command reloads any needed font and reactivates the font. The syntax for MODE REFRESH is

        dc:pathc MODE device CODEPAGE REFRESH

device is the name of the device whose code page should be reestablished. Don't give a code page number. MODE uses the last code page used in the MODE SELECT command.

To use MODE REFRESH, you must have used MODE PREPARE and either MODE SELECT for the device, or the CHCP command. MODE REFRESH can be issued as often as needed. Examples of the shorthand form of MODE REFRESH are

        MODE LPT1 CP REF

and

        MODE CON CP REF

Checking Code Pages with MODE /STATUS

You can use the MODE /STATUS command to display various code page information about a device. MODE /STATUS lists this information:

The number of the active code page, if any
The number of the hardware code page
The numbers of any prepared code pages

The syntax for MODE /STATUS is

dc:pathc\MODE device CODEPAGE /STATUS

device is the name of the device whose code page information you want displayed. Notice that this command is a switch. You must give the switch character (the slash), followed by the word STATUS.

The following sample session displays the MODE /STATUS command for the console. Before the session, DOS was started with this command in the CONFIG.SYS file:

DEVICE = C:\SYS\DISPLAY.SYS CON = (EGA, 437, 4)

The DISPLAY.SYS file has been set up for an EGA or VGA display (EGA), a hardware code page of 437, and 4 additional usable code pages.

```
C>MODE CON CODEPAGE PREP = (850, 860) C:\EGA.CPI
MODE Prepare Codepage function completed

C>MODE CON CODEPAGE SELECT = 850
MODE Select Codepage function completed

C>MODE CON CODEPAGE /STATUS
Active codepage for device CON is 850
hardware codepages:
   Codepage 437
prepared codepages:
   Codepage 850
   Codepage 860
   Codepage not prepared
   Codepage not prepared
MODE Status Codepage function completed

C>
```

The first MODE command sets up the console to use the 850 and 860 code pages, in addition to the 437 code page built into the display adapter. The second MODE command activates the 850 code page.

The first line of the MODE /STATUS command shows the active code page. If no code has been selected via the MODE SELECT or CHCP command, MODE /STATUS displays this line instead:

```
No codepage has been SELECTED
```

The next two lines give the hardware code page based on the DISPLAY.SYS or PRINTER.SYS line in the CONFIG.SYS file. The next lines show the software code pages. The number of lines is based on the *added_codepages* number given to DISPLAY.SYS or PRINTER.SYS. If a code page is prepared, you'll see the number listed. The message Codepage not prepared means that additional areas for code pages are available, but no code page has been prepared for this slot.

You can use MODE /STATUS at any time. However, you get an error message if the appropriate device driver has not been installed for the device. MODE /STATUS can be abbreviated to

MODE CON CP /STA

for the console or

MODE LPT1 CP /STA

for the first line printer.

You need the MODE CODEPAGE commands if you want to use a device or switch fonts. Some of the commands also are required if you are using the KEYB program. Remember: if you need to switch code pages, you need these commands. If you don't need to, you can safely ignore these commands.

Solving Display Problems Using GRAFTABL

There is a minor problem with displaying non-English characters on the IBM Color/Graphics Adapter (CGA). When you attempt to display characters in the ASCII range of 128 to 255 while in graphics mode, the characters are smeared and almost unreadable. Unfortunately, the non-English language characters are in the range of 128 to 255. This problem affects only the CGA. And the problem occurs only in medium-resolution, 320-by-200, 4-color mode, not in normal alphanumeric text mode or in the high-resolution, 640-by-200, 2-color mode.

To get a legible display in medium-resolution graphics mode, use
GRAFTABL. This command loads the alternate character set into the
computer's memory and then directs the CGA to use this set when it is in
graphics mode. The ASCII characters in the 128 to 255 range are thus
displayed legibly.

To use GRAFTABL, type

   dc:pathc\GRAFTABL

This external command must be loaded from the disk. When GRAFTABL
loads into memory, the program steals about 1,200 bytes of RAM.
Therefore, you should run GRAFTABL only once after you start DOS.
Running GRAFTABL more than once simply wastes 1,200 bytes of memory
each time you run it. This memory remains trapped until you either restart
DOS or turn off the computer.

Run GRAFTABL before you run other programs that use the medium-
resolution graphics mode of the Color/Graphics Adapter. If a program you
frequently run requires GRAFTABL, simply add the command to your
AUTOEXEC.BAT file.

Using SELECT To Automate Your Selection

SELECT is a program that automates the selection of the country code and
keyboard program. Read the section on SELECT first. SELECT for pre-DOS
V3.2 destroys any previously established CONFIG.SYS and AUTOEXEC.BAT
files. SELECT for V3.2 and V3.3 runs FORMAT and destroys all the files on
the disk! If you have already set up your disk, you accomplish more by
simply editing the CONFIG.SYS and AUTOEXEC.BAT files than by running
SELECT.

If you will use SELECT with diskettes, you need the correct blank diskette
for your disk drive. If you have a 1.2M disk drive, you need a 1.2M
diskette. If you have a 1.44M disk drive, you need a 1.44M diskette. Using
the wrong capacity diskette can cause SELECT to fail.

SELECT for DOS V3.1 and Earlier

SELECT versions for DOS V3.1 and earlier work only on diskettes. These
versions of SELECT do not work on the fixed disk. The syntax for SELECT
DOS pre-V3.2 is

   dc:pathc\SELECT countrycode keyboardcode

where countrycode is the three-digit code for your country, and keyboardcode is the two-character code for your country.

To use this version of SELECT, you need a copy of your DOS master diskette and a blank diskette. Put the copy of the DOS diskette into drive A. If you use a system with two floppy disk drives, put the blank diskette into drive B. For a system with one floppy disk drive, you'll be exchanging diskettes in drive A shortly.

After the diskette or diskettes are in the disk drive, type the SELECT command with the country code and keyboard code for your locality. If you run SELECT before the diskettes are in the computer, you'll get a DOS error message. Simply put the DOS diskette into drive A and press R for Retry.

Under DOS V3.0, SELECT runs the DISKCOPY and DISKCOMP programs. Under DOS V3.1, SELECT runs only the DISKCOPY program. Because the wording is different for the two programs that SELECT is about to run, the terms should be explained. The terms "FIRST" and "SECOND" apply to SELECT V3.0. The terms "source" and "target" apply to SELECT V3.1. The source or FIRST diskette is the DOS master diskette. The target or SECOND diskette is the blank diskette.

First, SELECT runs DISKCOPY, copying the DOS diskette to the blank diskette. You won't see DISKCOPY's name on the screen, nor will you see DISKCOMP's name later. If you have one disk drive, change the diskettes when DISKCOPY prompts you. When the computer asks whether you want to make another copy, answer N for no.

For DOS V3.0 only, SELECT also runs DISKCOMP to ensure that your copy is correct. For DISKCOMP, the FIRST diskette is the DOS diskette, and the SECOND diskette is the fresh copy of DOS that DISKCOPY has just made. When it's finished, DISKCOMP asks whether you want to compare more diskettes; answer N for no.

SELECT then creates one or two additional files on the freshly copied and compared diskette. SELECT creates a CONFIG.SYS file with the COUNTRY command in it. If you designate a keyboard code other than US (United States), SELECT creates an AUTOEXEC.BAT file with the line KEYBxx, in which xx are the two letters for your keyboard code. The Personal Computer has the American English character set built in and does not need a KEYBxx program for this set.

If you run SELECT, the diskette you produce should become your new DOS working copy. Put any additional CONFIG.SYS or AUTOEXEC.BAT command lines you want into the files. If you have done the steps in

Chapter 12 (Understanding Batch Commands) and in Chapter 14 (Customizing DOS), you won't want to run SELECT. At the end of this chapter are directions on the lines you can add to your CONFIG.SYS and AUTOEXEC.BAT files.

SELECT for DOS V3.2 and V3.3

SELECT for DOS V3.2 and V3.3 can work on diskettes or fixed disks. This version of SELECT runs the FORMAT command. If you use SELECT on your fixed disk, you will destroy all information on the disk. For this reason, I strongly suggest that you do not run SELECT unless the fixed disk has no files. You'll gain more by just creating or editing your CONFIG.SYS and AUTOEXEC.BAT files than by copying everything back to your fixed disk after FORMAT has run.

The syntax for SELECT V3.2 and V3.3 is as follows:

   dc:pathc SELECT *ds: dd:pathd* countrycode keyboardcode

ds: is the name of the disk drive that holds the *source* disk and should hold the DOS Startup or Startup/Operating diskette. *ds:* must be a floppy disk drive (either A or B). If you don't specify the source disk drive, SELECT uses drive A.

dd: is the optional *destination* disk, the disk to be set up. The destination disk must be different from the source disk. If you don't give *dd:* and the current disk is not the source disk, SELECT uses B. If you don't give *dd:* and the current disk is the source disk, SELECT displays an error message and aborts. To use SELECT on a fixed disk, you must specify the fixed disk's drive name.

\\pathd is the path to the directory that SELECT copies the DOS files to. You must use an *absolute* path name—that is, you must start with the root directory (\\); the . and .. names are not allowed.

If you don't give *\\pathd*, DOS copies the files to the root directory of *dd:*. If the destination is a diskette, you generally can omit *\\pathd*. Because of the limited memory, don't use a destination path if the destination is a 360K diskette. If the destination is a fixed disk, you should give *\\pathd*. The name I suggest is either BIN or DOS.

The last two parameters are identical to the DOS pre-V3.2 versions of SELECT. countrycode is the three-digit code for your country, and keyboardcode is the two-character code for your country.

Unlike earlier versions of SELECT, SELECT for V3.2 and V3.3 first runs the FORMAT /S command, to format the destination disk and place the DOS system files on the destination disk. This command destroys the information on the destination disk. Therefore, don't run SELECT on a diskette or fixed disk that holds useful files. Those files are "dead meat" after FORMAT is done.

If you run SELECT to prepare a fixed disk, you will be asked for a volume label. Putting volume labels on fixed disks is a good processing practice. FORMAT requests the existing volume label before it formats a fixed disk, so inadvertently formatting a fixed disk that has a volume label is almost impossible.

After FORMAT has run, SELECT runs XCOPY, to transfer the files from the startup diskette to the destination diskette or fixed disk. If you specified a destination path (*pathd*), XCOPY copies the files to the directory. SELECT then creates any needed directories. If you did not specify a destination path, XCOPY copies the files to the root directory of the destination disk.

Finally, SELECT creates a CONFIG.SYS file and an AUTOEXEC.BAT file. The CONFIG.SYS file for SELECT V3.2 and V3.3 holds the single line

```
COUNTRY = countrycode,codepage
```

or else

```
COUNTRY = countrycode,codepage,d:path\COUNTRY.SYS
```

This line sets up the COUNTRY directive. The correct code page is based on the country code you gave to SELECT. Use the first line if you do not give a destination path. Use the second line, which has the full file name for COUNTRY.SYS, if you give a destination path. The d:path is the destination drive and path name.

If the destination is a diskette, the AUTOEXEC.BAT file for V3.2 and V3.3 holds the following lines:

```
PATH \;\path
KEYB keycode codepage
ECHO OFF
DATE
TIME
VER
```

If the destination is a fixed disk, AUTOEXEC.BAT holds these lines:

```
PATH d:\;d:\path
KEYB keycode codepage
ECHO OFF
DATE
TIME
VER
```

d: is the name of the destination disk drive. If you gave a destination path (*pathd*) to SELECT, the first line substitutes the destination path for path. If you did not give a destination path to SELECT, the first line drops the second directory path. The line becomes either PATH \ or PATH d:\).

The AUTOEXEC.BAT file runs the KEYB program with the keyboard code you gave and inserts the compatible code page for the keyboard code. The batch file then turns echo off, asks for the date and time, and displays the DOS sign-on message. The last three commands approximate what DOS does if no AUTOEXEC.BAT file is on the disk.

If you run SELECT on a diskette, the diskette you produce should be your new DOS working copy. If you run SELECT on a fixed disk, your DOS files are copied to the disk. Put any additional CONFIG.SYS or AUTOEXEC.BAT command lines into the files. Again, if you have done the steps in Chapters 12 and 14, you shouldn't run SELECT.

A Sample COUNTRY Setup

To use the international features of DOS, you must add the COUNTRY line to the CONFIG.SYS file. If you will use code page switching, you will need the DISPLAY.SYS file. If your printer is compatible, you'll also need the PRINTER.SYS file.

The alterations to your AUTOEXEC.BAT file include NLSFUNC, CHCP, MODE, and possibly KEYB. If you use the Color/Graphics Adapter in medium-resolution graphics mode, you'll need to add the GRAFTABL line to the file as well.

If your CONFIG.SYS and AUTOEXEC.BAT files are already established, use a text editor to add the necessary lines to your boot diskette or fixed disk.

In these examples, I'll presume that you have a fixed disk and that all of the DOS program files are copied to a subdirectory called C:\BIN. I'll also presume that all .SYS files have been copied to C:\SYS. If this is not true, change the disk drive and path name to match your system. Floppy disk users should omit the path name and use A: in place of C:.

I make one exception to the placement of files. If you frequently use KEYB on your fixed disk, copy the KEYBOARD.SYS file to the root directory and issue the ATTRIB +R command to change the file to read-only. The reason is because KEYB does not remember where the keyboard file is kept. Typing a long path name for KEYBOARD.SYS is boring. Instead, I use this command to copy KEYBOARD.SYS from C:\SYS to the root directory:

```
C>COPY \SYS\KEYBOARD.SYS \
```

Then I use the ATTRIB command to mark the file as read-only, thus protecting the file from being altered or erased accidentally. The command is

```
ATTRIB +R C:\KEYBOARD.SYS
```

You now cannot alter or erase KEYBOARD.SYS. See the *Command Reference* for an explanation of ATTRIB.

The examples shown here are for DOS V3.3 only. Consult your DOS manual for your correct setup if you are using an older version of DOS.

Adding the International Directives to Your CONFIG.SYS File

To use DOS's international features, start by adding the following line to your CONFIG.SYS file:

```
COUNTRY = countrycode, codepage, d:path\COUNTRY.SYS
```

Here, countrycode is the country code that matches your locality. If your country is not listed, use the country whose date and currency formats most closely resemble yours. codepage is the starting code page for DOS, as listed in table 15.2 (437 is the usual choice). d:path\COUNTRY.SYS is the full file name for COUNTRY.SYS. Because I keep the file in a directory called C:\SYS, the line I use is

```
COUNTRY = 001, 437, C:\SYS\COUNTRY.SYS
```

If 437 is not the correct code page, use either the existing code page (if you don't plan to switch code pages) or the 850 code page (if you do). If you plan to switch code pages, you must use the appropriate device driver also.

If you have a PC Convertible LCD display, an EGA, or a VGA, use the DEVICE=DISPLAY.SYS. Here is the line I use for my EGA/VGA systems that have an EGA or a VGA:

DEVICE = C:\SYS\DISPLAY.SYS CON = (EGA, 437, 1)

This line sets up the display for the 437 code page and 1 additional code page. For a Monochrome Adapter, I use the line

DEVICE = C:\SYS\DISPLAY.SYS CON = (MONO, 437, 0)

You can't use added code pages on the Monochrome Adapter (MDA) or on the Color/Graphics Adapter. The number of added code pages is always 0.

Remember that if you use ANSI.SYS, the DRIVER.SYS line must appear after the ANSI.SYS line. Reversing this order causes you to lose the features that ANSI.SYS offers.

If you have either the IBM ProPrinter or the Quietwriter III, you should use PRINTER.SYS. The line I use for the ProPrinter is as follows:

DEVICE = C:\SYS\PRINTER.SYS LPT1 = (4201, 437, 1)

This line sets up the ProPrinter for the first parallel port (LPT1), the 437 code page, and one additional code page.

In the preceding lines, if 437 weren't my existing code page, I would use the existing code page and specify 2 instead of 1 for the added code pages to be used. For example, the DISPLAY.SYS line could be

DEVICE = C:\SYS\DISPLAY.SYS CON = (EGA, 863, 2)

meaning that the French Canadian code page (863) is built into the adapter and that I will use two additional code pages.

Remember that the CONFIG.SYS file must be in the root directory of the boot diskette or fixed disk, and that you must restart DOS before the change takes place.

Adding the International Commands to Your AUTOEXEC.BAT File

Add following lines to the AUTOEXEC.BAT file of your startup disk. If the startup disk is a fixed disk, place these additional commands after the line that holds your PATH command. When the commands occur after PATH, DOS automatically finds the commands.

The first step is to add the NLSFUNC command to AUTOEXEC.BAT. The line to add is simply

NLSFUNC

The next step is to use MODE PREP on each device. If DISPLAY.SYS is installed, use the MODE CON CODEPAGE PREPARE command. I use this line:

MODE CON CP PREP = (850) C:\BIN\EGA.CPI

This command prepares the 850 code page for use with my EGA/VGA-type displays. If your hardware code page is 437, use 850 as the prepared code page. If your hardware code page is not 437, use 850 and the existing code page, such as

MODE CON CP PREP = (850, 863) C:\BIN\EGA.CPI

This command adds the French Canadian code page to the multilingual code page.

If PRINTER.SYS is installed, use the MODE LPTx CODEPAGE PREPARE command. The line I use for the ProPrinter is

MODE LPT1 CP PREP = (850) C:\BIN\4201.CPI

which prepares the 850 code page for use with the model 4201, the ProPrinter. If the hardware code page is not 437, I prepare the 850 but add another code page, such as

MODE LPT1 CP PREP = (850, 863) C:\BIN\4201.CPI

which adds the French Canadian code page to the multilingual code page.

If you gave two hardware code pages for the Quietwriter III, you don't need to issue the MODE PREPARE command for this printer. Otherwise, follow the same form for the ProPrinter, but use 5202.CPI for the code page information file name.

After you add the commands to prepare the code pages, use the CHCP command to activate the pages. The line to be added to AUTOEXEC.BAT is as follows:

CHCP codepage

codepage is the existing code page. In my case, the command I type into my AUTOEXEC.BAT is

CHCP 437

If you are a new user of DOS, you can use 850 instead of 437.

Finally, add this line to enable switching of your keyboard:

> **KEYB keycode,,d:path\KEYBOARD.SYS**

The *keycode* is the two-letter code from table 15.4. For me, the line is

> **KEYB US,,C:\SYS\KEYBOARD.SYS**

If you use KEYB frequently on the fixed disk and follow the suggestion to copy the file to the root directory, add this command to the AUTOEXEC.BAT file instead:

> **KEYB US,,C:\KEYBOARD.SYS**

If you have a Color/Graphics Adapter and use the medium-resolution graphics mode frequently, add the line

> **GRAFTABL**

You're done! Now restart DOS and watch your display. If you see any error messages, check the lines in your CONFIG.SYS file and AUTOEXEC.BAT file. You probably simply misspelled a command or forgot to give the correct file name. Correct the mistake and try restarting DOS.

Summary

Although English is the international language of aircraft pilots and computers, computers must adapt themselves to other languages. The concept of code pages, the COUNTRY command, the NLSFUNC/CHCP combination, the MODE CODEPAGE subcommands, the KEYB program, and DOS's international function call are IBM's and Microsoft's response to help serve this need. In this chapter, you learned the following important points:

1. Code pages are fonts. Some code pages are built into hardware, and some are loadable from a file.

2. You use the CONFIG.SYS COUNTRY directive to tell DOS which international country code and which code page to use.

3. DOS adapts the format for the date and time based on the country code. DOS can also provide necessary information to a program so that the program can adapt to non-English conventions.

4. The DISPLAY.SYS device driver is used to allow code page switching on some video displays.

5. The PRINTER.SYS device driver is used to allow code page switching on some printers.

6. The NLSFUNC command provides additional functions that make DOS go international and allows the CHCP command to be used.

7. The CHCP command switches code pages for DOS and all devices at one time.

8. The MODE CODEPAGE PREPARE subcommand loads code pages for a device into memory.

9. The MODE CODEPAGE SELECT subcommand activates a prepared code page for a device.

10. The MODE CODEPAGE REFRESH subcommand reloads and reselects a previously selected code page for a device.

11. The MODE CODEPAGE /STATUS subcommand shows the selected code page, the hardware code page, and the prepared code pages for a device.

12. The KEYB command alters the keyboard for any of 17 different languages.

13. The GRAFTABL command enables you to display legibly non-English language characters and certain graphics characters when you use the Color/Graphics Adapter in medium-resolution mode.

Chapter 16 discusses additional uses of COPY, and shows how to gain more control over copying using the XCOPY command.

Part V

Managing Your System

INCLUDES

Managing Your Files
Gaining Control of Drives, Devices, and the Printer
Backing Up and Restoring the Fixed Disk
Gaining More Control of the Fixed Disk
Migration between Minifloppy and Microfloppy Systems
Some Final Thoughts

16

Managing Your Files

Now that you have learned and tried many commands, functions, and features of DOS V3, let's look at an old command, COPY, and at a new command, XCOPY.

Expanding Your Use of the COPY Command

As you learned earlier in this book, COPY copies files. With it, you can copy files between disk drives, between devices, or between a disk drive and another device. In fact, COPY demonstrates how a file can actually be a device. Instead of copying just from one disk file to another, you can copy from a disk file to a device, from a device to a disk file, or from a device to another device.

Understanding ^Z, the End-of-File Marker

ASCII files, usually called text files, use a special character to signal the end of a file. This character is represented as ^Z, CHR$(26), or 1A in the hexadecimal numbering system. The character is called the *end-of-file* marker.

Every program recognizes that Ctrl-Z marks the end of an ASCII text or data file. Anything beyond the end-of-file marker is considered invalid and is not used. If you press the F6 key at the system prompt, a ^Z, the end-of-file indicator, will appear on-screen.

COPY makes one assumption about the files being copied: if a file does not come from a character-oriented device, the file is considered a binary file. When DOS copies binary files, it uses the file size from the directory to determine how much information to copy. Thus, DOS copies everything in a disk file.

Copying files on the basis of their directory length works also for ASCII files. The end-of-file marker, which is reflected in the directory size, is copied with the rest of the file's information. Therefore, a copied text file keeps the end-of-file marker, and programs work correctly with this kind of file.

Working with nondisk devices is different. DOS has no way of knowing how many characters will be involved in copying with these devices. The indicator is the Ctrl-Z. When DOS receives a Ctrl-Z from the console, the serial port, or another nondisk device, DOS knows that all information has been received or sent. When you copy from the keyboard to a disk file, you press the F6 function key to inform COPY you have reached the end of your typing. When you press Ctrl-Z, COPY saves what you typed.

Using COPY's Switches (/A, /B, /V)

COPY has three switches, /A, /B, and /V. You can use the switches to force conditions on the COPY command. The switches /A and /B specify to COPY how much information is to be copied:

/A   an *ASCII* file
/B   a *binary* file

The /A switch makes DOS handle the file transfer as ASCII text. For source files, DOS copies all information up to, but not including, the first Ctrl-Z. For a destination file, DOS adds a Ctrl-Z to the end of the file. This method of copying files ensures that a good end-of-file marker is placed in the file. When you copy a file from a device other than a disk drive, DOS assumes that the /A switch is to be used.

The /B switch is the opposite of the /A switch. The /B switch tells DOS to copy binary (program) files. Source files are copied on the basis of directory size, and Ctrl-Z is treated as an ordinary character. For destination files, no Ctrl-Z is added. When you copy files from one disk to another, DOS assumes that the /B switch is to be used.

You cannot force DOS to copy a binary file from a nondisk device. DOS will have no way of knowing when the information has ended. If you type the /B switch with the source device name, DOS gives an error message and halts the command.

The COPY switches illustrate well how the position of switches affects DOS's operation with some commands. The placement of COPY's switches is important. A COPY switch affects the file or device name that precedes the switch and all file and device names after the switch, until contradicted by another switch. For example, if you use the /A switch after the first file or device name, you affect all files in the command line. If, however, you use the /A switch after the second file name, the switch affects only the second file and files after that. Look at the following examples:

1. COPY /A ONEFILE.TXT TWOFILE.TXT

   COPY treats ONEFILE.TXT and TWOFILE.TXT as ASCII text files. ONEFILE.TXT is copied up to, but not including, the first Ctrl-Z. A Ctrl-Z is added to the end of TWOFILE.TXT.

2. COPY ONEFILE.TXT /A TWOFILE.TXT

   This example's effect is identical to that of the first example. The /A switch affects the file in front of it (ONEFILE.TXT) and all files after the switch (TWOFILE.TXT).

3. COPY ONEFILE.TXT TWOFILE.TXT /A

   COPY treats ONEFILE.TXT as a binary file. All information from ONEFILE.TXT (determined by its length in the directory) is copied to TWOFILE.TXT. A Ctrl-Z is added to the end of TWOFILE.TXT.

4. COPY COM1: TWOFILE.TXT /B

   COPY takes information from the first communications adapter (COM1:) until it encounters the Ctrl-Z. COPY places this information, excluding the Ctrl-Z, in a disk file called TWOFILE.TXT. No additional Ctrl-Z is added.

5. COPY COM1: /B TWOFILE.TXT

   This command line is illegal. The /B switch affects the file or device in front of the switch and all files or devices after it. The problem with this command line is that the /B switch will affect the communications port, COM1:. COPY does not allow "binary" copies from a nondisk device, and DOS displays an error message if you try such an action.

A third switch used with COPY is /V, which verifies that the copies are correct. (You have used this switch throughout the book.) When you use /V, you must place it after the last file name. Although the /A and /B switches affect one another, /V does not affect the /A and /B switches.

Using COPY To Join Files

COPY does more than copy files. The command can also *concatenate* (join) files. The syntax is

COPY /A/B *d1:path1*\filename1.*ext1*/A/B +
d2:path2*filename2.ext2*/A/B + . . . *dd:pathd**filenamed.extd*
/A/B/V

d1:, *d2:*, and *dd:* are valid disk drive names. *path1*\, *path2*\, and *pathd*\ are valid path names to the files. filename1.*ext1*, *filename2.ext2*, and *filenamed.extd* are valid file names. Wildcards are acceptable. The . . . represents additional files in the form *dx:pathx**filenamex.extx*.

The numbers and the letter *d* are special notations. The numbered file names, marked 1 and 2, are the source files. Names followed by *d* represent destination files. The source files are those you want to join. The destination file or files will hold the product of this concatenation.

Can there be more than one destination? Yes, COPY can produce several destination files. This tricky and potentially dangerous process involves wildcard characters and is discussed later in the chapter.

Source files can be binary files (program files or non-ASCII data files) or ASCII files. When you concatenate, COPY assumes that you are joining ASCII files and issues an invisible /A switch. This assumption is not true when you copy disk-based files. But because non-ASCII files are rarely concatenated, the assumption is helpful.

The following screen shows an example of this command:

```
C>COPY FILE1.TXT + FILE2.TXT + FILE3.TXT FILE.ALL /V
```

The contents of FILE1.TXT are moved to a file called FILE.ALL. The contents of FILE2.TXT are added to the end of FILE.ALL. The contents of FILE3.TXT are appended also to FILE.ALL. The /V switch verifies the concatenation. Because no disk drive or path names are given, the entire activity takes place in the current directory on drive C.

Each source file name can have a disk drive name and a path name. The normal rules about current disk drives and current directory file names apply here.

You can use wildcard characters in the file names. Such characters force COPY to join any files that match the given wildcard name. With one file name, therefore, you can join several files.

If you must give additional file names, separate them with a plus sign (+). This sign tells DOS you are joining files. Give disk drive names and path names, as needed, for these additional files.

The destination file is the last file name on the command line that does not have a plus sign in front of its name. If you look at the preceding example, you will see a space, not a plus sign, between FILE.ALL and the last file to be concatenated (FILE3.TXT).

If you don't give an explicit destination file name, the last file name without a + in front of it is the destination file. That is, the first source file name becomes the destination file. DOS adds the second and subsequent files to the end of the first file. If you find this order confusing, just remember that the last file without a plus sign in front of its name is the destination file.

If you use matching wildcards for the root names of both the source and destination file names, you can create multiple destination files. Look at this example:

COPY *.LST + *.REF *.PRN

This line takes each root name that has a .LST extension and joins that file to each file that has a .REF extension. The command line then places the joined result into a file with the same root name but with a .PRN extension. This process allows you to produce multiple destination files. If you use a wildcard in the destination file name, the destination files have the same root names as the source files.

Now look at the following set of files:

MYFILE.LST	MYFILE.REF
APROG.LST	APROG.REF
FILE3.LST	FILE3.REF

The command COPY *.LST + *.REF *.PRN will combine these files in the following way:

MYFILE.LST	+	MYFILE.REF	→	MYFILE.PRN
APROG.LST	+	APROG.REF	→	APROG.PRN
FILE3.LST	+	FILE3.REF	→	FILE3.PRN

Each set of files with matching root names and the extensions .LST and .REF is combined and placed into a .PRN file.

The next example concerns using wildcards with a destination file that is also a source file. I'll discuss a common mistake that occurs in copying files in this manner. The following list shows the program files in the order in which they appear in the directory:

COUNT.C
PREP.C
DSKTIME.C
VERTEST.C
ALL.C
SWITCHAR.C

To combine these source files into one destination file called ALL.C, I used the command line:

COPY *.C + ALL.C

This command gave me an error message, but the message came too late. COUNT.C had already been placed in the file called ALL.C, followed by PREP.C, DSKTIME.C, and VERTEST.C. Then the error message appeared.

Why? The destination file is ALL.C. But ALL.C is also a source file. Let's examine the sequence of events.

Because the destination file and the first source file have different names, DOS copies the first source file to the destination file. This copy is destructive because the contents of the destination file are lost before the copy is made. Each additional source file is appended to the destination file.

DOS then encounters a source file name that is identical to the destination file name. But DOS already destroyed the old contents of the original destination file, so DOS cannot copy this file. DOS displays the message

```
Contents of destination lost before copy
```

and proceeds to concatenate the rest of the source files.

When you use wildcard names, DOS scans the directory from beginning to end. When DOS encounters a file that matches the wildcard name, DOS operates on the matching file. ALL.C was not the first file in the directory. The first file was COUNT.C. DOS saw that this file name was not the same as ALL.C, the destination file, and created a new ALL.C. Four files later, DOS discovered that ALL.C was also a source file. DOS had already altered this file—hence, the problem and the error message. The command used was not correctly phrased. Unfortunately, the error message came too late.

The correct command for copying all the *.C files into ALL.C is

COPY ALL.C + *.C

The last file without a plus sign in front of it is ALL.C. It becomes the destination file. Because ALL.C is also the first source file, DOS skips copying ALL.C. DOS appends all other .C files to ALL.C. Traveling down the list of files, versions of DOS prior to V3.3 find ALL.C a second time, know that this file has already been "copied," and skip the file again. DOS V3.3 finds the file a second time and gives the Contents lost warning, but ALL.C is intact and correct. The message is a lie.

You can change the date and time of a file when you copy it to a different disk. When you copy a file, DOS preserves the date and time. To change B:ALL.C's date and time, you type the following:

C>COPY B:ALL.C+

DOS joins all files by the name ALL.C (in this case, only one) on drive B and places the results on drive C, the default disk drive in this example. The date and time are changed because the file on drive C is a "new" file—the product of all the files named ALL.C on drive B. In reality, the contents of the file are unchanged. This DOS quirk is useful.

To "copy" the file B:ALL.C without moving it and to change the date and time, you type the following line:

C>COPY B:ALL.C+,, B:

The two commas tell DOS that no other file name is given after the plus sign. You must specify B: to keep the file on drive B. B: is the destination file name. No source file, however, is specified to be joined to ALL.C.

With the MODE command (discussed in the next chapter), a comma tells DOS to leave something alone. The two commas here do almost the same thing. They tell DOS that it has reached the end of the source file name. DOS usually expects a file name after the + sign. To ensure that DOS does not confuse the destination file name with the nonexistent additional source file name, two commas designate the end of the source file name.

The preceding COPY command appends B:ALL.C to a file by the same name on the same drive. When no file name and extension are used for the destination, DOS uses the same file name as that of the source file. What really happens is that DOS leaves the file in place and just changes the date and time.

If you want to concatenate program or non-ASCII data files, don't forget to use the /B switch. If you try either of the preceding command lines on a nontext file, you will not get what you want.

Be careful with wildcard names when you use concatenation to change a file's date and time. If you type

COPY B:*.* + ,, B:

DOS will combine all the files on drive B into the first file found on B! You probably don't want to combine these files.

If you want a quick way to add lines to the end of a batch file, try the following command:

COPY filename.BAT+CON

First create a batch file with the command COPY CON TESTCOPY.BAT. Type this line into the batch file:

ECHO This is the original line

Press Enter, press F6, and then press Enter again. Now type

COPY TESTCOPY.BAT+CON

This line tells DOS to copy the contents of TESTCOPY.BAT and the contents of CON, the keyboard, to the destination file. Because no destination file is stated, DOS assumes that the destination is TESTCOPY.BAT. After you see the word CON appear on the screen, type

ECHO This is the added line

Again, press Enter, press F6, and then press Enter. Use the TYPE command to view the TESTCOPY batch file. You should see the following lines:

```
C>TYPE TESTCOPY.BAT
ECHO This is the original line
ECHO This is the added line
```

You can use this technique when you want to add a few lines to an established .BAT file. COPY CON is a crude way to capture lines from the keyboard, however. If you make a mistake and press Enter, you cannot go back to correct a line. To add more than a few lines, use a text editor such as EDLIN.

Using COPY to concatenate files may seem difficult to understand at first. But once you learn the procedure and all the quirks, COPY is easy to use.

Gaining More Control of Copying with XCOPY

Beginning with V3.2, DOS introduced an *extended* copy command called XCOPY. XCOPY addresses the needs of three principal users: users who have more than one computer, users who have fixed disks, and users who need more selectivity than the standard COPY command offers. Almost all PC users fit one or more of these categories, so XCOPY is an important command to know and use. I have included a detailed explanation of how to use XCOPY in each of the examples presented later in this chapter.

XCOPY is best described as a hybrid between COPY and BACKUP/RESTORE, the disk-backup commands discussed in Chapter 18. XCOPY and COPY both copy files between disks. But unlike COPY, XCOPY does not copy files to a nondisk device, like the printer (PRN) or the console (CON). Like BACKUP and RESTORE, XCOPY can selectively copy files and traverse the directory tree to copy files from more than one directory. Like COPY but unlike BACKUP, XCOPY copies files that are directly usable: You cannot use files processed by BACKUP until you have processed them with RESTORE.

XCOPY's syntax is similar to COPY's syntax, but the switches are more complex. XCOPY's syntax is

> *dc:pathc*XCOPY *ds:paths\\filenames.exts*
> *dd:pathd\\filenamed.extd /V /P /W /S /E /A /M /D:date*

dc:pathc is the XCOPY command's optional path name. The *source* files, designated by an *s*, are the files to be copied. If you omit the disk drive name (*ds:*), the current disk drive is used. If you omit the path name (*paths*), the current directory on the drive is used. You may use wildcards in the file name (*filenames.exts*). If you omit the file name, XCOPY assumes that you want to specify a wildcard *.*, and all files in the given path will be copied. If you specify no path and file name, XCOPY issues an error message.

With XCOPY, the *destination* files are designated with a *d* in the name. File names, disk drives, and path names follow the *rule of currents*. If you do not specify a drive name (*dd:*), XCOPY uses the current disk drive. If you do not specify a path name (*pathd*), XCOPY uses the current disk's directory. If you omit the file name (*filenamed.extd*), the copied files retain their previous names.

If you give a destination name that might be a path name or a file name and the potential path does not exist on the destination, XCOPY asks you whether the destination is a file name or path name. This message is new to XCOPY V3.3. To illustrate XCOPY's operation, use the sample hierarchical directory in Appendix B. If you give the command

    XCOPY C:\WORDS*.* A:\WORDS

to copy the files from C:\WORDS to the diskette in drive A, and the diskette does not have a directory called WORDS, XCOPY will display this message:

```
Does WORDS specify a file name
or directory name on the target
(F = file, D = directory)? _
```

If the destination is a file name, you would answer F. If the destination is a directory, you would answer D. Unlike COPY, XCOPY creates directories on the destination disk as needed.

XCOPY's Switches

XCOPY has eight switches, as shown in table 16.1. Mastering the use of the switches is the key to mastering this powerful command.

/V is the familiar *verify* switch. XCOPY verifies that XCOPY has copied the files correctly.

/W causes XCOPY to prompt and *wait* for you to insert the source diskette. This switch is particularly important to floppy disk drive users. XCOPY is an external program that must be loaded from a disk, which normally starts the copying process after the program loads. If you want to copy files between diskettes that do not have the XCOPY program, use the /W switch. After XCOPY starts, the program prompts you to insert the correct diskette. Remove the diskette that holds XCOPY, insert the correct diskette, and tap any key to start the actual copying process.

/P is the *pause and ask* switch. XCOPY displays the name of the file it will copy and asks if the file should be copied. You answer Y to copy the file and N to skip the file. When you answer Y, XCOPY immediately copies the file.

Table 16.1
XCOPY's Switches

Switch	Function
/V	*Verifies* that the files have been copied correctly (identical to COPY's /V switch).
/W	*Waits* until the disk has been changed. XCOPY prompts you to change diskettes before it searches for the files to copy.
/P	*Pauses* and asks for confirmation before copying each file.
/S	Copies the files in the source directory and all files in subsequent *subdirectories*. This option is identical to BACKUP's and RESTORE's /S switch.
/E	When given with the /S switch, causes XCOPY to create *empty* subdirectories on the destination if the subdirectory on the source is empty. If you do not give the /E switch, /S ignores empty directories.
/A	Copies files with *archive* flags set to on (the file has been created or modified since the last running of BACKUP or XCOPY). /A does not reset the file's archive flag.
/M	Copies files with archive flags set to on (the file has been created or *modified* since the last running of BACKUP or XCOPY). /M resets the file's archive flag.
/D:date	Copies files created or modified since *date*. This option is identical to BACKUP's /D switch.

The next two switches, *∕S* and *∕E*, affect how XCOPY handles additional subdirectories. These two switches show the true power behind XCOPY. COPY limits itself to handling the files from one directory. XCOPY starts with the named or current directory and can process the files in all additional subdirectories of the directory, and all subdirectories of these subdirectories, and so on. XCOPY *traverses* the subdirectory tree and can copy complete directory branches from one disk to another.

The /S switch affects the source and destination directories. If you give the /S switch, you are instructing XCOPY to copy all designated files from the current and subsequent *subdirectories* to a parallel set of subdirectories on the destination disk drive. If you use the sample directory system shown in Appendix B, giving the command

XCOPY C:\WORDS*.* A: /S

first copies all files in WORDS to the current directory on drive A. The command then copies all files from WORDS\LETTERS to a subdirectory of the current directory called LETTERS on drive A and then copies all files from the subdirectory WORDS\CONTRACT to the subdirectory of the current directory on drive A called CONTRACT. In essence, XCOPY lifts a copy of the subdirectory tree starting at the source directory and transplants the copy onto drive A.

Note that XCOPY does not place the copied files from the subdirectories into a single directory. XCOPY places files from one subdirectory into a parallel subdirectory. If the subdirectory does not exist on the destination, XCOPY creates the subdirectory.

The /E switch affects the way the /S switch works. If XCOPY encounters an *empty* subdirectory on the source drive, XCOPY /S skips the empty subdirectory. If you give the /S and /E switches, XCOPY also creates empty subdirectories on the destination drive. If you give the /E switch without giving the /S switch, the /E switch has no meaning.

The next three switches, */A*, */M*, and */D:date*, control which files that match the source file name will be copied. The /M switch tells XCOPY to copy any file that has been *modified*. This switch really tells XCOPY to copy a file you have not before backed up or copied with XCOPY. Remember the archive attribute? It is stored in the directory with each file name. When you create or change a file, this attribute is turned on. XCOPY checks whether the archive attribute has been set. When you give the /M switch, XCOPY processes this file. If the attribute is not set, XCOPY skips the file.

The /A switch works like the /M switch. XCOPY will process only those files that have the *archive* flag turned on. However, whereas /M clears the archive attribute after XCOPY has copied a file, /A does not. This difference can be important. As discussed later in this book, the BACKUP command can select files based on the archive attribute. However, if XCOPY has cleared this flag, BACKUP will not process the file. Therefore, if you use XCOPY /M and BACKUP /M (the switches have identical meaning for the two commands), you can cause DOS to be confused. More importantly, the backup you make using BACKUP may not be complete. Unless you customarily use XCOPY as a backup program, avoid using the /M switch; use the /A switch instead.

The /D:date switch selects files based on their directory *date*, which is the date of the file's creation or modification. XCOPY copies files that have been created or modified on or after the *date* specified. The format of *date* depends on the convention for your location (the COUNTRY command of CONFIG.SYS). The COUNTRY command's settings options are

mm-dd-yy North American
dd-mm-yy European
yy-mm-dd East Asia

mm represents the month; *dd* represents the day; and *yy* represents the year. The character that separates the parts of the date depend on the COUNTRY command's setting and vary among the hyphen, the period, and the slash. North American users can substitute a slash (/) in place of the hyphen (-).

For North American users, *date* is *mm-dd-yy* (or *mm/dd/yy*) where you give the month, day, and year, respectively.

Using XCOPY Effectively

Because XCOPY can control which files should be copied by date or archive attribute, copy complete subdirectory trees, and confirm which files should be copied, the command has several ideal uses. One use is to selectively copy files between disks or directories. A second major use is as a "quickie" fixed-disk back up command if you want to back up only a few critical files in several subdirectories. The third major use is to keep the directories of more than one computer synchronized—a task that affects more and more computer users each day, including me.

With COPY, control is limited: The only control you have over the files that COPY will process is the source file name. COPY copies all files that match the given name, which is an all-or-nothing approach. If you use the /P switch with XCOPY, you can select all the files that match the source file name, and then XCOPY will ask you if each file should be copied. This *query* capability is a welcome feature. You can give a single "larger" file name (a name that selects more files than necessary but covers all the files you may want to copy), and then you can select individually which files you really want to copy.

The only bugaboo I have found with the /P switch is that XCOPY immediately begins copying after you answer Y to its query, meaning that you have to wait for XCOPY to finish copying each file before XCOPY presents the next file name. My patience exhausts as I wait for XCOPY to process a long file. Although I like XCOPY, for this reason, I would use any other program that first presents all the file names for you to select from at once, accepts all the selections, and then copies the selected files.

As a mini-backup program, XCOPY is practical to use if you want to copy less than a diskette full of files from several directories. You may frequently work intensively in one or two related subdirectories and not other directories. Rather than using BACKUP, you might prefer to use XCOPY to make a fairly quick copy of your files. I recommend using XCOPY /A to select files that have changed since the last backup.

This technique has one drawback: I recommend that you ensure that the files will fit on one diskette. When the destination diskette fills, XCOPY stops. XCOPY cannot gracefully handle full diskettes. You must change diskettes and restart the XCOPY process using the /A *and* /P switches to skip the files you have already copied. Also, XCOPY cannot handle files that occupy more than one diskette. That's why DOS offers the BACKUP command. If you need to back up files larger than a diskette, use BACKUP instead.

My favorite use of XCOPY is to keep the contents of computers' hard disks synchronized. More and more people use multiple computers today, especially many people who have one computer at work and another at home. If both computers have fixed disks, keeping your copies of programs and data files current is a major task. Which files did you change today? Which machine has the more current version?

XCOPY is a godsend. You'll find especially useful the /A switch or the /D:date switch if you use the /S switch on the donor and recipient (source and destination) computers. The /S switch forces XCOPY to play a hunt-and-seek game you would otherwise need to perform manually. Which switch you use, /A or /D, depends on how often you copy files between the machines. If you copy files between the machines frequently, you will find that the /A switch is preferable. If you let many days lapse between synchronizing your computers' contents, you may find that the /D switch works better. If you run BACKUP on the source machine between the times you use XCOPY, you must use the /D switch. BACKUP resets the archive attribute, and XCOPY will not catch all files that have changed.

If you have a base computer and a laptop computer, XCOPY works its magic well. Because most laptops are floppy disk-based computers, the /A and /D switches are important. Taking your work on the road means getting the new or changed files back onto your base computer. When you are moving files from the laptop to the base computer, use the /A switch. This switch copies only the new or changed files back to the base computer. When you are copying files to the laptop, look at the floppy disk's directory and use the latest date you can find with the /D switch.

Because I back up my fixed disk more frequently than I update the floppy diskettes for roadwork, the /D switch's date approach works better for me.

XCOPY is a major improvement over the COPY command in several areas. If you need selective copying, the /P switch forces XCOPY to ask you about copying a file before it copies the file. The process is slower than I like, but it's worthwhile. The /M, /A, and /D switches allow selective copying based on the file's directory date archive attribute. XCOPY can traverse subdirectory trees, allowing one command to copy files from many directories. Although XCOPY's speed in searching files leaves room for improvement, the time spent learning to use XCOPY effectively is worthwhile.

Summary

In this chapter, you learned these important points:

1. When you use COPY to copy files, you can specify the /A (ASCII file) and /B (binary file) switches.

2. You may use COPY to join, or concatenate files. The command **COPY filename.ext+CON** is a quick method of adding lines to an established file.

3. XCOPY can copy files between disk devices. The command can traverse the subdirectory tree, select files based on their archive attribute or date, and confirm individual files for copying.

Chapter 17 discusses recovering files with bad sectors, controlling devices, and printing from the background.

17

Gaining Control of Drives, Devices, and the Printer

This chapter discusses some of DOS V3's fundamental and advanced commands—RECOVER, MODE, and PRINT. RECOVER salvages files that have bad sectors. MODE controls your screen, serial ports, and printer. The PRINT command prints files while you continue performing other work with your computer.

Recovering Files and Disks (RECOVER)

The RECOVER command works with one file or with a complete disk. The form of RECOVER that works with a complete disk is dangerous and should not be run unless you read and heed the precautions. Don't run this form of the command unless you have no alternative. Once DOS has "fixed" the directory, you may spend hours trying to recover from RECOVER. The form of RECOVER you use on a single file is not risky.

How do you recover a file with defective sectors on the fixed disk? RECOVER is the program to use. With RECOVER, you can make a new copy of a file, minus the data held in the bad sectors. A bonus is that the bad sectors are marked "in use" so that they won't be used again.

The syntax for this form of RECOVER is

   *dc:pathc*RECOVER *d:path*filename.*ext*

The *dc:pathc* part of the command line is the optional disk drive and path name to the RECOVER command. *d:* is the optional disk drive name if the file is not on the current disk drive. *path* is the optional path name if the file is not in the current directory. filename is the root name of the file to RECOVER, and *.ext* is the extension if the file has a suffix. You may use wildcards in the file name, but you can recover only one file at a time. If you include a wildcard, DOS examines the directory and uses only the first file found that matches the wildcard name.

After RECOVER has finished, the file you are recovering has the same name as before. The bad sectors on the disk will be "removed" from use, but the material in them will be lost. This recovery method means that the total capacity of the disk is decreased by the capacity of the bad sectors that have been removed.

The only files you should recover are text and data files. Don't bother recovering program files. When information is lost from such a file, the program may not run at all or, worse, may run erratically when you recover it. Use a backup copy of the program instead.

You will need to edit text or data files after you recover them. For text or ASCII data files, use a text editor to get rid of any garbage or to add lost information. For non-ASCII data files, you may need to write special programs to restore files to their original states.

There is little reason for having to recover a file with RECOVER. If you make frequent backup copies of your fixed disk or diskettes, you can usually restore files easily from the backup copies and then reedit as necessary. You should run RECOVER, though, to "hide" the bad sectors on the disk.

The only way to remove bad sectors is to reformat the disk. If the disk is physically damaged, formatting will not help, however. If the disk is a floppy diskette, you should retire it. Fixed disks, however, are difficult to retire. You'll have to live with any flaws.

Bad sectors are a bad sign. Either the magnetic coating on the disk is damaged, or you have a problem with the electronics of the disk drive. The most likely reasons—in order—are these: (1) mishandling of the diskette or fixed disk; (2) physical wear from normal use of the diskette (seldom applicable to a fixed disk because its recording heads do not touch the surface when the drive is in use); (3) mechanical or electronic failure of the disk drive; (4) electronic failure of the disk interface or controller card (the board inside your computer); (5) a damaged disk drive cable; (6) bad random-access memory in the computer.

Bad RAM occurs infrequently. If the memory holding DOS goes bad, the machine language instructions executed by the CPU change. This change can cause erratic or disastrous disk performance. The best you can hope for is that nothing will happen—that DOS will just go "dead in the water." The worst that can happen is that DOS will reformat the disk or make garbage of directories. That's why a *memory-parity error* makes your computer "lock up." IBM wisely chose to stop the computer "dead in the water" so that only work in progress is destroyed and not your previous work, programs, and data stored on the disks.

If a diskette is physically worn, the time has come to retire it. Look through the access holes at the diskette's surface. Dark grooves indicate wear. Dark or dull splotches may indicate spots where the diskette has been mishandled or contaminated. If you see a fold or crease, retire the diskette.

Mechanical or electronic problems are more difficult to analyze. Run your diagnostics program. For floppy disk drives, use a diskette formatted on a drive you know is good. If the problem is in the fixed disk, back the disk up immediately!

If problems show up when you run the diagnostics, have your computer or disk drive repaired right away, before other diskettes are harmed. If a problem with a disk drive shows up in the diagnostics, the entire computer should be suspected. The problem may be caused by the disk drive, the interface board inside the computer, the cable that connects the board and the disk drive, the power supply of the disk drives, or possibly something else in the computer's main circuitry. Whatever the problem, have it repaired immediately.

Seldom do you electronically damage a diskette or fixed disk when you read information. If the problem is not in the diskette itself, and you have not written information to it, the diskette and its files are probably still intact. There is always a small chance that the disk drive wrote some garbage instead of reading information. Check out all the files or floppies you've used since you first detected the problem. Make sure that the information is intact.

What about bad sectors that can develop in directories? This problem is a serious one. If a bad sector is in the root directory, the problem is grave. The root directory is located in a fixed position on the fixed disk or diskette. Because DOS cannot relocate the root directory, this condition can be fatal. The second form of RECOVER, the potentially dangerous form, recovers damaged root directories.

If a subdirectory has bad sectors, the problem is serious, but not fatal. CHKDSK can cope with it. (For more information about CHKDSK, see the *Command Reference*.) Before you run CHKDSK, take the following steps for copying the diskette or fixed disk. If CHKDSK does not work, RECOVER is your final choice.

First, you should copy and/or back up all the files you can. Use a different set of diskettes than the set you used for your last backup copies. Keep your last backup diskettes intact. You may need to use them if all else fails.

For a faulty diskette, use the COPY command to copy each file to a second diskette. Then use the DISKCOPY command to copy the bad diskette to a third diskette. If the offender is the fixed disk, use a different set of backup diskettes. Run BACKUP, keeping your master backups and last daily backups intact.

Because you do not know at this point the cause of any bad sectors, you should suspect the backed-up or copied files you have just made. Whatever caused the directory to develop bad sectors may have damaged other areas on the diskette or fixed disk. Make sure that the files you just copied or backed up are correct before you fully trust them.

(If the problem is in a subdirectory, use CHKDSK first. If CHKDSK does not work, use RECOVER. In either case, you should continue reading the rest of this section.)

The next step is to use RECOVER. The syntax for this form of RECOVER is

   *dc:pathc**RECOVER *d:*

dc:pathc is the optional disk drive and path name to the RECOVER command. The second *d:* is the optional disk drive name. If the current drive does not hold the disk you want to recover, give the appropriate disk drive name.

DOS will run through the file allocation table (FAT). Remember that the FAT knows the disk clusters (sectors) where each file is stored. But the FAT does not know the previous file name, the file's attributes (system, hidden, etc.), or the file's date and time.

DOS first re-creates the root directory. Then DOS begins to create files with the name FILEnnnn.REC in the root directory. The nnnn is a number from 0000 to 9999. Each file that DOS creates represents one of the recovered files from the disk. Every file on the disk becomes a FILEnnnn.REC file: program files, data files, and subdirectories.

Now the detective work begins. Each FILEnnnn.REC can be anything—a normal file or a subdirectory. You must now find which FILEnnnn.REC files hold the information you need to keep and which FILEnnnn.REC files (such as subdirectories) hold information you can discard. The files' previous names are lost. Their dates and times are also lost. The major clue to what is in each file is the file itself.

You will need several tools to help you. The TYPE command can type the characters in a file. This command will help you locate ASCII text files. Program files and subdirectories are different, however. Most of their information is displayed as gibberish. To display the contents of these files, you will need DOS's DEBUG, NU from the Norton Utilities™, DUMP.EXE from Phoenix Associates, or a similar program.

With one of these tools, you can locate the files you were not able to copy or backup. Copy these files to another diskette and change their names back to what they were. Make sure that the files are intact. There is a small chance that whatever caused the directory to develop bad sectors may have affected other areas of the diskette or fixed disk, making other files bad also.

The task of identifying each file is difficult. For practice, I took a backup copy of a good diskette and ran RESTORE on the diskette. (I also had another backup copy.) I then tried to locate the files, using TYPE to type the files and DEBUG and DUMP to identify them. This tedious task took several hours, even though I wrote a utility or two to help.

Using RECOVER on a disk is extremely difficult. I spent several hours trying to decipher a 360K diskette. A full 1.2M or 1.44M diskette takes many hours to restore. You should use RECOVER only as a last resort. Unless your backup copies are extremely out-of-date, you'll find that re-creating or reediting files is better than trying to use RECOVER on a fixed disk or diskette.

Before you use RECOVER on a disk, practice first on a copy of any diskette. Then work with a copy of the disk you are attempting to recover. If you botch up the copy, nothing is really lost.

When you try to recover a diskette with a flawed directory, again use a copy. If you make a mistake with the copy, you can make another copy of the original, flawed diskette. If you work with the flawed diskette and don't have a copy, a mistake can be costly.

Remember that this discussion does not apply to RECOVER filename, in which the RECOVER command is used on a single file. Because this process works on one file at a time, the worst that can happen is that you'll lose part of the file.

After you have re-created your files, you should reformat your diskette or fixed disk. FORMAT gives a message when it cannot properly format any system area, including the areas for the boot record, the root directory, and the FAT. If you use FORMAT's /S switch, IBMBIO.COM's and IBMDOS.COM's areas are also checked, and DOS gives error messages if these areas are bad. The error messages indicate that the diskette or fixed disk is currently unusable. You can retire a diskette, but you must have a fixed disk repaired.

Remember to back up your data frequently. You will have less work and experience less frustration if you back up your diskettes and fixed disk instead of trying to re-create them with RECOVER.

Changing Modes of Operation (MODE)

The MODE command is unique to PC DOS. MODE serves several purposes. In fact, you could say that MODE is eight commands in one. (MODE is treated this way in the *Command Reference*.)

MODE enables you to customize your computer's setup. The major difference between using MODE and using the CONFIG.SYS file to customize DOS is that what you do with MODE is lost when you turn off your computer or reboot DOS. In other words, the effects of MODE disappear. If you find yourself issuing a MODE command whenever you boot DOS, it's time to put this command in the AUTOEXEC.BAT batch file.

MODE handles printers, serial adapters, and display adapters. MODE also prepares, selects, and displays font files for international computer users. The information on the international uses of MODE was given in Chapter 15. This chapter covers the other uses of MODE, important for all users of PCs and PS/2 computers.

Controlling Your Printer

For printing, MODE sets the lines per inch and characters per inch, handles timeouts, and indicates whether you are using a serial printer. (*Timeout* is the technical name used when the printer is not ready in a given length of time.) Remember, you can have as many as three printers. The first printer, the primary one, is called LPT1:. (PRN is the pseudonym for whatever printer is LPT1:. When you use PRN, you are telling DOS to use whatever has been assigned as LPT1:.)

The syntax for this form of MODE is

   MODE LPTx *cpl, lpi, P*

The **x** is the *number* of the printer (1, 2, or 3), and *cpl* is the number of *characters per line*, based on an eight-inch wide line. This number can be either 80 (10 characters per inch) or 132 (16.5 characters per inch). The *lpi* stands for *lines per inch*, which can be either 6 or 8. And *P* tells DOS to "keep trying" when the printer is not ready.

DOS starts with the printer at 80 characters per line and 6 lines per inch. To see how your printer is set up, type

MODE LPTx

Substitute the number of the printer (usually 1) for the x.

This form of MODE works best with IBM and EPSON® printers or with printers that act like EPSON printers. If you don't have such a printer, MODE cannot set the characters per line or the lines per inch. In fact, MODE gives a printer-error message when you use MODE with some other type of printer.

As just indicated, the *P* is the "keep trying" option. If you want DOS to keep trying to send characters to the printer when something is wrong, you must give the full command with the P whenever you use MODE LPTx:. If you give MODE LPTx: without the P, DOS will not retry but will give an error message when the printer "times out."

If you give the P and your printer "hangs up," your computer will lock up. You can get the computer out of this situation by typing Ctrl-C or Ctrl-Break. The computer should respond within 20 to 40 seconds.

If you are using a network in which the printer is shared, you should omit the P option. If the printer is busy because another computer is using the printer, the performance of your computer will degenerate almost to a standstill until the printer is free.

If you don't want to change all the options, either drop the optional elements from the command line or just use the comma and leave out the number.

The command line

MODE LPT1 132, 8

changes the characters per line to 132 and the lines per inch to 8.

The line

MODE LPT1 80

sets the characters per line to 80 but leaves the lines per inch unchanged.

Finally, the command line

    MODE LPT1, 6

leaves the characters per line unchanged and changes the lines per inch to 6. In these three examples, DOS will not retry on a timeout because the P has been omitted. To get continuous retries, you must add ,P to the first and third examples and ,,P to the second example.

Using a Serial Printer

The second form of MODE also involves the printer. The syntax is

    MODE LPTx: = COMy:

Here, x is the number of the printer you are reassigning, and COMy: is the communications adapter for your serial printer. This form of MODE tricks DOS into using the serial printer connected to a communications adapter instead of using the normal parallel printer. You may need to check what number is correct for the communications adapter because the number can be either 1, 2, 3, or 4. Use 1 if you have only one communications adapter (serial port). PS/2 users can use as many as four adapters. If you have more than one adapter, check with your dealer or experiment with this command.

Typing the line

    MODE LPT1 = COM1

directs DOS to use the printer connected to the first communications adapter. To reverse this setting, you use MODE LPTx. No other information is required.

Before you use this form of the command, you should set up the asynchronous adapter, using the form of MODE discussed in the next section.

Controlling the Serial Adapter

This form of MODE sets the communications adapter's characteristics: baud rate, parity, data bits, stop bits, and retries. The syntax is

    MODE COMy: baud rate, *parity, data bits, stop bits, P*

where **y** is the number of the communications adapter (1 through 4 for PS/2s; 1 or 2 for PCs). The colon after the number is optional. The baud rate is mandatory: It can be 110, 300, 600, 1200, 2400, 4800, or 9600. If you are using a PS/2, the baud rate can also be 19200. You can abbreviate the baud rate to just two numbers, such as 30 for 300 baud, 96 for 9600 baud, or 19 for 19200.

The rest of the command's syntax is optional. If you don't include a characteristic, you should use a comma in place of the characteristic. If you use parity, for example, and then skip to stop bits, don't forget to use a comma for each characteristic you skip (in this case, one comma). DOS also expects these parameters to be in the order shown on the syntax line.

The parity can be **Odd**, **Even**, or **None**. Parity starts as even. The number of data bits is either 7 or 8; the number starts as 7. And the number of stop bits is either 1 or 2. If you use 110 baud, the default is 2 stop bits. Any baud rate faster than 110 will default to 1 stop bit.

As with MODE LPTx:, the *P* is the retry option. If you don't set P, then the option is off. It you forget to set it, the option is also off. Retry is good to use with printers (when the printer is not used on a network) but not as good when the adapter is used with a modem. You can also use Ctrl-C or Ctrl-Break to get out of a retry loop.

Look at the following command lines:

    MODE COM1 1200

    MODE COM1 12

Either line sets the baud rate at 1200 for the first communications adapter. Everything except the retry remains the same. If retry were set before, it is now off because it isn't given here.

The command line

    MODE COM1 19,,7

sets the first adapter to 19200 baud and 7 data bits. Everything else except the retry is unchanged. Retry will be turned off.

Typing the line

    MODE COM1 48,,,,P

sets the adapter to 4800 baud and to continuous retries. As before, nothing else is changed.

Controlling the Video Display

The last form of MODE controls the video display. The primary use for this form of MODE is to reset the display or to change displays when you have more than one type of video adapter. If you use just the monochrome display, this command will not work for you.

The syntax for this form of MODE is

MODE *display type, shift, T*

The display type can be any of the displays indicated in table 17.1. You can use MODE with either a television set or a monitor. With some monitors, characters "fall off" the edge of the screen. *shift* lets you shift the line back into position. This command shifts the display left or right by one character position. You enter either L or R to accomplish the movement. *T* stands for test pattern. When you request it, MODE shows a line of 40 or 80 characters and asks whether the display is okay. You press Y for Yes if it is. If you press N, MODE again shifts the display by one character and repeats the question. In this way, you can adjust your screen without having to use the MODE command repeatedly.

Table 17.1
Types of Video Display

Display Type	Function
40	Uses 40-column lines for the C/G display
80	Uses 80-column lines for the C/G display
BW40	Makes the C/G display the active display, turns off color, and uses 40-character lines
BW80	Makes the C/G display the active display, turns off color, and uses 80-character lines
CO40	Makes the C/G display the active display, turns on color capabilities, and uses 40-character lines
CO80	Makes the C/G display the active display, turns on color capabilities, and uses 80-character lines
MONO	Makes the Monochrome Display the active display

Note: C/G display refers to the monitor or television attached to the Color/Graphics Adapter [CGA], Enhanced Color/Graphics Adapter [EGA], or Video Graphics Array [VGA]. The term Color/Graphics can refer to any of these adapters.

An active display is the display that DOS and your programs use to show information. If you have two displays, such as a monochrome display and another monitor attached to a C/G board, you can use either display with this command.

Selecting the CO40 or CO80 display enables DOS to display color. Specifying CO40 or CO80 does not guarantee that your programs will be in color, because some programs use color and others do not. It's up to you and your programs to make color appear.

Using a MODE color command doesn't affect BASIC either. If you use a color command in BASIC, specifying BW40, BW80, CO40, or CO80 to MODE makes no difference. BASIC still tries to send colors. Whether or not you see colors will depend on the monitor or TV you use. The size of the screen (40- or 80-column) will remain in effect, however.

MODE has the same effect on the Color/Graphics Adapter (CGA), the Enhanced Color/Graphics Adapter (EGA), and the Video Graphics Array (VGA). MODE does not change the character set on the Enhanced Color/ Graphics Adapter or the Video Graphics Array. The EGA can use the same character set (9×14 dot) that the Monochrome Display uses. The VGA can use the sharper 9×16-dot character set. To use the enhanced character sets, you must correctly set the switches on the EGA. Check the installation manual that comes with the Enhanced Color/Graphics Adapter for more information. Fortunately, the VGA automatically adapts to the monitor used and gives the 9×16-dot character sets if the appropriate monitor is used.

The most frequent use for this form of the MODE command is to clear the video display and reset the colors after a graphics program has gone awry. Type MODE CO80 to restore a sense of sanity to the color display.

Printing Your Files in the Background (PRINT)

The PRINT command is DOS V3's background printing facility. PRINT allows you to print a disk file while you are running another program. Essentially, PRINT is a primitive form of multitasking—having your computer do two or more activities at the same time.

You can print any disk-based file. The only file you can background print, however, is a disk file. You should use the PRINT command only with ASCII text files. Program or non-ASCII data files usually have control characters in them. If you use PRINT on these files, the results are similar to using TYPE on the files: the characters appear as nonsense. These control characters can drive your printer crazy.

Understanding the PRINT Command

The first time you use PRINT, DOS loads part of the PRINT program into memory and hooks the program into DOS. As a result, PRINT steals about 3K of memory. When you reboot DOS or turn your computer off and then on again, this memory will be freed.

The PRINT command works by sharing CPU working time with another program. PRINT V3 is different from PRINT V2. PRINT V2 stole idle time from the CPU. While your programs were running, the computer sometimes waited for you. During these times, PRINT V2 briefly diverted the CPU's attention to the PRINT program, and PRINT sent some characters to the printer.

Whereas PRINT V2 waited until your computer had nothing else to do, PRINT V3 demands some attention from the CPU. PRINT V3 "installs" a time-slicing module into DOS to get some of your computer's CPU time. PRINT V2 printed little when the CPU had little idle time. PRINT V3 prints more consistently.

Before you use PRINT, you should be familiar with a related term: queue. A *queue* is simply a line in which one waits for a turn. When you PRINT a file, you place it in a queue to await printing. DOS handles the queue one file at a time. The first file you place in PRINT is put at the front of the queue and is the first file printed. Any files that follow are printed in the order in which they were placed into the line. When we talk about a queue, we are referring to this lineup of files.

The syntax for the PRINT command is

> **PRINT** */B:bufsize /D:device /M:maxtick /Q:maxfiles*
> */S:timeslice /U:busytick d:path\filename.ext /T/C/P . . .*

in which *d:path\filename.ext* is the name of the file to print and the optional disk drive and path to the file. If you use wildcard characters, one "file name" can queue up several files. The rest of PRINT's syntax is discussed in the following section.

Using PRINT's Switches

PRINT has nine switches (see table 17.2). You can give the first six switches to PRINT, in the form */letter:option*, when you first use the command. PRINT displays an `Invalid parameter` warning if you use these switches at any other time. The other three switches can be given any time you use the PRINT command.

Table 17.2
Switches for the PRINT Command

Switches Used When PRINT Is First Issued	
/B:bufsize	The size of the *buffer*
/D:device	The *device* to use
/M:maxtick	The *maximum* number of clock ticks to use
/Q:maxfiles	The maximum number of files to *queue*
/U:busytick	The number of clock ticks to wait for the printer
/S:timeslice	The number of times per second that PRINT can print (number of *timeslices*)
Switches Used Any Time You Issue PRINT	
/T	*Terminates* printing
/C	*Cancels* the printing of the file
/P	*Prints* this file

Each of the switches starts with the switch character, the slash (/). For the first six switches, after the slash, you add the letter for the option, a colon, and then the appropriate information. Do not use any spaces between any of these elements.

/B: sets the PRINT command's internal buffer size, which holds sections of the file to be printed. The buffer's size, *bufsize*, is specified in bytes. The default is 512 bytes. Increasing the buffer size improves performance and the amount of space PRINT takes from DOS.

/D: determines the DOS *device* to be used for printing. You can use any DOS device name, such as LPTx or COMy. Obviously, you should not use

devices such as CON that aren't connected to printers. UNIX/XENIX-like names are not allowed. If you do not give the /D switch, PRINT asks for this switch the first time the program runs:

```
Name of list device [PRN]: _
```

If you press Enter, PRINT uses PRN. You could enter LPT1, LPT2, LPT3, COM1, COM2, COM3, COM4, AUX, or PRN. Don't give a device that is not on your system, however. DOS acts erratically if you do. Until you restart DOS, PRINT uses PRN (or whatever device you specify). To change this device, you must restart DOS.

The next three switches are for performance-tuning. Unless you are dissatisfied with the way PRINT operates, you can ignore the next three switches.

/M: determines the maximum number of clock ticks (*maxtick*) that PRINT uses each time it prints. A *clock tick* is 1/18.2 of a second, about 55 thousandths of a second. /M: tells PRINT how much time it has in which to send characters to the printer whenever it is PRINT's turn. For a 9600-baud serial printer, PRINT can send approximately 17 characters during each clock tick. PRINT can send two characters in one clock tick to a 1200-baud serial printer. A 240-cps parallel printer can get about 4 characters in a clock tick.

/M: starts at 2. The range is from 1 to 255. Increasing this number boosts the number of characters that PRINT sends to the printer. If you increase this number too much, however, the keyboard becomes sluggish when PRINT gets control.

/S: determines how many of the available timeslices per second that PRINT will get. The starting value is 8. The possible values are from 1 to 255. A second is divided into a number of turns. PRINT gets one turn out of every *timeslice* number of these turns. Timeslice's effect is opposite that of maxtick. Increasing the timeslice gives PRINT fewer turns to PRINT each second. Decreasing this value increases the number of times that PRINT is activated each second. If, however, you decrease this number too much, the keyboard becomes sluggish, and your programs will slow down because PRINT will be called more frequently.

If you are wondering whether to use /M or /S, the following formula determines how much of the CPU's time per second PRINT should get:

$$\text{PRINT's percent of CPU time} = \frac{\text{maxtick}}{(1 + \text{timeslice})} * 100$$

At 2 *maxticks* and 8 *timeslices*, PRINT's use of CPU time is

$$\frac{2}{(1 + 8)} * 100 = 22\%$$

Increasing maxtick by 2 gives PRINT 44 percent of the CPU's time each second. Keeping maxtick at 2 and increasing timeslice to 10 gives PRINT 18 percent of the CPU's time each second. As you can see, the /M and /S switches give you a wide range of control over the amount of time PRINT can steal.

/U: is the maximum number of clock ticks PRINT will wait for a busy printer. The starting value is 1. The possible values are from 1 to 255. When PRINT gets control, it waits *busytick* number of clock ticks for the printer to accept more characters. If the printer is not ready in busytick time, PRINT relinquishes its turn. The computer can then continue with productive work if PRINT cannot do anything in its turn. You should increase busytick when you have a slow printer—one that works at less than 4800-baud serial or less than 100 cps.

/Q: is the maximum number of files (*maxfiles*) you can place in the queue. The default value is 10. The possible values are from 1 to 32. Increasing this number increases slightly the size of PRINT but allows more files to be put in line for printing.

Unlike PRINT V2, PRINT V3 is gracious when you exceed the queue limit. If you overload PRINT V3, especially when you give wildcard file names, PRINT accepts up to the *maxfiles* number of files and then issues a warning message that it cannot print the additional files. When the queue empties, give the PRINT command again with the files you could not print the preceding time.

Remember, you give the preceding six switches only when PRINT is first used. You can give the following three switches whenever you use PRINT:

/T   *Terminates* printing

/C   *Cancels* the printing of the file

/P   *Prints* this file

If you don't give a switch but do give a file name, DOS assumes that you want to use the */P* switch and prints the files on the command line.

The three periods (. . .) in the command represent other files and switches on the command line. You can have several files and switches on the same line.

PRINT's switches work like COPY's switches. A switch affects the file name given before the switch and all files after the switch—until DOS finds another switch. For the next example, assume that you have several ASCII files on the current disk drive and in the current directory. Look at the following line:

PRINT MYFILE.TXT /P NEXTFILE.TXT

The line tells DOS to background print MYFILE.TXT and NEXTFILE.TXT. The /P switch affects the file before the switch (MYFILE.TXT) and the file after the switch (NEXTFILE.TXT).

The order of the switches in the following line has a different effect:

PRINT MYFILE.TXT /C NEXTFILE.TXT FILE3.TXT /P

The command cancels the printing of MYFILE.TXT and NEXTFILE.TXT and puts FILE3.TXT in the queue. The cancel switch, /C, works on the file names before and after it. The /P switch works on the file name before the switch (FILE3.TXT). If you typed additional file names after the /P switch, PRINT would print them as well.

Sometimes, giving file names with switches or switches with file names makes no sense. For instance, giving a file name when you use the /T switch makes no sense. This is the "stop everything you're printing and forget it" switch. Giving the /P switch when you are only adding files to the queue is a waste of typing four characters—the two spaces and the /P switch. PRINT would automatically add the files to the printing queue without the switch.

Changing disk drives and directories has no effect on PRINT. You can queue up additional files or cancel them regardless of changing your current disk or directory. Do not, however, change a floppy diskette that holds a file on which PRINT is being used. If you remove the diskette prematurely, PRINT will print an error message on the printer and skip the file.

Don't try to use the printer again until PRINT has finished. If you do, the program you are using will issue a Device not ready message or a similar error message. Pressing Shift-PrtSc should produce a similar error message. When you get such an error message from DOS, press A to abort, and DOS will continue.

PRINT is not a sophisticated function. It is not designed to underscore, do boldface printing, set margins, or number pages as a word-processing program can do. PRINT prints only what is in a disk file, exactly as it is. (PRINT does expand tabs to every ninth column.) For more information on PRINT, see the *Command Reference*.

Summary

In this chapter, you learned these important points:

1. RECOVER can recover a damaged file or a damaged disk. Use extreme caution in running RECOVER on a complete disk.

2. The MODE command sets the characteristics of the printer and the serial adapter and controls the active display and its characteristics.

3. You use the PRINT command for background printing of a file.

4. PRINT has nine switches: /D, /B, /M, /Q, /U, /Z, /T, /C, and /P. The first six switches must be specified the first time you use PRINT.

Chapter 18 discusses how to back up and restore the fixed disk.

18

Backing Up and Restoring the Fixed Disk

This chapter and the next are mainly directed to fixed disk users. Because many systems use a fixed disk, these chapters are for most readers. Fixed disks present certain problems. In this chapter we'll examine the procedure for backing up the entire disk, restoring disks from backup files, and updating a fixed disk to a new version of DOS.

Backing Up Your Fixed Disk (BACKUP)

BACKUP is a versatile command that can back up either a diskette or a fixed disk. You can back up a fixed disk onto another fixed disk or onto diskettes, or you can back up diskettes onto other diskettes. The most frequent use of BACKUP is to back up the fixed disk onto diskettes.

Earlier versions of BACKUP, V3.0 and V3.1, have quirks. BACKUP V3.0 has an occasional fatal problem filling out the *header* file, which contains the backup diskette number and the date. In a directory of a backup diskette created under pre-DOS V3.3, the first file name should be BACKUPID.@@@. Look at the length of the file. If the length of BACKUPID.@@@ is zero, BACKUP V3.0 goofed, and the backup copy is unusable. You will need to back up again.

Most problems with BACKUP occur when another program is "resident" in memory. BACKUP V3.1's ailment is an allergic reaction to the old versions of Borland's SideKick® V1.1. If you have SideKick V1.1 loaded and give a properly phrased BACKUP command, BACKUP reports Invalid drive specification and exits immediately. You must remove SideKick before you can use BACKUP. (The current version of SideKick, 1.5x, works with all versions of BACKUP.)

429

To get rid of SideKick, you must either reboot DOS or disconnect SideKick. If SideKick is the last "resident" program you used since booting DOS, you can use the disconnect keys. Press Ctrl-Alt. This brings up the SideKick menu. Press Ctrl-Home and then Ctrl-End. The Home and End keys share positions with the 7 and 1 keys, respectively, on the numeric keypad. The SideKick menu should disappear. Press Ctrl-Alt once more. You have just disconnected SideKick, and BACKUP should now work properly.

If SideKick is not the last resident program that you used since starting DOS, restart DOS.

BACKUP V3.2 and V3.3 have no reported problems to date. However, DOS V3.3 uses a different method than earlier versions to back up files. With the new technique, only two files are placed on the backup disks: a control file and a data file. The control file holds the housekeeping information about the data files. The single data file holds the backup files. The two-file technique makes BACKUP V3.3 40 percent faster than previous versions and more diskette-efficient, meaning you'll use fewer diskettes for backing up.

An unlikely problem may occur if you bring up DOS V3.3 and then need to return to a previous version of DOS. RESTORE V3.3, the counterpart to BACKUP, can read diskettes created under all versions of DOS. However, earlier versions of RESTORE cannot read files produced by BACKUP V3.3. For this reason, if you are upgrading to DOS V3.3, back up your fixed disk with the earlier version of BACKUP. If for any reason you must revert temporarily to an earlier version of DOS, then your earlier version of RESTORE can still read the backup diskettes. If you use the later version of BACKUP, your files will be trapped until you can run DOS V3.3 again.

Preparing Your Diskettes (FORMAT, CHKDSK)

The first step in backing up your fixed disk is having enough diskettes on hand to hold the backup files. Unless you are using BACKUP V3.3—which can format diskettes on-the-fly—these diskettes *must* be formatted before you run BACKUP. Once BACKUP starts, you don't want to stop the process until it is finished. If you don't have enough formatted diskettes on hand, you will have to stop and format more, which usually means starting the BACKUP command again from the beginning.

When you format the backup diskettes manually, don't use switches. You want the maximum storage capacity from your floppies. Therefore, don't decrease this capacity by placing DOS on the diskettes or by otherwise limiting the amount of disk space that can be used. You can, however, use the /V switch with FORMAT to create a volume label if you like. A volume label takes a directory entry but does not take up any other space on the diskette. BACKUP ignores volume labels.

If you are formatting diskettes or just stacking new diskettes in a pile to be used later, place a numbered label on each diskette. Start with #1 and number each diskette sequentially. If you are using several boxes of diskettes, label each group of ten diskettes with a letter as well. Use A for the first group, B for the second group, and so on. Indicate the letter on the label of each diskette as well as on the box or holder in which you keep the diskettes. If you are backing up more than one disk drive, also place the letter of the disk drive (such as C: or D:) on the label. You should always keep a group of diskettes together. It's quite frustrating to lose the diskette that holds the file you need to restore.

How many diskettes will you need to back up your fixed disk? The only answer is two more questions. What exactly are you backing up? And what is the capacity of the diskettes you are using? If you are backing up a full 10M fixed disk, you will need 29 360K diskettes. If each diskette holds less than 360K, you will need more. Backing up a full 20M Personal Computer AT drive onto HC diskettes requires 18 diskettes. The 30M AT disk drive requires 26 HC diskettes. A 20M PS/2 Model 30 needs 29 diskettes with a capacity of 720K. A 40M Model 50 or 60 needs 29 diskettes with a capacity of 1.44M. Bigger fixed disk drives and lower capacity diskettes mean that you need more diskettes.

Table 18.1 shows the maximum number of the various diskettes needed to back up different sizes of fixed disk drives. The figures include "fudge factor" calculations that are necessary to back up a full fixed disk.

Table 18.1
Number of Diskettes Needed for Backup

Fixed Disk Capacity	Diskette Capacity			
	360K	720K	1.2M	1.44M
10M	29	15	9	8
20M	59	29	18	15
30M	83	44	27	22
40M	116	58	35	29
70M	200	100	60	50

Are you backing up only part of the fixed disk? If so, you will need to approximate the number of diskettes you'll need. If you are backing up just one or two files or directories, run DIR and add up the number of bytes in the files. Divide this number by 362,496 for 360K diskettes; 1,228,800 for 1.2M diskettes; 730,112 for 720K diskettes; or 1,457,664 for 1.44M diskettes. Round off the result to the next highest number to determine approximately how many diskettes you will need. Because BACKUP stores some housekeeping information with the disk files, you may need one more diskette than your figure indicates.

If you are backing up all or most of the fixed disk, use the following formula to help you determine the number of diskettes you'll need. First, run CHKDSK to see the number of bytes in user files and in hidden files. If the space devoted to hidden files is less than 100K, ignore the hidden files. Round the number of bytes in your user files to the nearest thousand and divide this number by 1000. Then divide the result by the capacity in Ks of the diskettes you will use. The result, always rounded up, is the number of diskettes needed. A pocket calculator or SideKick can make this job easy. If you have two or more logical disk drives on the fixed disk, don't forget to repeat the process for the additional disk drives.

Suppose, for example, that CHKDSK reports these holdings for a disk on a PC XT:

```
10592256 bytes total disk space
   28672 bytes in 3 hidden files
   73728 bytes in 18 directories
 4894720 bytes in 331 user files
 5595136 bytes available on disk
```

The hidden files are less than 50K, and you simply ignore them. To achieve an approximate calculation, round off the space in your user files to the nearest thousand. The 4,894,729 becomes 4,895,000. Divide the result by 1,000. The approximate (~) amount of disk space in user files is 4,895 Kbytes.

To calculate the number of diskettes needed, divide the approximate number of bytes by the backup diskette capacity in Ks. For 360K diskettes, the calculation is

$$\frac{\text{~4895 Kbytes used}}{\text{~360 Kbytes per diskette}} = 13.60 \text{ diskettes}$$

Rounded up, the number of 360K diskettes needed is 14.

The actual number of diskettes needed is fairly close. The fixed disk required 13 diskettes to back up, just one diskette less than the approximation.

In another example for a Personal Computer AT with a 20M drive, suppose that CHKDSK reports the following holdings:

```
21213184 bytes total disk space
   49152 bytes in 5 hidden files
  241664 bytes in 107 directories
19556352 bytes in 1866 user files
 1366016 bytes available on disk
```

If you use 1.2M high-capacity disks, the calculation becomes the following:

$$\frac{\sim 19{,}556 \text{ Kbytes in user files}}{\sim 1{,}200 \text{ Kbytes per diskette}} = 16.30 \text{ diskettes}$$

Rounded up, the approximate number of diskettes needed is 17. Interestingly, it took 16 diskettes to back up under DOS V3.2 and 14 diskettes under DOS V3.3. BACKUP V3.3 is usually more efficient in storing files than previous versions of BACKUP; therefore, your diskette approximations with V3.3 may result in a higher number of diskettes than you actually need.

The final example is backing up a PS/2 Model 60 using a 40M disk drive and 1.44M floppy diskettes. The fixed disk is divided into two logical disk drives.

```
33419264 bytes total disk space
   53248 bytes in 3 hidden files
  137216 bytes in 66 directories
18536448 bytes in 1021 user files
   30720 bytes in bad sectors
14461632 bytes available on disk
```

```
10993664 bytes total disk space
       0 bytes in 1 hidden files
   40960 bytes in 10 directories
 2985984 bytes in 195 user files
   36864 bytes in bad sectors
 7929856 bytes available on disk
```

Although hidden file space is less than 100K, I demonstrate how to handle the hidden files. For the two disks, the calculations are as follows:

18,536	2,986	Kbytes in user files
+ 53	0	Kbytes in hidden files
18,589	2,986	Kbytes to back up

18,589	2,986	Kbytes to back up
1,440	1,440	Kbytes per diskette
= 12.91	2.07	Number of diskettes

Round up each figure; then combine the two. The result is 13 plus 3 diskettes, a total of 16 diskettes needed. It took exactly 13 diskettes to back up the first drive; BACKUP took two diskettes for the second drive. I'd rather err on the high side and have too many diskettes ready than find myself rushing to find one more formatted diskette because I didn't give the /F (format) switch to BACKUP.

If your hidden files exceed 100K, the number of diskettes you'll use can change. For less than 100K of hidden file space, however, using just the user file space is close enough. Additional precision is not required because the approximation has enough "fudge factor" to handle less than 100K of hidden files.

If you are unsure or nervous about the number produced by the approximation, have on hand the number of diskettes indicated by table 18.1.

Starting the Backup Process

When you first use BACKUP, you should back up the entire fixed disk. Make the current directory for the fixed disk the root directory. Start with this directory by typing:

CD C:\

As you become accustomed to the BACKUP command, you can start with a different directory and back up only sections of the fixed disk. However, for the examples that follow, if you make the fixed disk (drive C) the current drive, the next steps will be easier.

Using the BACKUP Command

The complete syntax for the BACKUP command is

dc:pathc BACKUP ds:*paths\\filenames.exts* dd:
　　/S /M /A /D:*mm-dd-yy* /T:*hh:mm:ss* /F /L:*dl:pathl\\filenamel.extl*

As with all other DOS commands, you may give a drive name and a path name before the word BACKUP. If BACKUP is not in your current directory or on the PATH, give the drive and/or path name (*dc:pathc*) before the word BACKUP.

ds: is the disk to be backed up, the *source*.

paths tells DOS which directory to start the backup with. If you begin with the right directory, you can omit the path name. (This is why I always move to the root directory of the fixed disk.)

filenames.ext is the name of the file(s) you want to back up. Wildcards are allowed.

For DOS V3.3, you must give a disk drive name for the source. For other versions of BACKUP, you must give at least one part of the full source file name, which can be either the disk drive, path name, or file name. For the older versions of BACKUP, the current drive is used if you omit the disk drive name.

If you omit the path, BACKUP starts with the current directory of the disk. If you omit the file name, BACKUP assumes the name *.*.

dd: is the disk drive, or *destination*, to receive the backup files. You should always give the name of the disk drive that will hold the backup, either the destination fixed disk or the floppy disk drive. DOS makes no assumptions about this name. When you back up the fixed disk onto diskettes, you will usually type A: as the destination drive name.

Using BACKUP's Switches

The versatility of BACKUP is shown by its switches. Note that some switches can be used together. BACKUP V3.3 has seven switches, whereas earlier versions have four switches. Table 18.2 briefly outlines the switches and their functions for BACKUP V3.3.

Table 18.2
Switches for the BACKUP Command

Switch	Function
/S	Backs up all *subdirectories*, starting with the specified or current directory on the source disk and working downward.
/M	Backs up all files *modified* since the last time they were backed up.
/A	*Adds* the file(s) to be backed up to the files already on the specified floppy disk drive.
/D:*date*	Backs up any files that were created or changed on or after the specified *date*.
/T:*time*	Backs up any file that was created or changed on or after the specified *time* on the specified date (given with the /D switch). This switch is new for DOS V3.3.
/F	*Formats* the destination diskette if the diskette is not formatted. This switch is also new to DOS V3.3
/L:*dl:pathl\filenamel.extl*	Creates a *log* file.

The Subdirectory (/S) Switch

If you have been wondering why you should start at the root directory, the /S switch provides the answer. BACKUP works with the specified directory or the current directory if a directory is not indicated. BACKUP backs up the specified files in that directory. If you give the /S switch, BACKUP uses the directory as a starting point, moves to the subdirectories of the directory and backs up the files, and then moves to the subdirectories of the subdirectory and backs up these files. With the /S switch, BACKUP moves down through all subdirectories on this branch of the directory tree and backs up all the specified files.

If you start with a subdirectory and use the /S switch, you will get all the files in the chain of subdirectories for that side of the directory tree, but you won't get the whole fixed disk. For example, look at the sample directory in Appendix B. If you start at the root directory and use the /S switch, you will back up the entire disk. But if you start in the WORDS directory, you will back up the files in WORDS, LETTERS, and CONTRACTS, but not the files on the DOS subdirectory side of the tree. If you start with DOS, you will back up all the files on that side of the tree, but the WORDS subdirectory side of the tree will not be backed up.

To back up the entire fixed disk onto diskettes, begin with the root directory. Type

    BACKUP C:\ A: /S

This command tells DOS to back up the files in the root directory, any subdirectories, any subdirectories of these subdirectories, and so on.

A common mistake I made when I first used the BACKUP command was to start in a subdirectory, not specify a path, and think that I had backed up the entire disk. I was wrong. DOS started with the directory I was in and backed up only about a third of my fixed disk. When you use BACKUP, watch your starting directory and the path name you give, if any. Make sure that you tell DOS exactly what you mean.

The FORMAT (/F) Switch

The /F switch is the savior of those who do not format enough diskettes to hold the backup files. When the /F switch is given, BACKUP tests the diskette to see if the diskette is formatted. If the diskette is not formatted, BACKUP runs FORMAT. When FORMAT is invoked, you can format as many diskettes as you like. FORMAT acts as though you had invoked the command from the keyboard, but there are two differences. For one, FORMAT invoked by /F does not display any information or warning message about placing a diskette into the drive. The only message about changing diskettes comes from BACKUP. The other difference is that when you leave FORMAT, you return to BACKUP, which continues the backup process.

I have mixed feelings about using the /F switch. Giving the /F switch is the "safety play." If you have omitted the /F switch and you happen to run out of formatted backup diskettes, you're out of luck. You will need to invoke BACKUP again, and you may need to restart the process from the beginning. Using the /F switch whenever you back up the fixed disk is reasonable and will prevent the formatting problem.

On the downside, I dislike losing control of the options to FORMAT. FORMAT will be run without any switches being set when you use the /F switch. In a previous section I stated that you should use FORMAT without any switches, except the /V volume label switch. I can see an occasion when you might use the /N:9 switch, if you are trying to format a 720K diskette on a 1.44M disk drive.

Why format a 720K diskette on a 1.44M disk drive? At the time of this writing, the price of 720K diskettes was just under a dollar, and 1.44M diskettes (if you could find any) were priced at over six dollars. My occasionally frugal instincts tell me that paying six times the price for twice the capacity is currently not worthwhile. Therefore, until the price of the 1.44M diskette declines significantly (which should happen by late-1987 or mid-1988), I'm using 720K diskettes for backups.

If I use the /F switch and BACKUP encounters an unformatted diskette, it will invoke FORMAT without the /N:9 switch. This means that PS/2s with 1.44M disk drives will format 720K diskettes at a 1.44M capacity. Experience has indicated that this operation is risky. I have seen too many diskettes that have been pushed to a higher capacity fail at a later date, if the diskette formats at all (currently a fifty-fifty chance). My response to trashing that backup diskette will be less than cordial, because the only way I'll discover the problem is when I need the files on the backup diskette.

Another misfortune that can happen when you depend on the /F switch to format your diskettes occurs when FORMAT is not in the current directory or on the PATH. This problem may strike when you use a batch file to invoke FORMAT (discussed in chapter 12) and expect an option that BACKUP cannot give, or when FORMAT is not placed in a directory on the path. You will find yourself in a "fine kettle of fish" when you have to stop BACKUP, format diskettes, and repeat the BACKUP process.

For these reasons, I recommend that you give the /F switch only if certain conditions are met. Use the /F switch anytime you are unsure you have enough formatted diskettes *and* FORMAT is in a PATHed directory *and* you use the right capacity diskettes for the floppy disk drive. Otherwise, I recommend omitting the /F switch and formatting enough diskettes before you run BACKUP.

The Modified (/M) and Add (/A) Switches

The /M switch tells DOS to back up any file that has been *modified*. This switch really tells DOS to back up a file you have not backed up before. Remember the archive attribute? It is stored in the directory with each file name. When you create or change a file, this attribute is turned on. DOS checks whether the archive attribute has been set. When you give the /M switch, DOS backs up the file. Otherwise, DOS skips the file.

This switch enables you to choose the files you want to back up, but there are two hitches. First, the XCOPY command, which was discussed in Chapter 16, also uses the archive attribute and can clear this flag. If you use the /M switch with XCOPY and do not change a file before you back it up, BACKUP /M will not back up the file. That means your backup will be incomplete. If you did not preserve the XCOPYed version of the file and the original file is destroyed, the file will be lost.

The other hitch occurs when you use BACKUP /M several times a month. Suppose that on the first day, you back up your entire fixed disk. Then on the second day, you use the /M switch to back up files selectively. During the next three days, you do the same. Did all your files get backed up each time? Maybe. If a file changed each day, it was backed up each day. But what happens if the file changed only on the second and third days? It was backed up on those days only.

Unless you give the /A *switch*, DOS erases all files on the backup diskettes before recording the new files. This provision may be helpful when you have only a few files in one directory or when you have a complete subdirectory chain to back up. But what if you need to restore a file, after using the same backup diskettes each day, and you haven't given the /A switch? Each day, DOS erases the files backed up on the preceding day before backing up the new files. You will succeed in backing up the file twice, but you'll still lose the file from the backup diskettes.

To prevent this loss, you should have two sets of backup diskettes, or you should give the /A switch whenever you back up. If you give the /A switch, DOS expects the previously used backup diskettes to be in the floppy disk drive you specify. Otherwise, DOS will prompt you to put the appropriate diskette into the disk drive and press a key to start.

You may still have problems, though. How will BACKUP know which file version is the most recent if you have backed up the file more than once? Which set of backup diskettes has the most recent version of the file? To avoid these questions, I generally don't use either the /M switch or the /A switch.

There is one occasion when the /A switch should be used, however. When a file is being used by another program or computer, BACKUP cannot back up the file. DOS gives a warning message when a file cannot be backed up. If this happens, I run BACKUP as many times as necessary, using the /A switch to add the files that were not backed up the first time. After the other program or computer is finished, I rerun BACKUP to add the files to my set of backup diskettes. Usually the command

    BACKUP C:\ A: /S/A

backs up only those files that were not backed up on the first run of the BACKUP program.

The Date (/D) and Time (/T) Switches

The */D* and the */T* switches are an alternative to the /M and the /A switches. You enter a date with the /D switch. You can also enter a time with the /T switch. BACKUP then backs up all files that have been created or changed on or after the specified date and time. Because of this switch, you should always answer the date and time questions when DOS boots. DOS uses the date and time in the directory in searching for files to back up.

The */D* (date) switch tells BACKUP to grab any file that has been created or changed on or after the given date. Although this switch enables you to copy the same files each day, the switch also makes BACKUP run longer. This increase in time, however, makes restoring the fixed disk easier.

The form of *date* depends on the setting of the COUNTRY command in CONFIG.SYS and can be

    mm-dd-yy North American
    dd-mm-yy European
    yy-mm-dd East Asia

mm is for the month; *dd*, for the day, and *yy*, for the year. The character separating the parts of the *date* depends on the setting of the COUNTRY command and varies among the hyphen, period, and slash. North American users can substitute a slash (/) in place of the hyphen (-).

The new /T switch can make the BACKUP process more selective. You can tell DOS to grab any file specified by the date and the time. This switch is most helpful when you must perform the backup process more than once in the same day. You simply give the date and the time of your backup, and BACKUP will find any files created or changed since the time of your last backup.

The form of *time* is *hh:mm:ss* where *hh* is the hour, *mm* the minutes, and *ss* the seconds. A colon usually separates the parts of the *time* switch, but a period (.) may be used if the COUNTRY command in CONFIG.SYS has been set to Denmark, Finland, or Germany. The /T switch is new to DOS V3.3.

You should not use the /T switch without also giving the /D switch. If you do use the /T switch by itself, you will back up any file created or changed from the time of day you specify to the following midnight, regardless of the day. The result will be a scattering of files that just happen to have been created or modified after the given time on *any* date, not on or after a desired date. DOS will do as bidden; what you get will not be what you want backed up.

Another switch new to BACKUP is the /L switch. It produces a *log file*, a file that reports the files processed by BACKUP. The first line of the log file holds the date and time of the backup. The remaining lines contain the diskette number of the backed up files with the full path and file name of the backed-up file.

The log file can be displayed by TYPE or MORE, or it can be used with any text editor. RESTORE does not use the file. The only reasons to produce a log file are to check what files BACKUP processed and to find which backup diskette holds the file you want to restore. Rather than processing each diskette through RESTORE, you can search quickly through the log file for the correct starting diskette. This process can save some time when you restore a few files.

Previous versions of BACKUP stored the files under their existing file name. Upon finding a name conflict, the earlier versions renamed the extensions of the files. The new BACKUP consolidates all files into one file called BACKUP.nnn, where nnn is the number of the diskette. Because you cannot examine directly and ascertain the files that are recorded on the diskette, preserving log files may be important to you. BACKUP, upon finding a previous log file, does not erase the log file but adds (appends) the new information to the old file.

/L:dl:pathl\filenamel.extl creates a log file. *dl:pathl\filenamel.extl* is the drive path/file name of the log file.

When you use the /L switch, you can omit the complete file name, and
the log file will be placed in the root directory of the source disk and
given the name BACKUP.LOG. If you omit the full file name, do not give a
colon after the /L.

If you do give a file name, a colon must appear directly after the L and
before the full file name. Using an argument like /L:C:\BIN\BACKUP.LOG,
with colons before and after the disk drive name, may look funny, but it is
the only way BACKUP will accept a file name with a disk drive.

The rules about the full file name for the /L switch are slightly different
from the normal rules. If you omit the disk drive or the path name, the
source disk drive and the current directory are used, respectively.
However, DOS makes no presumption about the file name. You must
specify at least the name of the log file. Unlike most DOS commands, the
disk drive and the path names cannot be used without specifying the file
name, which means that switches like /L:D: or /L:\WORDS (when
WORDS is a subdirectory of the root) won't work. For the latter example,
if WORDS were not a subdirectory of the root directory, the log file
would be called WORDS and placed in the root directory of the source
disk drive. In this example DOS does what you directed, but not what you
might have intended.

Making BACKUP a Routine Procedure

You should keep three sets of backup diskettes for each fixed disk, and
each set should be kept in a separate box or bin. Each set should also
have enough diskettes to hold the entire fixed disk.

Once every month, back up the entire fixed disk, using the first set of
diskettes. Try to do the backup on the same day each month. If your fixed
disk is subdivided into two or more logical disk drives, make sure you
back up all of the drives.

Each day (or every few days, depending on how often you use the
computer), back up the fixed disk, using the /D switch. Use the second
and third sets of diskettes for this procedure; alternate the sets each time.
The date you give BACKUP should be the day you backed up the entire
fixed disk. This way, you will back up each file that has changed since the
"master" backup of the fixed disk.

The monthly backup takes the most time, and the time required for daily
backup increases each day. Once you have completed the backup process,
the entire fixed disk and every file that has changed will be on two sets of

diskettes. The third set is for safety. If you have a problem with a file on a "daily" diskette, you can go to the other set. You will lose some work on the file, but that's better than losing a month's work.

BACKUP follows the status of VERIFY. If VERIFY is OFF, BACKUP does not check your backup files to see whether they have been recorded properly. If VERIFY is ON, BACKUP checks the files. Before you do a monthly backup, turn VERIFY on to ensure that your backup files will be recorded correctly. Be sure to turn VERIFY off afterward. VERIFY slows down DOS by more than 90 percent on the diskette. That's why I turn VERIFY on only when necessary. You may turn VERIFY off for daily backups because the operation is usually safe. You will be the best judge of whether you should turn VERIFY on or off while you are backing up your fixed disk.

An important step before you run BACKUP is to disconnect any unneeded resident programs, such as SideKick, before you run BACKUP. This step is necessary with DOS V3.1 and advisable with later versions of BACKUP. Also, break any JOIN, SUBST, or ASSIGN commands that are in effect. These commands are covered in Chapter 19. If any of these commands are in effect, your backup copies may not contain the files you think.

BACKUP V3.0 users should run DIR to get a directory listing of each backup diskette after finishing the BACKUP process. Check the BACKUPID.@@@ file. If the file has a size of 0, the backup is no good, and you'll need to back up again.

Running a backup like the one outlined here requires a little more work each day, but a lot less work when a crisis comes. And a crisis will come some day, from one of two different hardware failures.

First, all disk drives fail eventually. When I first used a fixed disk in 1979, my disk failed after two months. The last good backup copy I had was several weeks old. It took me more than a week to restore most of the files. Some files were lost permanently. Experienced? Yes, I am.

I am pleased to say that I have had only one other fixed disk failure since 1979 and lost only a few unimportant files. Fixed disks are increasingly reliable, but they are not everlasting. Do not get lured into a false sense of security.

The more common hardware failure, a "screw loose in the operator," has caught me more frequently. My failures range from overwriting good files with out-of-date files to erasing all files in the wrong directory. I have found this personal failure to be more frequent, more insidious (you typically don't discover the mistake until later), and almost as devastating as losing the entire fixed disk. For this reason, BACKUP has even more importance.

Restoring Backup Files (RESTORE)

The RESTORE command is the opposite of BACKUP. RESTORE takes the files from your backup diskettes or fixed disk and places (restores) these files on the destination diskette or fixed disk. To restore the entire fixed disk, you should run RESTORE twice—first with the monthly set of backups and then with the daily set. If you have lost a file or two, try to restore the file from the last daily backup. If the file is not there, it has not changed all month. Using the monthly backup set, run RESTORE again to retrieve the missing file.

Several switches have been added to the command to make the restoration process faster and more convenient.

The syntax for RESTORE is similar to BACKUP's:

*dc:pathc*RESTORE **ds:** *dd:pathd\\filenamed.extd*
/S /P /M /N /B:date /A:date /L:time /E:time

As with all other DOS commands, if RESTORE is not in your current directory, you can give a disk drive and path name before the word RESTORE (the *dc:pathc*).

ds: is the disk drive that holds the backup information (usually the drive for the backup diskettes), and *dd:* is the fixed disk drive. (If the current disk drive is the fixed disk drive, you can omit *dd.*)

The *pathd* is the optional path to the directory that will receive the restored files. RESTORE uses the current directory for the fixed disk if you don't specify a path.

The *filenamed.extd* is the name of the file(s) to be restored. Wildcards are permitted. For DOS V3.3, DOS assumes all files (*.*) if you don't give a file name *and* a path name. If you give a path name, then you must give a file name. Otherwise BACKUP does not find any file to restore.

The switches shown in table 18.3 can be used with the RESTORE command.

The /S switch is helpful when you restore the entire disk or many subdirectories. The /S switch tells RESTORE to travel through the starting directory and subsequent subdirectories to restore files.

The /P, the /N, and the /M switches selectively restore files based on the archive or read-only flags kept by DOS.

The /P switch causes RESTORE to ask if a read-only or subsequently modified file should be replaced with its backup copy. You answer Y for yes or N for no.

Table 18.3
Switches for the RESTORE Command

Switch	Function
/S	Restores files in the directory specified and all other *subdirectories* below it. This switch is identical to BACKUP's /S switch.
/P	*Prompts* and asks whether a file should be restored if it is marked as read-only or has been changed since the last backup.
/N	Restores all files that *no longer* exist on the destination. This switch is like the /M switch, but /N processes only the files deleted from the destination since the backup set was made. This switch is new to DOS V3.3.
/M	Restores all files *modified* or deleted since the backup set was made. This switch is like the /N switch because /M processes files that no longer exist on the destination, but /M also restores files that have been modified since the last backup. This switch is new to DOS V3.3.
/A:date	Restores all files created or modified on or *after* the *date*. The format of *date* is the same as the /B switch. This switch is new to DOS V3.3.
/B:date	Restores all files created or modified on or *before* the *date*. This switch is new for DOS V3.3.
/L:time	Restores all files modified at or *later* than the specified *time*. The form of *time* is *hh:mm:ss*, where *hh* is the hour; *mm*, the minutes; and *ss*, the seconds. This switch is new for DOS V3.3.
/E:time	Restores all files modified at or *earlier* than the specified *time*. This switch is new for DOS V3.3.

If a file is set to read-only, it has probably not been altered—and probably won't be. IBMBIO.COM and IBMDOS.COM are two examples of read-only files. However, RESTORE V3.3 no longer processes these files or the third system file, COMMAND.COM. If you are using RESTORE V3.3, these names should not appear when you restore files.

If a file has changed since it was last backed up, you usually won't want to restore the file. The backup copy is probably out-of-date. The only reason to restore an out-of-date file is if the current file is trashed (corrupted). In any case, DOS will ask whether you want to restore such a file.

The /P switch does not limit the selection of files; all files matching the destination name are eligible for restoration. The /P switch allows you to choose which updated or read-only files should or should not be replaced.

The /N switch, which is new to DOS V3.3, instructs RESTORE to search for files on the backup diskettes that have been erased or renamed since the backup was made. If you have deleted a set of files you need to restore, /N is the switch to use. Only the files on the backup diskette that have been erased will be restored. Watch out for renamed files, however. If you rename a file after the last time you backed up, DOS will not see that name in the directory and will restore the version of the file with the previous name. If this happens, simply delete the unwanted file.

The /M switch, which is also new in DOS V3.3, acts like the /N switch in that /M restores deleted files, but /M also selects files in the backup set that have been modified since the last backup. The /M switch replaces those files that were backed up but have been changed. I nicknamed the /M switch the surprise switch when some "surprise" has corrupted several files in a directory or two of mine. Generally, I wouldn't replace current files with out-of-date files unless the current files are worthless (that's the surprise!). If something has undesirably altered your files, as it did mine, you can replace the current, but worthless files, with the out-of-date, but worthwhile files. In this case, give the /P switch with the /M switch. This way RESTORE will ask before replacing files, reducing the chances of destroying a good file.

The next four switches, /A, /B, /L, and /E, control which files will be restored, based on the file's date and time. These switches are additions to DOS V3.3.

The /A:date switch selects files created or modified on or *after* a given date. The /B:date switch selects files created or modified on or *before* the given date. These switches limit the files that RESTORE processes, particularly if you have been using the /A and /M switches with BACKUP.

The form of *date* depends on the setting of the COUNTRY command in CONFIG.SYS and can be

   mm-dd-yy North America
   dd-mm-yy Europe
   yy-mm-dd East Asia

where *mm* is for the month, *dd* for the day, and *yy* for the year. The character separating the parts of the *date* depends on the setting of the

COUNTRY command and varies among the hyphen, period, and slash. North American users can substitute a slash (/) in place of the hyphen (-).

The /A switch prevents RESTORE from processing several previous revisions of the files. Specify the date that you last changed the file, and RESTORE processes only the copies that were backed up on or after that date. It is better to be too early with the date than too late. If too early, RESTORE restores several versions of the file, but only the most recent version remains. RESTORE will overwrite previous versions.

I think the /B switch is the tragic-accident-recovery switch. When something "explodes" unnoticed inside the computer and corrupts your files, the /B switch works well. Use the /B switch when the current or more recent backup files are wrong and you need an earlier backed up version. First, specify the date of the file you know is good. RESTORE processes all backup files that were modified or created on or before the given date for that file name. The given date should be your best guess of when the problem occurred. Unfortunately, you may need to use RESTORE several times before you can get the "best" out-of-date copy.

The /A and /B switches can be used together to form a range of dates. Give the earlier date to the /A switch and the later date to the /B switch. For example, to restore the files modified or created between June 1 and July 15, 1987, the switches would look like the following:

   /A:06-01-87 /B:07-15-87

The /L:time and the /E:time switches permit the fine-tuning of the /A and the /B switches. The /L switch includes files that were created or modified at or later than the given time; the /E switch works on those files created or modified at or earlier than the given time. These switches are new to DOS V3.3.

As with the /T switch of BACKUP, using either the /L or the /E switch without the /A or the /B switch is usually meaningless. If you do use the time switches alone, you'll get a scattering of files that were created or modified before, on, or after the given time, with no consideration for dates.

As with BACKUP, the starting directory is important when you use the RESTORE program. You must be in the right part of the directory tree to restore a file.

When a file is backed up or restored, the path and the file name appear on the screen. This information is stored in each backup file and is used when you restore files. If you have erased a subdirectory, DOS re-creates it.

This feature is useful when you are restoring a faulty section of the disk drive or when the fixed disk has been erased.

When you use RESTORE, you must always start with the first backup diskette of the set and work sequentially even if you are restoring only a few files. DOS prompts you to change diskettes.

Caution: RESTORE and APPEND do not mix. If you must use APPEND, give the command **APPEND;** before you RESTORE your files, particularly if you use the /M or the /N switches. If you do not clear APPEND first, RESTORE may search the directories given to the APPEND command for files rather than the real directory it should search. This potential confusion is avoided by clearing the APPEND command before using RESTORE.

BACKUP and RESTORE are two powerful utility programs for fixed disk users. Study them carefully and use BACKUP frequently. If you are lucky, you will need to use RESTORE only a few times.

Knowing When To Use BACKUP

The suggestion that you back up your diskettes frequently to protect your files applies also to the fixed disk. You should also back up your complete fixed disk at two other times: (1) when you reorganize your fixed disk, and (2) when you have heavy fragmentation of the fixed disk.

Reorganizing a fixed disk involves copying many files to different directories. Reorganizing may also involve creating new directories, deleting unused directories, and deleting old copies of files. After you have reorganized the fixed disk, you will want to make a "snapshot" (a captured image; in this case, a binary image) of the fixed disk. In other words, you'll want to back up your fixed disk. By backing up the fixed disk, you will not need to repeat the work you did in reorganizing the fixed disk in case the disk should "crash."

Fragmentation occurs when a file is not stored in contiguous sectors on the surface of the fixed disk. After you have deleted and added many files, a new file can be scattered across the entire fixed disk. This hurts neither DOS nor the file, but DOS must work longer to retrieve such a file. The fixed disk's recording heads must move across the disk several times to read the file. As a result, the performance of the fixed disk decreases. Fragmentation can also occur after a major reorganization of the fixed disk.

The solution to the problem of fragmentation is to back up your entire fixed disk, reformat it, and then restore your files. Formatting will erase from the fixed disk all the files and subdirectories. As you restore each file and subdirectory, the information will be stored on consecutive sectors, thus increasing the performance of the fixed disk.

To accomplish this task, you'll need to complete the following steps. These steps back up the fixed disk completely, reformat it, and then restore all the files.

Step 1. *Make certain that you have a diskette that contains the operating system (formatted with the /S switch) and the following programs and files:*

    COMMAND.COM
    BACKUP.COM
    FORMAT.COM
    RESTORE.COM

If BACKUP.COM is already on the fixed disk, you may use the version on the fixed disk instead. But you'll still need a diskette-based copy of FORMAT.COM and RESTORE.COM.

Step 2. *Be sure that you have a sufficient number of diskettes. Use the guidelines given in table 18.1 to determine the number of diskettes you will need. If you are using BACKUP pre-V3.3, the diskettes must be formatted before you start BACKUP.*

Step 3. *Uninstall any copy-protected programs such as dBASE III® or Javelin®. Backed up, copy-protected programs will not work after the programs have been restored. You must uninstall the programs and then reinstall these programs after you have restored the fixed disk. Follow the publisher's directions for uninstalling a particular program.*

Step 4. *Turn VERIFY on. This will almost double the time required for the backup, but you don't want anything to go wrong. Skipping this step can be risky.*

Step 5. *Make sure that you have turned off any resident programs like SideKick and any ASSIGN, JOIN, or SUBST commands. These can interfere with the BACKUP. Also, clear APPEND if you are using the command.*

Step 6. Run BACKUP by typing

> C>BACKUP C:\ A: /S /F

You can use this command line if BACKUP is in the current directory or in one of the subdirectories specified by the PATH command. In any other instance, you should invoke BACKUP from the diskette or specify the directory holding BACKUP. If you are using a previous version of BACKUP V3.3, omit the /F switch.

On one of my fixed disks, BACKUP is in a subdirectory called \BIN\DISK. For my backups, I type a slightly different command:

> C>\BIN\DISK\BACKUP C:\ A: /S /F

Regardless of where BACKUP is located, you should specify the fixed disk and root directory, which is where you want BACKUP to start.

DOS will prompt you to put your first diskette into the floppy disk drive A. Insert your backup diskette #1 (the diskette with the number 1 on the gummed label), close the door if you are using minifloppy disk drives, and press a key. Coordinate the numbers on the labels of the backup diskettes with the numbers that DOS assigns. That way, the diskettes will be easy to store and use.

When DOS prompts for the next diskette, take out of the drive diskette #1 and put it back in the envelope. Insert diskette #2 and repeat the procedure, continuing with each additional diskette until you are finished. (You can stack the diskettes at the side of the computer as you use them.) When you are finished, the stack of diskettes make up the copy of your fixed disk.

If you get an error message from the floppy disk drive during the backup procedure, abort the program and reformat the offending diskette. If any bad sectors show up, retire the diskette and format a replacement. If you get an error message indicating that a file cannot be backed up, correct the problem and restart BACKUP. If you run out of formatted diskettes and use DOS V3.3, FORMAT automatically runs and you can format additional diskettes.

Remember that the backup copy of the fixed disk must be correct. If you allow errors, information will be lost.

Step 7. *(For BACKUP V3.0 users.) Check the BACKUPID.@@@ file on each diskette. Starting with diskette #1, put each diskette into the floppy disk drive and type*

    C>DIR A:BACKUPID.@@@

Look at the length of each file. If one of these files has a length of zero or if DOS reports that no file was found, you have a "trashed" backup set. Go back to step 5 and again back up your fixed disk. You should also check to be sure that you don't have a resident program running that is causing interference.

By the way, after you have typed this directory line the first time and have looked at its results, change diskettes, press the F3 special-function key on the left side of the keyboard, and press Enter. You will see why I like the DOS editing keys (see Appendix F).

Step 7. *(For DOS V3.2 or later users.) Know the volume label of the fixed disk you will format. If necessary, perform a DIR or CHKDSK and write down the volume name.*

Step 8. *Now reformat the fixed disk.*

This is the point of no return. You must have a good backup copy of the fixed disk, or you will lose information.

Put the diskette that contains DOS, FORMAT.COM, and RESTORE.COM into drive A. Make drive A the current disk drive (type A:) and then type

    A>FORMAT C: /S /V

This command reformats the fixed disk, takes DOS from the diskette and puts DOS onto the fixed disk, and allows you to put a volume label on the fixed disk drive. Remembering the rules for volume labels (see Chapter 8), type your volume label when DOS prompts you.

Starting with DOS V3, FORMAT will warn you that you are formatting a fixed disk. The message is a reminder that 10 or 20 megabytes of information are about to be destroyed. This is also your last chance to back out of the procedure.

If you are using DOS V3.2 or later, FORMAT will ask for the volume label of the fixed disk you are formatting. This is a triple check that indeed you are formatting the fixed disk. Enter the volume label and press Enter.

Step 9. *To restore the fixed disk, type*

A> RESTORE A: C:\ /S

This command tells DOS to start at the root directory of the fixed disk drive and restore all files in this directory as well as all files in the subdirectories. You do not have to make subdirectories again. DOS will do it for you when the first file from an erased subdirectory is restored. That's why the path name is included in each backed-up file.

Remove the DOS and program diskette from drive A, put in the backup diskette #1, and press a key. Then, following DOS's prompts, take the next diskette from the pile and restore the next series of files. Continue this process until the system prompt reappears.

Step 10. *Turn VERIFY off. (This step is optional.)*

Step 11. *Reinstall any copy-protected programs that were on the fixed disk. Again, follow each publisher's directions.*

You are done! You have backed up the entire fixed disk, erased it, and restored it. This procedure takes from thirty minutes to two hours, depending on how full your fixed disk is.

If you get a diskette out of order while using RESTORE, the command prompts you to put the correct diskette into the disk drive. If you number your diskettes, you should not have this problem. You can tell by the label whether the diskettes are in the correct numerical sequence. Remember also to store your backup diskettes in a safe place.

You now have a complete backup of your fixed disk. The diskettes will be your monthly backup set until the next time you back up the entire fixed disk. If you use the /D switch for both monthly and daily backup procedures, change the switch's date to reflect the current date.

Updating a Fixed Disk to a New Version of DOS (REPLACE)

When DOS V3.0 came out, I was using an XT. When DOS V3.1 was released, I was using an AT. DOS V3.2 found me on the same AT, but V3.3 and I went to the PS/2s. In each case, I had to change versions of DOS. If you are in the same position, the technique I use may be of interest to you.

First, I boot the new DOS version from a diskette. Then I use DISKCOPY to make another copy of the DOS Startup diskette. Because I have a computer with one floppy disk drive, I use

A>DISKCOPY A: A:

Next, I copy my current CONFIG.SYS file from the fixed disk to the new copy of my DOS master diskette and edit the file appropriately. I change the disk drive names of the DOS device drivers and the SHELL command from C: to A:. I immediately reboot DOS so that the BUFFERS command takes effect. I then test my most frequently used programs to make sure that they work with the new DOS. This testing takes about two hours. (A few programs have problems moving from DOS V2 to V3. No program I use has problems moving between versions of DOS V3.)

Incidentally, be cautious about using any of the previous DOS utility programs. Mixing new DOS utilities with old ones, or old utilities with new versions of DOS, can cause the loss of data! Be careful about this potential problem.

The next task is to replace old DOS programs with their new versions. I'll mention both the method I use for DOS V3.0 and V3.1 and the newer way with DOS V3.2 and subsequent versions. The newer method uses the REPLACE command.

For DOS V3.0 and V3.1, I simply copy the files from the DOS master diskette and supplemental diskettes to \BIN. I keep all DOS utility programs in \BIN or in one of the \BIN subdirectories. The copying wipes out the out-of-date versions of the same files. Then I begin rearranging files.

To distribute copied programs in \BIN to other subdirectories, I copy the programs from \BIN to the other subdirectories and then erase the files in \BIN. (Because you can run a program from anywhere, keeping around two copies of the same DOS utility doesn't make much sense.) I also shove the BASIC programs on the DOS Supplemental Programs diskette into their own subdirectory and erase these files from \BIN.

With DOS V3.2 and later, you can use the REPLACE command. REPLACE replaces old files with newer versions or can add files that do not already exist on a disk. REPLACE is discussed in the *DOS Command Reference*.

With the Startup or Master diskette in the disk drive, issue the following command:

A>REPLACE A:*.* C:\BIN /S

This command causes REPLACE to search the subdirectory \BIN on drive C and all subsequent subdirectories for files that match those on drive A. (The /S switch causes the search of subdirectories.) If files with matching names are found, the files on drive C are replaced with the files from drive A.

The next step is to copy the new files to the \BIN directory. The command is

A>REPLACE A:*.* C:\BIN /A

REPLACE examines the names of files in the \BIN directory and on drive A. If a file exists on drive A but not in \BIN, the file is copied to \BIN. The /A flag *adds* files to the destination.

If you are using minifloppy diskettes, insert the Supplemental or Operating diskette into drive A and issue the two commands again.

This technique is ideal for users who keep all DOS files in one subdirectory or subdirectory branch. The first REPLACE command replaces old DOS files with their new counterparts. Because the REPLACE command can examine all subdirectories of the given subdirectory, REPLACE automates the "search and replace" mission that is needed. The second command adds the new files to the \BIN subdirectory.

The flaw of using the REPLACE command comes in the second step, however. If you place device drivers (.SYS) or similar files in a separate subdirectory and not in \BIN, you will still be required to move some files from \BIN to the other subdirectories. When you give the second command, which updates the directory, REPLACE adds all files that are not located in \BIN. If the files are in other subdirectories, REPLACE still adds the files. REPLACE does not search the other directories for files that already exist. Hence, using the REPLACE command still requires additional work to copy additional files into the correct location and to erase redundant files, which were processed by the first REPLACE command.

Because my .SYS and .CPI files go into a subdirectory called \SYS, and my .PIF (program information files for Windows and TopView) go into \BIN with my other DOS files, my solution for DOS V3.3 is to issue five REPLACE commands in place of the second REPLACE command. The commands are as follows:

```
REPLACE A:*.EXE C:\BIN /A
REPLACE A:*.COM C:\BIN /A
REPLACE A:*.PIF C:\BIN /A
REPLACE A:*.SYS C:\SYS /A
REPLACE A:*.CPI C:\SYS /A
```

The first three commands add any new executable (.EXE), command (.COM), or program information (.PIF) files to \BIN, where I keep these files. The last two commands add any .SYS or .CPI (code page information) files to \SYS. Although I issued a total of six commands instead of the original two REPLACE commands, the process takes less time than copying and erasing the redundant or misplaced files in the original step two.

The next step requires the SYS command. With my copy of the DOS master diskette in drive A, I type

   C>A:SYS C:

This command places the operating system on the fixed disk. I also copy COMMAND.COM from the diskette in drive A to the root directory by typing

   C>COPY A:COMMAND.COM C:\ /V

At this point, the fixed disk is ready with the new version of DOS. I remove the diskette from the disk drive and reboot DOS from the fixed disk. If all is well, the new DOS boots properly.

Because I have reorganized the disk, it is time to make a master backup of the fixed disk. I follow the steps in the previous section (including reformatting and restoring the entire fixed disk). The only difference involves the RESTORE command. I use

   C>RESTORE A: C:\ /S/P

The reason for the /P switch is that replacing IBMBIO.COM and IBMDOS.COM is not necessary when you restore the fixed disk. FORMAT places these files on the fixed disk when you reformat it. For RESTORE pre-V3.3, I simply answer N for no when DOS asks whether I want to restore these files. For DOS V3.3, the /P switch is unnecessary because RESTORE V3.3 does not process either file.

One last piece of advice—the BUFFERS command in the CONFIG.SYS file has a dramatic effect when you use BACKUP and RESTORE pre-V3.3. I made the mistake of booting from a copy of the PC DOS V3.1 master diskette when restoring my fixed disk. This diskette did not have a CONFIG.SYS file with the BUFFERS command. I was using only the 3 native buffers that DOS V3.0 though V3.2 gives when you do not use the BUFFERS command. With 20 buffers, about and hour and a half is required to back up and restore a nearly full 20M fixed disk. With only 3 disk buffers, the process took 3 hours!

Summary

In this chapter, the following key points were covered:

1. The BACKUP command makes backup copies of diskettes or the fixed disk.

2. The RESTORE command restores files that have been backed up. You use RESTORE after you use BACKUP.

3. To prevent the loss of information, you must follow certain procedures for backing up and restoring a fixed disk.

4. The REPLACE command can replace existing files on a disk or add new files to the disk in one of many subdirectories.

Chapter 19 covers more DOS commands for fixed disk users. Some of the commands are also beneficial to users with floppy disk drive computers.

19

Gaining More Control
of the Fixed Disk

This chapter covers ASSIGN, JOIN, and SUBST—three commands especially
worthwhile for users whose computers have fixed disks. Computer users
with floppy disk systems will occasionally have use for these commands as
well. This chapter also covers DOS V3.3's FASTOPEN command, a
command that can improve the speed of locating and using files.

Using the Pretender Commands

ASSIGN, JOIN, and SUBST are DOS's "pretender" commands. In Chapter 2,
you saw how DOS could use a single physical floppy disk drive as two
logical disk drives. In Chapter 14 you saw how the DRIVER.SYS file could
extend this capability. ASSIGN, JOIN, and SUBST use a similar type of
trickery to "reroute" programs.

When you use these commands, the disk drive or the disk's subdirectory
masquerades as a different disk drive. The program you are running
"thinks" that it is using a certain disk drive, even though it is using a
different physical disk drive or subdirectory. With this capability, you can
get the performance from the program you want, and the program works
happily in "ignorance." ASSIGN originated with DOS V2. SUBST and JOIN
started with DOS V3.1.

Why use these commands? Some accounting and word-processing
programs, dating back to DOS V1.1, assume that a computer uses only two
disk drives: the minifloppy disk drives A and B. Some programs are
ignorant of fixed disk drives (drives C and D), RAM disks, external floppy
disk drives, and the hierarchical directory system that makes managing files

on a fixed disk easier. You need a way to trick some programs into using different disk drives.

The pretender commands are usually effective; however these commands can have side-effects that are not always benign. Read the set of cautions at this chapter's end, which covers these three commands and the APPEND and PATH commands. The discussion includes why the pretender commands can cause confusion.

Pretending That a Whole Disk Drive Is Another (ASSIGN)

ASSIGN is the whole-disk reroute command. The syntax for ASSIGN is

> *dc:pathc*ASSIGN *d1=d2 . . .*

Because ASSIGN is an external command, *dc:pathc* is the disk drive and path name to the command. *d1* is the single-character name of the disk drive to be rerouted. *d2* is the single-character name of the disk drive that will be used in place of *d1*. You should not use a colon after either disk drive name, but you must use an equal sign between the disk drive letters. Whether you put a blank space before and after the equal sign is optional.

You can give more than one assignment in a single line. If you do, separate each additional assignment from the others with a space. The most frequent assignment is

> ASSIGN A=C B=C

This line assigns drives A and B to drive C, the fixed disk. Whenever a program tries to use either of the two floppy disk drives, DOS will trick the program into using the fixed disk instead.

My most frequent use of ASSIGN is to redirect a program to use my RAM disk, drive E. I use the line

> ASSIGN A=E

Any program attempting to use drive A, the floppy disk drive, is rerouted and uses the RAM disk instead.

To undo the assignments, type

> ASSIGN

without any drive assignments. This command clears all assignments.

Pretending That a Subdirectory Is a Disk Drive (SUBST)

SUBST, the second pretender command, works similarly to ASSIGN. But for hierarchical directory users, SUBST is more useful than ASSIGN. The difference between the two commands is that ASSIGN reroutes all disk activity to another disk. SUBST reroutes the activity to a subdirectory on another disk. SUBST is the better choice for programs that know nothing about subdirectories, usually programs written to run under DOS V1. The SUBST command tricks a program into thinking that a subdirectory of one disk is a physical disk drive.

SUBST lets you nickname a subdirectory name using a disk drive name. The nickname or *alias* is used like any disk drive name. While SUBST is in effect, you can still access the subdirectory normally (by its "real" disk drive/path name) or by its disk drive name alias.

SUBST's syntax is

   dc:pathc\SUBST da: d:path

in which da: is the *alias disk drive name* by which you can additionally access the subdirectory. d:path is the optional disk drive name and the mandatory path name to the directory you want to use. Do not use a file name in the path. You may use only the names of a subdirectory.

To see the current active substitutions, type SUBST with no other parameters. You will see a list of each current alias with the corresponding "real" disk drive and subdirectory.

To remove a substitution, type

   dc:pathc\SUBST da: /D

Give the alias disk drive name and the /D switch to *disconnect* the substitution.

You can also use SUBST to substitute an alias for a real disk drive. Give the disk drive letter with the name of the path to the subdirectory for which you want an alias. For example, giving the command

   SUBST A: C:\WORDS

reroutes any activity intended for drive A to the subdirectory WORDS on drive C. However, until you disconnect the substitution with the /D switch, you cannot use the real disk drive, and you can use only the substituted disk drive and subdirectory. In this example, the floppy disk drive A would be unusable until you disconnected the alias.

If the disk drive name you give to SUBST is higher than E, you must use the LASTDRIVE directive in your CONFIG.SYS file. This command enables you to use disk drive names F through Z.

To see how SUBST works, take a look at this example that uses my favorite spelling program, MicroSpell. MicroSpell in an earlier version required that the dictionary files be in the disk drive's current directory. To run the program from any subdirectory, I used SUBST to tell MicroSpell where its dictionary files reside.

First, I added the LASTDRIVE directive to the CONFIG.SYS file by typing

```
LASTDRIVE = I
```

Although I planned to use only drive F with MicroSpell, issuing this directive allowed me three additional drives to use with SUBST.

After rebooting the system, I typed

```
SUBST F: C:\WORDS\SPELL\LEX
```

This command made drive F the LEX subdirectory on drive C. When I typed SUBST without any arguments, I saw the following:

```
C>SUBST
F: => C:\WORDS\SPELL\LEX

C>
```

Using the pretender command, I ran MicroSpell. MicroSpell reported that it couldn't find its dictionary and asked what disk drive held the dictionary files. I specified F:. DOS tricked MicroSpell into using C: with \WORD\SPELL\LEX as drive F. MicroSpell was happily deceived and never knew that it was using a subdirectory, not a real disk drive. The program worked.

If you organize similar disk files into subdirectories, you'll find the SUBST command to be more useful than the ASSIGN command. ASSIGN is useful when you reroute all of one disk's activity to another disk's current directory. When you need to use more than one subdirectory, however, SUBST is the only command that allows this kind of rerouting.

Pretending That Two Disk Drives Are One (JOIN)

On a computer that has only one floppy disk drive, DOS uses the single disk drive as if it were two different disk drives: A and B. The JOIN command works in the opposite way, letting you combine two different disk drives into one larger disk drive.

The most frequent use of JOIN is to join two "logical" fixed disk drives into a larger combined drive. However, you can join any two disk drives, including joining a floppy disk drive to another disk drive. If you have a computer with two physical or logical fixed disks, such as the PS/2 with a 40M or larger disk drive, (or one fixed disk and one floppy disk drive), you can join them. You use the JOIN command to join the second disk to an empty subdirectory on the first.

The syntax for JOIN is similar to that for SUBST. To join two disk drives, use:

dc:pathc JOIN **d1:** *d2:* path

As with all external commands, the *dc:pathc* is the optional disk drive and path name to the JOIN command. To clarify the designations, I'll use the terms *guest* and *host*. The guest disk drive (**d1:**) is the disk drive that will be joined to another drive. The host is the disk drive that will logically make the guest drive look like part of the host. In the syntax phrasing, *d2:* represents the host disk drive's optional name. The *path*, which is mandatory, is an empty subdirectory at which point the two disk drives are logically connected.

The following example shows what happened when I joined my floppy disk drive (drive A) to my fixed disk.

```
C>DIR A:                          {Get a directory of the
                                   floppy disk.}

   Volume in drive A has no label
   Directory of A:\

CØ2    PCD    46336    4-22-85    4:55p
CØ3    PCD    15744    4-16-85    7:12p
CØ4    PCD    44288    4-22-85    3:57p
```

```
CØ5      PCD      35968     4-23-85   1Ø:44a
CØ6      PCD       8192     4-23-85   11:Ø3a
CØ7      PCD      12288     4-23-85   11:58a
CØ8      PCD      5312Ø     4-25-85    8:42a
        7 File(s)      143360 bytes free
```

C>MD C:\JOIN   {Make the subdirectory.}

C>DIR C:\JOIN   {Show the JOIN directory.}

```
 Volume in drive C is MORE DOS
 Directory of  C:\JOIN


 .          DIR       5-24-85   2:55p
 ..         DIR       5-24-85   2:55p
        2 File(s)      2101248 bytes free
```

C>JOIN A: C:\JOIN   {Do the JOIN.}

C>JOIN   {Have JOIN display the
                                       connection.}

```
A: => C:\JOIN
```

C>DIR C:\JOIN   {Show the new directory.}

```
 Volume in drive C is MORE DOS
 Directory of  C:\JOIN


CØ2      PCD      46336     4-22-85    4:55p
CØ3      PCD      15744     4-16-85    7:12p
CØ4      PCD      44288     4-22-85    3:57p
CØ5      PCD      35968     4-23-85   1Ø:44a
CØ6      PCD       8192     4-23-85   11:Ø3a
CØ7      PCD      12288     4-23-85   11:58a
CØ8      PCD      5312Ø     4-25-85    8:42a
        7 File(s)      2101248 bytes free
```

C>DIR A: {DOS no longer recognizes A:.}
Invalid drive specifier

```
C>JOIN A: /D                       {Break the connection.}

C>DIR A:                           {Show the diskette
                                    directory again.}


Volume in drive A has no label
Directory of  A:\

C02    PCD     46336    4-22-85     4:55p
C03    PCD     15744    4-16-85     7:12p
C04    PCD     44288    4-22-85     3:57p
C05    PCD     35968    4-23-85    10:44a
C06    PCD      8192    4-23-85    11:03a
C07    PCD     12288    4-23-85    11:58a
C08    PCD     53120    4-25-85     8:42a

       7 File(s)    143360 bytes free

C>_
```

In this process, my first step was to create an empty directory, which I called JOIN. Then I JOINed A: to C:\JOIN, the empty subdirectory. I performed the DIR command before and after the action to prove that DOS had made the two disks into one larger disk.

Notice that while JOIN was active, I attempted to get a directory of drive A. DOS denied this request. While you use JOIN to connect one disk to another, you cannot access the joined disk except through the connecting subdirectory. In this example, the only way to use drive A is to use its new alias, \JOIN.

Like SUBST, when you issue the JOIN command without any arguments, JOIN prints the current subdirectory and disk drive on which you have used JOIN. JOIN also recognizes the /D *disconnect* switch. To undo the action, you give the real disk drive name with the switch.

JOIN has some restrictions on the subdirectory you can use as the host. The subdirectory must be empty; that is, it can hold neither files nor additional subdirectories. The subdirectory must be held by the root directory. You cannot use a subdirectory of a subdirectory.

If the subdirectory you name does not exist, JOIN will create the subdirectory for you. JOIN does not remove the subdirectory, however. You must remove the subdirectory by using the RMDIR command.

As I mentioned earlier, a frequent use of JOIN is not to join a floppy disk to a fixed disk, but to join a second fixed disk drive to the first, or a RAM disk to a fixed disk. To join the second fixed disk to the first via a subdirectory called JOIN, the command would be

JOIN D: C:\JOIN

Presuming the RAM disk is drive E, the command to join the RAM disk to drive C using a subdirectory called VDISK is

JOIN E: C:\VDISK

Important Warnings about All Pretender Commands

ASSIGN, JOIN, SUBST, and the PATH and APPEND commands, discussed in Chapters 10 and 11, are five commands that trick DOS and other programs into using different disk drives and/or subdirectories. Because of the chicanery of the rerouting, I should mention certain warnings. Most of these are common sense, but some are not obvious.

The APPEND, ASSIGN, JOIN, and SUBST commands do not work with all programs, especially those that are copy protected. These programs are not fully tricked by the commands. Such a program makes a DOS special request to read a specific part of the diskette in the floppy disk drive. APPEND, ASSIGN, JOIN, and SUBST cannot intercept and reroute this special request. In this case, your only choice is to have the correct diskette, which the program wants, in the correct disk drive.

You should not use ASSIGN, SUBST, or JOIN to reroute a real disk drive to a nonexistent disk drive. If you try, most DOS V3 commands immediately display the error messages

    Invalid parameter

or

    Invalid drive specification

The highest disk drive on which you can use ASSIGN or SUBST is based on the LASTDRIVE directive you have in your CONFIG.SYS file. You must properly set up the LASTDRIVE command to use higher letter disk drive names.

Although JOIN creates a host subdirectory if one does not exist, SUBST needs an existing subdirectory. You'll get an error message if you try to use SUBST with a nonexistent subdirectory. Create a subdirectory first, if you need one, and then use SUBST.

While ASSIGN, SUBST, and JOIN are active, you should use some DOS commands with caution and avoid others altogether. Be cautious with the following commands when you specify an ASSIGN, SUBST, or JOIN command:

CHDIR	LABEL
MKDIR	APPEND
RMDIR	PATH

When you are changing, creating, and removing subdirectories, you are operating on the physical disk drive that is the recipient of the rerouting. Although you specify one disk drive to create or remove a subdirectory, DOS actually uses another disk drive if you have used a pretender command. Keep in mind the physical disk drive that is being affected by these commands.

If you attempt to use LABEL on a disk drive on which you have used ASSIGN, SUBST, or JOIN, you can receive some astonishing results. The "real" disk drive is actually labeled, despite the alias disk drive you specified. Remember that the search paths specified by the program and batch PATH command and/or APPEND command for program overlays and data files follow ASSIGN, JOIN, and SUBST. Using these commands to hide a path used by PATH causes DOS to display a warning message about invalid paths in DOS versions prior to DOS V3.2. For PATH and APPEND in DOS versions after DOS V3.2, no warning is given at all. DOS simply won't find your programs or data files.

The DIR and CHKDSK commands work differently (or not at all) with ASSIGN, SUBST, and JOIN. DIR gives an error message when you attempt to display the directory of the JOIN command's guest disk drive. You must break the JOIN before you can get a directory of the JOINed drive, or get a directory using the alias path name.

When you use DIR with a SUBST directory, DIR displays a proper list of files. The volume label reflects the real disk drive used. The disk drive name and the directory reflect the rerouting. For the ASSIGN command, DIR always displays the rerouted disk drive's files. For example, if drive A is assigned to drive B, a directory of either drive shows the files on drive B.

CHKDSK will not process the rerouted disk drive involved in the ASSIGN or JOIN command. Nor will CHKDSK process the substituted disk drive (which is actually a directory). CHKDSK will process the host disk drive of a JOIN command but skip the guest portion of the disk drive. You can use CHKDSK to analyze the subdirectory you have used in a SUBST command, provided that you use the subdirectory name instead of the alias disk drive name.

Both DIR and CHKDSK show the free disk space on the "real" disk. DOS does not attempt to give new statistics on the combined disk space for JOIN. DIR and CHKDSK will report free space and similar statistics on the joined-to (host) disk drive only. You have no way to find the free space on the disk that has been joined (the guest) unless you disconnect it from the second disk, and then run DIR or CHKDSK.

Do not use the following commands on the disk drives involved in an ASSIGN, SUBST, or JOIN command:

DISKCOPY   FORMAT
DISKCOMP   BACKUP
FDISK   RESTORE
PRINT

Most of these commands immediately issue an error message when you attempt to use them with ASSIGN, SUBST, or JOIN. The reason is that you may operate inadvertently on a disk drive that is physically different from the drive that you specify on the command line. DOS simply protects you (and itself) from such operations. PRINT, BACKUP, and RESTORE do not issue warning messages. You can use these commands while rerouting is in effect at your own risk. Depending on which command you have used, the results may be surprising. To use these commands, first break the assignment, joining, or substitution. Then run the commands.

Finally, you should not mix the pretender commands so that you reroute the rerouting. You can JOIN a disk drive, use SUBST on the JOINed directory, and then use ASSIGN to direct the whole thing to a different disk drive. DOS happily reroutes the disk activity. Where the rerouted activity ultimately goes may be difficult to determine, though. To avoid "spaghetti" rerouting, don't reroute something that is already rerouted.

Gaining More Speed with FASTOPEN

FASTOPEN is a command new to DOS V3.3. This command is applicable only to fixed disk drives. FASTOPEN partially solves a performance problem not solved by CONFIG.SYS's BUFFERS command. BUFFERS helps when your computer is reading and writing information to several files. BUFFERS helps most when the disk activity is isolated to a file's few key portions.

If you use many of the same files during the day, particularly small files that DOS can read or write in one cluster, BUFFERS is not a major benefit. The time DOS spends traversing the subdirectory system and opening the files may take more time than actually reading or writing the files.

FASTOPEN basically caches directory information, holding in memory the frequently used files' and directories' disk locations. Directories are a type of file, not accessible by users, which DOS reads and writes in a manner similar to other files. A part of the directory entry for a file or subdirectory holds the starting point for the file in the FAT. Because DOS typically holds the FAT in the disk buffers, one major improvement that could be made of DOS was to hold directory entries in memory. This purpose is FASTOPEN's purpose.

FASTOPEN is not a complex command, but you'll have to do a small amount of work before you can effectively use it. FASTOPEN's syntax is

> *dc:pathc*\FASTOPEN d: = *nnn*

dc:pathc\ is the disk drive and path to the FASTOPEN command. d: is the name of the fixed disk drive you want FASTOPEN to aid. *nnn* is the number of directory entries that FASTOPEN should cache. Each file or subdirectory requires one entry. If you do not specify *nnn*, the number defaults to 34. *nnn*'s allowable range is 10 to 999.

You can use FASTOPEN on as many disk drives as you desire. Note, however, that the total number of directory entries that FASTOPEN can handle is 999. If you issue the command for several disk drives, *nnn*'s sum for the commands cannot exceed 999. This limit is FASTOPEN's physical limit.

nnn's practical limit is between 100 and 200 per disk drive. If you use many entries above this number, DOS will wade through the internal directory entries slower than it reads information from the disk. Also, each directory entry stored in memory takes 35 bytes. Considering the speed-versus-memory tradeoff, the 100-to-200 limit yields adequate performance.

However, using too small a number for *nnn* can be a disadvantage. Directory entries are recycled in a manner similar to disk buffers, meaning the least recently used entry is discarded if a new entry is needed. The object is to have enough entries in memory so that FASTOPEN operates efficiently, but not so many that the time FASTOPEN spends wading through directory entries exceeds its performance increase.

Another rule is that *nnn* must exceed the number of subdirectories you must travel through to get to your "deepest" subdirectory. In Appendix B's model directory system, the deepest "level" used is three (\DOS\BASIC\TESTS and \DOS\BASIC\SAMPLES). The absolute minimum number of directory entries you should use is four, which is less than the minimum number of 10 that FASTOPEN accepts. If the deepest level were nine, you could use ten, but using this small a number defeats the improvements that FASTOPEN can offer. My not terribly scientific guideline is start with 100 and fine-tune up or down by 5 until you "feel" the right performance.

You should observe a few restrictions about using FASTOPEN. The disk drive you name to FASTOPEN cannot be one on which you have used JOIN, SUBST, or ASSIGN. In other words, FASTOPEN cannot be an alias disk drive used with SUBST; it cannot be the guest disk drive in a JOIN operation, nor can it be the redirected disk drive in an ASSIGN command.

If you use a disk drive device driver that is loaded through your AUTOEXEC.BAT file by something other than the CONFIG.SYS file (some manufacturers provide a driver in the form of a program other than a usual device driver), you must use FASTOPEN after you have defined all disk drives. FASTOPEN can become confused if you add additional disk drives after you have invoked the program.

The command I use for FASTOPEN on my fixed disk is

    FASTOPEN C: = 90

Because I typically use 30 program and data files in a single computer session and my subdirectories typically run four levels deep, I use the number 90. My number is based on the 30 files (needing 30 entries), plus the number of subdirectory levels divided in half (30 * 4 levels / 2 = 60). Approximately half the files I use are in the same subdirectory as some other files I use, so I chop my subdirectory estimate in half. The estimate is close enough and the performance improvement makes using FASTOPEN adequate.

If you use deeper subdirectory levels or if you use more files in a session, increase the number you give to FASTOPEN. If you keep more files in fewer directories or you use fewer files, decrease the number that you give to FASTOPEN.

Give FASTOPEN only once per disk drive. The best way to invoke FASTOPEN is to place the command in your AUTOEXEC.BAT file. In this way, the command runs automatically whenever you invoke DOS.

Summary

In this chapter, you learned the following important points:

1. The ASSIGN command reroutes the activity for one disk drive to another disk drive.

2. The SUBST command enables you to give a disk drive name to a subdirectory.

3. The JOIN command joins two disk drives into a single disk drive.

4. The FASTOPEN command speeds the finding of files on the fixed disk.

In Chapter 20, we'll discuss transferring information between minifloppy and microfloppy systems.

20

Migrating between Minifloppy and Microfloppy Systems

This chapter describes a new problem: *migration*, the transfer of information between computers that use 5 1/4-inch diskettes (minifloppies) and computers that use 3 1/2-inch diskettes (microfloppies). I examine the problem and suggest some solutions. This chapter also discusses using a minifloppy-based "base" computer (the computer at your office or home) and a microfloppy-based laptop or portable.

When the PC Convertible was announced in August of 1986, few industry watchers were surprised that the machine used microfloppy disk drives and diskettes. Although IBM did not announce that other new machines would use microfloppy disk drives, sharp-eyed computer users could see the writing on the wall. Actions speak louder than words.

When the PS/2 systems were announced in April of 1987, suspicions were confirmed. Every machine used microfloppy disk drives. All subsequent new machines would have microfloppy disk drives, too, was the educated guess. The current PC family someday would be withdrawn.

If you have a PC XT, Personal Computer AT, XT-286, PC*jr*™, or PC Portable, your machine uses 5 1/4-inch minifloppy diskettes. If you have a PC Convertible or a PS/2 computer, your machine uses 3 1/2-inch diskettes. Because you can't use minifloppy diskettes in a microfloppy disk drive or use microfloppy diskettes in a minifloppy disk drive, you face some challenges.

If your first computer is a PS/2 and you don't use any other computer, this chapter probably is not for you. If you don't need any information stored on minifloppy-based computers, you could skip this section. You might want to skim it, however, because almost everyone I know has some need to get information from a minifloppy-based machine.

Determining Your Migration Needs

Assume that you do need to transfer files from one system to another. The first logical step in satisfying your needs is determining those needs. Here are some questions to ask yourself:

- What and how much information must be moved?
- Will you continue to use your old computer?
- How frequently will you move information?

Finding the answers to these questions involves looking at both your minifloppy-based and microfloppy-based systems and planning the future use of your computers. These answers are the key to which migration solution works best.

What and How Much Information Must Be Moved?

If you answer "everything" to the question asking what information must be moved, you fail the test. After examination, you may find that a small percentage of files must be moved. Amazingly, a study of corporate management information services departments shows that only 5 percent of a computer's files are moved when a new system is brought in. I suspect that a greater number of files are moved when a new personal computer arrives but that the number of files is less than 50 percent.

You don't need to move all your files. First, you don't need to move DOS itself because you have a microfloppy copy of DOS. Second, you don't have to move copy-protected software because you'll need new microfloppy versions of the software. (However, you may have to move the data files you use with this software.) Third, you may have to replace older versions of programs with new versions. As with copy-protected software, only the data files may need to be moved.

Fourth, some utilities fall by the wayside. Some programs that fit only your old computer may not or will not work with your new system. If you have a new printer, for example, some older printer utilities do not need to be moved. Examine your old utilities to determine what should be moved and what should stay.

Fifth, you may have some old data files you don't use any more. I haven't met the fixed disk on a mature computer (one that's more than six months old) that does not have some abandoned relics. Look at your spreadsheet or word-processing directories. Look for files more than six months or one year old. Do you still need those files? If the answer is no, don't bother bringing them to your new system.

Two of your best aids in determining the files that need to be moved are the TREE /F and DIR commands. Get a complete road map of your fixed disk by entering TREE /F >PRN. Use the resulting list to see what files you have. Then, use the DIR command and look at each file's date and time stamp for clues to the use of that file. Data files more than one year old should be suspect. Don't apply this same standard to program files, however, because the dates of these files don't change when you use the program. Therefore, you must run the programs to determine whether they have a life on your new machine. (On my system, I still use programs from 1983.)

How many files do you think you need to move to your new computer? If your files will fit on one or two 360K diskettes, almost any method can work. I'd choose the lowest-cost method. If the number is larger—as many as ten diskettes—your choices are more limited. You might spend a little more money to make the transfer process faster and more convenient. If the number is larger than ten 360K diskettes, or if you don't plan to abandon your old computer, only a few choices are available.

Will You Continue To Use Your Old Computer?

Before I explain the methods of migration, you need to consider another question: what are your plans for your old machine? The answer to this question helps you choose your "ideal" solution. After your new computer is set up and running, will you abandon your old computer? Will you keep your old system as a backup? Will you take it home or give it to your children? Will it stay at work and move to a coworker's office?

Basically, you have three possible answers. One, you'll never see your minifloppy-based system again—your old workhorse is going to pasture. Two, your old machine will supplement your new computer. You will have constant access to your old computer. Three, your computer is going to another person nearby, or it is going to your home. You'll have occasional access to your old machine.

If you will never see your minifloppy-based system again, you just need to move files to your new computer. The transfer is one-way: old computer to new. After you complete that task, the files on your minifloppy diskettes or old fixed disk won't matter; both will disappear.

In one-way migration, if you have any question about whether a file should be moved to your new computer, move the file. After the files have been moved and your other machine is gone, discoveries about large files you need but forgot to move will be unpleasant. Moving too many files is better than moving too few.

If you will be using both machines, chances are good that the file movement will be bidirectional. In this case, you must find a convenient—almost casual—method of moving files between your computers. If you keep both machines, you can be more lax about what files must be moved. If you need a file on your other computer later, you can move that file then.

If your minifloppy-based computer is staying "in the family" (going to a coworker or to your home), you have several options. If your former computer will be located nearby at the office, you still have access to the machine. If your old system is going to your home, you still have access to your computer, but tying the old and new computers together may not be convenient. Basically, your margin for error in moving files to your new computer is acceptable. You still will have opportunities later to get those files, although your old computer will be less convenient at home than at the office.

How Often Will You Move Information?

How often will you move files between the systems? Obviously, if your old computer is going away, the answer is "once." You may have to spend several hours or days moving all the needed files; but afterward, your old machine is gone and will not be used again.

If you plan to move files occasionally from your old machine to your new one, the procedure for the "one-shot" move still works. You may have to grab the system from your coworker or bring your computer from home, but after the two machines are together again, you can transfer files from your old one to your new one.

If you plan to move files in both directions, the question of frequency becomes an issue. If the frequency is high, convenience is important. If you spend more time or energy moving your files than creating or editing them, why bother moving them? You'd be better off re-creating the edited file than moving the file.

Examining the Migration Solutions

To summarize, here are the migration issues:

- What and how much information must be moved?
- Is the movement one-way or two-way?
- How often will the movement take place?

Based on the answers to these questions, you have three choices:

- the IBM Migration Aid
- communications programs
- dual floppy disk drives

The IBM Migration Aid

The IBM Migration Aid is a software/hardware combination that moves files through the parallel ports of two computers. One of your computers must be a PS/2, and you must have the parallel cable. The package comes with a diskette and a device that plugs into the parallel port of the PS/2 computer and accepts the 36-pin "printer" end of the cable. The other end of the cable is plugged into the 25-pin parallel port of your minifloppy-based computer.

A program called RECV35.COM is on the PS/2 Reference diskette, and a program called COPY35.COM is on the diskette provided with the Migration Aid. You run RECV35 on your PS/2, and you run COPY35 on your minifloppy-based machine. The result is a fast and fairly convenient method of moving files from your minifloppy-based machine to your PS/2.

The Migration Aid, like the other solutions, has both advantages and disadvantages. If you already have the parallel cable, the Migration Aid, at less than $40, is inexpensive. Its information transfer is fast, and the copy-receive programs send information over parallel ports several times faster than files are sent over serial adapters. The copy-receive programs are fairly easy to use. The COPY35 program works in a manner similar to the DOS COPY command. You can use wildcard file names and with one command send all the files from a directory. You also specify the destination name to COPY35. You start RECV35 on your PS/2 and tell COPY35 on your minifloppy-based computer where the files should go on your new machine. You can send the files to a microfloppy or fixed disk. The entire process is fairly convenient.

The Migration Aid has only one major limitation. Its file movement is only from your minifloppy-based computer to your PS/2. You can't reverse directions. Although the PS/2 parallel port is bidirectional—capable of sending or receiving information—the parallel ports on the other computers can only send information. If you want to send information from your PS/2 to your minifloppy-based computer, the Migration Aid is not the solution for you.

The Migration Aid has some minor disadvantages, too. The process is convenient, but not exceptionally convenient. After you start RECV35 on your PS/2, the program stays active and does not return to DOS until you press Esc on your PS/2. Therefore, you can run COPY35 several times and not touch your PS/2. RECV35 actively receives all files sent by COPY35. But this advantage is offset by the fact that RECV35 does not make subdirectories automatically on your PS/2. You must manually create any needed directories on your PS/2. Although the transfer commands are issued on the minifloppy computer, you must occasionally leave RECV35 on your PS/2 and make subdirectories on the disk.

The Migration Aid copies only one subdirectory at a time. COPY35 has no /S (subdirectory) switch. Because RECV35 can't make needed subdirectories, the program can't copy files from multiple directories with one command.

Another disadvantage is that your machines must be within cable reach. Parallel cables are usually 25 feet long or less. Distance usually is no problem when you first transfer files. When you want to move files later and your other machine is in a different location, however, you must retrieve the other computer. This hassle may be more work than you'd like to do frequently.

Basically, the Migration Aid is good for moving information from a minifloppy computer to a PS/2. You can move any amount of information. The program is fairly painless to use. However, the file movement is one-way. If you need bidirectional file movement, the two other solutions are better.

Communications Programs

A second choice is the communications solution, which uses the serial ports of the two machines to move files between computers. The communications solution involves both hardware and software. The software is the communications program which makes possible the two-way flow of information. The hardware consists of the cable and modems.

If your machines are located within a few feet of each other, all you need is the right communications program on each machine and a serial cable. If your machines are farther apart, you may need modems on both.

Like the Migration Aid, the communications solution has both advantages and disadvantages. The principal advantage is that files can be moved both ways. Another advantage is that this method can be used if the machines are not near each other. Serial cables can be as long as 200 feet, so the distance between the systems can be greater. If modems are used on both machines, the two machines can be located almost anywhere.

You will find some tradeoffs with this solution, however. First, serial communications are slower than parallel communications. Unless a very high baud rate for the serial ports is used, the file transfer takes longer. Because you can't use very high baud rates with modems, only computers connected directly by a serial cable are fast. If you want to move several files, you may spend several minutes or hours waiting for your two computers to finish their conversation.

The ease of use for this method depends on your communications software. With most programs, you can send a group of files at one time. If you can send only one file at a time on your communications program, you must endure the tedious process of typing at both computers the name of every file you transmit.

Communications programs do not create subdirectories on the receiving machine. For this reason, you must manually create the needed subdirectories on your receiving machine. With some communications programs, you can control your receiving computer. If you use this type of program and transfer files only to your fixed disk, you can issue the necessary commands at your sending machine only. If you send information to microfloppy diskettes, however, someone must be at the receiving machine to change diskettes. Unattended operation of your receiving computer is not an option.

The communications solution can range from inexpensive to expensive. You will have to acquire a special serial cable, called a *null modem* cable. Basically, the second and third lines on the cable are reversed so that the two computers "talk" and receive on separate lines. Using the wrong type of cable is an exercise in futility because neither machine will "hear" the other. Fortunately, a null modem cable costs about the same amount as any other serial cable.

Communications programs can cost almost nothing, or they can be very expensive. You can use public-domain programs, which are available free from many user groups and community bulletin boards. Also available are shareware programs, which cost virtually nothing to acquire. (If you find the program useful, however, the author requests a donation, which you are morally bound to send.) Shareware programs are usually cheaper than their commercial counterparts, and are usually of good quality.

The other solution is to use commercial communications programs, which range in price from $50 to $400. The programs are worth the money, but they may be more than you need. Remember that you need compatible communications programs on both machines. This requirement can double the cost of the programs.

You don't have to have the same program on both machines, but the programs must understand how to talk to each other and must use the same type of special protocol to handle program files. If the programs don't agree, you cannot move the files.

The communications solution is an inexpensive-to-more-expensive solution. Files can be moved both ways, but the process is slower and may require more effort. The distance between machines is unlimited if you increase the cost by buying and using modems. The more cost-effective method is to use a long serial cable. The ease of use depends on the communications programs you use.

The Floppy Disk Drive Solution

The third solution is installing an additional floppy disk drive on your computer. This solution, which may be the most expensive (from $160 to $500), has some exclusive advantages.

Basically, you put on your computer an internal or external disk drive opposite the type you have: a minifloppy disk drive on your PS/2 or a microfloppy disk drive on your Personal Computer. After the disk drive is installed properly, the drive becomes a regular part of your computer. You use the disk drive like any other, to copy files to and from the diskettes.

To move files between your computers, you copy files to the diskette by using XCOPY, COPY, or BACKUP. Then you take the diskette from the disk drive and put it in the disk drive of your other computer. You use XCOPY, COPY, or RESTORE to retrieve the files. You can move files in either direction.

The advantage is that the new drive is a regular part of your system. All DOS commands work with the disk drive. You don't need any other programs, you get the additional use of the drive to store and retrieve files, and the computers can be located anywhere. You have only to transport the floppy diskettes between your computers—not bring the computers to each other.

The major disadvantage of this solution is cost. The price of the disk drive and any needed adapter is more than the price of the Migration Aid and can be more than that of the communications solution.

The minor disadvantage is storage capacity. IBM sells a 360K minifloppy disk drive for the PS/2. But if you use high-capacity disk drives, reverting to 360K floppies is a painful pullback. Some outside vendors sell 1.2M floppy disk drives, which appear to be the best solution. IBM also sells a 720K microfloppy disk drive for Personal Computers. Fortunately, the 720K microfloppy has enough capacity. The cost of 1.44M disk drives makes the 720K drive attractive.

If the disk drive solution seems desirable, you have two other considerations. Which machine gets the disk drive? Will the drive be internal or external?

The machine you choose as your workhorse will be the base computer for your operations. Most files will either originate on or return to this machine. Also, this machine is the one you will keep for the longest time. For this reason, your best investment is complementing your workhorse with the opposite type of disk drive.

My inclination is to put the disk drive on the computer I'll be using most a year from now. If you intend to use your PS/2 the most, choose a minifloppy disk drive on your PS/2. If your PC will be your workhorse, buy a microfloppy disk drive for that computer. If you plan to use both machines for more than a year, cost may be your deciding factor.

Do you need an internal or an external drive? External disk drives are slightly more expensive (from $30 to $100 more) than internal disk drives because external disk drives may require a separate power supply and cabinet for the disk drive.

Can you use an internal disk drive in your computer? If you have a PC that already has two floppy disk drives, the answer is yes. You can replace the second minifloppy disk drive with a microfloppy disk drive. If you don't want to remove a floppy disk drive, however, you need an external disk drive.

Are you placing a minifloppy disk drive on your PS/2? You may have a choice between internal and external disk drives also. IBM's minifloppy disk drive for the PS/2 is an external disk. Third-party vendors, however, have developed a minifloppy disk drive that fits in the slot for a second fixed disk on the Models 60 and 80. If you won't use a second fixed disk on one of these models, you can buy an internal minifloppy drive. If you have a different PS/2 model or will use both fixed disks, your only option is an external disk drive.

This solution has one problem. You must maintain two different types of diskettes—minifloppy and microfloppy. If you plan to use both computers, you still need both types of diskettes. The problem is a natural consequence of using both machines.

Installing a disk drive involves some hardware and software tinkering. You may have to install an adapter in your computer. You must connect the disk drive, which could involve opening your computer and playing around with the cables. On a Personal Computer, you alter your CONFIG.SYS file. If your disk drive is external, you copy a file or two from the diskette provided with the disk drive. On your PS/2, you run the configuration option from the Reference diskette. The process of installing a disk drive is not difficult or very complex, but if you are wary of these steps, have your dealer or a computer-literate friend install the drive for you.

The disk drive approach may be the most expensive, but it is the most natural to use. The speed of the transfers is the time needed to copy the diskette twice—once from your sending machine to the diskette and once from the diskette to the receiving machine.

Choosing the Best Migration Solution

Based on your needs and your budget, your migration problem can be solved in several ways. The following are my suggestions. Base your final decision on the number of files you will move, the frequency with which you will move files, and whether your files will be moved both ways.

The Migration Aid is the best solution if you are abandoning your minifloppy-based computer. You need to move information only one way, and you can move any amount of information. The cost of the Migration Aid is small, and the speed is acceptable.

The communications solution is best if you need to move several files to your microfloppy-based computer and later must occasionally move small files or a few files back to your minifloppy-based computer. Because you need to move files both ways, you need a bidirectional link between your machines. This link is furnished by the communications solution.

This solution is good if both machines usually are connected, will remain close, or will be used for other types of computer-to-computer communications. To talk to other computers, you must make an investment in communications software. You get the additional capability from the communications software to talk to your old computer also.

If you frequently must move many files between your machines, installing **floppy disk drives** is the solution for you. It is good also if your machines are in different locations—when you have a laptop computer, for example.

Transfer frequency and the number of files is the key. If you move files between your machines frequently, you want the most casual method possible. The extra disk drive makes the copying process easy, and your two machines can be anywhere. Instead of transporting your computers, you simply transport the information on diskettes.

I have all three methods available. My own choice is an additional disk drive. I put a microfloppy disk drive in my PC AT-clone because I use this computer more than any other one. With this disk drive in my system, I can produce diskettes that move to my PS/2 or to my Toshiba T1100 laptop computer. All files come home to my AT-clone, so this solution is the best one for me.

By the way, I should mention an even less expensive solution than the three I have given. Find a friend, a company, or a users group that has one of these setups, and use it. (One of the technical editors of this book calls this the "Mooch Solution.") If you need the setup only occasionally, borrowing someone else's hardware and software makes sense.

Recommended Migration Techniques

My favorite technique for the whole computer-file transfer is to use BACKUP or XCOPY. I back up on microfloppy diskettes the directories holding the files to be moved, and then I use RESTORE to transfer them to my other machine. This solution is the fastest. Afterward, however, be careful to remove files you don't need, and be sure not to wipe out new versions of software when you RESTORE. If you are unsure, back up your receiving fixed disk before you move the software. If you make a mistake, you can restore the right file.

BACKUP works best when you first buy a new computer and want to move almost all your files to a new fixed disk. If you copy only a few files or subdirectories, use XCOPY to copy the files and their subdirectories to the floppy diskette. Then take the diskette to your other computer and use

XCOPY again. If you copy more than one subdirectory, you can use the /S switch on XCOPY each time.

If I think that I might fill up my transfer diskette, I use ATTRIB and XCOPY. ATTRIB turns on the archive attribute for the files I copy. The command is

    ATTRIB +A filename

in which filename is the full name for the files to be moved. Then, I copy the files in which the archive attribute is turned on by giving the command

    XCOPY filename B: /M

If the diskette fills up, I move to my other computer, issue XCOPY to copy the files from the diskette to the fixed disk, erase the files on the diskette, and then return the diskette to my original computer. I give the same XCOPY command again. Because XCOPY turned off the archive attribute on the files it copied, only uncopied files are processed. The trick works well.

If you copy from more than one subdirectory, add the /S switch to the ATTRIB and XCOPY commands. To avoid copying more files than you want, add the /P switch to the XCOPY command. XCOPY asks which files should be copied. Answer Y to any files that should be copied and N for files that should not be transferred.

Migration appears to be a temporary and very solvable problem. As with most computer decisions, some planning is needed. You must judge your future use of your old computer and decide whether files will be moved one way or both ways. You must determine how many files should be moved. After you have reached these conclusions, only your budget and the ease of use affect which solution you should use.

Summary

This chapter discussed the migration of information between minifloppy and microfloppy diskettes. To solve migration problems, you learned to first determine your migration needs by answering the questions:

- What and how much information must be moved?

- Will you continue to use your old computer?

- How often will you move information?

The chapter then examined the three solutions to migration problems:

- the IBM Migration Aid

- communications programs

- the floppy disk drive solution

You learned how to decide which solution is the best for you, and you also learned some migration techniques. Chapter 21 provides some final tips on using PC-DOS and introduces a few of my favorite programs.

21

Some Final Thoughts

This final chapter looks at many subjects already discussed in this book. I offer some thoughts about how to make DOS easier to use and how to avoid certain pitfalls. The "pitfall" experiences are based on my own encounters, and if humor is a reaction to pain, you will find some laughter in this chapter.

Avoiding Dangerous Commands

In several chapters in this book, some commands are labeled "dangerous." Such commands are not dangerous to you personally, of course, but to the data recorded on your disk. If you don't use these commands properly, they can erase or destroy files.

Recording any material on a disk takes time and work. Even though the data takes only seconds to copy or change, it still may represent the heart of your business or livelihood. Common sense should tell you that this data must be protected. If you apply this common sense, you should have few problems.

FORMAT and DISKCOPY are the two most dangerous commands. If you use FORMAT or DISKCOPY on the wrong disk, you can destroy several files in just a few seconds. ERASE (DEL) is dangerous also because it deletes files. Although these three commands appear to do the same thing, they have differences.

When you erase a file, you don't remove it from your disk. DOS simply marks the directory entry holding this file name as "erased" and frees the FAT sectors that held this file. When you add or extend a file, the new file either takes over the directory entry for your erased file or uses the sectors that held the erased file. With an appropriate program, you can unerase a file as long you have not added anything else to your disk. (The best unerase program I have seen is part of the Norton Utilities by Peter Norton, discussed later in this chapter.)

FORMAT and DISKCOPY record new information on the entire diskette and, depending on your version of DOS, FORMAT may wipe clean your fixed disk. When you format a disk, dummy information is recorded. When you use DISKCOPY, every bit of information from your first disk is copied to your second disk. If you use either FORMAT or DISKCOPY on a disk that has useful files, the information is no longer usable; it is lost.

In early versions of DOS, if you run FORMAT while the fixed disk is the current disk drive and you don't specify a disk drive name to FORMAT, you see the following emphatic message:

```
WARNING, ALL DATA ON NON-REMOVABLE DISK
DRIVE C: WILL BE LOST!

Proceed with Format (Y/N)?_
```

Needless to say, ignoring the message given by FORMAT V3 and earlier versions can destroy up to 32M of fixed disk information—the easy way. DOS V3.2 and later versions insist emphatically that you type the volume label of the fixed disk before you format the disk drive. The additional precaution is welcome. *Carefully read the messages on your screen whenever you use FORMAT.* A momentary lapse can have disastrous results.

SELECT is also a dangerous command because it runs FORMAT. Do not use SELECT on a fixed disk that holds any useful files. The files will be gone after SELECT has run.

COPY and XCOPY too can be problematic commands. If you use either command to copy an old version of a file to a disk holding a new version and you don't change the file name, you are in trouble. The new version of your file will be destroyed. Be careful when you use COPY or XCOPY.

The RECOVER command can be troublesome also. For a single file, RECOVER is easy and simple to use, but when you use RECOVER to recover a complete disk, you may need hours or days to recover files. Practice before you use RECOVER on live disks.

Knowing the Secret

Hierarchical directories and I/O redirection are difficult concepts to grasp at first. With a little practice, these facilities are easily mastered once you "know the secret."

A professional magician used to appear on television commercials all over the United States for a product called "TV Magic Cards." After performing a few tricks, he told viewers that they could easily do the card tricks "once you know the secret."

I feel the same way about computers and DOS. After you know how a command operates, you know the secret. After you've learned how to use the commands and know a little about how your computer operates, you can imagine what actually goes on when you invoke DOS and use its commands. Computers are "mystical" only when no one bothers to explain what really happens inside them. I hope that this book has provided you with some helpful ideas about how your computer operates.

DOS really is a friendly operating system. You can learn by doing. Just be sure to watch what you are doing. Even experienced users make mistakes, which occur most often when users get overconfident or sloppy.

After a while, you may develop "advanced user's syndrome." Your fingers fly across your keyboard. You know exactly what you want to do before you do it. Then you make an "experienced mistake." You use FORMAT or DISKCOPY on the wrong disk or copy the wrong files over good ones. You don't check to see whether the proper diskettes are in the disk drives. You don't read the messages completely, or you make a typing error and don't see it. You'll get so good at using your computer that you don't notice a mistake until it's too late.

To avoid some of these problems, always proofread your typing and check your messages. Take the time to be certain. Make sure that the correct diskettes are in the right disk drives. Write-protect an important diskette, even if you plan to remove the tab after you have formatted or used DISKCOPY on the diskette. Run DIR to be certain that no useful files will be destroyed by COPY, XCOPY, DISKCOPY, or FORMAT. Label your diskettes.

Forgetting to save frequently while you revise a copy of a document, a spreadsheet, or a program also can be an "experienced mistake." You may be confident you won't forget to save your information before you are finished, so you keep adding to, editing, or revising your document, spreadsheet model, or program without saving—even though the last time you saved a revision to the disk may have been more than an hour ago. An annoying feeling that you should save your revision gnaws at you, but you carry on. This is the time that Murphy strikes.

Let me relate both an old and a new story. I told the first story in the first edition of this book.

I once worked on a spreadsheet model for more than an hour. Several times I felt my nagging subconscious reminding me to save my work. I ignored the feeling and kept on refining the model. True to Murphy's never-ending mischievousness, in a half-second loss of power, the model I had been working on was destroyed. Restoring the model took only half an hour, but that time would not have been wasted if I had taken just 10 seconds to save the model.

Lesson One: Save your work frequently.

Lesson Two: Save your work more frequently if a storm is near.

I learn lessons the hard way. The next few lessons came during the summer I was writing this edition.

Waves of strong thunderstorms swept across Indianapolis late one afternoon. When I noticed the sky darkening and the wind growing stronger, I immediately marked my place in the text, saved my work, and turned off my computer. Within minutes, torrential rains soaked the area—and my car, on which the sunroof was wide open. After dashing the 20 feet from my door to my car, I was thoroughly drenched and found I could squeegee water from the car seats. Needless to say, my general humor when I returned to my desk was darker than the skies.

The power flickered several times. I felt relieved for having had the foresight to abandon my work during the height of the storm. Then, as quickly as the storms came, the skies cleared.

Impatient to begin working again, I started my computer and continued writing. The skies were almost clear when a brief power flicker paralyzed my computer. I lost 15 minutes of work. After impugning my computer, the local power company, and my stupidity for not following my own advice, I quickly reentered the lost material.

Lesson Three: You can't beat Mother Nature if she's out to get you.

Later that evening, a friend diverted me from work to go to dinner. After returning home, I felt I could squeeze in a couple more hours of work. When I write, time passes quickly. My last glance at my watch told me that it was 10:45 p.m. The next time I looked at my watch, I was in total darkness. The power had gone out for five seconds. All my computers went to sleep—where I should have been. My watch read 12:10 a.m. I restarted my computer and checked the time for the chapter I was working on: 11:14 p.m. Another hour of work had been blissfully slung into the bit-bucket. I resisted my strong desire to drown my system and myself in the pond outside my window and began to reenter my work.

Lesson Four: If you work late, keep a clock in sight so you'll remember when to save your work.

Lesson Five: If you don't save your work every 10 to 15 minutes, regardless of weather conditions, you deserve to be up until 2 a.m. reentering your work.

Lesson Six: Profanity is the language that computerists know best.

The Most Important Lesson: Save your work "frequently and often."

Finally, always back up your fixed disk and diskettes. Let me relate two true "horror" stories. Both stories demonstrate that the impossible can happen.

A computer user had issued an ASSIGN command on a non-IBM computer. Remember that this command tricks your programs into using a disk drive different from the one that the programs intend to use. The command was

ASSIGN A=C

The command tricked all his programs into using the fixed disk instead of the floppy disk drive A.

A half hour later, he issued the command

FORMAT A:

The normal DOS messages appeared. He put a diskette in drive A and then pressed Enter. After 30 seconds, he noticed that the light on his floppy disk drive had not gone on, which meant that the floppy drive was not in use. He then looked at the light on his fixed disk: it was on.

He quickly pressed Ctrl-C and looked at his fixed disk directory, which reported that his 10M fixed disk "thought" it was a 360K floppy. He had lost more than 8 megabytes of data, and I had no way to help him. FORMAT had written over his directory and his file allocation table. Recovering his data would be like rebuilding the side of a mountain after it had been dynamited.

The tragedy was not that FORMAT did something it should never do. FORMAT, under IBM PC DOS, is never fooled by the ASSIGN command, although the computer manufacturer was fooled in the command's MS-DOS® V2 implementation. The real tragedy was that the man had to spend three weeks recovering his files from a 30-second mistake because he had never made a backup of his fixed disk.

Now, I remind you that I am a very experienced computer user. I entered the homestretch of writing this book after returning from a trip to the West Coast. Cautious person that I am, I backed up my fixed disk before I left. After I returned, I worked furiously at my machine for 10 to 12 hours a day. The end was in sight.

Something had my end in sight also. To this day, I do not know what happened, although I use some experimental and rather exotic software combinations that may have been the cause. The temperature on those sunny days was high, and my air conditioning was not handling the problem well. Maybe the heat caused the failure. My machine is trustworthy, and the problem has not recurred since. Whatever the electronic mischief was, the outcome was a scrambled file allocation table on the fixed disk holding my book.

I first noticed the problem when I found a file that contained the wrong information. I corrected the problem file. I then ran a disk test program, which reported that the disk had no bad sectors. After finding nothing wrong, I continued my work.

The problem was insidious. No physical damage had occurred, but parts of my file allocation table had become electronic spaghetti. The damage was purely logical, affecting only the electronic information that DOS stored on files. The housekeeping information was stored correctly, but the information was wrong. The problem showed on only a few files I was using. As I continued to use my computer, I created more havoc on my disk.

When I discovered the extent of logical damage to my disk, I was shocked. CHKDSK reported so many crossed-up files that it actually aborted. When I cleaned up this mess, rerunning CHKDSK caused it to lock up my system. CHKDSK, which had found a circular chain in my file allocation table, was endlessly chasing its tail. I had to restart DOS to get to my disk. I finally was able to back up a few changed files before I had to reformat my fixed disk. However, most of my work from the past three weeks was ruined.

The only damage in this event was self-inflicted. I had not made a backup for more than three weeks. I spent the next four weeks recovering from my mistake. Even my 12-year-old nephew berated me for not following my own advice.

Yes, there is also a chance that one of the backups you make may be bad. For this reason, you should rotate sets of backup disks. If you have a bad backup set, you can restore from your previous set. The goal is to lose as little work as possible.

Back up, back up, back up, back up! Backups are your cheapest form of insurance. I cannot emphasize enough the need to back up your fixed disk. If your business or personal life depends on the information on your computer, you can't afford not to back up.

Introducing Some Favorite Programs

I have found that a few programs are indispensable in my daily DOS use. These programs are described in this section.

The "granddaddy" of the DOS add-on utility programs is the Norton Utilities by Peter Norton, who is a regular columnist for *PC Magazine, PC Week,* and *PC Tech Journal,* as well as a respected book author (and a respected competitor, I might add).

The Norton Utilities, which have undergone several revisions, are a set of programs that can sort the names of your files in a directory, set the foreground and background colors for your screen, test floppy diskettes and disk drives for bad sectors, report technical information about your system, display or change a file's attributes, time a program or an activity, and search for text among all the files in a directory or on a disk.

The most important program in the set is called NU. With this program, you can examine the contents of a file, directly alter the file, examine the directory, and unerase files. NU is menu-driven, simple to operate, and effective. I took a copy of a 360K disk and erased all the files on it. Using NU, I needed only 10 minutes to restore 20 files.

The latest version, V4.1, includes a quick unerase program. If you have a previous version, Version 4.1 is worth the small update fee. An Advanced Version, which includes even more useful programs, also is available.

The program price is about $100 for the regular utilities; the advanced version is more. However, either version is well worth five times that amount if you ever have to unerase even one file. The Norton Utilities is a must for every PC owner. You'll find the program in many computer and software stores. If you don't have and can't find the Norton Utilities, you can write to the author:

Peter Norton
2210 Wilshire Blvd.
Santa Monica, CA 90403

Another excellent group of utilities comes from SDA Associates, of San Jose, California. One set of programs is called FilePaq© ($39.95); another set is called FilePath© ($34.95).

FilePaq has four utility programs. One of these, SDADIR, is a directory program that can show normal files, hidden and system files, and subdirectories; or subdirectories only. The actual file size and the allocated file size (based on clusters) are shown, and SDADIR totals the figures for all displayed files. Like the /S switch for BACKUP and RESTORE, the /T switch for SDADIR traverses subdirectories.

SDADEL erases files. This command has a /P switch that tells SDADEL to display each matching file name, one by one, and to ask whether the file should be deleted. This utility is one of the few I know about that allows you to erase selected files.

SDARD removes subdirectories. Unlike RD, SDARD erases all files in the subdirectory (and all subdirectories in the subdirectory) before the command removes the subdirectory. With SDARD, you can type one command to remove a directory without first having to erase all your files and subdirectories. Needless to say, use SDARD with caution.

SDACHMD is a program that can change a file's attributes. Unlike ATTRIB (before 3.3), in which you can change only the read-only attribute, SDACHMD and Norton's FA (File Attribute) program can flip the hidden, read-only, system, and archive attributes for any file. Although some of FilePaq's functionality is duplicated in the Norton Utilities, FilePaq is a useful addition on any computer.

FilePath is an extensive version of the APPEND command. For machines that are not running DOS V3.3, you load FilePath through your AUTOEXEC.BAT file whenever you boot DOS. FilePath sits in memory and tricks the program into looking for the file in a different directory.

FilePath is a worthy addition for any fixed disk user who doesn't use DOS V3.3. Because these products may not be available in computer stores, you can call or write the company:

SDA Associates
P.O. Box 36152
San Jose, CA 95158
(408) 281-7747

A "resident" program, SideKick, from Borland International, is one of my favorites. The program has a calculator, an appointment calendar, a phone dialer, a WordStar-like memo pad, and an ASCII chart. Admittedly, I use only the calculator (which has a binary and hexadecimal—base 16—

mode) and the ASCII chart. The rest are just frills for me. When I move to a UNIX or OS/2 system, however, I usually miss SideKick within a few minutes. I recommend SideKick. The program costs $89.95, and you can buy it at many computer and software stores or directly from Borland:

Borland International
4113 Scotts Valley Drive
Scotts Valley, CA 95066
(408) 438-8400

You also can buy many different backgrounders or resident programs. Software Arts, now part of Lotus Development Corporation (of 1-2-3 fame), offers Metro™. BELLESOFT of Bellevue, Washington, has Pop-Up™ programs. Both programs have an alarm clock, which SideKick does not have.

I mention these particular programs because I spend a fair amount of time writing and programming. SideKick suits my style. Because your needs will vary from mine, a different backgrounder may suit you better. You may want to check these and similar programs at your local computer or software store. One of these backgrounders will make your life easier.

The final must-have-if-you-have-a-fixed-disk program is one I stumbled on at the 1985 National Computer Conference (NCC), in Chicago. I've been using the program ever since then.

I bumped into Jerry Pournelle, a fellow author-columnist. He and I walked the floors at McCormick Place and looked for interesting products. The one jewel we found is FASTBACK.

Jerry and I agree that if Winchester disk drives have any problem, it's the problem of backup. Neither of us backs up our disks as frequently as we should because of the time required for backing up. We recognize the danger of this attitude—witness my earlier confession. If one mistake is made, valuable work is lost. And we know that we are not alone in our attitude. After using FASTBACK, though, our thinking has changed.

FASTBACK is a hard-disk backup utility from Fifth Generation Systems. The utility works with all PC and PS/2 computers and many close clones. FASTBACK is simply an extremely fast backup program. It presents a series of questions about which files should be backed up, which floppy disk drives to use, and whether to back up all files or only changed files.

You stick a diskette in the drive and let the program go. If you have two floppy disk drives, the program uses both drives to back up your fixed disk.

The results of FASTBACK are spectacular. The program took 20 minutes and 15 seconds to back up almost 19 megabytes of files (a total of 1,940 files) on 14 HC diskettes. At least 1 minute of that time was spent changing diskettes. I also had used unformatted diskettes, which FASTBACK formatted "on the fly." When I ran FASTBACK a second time, on formatted diskettes, the backup time dropped to just less than 12 minutes.

With DOS's BACKUP, the fixed disk backup took about an hour and a half. If you include the time for formatting the diskettes, add about 15 minutes. FASTBACK, even when it formatted diskettes, was more than 5 times faster than FORMAT and BACKUP. When FASTBACK was not formatting diskettes, it was 7 1/2 times faster than BACKUP.

FASTBACK costs $179, and site licensing and dealer discounts are available. Although FASTBACK is more expensive than DOS's BACKUP (BACKUP is included with DOS), I consider FASTBACK infinitely more valuable. By using the program just four times, I have already saved the equivalent of its cost in time.

FASTBACK is available in many computer stores, or you can write directly to:

Fifth Generation Systems
11200 Industriplex Boulevard
Baton Rouge, LA 70809
(800) 225-2775

This outstanding program is for anyone who must back up a fixed disk on floppies. FASTBACK requires no additional equipment for performing this crucial but tedious housekeeping chore, and the improvement in speed is startling.

FLASH™ is a program that can improve your disk performance. DOS provides three tools to improve disk performance: the BUFFERS directive, provided with DOS Versions 2.0 and later; FASTOPEN, provided with DOS V3.3; and IBMCACHE, provided with the some PS/2 models. If you want to get more performance out of your disk drives, I strongly suggest a third-party disk-cache program. Disk-cache programs greatly outperform the DOS-provided tools. My personal favorite disk-cache program is FLASH.

FLASH is more versatile than the three DOS tools. FLASH can cache floppy or fixed disks; IBMCACHE handles only fixed disks. FLASH buffers directories better than FASTOPEN can. FLASH is faster than DOS's disk buffers.

FLASH, like any good disk-cache program and like DOS disk buffers, buffers as much information from the disk as possible into its cache. When a program wants information that resides in the cache, FLASH hands this information to DOS, which relays the information to the program. FLASH, like DOS disk buffers, minimizes the number of times the disk must be read. FLASH, however, regulates the cache more efficiently than DOS regulates its disk buffers. The result is that FLASH is fifty percent faster than DOS.

Another attractive feature of FLASH is that the program overrides DOS when it attempts to write disk sectors that have not changed. For example, a program reads four sectors into memory. The contents of two sectors are altered. The program instructs DOS to write all four sectors back to the disk. FLASH looks at the disk sectors to be written. If the information has not changed, FLASH instructs DOS not to write the unchanged sectors. Since writing information to the disk is more time-consuming than reading information, this feature vastly improves disk performance.

I enjoy several other features of FLASH. The cache can be placed in expanded (EMS) memory or extended (80286/80386) memory. If you have either type of memory, you can use a very large cache area and not impinge heavily on the precious 640K of DOS memory. FLASH automatically employs full-track reading and writing of disk information, which greatly speeds sequential disk operations without greatly slowing random disk operations.

(IBMCACHE handles multiple disk sector reading and writing, but cannot automatically adapt as FLASH does. The result is that sequential disk operations are faster and random operations are much slower.)

FLASH has other features I won't mention. I will mention that several other disk-cache programs are available. The price and major features of all disk-cache programs vary only slightly. I will also state that FLASH boosts my disk performance by thirty-five percent. FLASH is the disk-cache program I use.

FLASH costs $69.95 and is available from

Software Masters
6352 Guilford Avenue
Indianapolis, IN 46220
(317) 253-8088

Looking Ahead

This book has described most DOS commands, features, and functions. You have learned how to use DOS effectively, and you also have had some hands-on practice. You now should feel comfortable with your system.

In addition to the switches described in the main chapters, some additional switches appear in the DOS Command Reference, which provides helpful hints. The *Command Reference* also has some additional information about several commands not covered in the first parts of the book. Read this section, and return to it whenever you are "stuck" on a command.

Getting More Information

User groups are invaluable resources. You may find you are not the first person to have a problem with a program. Members of user groups can often help each other with problems or projects. Find a group in your area and join it. The benefits of membership will be worth your money.

If you are looking for more information about using your fixed disk, I recommend *Managing Your Hard Disk*, written by Don Berliner and me (and published by Que Corporation). The book has detailed discussions about fixed-disk organization and DOS tools and describes a number of outside programs that make using your fixed disk more enjoyable and effective.

Finally, try to enjoy. You learn by doing, as well as from friends, classes, user groups, and books. I hope that the time you have spent with this book was both useful and enjoyable. Here's to pleasant experiences.

Part VI

DOS
Command Reference

DOS Survival Guide

Note: An asterisk (*) designates a CONFIG.SYS directive.

To:	Use
Analyze a disk	CHKDSK
Automatically find files	APPEND, PATH
Automatically run a file at startup	AUTOEXEC.BAT
Print from the background	PRINT
Back up files	BACKUP, COPY, XCOPY
Back up disks	BACKUP, DISKCOPY
Change a code page	CHCP, KEYB, MODE
Change the active display	MODE
Change the baud rate	MODE
Change the console	CTTY
Change the current directory	CHDIR (CD)
Change the current disk drive	d:
Change disk buffers	BUFFERS*
Change the disk label	LABEL
Change the environment	SET
Change file attributes	ATTRIB
Change a file name	RENAME (REN)
Change/set location of the command interpreter	SHELL*
Change program input	<
Change program output	>, >>
Clear the video display	CLS
Combine disks	JOIN
Combine files	COPY
Compare diskettes	DISKCOMP
Compare files	COMP
Concatenate files	COPY
Connect disk drives	JOIN
Control Ctrl-Break	BREAK, BREAK*
Control verification of files	VERIFY
Copy diskettes	DISKCOPY,COPY, XCOPY
Copy backup files	RESTORE
Copy files	COPY, REPLACE, XCOPY
Create a subdirectory	MKDIR (MD)
Display available RAM	CHKDSK
Display the current code page	CHCP, MODE
Display the date	DATE
Display the version of DOS	VER
Display environmental variables	SET
Display contents of a file	MORE, TYPE
Display a list of directories	CHKDSK /V, TREE
Display a list of files	DIR, CHKDSK /V, TREE /F

Display national-language characters	CHCP, GRAFTABL, KEYB, MODE
Display the time	TIME
Display the volume label	VOL, LABEL, DIR, CHKDSK
Erase a character	←
Erase a directory	RMDIR (RD)
Erase a disk label	LABEL
Erase files	DEL, ERASE
Ignore a line	Esc
Execute several DOS commands with one command	Batch file
Find disk free space	CHKDSK, DIR
Find a file	CHKDSK /V, TREE /F
Find a word or phrase in a file	FIND
Freeze the video display	Ctrl-NumLock, Pause
Load file-sharing software	SHARE
Pause the display	Ctrl-Num Lock, Pause, Ctrl-S
Pipe output between programs	|
Place DOS on a disk	SYS, FORMAT /S
Prepare a disk	FORMAT, FDISK
Print graphics	GRAPHICS
Print the display	Shift-PrintSc, GRAPHICS
Print on the display and the printer	Ctrl-PrintSc
Print a file	PRINT, >, >>
Reassign disk drives	ASSIGN, JOIN, SUBST
Reassign printers	MODE
Restore backup files	RESTORE
Repair a file	RECOVER
Repair a disk	RECOVER, CHKDSK
Remove a directory	RMDIR (RD)
Remove files	DEL, ERASE
Run a program	program_name
Set alternative directories for programs	PATH
Set alternative directories for data files	APPEND
Set the country code	COUNTRY*
Set/change a code page	MODE, KEYB
Set/change checks on file writing	VERIFY
Set/change communications ports	MODE
Set/change displays	MODE
Set/change an environmental variable	SET
Set/change printers	MODE
Set/change internal stacks	STACKS*
Set/change the system date	DATE
Set/change the system prompt	PROMPT
Set/change the system time	TIME
Sort a file	SORT
Speed DOS	BUFFERS*, FASTOPEN
Stop a running program	Ctrl-Break, Ctrl-C
Stop a running program and reset the computer	Ctrl-Alt-Del
Unfreeze the video display	Any key
Update files	REPLACE
Use a different disk drive	d:, ASSIGN, SUBST
Use a new device	DEVICE*
Use a subdirectory in place of a disk	SUBST

Introduction to the Command Reference

This *DOS Command Reference* explains in reference form all of PC DOS's commands. Each command is presented in this format: the command name appears first, followed by the version of DOS to which the command applies. Asterisks (**) indicate that the command's functions are different in the newest versions of DOS.

The terms *Internal* and *External* indicate whether the command is built into DOS (internal) or is disk-resident (external).

Each command entry discusses the command's purpose, followed by the syntax required to invoke the command. Exit codes, if the command produces the codes, are listed.

Also listed are the rules governing the command's use. A single asterisk (*) before a rule designates a warning.

Examples demonstrate each command's use. The examples show the exact dialogue between the operator and the computer. Comments appear on the right side of the page.

The "Notes" section contains additional comments, hints, or suggestions on the command's use.

The "Messages" section is an alphabetical listing of the messages that the command produces. These commands produce three types of message:

INFORMATIONAL: This message simply informs the operator that an activity is taking place, or the message prompts the operator for a response.

WARNING: This message warns the operator of a possible problem. The command continues to function.

ERROR: This message indicates that an error has occurred. The error may be caused by the way the information on the command line was invoked (a command error) or may occur during an operation (a disk or other hardware error). The command terminates (aborts) after an error message.

Notation

The common notation used to represent a file specification is

d:path\filename.*ext*

d: is the name of the disk drive that holds the file, and *path*\ is the directory path to the file. filename is the root name of the file, and .*ext* is the file name extension.

If any part of this notation does not appear in the file specification (under "Syntax"), the omitted part is not allowed with the command. For example, the notation d:filename.ext indicates that path names are not allowed in the command.

In most cases, a device name may be substituted for a full file specification.

If a notation under "Syntax" appears in this type face, the notation is mandatory and must be entered. If a notation appears in *this type face*, the notation is optional and is entered only when appropriate.

Notation for External Commands and Batch Files

Starting with DOS V3, external commands (which are simply program files) and batch files residing in different subdirectories can be executed, just as program and batch files on different disks can be executed. The syntax used in this summary has a *c* added to the disk drive name and path. The notation is

dc:pathc\command_name

dc: is the name of the disk drive holding the command, *pathc*\ is the directory path to the command, and command_name is the name of the program or batch file to execute.

This notation is valid only for external commands—those disk-resident commands that are not part of COMMAND.COM (DOS's Command

Processor). The notation may be used also for batch files. But the notation is not valid for internal commands, those that are part of COMMAND.COM.

In this command notation, the following rules apply:

1. If you do not give a disk drive name for the command (*dc:*), DOS will search for the command on the current disk drive.

2. If you do not give a path (*pathc*), DOS will search for the command on the current directory of the current disk (or the current directory of the specified disk drive if one was given).

3. If you do not give a drive name and a path name, DOS will search the current directory of the current disk for the command. If the command is not found, DOS will search the list of paths specified by the PATH command. If DOS does not find the command after searching the path, DOS displays the error message

   ```
   Bad command or file name
   ```

   and gives the DOS system prompt (usually A>).

Using Upper- and Lowercase Letters

Words that appear in uppercase letters under "Syntax" are the words you type. Words that appear in lowercase letters are variables. Be sure to substitute the appropriate disk drive letter or name, path name, file name, etc., for the lowercase variable when you type the command.

Commands, as well as all parameters and switches typed with commands, may be entered in either upper- or lowercase. The exceptions are FIND and the batch subcommands; for these commands, the use of upper- or lowercase for certain parameters may be important. (See the sections on FIND and the batch subcommands for further information.)

DOS Messages

DOS messages fall into two groups: general DOS messages and DOS device error messages. The larger group, general DOS messages, is listed here alphabetically, followed by the device error messages.

General DOS Messages

The following messages may appear when you are starting DOS or using your computer. Messages that occur only when you are starting DOS are marked (start-up). Most start-up errors mean that DOS did not start and you must reboot the system. Most of the other error messages mean that DOS terminated (aborted) the program and returned to the system prompt (A>). The messages are listed in alphabetical order for easy reference.

Bad command or filename

ERROR: The name you entered is not valid for invoking a command, program, or batch file. The most frequent causes are the following: (1) you misspelled a name; (2) you omitted a needed disk drive or path name; or (3) you gave the parameters without the command name, such as typing myfile instead of ws myfile (omitting the ws for WordStar).

Check the spelling on the command line. Make sure that the command, program, or batch file is in the location specified (disk drive and directory path). Then try the command again.

Bad or missing Command Interpreter

ERROR (start-up): DOS cannot find COMMAND.COM, the command interpreter. DOS does not start.

If you are starting DOS, this message means that COMMAND.COM is not on the start-up disk, or that a version of COMMAND.COM from a previous DOS is on the disk. If you have used the SHELL directive in CONFIG.SYS, the message means that the SHELL directive is improperly phrased or that COMMAND.COM is not where you specified. Place another diskette that contains the operating system (IBMBIO.COM, IBMDOS.COM, and COMMAND.COM) in the floppy disk drive, and then reset the system.

After DOS has started, copy COMMAND.COM to the original start-up disk so that you can boot DOS.

If this message appears while you are running DOS, there are several possible explanations: COMMAND.COM has been erased from the disk and directory you used when starting DOS, a version of COMMAND.COM from a previous DOS has overwritten the good version, or the COMSPEC entry in the environment has been changed. You must restart DOS by resetting the system.

If resetting the system does not solve your problem, use a copy of your DOS master diskette to restart the computer. Copy COMMAND.COM from this diskette to the offending disk.

Bad or missing filename

WARNING (start-up): The device driver `filename` was not found; an error occurred when the device driver was loaded; a break address for the device driver was out of bounds for the size of RAM memory being used in the computer; or DOS detected an error while the driver was being loaded into memory. DOS will continue its boot but will not use the device driver `filename`.

If DOS loads, check your CONFIG.SYS file for the line `DEVICE=filename`. Make sure that the line is spelled correctly and that the device driver is where you specified. If this line is correct, reboot the system. If the message appears again, copy the file from its original diskette to the boot disk and try starting DOS again. If the error persists, contact the dealer or publisher who sold you the driver, because the device driver is bad.

Batch file missing

ERROR: DOS could not find the batch file it was processing. The batch file may have been erased or renamed. For DOS V3.0 only, the diskette containing the batch file may have been changed. DOS aborts the processing of the batch file.

If you are using DOS V3.0 and you changed the diskette containing the batch file, restart the batch file and do not change the diskette. You may need to edit the batch file so that you won't need to change diskettes.

If you renamed the batch file, rename it again, using the original name. If required, edit the batch file to ensure that the file name does not get changed again.

If the file was erased, recreate the batch file from its backup file, if possible. Edit the file to ensure that the batch file does not erase itself.

Cannot load COMMAND, system halted

ERROR: DOS attempted to reload COMMAND.COM, but the area where DOS keeps track of available and used memory was destroyed, or the command processor was not found in the directory specified by the COMSPEC= entry. The system halts.

This message indicates either that COMMAND.COM has been erased from the disk and directory you used when starting DOS, or that the COMSPEC= entry in the environment has been changed. Restart DOS from your usual start-up disk. If DOS does not start, the copy of COMMAND.COM has been erased. Restart DOS from the DOS start-up or master disk and copy COMMAND.COM onto your usual start-up diskette.

Another possible cause for this message is that an erroneous program corrupted the memory allocation table where DOS tracks available memory. Try running the same program that was in the computer when the system halted. If the problem occurs again, the program is defective. Contact the dealer or publisher who sold you the program.

Cannot start COMMAND, exiting

ERROR: You or one of your programs directed DOS to load an additional copy of COMMAND.COM, but DOS could not load it. Either your CONFIG.SYS FILES directive is set too low, or you do not have enough free memory for another copy of COMMAND.COM.

If your system has 256K or more and FILES is less than 10, edit the CONFIG.SYS file on your start-up disk and use FILES = 15 or FILES = 20. Then restart DOS.

If the problem occurs again, either you don't have enough memory in your computer, or you have too many resident or background programs competing for memory space. Restart DOS again and do not load any resident or background programs you do not need. If necessary, eliminate unneeded device drivers or RAM-disk software. Another alternative is to increase the amount of RAM memory in your system.

Configuration too large

ERROR (start-up): DOS could not load itself because either you specified in your CONFIG.SYS file too many FILES or BUFFERS, or you specified too large an environment area (/E switch) to the SHELL command. This problem should occur only on systems with less than 256K.

Restart DOS with a different diskette; then edit the CONFIG.SYS file on your boot disk, lowering the number of FILES and/or BUFFERS. You could also edit the CONFIG.SYS file to reduce the size of the environment, either in addition to lowering the number of FILES and BUFFERS, or as an alternative solution. Restart DOS with the edited disk. Another alternative is to increase the RAM memory in your system.

Current drive is no longer valid

WARNING: You have set the system prompt to PROMPT $p. At the DOS system level, DOS attempted to read the current directory for the disk drive and found the drive no longer valid.

If the current disk drive is set for a floppy disk, this warning appears when you don't have a diskette in the disk drive. DOS reports a Drive not ready error. You give the **F** command to fail or the **I** command to ignore the error. Then insert a floppy diskette into the disk drive.

The invalid drive error also can happen if you have a current networked or SUBST disk drive that has been deleted or disconnected. Simply change the current disk to a valid disk drive.

Disk boot failure

ERROR (start-up): An error occurred when DOS tried to load itself into memory. The disk contained IBMBIO.COM and IBMDOS.COM, but one of the two files could not be loaded. DOS did not start.

Try starting DOS from the disk again. If the error recurs, try starting DOS from a diskette you know is good, such as a copy of your DOS start-up or master diskette. If this action fails, you have a hardware disk drive problem. Contact your local dealer.

Divide overflow

ERROR: A program attempted to divide by zero. DOS aborts the program. Either the program was incorrectly entered, or it has a logic flaw. With well-written programs, this error should never occur. If you wrote the program, correct the error and try the program again. If you purchased the program, report the problem to the dealer or publisher.

This message can also appear when you are attempting to format a RAM disk under DOS V3.0 and V3.1. Make sure that you are formatting the correct disk, and try again.

Error in COUNTRY command

WARNING (start-up): The COUNTRY directive in CONFIG.SYS is either improperly phrased or has an incorrect country code or code page number. DOS continues its start-up but uses the default information for the COUNTRY directive.

After DOS has started, check the COUNTRY line in your CONFIG.SYS file. Refer to Chapter 16 and ensure that the directive is correctly phrased (using commas between country code, code page, and COUNTRY.SYS file) and that any given information is correct. If you detect an error in the line, edit the line, save the file, and restart DOS.

If you do not find an error, restart DOS. If the same message appears, edit your CONFIG.SYS file. Reenter the COUNTRY directive and delete the old COUNTRY line. The old line may contain some nonsense characters that DOS can see but are not apparent to your text-editing program.

Error in EXE file

ERROR: DOS detected an error while attempting to load a program stored in an .EXE file. The problem is in the relocation information DOS needs to load the program. This problem can occur if the .EXE file has been altered in any way.

Restart DOS and try the program again, this time using a backup copy of the program. If the message reappears, the program is flawed. If you are using a purchased program, contact the dealer or publisher. If you wrote the program, use LINK to produce another copy of the program.

Error loading operating system

ERROR (start-up): A disk error occurred while DOS was loading itself from the fixed disk. DOS does not start.

Restart the computer. If the error keeps occurring after several tries, restart DOS from the floppy disk drive. If the fixed disk does not respond (that is, you cannot run DIR or CHKDSK without getting an error), you have a problem with the fixed disk. Contact your local dealer. If the fixed disk does respond, use the SYS command to put another copy of DOS onto your fixed disk. You also may need to copy COMMAND.COM to the fixed disk.

EXEC failure

ERROR: Either DOS encountered an error while reading a command or program from the disk, or the CONFIG.SYS FILES directive has too low a value.

Increase to 15 or 20 the number of FILES in the CONFIG.SYS file of your start-up diskette. Restart DOS. If the error recurs, you may have a problem with the diskette. Use a backup copy of the program and try again. If the backup copy works, copy it over the offending copy.

If an error occurs in the copying process, you have a flawed diskette or fixed disk. If the problem is a diskette, copy the files from the flawed diskette to another diskette and reformat or retire the original diskette. If the problem is the fixed disk, immediately back up your files and run RECOVER on the offending file. If the problem persists, your fixed disk may have a hardware failure.

File allocation table bad, drive d
Abort, Retry, Fail?

WARNING: DOS encountered a problem in the file allocation table of the disk in drive d. Enter **R** for Retry several times. If this does not solve the problem, use **A** for Abort.

If you are using a diskette, attempt to copy all the files to another diskette and then reformat or retire the original diskette. If you are using a fixed disk, back up all files on the disk and reformat the fixed disk. The disk is unusable until reformatted.

File creation error

ERROR: A program or DOS attempted to add a new file to the directory or to replace an existing file, but failed.

If the file already exists, use the ATTRIB command to check whether the file is marked as read-only. If the read-only flag is set and you want to change or erase the file, use ATTRIB to remove the read-only flag; then try again.

If the problem is not the read-only flag, run CHKDSK without the /F switch to determine whether the directory is full, the disk is full, or some other problem exists with the disk.

File not found

ERROR: DOS could not find a file that you specified. Either the file is not on the correct diskette or in the correct directory, or you misspelled the disk drive name, path name, or file name. Check these possibilities and try the command again.

Incorrect DOS version

ERROR: The copy of the file holding the command you just entered is from a different version of DOS.

Get a copy of the command from the correct version of DOS (usually from your copy of the DOS start-up or master diskette), and try the command again. If the disk or diskette you are using has been updated to hold new versions of the DOS programs, copy the new versions over the old ones.

Insert disk with batch file and strike any key when ready

INFORMATIONAL: DOS is attempting to execute the next command from a batch file, but the diskette holding the batch file is not in the disk drive. This message occurs for DOS V3.1 and later versions. DOS V3.0 gives a fatal error when the diskette is changed.

Put the diskette holding the batch file into the disk drive and press a key to continue.

Insert disk with \COMMAND.COM in drive d and strike any key when ready

INFORMATIONAL and WARNING: DOS needed to reload COMMAND.COM but could not find it on the start-up disk.

If you are using diskettes, the diskette in drive d (usually A:) probably has been changed. Place a diskette holding a good copy of COMMAND.COM in drive d and press a key.

Insert diskette for drive d and strike any key when ready

INFORMATIONAL: On a system with one floppy disk drive or a system using DRIVER.SYS that makes more than one logical disk drive out of one physical disk drive, you or one of your programs specified the tandem disk drive d (such as A: or B:). This drive is different from the current disk drive.

If the correct diskette is in the disk drive, press a key. Otherwise, put the correct diskette into the floppy disk drive and then press a key.

Insufficient disk space

WARNING or ERROR: The disk does not have enough free space to hold the file being written. All DOS programs terminate when this problem occurs, but some non-DOS programs continue.

If you think that the disk has enough room to hold this file, run CHKDSK to see whether the disk or diskette has a problem. Sometimes when you terminate programs early by pressing Ctrl-Break, DOS isn't allowed to do the necessary clean-up work. When this happens, disk space is temporarily trapped. CHKDSK can "free" these areas.

If you simply have run out of disk space, free some disk space or use a different diskette or fixed disk. Try the command again.

Insufficient memory

ERROR: The computer does not have enough free RAM memory to execute the program or command.

If you loaded a resident program like PRINT, GRAPHICS, SideKick, or ProKey, restart DOS and try the command before loading any resident program. If this method fails, remove any unneeded device driver or RAM-disk software from the CONFIG.SYS file and restart DOS again. If this action fails, your computer does not have enough memory for this command. You must increase your RAM memory to run the command.

Intermediate file error during pipe

ERROR: DOS is unable to create or write to one or both of the intermediate files it uses when piping (|) information between programs. The disk is full, the root directory of the current disk is full, or DOS cannot locate the files. The most frequent cause is running out of disk space.

Run the DIR command on the root directory of the current disk drive. Make sure that you have enough free space and enough room in the root directory for two additional files. If you don't have enough room, create room on the disk by deleting, or copying and deleting, files. You may also copy the necessary files to a different diskette with sufficient room.

One possibility is that a program is deleting files, including the temporary files DOS uses. If this is the case, you should correct the program, contact the dealer or program publisher, or avoid using the program with piping.

Internal stack overflow
System halted

ERROR: Your programs and DOS have exhausted the stack, the memory space that is reserved for temporary use. This problem is usually caused by a very rapid succession of hardware devices demanding attention (interrupts). DOS stops, and the system must be turned off and on again to restart DOS.

The circumstances that cause this message are generally infrequent and erratic, and may not recur. If you want to prevent this error from occurring at all, add the STACKS directive to your CONFIG.SYS file. If the directive is already in your CONFIG.SYS file, then increase the number of stacks specified. See Chapter 14 for more information on the STACKS directive.

Invalid COMMAND.COM in drive d

WARNING: DOS tried to reload COMMAND.COM from the disk in drive d and found that the file was from a different version of DOS. You will see a message instructing you to insert a diskette with the correct version and press a key. Follow the directions for that message.

If you frequently use the diskette that was originally in the disk drive, copy the correct version of COMMAND.COM to that diskette.

Invalid COUNTRY code or code page

WARNING (start-up): Either the COUNTRY code number or the code page number given to the COUNTRY directive in the CONFIG.SYS file is incorrect or incompatible. DOS ignores the COUNTRY directive and continues to start.

Check the COUNTRY directive in your CONFIG.SYS file. Refer to Chapter 15 and ensure that the correct and compatible country code and code page numbers are specified. If you detect an error, edit and save the file, and restart DOS.

Invalid COMMAND.COM, system halted

ERROR: DOS could not find COMMAND.COM on the fixed disk. DOS halts and must be restarted.

COMMAND.COM may have been erased, or the COMSPEC variable in the environment may have been changed. Restart the computer from the fixed disk. If you see a message indicating that COMMAND.COM is missing, the file was erased. Restart DOS from a diskette and recopy COMMAND.COM to the root directory of the fixed disk or to wherever your SHELL directive directs, if you have used this command in your CONFIG.SYS file.

If you restart DOS and this message appears later, a program or batch file is erasing COMMAND.COM or is altering the COMSPEC variable. If a batch file is erasing COMMAND.COM, edit the batch file. If a program is erasing COMMAND.COM, contact the dealer or publisher who sold you the program. If COMSPEC is being altered, either edit the offending batch file or program, or place COMMAND.COM in the subdirectory your program or batch file expects.

Invalid directory

ERROR: One of the following errors occurred: (1) you specified a directory name that doesn't exist, (2) you misspelled the directory name, (3) the directory path is on a different disk, (4) you forgot to give the path character (\) at the beginning of the name, or (5) you did not separate the directory names with the path character. Check your directory names, ensure that the directories do exist, and try the command again.

Invalid disk change

WARNING: The diskette in the 720K, 1.2M, or 1.44M disk drive was changed while a program had open files to be written to the diskette. You will see the message `Abort, Retry, Fail`. Place the correct diskette in the diskette drive and type `R` for Retry.

Invalid drive in search path

WARNING: Either a specification you gave to the PATH command has an invalid disk drive name, or a named disk drive is nonexistent or hidden temporarily by a SUBST or JOIN command.

Use PATH to check the paths you instructed DOS to search. If you gave a nonexistent disk drive name, use the PATH command again and enter the correct search paths. If the problem is temporary because of a SUBST or JOIN command, you can again use PATH to enter the paths, but leave out or correct the wrong entry. Or you can just ignore the warning message.

Invalid drive or file name

ERROR: Either you gave the name of a nonexistent disk drive, or the disk drive and/or file name is mistyped.

Remember that certain DOS commands (such as SUBST and JOIN) temporarily hide disk drive names while the command is in effect. Check the disk drive name you gave, and try the command again.

Invalid drive specification

ERROR: This message is given when one of the following errors occurs: (1) you have entered the name of an invalid or nonexistent disk drive as a parameter to a command; (2) you have given the same disk drive for the source and destination, which is not permitted for the command; or (3) by not giving a parameter, you have defaulted to the same source and destination disk drive.

Remember that certain DOS commands (such as SUBST and JOIN) temporarily hide disk drive names while the command is in effect. Check the disk drive names. If the command is objecting to a missing parameter and defaulting to the wrong disk drive, explicitly name the correct disk drive.

`Invalid drive specification`
`Specified drive does not exist,`
`or is non-removable`

ERROR: One of the following errors occurred: (1) you gave the name of a nonexistent disk drive, (2) you named the fixed disk drive when using commands for diskettes only, (3) you did not give a disk drive name and defaulted to the fixed disk when using commands for diskettes only, or (4) you named or defaulted to a RAM-disk drive when using commands for a "real" floppy diskette only.

Remember that certain DOS commands (such as SUBST and JOIN) temporarily hide disk drive names while the command is in effect. Check the disk drive name you gave, and try the command again.

`Invalid environment size specified`

WARNING: You have given the SHELL directive in CONFIG.SYS. The environment-size switch (*/E:size*) contains either nonnumeric characters or a number that is less than 160 or greater than 32768.

If you are using the SHELL */E:size* switch of DOS V3.1, *size* is the number of 16-byte paragraphs, not the number of bytes.

Check the form of your CONFIG.SYS SHELL directive; the form needs to be exact. There should be a colon between */E* and *size*; there should be no comma or space between or within the */E:* and the *size* characters; and the number in *size* should be greater than or equal to 160, but less than or equal to 32768.

`Invalid number of parameters`

ERROR: You have given either too few or too many parameters to a command. One of the following errors occurred: (1) you omitted required information, (2) you forgot a colon immediately after the disk drive name, (3) you put a space in the wrong place or omitted a needed space, or (4) you forgot to place a slash (/) in front of a switch.

`Invalid parameter Incorrect parameter`

ERROR: At least one parameter you entered for the command is not valid. One of the following errors occurred: (1) you omitted required information, (2) you forgot a colon immediately after the disk drive name,

(3) you put a space in the wrong place or omitted a needed space, (4) you forgot to place a slash (/) in front of a switch, or (5) you used a switch that the command does not recognize. For more information, check the explanation of this message in the *Command Reference* under the command you were using when the message occurred.

Invalid partition table

ERROR (start-up): While you were attempting to start DOS from the fixed disk, DOS detected a problem in the fixed disk's partition information.

Restart DOS from a diskette. Back up all files from the fixed disk, if possible. Run FDISK to correct the problem. If you change the partition information, you must reformat the fixed disk and restore all its files.

Invalid path

ERROR: One of the following errors has occurred to a path name you have entered: (1) the path name contains illegal characters, (2) the name has more than 63 characters, or (3) one of the directory names within the path is misspelled or does not exist.

Check the spelling of the path name. If needed, do a DIR of the disk and ensure that the directory you have specified does exist and that you have the correct path name. Be sure that the path name contains 63 characters or less. If necessary, change the current directory to a directory "closer" to the file and shorten the path name.

Invalid STACK parameter

WARNING (start-up): One of the following errors has occurred to the STACKS directive in your CONFIG.SYS file: (1) a comma is missing between the number of stacks and the size of the stack, (2) the number of stack frames is not in the range of 8 to 64, (3) the stack size is not in the range of 32 to 512, (4) you have omitted either the number of stack frames or the stack size, or (5) either the stack frame or the stack size (but not both) is 0. DOS continues to start but ignores the STACKS directive.

Check the STACKS directive in your CONFIG.SYS file. Edit and save the file, and restart DOS.

Invalid switch character

WARNING: You have used VDISK.SYS in your CONFIG.SYS file. VDISK encountered a switch (/) but the character immediately following it was not an *E* for *extended* memory. DOS loads VDISK and attempts to install VDISK in low (nonextended) memory. Either you have misspelled the /E switch, or you have left a space between the / and the *E*. Edit and save your CONFIG.SYS file, and restart DOS.

Memory allocation error
Cannot load COMMAND, system halted

ERROR: A program destroyed the area where DOS keeps track of in-use and available memory. You must restart DOS.

If this error occurs again with the same program, the program has a flaw. Use a backup copy of the program. If the problem persists, contact the dealer or program publisher.

Missing operating system

ERROR (start-up): The DOS fixed disk partition entry is marked as "bootable" (able to start DOS), but the DOS partition does not have a copy of DOS on it. DOS does not start.

Start DOS from a diskette. Use the SYS C: command to place DOS on the fixed disk, and then copy COMMAND.COM to the disk. If this fails, you must back up the existing files, if any, from the fixed disk; then issue FORMAT /S to put a copy of the operating system on the fixed disk. If necessary, restore the files that you backed up.

No free file handles
Cannot start COMMAND, exiting

ERROR: DOS could not load an additional copy of COMMAND.COM because no file handles were available.

Edit the CONFIG.SYS file on your start-up disk to increase the number of file handles (using the FILES directive) by five. Restart DOS and try the command again.

```
Non-System disk or disk error
Replace and strike any key when ready
```

ERROR (start-up): Either your diskette or fixed disk does not contain IBMBIO.COM and IBMDOS.COM, or a read error occurred when you started the system. DOS does not start.

If you are using a floppy disk system, put a startable diskette in drive A and press a key.

The most frequent cause of this message on fixed disk systems is that you left a nonstartable diskette in disk drive A with the door closed. Open the door to disk drive A and press a key. DOS will boot from the fixed disk.

```
Not enough memory
```

ERROR: The computer does not have enough free RAM memory to execute the program or command.

If you loaded a resident program like PRINT, GRAPHICS, SideKick, or ProKey, restart DOS and try the command again before loading any resident program. If this method fails, remove any unneeded device driver or RAM-disk software from the CONFIG.SYS file and restart DOS again. If this option fails also, your computer does not have enough memory for this command. You must increase your RAM memory to run the command.

```
Out of environment space
```

WARNING: DOS is unable to add any more strings to the environment from the SET command. The environment cannot be expanded. This error occurs when you load a resident program, such as MODE, PRINT, GRAPHICS, SideKick, or ProKey.

If you are running DOS V3.1 or later versions, refer to the SHELL directive in Chapter 14 (on customizing DOS) for information about expanding the default space for the environment. DOS V3.0 has no method to expand the environment.

Path not found

ERROR: A file or directory path that you named does not exist. You may have misspelled the file name or directory name, or you may have omitted a path character (\) between directory names or between the final directory name and file name. Another possibility is that the file or directory does not exist where you specified it. Check these possibilities and try again.

Path too long

ERROR: You have given a path name that exceeds the 63 character limit of DOS. Either the name is too long, or you omitted a space between file names. Check the command line. If the phrasing is correct, you must change to a directory that is closer to the file you want and try the command again.

Program too big to fit in memory

ERROR: The computer does not have enough memory to load the program or the command you invoked.

If you have any resident programs loaded (such as PRINT, GRAPHICS, or SideKick), restart DOS and try the command again without loading the resident programs. If this message appears again, reduce the number of buffers (BUFFERS) in the CONFIG.SYS file, eliminate unneeded device drivers or RAM-disk software, and restart DOS again. If these actions do not solve the problem, your computer does not have enough RAM memory for the program or command. You must increase the amount of RAM memory in your computer to run this command.

Sector size too large in file filename

WARNING: The device driver `filename` is inconsistent. The device driver defined a particular sector size to DOS but attempted to use a different size. Either the copy of the device driver is bad, or the device driver is incorrect. Copy a backup copy of the device driver to the boot diskette and then reboot DOS. If the message appears again, the device driver is incorrect. If you wrote the driver, correct the error. If you purchased the program, contact the dealer or software publisher.

Sharing violation

WARNING: With the file-sharing program (SHARE.EXE) loaded, you or one of your programs attempted to access a file by using a sharing mode not allowed at this time. Another program or computer has temporary control over the file.

You'll see the message Abort, Retry, Fail. Choose R for Retry several times. If the problem persists, choose A for Abort. If you abort, however, any data currently being manipulated by the program is lost.

Syntax error

ERROR: You phrased a command improperly by (1) omitting needed information, (2) giving extraneous information, (3) putting an extra space in a file name or path name, or (4) using an incorrect switch. Check the command line for these possibilities and try the command again.

Too many block devices

WARNING (start-up): There are too many DEVICE directives in your CONFIG.SYS file. DOS continues to start but does not install any additional device drivers.

DOS can handle only 26 block devices. The block devices created by the DEVICE directives plus the number of block devices automatically created by DOS exceeds this number. Remove any unnecessary DEVICE directives in your CONFIG.SYS file and restart DOS.

Top level process aborted, cannot continue

ERROR (start-up): COMMAND.COM or another DOS command detected a disk error, and you chose the A (abort) option. DOS cannot finish starting itself, and the system halts.

Try to start DOS again. If the error recurs, use a floppy diskette (if starting from the fixed disk) or a different floppy diskette (if starting from floppy diskettes) to start DOS. After DOS has started, use the SYS command to put another copy of the operating system on the disk, and copy COMMAND.COM to the disk. If DOS reports an error during the copying, the disk or diskette is bad. Either reformat or retire the floppy diskette, or back-up and reformat the fixed disk.

Unable to create directory

ERROR: Either you or a program has attempted to create a directory, and one of the following has occurred: (1) a directory by the same name already exists; (2) a file by the same name already exists; (3) you are adding a directory to the root directory, and the root directory is full; or (4) the directory name has illegal characters or is a device name.

Do a DIR of the disk. Make sure that no file or directory already exists with the same name. If adding the directory to the root directory, remove or move (copy, then erase) any unneeded files or directories. Check the spelling of the directory and ensure that the command is properly phrased.

Unrecognized command in CONFIG.SYS

WARNING (start-up): DOS detected an improperly phrased directive in CONFIG.SYS. The directive is ignored, and DOS continues to start; but DOS does not indicate the incorrect line. Examine the CONFIG.SYS file, looking for improperly phrased or incorrect directives. Edit the line, save the file, and restart DOS.

filename device driver cannot be initialized

WARNING (start-up): In CONFIG.SYS, either the parameters in the device driver `filename` are incorrect, or the DEVICE line is in error. Check for incorrect parameters, and check for phrasing errors in the DEVICE line. Edit the DEVICE line in the CONFIG.SYS file, save the file, and restart DOS.

DOS Device Error Messages

When DOS detects an error while reading or writing to disk drives or other devices, one of the following messages appears:

>*type* error reading *device*

>*type* error writing *device*

type is the type of error, and *device* is the device at fault. If the device is a floppy disk drive, do not remove the diskette from the drive. Refer to the possible causes and corrective actions described in this section, which lists the types of error messages that may appear.

Bad call format

A device driver was given a requested header with an incorrect length. The problem is the application software making the call.

Bad command

The device driver issued an invalid or unsupported command to *device*. The problem may be with the device driver software or with other software trying to use the device driver. If this is a program you have written, the program needs to be corrected. For a purchased program, contact the dealer or publisher that sold you the program.

Bad format call

The device driver at fault passed an incorrect header length to DOS. If you wrote this device driver, you must rewrite it to correct the problem. For a purchased program, contact the dealer or publisher who sold you the driver.

Bad unit

An invalid subunit number was passed to the device driver. The problem may be with the device driver software or with other software trying to use the device driver. Contact the dealer who sold you the device driver.

Data

DOS could not correctly read or write the data. Usually the disk has developed a defective spot.

Drive not ready

An error occurred while DOS tried to read or write to the disk drive. For floppy disk drives, the drive door may be open, the microfloppy diskette may not be inserted, or the diskette may not be formatted. For fixed disk drives, the drive may not be properly prepared—you may have a hardware problem.

FCB unavailable

With the file-sharing program (SHARE.EXE) loaded, a program that uses the DOS V1 method of file handling attempted to open concurrently more file control blocks than were specified with the FCBS directive.

Use the Abort option (see the end of the section). Increase the value of the FCBS CONFIG.SYS directive (usually by four), and reboot the system. If the message appears again, increase the number again and reboot.

General failure

This is a catchall error message not covered elsewhere. The error usually occurs for the following reasons: (1) you are using an unformatted diskette or fixed disk; (2) the disk drive door is open; (3) the diskette is not seated properly; or (4) you are using the wrong type of diskette in a disk drive, such as formatting a 360K diskette in a 1.2M disk drive.

Lock violation

With the file-sharing program (SHARE.EXE) or the network software loaded, one of your programs attempted to access a file that is locked. Your best choice is Retry. Then try Abort. If you choose A, however, any data in memory is lost.

No paper

The printer is either out of paper or not turned on.

Non-DOS disk

The FAT has invalid information. This diskette is unusable. You can Abort and run CHKDSK on the diskette to see whether any corrective action is possible. If CHKDSK fails, your other alternative is to reformat the diskette. Reformatting, however, will destroy any remaining information on the diskette.

If you use more than one operating system, the diskette has probably been formatted under the operating system you're using and should not be reformatted.

Not ready

The device is not ready and cannot receive or transmit data. Check the connections, make sure that the power is on, and check to see whether the device is ready. For floppy disk drives, check that the diskette is formatted and is properly seated in the disk drive.

Read fault

DOS was unable to read the data, usually from a fixed disk or diskette. Check the disk drive doors, and be sure that the diskette is inserted properly.

Sector not found

The disk drive was unable to locate the sector on the diskette or the fixed disk platter. This error is usually the result of a defective spot on the disk or of defective drive electronics. Some copy-protection schemes also use this method (a defective spot) to prevent unauthorized duplication of the diskette.

Seek

The disk drive could not locate the proper track on the diskette or the fixed disk platter. This error is usually the result of a defective spot on the diskette or the fixed disk platter, an unformatted disk, or drive electronics problems.

Sharing violation

With the file-sharing program (SHARE.EXE) or network software loaded, your programs attempted to access a file by using a sharing mode not specified for that file. Your best response is Retry. Then try Abort.

Write fault

DOS could not write the data to this device. Perhaps you inserted the diskette improperly, or you left the disk drive door open. Another possibility is an electronics failure in the floppy or fixed disk drive. The most frequent cause is a bad spot on the diskette.

Write protect

The diskette is write-protected.

Note: One of the previously listed messages (usually `Data`, `Read fault`, or `Write fault`) appears when you are using a double-sided diskette in a single-sided disk drive or a 9-sector diskette (V2 and later) with a version of DOS V1. DOS will display one of these error messages, followed by the line

```
Abort, Retry, Fail?
```

for DOS V3.3 or

```
Abort, Retry, Ignore?
```

for pre-DOS V3.3.

If you press A for Abort, DOS ends the program that requested the read or write condition. Typing R for Retry causes DOS to try the operation again. If you press F for Fail or I for Ignore, DOS skips the operation, and the program continues. Some data may be lost, however, when Fail or Ignore is used.

The order of preference, unless stated differently under the message, is R, A, and F or I. You should retry the operation at least twice. If the condition persists, you must decide whether to abort the program or ignore the error. If you ignore the error, data may be lost. If you abort, data still being processed by the program and not yet written to the disk will be lost. Remember that F and I are the least desirable options and that A should be used after Retry has failed at least two times.

APPEND
(Set directory search order)   *V3.3—External*

Purpose

Instructs DOS to search the specified directories on the specified disks if a nonprogram/nonbatch file is not found in the current directory

Syntax

To establish the data file search path the first time, use

    *dc:pathc*APPEND *d1:path1;d2:path2;d3:path3;* . . .

To use either of APPEND's switches, use

    *dc:pathc*APPEND */X /E*

To change the data file search path, use

    APPEND *d1:path1;d2:path2;d3:path3;* . . .

To see the search path, use

    APPEND

To disconnect the data file search, use

    APPEND;

dc: is the name of the disk drive that holds the command.

pathc is the path to the command.

d1:, d2:, d3 are valid disk drive names.

path1, path2, path3 are valid path names to the directories you want DOS to search for nonprogram/nonbatch files.

The three periods (. . .) represent additional disk drive and path names.

Switches

/X   Redirects programs that use the DOS function calls SEARCH FIRST, FIND FIRST, and EXEC.

/E   Places the disk drive paths in the *environment*.

Exit Codes   None

Rules

1. The first time you execute APPEND, the program loads from the disk and installs itself in DOS. APPEND then becomes an internal command and is not reloaded from the disk until you restart DOS.

2. You can only give the /X and /E switches when you first invoke APPEND. You cannot give any path names with the switches.

3. If you do not enter a disk drive name for a path, APPEND uses the current disk drive.

4. Each path can be any valid series of subdirectories, separated by the path character (the backslash).

5. If you specify more than one set of paths, the following rules apply:

   a. The path sets must be separated by semicolons.

   b. The search for the nonprogram files is made in the order in which you gave the path sets. First the specified directory (or current directory if none is specified) is searched. Then *d1:path1* is searched, followed by *d2:path2*, and so on, until the file is found, or until APPEND exhausts the list of directory paths.

6. APPEND's total length of the paths given cannot exceed 127 characters (including the length of the APPEND command).

7. If an invalid path is encountered (for example, if you misspelled the name, or the path no longer exists), DOS skips this path and does not display any message.

8. If you use the /X switch, APPEND processes DOS function calls SEARCH FIRST, FIND FIRST, and EXEC.

*9. Do not use RESTORE while you are using the /X switch.

10. To disable APPEND, give the command followed by a semicolon. APPEND remains resident but inactive until you issue another APPEND command with path names.

11. If you use the /E switch, DOS establishes an environmental variable called APPEND. The variable holds the current paths that APPEND uses.

*12. The file found by APPEND can be safely read by the program. However, any changes to the file will be saved in a copy of the file placed in the current directory. The original file remains intact.

13. If you are using TopView or the ASSIGN command with APPEND, you must issue the APPEND command before you start TopView or use ASSIGN.

14. To see the current search path used by APPEND, type **APPEND**.

Examples

A. APPEND /X /E

Loads the APPEND command and establishes APPEND to intercept the SEARCH FIRST, FIND FIRST, and EXEC DOS function calls (the /X switch). DOS places in the environment the paths you give to APPEND (the /E switch). This example presumes that APPEND is in the current directory or on the PATH.

B. **APPEND C:\BIN;C:\BIN\OVR**

Instructs APPEND to search the specified or current directory for nonprogram files and then search the directories C:\BIN and C:\BIN\OVR.

C. **APPEND;**

Disables the APPEND command. The APPEND command stays in memory until you restart DOS. To reactivate APPEND, simply give a set of path names to the command.

Notes

APPEND is the PATH command for data and other nonprogram files. The command is especially useful for those users whose programs do not support hierarchical directories. With the APPEND command, you can place additional program files (such as those used with WordStar Release 3) or data files in any directory.

APPEND has two "levels." To use the first level, use APPEND with the /X switch to trick programs that attempt to "open" files. To use the second level, use APPEND with the /X switch to trick programs that search the directory for files. The /X switch also tricks programs that automatically run other programs (called *execing* or executing).

The /E switch places the paths fed to APPEND in the environment, under the variable named APPEND. If you use the /E switch, programs can examine the environment for the APPEND variable and use the contents to find their files. However, do not use APPEND from within a program if you have used the /E switch. The changes that APPEND makes to the environment are temporary—the copy of COMMAND used to run APPEND is temporary. When you return to the program, changes made by APPEND will be lost.

APPEND /X can cause problems with certain programs. If you suddenly discover a problem locating files, first deactivate APPEND using the command APPEND;. If the problem persists, use APPEND without the /X switch. If the problem continues, look for some other cause. If APPEND is deactivated, it should not affect any running program.

Do not use APPEND /X with RESTORE. RESTORE will search for files in the directories on which you have used APPEND. If you are using the /N or /M switch with RESTORE, RESTORE may not process the correct files. Before you use RESTORE, be sure you have deactivated APPEND.

Be cautious if you are writing to files that APPEND has found. APPEND tricks programs into reading files from anywhere. APPEND does not trick programs when they write files. DOS saves any changes you make to a file in a copy of that file, which it places in the current directory. The original file in the directory on which you used APPEND remains unchanged. This problem can be especially confusing if you use a file in one directory, save a new version of the file, move to another directory, and attempt to use the file again. You will be working with the original file without the changes. The changed file will be in the directory from which you made the changes.

APPEND is an "open-me-first" type command if you use it with TopView, IBM's windowing package, or with the ASSIGN command. You must start APPEND first, before you use TopView or the ASSIGN command. Reversing the order causes APPEND to deliver an error message, and the command does not load.

APPEND is the counterpart of the PATH command, which works with program files. For more information, see the PATH command in the *Command Reference*.

Messages

1. APPEND/ASSIGN Conflict

   APPEND/TopView Conflict

   ERROR: You have attempted to use APPEND after you have loaded either TopView or ASSIGN. If you are using TopView, exit TopView, give the APPEND command, and then restart TopView. If you are using ASSIGN, break the assignment, issue the APPEND command, and then issue the ASSIGN command again.

2. APPEND already installed

   WARNING: You have attempted to load APPEND again by giving a disk drive or path name for the command. You need to load APPEND only once. Give the command again without the command's drive or path name.

3. Incorrect APPEND Version

   ERROR: You are using a version of APPEND from a different version of DOS. Check that you are not using the version of APPEND from the IBM Local Area Network program. The problem may be that the wrong version of APPEND is being loaded first from a PATHed directory.

4. Invalid parameter

   ERROR: You used a switch that APPEND does not recognize when you first ran the command. The only valid switches are /X and /E. Try the command again using the correct switches.

5. Invalid path

   ERROR: The path you gave to APPEND was not valid for one of these reasons: (1) you gave illegal characters, (2) you forgot to separate each path set with a semicolon, or (3) you gave a path name that exceeded 63 characters. Check the spelling of each path set, the semicolons that separate multiple paths, and the lengths of each path. Then try the command again.

6. Invalid path or parameter

ERROR: After you installed APPEND, you made one of the
following errors: (1) you used a switch with the command,
(2) you used a misspelled path name, or (3) you used a
path that exceeded 63 characters. Check the spelling of the
paths and the semicolons that separate each path. Then try
the command again. To use a different switch with APPEND,
you must restart DOS and give the APPEND command with
the appropriate switch.

7. No Append

INFORMATION: You typed APPEND to see the current path
and APPEND is currently inactive.

ASSIGN
(Assign disk drive)   *V2, V3—External*

Purpose   Instructs DOS to use a disk drive other than the one specified by a
program or command

Syntax   To reroute drive activity, use

$dc{:}pathc\backslash$ ASSIGN d1=d2 . . .

dc: is the name of the disk drive that holds the command.

pathc is the path to the command.

d1 is the letter of the disk drive that the program or DOS normally
uses.

d2 is the letter of the disk drive you want the program or DOS to
use, instead of the usual drive.

The three periods (. . .) represent additional disk drive assignments.

To clear the reassignment, use

$dc{:}pathc\backslash$ ASSIGN

Exit Codes   None

Rules
1. You may reassign any valid DOS drive to any other drive, but
   not to itself.

2. Do not use a colon after the disk drive letter **d1** or **d2**. You
   may use a space on either side of the equal sign.

3. You can give more than one assignment on the same
   line. Use a space between each set of assignments
   (ASSIGN B=C A=C).

4. Some copy-protection schemes and programs (including
   DOS's DISKCOMP, DISKCOPY, and FORMAT) completely or
   partially ignore the ASSIGN command.

5. Use ASSIGN only when necessary.

6. Do not ASSIGN a disk drive to a drive that is not on your system. If you make this mistake, DOS will return an error message.

Examples

A. ASSIGN A = C or ASSIGN A=C

DOS reroutes to drive C any activity for drive A. You may use a space on either side of the equal sign.

B. ASSIGN A=C B=C

DOS reroutes to drive C any activity requests for drives A and B.

C. ASSIGN

Clears any previous drive reassignment.

Notes

ASSIGN is a "pretender" command for DOS. ASSIGN reroutes a program, causing it to use a disk drive that is different from the one the program intends. A program "thinks" that it is using a certain disk drive, but the program really is using a different disk drive.

You should use ASSIGN primarily for programs that do not allow you to specify the disk drive. Some accounting and word-processing programs "assume" only two possible disk drives: the minifloppy disk drives A and B. You use ASSIGN to "trick" programs into using the fixed disk (drive C). Computer users need to use this command less frequently now because most programs allow users to specify the disk drives that programs should use.

The ASSIGN command does not work with all programs. Some programs make a special DOS request to read a specific part of the diskette in the floppy disk drive. ASSIGN cannot intercept and reroute these special requests. In such cases, your only choice is to place in the correct disk drive the diskette requested by the program.

Don't ASSIGN a real disk drive to a nonexistent drive. If you attempt such an assignment, the DOS V3 ASSIGN command immediately displays the error message:

```
Invalid parameter
```

If you have not used the LASTDRIVE command in CONFIG.SYS, when you type the line

   ASSIGN A=F

DOS immediately displays an error message and does not change any current assignments.

For DOS V3.1 and later versions, an alternative to ASSIGN is SUBST (discussed later in the *Command Reference*).

ASSIGN can interfere with certain DOS commands, such as DIR (directory), CHKDSK (check disk), DISKCOMP (compare diskettes), and DISKCOPY (copy diskettes). When ASSIGN is in effect, these DOS commands will not work on the drive on which you have used ASSIGN. You must break the assignment (by issuing ASSIGN with no parameters) before you can perform these commands on the disk.

Messages

1. `Invalid parameter`

   ERROR: You made one of the following errors: (1) you put a colon after one or more drive letters, (2) you did not type all the information that ASSIGN required, (3) you used a letter for a nonexistent disk drive, or (4) you did not correctly phrase the command.

2. `Incorrect DOS Version`

   ERROR: The version of ASSIGN you are using does not match the version of DOS the computer is using. Ensure that your machine is running the correct version of DOS and that the proper version of your utility programs is on your disk.

ATTRIB
(Change/show a file's read-only and archive attributes)   *V3**—External*

Purpose   Displays, sets, or clears a file's read-only and archive attributes

---

Syntax   To set the file's attributes on, use

dc:pathc\\ATTRIB +R +A *d:path*\\filename.*ext* /S

To clear the file's attributes, use

dc:pathc\\ATTRIB -R -A *d:path*\\filename.*ext* /S

To display a file's read-only and archive status, use

dc:pathc\\ATTRIB *d:path*\\filename.*ext* /S

dc: is the name of the disk drive that holds the command.

pathc\\ is the path to the command.

R is the read-only attribute.

A is the archive attribute (DOS V3.2 and later).

+ turns on the attribute (the file becomes read-only or marked as created/changed).

- turns off the attribute (the file is writeable or marked as not created/changed).

d: is the name of the disk drive that holds the files for which the read-only or archive attribute will be displayed or changed.

path\\ is the starting path to the files for which the read-only or archive attribute will be displayed or changed.

filename.*ext* is the name of the file(s) for which the read-only or archive attribute will be displayed or changed. Wildcards are allowed.

Switch   /S   Sets or clears the attributes with the files in the current or specified directory and all subsequent *subdirectories*, continuing downward through the subdirectories (DOS V3.3).

Exit Codes   None

Rules

1. If you do not give a disk drive name (*d:*), ATTRIB uses the current disk drive.

2. If you do not give a path name (*path*), ATTRIB uses the current directory.

3. If you do not give a **filename**, DOS displays an error message.

4. To mark a file as read-only, insert a +R (for *add read-only*) between the command and the file name. To remove the read-only flag from the file, insert a -R (for *subtract read-only*) between the command and the file name.

5. To mark a file's archive attribute, insert a +A (for archive on) between the command and the file name. To clear the archive attribute from the file, insert a -A (for *archive off*) between the command and file name or after the file name.

6. To display the read-only and archive attribute status of a file, do not use +R, -R, +A, or -A. ATTRIB displays an A in the third column before the file names if the archive attribute is on. An R is displayed in the seventh column if the read-only attribute is on for the file. If the attribute is not on, a space appears in place of the letter.

7. You can use both the R and the A characters, or either character, in the command. You can mix the plus and minus attributes of the commands (for example, +R -A), but you cannot use plus and minus the same character in the command (for example, +R -R).

8. When a file is marked as read-only, you cannot alter or delete it.

9. When a file's archive attribute is on, BACKUP and XCOPY with the /M or /A switch will process the file.

Notes

With DOS V3's addition of ATTRIB, users have more control over the DOS read-only and archive file attributes. ATTRIB sets or clears these attributes. When the file is marked as read-only, it cannot be altered or deleted. When the archive attribute is on, the file can be processed by BACKUP /M or XCOPY /A.

ATTRIB does not affect any other DOS file attribute, including those for system and hidden files. To change these file characteristics, you must use a different program, such as the Norton Utilities or SDACHMD (by SDA Associates).

Although you cannot alter or erase a read-only file, you can rename the file. If you change the name of a read-only file, you may cause some problems with certain programs, however.

Messages

1. Access denied

   ERROR: You cannot change the read-only attribute of this file. The file may be temporarily unavailable because another computer or program is using the file, or the file may be in a directory on a networked disk for which you do not have permission to change files. If another program or computer has control of the file, try the command again later. If you do not have permission to change the file on the networked disk, ask the computer network manager to make the change for you.

2. Incorrect DOS Version

   ERROR: The version of ATTRIB you are using does not match the version of DOS the computer is using. Ensure that your machine is running the correct version of DOS, and that the proper version of your utility programs is on your disk.

3. Invalid drive specification

   ERROR: You specified a disk drive that does not exist. Check your phrasing of the command and try again.

4. Invalid number of parameters

   ERROR: You did not specify a file name.

5. `Invalid path or file not found`

   ERROR: You specified a directory or file name that does not exist. Check the spelling of the names and be sure that the files are in the directory you specified.

6. `Syntax error`

   ERROR: One of the following errors occurred: (1) you gave a switch other than /S to ATTRIB; (2) you gave an ill-formed **R** and/or **A** command (omitting the + or -, or the **R** or **A** itself, or giving both the + and - for an attribute); or (3) you gave more than one file name.

BACKUP
(Back up diskettes or fixed disks)   *V2, V3**—External*

Purpose

Backs up one or more files from a fixed disk or diskette onto a diskette or another fixed disk

---

Syntax

*dc:pathc***BACKUP** *d1:path\\filename.ext d2: /S /M /A /D:date /T:time /F /L:dl:filenamel:extl*

dc: is the name of the disk drive that holds the command.

pathc is the path to the command.

d1: is the name of the fixed disk or floppy disk drive to be backed up.

path is the starting directory path for backup.

filename.ext specifies the name(s) of the file(s) you want to back up. Wildcards are allowed.

d2: is the fixed disk or floppy disk drive that will receive the backup files.

Switches

/S   Backs up all *subdirectories*, starting with the specified or current directory on the disk and continuing down through the subdirectories.

/M   Backs up all files that have been *modified* since the last time you backed up. This switch backs up any file that has been changed or created since the last time you used BACKUP.

/A   *Adds* the file(s) to previously backed-up files. Without this switch, DOS erases the files already on the backup disk. If you are using a diskette to receive backup files, DOS expects the correct diskette to be in the drive whenever you use this switch.

/D:date   Backs up any files that were changed or created on or after the specified *date*. The form of *date* depends on the setting of the COUNTRY command in CONFIG.SYS and can be

mm-dd-yy	North America
dd-mm-yy	Europe
yy-mm-dd	East Asia

where: *mm* is the month (1 - 12)
dd is the day (1 to 31)
yy is the year (00 - 99)

The character separating the parts of the *date* depends on the setting of the COUNTRY command; the character can be either the hyphen (-), the period (.), or the slash (/). You can substitute any of the three characters for the character set by the COUNTRY command; for example, North American users can substitute a slash in place of the hyphen. Do not put spaces between the */D:* and the date.

/T:time   Backs up any files that were changed at created at or after the specified *time* on the specified date (given with the /D switch). The form of *time* is *hh:mm:ss*, where:

hh is the hour (0 - 23)
mm is the minutes (0 - 59)
ss is the seconds (0 - 59)

The character separating the parts of *time* is usually the colon, but certain countries may use the period (.). (DOS V3.3)

/F   *Formats* the destination diskette, if unformatted. Invokes the FORMAT command with the /H switch. Be sure to use high capacity diskettes in 1.2M disk drives. (DOS V3.3)

/L:dl:pathl\filenamel.extl   Creates a *log* file.

dl:pathl\filenamel.extl is the full file name of the log file. (DOS V3.3)

Exit Codes   0 = Successful backup
1 = No files found to be backed up
2 = Some files not backed up because of sharing problems
3 = Aborted by the user (Ctrl-Break or Ctrl-C)
4 = Aborted because of an error

Rules

1. You must give both a source and a destination for BACKUP. Neither disk can be a networked disk, and neither disk can be used in an ASSIGN, SUBST, or JOIN command.

2. The source name must specify the valid name of the disk drive to be backed up and can also include either or both of the following:

   a. a valid directory path containing the files to be backed up

   b. a file name with appropriate extensions, if desired. Wildcards are allowed.

3. The destination is any valid name for a floppy or fixed disk drive.

4. If you do not give

   a. a source drive name, a No source drive specified error message is given;

   b. a source directory path, the current directory is used;

   c. a source file name, all files in the specified directory are backed up;

   d. any of these, a No source drive specified error message is displayed.

5. If you are backing up onto diskettes with BACKUP from a version of DOS prior to V3.3, you must have a sufficient number of diskettes formatted before you invoke the BACKUP command. BACKUP does not work on unformatted or non-DOS diskettes. If you do not have enough formatted diskettes, you will have to stop and restart BACKUP after you format more diskettes.

   If you are backing up onto diskettes with BACKUP V3.3, you may give the /F switch, which causes BACKUP to run FORMAT for any unformatted diskettes. If you run out of formatted diskettes and have not given the /F switch, you will have to restart BACKUP after you stop to format more diskettes.

6. If you are backing up onto a fixed disk, you must have sufficient room to hold the backup files. If you run out of room on the fixed disk, you will need to delete files from the backup fixed disk and start BACKUP again.

7. To keep the files on a previously backed-up disk, use the /A option. If you do not use this switch, all files previously stored on the receiving diskette are destroyed, or all files in the \BACKUP subdirectory of the fixed disk are destroyed.

   To use the /A option with diskettes, you must start with a diskette that contains the special files created by BACKUP, named CONTROL.xxx and BACKUP.xxx (the xxx is the number of the diskette). Otherwise, BACKUP displays the message `Last backup diskette not inserted` and aborts.

8. If you do not use the /A option and are backing up onto diskettes, DOS prompts you to insert the first backup diskette. If you use the /A option, the backup diskette should be in the correct drive before you type the command line; otherwise, DOS requests that you `Insert last backup diskette`.

9. When you are backing up with diskettes, DOS prompts you to change diskettes. Make sure that you insert the correct diskette in the disk drive when you are prompted.

10. You can retrieve backed-up files only with the RESTORE command. Otherwise, these files are unusable.

11. BACKUP follows the VERIFY command. If VERIFY is OFF, DOS does not check the newly created BACKUP files on the diskette to see whether they were recorded correctly. If VERIFY is ON, DOS checks to ensure that the files were stored correctly.

12. If you are backing up onto diskettes, all files are placed in the root directory. If you are backing up onto another fixed disk, the files are stored in the subdirectory \BACKUP.

13. To create a log of the files that BACKUP processed, give the /L switch. If you do not specify a full file name, BACKUP creates the log file under the name BACKUP.LOG in the source disk's root directory. If you do not specify for the log file name

    a. a disk drive (*dl:*), the source disk is used;

    b. a directory path (*path*), the current directory is used;

    c. a file name (*filenamel.extl*), BACKUP displays an error message and aborts.

If you give a log file name, you must use a colon between the *L* and the first character in the log file name. Do not use spaces from the beginning of the switch to the end of the log file name. If you do not give a log file name, do not use a colon after the *L*.

If a log file already exists, BACKUP will add to the log file. If a file does not exist, a new file is created.

You cannot place the log file on the destination disk (the disk used to store the backup files).

Examples

For the following examples, refer to the sample hierarchical directory in Appendix B. The directory is used with these examples (as the directory of the fixed disk) to show the effects of the different commands. For each set of examples (lettered A through J), the current directory is indicated.

Example A. *Current directory: root*

Commands

(1) BACKUP C: A:
(2) BACKUP C:*.* A:
(3) BACKUP C:\ A:
(4) BACKUP C:*.* A:

What They Back Up

IBMBIO.COM, IBMDOS.COM, AUTOEXEC.BAT, CONFIG.SYS, VDISK.SYS, COUNTRY.SYS, and KEYBOARD.SYS

These four commands all have the same effect. They back up the files only in the root directory.

Example B. *Current directory: \WORDS\LETTERS*

Commands

(1) BACKUP C: A:
(2) BACKUP C:*.* A:
(3) BACKUP C:.*.* A:
(4) BACKUP C:\WORDS\LETTERS A:
(5) BACKUP
     C:\WORDS\LETTERS*.* A:
(6) BACKUP . A:

What They Back Up

IBM.BAK, IBM.LET, JACK.BAK, JACK.LET, and DOUG.LET

These six commands all have the same effect. They back up all files in the directory LETTERS.

Examples A-1 and B-1 tell DOS to back up onto drive A all the files in the current directory on drive C. These examples are based on the assumption that you are using the directory you want to back up. Because you have not given a file name, BACKUP "assumes" that all files should be backed up.

The only difference between A-1/B-1 and A-2/B-2 is that the *.* wildcard is given in A-2 and B-2. Giving the *.* in these commands is the same as not giving a file name. If you do not give a drive name or path name, you must use **BACKUP** *.* **A:** because BACKUP must have a source name.

Examples A-3 and B-3 are phrased differently and have different meanings, although the apparent effect is the same. Example A-3 explicitly tells DOS to back up all files in the root directory. A backslash (\ ) at the beginning of the path name tells DOS to start with the root directory of the disk. Because the root directory is the only specified directory on the path, only the root directory's contents are backed up. Example B-3 tells DOS to back up the files in the current directory. When a period (current directory symbol) is used as a path name, the effect is the same as giving no path.

The major difference between A-3 and B-3 is that A-3 is an absolute path reference and B-3 is a relative reference. No matter what directory you are using on drive C, A-3 always backs up the root directory, and B-3 always backs up the current directory.

Example A-4 is the same as A-3, except that in A-4 the *.* wildcard file name is used. Examples B-5 and B-4 are also the same. Both back up all files in the LETTERS subdirectory on the disk. Examples B-4 and B-5 have the same characteristics as A-3. All three commands explicitly state the directory to be used for the backup (the last named directory in the chain, or path).

Example C. *Current directory: LETTERS*

Commands	*What They Back Up*
(1) **BACKUP C:*.LET A:**	⎰ IBM.LET, JACK.LET,
(2) **BACKUP C:\WORDS\LETTERS*.LET A:**	⎱ and DOUG.LET

Examples C-1 and C-2 back up all files with the file name extension .LET in the directory LETTERS. The difference between C-1 and C-2 is that C-2 can be issued while you are using a directory other than LETTERS. To use C-1, however, your current directory must be LETTERS.

Example D. *Current directory: root*

Commands	What They Back Up
(1) BACKUP C: A: /S	{ All files on drive C
(2) BACKUP C:\ A: /S	

These examples use the /S switch, which tells DOS to start with the directory indicated and move down through all the subdirectories. Examples D-1 and D-2 perform the same action: they back up all the files on drive C. The commands have one major difference, however. Example D-2 works the same way regardless of the current directory, but D-1 backs up all the files on drive C only if the current directory is the root directory.

Example E. *Current directory: DOS*

Commands	What They Back Up
(1) BACKUP C:\ A: /S	{ All files on the disk
(2) BACKUP C: A: /S	{ All files in the DOS, BASIC, UTIL, HARDDISK, SAMPLES, and TEST directories

Examples D-2 and E-1 are identical, as are D-1 and E-2. D-2 and E-1 back up all the files on the disk. The key is the indicated path. In D-2 and E-1, the root directory symbol is given for the path. No matter which directory is current on drive C, BACKUP starts at the root directory. This condition is not true in D-1 or E-2. Because no path is given, BACKUP starts with the current directory and works downward through any additional subdirectories.

A common mistake occurs when you are working in a subdirectory and you try to use D-1 or E-2 to back up the entire disk. To back up the entire disk, use D-2 or E-1.

Example F. *Current directory: root*

Commands	What They Back Up
(1) BACKUP C:\ A: /S /D:08/21/87	{ All files created or changed since August 21, 1987
(2) BACKUP C:\ A: /S /D:08-21-87	

In both lines, BACKUP backs up in every directory on drive C all files created or changed since August 21, 1987. Examples F-1 and F-2 are different forms that achieve the same result. Slashes or hyphens are acceptable between the numbers, and leading zeros are not necessary with one-digit months or days. You can have no spaces between the starting slash of the switch and the ending number in the *date*.

Example G. *Current directory: root*

Commands	*What They Back Up*
(1) BACKUP C:\ A: /S /D:08/21/87	{ All files created or changed since August 21, 1987
(2) BACKUP C:\ A: /S /D:08-21-87 /T:12:45	{ All files created or changed since 12:45 p.m., August 21, 1987

In both lines, BACKUP backs up in every directory on drive C all files created or changed since August 21, 1987. However, G-2 processes files changed or altered after 12:45 p.m.; G1 processes files changed or altered any time during August 21. The /T switch restricts BACKUP to finding files changed or altered after a given time. The time is based on a 24-hour clock. For example, 2:00 p.m. would be entered as 14:00.

Example H. *Current directory: root*

Command	*What It Backs Up*
BACKUP C:\ A: /S /D:08-21-87 /A	{ All files created or changed since August 21, 1987

Like F-1, this command backs up all fixed disk files created or changed since the given date. The difference is that the /A switch directs BACKUP to add these files to the backup diskette without deleting the old files. Without the /A switch, any files in the \BACKUP subdirectory (if you are backing up onto another fixed disk) or on the backup diskette will be erased.

When you give the /A switch and back up onto diskettes, you should have a backup diskette in the disk drive; otherwise DOS requests that you Insert last backup diskette. The diskette must be a backup diskette. BACKUP checks the diskette for the special file BACKUP.xxx (xxx is the number assigned to backup disks in order of insertion during a backup). If this file is not on the diskette, BACKUP notifies you that you have the wrong diskette and then aborts.

Example I. *Current directory: root*

Command	What It Backs Up
BACKUP C:\ A: /S /M	{ All files created or changed since the last time you ran BACKUP

The */M* switch tells BACKUP to back up any files that do not have the *archive bit* set. An archive bit is a special area kept in the directory for each file. When you create or modify a file, the archive bit is off. When you back up a file, BACKUP turns on the archive bit.

When you use the */M* switch, BACKUP skips any file with an archive bit that is turned on. This switch setting allows BACKUP to back up any file or version of a file you have not previously backed up.

Obviously, if you create a file, BACKUP selects that file for backup. If you change a file, BACKUP selects that file. However, backing up a portion of a fixed disk may cause confusion later. Suppose that you back up only part of the disk and later back up the complete disk, using the */M* switch. In this case, BACKUP will back up the following:

1. all files in the portion of the disk you had not backed up earlier;

2. all files in the previously backed-up portion that were modified or created since you first used BACKUP.

On the second running (backing up the complete disk), BACKUP will probably select more files than on the first running (backing up only a part of the disk). Don't be alarmed; BACKUP is simply doing what you requested.

Example J. *Current directory: root*

Commands	What They Back Up
(1) BACKUP C:\ A: /S /F	{ All files on the disk, running FORMAT if a backup diskette is not formatted
(2) BACKUP C:\ A: /S /F /L	{ Same as J-1 but creates a log file
(3) BACKUP C:\ A: /S /F /L:082187.LOG	{ Same as J-2 but places the log in a file called 082187.LOG

J-1 through J3 show examples of backing up the entire disk, using the /F and /L switch. Use J-1 when you want to back up the entire disk, but you are unsure you have enough formatted diskettes. If BACKUP encounters an unformatted diskette, BACKUP will automatically run FORMAT.

J-2 and J-3 show how to create a log file. For J-2, BACKUP places the log in the C drive's root directory (the source directory), under the name BACKUP.LOG. For J-3, BACKUP places the log on drive C in the current directory under the name 082187.LOG, the specified name. If you specify a disk drive, the log file will be placed on the specified disk. If you specify a path, the log file will be placed in the specified directory.

When you give the /F switch to run FORMAT from BACKUP, DOS does *not* give the customary message to place a diskette in the drive. BACKUP and FORMAT assume that the diskette you have placed in the disk is the correct diskette. When FORMAT runs, you may FORMAT as many diskettes as you wish; remember, however, to change diskettes before you format another diskette.

Notes

BACKUP in DOS V3.3 is different in several ways from BACKUP in versions of DOS prior to V3.3. In DOS versions before V3.3, BACKUP creates a heading file called BACKUPID.@@@ on each diskette. This file contains the date, time, and diskette number of the backup. BACKUP stores each backed-up file individually on the diskette. Each file contains a 128-byte heading that identifies the path, file name, the file's original directory attributes, and whether the file is complete or the backup diskette contains only part of the file.

BACKUP V3.3 uses a different approach for the diskette that holds the backup files. A file called CONTROL.nnn holds the directory, file names, and other housekeeping information. All the backed-up files are placed in one large file called BACKUP.nnn. (For both files, the nnn represents the number of the backup diskette.) The two files are marked as read-only so that you cannot inadvertently erase or alter them.

By placing all the files into a larger file, BACKUP V3.3 gains speed over its predecessors. Its backup process takes less than half the time that earlier versions of BACKUP required. You have no way to tell, however, what diskette holds what file. DOS V3.3's log file is the only clue you have to locate a file.

For more information on the BACKUP command, see Chapter 18.

Messages

1. ***Backing up files to target drive d: ***
   Diskette Number: nn

   INFORMATION: BACKUP displays this message as the
   program archives the files from the source disk to the
   receiving diskette in disk drive d or to the receiving fixed
   disk drive d. If you are using diskettes to back up, nn is the
   backup diskette's sequential number, starting with 1. After
   you see the message shown in item 1, DOS will display a list
   of the files that it is backing up. DOS displays the complete
   path and file name for each file.

2. Cannot execute FORMAT

   WARNING: BACKUP could not execute FORMAT because
   (1) FORMAT is not in the current directory or in a
   directory specified to the PATH command, or (2) you do
   not have enough memory to run FORMAT. When you see
   this error message, FORMAT does not run. If you have no
   formatted diskettes, abort BACKUP, format additional
   diskettes, and rerun BACKUP. If you have formatted
   diskettes, insert one into the disk drive and continue the
   backup process.

3. Cannot FORMAT nonremovable drive d:

   ERROR: The destination disk to receive the backup files is a
   fixed disk or networked disk drive, and you used the /F
   switch to request formatting. When you see this message,
   BACKUP aborts. To recover from this error, issue the
   BACKUP command again without the /F switch, or use a
   floppy disk drive as the destination.

4. Disk full error writing to BACKUP Log File
   Strike any key to continue

   WARNING: The disk that holds the BACKUP log file is full.
   Press any key to continue backing up your files; however
   BACKUP will not write any new information to the log file.

5. Error opening logfile

   ERROR: BACKUP could not open the log file. You may have
   made one of the following errors: (1) you may have omitted
   the file name; (2) you may have given an improperly
   phrased file name; (3) you may have given an incorrect disk

drive name (remember that you cannot place the log file on the destination disk); (4) you may have given an incorrect path; (5) the log file may be in use by another program; or (6) the disk's root directory may not have available additional directory entries.

If you have used the /L switch without a file name, check to see if you have sufficient room in the root directory for the log file. If necessary, delete or move a file from the root directory, and try again. If you specified a file name, make sure that you spelled and punctuated the name correctly. Ensure that the file name is correct, and try the command again.

6. `Fixed Backup device is full`

   ERROR: The fixed disk you specified to receive the backed-up files is full. To remedy the error, begin the backup process again using diskettes, or delete unwanted files from the target fixed disk. Then try BACKUP again.

7. `Insert backup diskette nn in drive d:`
   `Strike any key when ready`

   INFORMATION: This message appears when the source of the backup is a diskette, not a fixed disk. Insert the proper diskette number nn in drive d: and press a key to start or continue the backup process.

8. `Insert backup diskette nn in drive d:`

   `Warning! Files in the target drive`
   `d:\ root directory will be erased`
   `Strike any key to continue`

   INFORMATION and WARNING: This message appears during the backup process when you are backing up onto diskettes. When you use the /A switch, the message does not appear for the first target diskette but appears for subsequent diskettes. This message appears for all diskettes when you are not using the /A switch.

   The message instructs you to put the first or next backup diskette (diskette number nn in the series) into drive d: and press any key to continue. The message also warns that BACKUP will delete any existing files in the root directory of the receiving diskette before transferring any files. Be sure that the proper diskette is in the disk drive, and then press any key to start.

9. `Insert last backup diskette in drive d:`
   `Strike any key when ready`

   INFORMATION: This message appears only when you are using the /A switch and invoking BACKUP without having placed the backup set's final diskette in the correct disk drive. Put the proper diskette into the disk drive, and press any key to start.

10. `Insert backup source diskette in drive d:`
    `Strike any key when ready`

    INFORMATION: You have specified a floppy disk drive as the source for BACKUP. BACKUP is requesting you to insert the source diskette, and press any key when you are ready to begin the backup process.

11. `Invalid date`

    ERROR: You made one of two errors: (1) you inserted a space between the /D switch and the date, or (2) you gave an impossible date. Check that the date you gave is correct and try the command again.

12. `Invalid path`

    ERROR: You made one of two errors: (1) you specified a directory path for the source drive that contains invalid characters, or (2) your directory path is too long. Check the PATH command's spelling and phrasing, and try the command again.

13. `Invalid time`

    ERROR: You made one of two errors: (1) you inserted a space between the /T switch and the time, or (2) you gave an impossible time. Check the time you gave, and try the command again.

14. `Invalid drive specification`

    ERROR: You made one of the following errors: (1) you specified a nonexistent disk drive as the source or destination for BACKUP; (2) you did not specify a source disk drive name; (3) you specified a disk drive that is currently being used by an ASSIGN, SUBST, or JOIN command; (4) you allowed a resident program like SideKick to remain active and thus interfere with BACKUP. Check the disk drive names that you specified and inactivate any interfering memory-resident programs. If necessary, restart DOS and try the command again.

15. `Last backup diskette not inserted`

   WARNING or ERROR: This message appears when you use the /A switch and the diskette in the disk drive is not the last diskette from a previously made backup set. If you used a diskette previously processed by BACKUP, this message appears with the `Insert last backup diskette in drive d:` message. If the diskette has not been processed by BACKUP before, BACKUP aborts.

16. `*** Last file not backed up ***`

   ERROR: The fixed disk used as the recipient for the backed-up files is full. The file not backed up is the last file in the list that is displayed on the screen. BACKUP deletes this backup file. The original source file is left intact and not marked as having been backed up.

   To correct the problem, you should either back up onto floppies or delete unwanted files from the target fixed disk. Then try the backup again.

17. `Logging to file filename`

   INFORMATION: You have used the /L switch, and BACKUP is recording information to the log file called `filename`.

18. `No source drive specified`

   ERROR: You did not give a disk drive name for the source. Retry the command and give a disk drive name for the source and destination.

19. `No target drive specified`

   ERROR: You did not give a disk drive name for the destination disk, or you forgot to give the source disk drive name. Retry the command and give a disk drive name for the destination.

20. `*** Not able to back up file ***`

WARNING: The file that was listed just before this message is displayed could not be backed up because of a file-sharing conflict. The file is being used by another program, and BACKUP cannot read this file. BACKUP simply skips this file and continues.

Try backing up this file later when the file is not in use by another computer. You can do the entire backup again or use the /M and /A switches (backing up only modified files and adding to the backup set) to add the skipped file to the backup set.

21. `Source and target drives are the same`

ERROR: You specified the same disk drive to be the source of the backup and to receive the backup files. Issue the command again and use a different disk drive for either the source or the target.

22. `Target can not be used for backup`

ERROR: BACKUP could not place files on the destination disk. The disk is flawed. If you are using diskettes, try a different diskette. If you are using a fixed disk, try backing up to a different disk drive, or restart DOS and reissue the BACKUP command.

23. `Warning! Files in the target drive`
`d:\BACKUP directory will be erased`
`Strike any key when ready`

INFORMATION and WARNING: This message appears during the backup process when you are backing up onto a fixed disk. You have not used the /A switch, and BACKUP will erase the files in the BACKUP subdirectory. Before you proceed, check to be sure that you have selected the proper directory.

24. `Warning! No files were found to back up`

WARNING: No files on the disk you designated for BACKUP matched the file specifications you gave. Check the spelling of the path and file names. Then get a listing of the disk's directory to see whether the files you want to back up are located there.

Batch Command

V1, V2, V3—Internal

Purpose	Executes one or more commands contained in a disk file

Syntax

    dc:pathc\filename *parameters*

dc: is the name of the disk drive that holds the batch file.

pathc is the path to the batch file.

filename is the batch file's root name.

parameters are the parameters to be used by the batch file.

Exit Codes   None

Rules for Executing Batch Files

1. A batch file must have the extension .BAT.

2. If you do not give a disk drive name, the current disk drive is used.

3. If you do not give a path name, the current directory is used.

4. To invoke a batch file, simply type its root name. For example, to invoke the batch file OFTEN.BAT, type **OFTEN**, and then press Enter.

5. DOS executes each command one line at a time. The specified parameters are substituted for the markers when the command is used.

6. DOS recognizes a maximum of ten parameters. You may use the SHIFT subcommand to get around this limitation.

7. If DOS encounters an incorrectly phrased batch subcommand when you run a batch file, DOS displays a `Syntax error` message, and then continues with the remaining commands in the batch file.

8. You can stop a running batch file by pressing Ctrl-Break. DOS will display this message:

```
Terminate batch job (Y/N)?_
```

If you answer Y for yes, the rest of the commands are ignored, and the system prompt appears. If you answer N for no, DOS skips the current command but continues to process the other commands in the file.

9. DOS remembers which directory holds the batch file. Your batch file may cause the current directory to change at any time.

10. DOS remembers which diskette holds the batch file, and you may change diskettes at any time. DOS will prompt you to insert the diskette that holds the batch file, if necessary. However, for DOS V3.0, if the batch file is on a diskette, you may not remove the diskette. If you remove it, DOS displays an error message and stops processing the batch file.

11. You can make DOS execute a second batch file immediately after the first one is finished. Simply enter the name of the second batch file as the last command in the first batch file. You can also execute a second batch file within the first batch file and return to the first batch file by using the CALL subcommand.

12. Batch subcommands are valid only for batch files. You cannot execute batch file subcommands as normal DOS commands. (See the "Notes" section.)

13. You may not redirect the input or output of a batch file. However, you can use redirection in the lines within a batch file.

Rules for the AUTOEXEC.BAT File

1. The file must be called AUTOEXEC.BAT and reside in the boot disk's root directory.

2. The AUTOEXEC.BAT file's contents must conform to the rules for creating batch files.

3. When you boot DOS, DOS automatically executes the AUTOEXEC.BAT file.

4. When DOS executes the AUTOEXEC.BAT file after the computer boots, the system doesn't automatically request the date and time. To get the current date and time, you must put the DATE and TIME commands in the AUTOEXEC.BAT file.

Rules for
Creating
Batch Files

1. A batch file contains ASCII text. You may create a batch file by using the DOS command COPY, EDLIN (the DOS line editor), or another text editor. If you use a word-processing program, make sure that it is in programming, or nondocument, mode when you create the batch file.

2. The batch file's root name can be from one to eight characters long and must conform to the rules for creating file names.

3. The file name extension must be .BAT.

4. A batch file should not have the same root name as that of a program file (a file ending with .COM or .EXE) in the current directory. Nor should you use an internal DOS command, such as COPY or DATE, as a root name. If you use one of these root names to name a batch file, and then try to run the batch file, DOS will execute the program or the command instead.

5. You may enter any valid DOS system-level commands. You also may use the parameter markers (%0–%9), environmental variables by enclosing the variable name in percent signs (such as **%COMSPEC%**), and the batch subcommands.

6. You may enter any valid batch subcommand. (The batch subcommands are included in the *Command Reference.*)

7. To use the percent sign (%) for a file name in a command, enter the percent symbol twice. For example, to use a file called A100%.TXT, you enter **A100%%.TXT**. This rule does not apply to the parameter markers (%0–%9) or environmental variables.

8. You may suppress the display of any line from the batch file if an @ is the first nonspace character on the line.

Notes

Two batch subcommands, ECHO and PAUSE, are accepted by DOS as system commands. At the command level, however, the usefulness of these two commands is dubious.

All DOS versions except V3.0 will allow you to change the diskette that holds the batch file. For DOS V3.0, if you change the diskette that holds the batch file, DOS displays an error message and quits processing the file.

For additional information on batch files and subcommands, refer to Chapters 12 and 13.

Batch Subcommands
CALL   *V3.3*

Purpose   Runs a second batch file, and then returns control to the first batch file

Syntax   CALL *dc:pathc*filename *parameters*

dc: is the name of the disk drive that holds the called batch file.

pathc is the path to the called batch file.

filename is the root name of the called batch file.

parameters are the parameters to be used by the batch file.

Rules   1. If you do not give a disk drive name, the current disk drive is used.

2. If you do not give a path name, the current directory is used.

3. The named batch file is run as if invoked from the keyboard. Parameters are passed to the called batch file as if the file were invoked from the keyboard.

4. You may not redirect the input or output of the batch file which you have called using CALL. However, you can use redirection on the lines within the batch file which you have called using CALL.

5. When the second batch file finishes, DOS executes the next line of the first batch file.

Notes   Use the CALL command to run a second batch file from another batch file. When the second batch file is finished, DOS continues processing the remaining commands in the first batch file.

If CALL is not used to run the second batch file, DOS concludes batch file processing when the second file finishes. DOS does not normally return to the first batch file.

You can duplicate the same procedure in versions of DOS prior to V3.3 by using COMMAND in the form

COMMAND /C *dc:pathc*filename *parameters*

where **filename** is the root name of the second batch file.

Batch Subcommand
ECHO

Purpose

Displays a message and allows or inhibits the display of batch commands and messages by other batch subcommands as DOS executes these subcommands

---

Syntax

To display a message, use

ECHO *message*

To turn off the display of commands and messages by other batch commands, use

ECHO OFF

To turn on the display of commands and messages, use

ECHO ON

To see the status of ECHO, use

ECHO

message is the text of the message to be displayed on the video screen.

Rules

1. For unconditional display of a message on the video screen, use ECHO *message*.

2. When ECHO is on, the batch file displays each command as DOS executes each line. The batch file also displays any messages from the batch subcommands.

3. When ECHO is off, the batch file does not display its commands as DOS executes them. The batch file also does not display messages produced by other batch subcommands. The exceptions to this rule are the Strike a key when ready message generated by the PAUSE subcommand and any ECHO *message* command.

4. DOS starts the system with ECHO on.

5. An ECHO OFF command is active until batch processing is finished or an ECHO ON command is encountered. If one batch file invokes another, ECHO is not turned back on by DOS when the second batch file is invoked. ECHO is turned on after the final batch file is processed.

6. ECHO affects messages produced only by batch subcommands. The command does not affect messages from other DOS commands or programs.

Notes

The ECHO message is not the same as the REM message. REM is affected by an ECHO OFF command. The message on the line with the REM subcommand is not displayed if ECHO is off. The message on the line with ECHO is always displayed.

You can suppress the display of a single batch file line by using the @ as the first character in a line. By using the line

@ECHO OFF

the command ECHO OFF is not displayed on the screen.

To suppress the output of a command, use I/O redirection to the null device (NUL). For example, to suppress the file(s) copied message when you are using COPY, use the form:

COPY file1.ext file2.ext >NUL

The command's output is sent to the null device and is not displayed on the screen.

Message

ECHO is *status*

INFORMATION: ECHO's *status* is displayed as either ON or OFF.

Batch Subcommand
FOR..IN..DO   *V2, V3*

Purpose   Allows iterative (repeated) processing of a DOS command

Syntax   FOR %%variable IN (set) DO command

variable is a single letter.

set is one or more words or file specifications. The file specification is in the form *d:path*\filename.*ext*. Wildcards are allowed.

command is the DOS command to be performed for each word or file in the set.

Rules
1. You may use more than one word or a full file specification in the **set**. Separate words or file specifications by spaces or by commas.

2. **%%variable** becomes each literal word or full file specification in the set. If you use wildcard characters, FOR..IN..DO executes once for each file that matches the wildcard file specification.

3. You may use path names.

4. You cannot nest FOR..IN..DO subcommands (put two of these subcommands on the same line). You may use other batch subcommands with FOR..IN..DO.

Notes   For the FOR..IN..DO subcommand, the major change between DOS V2 and DOS V3 is the use of path names for the file specification. DOS V2 does not allow path names, but DOS V3 does.

set can also contain literal words, separated by spaces. **set** replaces **%%variable** when the command executes. See Chapters 12 and 13 on batch commands and subcommands for more information.

Message   FOR cannot be nested

ERROR: More than one FOR command was found on a command line in the batch file. Edit the batch file to correct this problem and try executing the batch file again.

Batch Subcommand
GOTO   *V2, V3*

Purpose	Jumps (transfers control) to the line following the label in the batch file and continues batch file execution from that line

Syntax

GOTO label

label is the name used for one or more characters, preceded by a colon. Only the first eight characters of the label name are significant.

Rules

1. The label must be the first item on a line in a batch file and must start with a colon (:).

2. When GOTO label is executed, DOS jumps to the line following the label and continues execution of the batch file.

3. A label is never executed. DOS uses the label only as the jump-to marker for the GOTO subcommand.

4. If you issue a GOTO command with a nonexistent label, DOS issues an error message and stops processing the batch file.

Message

Label not found

ERROR: DOS cannot find the label specified in the GOTO command. The batch file is aborted, and the system prompt reappears.

Batch Subcommand
IF   *V2, V3*

Purpose   Allows conditional execution of a DOS command

Syntax   IF *NOT* condition command

NOT tests for the opposite of the **condition** (executes the command if the condition is false).

condition is what is being tested. It may be one of the following:

ERRORLEVEL number—DOS tests the exit code (0 to 255) of the program. If the exit code is greater than or equal to the **number**, the condition is true.

string1 == string2—DOS tests whether these two alphanumeric strings are identical.

EXIST *d:path\filename.ext*—DOS tests whether the file *d:path\filename.ext* is in the specified drive or path (if you give a drive name or path name), or is on the current disk drive and directory.

command is any valid DOS batch file command.

Rules   1. For the IF subcommand, if the condition is true, the command is executed. If the condition is false, the command is skipped, and the next line of the batch file is immediately executed.

2. For the IF NOT subcommand, if the condition is false, the command is executed. If the condition is true, the command is skipped, and the next line of the batch file is immediately executed.

3. The only DOS programs that leave exit codes are BACKUP, FORMAT, GRAFTABL, KEYB, REPLACE, and RESTORE. Using an **ERRORLEVEL** condition with a program that does not leave an exit code is meaningless.

4. For **string1** == **string2**, DOS makes a literal, character-by-character comparison of the two strings. The comparison is based on the ASCII character set, and upper- and lowercase letters are distinguished.

5. When you are using **string1** == **string2** with the parameter markers (%0–%9), neither string may be null (empty, or nonexistent). If either string is null, DOS displays a `Syntax error` message and aborts the batch file.

Batch Subcommand
PAUSE *(Pause execution)*   *V1, V2, V3*

Purpose

Suspends batch-file processing until a key is pressed, and optionally displays a user's message

Syntax

PAUSE *message*

message is a string of up to 121 characters.

Rules

1. The *message*, a series of up to 121 characters, must be on the batch file line with the word PAUSE.

2. When DOS encounters a PAUSE subcommand in a batch file, DOS displays the optional *message* if ECHO is on. If ECHO is off, DOS does not display the optional *message*.

3. Regardless of ECHO's setting, DOS displays the message Strike a key when ready . . .

4. DOS suspends the processing of the batch file until you press any key. Afterward, DOS continues processing the batch file's lines. To end a batch file's processing, press Ctrl-Break or Ctrl-C.

Batch Subcommand

REM *(Show remark)*   *V1, V2, V3*

Purpose   Displays a message within the batch file

Syntax

    REM *message*

message is a string of up to 123 characters.

Rules

1. REM must be the last batch file command on the line when you use REM with the IF or FOR..IN..DO subcommands.

2. The optional *message* can contain up to 123 characters and must immediately follow the word REM.

3. When DOS encounters a REM subcommand in a batch file, DOS displays the *message* if ECHO is on. If ECHO is off, DOS does not display the *message*.

4. The difference between **ECHO** *message* and **REM** *message* is that with ECHO, the message is always displayed. IF ECHO is off, the message with REM is not displayed.

Batch Subcommand
SHIFT *(Shift parameters)*   *V2, V3*

Purpose   Shifts one position to the left the parameters given on the command
line when the batch file is invoked

Syntax   **SHIFT**

Rules   1. When you use SHIFT, DOS moves the command line
                         parameters one position to the left.

                     2. DOS discards the former first parameter (%0).

                     See Chapter 13 for a discussion of the SHIFT command.

BREAK
(Control Break)   *V2, V3—Internal*

Purpose

Determines when DOS looks for a Ctrl-Break to stop a program (PC DOS uses Ctrl-Break, but MS-DOS uses Ctrl-C.)

Syntax

To turn on BREAK, use

  BREAK ON

To turn off BREAK, use

  BREAK OFF

To find out whether BREAK is on or off, use

  BREAK

Rules

1. BREAK is either on or off.

2. If BREAK is on, DOS looks for Ctrl-Break when performing any operation.

3. If BREAK is off, DOS checks for Ctrl-Break only when performing operations with the following equipment:

  a. the terminal or keyboard/screen

  b. the printer

  c. the RS-232 (asynchronous) adapters

4. When you set BREAK, DOS displays no messages.

Notes

The BREAK command determines when DOS will check for Ctrl-Break, which aborts, or stops, the running program. With programs that have little input and output to the keyboard, screen, or printer (computation-bound programs), you may not be able to stop the program if something goes wrong. BREAK ON tells DOS to check for Ctrl-Break before any DOS operation, including using the disk drives.

BREAK ON has little effect on disk performance. DOS works only one to two percent slower with BREAK turned on.

You are usually safe with BREAK OFF, unless you are running long programs with little display, keyboard, or printer activity. In these cases, turn BREAK on before you run the program and turn BREAK off after the program has finished running.

The Ctrl-Break (or Ctrl-C) command does not work while the computer is "number crunching" but does work when a program interacts with DOS. Using BREAK ON does not allow Ctrl-Break to stop a CPU-intensive, computative task.

This command is the same as the BREAK directive in the CONFIG.SYS file given in Chapter 14.

Message

Must specify ON or OFF

WARNING: You gave the BREAK command with some word other than ON or OFF.

CHCP
(Change code page)   *V3.3—Internal*

Purpose   For as many devices as possible, changes the code page (font) that DOS uses

Syntax   To change the current code page, use:

CHCP codepage

To display the current code page, use:

CHCP

codepage is a valid three-digit code page number.

Rules
1. You must use NLSFUNC prior to issuing this command.

2. When you have successfully selected a code page, the new code page becomes the specified code. If you have included CONFIG.SYS directives for devices that use code pages (directives such as **DEVICE=PRINTER.SYS** or **DEVICE=DISPLAY.SYS**), CHCP loads the correct code pages for the devices.

3. You may access the COUNTRY.SYS file to get new country information. If you did not specify the location of COUNTRY.SYS when you invoked the NLSFUNC, COUNTRY.SYS must exist in the current disk's root directory, or DOS returns a File not found message.

Exit Codes   None

Notes   CHCP is a system-wide code page (font) changer. CHCP sets all possible devices to use the new font. MODE works similarly but changes only one device at a time.

For more information, see Chapter 15, "Making DOS Go International," and MODE CODEPAGE and NLSFUNC in the *Command Reference*.

Messages

1. Code page nnn not prepared for all devices

ERROR: CHCP could not select the code page nnn because of one of the following errors: (1) you did not use MODE to prepare a code page for this device; (2) an I/O error occurred while DOS was sending the new font information to the device; (3) the device is busy (for example, a printer is in use or off-line); or (4) the device does not support code-page switching.

Check that the MODE CODEPAGE PREPARE command has been issued for the appropriate devices and that the devices are on-line and ready. Then try CHCP again.

2. Code page nnn not prepared for system

ERROR: CHCP could not select the code page nnn because of one of the following errors: (1) you have not yet run NLSFUNC; (2) you have specified an invalid code page (nnn) for your country; or (3) you have not prepared a code page, using the MODE command.

Ensure that you have run NLSFUNC and that you have used the MODE CODEPAGE PREPARE command to prepare the code page for the appropriate devices.

3. File not found

ERROR: CHCP could not find the COUNTRY.SYS file. One of two errors occurred: (1) you did not specify COUNTRY.SYS's location when you gave the NLSFUNC command; or (2) COUNTRY.SYS is not in the current disk drive's root directory.

CHDIR or CD
(Change directory)   *V2, V3—Internal*

Purpose   Changes the current directory or shows the path of the current directory

---

Syntax   To change the current directory, use either of the subsequent syntax forms:

CHDIR *d:*path

CD *d:*path

To show the current directory path on a disk drive, use either of the subsequent syntax forms:

CHDIR *d:*

CD *d:*

d: is a valid disk drive name.

path is a valid directory path.

Rules

1. If you do not indicate a disk drive, the current disk drive is used.

2. When you give a path name, DOS moves from the current directory to the last directory specified in the path.

3. If you want to start the move with the disk's root directory, use the backslash (\ ) as the path's first character. Otherwise, DOS assumes that the path starts with the current directory.

4. If you give an invalid path, DOS displays an error message and remains in the current directory.

Exit Codes   None

Examples

For the following examples, refer to the sample hierarchical directory in Appendix B.

Example A. *Starting from the root directory*

CHDIR DOS

DOS moves from the root directory to the directory named DOS.

Example B. *Starting from the root directory*

CHDIR DOS\HARDDISK

DOS moves from the root directory to HARDDISK.

Example C. *Starting from the \DOS\HARDDISK directory*

(1) CHDIR ..
(2) CHDIR \DOS

DOS moves from HARDDISK back to the DOS directory.

These two examples illustrate different ways to move between directories. CHDIR .. shows how to move up to a parent directory. DOS does not permit movement by parent directory name when you are working in a subdirectory. Therefore, you cannot move up a level from HARDDISK to DOS by typing the line CHDIR DOS. If you give this command, DOS "thinks" you are trying to move to a HARDDISK subdirectory named DOS instead of trying to move up a level. The only way you can move up one level is by using the parent directory symbol (..).

CHDIR \DOS shows how to move from the disk's root directory to the correct directory. Notice that the first character in the directory name is the path character, the backslash (\). When you use the backslash as a path name's first character, DOS returns to the root directory to begin movement. In this example, DOS returns to the root directory and then moves down one level to the DOS directory.

Example D. *Starting from the \DOS\HARDDISK directory*

(1) CHDIR ..\BASIC
(2) CHDIR \DOS\BASIC

DOS moves from HARDDISK to BASIC.

In the first example, DOS moves up to the parent directory of HARDDISK, which is the DOS directory, and then down to the BASIC subdirectory. In the second example, DOS begins the movement at the root directory and then moves down through the DOS directory to BASIC. Although you can use either method, you may find the first one easier to remember.

Example E. *Starting from the \DOS\HARDDISK directory*

(1) CHDIR ..\..\WORDS
(2) CHDIR \WORDS

DOS moves from HARDDISK to WORDS.

This example is almost the same as the preceding one. Notice that DOS moves up two directories (the DOS directory and the root) and then moves down to WORDS. The second method, returning to the root directory and moving down one level, is easier because it requires typing fewer characters and is simpler to remember.

Example F. *Starting from the \WORDS\LETTERS directory*

(1) CHDIR ..\..\DOS\BASIC\SAMPLES
(2) CHDIR \DOS\BASIC\SAMPLES

DOS moves from LETTERS to SAMPLES.

These two command lines accomplish the same thing, but the second method is simpler.

Notes

CHDIR, or the short form CD, is the command you use to maneuver through hierarchical directories. You can always use CD in place of CHDIR.

You have two ways to maneuver through the hierarchical directories: (1) starting at the root (top) directory of the disk and moving down; or (2) starting with the current directory and moving in either direction.

To start at the root directory of a disk, you must begin the path with the path character (\), as in \ or **B:**\ When DOS sees the path character (\) as the first character in the path, the system starts with the root directory. Otherwise, DOS starts with the current directory.

To start the move with the current directory, use one of the subdirectory names or a parent directory symbol (..). DOS knows you are starting with the current directory. To move up one level, use the double period (..). DOS moves to the *parent directory* (the directory that holds the name of the current directory). A disk drive name can precede the parent directory symbol (..). If you do not use this symbol, you must use a subdirectory name that appears in the current directory.

To move through more than one directory at a time, separate each directory name with the path character (\). You can chain together as many directories as you want, provided that the total number of characters for the path does not exceed 63.

You are not restricted to changing directories only on the current disk. For example, if the current drive is drive A and the disk with the sample directory is in drive B, you can add **B:** before each path name, and your commands will work the same way.

Message

```
Invalid directory
```

ERROR: A directory you specified does not exist. This error can occur for several reasons: (1) you may have spelled the directory name incorrectly, (2) you may have forgotten or misplaced the path character (\) between the directory names, or (3) the directory may not exist in the path you specified. When this error occurs, CHDIR aborts and remains in the current directory.

CHKDSK
(Check disk)

V1, V2, V3—External

Purpose

Checks the directory and the file allocation table (FAT) of the disk, and reports disk and memory status. CHKDSK can also repair errors in the directories or the FAT.

Syntax

*dc:pathc*CHKDSK *d:path\\filename.ext/F/V*

dc: is the name of the disk drive that holds the command.

pathc is the path to the command.

d: is the name of the disk drive to be analyzed.

path is the directory path to the files to be analyzed.

filename.ext is a valid DOS file name. Wildcards are allowed.

Switches

/F   *Fixes* the file allocation table and other problems if errors are found.

/V   Shows CHKDSK's progress and displays more detailed information about the errors the program finds. (This switch is known as the *verbose* switch.)

Rules

1. If you do not give a disk drive name, the current disk drive is used.

2. To check a diskette, make sure that the diskette you want to analyze is in the drive before you run CHKDSK. If you have a one-drive system and want to analyze a diskette that does not contain CHKDSK, specify a second drive (that is, B: instead of A:).

3. You must direct CHKDSK to make repairs to the disk by giving the /F switch. CHKDSK asks you to confirm that you want the repairs made before the program proceeds.

4. If you give a file name, with or without wildcards, CHKDSK checks the file(s) for continuity.

*5. Do not combine different versions of CHKDSK and DOS. For example, do not use CHKDSK V2.1 with DOS V3. You can lose files if you do.

6. CHKDSK will not process a directory on which you have used the JOIN command—that is, a second disk joined to a subdirectory. CHKDSK processes the "real" portion of the disk and then displays a warning message indicating that the command cannot process the directory on which you have used JOIN. CHKDSK then continues processing the real portion of the disk/directory.

7. CHKDSK will not process a disk on which you have used a SUBST command, which is a subdirectory using a disk drive name as an alias. To analyze the files in the alias subdirectory, you must give the full, real path name to the files. For example, if C:\WORDS\LETTERS is a subdirectory on which you have used SUBST to name the subdirectory drive E, the command **CHKDSK E:** produces an error message. You must use **CHKDSK C:\WORDS\LETTERS**, or **CHKDSK WORDS\LETTERS** if your current disk drive and directory is C:\.

8. CHKDSK will not process a disk drive on which you have used the ASSIGN command. If you have given **ASSIGN A=C**, you cannot analyze drive A unless you first unassign the disk drive with **ASSIGN**.

9. CHKDSK will not process a networked (shared) disk. You must run CHKDSK on the computer that owns the disk drive, and you must pause (using NET PAUSE) network processing or disconnect (using NET DISCONNECT) the PC from the network before you run CHKDSK.

Examples

a. **CHKDSK**

DOS analyzes the disk or diskette in the current drive.

b. **CHKDSK B:**

DOS analyzes the diskette in drive B.

c. **CHKDSK A: /F**

DOS analyzes the diskette in drive A and asks permission to repair the file allocation table (FAT) if CHKDSK finds a flaw. In case of a flaw, one message may be

```
xxxx lost clusters found in xxx chains
Convert lost chains to files (Y/N)?_
```

If you answer Y for yes, CHKDSK converts into files the lost areas of the disk. These files will appear in the disk's root directory, under the name FILExxxx.CHK, in which xxxx is a consecutive number between 0000 and 9999. If these files do not contain anything useful, you can delete them.

d. **CHKDSK /V**

DOS invokes the "verbose" mode, which lists each directory and subdirectory on the disk and all files in the directories. You can redirect this output to a file or printer.

e. **CHKDSK *.***

DOS checks all files in the current drive's current directory to see whether they are stored contiguously on the disk. Two messages may be displayed:

(1) `All specified file(s) are contiguous`

(2) `d:path\filename.ext`
    `Contains xxx noncontiguous blocks`

The first message means you are getting good disk performance. The second message means that the files you specified are not stored contiguously on the disk. The second message is displayed for each file not stored contiguously. If you are analyzing a diskette and many file names are listed, you will probably want to COPY (*not* DISKCOPY) the files to another diskette. In the case of the fixed disk, BACKUP your entire hard disk, reformat it, and RESTORE it.

What CHKDSK shows

1. Volume name and creation date (only disks with volume labels)

2. Total disk space

3. Number of files and bytes used for hidden or system files

4. Number of files and bytes used for directories

5. Number of files and bytes used for user (normal) files

6. Bytes used by bad sectors (flawed disk space)

7. Bytes available (free space) on disk

8. Bytes of total memory (RAM)

9. Bytes of free memory

For a diskette that holds the files listed in the sample directory in Appendix B, CHKDSK would show the following:

```
Volume EXAMPLE DSK created Jun 23, 1987 11:36a

   1457664 bytes total disk space
     78336 bytes in 3 hidden files
      9216 bytes in 9 directories
    323504 bytes in 31 user files
   1046608 bytes available on disk

    654336 bytes total memory
    522368 bytes free
```

Because this diskette had no bad sectors, CHKDSK did not display the Bytes in bad sectors message.

Notes

CHKDSK checks a disk's directories and the file allocation table. The command checks also the amount of memory in the system and determines how much of that memory is free. If CHKDSK finds any errors, it reports them on the screen before CHKDSK makes a status report.

When you first use a disk, the individual 512-byte sections of the program or data files are stored in contiguous sectors (one after the other). After you have erased files or added others, DOS attempts to store a new file in any open sector. This method of file storage means that DOS may store a large file in several noncontiguous sectors on the disk. DOS slows down when it reads this file because the system must move the disk's recording heads many times in order to read the entire file.

CHKDSK *filename* checks to see whether the specified file or files are stored contiguously on the disk. DOS reports any programs that are stored noncontiguously and how many different sections in which the file or files are stored. If CHKDSK reports that many files on a diskette are noncontiguous, you should format a new diskette. Use the COPY *.* command (*not* DISKCOPY) to consolidate your files from the old diskette to the new one.

CHKDSK processes only "real" disk drives or subdirectories. You cannot use any alias or substitution disk drives. CHKDSK will not process a networked disk (a disk belonging to another system on the network or being used by the network), a disk drive on which you have used the ASSIGN command (for example, drive A in the command ASSIGN A=C), a disk drive on which you have used the JOIN command, or a disk on which you have used a SUBST command (which is actually a subdirectory of a disk).

To run CHKDSK on a networked disk, you must run the command from the computer that owns the disk drive. You must pause or disconnect the computer from the network before you run CHKDSK.

For disk drives on which you have used the ASSIGN command, you must break the assignment by using ASSIGN. Then you can analyze the disk or diskette. You must break the JOIN command from a disk and its subdirectory on which you have used JOIN before you can analyze the disk. You may not use the disk drive letter given in the SUBST command for processing a subdirectory. You must give the real drive and path name to CHKDSK to analyze the files in the subdirectory.

For disks on which you have used JOIN or ASSIGN, CHKDSK reports the statistics of only the "true" disk or diskette and does not include the additional space offered by the JOIN or ASSIGN commands. For more information, see the SUBST and JOIN commands in Chapter 19 and also the listings for these commands in this *Command Reference*.

CHKDSK will process a RAM (virtual) disk drive, such as VDISK.SYS provided with DOS V3.

Messages

1. `All specified file(s) are contiguous`

   INFORMATION: The files you specified are stored in contiguous sectors on the disk, and you are getting the best performance from this diskette or disk subdirectory.

2. `filename`
   `Allocation error for file, size adjusted`

   WARNING: The file `filename` has an invalid sector number in the file allocation table (FAT). CHKDSK truncates the file at the end of the last valid sector.

Check this file to ensure that all information in the file is correct. If you find a problem, use your backup copy of the file. This message is usually displayed when the problem is in the FAT, not in the file. Your file should still be good.

3. `Cannot CHDIR to root`

ERROR: CHKDSK could not return to the root directory during its scan of the disk's subdirectories. When this message appears, CHKDSK aborts. Try CHKDSK again. If the message reappears, restart DOS and try CHKDSK again. If the message appears yet again, the disk is damaged, and CHKDSK cannot fix the damage. Try to copy as many files as possible to another disk, and then reformat or retire the damaged disk.

4. `Cannot CHKDSK a Network drive`

ERROR: You attempted to run CHKDSK on a disk drive that is part of a network. You must run CHKDSK on the computer attached to the disk drive, and pause or disconnect the computer from the network when you run CHKDSK.

5. `Cannot CHKDSK a SUBSTed or ASSIGNed drive`

ERROR: You attempted to run CHKDSK on a disk drive that is actually a subdirectory (SUBST) or a different disk drive (ASSIGN). If you are trying to analyze a subdirectory, rerun CHKDSK, giving the real disk drive and path name. You cannot analyze a disk on which you have used the ASSIGN command. You must break the assignment by giving the ASSIGN command without parameters and then rerun CHKDSK on the disk.

6. `directoryname`
   `Cannot recover direntry`
   `entry, processing continued`

WARNING: CHKDSK cannot recover `direntry`, which is either the . (current directory entry) or the .. (parent directory entry) in the named subdirectory, *directoryname*. This subdirectory may be so badly damaged that CHKDSK cannot recover the directory.

If possible, copy all the files from this subdirectory to another disk or subdirectory. Then erase the files in the original subdirectory and remove the subdirectory (using the

RD command). Most likely, you have lost the files in the subdirectory that CHKDSK reported to be faulty. You may need to restore the files from backup copies.

If the problem is in diskette's subdirectory, copy all the files from the offending diskette to another diskette. Either reformat or retire the offending diskette.

7. `CHDIR .. failed trying alternate method`

   ERROR: CHKDSK is confused and does not know how to return to a parent directory. This error is internal to CHKDSK or DOS (or both) and does not mean that your disk drive or diskette is bad.

   The best approach is to restart DOS and rerun CHKDSK. If you see this message a second time, get another copy of CHKDSK from your DOS master diskette. The copy of CHKDSK you are using is probably bad. Restart DOS and run CHKDSK a third time. If you still get this error, your disk has a serious flaw. Copy whatever files you can from the diskette or disk. Retire or reformat the diskette or reformat the fixed disk.

8. `filename`
   `Contains invalid cluster, file truncated`

   WARNING: The file `filename` has a bad pointer to a section in the FAT on the disk. If you gave the /F switch, CHKDSK will truncate the file at the last valid sector. If you did not use the /F switch, CHKDSK will take no action.

   Check this file to see whether all information is intact. If it is, usually CHKDSK can correct this problem without any loss of information in the file.

9. `filename`
   `Contains xxx noncontiguous blocks`

   INFORMATION: The file `filename` is not stored contiguously on the diskette or fixed disk but is stored in xxx number of pieces. If you find that many files on a diskette are stored in noncontiguous pieces, COPY the diskette to another diskette to increase disk performance. If you are using a fixed disk, BACKUP the fixed disk, format it, and then RESTORE it.

10. `directoryname`
    `Convert directory to file (Y/N)?`

    WARNING: The directory `directoryname` contains so much bad information that the directory is no longer usable as a directory. If you respond with Y, CHKDSK converts the directory into a file so that you can use DEBUG or some other tool to repair the directory. If you answer N, CHKDSK takes no action.

    Respond with N the first time you see this message. Try to copy any files you can from this directory to another disk. Check the copied files to see whether they are usable. Then rerun CHKDSK to convert the directory into a file and try to recover the rest of the files.

11. `directoryname`
    `Directory is joined,`
    `tree past this point not processed.`

    WARNING: CHKDSK encountered a directory that is actually a disk on which you have used JOIN to attach it to the currently processed disk. CHKDSK will not process this subdirectory but will continue to process the remaining portion of the real disk or diskette.

12. `Disk error reading FAT n`

    WARNING: CHKDSK encountered a disk error while attempting to get information from FAT 1 or FAT 2 (shown by the number n). The probable cause is a premature shutdown while the computer was trying to write to the disk (for example, a power failure, system lockup, or you pulled the diskette from the drive too soon).

    If this message appears for FAT 1 or FAT 2 on a diskette, copy all the files to another diskette. Then retire or reformat the bad diskette. If this message appears for the fixed disk, BACKUP all files on the fixed disk. Then reformat and RESTORE the fixed disk.

    If the message appears for both FAT 1 and FAT 2, the diskette is unusable. Copy the files to another diskette and retire or reformat the diskette after you have removed all the information you can.

13. `Disk error writing FAT n`

    WARNING: CHKDSK encountered a disk error while attempting to put information into FAT 1 or FAT 2 (shown by the number n).

    If this message appears for FAT 1 or FAT 2 on a diskette, copy all the files to another diskette. Then retire or reformat the bad diskette. If this message appears for the fixed disk, BACKUP all files on the fixed disk, reformat it, and then RESTORE it.

    If the message appears for both FAT 1 and FAT 2, the diskette is unusable. Copy the files to another diskette and retire or reformat the diskette after you have removed all the information you can.

14. `. or`
    `..`
    `Entry has a bad attribute or`
    `Entry has a bad size or`
    `Entry has a bad link`

    WARNING: The link to the parent directory (..) or the current directory (.) has a problem. If you gave the /F switch, CHKDSK will attempt to repair the problem. This procedure is normally a safe one and does not carry the risk of losing files.

15. `Error found, F parameter not specified`
    `Corrections will not be written to the disk`

    INFORMATION: CHKDSK found an error. This message tells you that CHKDSK will go through the motions to repair (fix) the disk but will not actually make any changes to it because you did not give the /F switch.

    If you see this message, you can freely answer yes to any CHKDSK message, knowing that the disk will not be changed. However, you can see what actions CHKDSK would have to take to correct the error.

    This message also means that your disk does have problems. You will have to run CHKDSK with the /F switch to fix the disk.

16. `filename`
    `First cluster number is invalid,`
    `entry truncated`

    WARNING: The file `filename`'s first entry in the FAT refers to a nonexistent portion of the disk. If you gave the */F* switch, the file will become a zero-length file (truncated).

    Try to copy this file to another diskette before CHKDSK truncates the file. You may not get a useful copy, however, and the original file will be lost.

17. `filename`
    `has invalid cluster, file truncated`

    INFORMATION and WARNING: A part of the file's (`filename`) chain of FAT entries points to a nonexistent part of the disk. If you gave the */F* switch, the file is truncated at its last valid sector. If you did not give the */F* switch, no corrective action is taken. Try to copy this file to a different disk and rerun CHKDSK with the */F* switch. You may lose part of the file.

18. `filename1`
    `Is cross linked on cluster x`
    `filename2`
    `Is cross linked on cluster x`

    WARNING: Two files—`filename1` and `filename2`—have an entry in the FAT that points to the same area (cluster) of the disk. In other words, the two files "think" that they own the same piece of the disk.

    CHKDSK will take no action on this problem. You must correct the problem yourself by completing the following steps: (1) Copy both files to another diskette; (2) Delete the files from the original diskette; (3) Edit the files as necessary. Both files may contain some garbage.

19. `Insufficient room in root directory`
    `Erase files from root and repeat CHKDSK`

    ERROR: CHKDSK has recovered so many "lost" clusters from the disk that the root directory is full. CHKDSK will abort at this point.

Examine the FILExxxx.CHK files. If you find nothing useful, delete them. Then rerun CHKDSK with the */F* switch to continue recovering "lost" clusters.

20. `directoryname`
    `Invalid current directory`

    WARNING: The directory `directoryname` has invalid information in it. CHKDSK will attempt to repair this directory. For more specific information about the problem with the directory, do *one* of the following:

    A. Enter **CHKDSK** /V

    B. Move into the faulty directory, if possible, and enter **CHKDSK *.* /V**

    The "verbose" mode will tell you more about what is wrong.

21. `directoryname`
    `Invalid sub-directory entry`

    WARNING: The directory `directoryname` has invalid information in it. CHKDSK will attempt to repair this directory. For more specific information about the problem with the directory, do *one* of the following:

    A. Enter **CHKDSK** /V

    B. Move into the faulty directory, if possible, and enter **CHKDSK *.* /V**

    The "verbose" mode will tell you more about what is wrong.

    If you need, copy the files from this directory and repeat CHKDSK with the */F* switch to fix the problem.

22. `Probable non-DOS disk`
    `Continue (Y/N)?`

    WARNING: The special byte in the FAT indicates that your disk is a DOS disk, but that the disk was not formatted, was formatted under a different operating system, or is badly damaged.

    If you used the */F* switch, answer **N**. Recheck the disk without the */F* switch, and then answer **Y** in response to the prompt. See what action DOS takes. Then, if your disk is a DOS disk, run CHKDSK again with the */F* switch.

If you did not use the */F* switch, press Yand watch what action DOS takes. Then decide whether you want to rerun **CHKDSK** */F*to correct the disk.

23. `Processing cannot continue,`
    `message`

    ERROR: This error message indicates that CHKDSK is aborting because of an error; `message` tells you what the problem is. The likely culprit is a lack of enough random-access memory to check the diskette. This message occurs most often with 64K systems. Because most systems have 256K or more, users should infrequently see the message. If DOS returns this message, you may have to increase the amount of memory in your computer or "borrow" another computer to check the diskette.

24. `Tree past this point not processed`

    WARNING: CHKDSK cannot continue down the indicated directory path because the system has found a bad track or the subdirectory is actually a disk on which you have used the JOIN command.

    If the fault is not that you have used the JOIN command, copy all files from the disk to another floppy. The original disk may not be usable any more, and you may have lost some files.

25. `xxxxxxxxxx bytes disk space freed`

    INFORMATION: CHKDSK regained some disk space that was improperly marked as "in use." `xxxxxxxxxx` tells you how many additional bytes are now available. To free this disk space, review and delete any FILExxxx.CHK file that does not contain useful information.

26. `xxx lost clusters found in yyy chains`
    `Convert lost chains to files (Y/N)?`

    INFORMATION: Although CHKDSK has found `xxx` blocks of data allocated in the FAT, no file on the disk is using these blocks. They are lost clusters, which CHKDSK normally safely frees if no other error or warning message is given.

If you have given the */F* switch and answer Y, CHKDSK will join each set of lost chains into a file placed in the root directory of the disk, called FILE0000.CHK. Examine the files and delete any that do not contain useful information.

If you answer N and have used the */F* switch, CHKDSK simply frees the lost chains so the disk space can be reused by other files. No files are created.

If you answer Y and have not given the */F* switch, CHKDSK displays the actions it would take, but does not take any action.

See the examples under "Notes" for additional information.

CLS
(Clear screen)   *V2, V3—Internal*

Purpose   Erases the display screen

Syntax   CLS

Rules   1. All information on the screen is cleared, and the cursor is
                        placed at the home position (upper left corner).

                     2. This command affects only the active video display.

                     3. If you have used the ANSI control codes to set the
                        foreground and background, the color settings remain in
                        effect.

                     4. If you have not set the foreground/background color, the
                        screen reverts to light characters on a dark background.

                     5. CLS affects only the screen, not memory.

COMMAND
(Invoke secondary command processor)   *V2, V3—External*

Purpose   Invokes a second copy of COMMAND.COM, the command processor

Syntax   *dc:pathc*COMMAND */E:size /P /C string*

dc: is the name of the drive where DOS can find a copy of COMMAND.COM.

pathc is the DOS path to the copy of COMMAND.COM.

string is the set of characters you pass to the new copy of the command interpreter.

Switches   */E:size*   Sets the *size* of the *environment*. Size is a decimal number from 160 to 32,768, rounded up to the nearest 16-byte multiple.

    /P   Keeps this copy *permanently* in memory (until the next system reset).

    /C   Passes the string of commands (the *string*) to the new copy of COMMAND.COM.

Rules   1. The *string* in the */C* option is interpreted by the additional copy of COMMAND.COM just as though you had typed the string at system level. The */C* must be the last switch used on the line. Do not use the form **COMMAND /C string /P**.

    2. You can exit from the second copy of the command processor by issuing the command EXIT if you have used the */P* option (permanent).

    3. If you issue the */P* and */C* switches together, the */P* switch is ignored.

COMMAND is an advanced DOS command not recommended for newcomers or novices. Consult the DOS *Technical Reference* manual for more information about this command.

COMMAND can be used to approximate the CALL batch subcommand. Use the form

COMMAND /C batchfile

where batchfile is the name of the batch file to run. When the second batch file is finished, COMMAND exits and returns control to the first batch file.

COMP
(Compare files)   *V1, V2, V3—External*

Purpose	Compares two sets of disk files to see whether they are the same or different

Syntax

dc:pathc\ COMP d1:path1\filename1.ext1
    d2:path2\filename2.ext2

dc: is the name of the disk drive that holds the command.

pathc is the path to the command.

d1: is the drive that contains the first set of files to be compared.

path1 is the path to the first set of files.

filename1.ext1 is the file name for the first set of files. Wildcards are allowed.

d2: is the drive that contains the second set of files to be compared.

path2 is the path to the second set of files.

filename2.ext2 is the file name for the second set of files. Wildcards are allowed.

d1 and *d2* may be the same.

path1 and *path2* may be the same.

filename1.ext1 and *filename2.ext2* may be the same also.

Special Terms   *d1:path1\filename1.ext1* is the *primary* file set.

d2:path2\filename2.ext2 is the *secondary* file set.

Rules

1. If you do not give a drive name for a set, the current disk drive is used. (This rule applies to *d1:* and *d2:*, as well as to *dc:*, the drive that holds the command itself.)

2. If you do not give a path for a file set, the current directory of the disk drive is used.

3. If you do not enter a file name for a file set, all files for that set (primary or secondary) are compared (which is the same as entering *.*). However, only the files in the secondary set with names matching file names in the primary set are compared.

4. If you do not enter a drive name, path name, and file name, COMP prompts you for the primary and secondary file sets to compare. Otherwise, the correct diskettes must be in the correct drive if you are comparing files on diskettes. COMP does not wait for you to insert diskettes if you give both primary and secondary file names.

5. Only normal disk files are checked. Hidden or system files and directories are not checked.

6. Files with matching names but different lengths are not checked. A message is printed indicating that these files are different.

7. After 10 mismatches (unequal comparisons) between the contents of two compared files, COMP automatically ends the comparison between the two files and then aborts.

Examples

a. COMP A:IBM.LET C:IBM.LET

The file in the current directory on drive A, IBM.LET, is compared to the file in the current directory on drive C, IBM.LET.

b. COMP *.TXT *.BAK

Files with the extension .TXT are compared to files that end with the extension .BAK on the current disk in the current directory.

c. COMP A:\WORDS\LETTERS\DOUG.LET B:DOUG.LET

The file DOUG.LET in the subdirectory LETTERS on drive A is compared to the file DOUG.LET in the current directory on drive B.

d. COMP C:\WORDS\DAVID C:\WORDS\MIKE

All files in the subdirectory DAVID on drive C are compared with the files on the subdirectory MIKE, also on drive C. Note that DAVID and MIKE must be directories, not files. Because no file name is given, COMP assumes *.* (all files).

Sample Session

In this sample session, COMP first compares one file with another and then compares a set of files on one diskette to a set of files having the same names on the fixed disk.

A>COMP

```
Enter primary file  name
FIXIT.C                              {Enter the first file name.}
Enter 2nd file name or drive id
FIXIT1.C                             {Enter the second file name or
                                      disk name.}

A:FIXIT   .C  and FIXIT1  .C         {DOS displays the file names.}

Compare error at offset 36A          {COMP has found a mismatch.
File 1 = 78                          The offset is the number of
File 2 = 62                          bytes into the file where the mismatch
                                     occurred. The displayed differences are
                                     in hexadecimal format (base 16). 78
                                     hex is the letter X; 62 hex is the letter
                                     B. These are the only differences
                                     between the two files.}

Compare more files (Y/N)? Y
Enter primary file name
*.C                                  {Now compare all files that end with .C
                                     against the files with the same names
                                     on drive C.}

Enter 2nd file name of drive id
C:
A:FIXIT   .C  and C:FIXIT   .C

Files compare ok

A:TEST87  .C  and C:TEST87  .C

Files compare ok

A:CHECKSUM.C  and C:CHECKSUM.C

Files compare ok                     {All files match.}

Compare more files (Y/N) N           {So quit.}
A>
```

Notes

COMP is the utility you use for comparing files. The command's ideal uses are to ensure that the files on which you have just used the COPY command are correct and to check a known good copy of a program against a questionable copy. If you have a program that once functioned properly but now is acting strangely, check a good backup copy of the file against the copy you are using. If COMP finds differences, copy the good program to the disk you are using.

Do not compare in-use files with copies you have archived with the BACKUP program. You will find differences because BACKUP places additional information at the beginning of each file. If your only backup copy of a program is in a backed-up file, use RESTORE to place the file in a directory and then use COMP to compare the files. If the program still resides in the directory where its backed-up copy is located, first copy the program to a different directory and then RESTORE the backed-up version. If you do not do this, the current copy of the program is replaced by the backed-up version.

When you try to find the last revision of a file, look at its date and time in the directory instead of using COMP. Often you can identify the most recent revision of a file with this method, which is much faster than using COMP. If you want to compare two entire diskettes on which you have used DISKCOPY, use DISKCOMP instead of COMP.

Messages

1. Compare error at offset xxxxxxxx

   INFORMATION: The files you are comparing are not the same. The difference occurs at xxxxxxxx bytes from the beginning of the file. (The number given is in hexadecimal format, base 16.) The values for the differing bytes in the files are displayed also in hexadecimal format.

2. EOF mark not found

   INFORMATION or WARNING: This message is information if the files you are comparing are program files, but the message is a warning if the files you are comparing are text files. The message indicates that COMP could not find the customary end-of-file marker (EOF marker, which is Ctrl-Z or 1A hex). COMP got to the end of the file before it found the EOF.

This problem does not occur when you compare program files and some data files. The absence of an EOF is a problem for text files. COMP always compares the files on the basis of each file's length in the directory. Sometimes files are saved with extraneous information after the end-of-file marker. As a result, you may get a compare error for the extra bytes. Check that the text files are intact. If the files are all right, COMP was comparing the extraneous part of the files.

3. `d:path\filename.ext - File not found`

    ERROR: The file `d:path\filename.ext` was not found. Check the spelling of the drive, path, and file names. Make sure that the correct diskette is in the disk drive and try the command again.

4. `d:path\filename.ext - File sharing conflict`

    ERROR: The file `d:path\filename.ext` is being used by another program or another computer on a network, and COMP cannot read the file. Check that the file is not in exclusive use by another process or computer. Retry the command later.

5. `Files are different sizes`

    WARNING: You have asked COMP to compare two files that are of different lengths. Because COMP compares only files that are the same size, COMP skips the comparison.

6. `Invalid drive specification`

    ERROR: You gave a disk drive name that does not exist. Check the disk drives and the command line you typed and try again.

7. `d:path\filename.ext - Invalid path`

    ERROR: You specified a directory path that does not exist. Check that your spelling is correct, the correct diskette is in the floppy disk drive, and the directory path you specified does exist. Then try the command again.

8. `1Ø Mismatches—ending compare`

    WARNING: COMP found 10 mismatches between the two files you were comparing. COMP therefore assumes that it has no reason to continue and aborts the comparison of the two files.

COPY
(Copy files)

V1, V2, V3—Internal

Purpose

Copies files between disk drives and/or devices, either keeping the same file name or changing it. COPY can concatenate (join) two or more files into another file or append one or more files to another file. Options support special handling of text files and verification of the copying process.

Syntax

To copy a file, use:

> COPY */A/B d1:path1*\filename1.*ext1/A/B d0:path2/*
> filename0.*ext0/A/B/V*

You may also use:

> COPY */A/B d1:path1*\filename1.*ext1/A/B/V*

To join several files into one file, use:

> COPY */A/B d1:path1*\filename1.*ext1/A/B* +
> *d2:path2*\filename2.*ext2/A/B* + . . .
> *d0:path0*\filename0.*ext0 /A/B/V*

d1:, *d2:*, and *d0:* are valid disk drive names.

path1\, *path2*\, and *path0*\ are valid path names.

filename1.*ext1*, filename2.*ext2*, and filename0.*ext0* are valid file names. Wildcards are allowed.

The three periods *(. . .)* represent additional files in the form *dx:pathx/*filenamex.*extx*.

Special Terms

The file that is being copied from is the *source* file. The names containing **1** and **2** are the source files.

The file that is being copied to is the *destination* file. It is represented by a **0**.

| *Switches* | /V | Verifies that the copy has been recorded correctly. |

The following switches have different effects for the source and the destination.

For the source file:

| /A | Treats the file as an ASCII (text) file. The command copies all the information in the file up to, but not including, the end-of-file marker (Ctrl-Z). Anything after the end-of-file marker is ignored. |

| /B | Copies the entire file (based on its size, as listed in the directory) as though it were a program file (*binary*1). Any end-of-file markers (Ctrl-Z) are treated as normal characters, and the EOF characters are copied. |

For the destination file:

| /A | Adds an end-of-file marker (Ctrl-Z) to the end of the ASCII text file after it is copied |

| /B | Does not add the end-of-file marker to this binary file |

| *Notes* | The meanings of the /A and /B switches are based on their positions in the line. The /A or /B switch affects the file immediately preceding the switch and all files after the switch *until* another /A or /B switch is encountered. When one of these switches is used before any **filename**, the switch affects all following files *until* contradicted by another /A or /B switch. |

| *Exit Codes* | None |

Rules for Copying Files with Both Source and Destination Given	1. The source name comes first, followed by the destination name.
	2. If you do not give a drive name, COPY uses the current drive.
	3. If you do not give a path, COPY uses the current directory.
	4. The following rules apply to the file name:

a. You must give either a path name or a file name. Wildcards are allowed in the source file name. If you do not give a file name but give a path name for the source, DOS assumes *.*.

b. If you do not give a destination file name, the copied file or files have the same name as the source file(s).

5. You may substitute a device name for the complete source or destination name.

6. When you copy between disk drives, COPY "assumes" that binary files are being copied (as though a /B switch were given).

7. When you copy to or from a device other than a disk drive, COPY assumes that ASCII files are being copied (as though the /A switch were given).

8. An /A or /B switch overrides COPY's default settings (rules 6 and 7).

Rules for Copying Files with Only One File Specified

1. The file specification you give (*d1:path1*\filename1.*ext1*) is the source. This specification must have one or both of the following:

   a. A valid file name. Wildcards are allowed.

   b. A drive name, a path name, or both. If only one is given, it must be different from the current drive name or path name; if both are given, at least one must be different from the current drive name or path name.

2. The source cannot be a device name.

3. The destination is the current drive and current directory.

4. The copied file(s) have the same name as the source file(s).

5. COPY "assumes" that binary files are being copied (as though a /B switch were given).

Rules for Concatenating Files

1. The destination file is the last file in the list unless you have a plus sign (+) before that file name. If you do not specify a destination file name, the first source name becomes the destination name.

2. If you do not give a drive name, the current drive is used.

3. If you do not give a path, the current directory is used.

4. The following rules apply to source files:

   a. You must give a valid file name. Wildcards are allowed, but their use may be dangerous. (See the descriptions of COPY in Chapters 2, 4, and 16.)

   b. After the first file name, any additional source file specifications must be preceded by a plus sign (+).

5. The following rules apply to the destination file:

   a. You can have only one destination file specification. If you give a destination without wildcards, only one destination file is used. If you give a destination file name with wildcards, one or more destination files are used.

   b. If you do not give a destination, the first source file is used also as the destination, with the following results:

      i. The first file that matches the wildcard file name is used as the destination file if you gave a wildcard as part of the first source file name.

      ii. The files to be joined are appended to the end of the first source file.

Messages

1. Cannot do binary reads from a device

   ERROR: This message tells you one of two things:

   a. You used a /B switch when you tried to copy something from a binary device. When DOS is copying from a device, it must have some way of determining the end of the information to be transferred. This indication is made with an end-of-file marker, the Ctrl-Z. DOS is acting intelligently. Without an end-of-file marker, DOS has no way of knowing when to complete the transfer and, therefore, will wait forever.

   b. You used a /B (binary) switch somewhere on the command line in front of the device name, probably just after the word COPY. Use the /B switch after the file name or omit the /B completely.

2. Content of destination lost before copy

WARNING: A destination file was not the first source file. The previous contents were destroyed. COPY continues concatenating the remaining files, if any.

For more information, see COPY in Chapters 2, 4, and 16.

3. File cannot be copied onto itself

ERROR: You attempted to COPY a file back to the same disk and directory containing the same file name. This usually happens when you misspell or omit parts of the source or destination drive, path, or file name. Check your spelling and the source and destination names, and then try the command again.

4. Invalid path or file name

ERROR: You gave a directory name or file name that does not exist, used the wrong directory name (a directory not on the path), or mistyped a name. COPY aborts when it encounters an invalid path or file name. If you used a wildcard for a file name, COPY transfers all valid files before it issues the error message.

Check to see which files already are transferred. Determine whether the directory and file names are spelled correctly and whether the path is correct. Then try again.

CTTY
(Change console)   *V2, V3—Internal*

Purpose	Changes the standard input and output device to an auxiliary console, or changes the input and output device back from an auxiliary console to the keyboard and video display

Syntax	**CTTY device**

device is the name of the device you want to use as the new standard input and output device. This name must be a valid DOS device name.

Exit Codes	None

Rules	1. The **device** should be a character-oriented device capable of both input and output.

2. Typing a colon (:) after the device name is optional.

3. Programs designed to work with the video display's control codes may not function properly if you redirect them.

4. CTTY does not affect any other form of redirected I/O or piping. For example, the < (redirect from), the > (redirect to), and the | (pipe between programs) work as usual.

Examples	a. **CTTY COM1**

This command makes the device attached to COM1 the new console. The peripheral connected to COM1 must be a terminal or a teleprinter (printer with a keyboard). After you give this command, DOS expects normal input to come from COM1 and sends anything for the video display to COM1.

b. **CTTY CON:**

This command makes the keyboard and video display the console. In effect, this command cancels the first example. The colon after CON or any other valid DOS device name is optional.

Notes

The CTTY command was designed so that a terminal or teleprinter, instead of the normal keyboard and video display, can be used for console input and output. This added versatility has little effect on most Personal System/2 and Personal Computer users.

You must specify a device that can both receive input and send output to the computer system. Using CTTY with a normal printer (an output-only device) is a mistake. DOS will patiently wait forever for you to type commands on the printer's nonexistent keyboard. In other words, the computer will "go West" and must be reset before you can use it again.

Message

```
Invalid device
```

ERROR: You specified an invalid device name. Your spelling may be incorrect, or DOS does not "know" the device by the name you entered.

DATE
(Set/show date)   *V1, V2, V3—Internal*

Purpose	Displays and/or changes the system date

Syntax

DATE *date_string*

date_string is in one of the following forms:

mm-dd-yy or *mm-dd-yyyy* for North America
dd-mm-yy or *dd-mm-yyyy* for Europe
yy-mm-dd or *yyyy-mm-dd* for the East Asia

mm is a one- or two-digit number for the month (1 to 12).

dd is a one- or two-digit number for the day (1 to 31).

yy is a one- or two-digit number for the year (80 to 99). The 19 is assumed.

yyyy is a four-digit number for the year (1980 to 2099).

The delimiters between the day, month, and year can be hyphens, periods, or slashes. The result that is displayed varies, depending on the country code set in the CONFIG.SYS file.

Exit Codes   None

Rules

1. When you enter a correctly phrased date with this command, DOS sets the date and returns to the system prompt.

2. If you do not enter a date, DOS displays one that may or may not be correct. If the date is incorrect, enter a correctly phrased date, which DOS then uses as the new date. If the date is correct, just press the Enter key. DOS continues to use the originally displayed date.

3. You may use a hyphen (-), slash (/), or period (.) between the month and day and between the day and year.

4. Entering an incorrectly phrased or nonsense date (such as 02/29/87, 06/31/88, or 06:03:1988) causes DOS to display an error message and a request to try again.

Sample Session

A>DATE 07/31/87
A>

{The DATE command was run with a correctly phrased date, July 31, 1987. DOS accepts the date and returns to the system prompt.}

A>DATE
Current Date is Sun 7-31-1987
Enter new date: 08/1/87
A>

{DATE is invoked, shows the current date, and allows you to reset the date. When a new date is entered, DOS returns to the system level.}

A>DATE
Current Date is Mon 8-Ø1-1987
Enter new date:
A>

{Check to see whether DOS did use the new date. In this case, DATE displayed the correct date. Therefore, you press Enter. DOS does not change the date but returns to the system prompt.}

Notes

When you boot DOS, it issues the DATE and TIME commands to set your system clock. If an AUTOEXEC.BAT file is on the boot disk, DOS does not display a prompt for the date or time. You may include the DATE or TIME commands in the AUTOEXEC.BAT file if you want these functions to be set when DOS is booted.

Computers such as the Personal Computer AT and the PS/2 computers have battery-operated clocks. After you set the clock when you first install the system, you should not have to enter the date or time unless the battery wears out.

DOS uses the date and time. When you create or update a file, DOS updates the directory with the date you entered. This date shows which copy is the latest revision of the file. The DOS BACKUP command uses the date in selecting files to back up.

The day-of-year calendar uses the time-of-day clock. If you leave your system on overnight, the day advances by one at midnight. DOS also knows about leap years and appropriately adjusts its calendar. However, you must access this clock once each day, or DOS does not advance the date properly. If you leave your computer on during the weekend but do not use it, when you return to the computer on Monday, DOS will be one day behind.

The time-of-day clock built into most PCs (but not the Personal Computer AT or the PS/2s) is a software clock. Its accuracy can vary. If you leave your system on constantly and do not reset it (system boot), the date usually is accurate, but the time may not be.

Message

`Invalid date`

ERROR: You gave an impossible date or used the wrong kind of character to separate the month, day, and year. This message is also displayed if you enter the date by using the keypad when the keypad is not in numeric mode.

DEL
(Delete files)   *V1, V2, V3—Internal*

Purpose   Deletes files from the disk

DEL is another term for ERASE. See ERASE for a complete
description.

DIR
(Directory)   *V1, V2, V3—Internal*

Purpose

Lists any or all files and subdirectories in a disk's directory

The DIR command displays the following:

Disk volume name (if any)
Name of the directory (its complete path)
Name of each disk file or subdirectory
Number of files
Amount, in bytes, of free space on the disk

The DIR command, unless otherwise directed, shows also the following:

Number of bytes occupied by each file
Date/time of the file's creation/last update

Syntax

DIR *d:path\filename.ext* /P/W

d: is the drive that holds the disk you want to examine.

path is the path to the directory you want to examine.

filename.ext is a valid file name. Wildcards are allowed.

Switches

/P   Pauses when the screen is full and waits for you to press any key

/W   Gives a wide (80-column) display of the names of the files. The information about file size, date, and time is not displayed.

Rules

1. If you do not give a drive name, the current drive is used.

2. If you do not give a path, the current directory is used.

3. If you do not give a file name, all files in the directory are displayed.

4. The DIR command shows the contents of only one directory at a time.

5. You cannot use the DIR command on a disk drive on which you have used the ASSIGN or JOIN command. You must break the assignment before you can see the directory on a drive on which you have used ASSIGN. You must use the path name of the disk used in the JOIN command. You may use the DIR command on the host disk drive involved in a JOIN command.

Exit Codes   None

Notes   The DIR command finds the disk files or subdirectories on the disk. This command shows only the files and subdirectories in the specified (or default) directory. To see a list of all the files on a disk, use CHKDSK /V or TREE /F.

If you use the /W switch, the file names and directory names are listed with five names on a line. The file date and size are not displayed, nor is the <DIR> for subdirectories. When you give the DIR /W command, you may have trouble determining which names refer to files and which names refer to directories.

DIR does not report statistics on disk drives on which you have used the ASSIGN or JOIN commands. For disk drives on which you have used JOIN, DIR reports the free space of the host disk drive (the disk drive to which the second disk drive is joined) but does not report the total of the two disk drives on which you have used JOIN. You must remove the ASSIGN command from the disk drive to find its amount of free space.

Message   File not found

ERROR: The path or file name you gave does not exist. The path may be incorrect, the file may not exist in the directory, or your spelling may be incorrect.

If you were listing a directory of another directory, you might move to the other directory (using CHDIR) and try the command again. If you still believe that the file is in the directory, enter DIR /P to display the complete directory and check the file name.

Hints

1. Before you ERASE files by using wildcard characters, run a DIR with the same file name.

   If names of files you do not want to erase are displayed, don't use that file name. Keep experimenting with the DIR command until you get the correct file name to use with the ERASE command. Or simply issue separate ERASE commands without wildcard characters.

2. I/O redirection is easy to use with the DIR command.

   You can print the directory by typing DIR >PRN, or you can put a copy of the directory into a file by typing DIR >filename1. Here, filename1 is the name of the file to hold the directory.

DISKCOMP
(Compare diskettes)

V1, V2, V3—External

Purpose

Compares two diskettes on a track-for-track, sector-for-sector basis to see whether their contents are identical

Syntax

dc:pathc **DISKCOMP** *d1: d2: /1 /8*

dc: is the name of the disk drive that holds the command.

pathc is the path to the command.

d1: and *d2:* are the disk drives that hold the diskettes to be compared. (These drives may be the same or different drives.)

Switches

/1   Compares only the first side of the diskette, even if the diskette or disk drive is double-sided

/8   Compares only 8 sectors per track, even if the first diskette has 9, 15, or 18 sectors per track (DOS V2 and V3 formats)

Rules

1. If you do not give a drive name, the first floppy disk drive (usually drive A) is used.

2. If you give only one valid floppy disk drive name, it is used for the comparison.

3. Giving the same valid floppy disk drive name twice is the same as giving only one disk drive name.

4. If you give a valid fixed disk drive name or an invalid disk drive name, DOS displays an error message and does not perform the comparison.

5. When you are using one disk drive (rules 1–4), DOS prompts you to change diskettes.

6. Only compatible diskettes should be compared. The two diskettes must be formatted with the same number of tracks, sectors, and sides.

7. Don't use DISKCOMP with a disk drive on which you have used the ASSIGN command. DISKCOMP ignores the effects of the ASSIGN.

8. Do not use DISKCOMP on a disk on which you have used JOIN, SUBST, or on a virtual (RAM) disk and networked disk drives. DOS displays an error message if you do.

Exit Codes   None

Examples   Example A.

DISKCOMP A: B:

DOS compares the diskette in drive A with the diskette in drive B.

Example B.

(1) DISKCOMP A: A:

(2) DISKCOMP

Both commands perform a single-drive comparison on drive A. DOS prompts you to insert and change diskettes at the appropriate times. Then DOS waits for you to press a key before it continues.

Example C.

DISKCOMP A: B: /1

DOS compares only the first side of the diskette in drive A with the first side of the diskette in drive B.

Example D.

DISKCOMP A: B: /8

DOS compares only eight sectors per track of the diskette in drive A with eight sectors of the diskette in drive B.

Sample Sessions

This session demonstrates two comparisons by DISKCOMP. The first comparison is successful, but the second one is not. In this example, a copy of the diskette is made with DISKCOPY and then with COPY. The original diskette is then compared to the two copies. The diskette has

been in use for some time, and several BASIC programs have been added
and deleted.

A>**DISKCOPY A: B:**   {First, copy the diskette.}

```
Insert source diskette into drive A
Insert target diskette into drive B
Strike any key when ready ↵

Copying 8Ø tracks
9 sectors per track, 2 side(s)        {It's a 1.2M diskette.}
Copy complete
Copy another (Y/N)?N
```

A>**COPY A:*.* B:**   {Now put a formatted diskette
                                                         into drive B and copy the files.}

```
   . . .
   . . .
   . . .

x file(s) copied
```

A>**DISKCOMP A: B:**   {Put the DISKCOPYed diskette back
                                                         into drive B.}

```
Insert first diskette into drive A
Insert the second diskette into drive B
Strike any key when ready ↵
Comparing 15 sectors per track, 2 side(s)

Diskettes compare OK
```

```
Compare more diskettes (Y/N)? Y       {Put the COPYed diskette
Insert first diskette into drive A     into drive B.}
Insert the second diskette into drive B
Strike any key when ready ↵
Compare error(s) on
Track 9, side 1

   . . .
   . . .
   . . .

Compare more diskettes (Y/N)? N
A>
```

This session shows that the destination diskette made with DISKCOPY is identical to the original diskette. The message `Diskettes compare OK` indicates that the two diskettes are identical.

Note, however, that the destination diskette made with COPY failed the DISKCOMP. This result was expected. When you COPY files from one diskette to another, they may not be placed in the identical spots on the new diskette. For this reason, DISKCOMP indicates that the diskettes are different. The message does not mean that the files on the destination diskette are bad or damaged, but simply that they are not in the same relative places on the two diskettes. To compare files that have been duplicated with the COPY command, use COMP rather than DISKCOMP.

If DISKCOMP reports any differences between diskettes that have been newly duplicated with DISKCOPY, the destination diskette is faulty. When this happens, DISKCOPY the diskette again. If DISKCOPY or DISKCOMP still shows that the destination diskette is faulty, the diskette itself is bad and should be discarded.

The next sample session illustrates a comparison, on a single-drive computer, of the original diskette and the destination diskette created by DISKCOPY. Drive A is used for the comparison.

A>**DISKCOMP A:**
```
Insert first diskette into drive A
Strike any key when ready ↵

Comparing 15 sectors per track, 2 side(s)

Insert second diskette into drive A
Strike any key when ready ↵

Insert first diskette into drive A
Strike any key when ready ↵

Insert second diskette into drive A
Strike any key when ready ↵

Diskettes compare OK

Compare more diskettes (Y/N)? N
A>
```

The number of times you change diskettes depends on how much memory you have and the type of diskette (8 versus 9, 15, or 18 sectors; 40 versus 80 tracks; and 1 versus 2 sides). The more random-access memory you have in your system, the less often you have to change diskettes. You change single-sided diskettes less often than double-sided ones. You change 40 track diskettes less frequently than 80 track diskettes. You change 8-sector diskettes less often than diskettes with 9 sectors; 9-sector diskettes less frequently than 15-sector diskettes; and 15-sector diskettes less often than 18-sector diskettes.

Notes

DISKCOMP compares the contents of two compatible diskettes. The command compares the files track-for-track. Although you can use this command with any two compatible (or nearly compatible) diskettes, its most effective use is in comparing original and duplicate diskettes that have been duplicated with DISKCOPY.

Using DISKCOMP to compare an original diskette with a duplicate that has been duplicated with the COPY command can be meaningless. Because COPY copies files one at a time, the copied files may not reside in exactly the same spots on the duplicated diskette and the source diskette. DISKCOMP seldom works because DOS reports that the contents of the tracks of each diskette are not the same when, in fact, the files themselves are identical. To compare diskettes that have been duplicated with COPY (not DISKCOPY), use the COMP command.

The switches, /1 for one-side comparison and /8 for eight-sector (DOS V1) comparison, affect only the portion that the program compares. If you try to compare two different types of diskettes, DOS aborts the comparison or displays a number or a message indicating that the two diskettes are not the same.

Remember: compare only diskettes that have been duplicated with DISKCOPY.

Don't attempt to use a "nonreal" floppy disk drive with DISKCOMP. If the floppy disk drive is part of a network or is a RAM disk (VDISK), or if the drive has been used with the SUBST or JOIN commands, DISKCOMP issues an error message and quits. DISKCOMP simply ignores the effects of the ASSIGN command.

If you DISKCOPY a 360K diskette on a 1.2M floppy disk drive and then compare the diskette on a 360K floppy disk drive, DISKCOMP may report that the diskettes are not the same. The 1.2M floppy disk drive records the information in a narrower band on the diskette than the band that a 360K floppy disk drive uses. If you have to run this copy on 360K floppy disk drives, make another copy of the original diskettes and use a 360K floppy disk drive. This is not true for 720K diskettes formatted on a 1.44M disk drive. 720K diskettes format correctly.

Messages

1. `Cannot DISKCOMP to or from`
   `a network drive`

   ERROR: You attempted to compare diskettes on a disk drive that is part of a network. You may use DISKCOMP only on the disk drives owned by the computer and only on the disk drives that are not part of the network. To correct this problem, use a different disk drive. Or you may want to pause or disconnect from the network and use DISKCOMP again.

2. `Compare error(s) on`
   `Track tt, side s`

   WARNING: The diskettes you are comparing are different at track number `tt`, side `s`. DISKCOMP does not specify which sectors are different, only that one or more sectors differ between the two diskettes.

   If you have just duplicated these diskettes with DISKCOPY and DISKCOPY did not report a problem, the second diskette probably has a flaw. Reformat this diskette and try DISKCOPY again. Otherwise, assume that the diskettes are different.

3. `Comparing tt tracks,`
   `xx sectors per track, s side(s)`

   INFORMATION: DISKCOMP states how many tracks (40 or 80), sectors per track (8, 9, 15, or 18), and how many sides (1 or 2) the program is comparing.

4. `Compare process ended`

   INFORMATION: DISKCOMP indicates that the comparison of the diskettes is completed.

5. disknumber diskette bad or incompatible

WARNING: The first or second diskette (disknumber) either is bad or is incompatible with the other diskette. The file allocation table of the disknumber diskette indicates that the diskette is the wrong type for this comparison.

6. Diskettes compare OK

INFORMATION: DISKCOMP compared the two diskettes and found that they match.

7. Drive or diskette types not compatible

ERROR: The disk drives or diskettes are different. The first diskette was read successfully on both sides. However, the second diskette or disk drive is not identical to the first diskette or drive.

You cannot compare 1.2M diskettes with non-1.2M diskettes or compare 1.2M diskettes on 360K floppy disk drives. You cannot compare 1.44M diskettes with non-1.44M diskettes or on 720K disk drives. You cannot compare double-sided diskettes with single-sided diskettes or compare double-sided diskettes on single-sided disk drives. You cannot compare 9-sector diskettes (DOS V2 and V3) with 8-sector diskettes (DOS V1).

Run a CHKDSK on both diskettes, and use the disk drive with the highest capacity. For each diskette, look at the number on the line bytes total disk space. If the numbers are different for the diskettes, you cannot compare them. If the numbers are the same, the disk drive that holds the second diskette is the wrong type or has a hardware problem.

If the numbers are the same, compare both diskettes on the same floppy disk drive. If this message appears again, you are using a bad copy of DISKCOMP, or the second diskette is faulty. If this message does not appear again and the second drive is the correct type for the diskette, you have a hardware problem.

8. `Invalid drive specification`
   `Specified drive does not exist,`
   `or is non-removable`

   ERROR: One (or both) of the disk drive names you gave for the comparison (1) does not exist on your system, (2) is a RAM disk, (3) is a disk drive used in a JOIN or SUBST command, or (4) is a networked drive or a fixed disk. You also may have omitted the colon following the disk drive letter. Check the disk drive name you entered. Make sure that the disk drive is "real" and try the command again.

9. `Invalid parameter`
   `Do not give filename(s)`
   `Command format: DISKCOMP d: d:[/1][/8]`

   ERROR: You gave on the command line a switch that DISKCOMP does not recognize, gave a file or path name after the disk drive name, or omitted a colon after a disk drive name. Check your typing and try the command again.

10. `Drive d: not ready`
    `Make sure a diskette is inserted into`
    `the drive and the door is closed`

    WARNING: DISKCOMP is having difficulty reading the diskette in drive d. The disk drive door may be open, a unformatted or non-DOS diskette may have been placed in the drive, or the diskette is not inserted properly in the disk drive. Check these conditions and then try DISKCOMP again.

11. `Unrecoverable read error on drive x`
    `Track tt, side s`

    WARNING: Four attempts were made to read the data from the diskette in the specified drive. The error is at track number tt, side s. If drive x is the diskette that holds the destination (copied) diskette, the copy probably is bad. (The diskette has a "hard" read error.) If drive x holds the original diskette, the diskette had a flaw when it was formatted, or the diskette has developed a flaw.

Run CHKDSK on the original diskette and look for the line bytes in bad sectors. If this line is displayed, the original diskette and the copy may actually be good. When you are formatting a diskette, FORMAT detects bad sectors and "hides" them. However, DISKCOMP does not check for bad sectors and attempts to compare the tracks even if bad sectors are present. If CHKDSK shows that the original diskette has bad sectors, the destination diskette may actually be good despite this message. In either case, you eventually should retire the original diskette.

If CHKDSK doesn't show anything for bad sectors, the original diskette has a bad spot or the disk drive that holds the diskette is faulty. The diskette probably is the source of the error. Run the diagnostics on your disk drive. If it passes this test, your diskette is faulty and should be retired.

DISKCOPY
(Copy entire diskette)   *V1**, V2**—External*

Purpose   Copies the entire contents of one diskette to another diskette on a
track-for-track basis (making a "carbon copy"). DISKCOPY works
only with diskettes.

Syntax   *dc:pathc* DISKCOPY *d1: d2: /1*

dc: is the name of the disk drive that holds the command.

pathc is the path to the command.

d1: is the floppy disk drive that holds the source (original) diskette.

d2: is the floppy disk drive that holds the target diskette (diskette to
be copied to).

Switch   */1*   Copies only the first side of the diskette

Special Terms   The diskette you are copying from is the *source* diskette.

The diskette you are copying to is the *target* diskette.

Rules
1. The source and destination disk drives must be real floppy
   disk drives. They cannot be fixed or networked disk drives,
   RAM disks, or disk drives on which you have used the JOIN
   or SUBST command. Giving or defaulting to a nonreal source
   or destination disk drive causes DOS to return an error
   message and abort the disk copy.

2. If you do not give a source disk drive name, DISKCOPY uses
   the default disk drive. If you give an improper source disk
   drive, DISKCOPY issues an error message and aborts. In
   other instances, DISKCOPY uses the current disk drive as
   the source disk drive.

3. If you give only one valid floppy disk drive name, it is used
   as both the source and destination disk drives for the copy
   (if your system has a single floppy disk drive). If your system

has two floppy disk drives, giving only one valid disk drive name results in an `Invalid drive specification` error.

4. Giving the same valid floppy disk drive name twice is the same as giving only one disk drive name.

5. If you have a system with a single floppy disk drive, drive A is used no matter what drive name you give.

6. When you copy on one floppy disk drive (rules 2–5), DOS prompts you to insert the appropriate diskette and then waits for you to press any key before the DISKCOPY continues.

7. After copying, DISKCOPY displays the following prompt:

`Copy another (Y/N)?`

Press **Y** to copy another diskette or **N** to stop the program. If you respond with **Y**, the next copy is performed on the same disk drive(s) as before.

8. If the target diskette is not formatted or is formatted differently from the source diskette, DISKCOPY automatically formats the target diskette and uses the same format as that of the source diskette. This formatting does not apply, however, to copying a double-sided diskette on a single-sided drive with the /1 switch.

*9. DISKCOPY destroys any information recorded previously on the target diskette. Do not use as the target diskette a diskette containing information you want to keep.

10. To ensure that the copy is correct, run DISKCOMP on the two diskettes.

*11. You cannot DISKCOPY a 360K or 1.2M diskette on a single-sided disk drive (regardless of whether you use the /1 switch). You cannot DISKCOPY a 1.2M diskette on a 360K disk drive, nor a 1.44M on a 720K disk drive. The copy of a single- or double-sided (180K or 360K) diskette produced on a HC drive may not be reliable when it is used with a single- or double-sided disk drive.

12. DISKCOPY ignores the effects of an ASSIGN command.

Exit Codes   None

Sample Session

This session involves using DISKCOPY on a two-drive, double-sided system. First, a double-sided, V3.3 diskette is copied and then a single-sided, V1 diskette. In both cases, two double-sided diskettes were formatted on the system.

```
A>DISKCOPY A: B:
Insert the SOURCE diskette in drive A    {Change diskettes before
Insert the TARGET diskette in drive B    you press Enter.}
Strike any key to begin. ↵
Copying 40 tracks,
9 Sectors/Track, 2 Side(s)
```

(Copying process continues . . .)

```
Copy another(Y/N)?   Y

Insert the SOURCE diskette in drive A    {Change diskettes before
Insert the TARGET diskette in drive B    you press Enter.
Strike any key to begin. ↵
Copying 40 tracks,
8 Sectors/Track, 1 side(s)

Formatting while copying

Copy another(Y/N)? N
A>
```

Notes

DISKCOPY makes identical copies of diskettes. The command automatically evaluates the size of the source diskette and makes an exact copy of it on another disk drive. If the target diskette is not formatted or is formatted differently, DISKCOPY reformats the diskette to the same size as the source diskette. For example, if the source diskette is double-sided with nine sectors per track and the target diskette is single-sided with eight sectors per track, DISKCOPY reformats the target diskette and makes it double-sided with nine sectors per track before it copies the information to the target diskette.

Always format your diskettes ahead of time. If FORMAT reports any bad sectors on a diskette, you cannot use that diskette as the target diskette with DISKCOPY. The command attempts to write to the target diskette's bad sectors and does not produce a good copy.

Fixed disk users should always give at least one floppy disk drive name with DISKCOPY. If the current disk is the fixed disk drive and you type the line

C>**DISKCOPY**

you see the message

```
Invalid drive specification
Specified drive does not exist,
or is non-removable
```

Interestingly, under DOS V3.1 on an AT with a single HC floppy disk drive, I gave the following command:

C> **DISKCOPY B: A:**

The message DOS gave was

```
Insert the SOURCE diskette into drive A:
```

DISKCOPY ignored the invalidly specified source drive B and proceeded to use drive A as the source drive. DOS V3.2 and V3.3 give a different message:

```
Insert SOURCE diskette in drive B:
```

which means that DISKCOPY would use the single disk drive as A and B and perform a single disk drive DISKCOPY. However, giving drive C (the fixed disk) or drive D (a RAM disk) results in the `Invalid drive specification` message.

As described earlier in this book, diskettes produced on a high-capacity disk drive do not work with all single-sided (180K) or double-sided (360K) disk drives. This restriction includes diskettes on which you have used DISKCOPY. If you have had problems with reading 360K diskettes produced on HC disk drives, use a 360K disk drive for copying 360K diskettes with DISKCOPY. This problem does not occur with 720K diskettes produced on 1.44M disk drives, which produce reliable 720K diskettes.

Hints

1. Write-protect your source diskette.

   Write-protecting your source disk is particularly important when you use only one floppy disk drive to make a copy of a diskette. DOS periodically prompts you to change the diskette. If the source diskette is write-protected, you cannot damage it if you put it into the drive when DOS tells you to insert the target diskette.

Write-protecting your source diskette can be important also for a system with two floppy disk drives in case you specify the wrong drives for the copy. An infrequent but fatal mistake is to put the source diskette into drive B and the target diskette into drive A, and then to type the following:

DISKCOPY A: B:

Now the source and target diskettes are reversed. If you do not stop DISKCOPY in time, the command destroys the information on the source diskette and replaces that information by whatever (if anything) is on the old target diskette.

For peace of mind, write-protect the source diskette.

2. If you have a system with two floppy disk drives and you don't write-protect your source diskette, watch the disk drive lights and be ready to flip open a disk drive door.

   If you don't write-protect your diskette on a two-drive system, watch to see which disk drive light comes on first when the copying starts. The light for the drive that holds the source diskette should be the first light to come on. If the other disk drive light comes on first, *immediately flip open the drive door* or *punch the eject button* of the source diskette and let DOS abort. If DOS starts to write to the wrong diskette, it's too late!

   Using the Ctrl-Break or Ctrl-C keystrokes to stop the action does not always work because DOS may not check for this action in time. Nor does flipping open the drive door on the "new" source diskette always work because DOS may already have read enough information on this diskette and may be on its way to copying onto the wrong diskette.

   Flipping open the disk drive door or pushing the eject button does not hurt either diskette. When DOS starts its copying process, only information from the first diskette is read. It is difficult to damage a diskette from which the system is only reading.

3. Have as much free RAM available as possible.

   When you are using DISKCOPY, DOS reads into memory as much information from the source diskette as possible. Then DOS copies this information to the target diskette and reads the next batch of information from the source diskette. The more free memory you have, the less time you will need to copy a diskette.

4. If you have used a diskette for a long time and have created and deleted many files on it, use COPY *.* rather than DISKCOPY.

DISKCOPY makes a "physical" image (exact copy) of a diskette. A diskette on which many files have been created and deleted becomes *fragmented*, which means that a single file is stored all over the diskette. This fragmentation happens frequently with word-processing programs that automatically create backup copies of files. The result is that DOS slows down when it uses the file because DOS must read the file from many different places.

Use CHKDSK *.* to determine whether this condition is true for a particular diskette. If CHKDSK *.* tells you that several files are noncontiguous, format a diskette and use COPY *.* from the old floppy to the new one to make the files contiguous and to speed searches for files.

If you have subdirectories on a diskette, be sure to create the same subdirectories (using MKDIR or MD) on the new diskette and to copy their contents.

Messages

1. `Cannot DISKCOPY to or from`
`a network drive`

ERROR: You specified a disk drive used by a network (attached to your computer or another one). You can use only disk drives attached to your computer for the DISKCOPY command, and the disk drives may not be used by the network.

If you "own" the disk drives and the drives also are part of a network, pause or disconnect from the network and then rerun DISKCOPY. If you still get the message, check the drive names you gave or use a different disk drive and try the command again.

2. `Drive d: not ready`
`Make sure a diskette is inserted into`
`the drive and the door is closed`

WARNING: DISKCOPY is having difficulty reading or writing the diskette in drive d. The diskette was not properly inserted, the source diskette was not formatted or is a non-DOS diskette, or the drive door is open. Check each of these possibilities and press a key to continue.

3. `Drive types or diskette types not compatible`

INFORMATION or ERROR: The disk drives or the diskettes are not compatible for the copying. If the problem is the disk drives, the message indicates an error. The message contains information if the problem is the diskettes.

For disk drives, the message indicates that the drive types you attempted to use are different and cannot handle the operation. The first diskette was read successfully, but the drive specified to make the copy (target) diskette is not the right type. You cannot DISKCOPY 1.2M diskettes on non-1.2M disk drives or copy 1.44M diskettes on 720K disk drives. See the identical message under DISKCOMP for remedial action.

If the destination diskette was formatted previously with a capacity that is different from that of the source diskette, this message precedes the `Formatting while copying` message. DISKCOPY reformats the destination diskette to match the source diskette's format. No other action is necessary.

4. `Invalid drive specification`
   `Specified drive does not exist,`
   `or is non-removable`

ERROR: You made an error in giving one or both of the disk drive names you gave for the copy. One of the following problems occurred: (1) the disk drive does not exist on your system, (2) the disk drive is a RAM disk, (3) the disk drive is a disk drive being used in a JOIN or SUBST command, (4) the disk drive is a networked drive on another computer, or (5) the disk drive is a fixed disk. You also may have omitted the colon after a disk drive name. Check the disk drive names you entered. Determine that each disk drive is "real" and try the command again.

5. Invalid parameter
   Do not specify filenames
   Command format: DISKCOPY d: d: [/1]

   ERROR: You gave a path and/or a file name with, or in place of, a disk drive name, or you gave a switch that DISKCOPY does not recognize. Check the command line to ensure that you typed the command correctly and try the command again.

6. Read error on drive d:
   Write error on drive d:

   WARNING: DISKCOPY is having difficulty reading or writing the diskette in drive d. The diskette is not properly inserted, the source diskette is not formatted or is a non-DOS diskette, or the drive door is open. Check these possibilities.

7. SOURCE diskette bad or incompatible
   TARGET diskette bad or incompatible

   WARNING: DISKCOPY has detected errors while reading the source diskette (first message) or writing the target diskette (second message). The error may be caused by bad sectors on either diskette, or the diskette may be in the wrong type of disk drive (a 1.2M diskette in a 360K drive or a 1.44M diskette in a 720K disk drive).

   Determine whether either diskette has bad sectors. If either diskette has bad sectors, use neither diskette with DISKCOPY. If the source diskette is bad, use COPY *.* to copy files from the source diskette. If the target diskette is bad, use a different diskette or try to FORMAT the diskette again, and then use DISKCOPY. If the problem is a suspect disk drive, determine which disk drive is the known, good drive, and use only that single disk drive to DISKCOPY the disks.

8. Target diskette is write-protected
   Press any key when ready...

   WARNING: The target diskette has a write-protect tab (for 5 1/4-inch minifloppies), or the write-protect switch is up (not covering the hole) for microfloppies.

Before removing or moving the tab, make sure that the correct diskettes are in the disk drives and check the manner in which you invoked the DISKCOPY command. If you used the write-protect notch to protect the wrong diskette, make sure that you DISKCOPY the intended source diskette to the right target diskette.

9. ```
Unrecoverable read error on drive d:
Side s, track tt
Target diskette may be unusable

Unrecoverable write error on drive d:
Side s, track tt
Target diskette is unusable
```

WARNING: These two messages indicate that the source diskette, destination diskette, or disk drives used for the DISKCOPY are flawed. The error occurred on d:, side s, track tt. The destination (target) diskette may not be an exact copy of the original and therefore is unusable.

When the message indicates a read error, the source diskette and the source drive are suspect. If you have not experienced any difficulties with the disk drive, the source diskette may have a bad sector or track.

A read error occurs on source diskettes with any bad sectors. A diskette that has been formatted and has shown bytes lost to bad sectors also produces a read error when you use DISKCOPY on the diskette. DISKCOPY attempts to copy the bad sectors even though no useful information resides in them. In this case, the target diskette is good and may be used. However, some disk space on the target diskette still is lost to the "bad sectors" on the source diskette. This loss occurs because the FAT of the source diskette, which has the bad sectors marked out, is copied to the target diskette. The corresponding sectors on the target diskette are good but are lost for use.

Run CHKDSK to see if the source diskette has bad sectors. If the source diskette shows no bad sectors when you run CHKDSK, a recent flaw in the source diskette has caused the bad sector. The target diskette probably is unusable.

You should use COPY rather than DISKCOPY on source diskettes that have bad tracks.
```

If the message indicates a write error, suspect the target diskette or disk drive that is holding the target diskette. If during previous use of the disk drive, you've experienced no other problems and if the disk drive is in good working condition, the problem is with the target diskette.

To solve the problem with the target diskette, exit from DISKCOPY and then FORMAT the intended target diskette. If the diskette has bad sectors when it is formatted, you cannot use this diskette with the DISKCOPY command. When FORMAT does not show any bad sectors, repeat the DISKCOPY. If more problems occur, try to DISKCOPY from drive B to drive A and suspect that one disk drive may be at fault.

ERASE
(Erase files)

Purpose	Removes one or more files from the directory

Syntax	**ERASE** *d:path\filename.ext*

or

DEL *d:path\filename.ext*

d: is the name of the disk drive that holds the file(s) to be erased.

path is the directory of the file(s) to be erased.

filename.ext is the name of the file(s) to be erased. Wildcards are allowed.

Rules	1. If you do not give a disk drive name, the current disk drive is used.

2. If you do not give a path name, the current directory is used.

3. If you give a disk drive name and/or a path name but no file name, DOS "assumes" that the file name is *.* (all files). If you do not give a disk drive name, path name, and file name, DOS issues an the error message Invalid number of parameters, and then it aborts the program.

4. If you specify *.* or no name for the file name (when you have given a disk drive name and/or path name), DOS displays the following prompt:

   Are you sure (Y/N)?

   If you answer **Y**, ERASE erases all files in the specified directory. If you answer **N**, ERASE erases no files.

5. You cannot erase a directory, including the . (the current directory) and the .. (the parent directory), from a subdirectory. To remove a directory, you must use RMDIR.

ERASE, or its short form DEL (delete), removes files. The directory entry for each erased file is altered to mean "not in use," and the space occupied by each file erased on the diskette or disk is freed.

As long as you do not place any more information on the diskette, you can recover the erased file with special utility programs, which are not provided with DOS. One such program is provided by the Norton Utilities. IBM's RECOVER does not recover erased files, however.

Remember that you may not be able to recover erased files if you put any more information on (write to) the diskette.

Hints

1. Using wildcards can be helpful when you erase a group of files, but inadvertently erasing the wrong file or files is easy to do.

   Use the DIR command with your intended wildcard file name to test-list the files that want to erase. If you find a file or files you don't want to erase in this directory listing, you must use a different file name. In other words, experiment with the DIR command to find the right file name(s) before you ERASE with wildcards. Don't forget that erasing the wrong file is always easier than recovering the erased file, even if you have the right utility program.

2. You should check for typing errors in the file name(s) before you press Enter to activate the erasing process.

   You can easily make a typographical error and erase the wrong file.

Messages

1. Access denied

   ERROR: Either you attempted to erase a file marked as read-only, or the file is being used by another program or computer and is marked temporarily as read-only.

   If the file you intend to erase has the read-only attribute set, use the ATTRIB command to turn off the read-only flag. If this file is being used by another program or computer, wait until the other program or computer is done and then erase the file. If the file is on another computer in a network and you do not have permission to erase the file, ask the operator to erase the file for you.

2. `File not found`

ERROR: The file name you gave does not exist on the current or specified disk drive or directory. You also receive this message if you have an incorrect directory name as part of the file name. Check your typing of the names, make sure that the correct diskette is in the drive, and try again.

3. `Invalid drive specification`

ERROR: You entered an ill-formed disk drive name (a colon is missing) or a nonexistent disk drive name. Check your spelling and try again.

4. `Invalid number of parameters`

ERROR: You made one of the following errors: (1) you did not specify a disk drive name, path name, or file name; (2) you have spaces in the file specification; or (3) you have extraneous characters on the command line.

EXE2BIN
*(Change .EXE files into .BIN
or .COM files)*   *V1.1, V2, V3—External*

Purpose   Changes suitably formatted .EXE files into .COM files

Syntax   *dc:pathc***EXE2BIN** *d1:path1*filename1*.ext1*
                    d2:path2\\filename2.ext2

dc: is the name of the disk drive that holds the command.

pathc is the path to the command.

d1: is the name of the disk drive that holds the file to be converted.

path1 is the directory of the file to be converted.

filename1 is the root name of the file to be converted.

.ext1 is the extension name of the file to be converted.

d2: is the name of the disk drive for the output file.

path2 is the directory of the output file.

filename2 is the root name of the output file.

.ext2 is the extension name of the output file.

Special Terms   The file to be converted is the *source* file.

The output file is the *destination* file.

Exit Codes   None

Rules

1. If you do not specify a drive for the source file, EXE2BIN uses the current drive as the source file.

2. If you do not specify a drive for the destination file, EXE2BIN uses the source drive.

3. When you do not specify a path, EXE2BIN uses the current disk's directory.

4. You must specify a root name for the source file (the file to be converted).

5. If you do not specify a root name for the destination file, EXE2BIN uses the root name of the source file.

6. If you do not specify an extension for the source file, EXE2BIN uses the extension .EXE.

7. If you do not specify an extension for the destination file, EXE2BIN uses the extension .BIN.

8. The .EXE file must be in the correct format (following the Microsoft conventions).

Notes

EXE2BIN is a programming utility that converts .EXE (executable) program files to .COM or .BIN (binary image) files. The resulting program takes less disk space and loads faster. This conversion, however, may be a disadvantage in future versions of DOS. Unless you use a compiler-based language, you probably will never use this command. For further information about EXE2BIN, see the DOS Technical Reference manual.

FASTOPEN
(Fast opening of files)

V3.3—External

Purpose

Keeps directory information in memory so that DOS can quickly find and use files you frequently need

Syntax

*dc:pathc*FASTOPEN **d:**=*nnn* . . .

dc: is the name of the disk drive that holds the command.

pathc is the path to the command.

d: is the name of the disk drive whose directory information should be held in memory.

nnn is the number of directory entries to be held in memory (10 to 999).

. . . designates additional disk drives in the form **d:**=*nnn*.

Exit Codes

None

Rules

1. You must specify the name of the disk drive whose entries are in memory. The drive cannot be a floppy disk drive.

2. You can use FASTOPEN on an unlimited number of nonfloppy disk drives. Simply give the additional disk drives, separated by a space, on the same command line, or repeat the command for each disk drive.

3. If you do not specify *nnn*, FASTOPEN uses the value of 34.

4. If you give *nnn*, the value must be between 10 and 999, inclusive. FASTOPEN's minimum value is the maximum level of your deepest directory plus 1 or 10, whichever is greater.

5. The sum of *nnn* for all successful FASTOPEN commands cannot exceed 999.

Notes

FASTOPEN is a DOS V3.3 addition that caches directory information on files. You can use the command on any disk drive. The value of using the command on a RAM disk is dubious, however.

FASTOPEN works by keeping directory information in memory. Because disk buffers already hold the file allocation table information, FASTOPEN allows DOS to search memory for the file's or subdirectories' directory entry, to locate quickly the corresponding FAT entry, and to open the file. If you effectively use FASTOPEN, you can increase DOS's performance significantly when you use many files.

FASTOPEN is not the same as the BUFFERS command, which works when DOS reads or writes a file. FASTOPEN works when you first open a file.

As with BUFFERS, there is no predetermined "best" number for you to use. The default value of 34 works well with many installations. If your subdirectories run many levels deep or if you use many files, specifying a larger number can improve performance. However, using a value for *nnn* that is too large (greater than 200) bogs the system. DOS spends more time examining in-memory directory entries than rereading the entries from the disk.

Messages

1. Cannot use FASTOPEN for drive d:

   ERROR: You have attempted to use FASTOPEN on drive d:, which is part of an ASSIGN, JOIN, or SUBST command. You cannot use FASTOPEN on these drives.

   Make sure you have given the correct disk drive name and try the command again.

2. FASTOPEN installed

   INFORMATION: The FASTOPEN command was successful.

3. FASTOPEN already installed

   ERROR: The FASTOPEN command already has been issued successfully and/or the command you gave was unsuccessful. This message may appear after another error message.

4. Incorrect number of parameters

   ERROR: You omitted the disk drive name given to the FASTOPEN command.

5. Insufficient memory

ERROR: Insufficient memory is available for issuing the FASTOPEN command. Either remove any unneeded resident programs or modify your CONFIG.SYS file to free more RAM. Then restart DOS.

6. Invalid drive specification

ERROR: You gave the name of a floppy disk drive to FASTOPEN. You can use FASTOPEN on only nonremovable disks. Check the command line and try the command again.

7. Invalid parameter

ERROR: You made one of the following errors: (1) you gave a switch to FASTOPEN, (2) you forgot the = between the disk drive name and the number of entries to hold, (3) you forgot to give a disk drive name, or (4) you forgot the colon after the disk drive name. Check the command line and try the command again.

8. Same drive specified more than once

ERROR: You already have issued the FASTOPEN command on the specified disk drive. After you have given the FASTOPEN command for a disk drive, you cannot alter the number of directory entries for that drive. To alter the number, you must restart DOS and give the FASTOPEN command with the desired number of entries to hold.

9. Too many drive entries

ERROR: You gave too many disk drive names to FASTOPEN. FASTOPEN was not installed for any of the disk drives named. Repeat the command and use fewer disk drive names.

10. Too many name entries

ERROR: Either the sum of directory entries for all FASTOPEN commands exceeds 999 or the command for a single drive exceeds 999. FASTOPEN is not installed for the disk drives you have just named. Try the command again and reduce the number of entries, or restart DOS and try the command again.

FIND

(Find string filter)   *V2, V3—External*

Purpose   Displays from the designated files all the lines that match (or do not match) the specified string. This command also can display the line numbers.

Syntax   *dc:pathc*FIND */V/C/N* "**string**" *d:path\\filename.ext* . . .

dc: is the name of the disk drive that holds the command.

pathc is the path to the command.

string is the set of characters for which you want to search. As indicated, **string** must be enclosed in quotation marks.

d: is the name of the disk drive for the file.

path is the directory that holds the file.

filename.ext is name of the file you want to search.

Switches

/V   Displays all lines that do *not* contain **string**

/C   Counts the number of times that **string** occurs in the file but does not display the lines

/N   Displays the line number (number of the line in the file) before each line that contains **string**

Rules

1. You may use more than one file specification. All file specifications must appear after **string** and be separated by spaces.

2. For each file specification,

   a. If you do not give a disk drive, the current drive is used;

   b. If you do not give a path name, the current directory is used.

3. If you do not give any file specifications, FIND "expects" information from the keyboard (standard input).

4. If you use switches with FIND, you must locate them between the word FIND and the string. (Most DOS commands require that you place switches at the end of the command line.)

5. You must enclose string in double-quotes. To use the double-quote character in the string, use two double-quote characters in a row.

Sample Session

For this session, two files were created: MEN.TXT and GETTY.TXT.

```
A>dir
  Volume in drive C is QUE_DISK
  Directory of C:\TEST

.                <DIR>      8-Ø1-87    1Ø:27a
..               <DIR>      8-Ø1-87    1Ø:27a
MEN     TXT         72      8-Ø5-87    3:29p
GETTY   TXT        18Ø      8-Ø5-87    3:31p
                    4 File(s)    3981312 bytes free
```

```
A>type men.txt                          {Show what's in the file.}
```

```
Now is the time for all good
men to come to the aid of
their party.
```

```
A>type getty.txt                        {Show what's in this file.}
```

```
Fourscore and seven years ago, our
fathers brought forth upon this
continent a new nation conceived in
liberty and dedicated to the proposition
that all men are created equal.
```

```
A>find "men" men.txt                    {Find the word "men" in MEN.TXT.}
```

```
---------- men.txt                      {The file name}
```

```
men to come to the aid of               {The lines from the file}
```

A>find "men" getty.txt   {Do the same thing for GETTY.TXT.}

---------- getty.txt
that all men are created equal.

A>find "men" men.txt getty.txt   {Find "men" in both files.}

---------- men.txt
men to come to the aid of

---------- getty.txt
that all men are created equal.

A>find /v "men" men.txt getty.txt   {Show which lines don't have "men".}

---------- men.txt
Now is the time for all good
their party.

---------- getty.txt
Fourscore and seven years ago, our
fathers brought forth upon this
continent a new nation conceived in
liberty and dedicated to the proposition

A>find /c "men" men.txt getty.txt   {Count the lines that contain "men" in
                                                 both files.}

---------- men.txt: 1   {The file name and the count}

---------- getty.txt: 1   {The file name and the count}

A>find /v/c "men" men.txt getty.txt   {Count the number of lines that don't
                                                 have "men".}

---------- men.txt: 3
---------- getty.txt: 5

A>find /n "men" men.txt getty.txt   {Number the lines with "men".}

---------- men.txt   {The count is always
[2]men to come to the aid of   relative to the file.}

```
---------- getty.txt
[5]that all men are created equal.
```

A>find /v/n "men" men.txt getty.txt   {Same thing, but lines without "men"}

```
---------- men.txt
[1]Now is the time for all good
[3]their party.
[4]
---------- getty.txt
[1]Fourscore and seven years ago, our
[2]fathers brought forth upon this
[3]continent a new nation conceived in
[4]liberty and dedicated to the proposition
[6]
```

A>find /n "t" men.txt getty.txt   {Search for any line with the letter "t".}

```
---------- men.txt
[1]Now is the time for all good
[2]men to come to the aid of
[3]their party.

---------- getty.txt
[2]fathers brought forth upon this
[3]continent a new nation conceived in
[4]liberty and dedicated to the proposition
[5]that all men are created equal.
```

A>find /n "th" men.txt getty.txt   {Got too many lines; wanted only lines with "th".}

```
---------- men.txt
[1]Now is the time for all good
[2]men to come to the aid of
[3]their party.

---------- getty.txt
[2]fathers brought forth upon this
[4]liberty and dedicated to the proposition
[5]that all men are created equal.
```

A>find /n "the" men.txt getty.txt   {Look for the word "the".}

```
---------- men.txt
[1]Now is the time for all good
[2]men to come to the aid of
[3]their party.

---------- getty.txt
[2]fathers brought forth upon this
[4]liberty and dedicated to the proposition
```

A>find /n "THE" men.txt getty.txt   {How about "THE"?}

```
---------- men.txt
```

```
---------- getty.txt
```
                                                     {Not in either file}

This last example shows one problem you may encounter when you try to find a string. FIND looks for the exact match of your search string. Upper- and lowercase letters are treated differently. FIND does not locate a word entered in lowercase letters if the word in the file has any capital letters. That's why *the* was found in the file, but *THE* was not found.

Notes

FIND is one of several filters provided with DOS V3. The command can find lines that contain **string** and those that do not. FIND also can number and count lines rather than display them.

This filter is useful when it is combined with DOS I/O redirection. You can redirect FIND's output to a file by using the > redirection symbol. Because FIND accepts a sequence of files to search, you do not have to redirect the input to FIND.

Messages

1. FIND: Access denied filename

    ERROR: The file named filename is being used by another program or networked computer that has an exclusive-use lock on the file. FIND cannot read the file. Try the command later.

2. FIND: File not found filename

WARNING: FIND cannot find the file named `filename` because of one of the following problems: (1) the file does not exist; (2) the file is not in the location you specified (you gave a wrong drive or path); or (3) you made a spelling error.

If you give a switch after **string** FIND thinks that the switch is a file name and gives you this warning message. Afterward, FIND continues to process any other files you have specified.

3. FIND: Invalid number of parameters

ERROR: You didn't give FIND enough information. You must type at least the following:

   FIND "string"

Most likely, you didn't supply a string.

4. FIND: Invalid parameter *x*

WARNING: You gave FIND an incorrect switch. FIND recognizes only the /C, /N, and /V switches. FIND prints this warning message and continues.

5. FIND: Read error in filename

ERROR: FIND encountered an error while it was reading the file named `filename`. Try FIND again. If the read error occurs a second time, COPY the file to a different disk or subdirectory and try the command again. If an error occurs during the COPY process, follow the directions under COPY to recover the file.

6. FIND: Syntax error

ERROR: You did not phrase the command correctly. You probably didn't put quotation marks around the string for which you were searching.

FORMAT
(Format disk)

V1, V2, V3**—External

Purpose

Initializes a disk to accept DOS information and files. FORMAT also checks the disk for defective tracks and (optionally) places DOS on the diskette or fixed disk.

Syntax

dc:pathc**FORMAT** d: */S/1/8/V/B/4/N:ss/T:tt*

dc: is the name of the disk drive that holds the command.

pathc\\ is the path to the command.

d: is a valid disk drive name.

Switches

/S	Places a copy of the operating *system* on the disk so that it can be booted
/1	Formats only the *first* side of the diskette
/8	Formats an *eight*-sector diskette (V1)
/V	Writes a *volume* label on the disk
/B	Formats an eight-sector diskette and leaves the proper places in the directory for any version of the operating system, but does *not* place the operating system on the diskette
/4	Formats a diskette in a 1.2M disk drive for double-density (320K/360K) use
/N:ss	Formats the disk with *ss number* of sectors. *ss* ranges from 1 to 99.
/T:ttt	Formats the disk with *ttt* number of *tracks* per side. *ttt* ranges from 1 to 999.

Rules

1. If you do not give a disk drive name, the current disk drive is used.

2. Before you can use a new diskette, you must format it. The only exceptions occur when you use a new diskette as the target for DISKCOPY (DISKCOPY also formats diskettes), or when you use BACKUP with the /F switch.

3. DOS checks the floppy disk drive. Unless otherwise directed through a switch, DOS formats the diskette to its maximum capacity: 2 sides if a double-sided drive is used; 9 sectors per track for normal disk drives; and 15 sectors per track for HC disk drives.

4. Some switches do not work together. For example, you cannot use the following switch combinations:

   a. /V or /S with /B;

   b. /V with /8;

   c. /N or /T with a 320/360K or fixed disk drive;

   d. /1, /4, /8, or /B with the fixed disk.

*5. FORMAT destroys any information previously recorded on the diskette or fixed disk. Do not FORMAT a diskette or fixed disk that contains any useful information.

6. To make a diskette usable with all versions of DOS and IBM computers, use the /B and /1 switches. (Format the diskette for any DOS version and format only one side.)

7. If you give the disk a volume name, the name can be 1 to 11 characters long and contain any character that is legal in a file name.

8. If you use the /S switch (to place the operating system on a disk) and the current directory does not have a copy of DOS, DOS prompts you to put the DOS diskette into drive A so that the system gets the copy of DOS before it formats the disk.

9. If DOS formats a fixed disk that has a volume label, it asks

   ```
   Enter current Volume Label for drive d:
   ```

   To continue formatting disk drive d:, enter the disk drive's current volume label. If you do not enter the exact volume label, FORMAT displays

```
Invalid Volume ID
Format failure
```

and aborts.

10. If you are formatting a fixed disk without a volume label,
    FORMAT displays the message:

    ```
    WARNING, ALL DATA ON NON_REMOVABLE DISK
    DRIVE d: WILL BE LOST!
    Proceed with Format (Y/N)?
    ```

    Answer **Y** for yes to format the fixed disk drive d:, **N** for no
    to abort FORMAT from formatting the fixed disk.

11. Although the /4 switch may be used to create double-
    density diskettes in a 1.2M disk drive, the formatted diskette
    is not reliable when it is used in double-density disk drives.

12. You cannot format a RAM disk (VDISK), a networked disk,
    or a disk drive on which you have used the ASSIGN, SUBST,
    or JOIN command.

Exit Codes		
	0	Successful completion of last format
	1	Not defined
	2	Not defined
	3	Aborted by user (Ctrl-Break)
	4	Aborted due to error
	5	Aborted due to **N** response on a fixed disk format

Sample Session

This session describes the formatting of six diskettes. The first two
diskettes are formatted on a 1.2M disk drive, the third diskette on a 1.44M
disk drive, the fourth diskette on a 720K disk drive, and the fifth diskette
on a 360K drive. The sixth diskette is a 720K diskette made on a 1.44M
disk drive. The operating system is placed on the third and fourth diskettes
(using the /S switch), and the last diskette has a volume label added
(using the /V switch).

```
A>FORMAT A:                              {Put a diskette in the
Insert new diskette for drive A:          drive and press Enter.}
and strike ENTER when ready
```

```
Format complete
    1213952 bytes total disk space
    1213952 bytes available on disk


Format another (Y/N)? Y                      {Now format the second
Insert new diskette for drive A:             diskette.}


and strike ENTER when ready


Format complete

1213952 bytes total disk space              {The diskette has several
    7680 bytes in bad sectors               bad sectors. It can
1206272 bytes available on disk             still be used for most operations but
                                            not for DISKCOPY or DISKCOMP.}


Format another (Y/N)? N                      {Rerun FORMAT to put the
A>FORMAT A: /S                               operating system on the next diskette.}


Insert DOS disk in drive A:                  {This message appears
and strike ENTER when ready                  only when you give the switch
Insert new diskette for drive A:             and the current disk does not contain
and strike ENTER when ready                  COMMAND.COM and the operating
                                             system.}
Format complete
System transferred

    1457664 bytes total disk space          {This diskette was a
      78336 bytes used by system            1.44M diskette.}
    1379328 bytes available on disk


Format another (Y/N)? N
A>FORMAT B: /S
Insert new diskette for drive B:
and strike ENTER when ready


Format complete
System transferred

     730112 bytes total disk space          {This diskette is a 720K disk.}
      78848 bytes used by system
     651264 bytes available on disk
```

```
Format another (Y/N)? N
A>FORMAT B: /V
Insert new diskette for drive B:
and strike ENTER when ready

Format complete

Volume label (11 characters, ENTER for none)? account dsk

    362496 bytes total disk space
    362496 bytes available on disk

Format another (Y/N)? N
A>DIR B:

 Volume in drive B is ACCOUNT DSK
 Directory of B:\

File not found

A>FORMAT B: /N:9
Insert new diskette for drive B:
and strike ENTER when ready


Format complete

    730112 bytes total disk space
    730112 bytes available on disk

Format another (Y/N)? N
A>
```

{This method is the way
to format a 720K diskette
on a 1.44M disk drive.}

Notes

You must format each diskette or fixed disk before you can use it. FORMAT actually performs several tasks. The program sets up each track and sector on the disk so that it accepts information. Special information is recorded, such as track headers (one for each track), sector headers (one for each sector), and CRC (cyclic redundancy check) bits to ensure that the recorded information is accurate.

FORMAT V3, like FORMAT V2, always records nine sectors per track even if you have used the /B or /8 switch for eight sectors per track. DOS simply marks the ninth sector "invisible" and unusable in the file allocation table (FAT).

As DOS completes the formatting of each track, DOS tests that track. If the track passes the test, DOS moves to the next track. If the track is bad, DOS remembers and marks the track as "reserved" in the FAT. DOS records no useful information on bad tracks.

DOS then establishes the area for the disk's root directory and file allocation table (FAT). If DOS has found any bad tracks, the FAT is marked appropriately.

Do not try to format a diskette on any type of virtual disk; on a disk that is part of an ASSIGN, SUBST, or JOIN command; or on a disk owned by a different computer (a networked disk). FORMAT usually gives an error message and does not attempt the operation.

Never attempt to format a RAM disk. Under the wrong circumstances, FORMAT "gets lost" in trying to format a RAM disk, particularly VDISK (the DOS V3 RAM disk program). The responses can range from DOS's displaying a `Divide overflow` message to your computer's taking a trip "west" (locking up). If the computer locks up, you must turn the computer off and then on again. Obviously, the RAM disk's contents are lost, but no other disks or diskettes are damaged.

An undocumented switch is /H, the *hide* prompt messages switch. /H suppresses the message to place a diskette in the drive and to press Enter to continue. This switch is used by BACKUP when it must format a diskette. I do not encourage using this switch manually because FORMAT immediately attempts to format the diskette in the disk drive. You do not have an opportunity to confirm that the correct diskette is in the disk drive.

Be especially cautious when you format fixed disks if you have used the disks before. If the disk has a volume label, DOS asks you to enter the exact volume label. If the disk does not have a volume label, DOS displays a emphatic warning message and asks for your yes/no confirmation. Before entering the label or typing Y for yes, be sure you are formatting the correct disk drive. A mistake can clear as much as 32M of files.

Hint

When you use a single-disk drive system (a floppy disk drive), write-protect the diskette that holds the FORMAT program. This action keeps you from accidentally erasing a good diskette that you might inadvertently leave in drive A. Nevertheless, you should always determine whether the proper diskette is in the drive before you press the key to begin formatting.

Messages

1. Attempted write-protect violation

   WARNING: The diskette you are trying to format is write-protected.

   You protect a minifloppy diskette by covering the write-protect notch with a tab. You protect a microfloppy diskette by sliding the write-protect tab up (so that you can see through a hole in the diskette).

   Check the diskette in the drive. If the diskette is the one you want to format, remove the write-protect tab (for minifloppies) or move the write-protect tab down (for microfloppies). If the diskette in the drive is the wrong diskette, put the correct diskette in the drive and try the command again.

2. Bad Partition Table

   ERROR: FORMAT displays this message only when it formats the fixed disk. FORMAT has detected that the fixed disk's partition table does not have a valid DOS partition or any DOS partition.

   If the fixed disk is new, the message indicates that you have not run FDISK on the disk. Run FDISK to establish a DOS partition, and then repeat the FORMAT command. If the fixed disk has been in use, the loss of the partition table is a grave sign. An error has caused the disk to lose the essential information at the start of the disk. Run FDISK, reestablish the DOS partition, and then rerun FORMAT. Another partition error indicates that the fixed disk is in error and needs repair.

3. Cannot FORMAT a Network drive

   ERROR: You are attempting to format a disk drive used by a network, either on your computer or on another computer. If you gave the wrong disk drive letter, repeat the command with the correct disk drive name. If your drive is used by the network, perform a NET PAUSE, format the disk, and then use the NET CONTINUE command.

4. Cannot format an ASSIGNed
   or SUBSTituted drive.

ERROR: This disk drive is being rerouted with the ASSIGN command or is being used as part of a SUBST command. You cannot format a diskette in a disk drive that is part of an assignment or a substitution.

If you are trying to format a drive on which you have used the ASSIGN command, clear the assignment by giving ASSIGN with no additional information. If you are trying to format a drive on which you have used a SUBST command, clear the substitution by entering SUBST d: /d, in which d: is the floppy disk drive. Then try formatting again.

5. Disk unsuitable for system disk

WARNING: FORMAT detected on the diskette one or more bad sectors in the area where DOS normally resides. Because DOS must reside on a specified spot on the disk and this portion is unusable, you cannot use the diskette to boot (load and start) DOS.

Try reformatting this diskette. Some diskettes format successfully the second time. If FORMAT gives this message again, you cannot use the diskette as a boot diskette.

6. Drive letter must be specified

ERROR: You did not give a disk drive name to FORMAT. Check the command line and try the command again.

7. Enter current Volume Label for drive d:

WARNING: You are attempting to format a fixed disk that has a volume label. Enter the exact volume label to proceed with the format; if you do not want to enter a volume label, press Enter.

8. Error reading partition table
   Error writing partition table

ERROR: FORMAT could not successfully read or write the fixed disk's initial sectors. The error probably is a hardware failure. Run FDISK again. Delete and reestablish the DOS partition. Run FORMAT again. If the problem recurs, the fixed disk has failed and needs to be repaired.

9. Format failure

WARNING: FORMAT encountered a disk error that the program could not handle. This message usually comes after another error message and indicates that FORMAT has aborted.

One cause of this error may be a diskette that has bad sectors where DOS normally records the boot sector, FAT, or root directory. You cannot use a diskette or disk with flaws in any of these areas.

10. Format not supported on drive d:

ERROR: The disk drive or RAM disk drive cannot be used by the DOS FORMAT command. This error should not occur if you are using IBM disk drives, but it does occur with most RAM disk programs.

If you are using an IBM-compatible disk drive, run a different copy of FORMAT. If the message reappears, reboot your system and try again. If the message appears a third time, you may have a hardware problem.

If your drive is not compatible, use the format program provided by your drive's vendor or simply use a different disk drive for FORMAT.

11. Insert DOS disk in d:
    and strike any key when ready

INFORMATION: Before formatting a diskette with the /S switch, FORMAT reads into memory the DOS system files IBMBIO.COM, IBMDOS.COM, and COMMAND.COM. This message indicates that DOS cannot find these files. To correct the problem, put a DOS diskette containing these three files into drive D and press any key to continue.

12. Insert new diskette for drive d:
    and strike ENTER when ready

INFORMATION: FORMAT is waiting for you to insert in drive d the diskette to be formatted. After you put the correct diskette in this drive, press Enter to start the formatting process. Before you press Enter, check the prompt again to ensure that d: is the drive you are using for FORMAT and that the correct diskette is in the drive.

13. Insufficient memory for system transfer

WARNING: The disk you were attempting to format had insufficient space to accept a copy of the DOS system files. Because no DOS diskette has a total capacity of less than 75K, this message indicates that something else is wrong. Your copy of the DOS system files may be in error, or the diskette may have so many bad sectors that it cannot be used.

Take the diskette out of the disk drive, reinsert the diskette, and try FORMAT again. If this message reappears, try a different diskette (if FORMAT reports a large number of bad sectors) or restart DOS and try again. If this message appears a third time, you have a disk drive failure.

14. Invalid characters in volume label

WARNING: At least one character in the label name you gave is invalid. Type the name again, and make sure that the characters are appropriate for a volume name. The most common mistake is to use a period (.) in the volume name. DOS asks you to try again.

15. Invalid device parameters from device driver

ERROR: When DOS was partitioning the fixed disk, the DOS partition did not start on a track boundary; it started in the middle of a track instead. DOS cannot handle a partition starting in the middle of a track. Because FDISK does not allow DOS to start in the middle of a track, either the disk has a problem or the program you used is defective.

Try running FDISK or the partitioning program again and make sure that the DOS partition starts on a track boundary. Run FORMAT again.

16. Invalid media or track 0 bad - disk unusable

WARNING: Track 0 holds the boot record, the FAT, and the directory. This track is bad, and the diskette is unusable. Try formatting the diskette again. If the error recurs, the diskette is bad, and you cannot use it.

This error can occur when you format 720K diskettes as 1.44M diskettes (if you forgot to give the /N:9 switch when you formatted on a 1.44M disk drive), or when you formatted 360K diskettes as 1.2M diskettes (if you forgot the /4 switch).

This error can occur also when you format 1.2M diskettes at lower capacities, such as 360K, and have given the /4 switch. In this case, try using a diskette rated for double-sided, double-density use.

17. `Invalid parameter`

   ERROR: You have given an invalid disk drive name or an unrecognized switch. Check the command line and try the command again.

18. `Parameters not compatible`

   ERROR: You gave two or more switches that are not compatible. Check FORMAT's rules to see which switches you can use together. Then try running FORMAT again.

19. `Parameter not compatible with fixed disk`

   ERROR: You gave the /1, /4, /8, /B, /N, or /T switch when you attempted to format the fixed disk. Be sure that you are formatting the correct disk drive. If you are formatting the fixed disk, don't use either switch.

20. `System transferred`

   INFORMATION: FORMAT has successfully written the DOS system files (IBMBIO.COM and IBMDOS.COM) and COMMAND.COM onto the formatted disk.

21. `Unable to write BOOT`

   WARNING: Either the first track of the diskette or the DOS portion of the fixed disk is bad. DOS cannot write the bootstrap loader (BOOT program) to the diskette or disk. The diskette or DOS portion of the fixed disk cannot be used. Try reformatting. If the error occurs again, you cannot use the diskette or fixed disk drive.

22. `Volume label (11 characters,`
    `ENTER for none)?`

   INFORMATION: FORMAT is requesting the volume name that you want to give to the newly formatted diskette or fixed disk. Enter a valid volume name (a maximum of 11 characters) and press Enter. If you do not want a volume label, simply press Enter.

23. ```
WARNING! ALL DATA ON NON-REMOVABLE
DISK DRIVE d: WILL BE LOST
Proceed with Format (Y/N)?_
```

WARNING: FORMAT is warning that you are about to format a fixed disk. Answer Y and press Enter if you want to format the fixed disk; if you do *not* want to format the fixed disk, press N and then press Enter. If you give the wrong answer to this question, you can destroy as much as 32 megabytes of information.
```

GRAFTABL
(Load graphics table)

V3, V3.3*—External

Purpose

Loads into memory the tables of additional character sets to be displayed on the Color/Graphics Adapter

Syntax

To install or change the table used by the Color/Graphics Adapter, use

  dc:pathc GRAFTABL *codepage*

To display the number of the current table, use

  dc:pathc GRAFTABL /STATUS

To show the options to GRAFTABL, use

  dc:pathc GRAFTABL ?

dc: is the name of the disk drive holding the command.

pathc is the path to the command.

codepage is the three-digit number of the code page for the display.

Exit Codes

0 = GRAFTABL installed successfully for the first time

1 = The code page used for GRAFTABL has been successfully changed, or, if no new code page was specified, there is an existing code page

2 = GRAFTABL has been installed, no previous code page was installed or is installed

3 = Incorrect parameter, no change in GRAFTABL

4 = Incorrect version of DOS

Rules

1. To display legible characters in the ASCII range of 128 to 255 when you're in APA (all-points-addressable) mode on the Color/Graphics Adapter, load GRAFTABL.

2. GRAFTABL increases the size of DOS by 1,360 bytes.

3. *codepage* is the appropriate code page; *codepage* can be any of the following:

437   United States
860   Portugal
863   French Canada
865   Norway and Denmark

If no page is specified, 437 is assumed.

4. Unlike previous versions of GRAFTABL, GRAFTABL can be used as often as necessary to change the code page displayed while a program is in APA mode.

5. GRAFTABL does not affect characters in the A/N (alphanumeric), or text, mode. GRAFTABL should be used only on systems that have the Color/Graphics Adapter.

6. After you invoke GRAFTABL, the only way to deactivate the command is to restart DOS.

Notes

The IBM Color/Graphics Adapter in graphics mode smears ASCII characters in the 128-to-255 range. National-language characters and many graphics characters are in this range. GRAFTABL produces a legible display of these ASCII characters.

IBM's world trade group developed GRAFTABL principally for national-language use. Before DOS V3 was released, GRAFTABL was available only for PCs sold outside the United States. Now, with DOS V3, this command is included for all systems worldwide.

GRAFTABL is useful only when your system is equipped with the Color/Graphics Adapter and when you use the Adapter in medium- or high-resolution graphics mode. Don't use the command with PCjrs, with systems using the Monochrome Display Adapter (MDA), with the Enhanced Color/Graphics Adapter (EGA), or with the Video Graphics Array (VGA). This command, which has no effect on these displays, wastes some of the computer's free memory. The memory used by the program is trapped until you restart DOS.

Messages

1. Incorrect parameter

   ERROR: You have used a code page that GRAFTABL does not recognize, forgotten the / in front of STATUS, or entered more than one code page.

2. name version of Graphics Character Set is already loaded name version of Graphics Character Set has just been loaded

   INFORMATION: GRAFTABL displays which character set was previously used and which set is now active. name is the name of the character set (Can. French, Nordic, Portuguese, USA, or No for none).

GRAPHICS
(Graphics screen print)   *V2, V3*—External*

Purpose   Prints the graphics-screen contents on a suitable printer

Syntax   *dc:pathc*GRAPHICS *printer /R /B /LCD*

dc: is the name of the disk drive holding the command.

pathc is the path to the command.

printer is the type of IBM Personal Computer printer you are using.
The *printer* can be one of the following:

COLOR1	Color Printer with a black ribbon
COLOR4	Color Printer with an RGB (red, green, blue, and black) ribbon, which produces four colors
COLOR8	Color Printer with a CMY (cyan, magenta, yellow, and black) ribbon, which produces eight colors
COMPACT	Compact Printer
GRAPHICS	Graphics Printer and IBM ProPrinter™
THERMAL	PC Convertible Printer

Switches

/R	*Reverses* print colors so that the image on the paper matches the screen (that is, produces a white-on-black image)
/B	Prints the *background* color of the screen. You can use this switch only when the *printer* type is COLOR4 or COLOR8.
/LCD	Prints the image as displayed on the PC Convertible's *LCD* display.

Exit Codes   None

Rules

1. If you use this command to print the graphics-screen contents, your printer must be compatible with the IBM Color Printer, Compact Printer, ProPrinter, or Graphics Matrix Printer, or with the Thermal Printer.

2. If you do not specify a *printer*, the Personal Computer Graphics Matrix Printer is assumed.

3. If you do not use the */R* (reverse) switch, an inverse image is printed black on white. White images on the screen are printed as dark colors, and black images are printed as white images. If you use the */R* switch, white images are printed as white, and black images are printed as black.

4. If you do not use the */B* switch, the background color of the screen is not printed. Giving the */B* switch causes the printing of the background color. The */B* switch has no effect unless you specify the printer type COLOR4 or COLOR8.

5. After you invoke the GRAPHICS command, you can print the graphics-screen contents by pressing the Shift and PrtSc keys (the print-screen feature).

6. If the program is in text mode, screen printing takes less than 30 seconds. In graphics mode, screen printing takes as much as 3 minutes.

7. When you choose the 320-by-200 (medium-resolution) mode, the printer prints in four shades of gray, corresponding to the four possible colors. When you specify the 640-by-200 (high-resolution) mode, the printer prints in black and white, but the printout is rotated 90 degrees to the left. (The upper right corner of the screen is placed on the upper left corner of the printout.)

8. After you give the GRAPHICS command, do not reissue it until after your next system reset or power-up. The GRAPHICS command increases the size of DOS by 3,268 bytes; every time you re-invoke GRAPHICS, it wastes at least this number of bytes.

9. The only way to deactivate GRAPHICS is to reset your computer.

The GRAPHICS command replaces many graphics screen-printing programs written for earlier versions of DOS. The command allows you to "dump" the graphics screen to the printer. Although GRAPHICS has no effect on systems that do not have the Color/ Graphics Adapter, the command, if invoked, still increases the size of DOS by 3,268.

GRAPHICS affects only the graphics screen dumps. If your display is in text mode (A/N mode), the print-screen function does not act differently. Only when medium- or high-resolution graphics are active does GRAPHICS print the screen differently.

The names COLOR4 and COLOR8 on the Color Printer are logical names. The red-green-blue-black ribbon produces four colors (five if you include the color of the paper itself). The cyan-magenta-yellow-black ribbon produces eight colors through combinations that overstrike one color on another. For the video display, the primary colors are red, green, and blue. For printing, the primary colors are cyan, magenta, and yellow.

If you frequently use the GRAPHICS command, make it part of the AUTOEXEC.BAT file for your DOS boot diskette.

Message

Invalid parameter

ERROR: One of the following errors occurred: (1) you gave a printer type that GRAPHICS does not recognize, (2) you used the /B switch with a printer other than COLOR4 or COLOR8, (3) you gave the /LCD switch on a computer other than the PC Convertible, or (4) you gave a switch that GRAPHICS does not recognize.

Check the command line to be sure that the correct printer type is specified and that the switches can be used with the printer. Try the command again.

JOIN
(Join disk drives)

Purpose	Produces a single directory structure by connecting a disk drive to a subdirectory of a second disk drive

Syntax

To connect disk drives, use

dc:pathc\JOIN d1: *d2:*\directoryname

To disconnect disk drives, use

dc:pathc\JOIN d1: /D

To show currently connected drives, use

dc:pathc\JOIN

dc: is the name of the disk drive holding the command.

pathc\ is the path to the command.

d1: is the name of the disk drive to be connected.

d2: is the name of the disk drive to which **d1:** is to be connected.

directoryname is the name of a subdirectory in the root directory of *d2:* (the host). **directoryname** holds the connection to **d1:** (the guest).

Switch

/D   *Disconnects* the specified guest disk drive from its host

Special Terms

The disk drive being connected is called the *guest disk drive*.

The disk drive and the subdirectory to which the guest disk drive is connected are the *host disk drive* and the *host subdirectory*.

Rules

1. You must specify the guest disk drive name.

2. If you do not give a host disk drive name, the current disk drive is used.

3. You must specify the host's subdirectory name. This subdirectory must be a level-one subdirectory. In other words, the subdirectory must belong to the host disk drive's root directory and not to another subdirectory.

4. For DOS V3.1 and V3.2, the host subdirectory must not be the current directory of the disk drive. For DOS V3.3, the host subdirectory may be the current subdirectory.

5. The host and guest disk drives must not be networked disk drives. DOS displays an error message and does not attempt the connection if either the host or the guest is a networked disk drive.

*6. The host and guest disk drives must not be part of a SUBST or ASSIGN command. The result of JOINing a SUBSTituted or ASSIGNed disk drive is unpredictable.

7. The guest disk drive must not be the current disk drive. In this case, DOS displays an error message and does not attempt the connection.

8. If the subdirectory does not exist, JOIN creates one. If the subdirectory exists, it must be empty (it must have only the . and .. entries), or DOS displays an error message and aborts the connection.

9. When the disk drives are JOINed, the entire directory tree of the guest disk drive is added to the host subdirectory. The guest's root directory is added to the host's subdirectory. All subdirectories of the guest's root directory become subdirectories of the host subdirectory.

10. While a guest disk drive is JOINed, it appears to be part of the host's subdirectory. You can access this disk drive only through its host's disk drive and subdirectory. If you attempt to access the guest disk drive by using the guest's normal disk drive name, you receive an Invalid drive specification error message, and DOS ignores the attempt.

11. To break the connection, specify the guest disk drive's normal name with the /D switch. You can use the guest's normal disk drive name only when you disconnect the drives.

12. To show the current disk drive connections, type JOIN with no parameters. JOIN shows all current connections. If no connections exist, JOIN does not display any message, and the system returns to the system prompt.

*13. Do not use the BACKUP, RESTORE, FORMAT, DISKCOPY, or DISKCOMP commands on the guest or host disk drive. The command may ignore the JOIN, or may issue an error message.

14. While JOIN is in effect, the DIR (directory) command works normally but reports the `bytes free` for only the host disk drive.

15. While JOIN is in effect, CHKDSK (check disk) will process the host disk drive but will not process or report information on the portion of the disk drive that is the guest. To process the guest disk drive, you must disconnect the disk drives (using the /D switch) and then run CHKDSK on the former guest disk drive.

Examples

For these examples, assume that drive C has the following directory structure and that all subdirectories have files except /MNT, which is an empty subdirectory that holds only the . and .. entries.

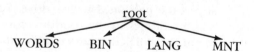

1. **JOIN A: C:\MNT**

    JOIN connects the disk in drive A to the subdirectory \MNT on drive C.

2. **JOIN B: C:\DRIVEB**

    JOIN connects the disk in drive B with the new subdirectory \DRIVEB on drive C. Because \DRIVEB did not exist before the JOIN command was issued, JOIN creates this subdirectory.

3. JOIN

JOIN displays the current assignments. You'll see this
message:

```
A: => C:\MNT
B: => C:\DRIVEB
```

4. JOIN B: /D

JOIN disconnects the disk in drive B from drive C. The
subdirectory created by JOIN (\DRIVEB) remains.

Notes

JOIN is a command introduced in DOS V3.1. The command
combines two disks into a single disk. The guest disk logically
(apparently) becomes a subdirectory to the host disk.

A good use for JOIN is to connect a RAM disk to a "real" disk. Then
you can use the RAM disk as though it were part of a floppy disk or
fixed disk drive. Another use is to connect two fixed disk drives.

Some programs allow only one disk drive to hold data or certain
pieces of the program itself. If these programs allow subdirectory
names (written for DOS V2 and later), you can use JOIN to trick the
programs into using one "very large" disk drive.

JOIN does not affect the guest disk drive; it affects only the way you
access the files on that disk drive. You cannot exceed the maximum
number of files in the root directory of a JOINed disk. The size of a
file in the JOINed subdirectory cannot exceed the size of the guest
disk used, nor can a single file span more than one disk.

When you give a nonexistent host directory name, JOIN creates a
new subdirectory in the host disk drive's root directory. When you
break the connection, the subdirectory remains. You can use this
subdirectory later for another JOIN command, or delete the
subdirectory by issuing the RMDIR (remove directory) command.

You must take some precautions when you use the JOIN command.
When a JOIN is active, certain DOS commands work differently; some
DOS commands should not be used at all. While JOINed, the guest
disk drive appears to be a host subdirectory. You cannot perform a
DIR (directory) or CHKDSK (check disk) using the guest's disk drive
letter. You must break the connection first and then use DIR or
CHKDSK on the former guest.

Do not use FORMAT, DISKCOPY, and DISKCOMP on any JOINed disk drive. Most of these commands recognize that a "pseudo" disk drive is in use and will abort.

When you use JOIN, don't use BACKUP and RESTORE. BACKUP backs up the joined disk drives as though the two drives were one, which is not a problem until you use RESTORE. If the two disk drives are not joined at the same directory, RESTORE puts the files of the "then" guest disk drive on the host disk drive. If the host disk drive does not have room for all the files, RESTORE issues a `Disk full` message and does not restore the remaining files. You must delete the "guest" files and rerun RESTORE as many times as necessary to bring back the additional files. This additional work is burdensome and frustrating. The solution to this potential problem is simple: don't use BACKUP when the disk you want to back up is JOINed to another disk drive.

Never JOIN a disk drive that is part of an ASSIGN or SUBST command. The results are unpredictable, never pleasant, and occasionally dangerous. The JOIN command appears to work on the ASSIGNed or SUBSTituted disk drives. DOS gets confused, however, when it tries to access the JOINed disk drives. The results range from DOS commands not working, to losing data written to the disk, to locking up the computer. If your computer locks up, you must reboot DOS.

You can JOIN two or more "real" disk drives or RAM disks. Do not JOIN a networked disk drive, however. DOS simply issues an error message and does not connect the disk drives.

Messages

1. `Cannot JOIN a network drive`

   ERROR: You attempted to connect a networked disk drive with another disk drive. If the disk drive you are trying to use is not a networked disk drive, check your spelling and try the command again.

2. `Directory not empty`

   ERROR: The host subdirectory you attempted to use is not empty (it contains files other than the . and .. entries). Either delete all files in the host subdirectory, specify a subdirectory that is empty, create a new subdirectory, or give a name for a host subdirectory that does not exist. Then try the command again.

3. Incorrect number of parameters

ERROR: You omitted the guest disk drive name or the host disk drive name and subdirectory name. Check the command line you typed and try again.

4. Invalid parameter

ERROR: One of the following errors occurred: (1) you omitted the colon after a disk drive name, (2) you gave the name of a disk drive that does not exist, (3) you failed to give a host subdirectory name or omitted the path character (\) before the name, (4) you gave a subdirectory name not owned by the root directory, or (5) you gave a subdirectory name or host disk drive name when you used the /D disconnect switch. Another possibility, for JOIN V3.1 or V3.2, is that the current directory of the host disk drive is the intended host subdirectory.

Check the command line to be sure that the proper parameters are given and that the current directory of the host disk drive is not the intended host subdirectory. Then try the command again.

KEYB
(Enable foreign-language keys)   *V1, V2, V3*—External*

Purpose   Changes the keyboard layout and characters to one of five non-American-English languages

Syntax   To change the current keyboard layout:

*dc:pathc***KEYB** *keycode, codepage, d:path\\KEYBOARD.SYS*

To display the current values for **KEYB**:

*dc:pathc***KEYB**

dc: is the name of the disk drive holding the command.

pathc is the path to the command.

keycode is the two-character keyboard code for your location.

*keycode*s supported by DOS V3.3 are

Australia	US	Netherlands	NL
Belgium	BE	Norway	NO
Canada (English)	US	Portugal	PO
Canada (French)	CF	Spain	SP
Denmark	DK	Sweden	SV
Finland	SU	Switzerland (French)	SF
France	FR	Switzerland (German)	SG
Germany	GR	United Kingdom	UK
Italy	IT	United States	US
Latin America	LA		

codepage is the three-digit code page to be used (437, 850, 860, 863, or 865)

d:path\\KEYBOARD.SYS is the drive and path to the KEYBOARD.SYS file.

Exit Codes	0 = KEYB ran successfully
	1 = Invalid keycode type, code page, or other syntax error
	2 = Bad or missing KEYBOARD.SYS file
	3 = KEYB could not create a keyboard table in memory.
	4 = KEYB could not communicate successfully with CON (the console).
	5 = The specified code page has not been prepared.
	6 = The internal translation table for the selected code page could not be found; the *keycode* and *codepage* is incompatible.

Rules

1. To type one of the foreign-language character sets, load the **KEYB** program and use the appropriate two-letter code for your country.

*2. Do not use the **KEYB** programs from earlier versions of DOS with DOS V3.3. The computer will act erratically, and you'll have to reboot DOS.

3. If you do not give a *codepage*, DOS uses the default code page for your country (the default code page established by the COUNTRY directive in CONFIG.SYS or, if the COUNTRY directive is not used, the DOS default code page). KEYB attempts to activate the default code page.

4. If you give a *codepage*, the code page must be compatible with your keyboard-code selection. The following combinations of keyboard codes and code pages are allowed:

437	FR, GR, IT, LA, NL, SP, SU, SV, UK, US
850	any keyboard code
860	PO
863	CF
865	DK, NO

If you use a combination that is not allowed, the system acts erratically until you either use a correct KEYB combination or restart DOS.

5. If you do not specify the keyboard definition file (*KEYBOARD.SYS*), DOS looks for this file in the root directory of the current disk. Otherwise, DOS uses the full file name to search for the file. If a disk drive is not specified, DOS searches the current disk drive; if a path is not specified, DOS searches the current directory. The name of the file (KEYBOARD.SYS) must be included.

6. After the program is loaded, it transforms the keyboard into the appropriate layout for the foreign language specified. The information for individual layouts is in the *Guide to Operations* manual that comes with your computer, or in the *Disk Operating System Reference* manual that comes with DOS V3.3 or later versions.

7. To use the American English layout, press Ctrl-Alt-F1 (press and hold down the Ctrl and Alt keys while you press the F1 function key also). To return to the foreign-language layout, press Ctrl-Alt-F2.

8. When KEYB is used the first time, it increases the size of DOS by approximately 2K. After that, you can use KEYB as often as you want; the size of DOS is not further increased.

9. To display the active keyboard and the display code pages, use **KEYB** without any additional parameters.

Notes

Previously, KEYB was a set of five programs—one program each for the five national languages supported. DOS V3.3 codifies the five programs into one program.

KEYB "hooks" into the ROM BIOS of the computer. When the program is loaded, it alters the keyboard layout; you can then type foreign-language characters. KEYB also alters the video display if the **DEVICE=DISPLAY.SYS** command has been included in CONFIG.SYS and you have issued the appropriate MODE commands to prepare and select a code page (font file) for your display.

When KEYB is active, it reassigns some alphanumeric characters to different keys and introduces new characters. The new layout and characters vary among the different supported languages.

Some new characters introduced are symbols or punctuation signs, such as the pound sterling sign (£) for the United Kingdom, or the inverted question mark (¿) for Spain. Most new characters introduced have *diacritics*: acute (´) or grave (`) accents, circumflex (^), or umlaut (¨). Some characters can be produced by one keystroke; some characters are created by pressing the acute or grave accent key and then the appropriate vowel. To get the accent, press and release the acute or grave accent key and then tap the space bar.

To accommodate certain "programming" characters, such as the path character (\), some keys produce three different characters. The characters are created by shifting or not shifting the key or by holding down the Ctrl and Alt keys while also pressing the character key. If you use the French Canadian keyboard, hold down the Alt and Shift keys and press the desired character.

When KEYB is loaded, it immediately takes control and switches the display and keyboard to the appropriate foreign-language character set. As indicated in rule 4, to switch to the American English character set, you press Ctrl-Alt-F1. To switch back to the foreign-language set, you press Ctrl-Alt-F2.

If you want to see the keyboard layouts for foreign languages, consult your *Guide to Operations* manual, which comes with your machine. For older machines that do not have this information, ask your computer dealer or supplier for a copy of these pages.

See the MODE CODEPAGE PREPARE and SELECT commands in the *Command Reference* for more information about code pages. If your computer has the Color/Graphics Adapter and you intend to use its graphics modes, see the GRAFTABL command in the *Command Reference*.

Messages

1. Active code page not available from CON device

   INFORMATION: The KEYB command, issued to display the current setting, could not determine what code page is being used. Either the DEVICE=DISPLAY.SYS directive has not been given in CONFIG.SYS or there is no currently loaded CON code page.

   If the DISPLAY.SYS line has been included in your CONFIG.SYS file, you must give the MODE CON CODEPAGE PREPARE command to load the font files into memory. See the MODE command for further information.

2. Bad or missing Keyboard Definition File

   ERROR: Either the keyboard definition file, usually KEYBOARD.SYS, has been corrupted or KEYB could not find the file. If you did not specify a disk drive and path name, KEYB looks for the file in the root directory of the current disk drive.

Either copy the file to the root directory, or give the full disk drive and path name for the file to KEYB. If this message reappears, the copy of KEYBOARD.SYS is bad. Copy the KEYBOARD.SYS file from your DOS startup diskette to the root directory of the startup disk, and try the command again.

3. `Code page requested (codepage) is not valid for given keyboard code`

ERROR: You have given a keyboard code to KEYB, but you did not give a code page. The keyboard code given does not match the currently active code page (`codepage`) for the console. KEYB does not alter the current keyboard or code page. Either choose a new code page for the console that matches the keyboard code by using the MODE CON CODEPAGE SELECT command or specify the appropriate matching code page when you give the KEYB command again.

4. `Code page specified is inconsistent with the selected code page`

WARNING: You have specified a keyboard code and a code page to KEYB. However, a different code page was active for the console (CON). The code page specified to KEYB is now active for the keyboard but not for the video display. You may notice that the characters you type are nonsense, because the keyboard and screen do not always "agree" on the characters you have typed.

Use the MODE CON CODEPAGE SELECT command to activate the correct code page (the one specified to KEYB) for the video screen.

5. `Code page specified has not been prepared`

ERROR: The **DEVICE=DISPLAY.SYS** directive has been included in your CONFIG.SYS, but the keyboard code you have used with KEYB needs a code page that has not been prepared. Use the MODE CON CODEPAGE PREPARE command to prepare the code page appropriate for the keyboard code you want to use.

6. `Current CON code page: codepage`

   INFORMATION: The current code page used by the "console" (video display) is designated by the number `codepage`.

7. `Current keyboard code: keycode`
   `code page: codepage`

   INFORMATION: The current *keycode* is the two-character `keycode`, and the code page (font file) used by the keyboard is the three-digit `codepage`.

8. `Invalid code page specified`

   ERROR: You have specified a code page that does not exist. Check the number you have used for the code page and try the command again.

9. `Invalid keyboard code specified`

   ERROR: You have specified a keyboard code that does not exist. Check the two-character keyboard code used and try the command again.

10. `Invalid syntax`

    ERROR: You have phrased the command in a manner that KEYB could not understand. Either you omitted part of the command (such as giving the code page but forgetting the keyboard code), forgot part of the punctuation for the KEYBOARD.SYS file, or forgot to place a space or comma between the keyboard code, the code page, and the full file name of the KEYBOARD.SYS file. Check your typing and try the command again.

11. `KEYB has not been installed`

    INFORMATION: You have used the KEYB command without any parameters (which requests the current status of KEYB) and KEYB reports that it has not yet been installed. If KEYB should be installed, give the command again with the appropriate parameters.

12. `One or more CON code pages invalid for given`
    `keyboard code`

WARNING: You have several code pages prepared for the console (CON) using the MODE command, and the keyboard code given to the KEYB command is not compatible with one or more console code pages. KEYB creates the necessary information to work with those keyboard and code pages that are compatible. The incompatible keyboard and code pages combinations are not honored.

13. Unable to create KEYB table in resident memory

ERROR: When KEYB is first installed, it fits within a predetermined amount of RAM memory. You have added additional code pages to the console (CON) using other commands, and you have attempted to use KEYB again. KEYB, which cannot expand past the predetermined amount of RAM memory, cannot adapt to the additional code pages. To use the additional code pages, restart DOS and give any needed MODE code page commands before you issue KEYB.

LABEL
(Volume label)

V3—External

Purpose

Creates, changes, or deletes a volume label for a disk

Syntax

dc:pathc LABEL *d:volume_label*

dc: is the name of the disk drive holding the command.

pathc is the path to the command.

d: is the name of the disk drive for which the label will be changed.

volume_label is the new volume label for the disk.

Rules

1. If you do not give a disk drive name, the current disk drive is used.

2. If you give a valid volume label, it immediately becomes the volume label for the disk drive.

3. If you do not specify a volume label, DOS prompts you to enter a new volume label. You may do one of the following:

   a. Enter a valid volume name and press Enter. DOS makes this name the new volume label. If a volume label existed, the old label is replaced by the new volume label.

   b. Press Enter to delete the current label without giving a replacement. DOS asks you to confirm the deletion.

4. If you enter an invalid volume label, DOS displays a warning message and asks for the volume label again.

5. Do not LABEL a disk drive that belongs to another computer (a networked disk drive). DOS displays an error message and does not label the disk drive.

*6. Do not LABEL a SUBSTituted or ASSIGNed disk drive. DOS labels the "real" disk drive instead. For example, if you have used the command ASSIGN A=C, entering the command LABEL A: changes the volume label of drive C.

Examples

1. **LABEL A:MYDISK**

   This command line creates the volume label MYDISK on the diskette in drive A. If a volume label existed previously, the old volume label is replaced by MYDISK.

2. **LABEL**

   The LABEL command requests a change in the volume label of the current disk drive, drive A. DOS responds with

   ```
   Volume in drive A is MYDISK
   
   Volume label (11 characters, ENTER for none)?_
   ```

   If you enter a valid volume label and press Enter, the old volume label MYDISK is replaced by the new label.

   If you press return, DOS asks

   ```
   Delete current volume label (Y/N)?
   ```

   Entering a Y removes the current volume label. Entering N causes LABEL to exit and leaves the current label intact.

Notes

A volume label is simply an electronic label for a diskette or fixed disk. Volume labels appear when you use the DIR (directory), TREE (print subdirectory tree), or CHKDSK (check disk) programs. Volume labels help you identify disks.

The volume label has one other use. When you format a fixed disk with a volume label, FORMAT requests that you type the label to confirm your intent. (If the disk has no volume label, FORMAT displays a warning message.) For this reason, LABELing a fixed disk offers some protection from inadvertently destroying megabytes of information from a FORMAT command.

Hint

A space is a valid character in a volume label.

Spaces (and underscores) can increase the readability of a volume label. However, LABEL V3.0 and V3.1 reject a space in a volume name when the name is given on the command line (such as **LABEL MY DISK**). To put a space in a volume label, type **LABEL**, a space, and the disk drive name, if needed; then press Enter. Don't enter a volume label on the command line. When LABEL asks for a new volume label, you can enter the label with spaces.

Messages

1. Cannot LABEL a Network drive

   ERROR: You attempted to put a volume label on a disk drive on your computer or on another computer used by a network. If this disk drive is "owned" by your computer, pause or disconnect from the network and try the LABEL command again.

2. Delete current volume label (Y/N)?

   INFORMATION and WARNING: You did not enter a volume label when you were requested to. DOS is asking whether the current label should be deleted or left unaltered. Pressing **Y** deletes the current label. Pressing **N** leaves the current label intact.

3. Invalid characters in volume label
   Volume label (11 characters, ENTER for none)?

   WARNING: You used a character not permitted in a volume label (usually some punctuation symbol such as the period or comma). Check to see whether the characters you entered for the label are valid, and then enter the volume label again.

4. Invalid drive specification

   ERROR: You gave the name of a disk drive that does not exist, gave a disk drive name that is part of a JOIN command, or omitted the colon in the disk drive name. Check these conditions and try the command again.

5. No room in root directory

   ERROR: The root directory of the disk is full and cannot hold the new volume label. This error should not occur when you change or delete a volume label—only when you add a new volume label. Delete, or copy and then delete, a file in the root directory of the disk, and try the command again.

6. Volume in drive d: is label_name
   Volume is drive d: has no label

   INFORMATION: The diskette in drive d: or disk drive d: has the volume label called label_name if the first message appears. If the second message appears, the diskette/disk drive has no volume label.

MKDIR or MD
(Make directory)   *V2, V3—Internal*

Purpose	Creates a subdirectory

Syntax

MKDIR *d:path*\ **directoryname**

or

MD *d:path*\ **directoryname**

d: is the name of the disk drive for the subdirectory.

path\ is a valid path name for the path to the directory that will hold the subdirectory.

directoryname is the name of the subdirectory you are creating.

Exit Codes   None

Rules

1. If you do not specify a disk drive name, the current disk drive is used.

2. If you do not specify a path name but give a disk drive name, the subdirectory is established in the current directory of the specified drive. If you do not specify a path name or a disk drive name, the subdirectory is established in the current directory of the current disk drive.

3. If you use a path name, separate it from the **directoryname** with the path character—the backslash (\ ).

4. You must specify the new subdirectory name. The **directoryname** must have from one to eight characters, with an optional extension, and it must conform to the rules for creating directory names.

5. You cannot use a directory name that is identical to a file name in the parent directory. For example, if you have a file named MYFILE in the current directory, you cannot create the subdirectory MYFILE in this directory. However, if the file is named MYFILE.TXT, the names do not conflict, and you can create the MYFILE subdirectory.

MKDIR, or the short form MD, makes subdirectories. You can make as many subdirectories as you want, but you must remember one caution: for the path name, DOS accepts no more than 63 characters, including backslashes. Don't create too many levels of subdirectories with long names, or else the path to the directory may exceed 63 characters.

You are not restricted to creating subdirectories in the current directory you are using. If you add a path name, DOS establishes a new subdirectory wherever you specify.

You can create subdirectories on a disk used in an ASSIGN, JOIN, or SUBST command. Remember that the subdirectory is created on the physical disk drive used and not on the logical disk that DOS "thinks" is in use. The result is that the subdirectory actually resides on a disk drive different from the one you specified.

For example, consider the following sequence of commands:

```
ASSIGN A = C
MKDIR A:\NEW
```

The subdirectory NEW is made in the root directory of drive C. The ASSIGN command tricks DOS into thinking that drive C is drive A. DOS goes to the ASSIGNed drive A (actually drive C) and makes the new directory.

For the sequence

```
JOIN A: C:\MNT
MKDIR C:\MNT\NEW
```

DOS physically creates the NEW subdirectory in the root directory of the diskette in drive A. While the JOIN command is in effect, NEW acts as a subdirectory on drive C:\MNT. When you use JOIN to break the connection, NEW remains as a subdirectory in the root directory of drive A.

The same logic applies to the SUBST command:

```
SUBST E: C:\WORDS\LETTERS
MKDIR E:\MEMOS
```

DOS physically creates a new subdirectory, called MEMOS, in C:\WORDS\LETTERS. You can access this subdirectory as C:\WORDS\LETTERS\MEMOS or as E:\MEMOS. When you remove the substitution, the MEMOS subdirectory remains in C:\WORDS\LETTERS.

DOS does nothing unpredictable in creating subdirectories on ASSIGNed, JOINed, or SUBSTituted disk drives. Remember, however, that when any one of these commands is in effect, the place where the subdirectory is created physically can be different from the place where the subdirectory "appears."

Message

Unable to create directory

ERROR: One of the following errors occurred: (1) the directory you tried to create already exists, (2) one of the path names you gave is incorrect, (3) the root directory of the disk is full, (4) the disk is full, or (5) a file already exists by the same name.

Check the directory in which the new subdirectory was to be created. If a conflicting name exists, either change the file name or use a new directory name. If the disk or the root directory is full, delete some files, create the subdirectory in a different directory, or use a different disk.

MODE
(Change/set mode)   V1, V2, V3, V3.3**—External

Purpose	Sets the mode of operation for the printers, the video display, and the Asynchronous Communications Adapter; controls code page switching for the console and printer

Notes

The MODE command is actually eight commands in one. The first four MODE commands set and control the characteristics for the printer, the video display and the display to use (when more than one display is in a system), and the Asynchronous Communications Adapter. The first four commands also set and control the redirection of printing between the parallel and serial printers.

The remaining four commands, which were added to DOS V3.3, concern code pages (font files) for international language use of your console (the keyboard and video display) and your printer. These MODE commands set and control the following: (1) the choice of the code pages to use (PREPARE), (2) the activation of the code pages (SELECT), (3) the reestablishment of code page information that has been lost (REFRESH), and (4) the display of the code page used currently (/STATUS).

Because of MODE's versatility, it is treated as eight separate commands.

MODE
(Set parallel printer characteristics)   *V1, V2, V3—External*

Purpose   Sets the IBM printer characteristics

Syntax   *dc:pathc*MODE LPTx: *cpl, lpi, P*

dc: is the name of the disk drive holding the command.

pathc is the path to the command.

x: is the printer number (1, 2, or 3). The colon is optional.

cpl is the number of characters per line (80 or 132).

lpi is the number of lines per inch (six or eight).

P specifies continuous retries on time-out errors.

Exit Codes   None

Rules

1. You must give a printer number. The colon following the printer number is optional. All other parameters are optional.

2. If you do not want to change a parameter, simply enter a comma for that parameter.

3. This command cancels the effect of MODE LPTx: = COMy:.

4. If you enter an invalid parameter or skip a parameter (other than the printer number), that parameter is not changed.

5. If you give a *P* for continuous retries, you can cancel the *P* only by repeating the MODE command without the *P*.

6. The *P* should not be used on networked printers.

7. The characters-per-line and lines-per-inch portions of the command affect only IBM and EPSON printers and any other printers that have EPSON-compatible control codes.

Notes

This command controls the IBM Matrix and Graphics Printers, all EPSON printers, and EPSON-compatible printers. The command may work partially or not at all on other printers.

When you change the column width, MODE sends the special printer-control code that specifies the normal font (80) or the condensed font (132). When you change the lines per inch, MODE sends the correct printer-control code for printing 6 or 8 lines per inch. MODE also sets the printer to 88 lines per page for an 8 lines-per-inch setting and to 66 lines per page for a 6 lines-per-inch setting.

If you give the *P* option and then attempt to print on a deselected printer, the computer does not issue a time-out error. Instead, the computer "internally" loops until the printer is ready (turned on, connected to the PC, and selected). For approximately one minute, the computer appears to be "locked up." To abort the continuous retry, press Ctrl-Break.

MODE
(Set display adapter/display characteristics)   V2, V3—External

Purpose

Switches the active display adapter between the Monochrome Display and a graphics adapter/array (Color/Graphics Adapter, Enhanced Color/Graphics Adapter, or Video Graphics Array) on a two-display system, and sets the characteristics of the graphics adapter/array

Syntax

*dc:pathc*MODE dt

or

*dc:pathc*MODE *dt,* s, *T*

dc: is the name of the disk drive holding the command.

pathc is the path to the command.

dt is the display type, which may be one of the following:

40	Sets the display to 40 characters per line for the graphics display
80	Sets the display to 80 characters per line for the graphics display
BW40	Makes the graphics display the active display and sets the mode to 40 characters per line, black and white (color disabled)
BW80	Makes the graphics display the active display and sets the mode to 80 characters per line, black and white (color disabled)
CO40	Makes the graphics display the active display and sets the mode to 40 characters per line (color enabled)
CO80	Makes the graphics display the active display and sets the mode to 80 characters per line (color enabled)
MONO	Makes the Monochrome Display the active display

s shifts the graphics display right (R) or left (L) one character.

T requests alignment of the graphics display screen with a one-line test pattern.

Special Terms   The *graphics display* is any display connected to the Color/Graphics Adapter (CGA), the Enhanced Graphics Adapter (EGA), PC Convertible, or Video Graphics Array (VGA). The type of video monitor connected to the adapter or array can be color or monochrome.

Exit Codes   None

Rules

1. For the first form of the command, you must enter the display type (**dt**). All other parameters are optional.

2. For the second form of the command, you must enter the shift parameter, **s** (which is an **R** or **L** for shifting right or left, respectively). The display type (*dt*) and test pattern (*T*) are optional.

3. If you do not have the correct display on your system, an Invalid parameter message appears.

4. If you use the CO40 or CO80 parameter for the display type, color is not automatically displayed. However, programs that use color can be displayed in color.

5. When you give any valid form of the command, the display is cleared.

6. The **s** (**R** or **L**) parameter works only with the Color/Graphics Adapter. If you use this command with any other adapter, the display does not shift. However, if you use the *T* parameter with any graphics adapter (Convertible, EGA, or VGA), the test pattern is displayed. If you use the command with the Monochrome Adapter, an error message is given.

7. When you use the shift and test pattern parameters, the screen is shifted, the test pattern is displayed, and DOS asks whether the screen is aligned properly. Answering **Y** for yes returns the cursor to the system prompt (A>). Answering **N** for no causes the shift and prompting process to be repeated.

8. When DOS is shifting the screen, the screen moves 1 character position left or right in 40-column mode and 2 character positions left or right in 80-column mode.

MODE
*(Set Asynchronous
Communications
Adapter characteristics)*   *V1.1, V2, V3, V3.3*—External*

Purpose   Controls the protocol characteristics of the Asynchronous
Communications Adapter

Syntax   *dc:pathc*MODE COM*y:* **baud**, *parity, databits, stopbits,* P

y: is the adapter number (1, 2, 3, or 4). The colon after the number
is optional.

baud is the baud rate (110, 150, 300, 600, 1200, 2400, 4800, 9600,
or 19200).

parity is the parity checking (None, Odd, or Even).

databits is the number of data bits (7 or 8).

stopbits is the number of stop bits (1 or 2).

P represents continuous retries on time-out errors.

Rules
1. You must enter the number of the adapter, followed by a
   space and a baud rate. If you type the optional colon, it
   must immediately follow the adapter number. All other
   parameters are optional.

2. If you do not want to change a parameter, enter a comma
   for that value.

3. If you enter an invalid parameter, no action takes place, and
   an Invalid parameter message appears.

4. You may use only the first 2 digits for the baud rate (for example, 11 for 110 baud and 96 for 9600 baud).

5. The 19200 baud rate is valid only for PS/2 computers. Using the 19200 baud rate on a PC family member results in an `Invalid parameter` message, and no action takes place.

6. If you want continuous retries after a time-out, you must enter the *P* whenever you use the MODE COMn: command.

7. If the adapter is set for continuous retries (*P*) and the device is not ready, the computer appears to be locked up. You can abort this loop by pressing Ctrl-Break.

MODE

*(Redirect printing from a parallel
printel to a serial printer)*   *V2, V3—External*

Purpose   Forces DOS to print to a serial printer rather than to a parallel
                     printer

Syntax   *dc:pathc*MODE LPT*x:* = COM*y:*

                     dc: is the name of the disk drive holding the command.

                     pathc is the path to the command.

                     x: is the parallel printer number (1, 2, or 3). The colon is optional.

                     y: is the Asynchronous Communications Adapter number (1, 2, 3
                     or 4).

Exit Codes   None

Rules   1. You must give a valid number for both the parallel printer
                        and the serial printer.

                     2. After you give the command, all printing that normally goes
                        to the parallel printer goes to the designated serial printer.

                     3. This command can be canceled by the MODE LPT*x:*
                        command.

Notes   This form of MODE is useful for systems that have only a serial
                     printer. When you type the line

                         MODE LPT1: = COM1:

                     all output usually sent to the system printer is sent to the serial
                     printer (assuming that the serial printer is connected to the first
                     Asynchronous Communications Adapter). This output includes the
                     print-screen (Shift-PrtSc) function.

                     You should use the MODE COM*n:* command to set up the serial
                     adapter used for the serial printer before you issue the MODE
                     LPT*x*=COM*y* command.

MODE
(Prepare code page for use)   *V3.3—External*

Purpose

Prepares (chooses) the code pages to be used with a device.

Syntax

dc:pathc\MODE device **CODEPAGE PREPARE** =
((codepage, *codepage, . . .*) *dp:pathp*\pagefile.*ext*)

or

dc:pathc\MODE device **CP PREP** = ((codepage, *codepage, . . .*)
dp:pathp\pagefile.*ext*)

dc: is the name of the disk drive holding the command.

pathc is the path to the command.

device is the name of the device for which code page(s) will be chosen. device may be:

CON:	The console
PRN:	The first parallel printer
LPTx:	The first, second, or third parallel printer (**x** is 1, 2, or 3)

codepage is the number of the code page(s) to be used with the device. The number(s) must be:

437	United States
850	Multilingual
860	Portugal
863	French Canadian
865	Denmark/Norway

. . . represents additional code pages

dp: is the name of the disk drive holding the code page (font) information.

pathp is the path to the file holding the code page (font) information.

pagefile.*ext* is the name of the file holding the code page (font) information. Currently, the DOS-provided code page files are:

4201.CPI	The IBM ProPrinter
5202.CPI	The IBM Quietwriter® III Printer
EGA.CPI	EGA/VGA type displays
LCD.CPI	IBM Convertible LCD display

Exit Codes   None

Rules

1. You must specify a device name (**device**)—either CON:, PRN:, LPT1:, LPT2:, or LPT3:. The colon after the device name is optional.

2. You must use the word **CODEPAGE** or **CP**, and **PREPARE** or **PREP**.

3. You must specify one or more code pages (**codepage**). If you give more than one code page, separate each number with a comma. The entire list of code pages must be enclosed in parentheses.

4. You cannot give more code pages than the number of *added_codepage* specified to the appropriate device driver.

5. When you add or replace code pages, enter just a comma for a code page that you do not want to change.

6. Do not use a hardware code page (the code page given to the DISPLAY.SYS for the console or PRINTER.SYS for the printers).

7. If you do not give a drive name (*dp:*), the current drive is used.

8. If you do not give a path name (*pathd*), the current directory is used.

9. You must specify the name of the code page information file (**pagefile.***ext*). If the file has an extension, it must be given.

10. If a code page number is invalid (it does not appear in the code page information file) or an invalid file is used (the file exists but is not a code page information file), all current code pages in the same position as code pages given to the command are removed.

Examples

1. MODE CON CODEPAGE PREPARE = (850, 863, 865)
    C:\EGA.CPI

    This command prepares the 850, 863, and 865 fonts for use
    with the EGA or VGA display. MODE gets its information on
    the fonts from the EGA.CPI file in the root directory of C:.

2. MODE LPT1 CP PREP = (850, 863) C:\4201.CPI

    This command prepares the 850 and 863 fonts for use with
    the IBM ProPrinter (Model 4201) connected to the first
    parallel port (LPT1:). The information file is 4201.CPI. The
    command shows the abbreviations for CODEPAGE and
    PREPARE.

3. MODE CON CP PREP = (,,437) C:\EGA.CPI

    This command shows how to replace one code page and
    retain previous code pages. You use a command to mark the
    position where a code page should not be replaced. In this
    example, the 437 code page replaces whatever code page
    held the third "position." If example 1 were used before this
    command, the 850 and 863 code pages would be retained,
    but the 865 code page would be replaced with the 437
    code page.

Notes

MODE CODEPAGE PREPARE is used to prepare code pages (fonts)
for the console (keyboard and display) and the printers. Issue this
subcommand before you issue the MODE CODEPAGE SELECT
subcommand. The exception is the IBM Quietwriter III printer, in
which font information is held in cartridges. If the needed code page
is in a cartridge and the code page has been specified to the
PRINTER.SYS driver, no PREPARE command is needed.

Example 3 shows how to replace some code pages but not others.
When you prepare code pages, they are held in memory in the order
you specified. When you give additional PREPARE commands, you
replace code pages only in the same position.

For more information about MODE PREPARE, see Chapter 15 about
internationalizing DOS.

MODE
(Select code page for use)   *V3.3—External*

Purpose   Activates the code page used with a device.

Syntax

   *dc:pathc*MODE device CODEPAGE SELECT = codepage

or

   *dc:pathc*MODE device CP SEL = codepage

dc: is the name of the disk drive holding the command.

pathc is the path to the command.

device is the name of the device for which code page(s) will be chosen. device may be:

CON:	The console
PRN:	The first parallel printer
LPTx:	The first, second, or third parallel printer (**x** is 1, 2, or 3)

codepage is the number of the code page(s) to be used with the device. The number(s) must be:

437	United States
850	Multilingual
860	Portugal
863	French Canadian
865	Denmark/Norway

Exit Codes   None

Rules

1. You must specify a device name (device)—either CON:, PRN:, LPT1:, LPT2:, or LPT3:. The colon after the device name is optional.

2. You must use the word CODEPAGE or CP, and SELECT or SEL.

3. You must specify a code page *codepage* The code page must be part of a MODE CODEPAGE PREPARE command for the device or the hardware code page specified to the appropriate device driver.

Examples

1. **MODE CON CODEPAGE SELECT = 863**

   This command activates the 863 font for use with the EGA or VGA display. The 863 code page must be part of a previous MODE CODEPAGE PREPARE command or the hardware code page for the EGA/VGA.

2. **MODE LPT1 CP SEL = 850**

   This command activates the 850 font for use with the printer attached to the first parallel port (LPT1:).

Notes

MODE CODEPAGE SELECT activates a currently prepared code page or reactivates a hardware code page. You can use MODE SELECT only on these two types of code pages.

MODE SELECT usually completes the downloading of any software font to the device. An exception, the Quietwriter III printer, uses cartridges. When you select a code page, the printer beeps, which indicates that you should check to see whether the proper cartridge is in the printer. DOS has no method of checking which cartridge is in use. Using the wrong cartridge can yield nonsense characters.

Another method of activating a code page is the CHCP command, which activates the code pages for all available devices. MODE SELECT activates code pages for individual devices.

For more information about CHCP and MODE SELECT, see Chapter 15 about internationalizing DOS. Also see CHCP in the *DOS Command Reference*.

MODE
(Reestablish the current code page)   *V3.3—External*

Purpose   Reloads and reactivates the code page used with a device

Syntax

*dc:pathc*MODE device **CODEPAGE REFRESH**

or

*dc:pathc*MODE device **CP REF**

dc: is the name of the disk drive holding the command.

pathc is the path to the command.

device is the name of the device for which code page(s) will be chosen. **device** may be:

CON:	The console
PRN:	The first parallel printer
LPTx:	The first, second, or third parallel printer (**x** is 1, 2, or 3)

Exit Codes   None

Rules

1. You must specify a device name (**device**)—either CON:, PRN:, LPT1:, LPT2:, or LPT3:. The colon after the device name is optional.

2. You must use the word **CODEPAGE** or **CP**, and **REFRESH** or **REF**.

Notes   MODE CODEPAGE REFRESH downloads, if necessary, and reactivates the currently selected code page on a device. This command should be used after you turn your printer off and on, or after a program leaves the video display in a "state of disgrace" and the console code page is ruined.

You do not give a code page to MODE REFRESH. REFRESH uses the last selected code page for the device.

For more information about MODE SELECT, see Chapter 15 about internationalizing DOS.

MODE
(Displays code page status)

V3.3—External

Purpose

Displays the status of code pages for a device

Syntax

*dc:pathc***MODE device CODEPAGE** */STATUS*

or

*dc:pathc***MODE device CP** */STA*

dc: is the name of the disk drive holding the command.

pathc is the path to the command.

device is the name of the device for which code page(s) will be chosen. **device** may be:

CON:	The console
PRN:	The first parallel printer
LPTx:	The first, second, or third parallel printer (**x** is 1, 2, or 3)

Switch

/STATUS displays the *status* of the device's code pages

Exit Codes

None

Rules

1. You must specify a device name (**device**)—either CON:, PRN:, LPT1:, LPT2:, or LPT3:. The colon after the device name is optional.

2. You must use the word **CODEPAGE** or **CP**.

3. You may use */STATUS* or */STA*. If you omit all other MODE keyboards and the switch, MODE assumes that you want the STATUS subcommand.

4. MODE /STATUS displays for the device:

   a. The selected (active) code page, or shows that no code page is selected.

   b. The hardware code page(s)

c. Any prepared code page(s)

d. Any available positions for additional prepared code pages

Examples

1. **MODE CON CODEPAGE /STATUS**

   This command displays the code page status of the console.

2. **MODE LPT1 CP**

   This command displays the code page status of the printer attached to the first parallel port (LPT1:). Notice that the /STATUS switch is optional. If you give no additional information in the command line other than the device name and the word **CODEPAGE** (or **CP**), MODE assumes that you want the status of the device displayed.

Notes

MODE CODEPAGE /STATUS shows the current code page status of the device.

Here is a sample output for the command:

```
Active codepage for device CON is 437
hardware codepages:
  Codepage 437
prepared codepages:
  Codepage 85Ø
  Codepage not prepared
MODE Status Codepage function completed
```

The first line displays the active code page for the device. If no code page has yet been selected, the command instead displays

```
No codepage has been SELECTED
```

and the device uses the hardware code page. The hardware code page is used until a different code page is selected via the MODE SELECT or CHCP commands.

The next lines display the hardware code page given to the DISPLAY.SYS driver for the console, or to the PRINTER.SYS driver for the printers. Usually, only one hardware code page is shown; however, two code pages may be shown for the IBM Quietwriter III printer.

The next lines in the message display the code pages available (prepared) for the device. Every code page is displayed, one per line. Additional lines that say Codepage not prepared mean that positions are available for additional code pages, but no code pages occupy these slots. You should see *added_codepages* number of lines for prepared codepages. (*added_codepages* is the number of additional code pages a device can use and is given to the DISPLAY.SYS or PRINTER.SYS driver.)

For more information about MODE STATUS, see Chapter 15 about internationalizing DOS.

MODE
(General)

Messages

1. `Active code page for device devicename is codepage`

   INFORMATION: The MODE /STATUS command displays the number of the active code page (`codepage`) for the device `devicename`.

2. `Codepage not prepared`

   INFORMATION or ERROR: If you used the MODE /STATUS command, it displays this message if a space is available for a prepared code page, but no code page has been prepared for this space.

   If you used the MODE SELECT command, the code page you have selected for this device is not prepared. If you issue the command for the console device (CON:), the selected code page may not have the correct font for the current video mode. MODE SELECT aborts.

   Use MODE PREPARE to reload the desired code page, and then reissue the MODE SELECT command. If the error reoccurs, edit the DEVICE=DISPLAY.SYS line to increase the number of *subfonts*, and restart DOS.

   This message may precede other MODE error messages.

3. `Codepage operation not supported on this device`

   ERROR: When you use either the MODE PREPARE or MODE SELECT command, one of the following has occurred: (1) you gave a nonsense device; (2) you misspelled the device name; (3) you gave the name of a device that does not exist on your system; (4) you gave the name of a device that does not have the proper device driver installed (DISPLAY.SYS for the console; PRINTER.SYS for the printer); (5) you incorrectly phrased the directive for the device driver; or (6) you gave the name of a device that cannot switch code pages.

   First check the spelling of the name of the device you specified to the MODE command. If the device name is correct, make sure you have the right phrasing for the device driver in CONFIG.SYS. Check the CONFIG.SYS file for the DISPLAY.SYS line (if the problem is in the CON device) or the PRINTER.SYS line (if the problem is in the LPTx or PRN devices). Make sure you have specified the number for LPT that is correct for your printer. If you change the CONFIG.SYS file, restart DOS and try the command again.

4. `Code pages cannot be prepared`

ERROR: You have used the MODE PREPARE command and have either specified more code pages than the device driver allows or duplicated a code page for the Quietwriter III printer. MODE does not prepare any code pages, and deletes the previously prepared code pages that are in the same position as the code pages in this command.

If you use the Quietwriter III, you cannot duplicate a hardware code page. If you use any other device, use the MODE /STATUS command to check the number of prepared code pages allowed. If you need more code pages than are listed in the prepared code page lines, edit the *added_codepages* parameter in the DISPLAY.SYS or PRINTER.SYS line in your CONFIG.SYS file. Restart DOS and try the command again.

5. `COMy bbbb,p,d,s,t initialized`

INFORMATION: The Asynchronous Communications Adapter was initialized successfully. y is the adapter number, bbbb is the baud rate, p is the parity, d is the number of data bits, s is the number of stop bits, and t is the retry on time-out.

6. `Current keyboard does not support this Codepage`

WARNING: You have issued the KEYB command previously. You have issued a MODE SELECT command, and a conflict exists between the current code page for the keyboard and the code page you just specified to MODE for the console. The code page for the console is set to the specified code page, but the keyboard code page is not changed. You get nonsense characters when you type on the keyboard.

To use this new code page on the console, issue the KEYB command with the correct, compatible keyboard code. When you issue the KEYB command, KEYB automatically switches the keyboard's code page.

7. `Device error during Prepare`
   `Device error during Refresh`
   `Device error during Select`
   `Device error during Status`
   `Device error during write of font file to device`

ERROR: During a MODE CODEPAGE operation, a device error was detected. The error occurs for one of the following reasons: (1) the device does not support code page switching, (2) the CONFIG.SYS file does not have the line for including the proper device driver, (3) the number of *added_codepages* is too low to allow for additional code pages, (4) the code page information file is ruined, (5) you forgot to give the full file name of the code page information file for a MODE PREPARE command, (6) an incorrect code page number was given, (7) the device detected a transmission error, (8) the device may be turned off or not selected, or (9) you used the MODE REFRESH command before you gave a MODE SELECT or CHCP command.

If you use MODE REFRESH, issue the MODE SELECT command instead. Be sure you have given the proper device name, code page number, and full file name for the code page file, and that the device is turned on and ready. Then try the command again.

If you get the error message again, first examine the CONFIG.SYS file to ensure that the proper device driver (DISPLAY.SYS for the console; PRINTER.SYS for the printers) has been included and that the proper parameters have been given. If the line is included and properly phrased, check the number of additional code pages. If this number is too low, edit the line, and increase the number of added code pages. Restart DOS and try the command again.

If the message reappears, you probably have a hardware problem. For the printer only, be sure that printer connections are secure and that the printer is receiving characters. Try Shift-PrintScreen. If nothing prints, your printer has a problem. If the screen's contents print and the MODE command still does not work, your printer has an internal electronics malfunction.

8. Device or codepage missing from font file

ERROR: By using the MODE PREPARE command, you have specified a correct possible code page, but the code page information file does not have the font. This error can come from attempting either to prepare a hardware code page or to use a font that the device does not support. All existing code pages for this device are discarded and must be prepared again.

Try the command again, and use a different correct code page number. If this step works, the device can use code pages, but the code page originally specified cannot be used. Also, be sure that you have specified the correct hardware code page to the appropriate device driver. If the hardware code page is incorrect, edit the CONFIG.SYS file, restart DOS, and try the command again.

9. Do you see the leftmost Ø? (Y/N)
   Do you see the rightmost 9? (Y/N)

INFORMATION: You are adjusting the display connected to the Color/Graphics Adapter. Answer N or press any other key to shift the display left or right (depending on how you invoked MODE). Answer Y if the display is centered properly. This answer ends the MODE command.

10. Error during read of font file

ERROR: DOS read the code page information file during a MODE PREPARE command and detected a disk error. The most likely cause is a bad sector on the disk. MODE aborts and does not change the prepared fonts.

Run RECOVER on the file. If RECOVER reports any bad sectors for a diskette, reformat or retire the diskette. If the problem is a fixed disk, RECOVER "hides" the bad sectors, and the code page information file is ruined. Copy the .CPI file from a copy of your DOS startup diskette to the fixed disk, and try the command again.

11. Failure to access Codepage Font File

ERROR: You have used the MODE PREPARE command, and MODE could not find the code page information file you specified. You omitted a drive or path name, misspelled the file name, or gave a nonsense file name. Be sure that the code page information file name is spelled correctly and that it is on the correct disk and directory. Try the command again.

12. `Failure to access device: devicename`

ERROR: MODE CODEPAGE could not open the device `devicename`. You have given the wrong device name, the proper device driver is not installed in CONFIG.SYS, or the device is turned off or disconnected.

If you gave the wrong device name, try the command again with the correct device name. If the device is a printer, make sure the printer is connected and turned on. Be sure that the proper device driver (DISPLAY.SYS for the console; PRINTER.SYS for the printer) is loaded via CONFIG.SYS and phrased properly. If you detect an error in CONFIG.SYS, edit the file, restart DOS, and try the command again.

13. `Font file contents invalid`

ERROR: During a MODE PREPARE command, MODE found the file you specified as the code page information file, but the file's contents are incorrect. Either you specified the name of an existing file that is not a code page information file or the code page information file has been ruined. All existing prepared code pages for the device are discarded.

Be sure that you have given the correct file name to MODE, and try the command again. If the error reoccurs, the code page file is damaged. Copy the code page information file from your copy of the DOS startup diskette, and try the command again.

14. `Illegal Device Name`

ERROR: One of the following errors occurred: (1) you did not specify a number with LPTx: or COMy:; (2) you used a number that is not in the correct range (1, 2, or 3 for LPTx:; or 1 or 2 for COMy: for the PC; 1, 2, 3, or 4 for PS/2 computers); (3) you put no spaces between LPTx: or COMy: and the next parameter; (4) you put more than one space between LPTx: or COMx: and the next parameter; or (5) the specified adapter is not connected to your system.

Check each possibility, make the needed correction in the command, and try again.

15. `Infinite retry on parallel printer timeout`
    `No retry on parallel printer timeout`

    INFORMATION: You have used the MODE LPTx or COM commands. The first message appears if you specify the ,P option. The second message appears if you do not specify the ,P option.

16. `Infinite retry not supported on Network printer`

    ERROR: You have used the ,P option of the MODE LPTx command, and the printer you specified is owned by another computer or is part of a network. You cannot use ,P on this printer. Either give the command again without the ,P or specify a printer owned by your computer and not used by a network.

17. `Invalid baud rate specified`

    ERROR: You gave an incorrect baud rate. The baud rate must be 110, 150, 300, 600, 1200, 4800, 9600, or 19200 (or the first two characters for one of these numbers).

18. `Invalid parameter 'string'`

    ERROR: MODE detected an error in your phrasing for a code page command. The objectionable word is `string`, which might be abbreviated to three or four letters. You may have (1) forgotten the equal sign or the code pages in parentheses in a MODE PREPARE command, (2) reversed the order of words, (3) forgotten to give the word CODEPAGE (or CP), (4) forgotten to give the device name, or (5) used a word that MODE does not recognize.

    Check your spelling and punctuation of the command, and try it again.

19. `Invalid parameters`

    ERROR: One of the following errors occurred: (1) you forgot to give a necessary parameter, (2) the first parameter (for the printer or communications adapter) did not start with L or C, (3) you gave a wrong parameter with the command, or (4) the display adapter you are referencing is not connected to your system. Check your spelling and punctuation, and try the command again.

20. `LPTx: not rerouted`

    INFORMATION: The specified printer adapter is getting its normal data. Any previous reassignment (LPTx: = COMy:) has been canceled. This message appears when you set or reset the characters per line or the lines per inch for the printer.

21. `LPTx: rerouted to COMy:`

    INFORMATION: The output that usually goes to the specified printer adapter now goes to the specified communications adapter.

22. `LPTx: set for 8Ø`
    `LPTx: set for 132`

    INFORMATION: The specified printer is set for 80 or 132 characters per line.

23. `MODE action Codepage function completed`

    INFORMATION: MODE has completed its function, `action`. This message appears after one of the MODE CODEPAGE functions have run successfully. `action` can be `Prepare`, `Refresh`, `Select`, or `Status`.

24. `Must specify COM1, COM2, COM3 or COM4`

    ERROR: You have given an invalid number for COMy in a MODE LPTx=COMy command. Check the number you gave and try again.

25. `No codepage has been SELECTED`

    INFORMATION: You have used the MODE /STATUS command, and you have not yet used the MODE SELECT command on this device.

26. `Printer error`

    ERROR: You used the MODE LPTx command, and MODE could not set the printer. The printer may be turned off, not selected, not connected, out of paper, or not IBM-compatible. Check your printer and try the command again.

27. `Printer lines per inch set`

INFORMATION: You specified a parameter for the lines per inch (six or eight). If your attempt to set the lines per inch fails, a `Printer error` message usually follows this message.

28. `Resident portion of MODE loaded`

INFORMATION: A section of MODE has been loaded and become a resident part of DOS. This message appears when you use the continuous retry option for MODE LPT#: or MODE COMx:, when you shift the display left or right, or when you reroute printers (MODE LPT#: = COMx). MODE stays resident until you restart DOS.

29. `Unable to shift screen left`
    `Unable to shift screen right`

ERROR: You used the MODE display command and requested the display to shift for a Monochrome Adapter, an Enhanced Color/Graphics Adapter, or a Video Graphics Display. You cannot shift the display connected to either of these adapters.

MORE

(More output filter)   *V2, V3—External*

Purpose   Displays one screenful of information from the standard input device and pauses while displaying the message --More--. When you press any key, MORE displays the next screenful of information.

Syntax   *dc:pathc*\MORE

dc: is the name of the disk drive holding the command.

pathc is the path to the command.

Exit Codes   None

Rules
1. MORE displays one screenful of information on the standard output (display).

2. After MORE displays a screenful of information, it pauses and waits for a keystroke before it displays the next screenful. This process is repeated until all output has been displayed.

3. MORE is useful with I/O redirection and piping.

Examples
1. MORE <TEST.TXT

   MORE displays a screenful of information from the file TEST.TXT. MORE then displays the prompt --More-- at the bottom of the screen and waits for a keystroke. When you press a key, MORE continues this process until all information has been displayed. The command does not display the prompt on the final screenful of information.

2. DIR | SORT | MORE

   MORE displays, 23 lines at a time, the sorted output of the directory command.

Notes

MORE is a DOS filter. With this command, you can display screenfuls of information and not manually "pause" the screen.

MORE is similar to the TYPE command, except MORE pauses automatically after each screenful of information.

A screenful of information is based on 40 or 80 characters per line and 23 lines per screen. MORE does not always display 23 lines from the file but instead acts intelligently with long lines. The program wraps lines that exceed the display width (40 or 80 characters). If one line from the file takes 3 lines to display, MORE displays a maximum of 21 lines from the file, pauses, and then shows the next screenful of lines.

NLSFUNC
(National language support)   *V3.3*—External*

Purpose	Provides support for extended country information in DOS and allows the use of the CHCP command.

Syntax

*dc:pathc*NLSFUNC *d:path*filename.*ext*

dc: is the name of the disk drive holding the command.

pathc is the path to the command.

d: is the name of the disk drive holding the country information file.

path is the path to the country information file.

filename.*ext* is the name of the file holding the country information. In DOS V3.3, this information is contained in the file COUNTRY.SYS.

Exit Codes   None

Rules

1. If you do not give a drive name for the country information file, the current disk drive is used.

2. If you do not give a path name, the current directory is used.

3. If you give a drive or path name, you must also give the name of the information file, which usually is COUNTRY.SYS.

4. If you omit the full file name, DOS searches for the file COUNTRY.SYS in the root directory of the current disk.

5. After NLSFUNC is loaded, it remains active until DOS is restarted.

Examples

a. **NLSFUNC**

Loads the NLSFUNC program. NLSFUNC expects the file COUNTRY.SYS to be in the root directory of the current disk drive.

b. NLSFUNC C:\BIN\COUNTRY.SYS

Loads the NLSFUNC program and directs NLSFUNC to find
the country information file, COUNTRY.SYS, in the directory
\BIN of C:.

Notes

NLSFUNC loads support for extended country information and allows
the use of the CHCP (Change Code Page) command. Loading
NLSFUNC increases the size of DOS by 2,672 bytes.

NLSFUNC contains the code used for DOS function number 66
hexadecimal (base 16). The function call provides information about
the conventions for items such as the date, time, numeric and
currency formatting, upper/lowercase translations, and the character
sorting order for the current country code (defined by the default
COUNTRY code for your system or the COUNTRY directive used in
CONFIG.SYS).

NLSFUNC also supports the CHCP command of DOS. NLSFUNC must
be loaded before CHCP can be used.

NLSFUNC is required only if your programs use the extended country
information that DOS can provide, or if you want to use the CHCP
command to change code pages. Your program's documentation
should state whether NLSFUNC is required.

DOS V3.3 has a problem. The documentation states that if you omit
the full file name of the COUNTRY.SYS file, NLSFUNC uses the name
supplied to the COUNTRY directive in CONFIG.SYS. Unfortunately,
DOS appears to "forget" the location of COUNTRY.SYS if you omit
the path. For this reason, either always give the full file name for
COUNTRY.SYS to NLSFUNC or place COUNTRY.SYS in the root
directory of your startup disk drive. NLSFUNC will find the
COUNTRY.SYS file if you follow either procedure.

For more information, see Chapter 15 about using DOS
internationally.

Messages

1. File not found

   ERROR: NLSFUNC could not locate the country information file, COUNTRY.SYS. Either you forgot to specify the disk drive, path, or file name for COUNTRY.SYS, or you omitted the complete full file name and COUNTRY.SYS is not in the root directory of the current disk drive. Either copy COUNTRY.SYS to the root directory of the disk, or give the full path and file name for the COUNTRY.SYS and try the command again.

2. NLSFUNC already installed

   WARNING: NLSFUNC has already been installed. NLSFUNC should be used only one time after DOS has started.

PATH
(Set directory search order)   *V2, V3—Internal*

Purpose

Tells DOS to search the specified directories on the specified drives if a program or batch file is not found in the current directory

Syntax

PATH *d1:path1;d2:path2;d3:path3; . . .*

d1:, d2:, and *d3:* are valid disk drives names.

path1, path2, and *path3* are valid path names to the commands you want to run while the system is logged to any directory.

The three periods (. . .) represent additional disk drives and path names.

Rules

1. If you do not enter a disk drive name for a path, the current disk drive is used.

2. Each path can be any valid series of subdirectories, separated by backslashes.

3. If you specify more than one set of paths, the following rules apply:

   a. The path sets must be separated by semicolons.

   b. The search for the programs or batch files is made in the order in which you give the path sets. First, the current directory is searched. Then *d1:path1* is searched, followed by *d2:path2, d3:path3,* and so on, until the command or batch file is found.

4. If you give invalid information (such as an invalid disk drive, a bad delimiter, or a deleted path), DOS does not display an error message. When searching the path for a program or batch file, DOS simply skips a bad or invalid path. If, however, you give an invalid disk drive name, DOS displays an Invalid drive in search path message when it searches the path for a program or batch file.

5. If the file cannot be found in the current directory and the given paths, a Bad command or filename message appears.

6. PATH affects the execution of only program (.COM or .EXE) files or batch (.BAT) files. This command does not work with data files, text files, or program overlays.

Notes

PATH is a useful command in hierarchical directories. Directories containing your utility programs, system programs, or batch files can be established and used from anywhere on the disk. PATH automatically causes DOS to search these directories to find your programs, and you don't have to type the path each time.

Note that only program files and batch files are located by the PATH command. After a program is invoked, your program—not DOS— must look in other directories for data files, text files, or program overlays. Programs such as WordStar Release 3 (not WordStar Release 4 or 2000) must have their overlay files in the same directory in which you are working. Future versions of programs will allow you to "install" a path. The DOS V3.3 APPEND command, however, can be used to trick programs into finding their overlays or data files in different directories.

To view the current path, use either the PATH or the SET command with no arguments.

Hint

Always specify an absolute path that starts with the root directory of a disk (\ ) instead of a relative path that starts with the current directory.

By specifying an absolute path, you won't have to be concerned about the current directory. For example, I keep my DOS programs for my computer in a level-two directory called BIN and in a level-three directory called UTIL. I set the path as

PATH C:\BIN;C:\BIN\UTIL

With this command, I can invoke a DOS command from anywhere on any disk—fixed, floppy, or RAM disk. If I used the PATH command and a relative path starting with the current or parent directory, I would have to change the path almost every time I changed subdirectories.

Because I also have started each path name with a disk drive name, DOS always searches the subdirectories \BIN and \BIN\UTIL on drive C, regardless of which disk drive is current. I can be working on any disk drive—not just the fixed disk—and invoke the DOS commands from BIN and UTIL.

Message

Invalid drive in search path

WARNING: You specified a nonexistent disk drive name in one of the paths. This message appears when DOS searches for a program or batch file, not when you give the PATH command.

Use PATH or SET to see the current path. If the disk drive temporarily is invalid because of a JOIN or SUBST command, you can ignore this message. If you have specified the wrong disk drive, issue the PATH command again and give the complete set of directory paths you want to use.

PRINT

(Background printing)   *V2, V3*—External*

Purpose   Prints a list of files on the printer while the computer performs other
                       tasks

Syntax   *dc:pathc***PRINT** */D:device /B:bufsiz /M:maxtick /Q:maxfiles*
                       /S:timeslice /U:busytick d1:path1*filename1.ext1 /P/T/C*
                       d2:path2*filename2.ext2/P/T/C* . . .

                       d1: and *d2:* are valid disk drive names.

                       path1\\ and *path2*\\ are valid path names to the files for printing.

                       filename1.ext1 and *filename2.ext2* are the names of the files you
                       want to print. Wildcards are allowed.

                       The three periods (. . .) represent additional file names in the form
                       dx:pathx*filenamex.extx.* They are valid file specifications.

Switches   You can specify any one of the following switches only the first time
                       you start PRINT:

                       /D:device   Specifies which device should be used for printing.
                                      device is any valid DOS device name. (When this
                                      switch is used, it must be listed first.)

                       /B:bufsiz   Specifies the size of the memory *buffer* to be used
                                      while the files are printing. *bufsiz* can be a number
                                      from 1 to 32767.

                       /M:maxtick   Specifies in clock ticks the maximum amount of time
                                      that PRINT has for sending characters to the printer
                                      every time PRINT gets a turn. *maxtick* can be a
                                      number from 1 to 255.

                       /Q:maxfiles Specifies the number of files that can be in the
                                      queue (line) for printing. *maxfiles* can be a number
                                      from 1 to 32.

                       /S:timeslice Specifies the number of slices in each second.
                                      timeslice can be a number from 1 to 255.

/U:busytick Specifies in clock ticks the maximum amount of time for the program to wait for a busy or unavailable printer. *busytick* can be a number from 1 to 255.

You can specify any one of the following switches whenever you use PRINT:

/P Queues up the file (*places* the file in the line) for printing

/T *Terminates* the background printing of any or all files, including any file currently being printed

/C Cancels the background printing of the file(s)

Special Terms A *tick* is the smallest measure of time used on Personal Computers and Personal System/2 computers. A tick happens every 1/18.2 (0.0549) seconds.

Exit Codes None

Rules
1. If you do not give a disk drive name, the current disk drive is used.

2. If you do not give a path name, the current directory is used.

3. If you do not give a file name, the status of the background printing is displayed.

4. You can give the first set of switches (/D, /B, /M, /Q, /S, and /U) only when PRINT is first used. If the /D switch is given, it must be the first switch on the line. You can give the other five switches in this group in any order before you specify a file name.

5. If you do not give the /D switch the first time you use PRINT, this prompt appears:

   ```
   Name of list device [PRN]:
   ```

   You have the following choices:

   a. Press Enter to send the files to PRN (normally LPT1:). If LPT1: is redirected (see the MODE command), the files are rerouted.

b. Enter a valid DOS device name. Printing will be directed to this device. If, however, you enter a device that is not connected to your system, unpredictable things happen.

You cannot change the assignment for background printing until you restart DOS.

6. If you do not give any of the other switches in the first set, the following values are assumed:

bufsiz	512 bytes
maxtick	2 ticks
maxfiles	10 files
timeslice	8 slices/second
busytick	1 tick

7. When you give a switch in the second set (*/P*, */T*, and */C*), the switch affects the file name preceding the switch and all succeeding files until the next switch on the line.

8. If you give a file specification without a switch, the */P* (print) switch is assumed.

9. Do not place more than *maxfiles* in the queue (10 if the */Q:* switch was not given). If you do, PRINT displays the message PRINT queue is full and ignores the command.

10. Files are printed in the order in which you enter the file names. If wildcards are used in a file name, the files are printed in the order in which they are listed in the directory.

11. If DOS detects a disk error in a file that PRINT is trying to print, DOS cancels the printing of that file, prints an error message, and then continues with any other files in line to be printed.

12. Entering **PRINT** /C has no effect.

13. To print on a networked printer, you must use NET PRINT instead of PRINT.

14. When you invoke PRINT the first time, the size of DOS increases by approximately 5,500 bytes. Increasing or decreasing certain default settings correspondingly changes the size of DOS. The only way to regain the memory space is to restart DOS.

PRINT controls the background printing feature of DOS V3. This command has been significantly improved compared to PRINT in DOS V2.

Background printing is simply the printing of a disk-based file while the computer is performing another task (usually running a program). Because the other task gets most of the computer's attention (or time), that task is considered to be "in the foreground." PRINT, which gets less attention from the computer, is a "background task."

The word *queue* comes from the Old French word for *tail* or *line*. When you invoke the PRINT command to print a file, you queue this file to be printed; that is, you add the file to the line of files to be printed. DOS prints the files in the line as free time becomes available.

Background printing is best used with program files stored in ASCII format. The PRINT command prints any disk file. All characters in the file are transmitted to the printer, including control characters. An exception is made for the tab character Ctrl-I, or CHR$(9), which DOS pads with spaces to the next eight-column boundary. If you attempt to background-print a .COM or an .EXE file, your printer does strange things.

The position of the */P*, */C*, and */T* switches on the command line is important. Each of these switches affects the immediately preceding file and all files following that switch until another switch is encountered. For example, the command

PRINT LETTER.TXT /P PROGRAM.DOC MYFILE.TXT /C TEST.DOC

places the files LETTER.TXT and PROGRAM.DOC in the queue to be background printed and cancels the background printing of MYFILE.TXT and TEST.DOC.

In this example, the */P* switch affects the file before the switch (LETTER.TXT) and the file that follows (PROGRAM.DOC). The */C* switch affects the file before the switch (MYFILE.TXT) and the file that follows (TEXT.DOC).

If you use the */T* switch, all files in the queue, including the file being background printed, are canceled. Giving the */T* switch with a file name is unnecessary because all files, including any file names given on the command line, are canceled.

If you cancel or terminate a file being printed, the following actions occur:

1. A cancellation message is printed on the printout. If you terminate (*/T*) all files, the message says All files canceled by operator. If you cancel (with */C*) the file currently being printed, the name of the file appears with the message File canceled by operator.

2. The printer does a form feed.

3. The printer's bell rings.

4. If all files have not been canceled, printing continues with the next queued file (the next one on the list).

If a disk error occurs during the background printing of a file, the following actions occur:

1. The current file is canceled.

2. A disk-error message appears on the printout.

3. The printer performs a form feed, and the bell rings.

4. DOS prints any remaining files in the queue.

Remember these warnings about the PRINT command:

1. When PRINT has control of the printer (is printing something), don't try to print anything else. If the program is in BASIC when you try to print, you get an out-of-paper error message. If you are at the system level, DOS displays a Device not ready error message.

   Press **A** for abort, and try later. If you attempt to print in the middle of a program, either the program is suspended (hung up), or an error message is displayed.

2. If you print files that reside on a floppy diskette, don't remove the diskette until PRINT finishes printing the files.

3. Do not edit, alter, or erase the file being PRINTed. DOS skips the file if the diskette is removed or if the file is deleted (as though DOS had a disk error), or DOS may not print the correct copy of the file (if the file is edited or altered).

PRINT V3 is sensible about handling the queuing of more than 10 files or exceeding *maxfiles*. PRINT V3 simply gives an error message and continues to work sanely. On the other hand, PRINT V2 acts erratically. If you queue more than ten files, you lose control over PRINT V2 until it finishes printing. Exceeding *maxfiles* with PRINT V3 is not as drastic an error as it is with PRINT V2.

When PRINT is first run, it increases DOS's size by 5,520 bytes. Changing the buffer size (with the /B switch) or the number of files that can be queued (with the /Q switch) alters DOS's size accordingly. You can regain this memory space by restarting DOS.

Hints

1. The use of the /D switch is obvious: it specifies to which device you will print.

   Unless you have a serial printer, PRN works well. The use of the other five switches is less obvious.

2. When the cursor sits at the system prompt (A>), PRINT gets almost all the computer's time.

   When you use any program, the remaining five switches control how fast PRINT will print.

3. /B:*bufsiz* acts like a disk buffer.

   PRINT reads into memory a portion of the document to print. Higher values for *bufsiz* decrease the number of times that PRINT reads the file from the disk; printing throughput is therefore increased. Always use a multiple of 512, such as 1,024, 2,048, etc., for /B:*bufsiz*. The default size (512 bytes) is adequate for most uses, but using /B:4096 increases performance for most two-page (or shorter) documents.

4. For the /M or /S switch, the following formula shows how much CPU time PRINT gets per second:

$$\text{PRINT's \% of CPU time} = \frac{maxtick}{(1 + timeslice)} * 100$$

   Using the default values, PRINT gets 22 percent of the computer's time. Increasing *maxtick* gives PRINT more time; increasing *timeslice* gives PRINT less time. Because the keyboard action becomes sluggish as PRINT gains more time, the default values for PRINT usually work well.

5. */U:* controls how long PRINT waits for a busy printer.

The default value is 1. Increase this number to range from 2 to 8 if you use a slow printer—that is, a printer that works at less than 4800 baud (a serial printer) or less than 100 cps (a parallel printer).

Messages

1. `Access denied`

   ERROR: You attempted to print a file for which another computer or program has exclusive use. Try the command later.

2. `All files canceled by operator`

   INFORMATION: You used the */T* switch to terminate all queued files.

3. `Cannot use PRINT - Use NET PRINT`

   ERROR: You attempted to print a file to a networked printer, either on your own computer or on another computer. You must use NET PRINT, not PRINT, to print to this printer. You may pause or disconnect from the network and use PRINT on your own printer.

4. `Errors on list device indicate that`
   `it may be off-line. Please check it.`

   WARNING: The device used for PRINT is probably not selected, connected, or turned on. Check your printer and cable, and check to see that all connections are correct.

5. `File filename canceled by operator`

   INFORMATION: This message appears on the printout to remind you that the printout of the file `filename` is incomplete because you canceled the printing of the file.

6. `filename File not found`

   WARNING: PRINT didn't find the specified file, `filename`. PRINT skips this file and processes any remaining file names on the command line. Check the disk drive, path, and file names for this file. Make sure that the file does exist where you specified, and then try the command again.

7. filename File not in PRINT queue

WARNING: You requested that PRINT cancel (with the /C switch) a file (filename) that PRINT did not have in its queue. Either the file has been printed already or the file name is misspelled. If you meant to cancel one or more files and to print others (that is, you intended to give both /C and /P), either you gave the /C switch out of order or you omitted the /P switch to print a file. Check each of these possibilities, and try the command again.

8. Invalid drive specification

WARNING: Either you specified a disk drive that doesn't exist or you omitted the colon after a disk drive name. PRINT skips this file and processes any remaining files named on the command line. Check your spelling of the file names, and try the command again.

9. Invalid parameter

ERROR: You gave a switch that PRINT does not recognize; or you gave the /B, /D, /M, /Q, /S, or /U switch when you ran PRINT the second or subsequent time. If you gave an unknown switch, try the command again. If you attempted to use one of the mentioned switches, you must restart DOS and run PRINT again with the switch.

10. filename is currently being printed
    filename is in queue

INFORMATION: This message tells you what file is being printed and what files are in line to be printed. This message appears whenever you use PRINT with no parameters or when you queue additional files.

11. List output is not assigned to a device

ERROR: The device you gave PRINT is not a recognized device; PRINT aborts. To solve this problem, reissue PRINT, and give a correct device name when requested.

12. filename Pathname too long

WARNING: The length of the file specification for filename exceeded the 63-character limit. PRINT skips this file and processes any other file name on the command line. You also may have omitted a space. In that case, type the command again. If the 63-character limit was exceeded, create a new subdirectory closer to the root subdirectory (fewer subdirectories in the chain to the file), move the files to the new subdirectory, and try the PRINT command again.

13. `PRINT queue is empty`

    INFORMATION: No files are in line to be printed by PRINT.

14. `PRINT queue is full`

    WARNING: You attempted to add too many files to PRINT and exceeded the maximum number accepted. The request to add more files fails for each file past the limit. You must wait until PRINT processes a file before you can add another file to the queue.

15. `Resident part of PRINT installed`

    INFORMATION: The first time you use PRINT, this message indicates that PRINT has installed itself in DOS and has increased the size of DOS by about 5,500 bytes.

16. `Disk-error-type error on file filename`

    WARNING: This message appears on the printout. A disk error (`disk-error-type`) occurred when DOS tried to read the file `filename`. PRINT uses its procedure for handling disk errors.

PROMPT
(Set the System Prompt)   *V2, V3—Internal*

Purpose   Customizes the DOS system prompt (the A>, or A prompt)

Syntax   **PROMPT** *promptstring*

promptstring is the text to be used for the new system prompt.

Exit Codes   None

Rules
1. If you do not enter the *promptstring*, the standard system prompt reappears (A>).

2. Any text entered for *promptstring* becomes the new system prompt. You can enter special characters by using the meta-strings.

3. The new system prompt stays in effect until you restart DOS or reissue the PROMPT command.

4. To see the text of PROMPT after it has been set, use the SET command.

5. To start the prompt with a character that is normally a DOS delimiter (blank space, semicolon, comma, etc.), precede the character with a null meta-string (a character that has no meaning to PROMPT, such as $A).

Meta-Strings A *meta-string* is a group of characters transformed into another character or characters. To use certain characters (for example, the < or > I/O redirection symbols), you must enter the appropriate meta-string to place the desired character(s) in your *promptstring*. Otherwise, DOS immediately attempts to interpret the character.

All meta-strings begin with the dollar sign ($) and have two characters, including the $. The following list contains meta-string characters and their meanings:

Character	*What It Produces*
$	$, the dollar sign
_ (underscore)	newline, (moves to the first position of the next line)
b	|, the vertical *b*ar
e	The *E*scape character, CHR$(27)
d	The *d*ate, like the DATE command
h	The backspace character, CHR$(8), which erases the previous character
g	>, the *g*reater-than character
l	<, the *l*ess-than character
n	The curre*n*t disk drive
p	The current disk drive and *p*ath, including the current directory
q	=, the e*q*ual sign
t	The *t*ime, like the TIME command
v	The *v*ersion number of DOS
Any other	Nothing or null; the character is ignored

Examples

1. **PROMPT**

   or

   PROMPT ng

   PROMPT sets the DOS system prompt to the normal prompt (A>). Here, the first example shows the default use of PROMPT. If you do not specify a *promptstring*, the standard system prompt is restored. In the second example the $n is the letter of the current disk drive, and the $g is the greater-than sign (>). The new prompt, if the current disk drive is A, becomes A + >, or A>.

2. **PROMPT The current drive is $n:**

   This command sets the new system prompt to

   ```
   The current drive is A:
   ```

3. **PROMPT $p**

PROMPT sets the system prompt to the current disk drive and the path to the current directory. If you are using the example disk in drive A and are in the SAMPLES directory, the system prompt in this command line displays

```
A:\DOS\BASIC\SAMPLES
```

4. **PROMPT $A;$t;**

PROMPT sets the system prompt to the system time, such as

```
;12:04:12.46;
```

Note that a semicolon normally separates items on the DOS command line. To make the first character of the system prompt a delimiter, a null meta-string must be used. Because $A does not have any special meaning for DOS, the system ignores this meta-string and makes the semicolon the first character of the new prompt.

5. **PROMPT $$**

This sets the system prompt to imitate UNIX's Bourne shell prompt:

```
$
```

Notes

The PROMPT command gives users greater control over their systems—in this case, the system prompt. With hierarchical directories, displaying the current path on your disk drive is helpful. For that reason, many DOS V3 users may want to set the system prompt to

PROMPT $p

This command displays the current disk drive and the current path as the prompt.

You can use any text in the prompt, including text you may not normally think of, such as your name. Because I am conscious of time and forgetful of dates, I have used in the past

PROMPT $d $t $p $_yes, Chris $

This command sets the system prompt to display the date, time, and current disk drive and path. On the next line, yes, Chris is displayed, as in the following:

```
Mon 11-15-1985   9:57:13.11 A:\DOS\BASIC
yes, Chris
```

I use the last dollar sign to ensure that a space appears between the s in Chris and whatever I type at this new system prompt. Some text editors strip away spaces after the last printable character on a line. (IBM's Personal Editor does this.) To keep the space, I use the dollar sign, which DOS ignores, as the last character. New versions of DOS may force me to use instead a complete null meta-string, such as the $A.

The system prompt I used had two disadvantages: it is a wordy two-line prompt that distracts other people who use my computer, and if a floppy disk drive is the current disk drive, I must always have a floppy in the disk drive.

I use several IBM Personal Computer and PS/2 family members and several workalikes. Normally, the current disk drive is the fixed disk, drive C. When I make drive A the current drive, DOS reads the diskette before it displays the system prompt. Therefore, if a diskette is changed, DOS resets the new diskette's current directory to the root directory and displays the correct path.

If no diskette is in the floppy disk drive (or if the disk drive door is open), I get a drive not ready error message. If you use the $p (drive/path) meta-string in your prompt, expect DOS to read the current disk drive before it displays your customized system prompt.

I have a newer prompt that is simpler:

   PROMPT p_yes,Chris? $

This prompt displays the path, goes to the next line, and writes yes, Chris? Now that I have a clock-calendar on my desk, I don't need the date and time, but I still need to know the disk and directory I am using. (I also like to demand "a sense of humility" from my computers.)

I have seen prompts that range from The check is in the mail > to

   PROMPT $e[s$e[24Ape[u-

This prompt places the cursor on the top line of the screen and prints the current path followed by a minus sign. The prompt depends on the display control codes from ANSI.SYS. You must have the **device = ansi.sys** line in your CONFIG.SYS file for this prompt to work.

Have fun experimenting with PROMPT. You can try it many times and not "hurt" anything. After you create a prompt you like, include it in your AUTOEXEC.BAT file, or create a separate batch file you can execute after DOS has started. To cancel your new prompt and restore the old A> prompt, just reissue PROMPT without a *promptstring*.

RECOVER
(Recover files or disk directory)   *V2, V3—External*

Purpose

Recovers a file that has bad sectors or a file from a disk that has a damaged directory

Syntax

To recover a file, use

   *dc:pathc*RECOVER *d:path/filename.ext*

To recover a disk that has a damaged directory, use

   *dc:pathc*RECOVER **d:**

dc: is the name of the disk drive holding the command.

pathc is the path to the command.

d: is the name of the disk drive holding the damaged file or diskette.

path is the path to the directory holding the file to be recovered.

filename.ext is the file to be recovered. Wildcards are allowed, but only the first file that matches the wildcard file name is recovered.

Exit Codes

None

Rules

  *1. Do not use this command on files or disks that do not need it!

  2. If you do not give a drive name, the current disk is used.

  3. If you do not give a path name, the current directory is used.

  4. If you give a file name, DOS skips the bad sectors and recovers as much information as possible from that file.

  5. If you give just a drive name, DOS attempts to recover the directory of the disk. (This rule applies to the second syntax line.)

6. If you do not give any disk drive name, path name, or file name, RECOVER displays an error message and immediately exits.

7. If you give a wildcard character in the file name, RECOVER works only on the first file that matches the ambiguous name.

8. RECOVER does not restore erased files.

9. Do not use RECOVER on a networked disk drive. RECOVER displays an error message if you try.

10. Do not use RECOVER on an ASSIGNed, SUBSTituted, or JOINed disk drive. The results are unpredictable.

Notes

RECOVER attempts to recover either a file with a bad sector or a disk with a directory containing a bad sector. To recover a file that has one or more bad sectors, you enter RECOVER d:filename.ext. (You know whether a file has bad sectors because DOS displays a disk-error message when you try to use the file.)

When RECOVER works on a file, DOS attempts to read the file's sectors, one at a time. After RECOVER successfully reads a sector, the information is placed in a temporary file. If RECOVER cannot successfully read the sector, it is skipped; but the FAT is marked so that no other program can use the bad sector. This process continues until the entire file has been read. The old file is erased, and the temporary file is renamed with the name of the damaged file. The new file is located in the same directory where the old file resides.

If the damaged file is a program file, the program probably cannot be used. If the file is a data or text file, some information can be recovered. Because RECOVER reads to the end of the file, make sure that any garbage at the end has been eliminated by a text editor or a word processor.

To recover a disk, enter the disk drive name after the command. DOS creates a new root directory and recovers each file and subdirectory. The system names the recovered files FILEnnnn.REC. (nnnn is a four-digit number.) Even good files are placed in FILEnnnn.REC files. The only way you can determine which original file corresponds to which FILEnnnn.REC file is to TYPE or print each file and use the last printed directory of the disk—or have a good memory. A disk editor that can display the ASCII and hexadecimal characters in a file is a big help. If you don't have a disk editor, TYPE each file and rename it after you have determined what it is. Then try to guess the names of any remaining files.

Remember that subdirectories also are recovered in FILEnnnn.REC files. When you TYPE a subdirectory file, you see that the first character is a period (.). About halfway across the screen is a double period (..). When you see these two symbols, you can safely guess that this file is a subdirectory.

RECOVER does not recover erased files. You need a separate utility program to recover them.

For more information about RECOVER, see Chapter 17.

Messages

1. `Cannot RECOVER a Network drive`

   ERROR: You attempted to run RECOVER on a disk drive that is part of a network. You must pause or disconnect from the network and then rerun RECOVER.

2. `File not found`

   ERROR: RECOVER cannot find the file you specified to be recovered. Check the spelling of the file name, make sure that the file exists on the specified disk drive and directory, and try the command again.

3. `Invalid drive or file name`

   ERROR: One of the following errors occurred: (1) you specified a disk drive that does not exist, (2) you omitted the colon in a disk drive name, (3) you misspelled the directory path to the file name, or (4) you failed to give a disk drive name or file name. Check each possibility and try the command again.

4. `Invalid number of parameters`

   ERROR: You specified more than one argument for RECOVER. Perhaps you inserted a space between the disk drive name and path name or between the path name and file name, or you used an illegal character. Check the command line and try the command again.

5. `Press any key to begin recovery`
   `of the file(s) on drive d:`

   INFORMATION and WARNING: RECOVER is asking you to confirm that you want to recover a file or all files on disk drive d. If you want RECOVER to attempt the recovery of the file(s) on the disk drive, press any key. If you don't want to RECOVER the file(s) from the disk drive, press Ctrl-Break or Ctrl-C. Be sure to check the command line before you press the key to begin. RECOVER displays this message for the recovery of a single file or all files.

6. `Warning - directory full`
   `nnn file(s) recovered`

   ERROR: The root directory on the disk is full. No more files can be recovered, and RECOVER stops. You should erase or copy to another disk the files in the root directory to free more directory space. Then rerun RECOVER.

RENAME or REN
(Rename file)   *V1, V2, V3—Internal*

Purpose   Changes the name of the disk file(s)

Syntax   RENAME *d:path*\ filename1.*ext1* filename2.*ext2*

or

REN *d:path*\ filename1.*ext1* filename2.*ext2*

d: is the name of the disk drive holding the file(s) to be renamed.

path\ is the path to the file(s) to be renamed.

filename1.*ext1* is the current name of the file. Wildcards are allowed.

filename2.*ext2* is the new name for the file. Wildcards are allowed.

Rules   1. If you do not give a drive name, the current disk drive is used.

2. If you do not give a path name, the current directory is used.

3. You can give a disk name and path name for the first file name only.

4. You must give both the old file name and the new file name with their appropriate extensions, if any.

5. Wildcard characters are permitted in the file names.

6. If a file in the same directory already has the new file name, a Duplicate file name or File not found message is displayed, and no further action is taken.

Notes   RENAME, or the short form REN, changes the name of a file on the disk. The form is

RENAME old_name → new_name

Because you are renaming an established disk file, any drive or path designation goes with the old name so that DOS knows which file you are renaming.

Wildcard characters are acceptable in either the old or the new name. These characters can be troublesome if you are not careful. For example, suppose that a directory has the following files:

LETTER.TXT
LETTER1.TXT
RENAME.DOC
RENAME.TXT

If you attempt to rename all .TXT files as .DOC files with the command

RENAME *.TXT *.DOC

RENAME stops when it encounters RENAME.TXT, because a RENAME.DOC already exists. All .TXT file names listed before RENAME.TXT, however, will be changed to .DOC file names.

Messages

1. Duplicate filename or File not found

   ERROR: You attempted to change a file name to a name that already exists, or the file to be renamed does not exist in the directory. Check the directory for conflicting names. Make sure that the file name does exist and that you have spelled it correctly. Then try again.

2. Invalid number of parameters

   ERROR: You gave too few or too many file names. You must give two file names. Possibly you used spaces between the disk drive name and path name or between the path name and file name for the first file. Or you may have used an invalid character in one or both file names.

3. Missing file name

   ERROR: You forgot to enter the new name for the file.

REPLACE
(Replace/update files)   *V3.2 and later—External*

Purpose   Selectively replaces files with matching names from one disk to another. Selectively adds files from one disk to another.

Syntax   *dc:pathc***REPLACE** *ds:paths***filenames.***exts dd:pathd* /A/P/R/S/W

dc: is the name of the disk drive holding the command.

pathc is the path to the command.

ds: is the name of the disk drive holding the replacement files.

paths is the path to the replacement files.

filenames.*exts* is the name of the replacement file(s). Wildcards are allowed.

dd: is the disk drive whose files will be replaced.

pathd is the path to the directory to receive the replacement file(s).

Special Terms   The file(s) that will be added to or that will replace another file(s) is the *source* represented by an *s* in the name (*ds:paths***filenames.***exts*).

The file(s) that is replaced or the disk and directory that will have the file(s) added is the *destination*, represented by the letter *d* (*dd:pathd*). However, DOS calls this the *target*.

Switches

/A   *Add* files from sources that do not exist on the destination.

/P   *Prompt* and ask whether the file should be replaced or added to the destination.

/R   Replace *read-only* files also.

/S   Replace files in the current directory and all other *subdirectories* beneath this directory.

/W   *Wait* for the source diskette to be inserted.

Exit Codes

REPLACE returns the DOS error code. A zero exit code indicates successful completion. A nonzero exit code indicates an error. Common exit levels are:

2 = No source files were found
3 = Source or target path is invalid
5 = Access denied to the file(s) or directory(ies)
8 = Out of memory
11 = Invalid parameter, incorrect number of parameters
15 = Invalid disk drive
22 = Incorrect version of DOS

Rules

1. If you do not give a disk drive name for the source (*ds:*), the current disk drive is used.

2. If you do not give a path name for the source (*paths*), the current directory is used.

3. You must specify a file name (filenames.*exts*). Wildcards are allowed.

4. If you do not specify a disk drive name for the destination (*dd:*), the files on the current disk drive will be replaced or added.

5. If you do not specify a path name for the destination (*pathd*), the files in the current directory will be replaced or added.

*6. REPLACE adds or replaces by file name. REPLACE does not care about the contents of files, which means that REPLACE can replace program or data files whose names match, even if the programs or data files are different.

7. The /A switch and /S cannot be used together. All other switches can be used with each other.

8. To add files to the destination directory, use the /A switch. REPLACE adds the files from the source that do not have a matching file name in the destination directory.

9. To replace files in more than one directory on the destination, use the /S switch. REPLACE replaces all files in the specified directory and all subsequent subdirectories whose names match files in the source directory.

10. To add or replace files selectively, use the /P switch. REPLACE asks whether each file should be added or replaced. Answer Y for yes, or N for no.

11. To replace read-only files, use the /R switch. If this switch is not used, REPLACE skips files marked with the read-only flag.

12. If the /W (*wait*) switch is used, REPLACE prompts you to insert the source diskette. This switch is useful when you must change diskettes before REPLACE searches for the source file names. If the /W switch is not used, REPLACE assumes that the correct diskette is in the drive and immediately begins the search for the source files.

13. REPLACE does not process hidden or system files.

Examples

a. **REPLACE A:*.COM C:\BIN**

Copies files that have a .COM extension in the current directory of A: over those files with existing, matching file names in C:\BIN. Any .COM file on A: whose name does not match a file in the directory C:\BIN is not copied.

b. **REPLACE A:*.COM C:\BIN /S**

Copies files that have a .COM extension in the current directory of A: over the files with the same name in the subdirectory C:\BIN and all subsequent subdirectories. This single command replaces all matching files in C:\BIN and lower subdirectories.

c. **REPLACE A:*.COM C:\BIN /S/R**

This example is identical to the second example, except that read-only files also are replaced. Note that REPLACE does not process hidden or system files. If you were processing the DOS Startup Diskette, which contains the two files IBMBIO.COM and IBMDOS.COM, REPLACE does not process these files. The two files are marked read-only, but they are marked also as hidden and system files. Hence, these system files would not be copied by the REPLACE command.

d. **REPLACE A:*.COM C:\BIN /P**

This command replaces the files on C:\BIN that match files on the current directory of A: drive, except that REPLACE asks for confirmation for each file to be replaced, one at a time. The */P* switch (prompt switch) is used when you need more control in determining which files should be replaced.

e. **REPLACE A:*.COM C:\BIN /A**

Copies files in the current directory of A: that have a .COM extension and that do not match the file names in C:\BIN. This command uses the add switch (*/A*) to add files that do not exist in the destination subdirectory.

f. **REPLACE A:*.* C:\ /S/W/P**

This command replaces all files on C: whose names match files in the current directory of A:. REPLACE prompts you to insert the diskette in A: before REPLACE reads the source files (the effect of the */W wait* switch). The */P* switch is used to confirm that individual files should be replaced. The command could inadvertently replace a different file in some directory of the disk if the file happens to have the same name as a file on the source diskette.

Notes

REPLACE is a command added in DOS V3.2. REPLACE is a semi-intelligent COPY program that can update or add files selectively to directories.

REPLACE has two ideal uses: replacing one or a few files duplicated in many subdirectories; or updating a major application program or DOS itself when the files have been placed in one part of the directory tree (when the files exist in a directory and its subdirectories).

REPLACE's decision to replace or add files is based on matching file names. The drive and directory names are not considered—only the root and extension name are. REPLACE does not care about the contents of the file, only the file name. Hence, older program and data files can be replaced quickly by their newer counterparts.

One of REPLACE's major advantages is also its key disadvantage. Be careful when you "unleash" REPLACE on several subdirectories, particularly when you use REPLACE /S on the entire disk. A dissimilar file with a matching name in a differenct directory might be replaced. For example, to update my DOS files, I unleashed REPLACE on my fixed disk with the command

REPLACE A:*.* C:\ /S

REPLACE successfully updated the DOS programs, but it replaced also a program called SORT.EXE in the subdirectory C:\UTILS with the DOS version of SORT.EXE. Because my version of SORT.EXE was more powerful than the DOS-provided version, the replacement was an unpleasant surprise.

To prevent replacing the wrong files, restrict the destination path name to cover only the directories that hold the files you want REPLACE to replace. Check the source and destination directories for matching file names. If you find any conflicts, or if you are unsure, use the /P switch. REPLACE asks before it replaces any files.

REPLACE also selectively adds files to a subdirectory. Using REPLACE /A *adds* files from the source directory that do not exist in the destination directory. However, this form of REPLACE cannot work with more than one destination subdirectory at a time. The /S switch cannot be used with the /A switch.

Note that REPLACE can handle files marked with the DOS read-only attribute by using the /R flag. However, REPLACE does not process files marked with the hidden or system attribute. Therefore, you cannot replace files such as the two DOS system files, IBMBIO.COM or IBMDOS.COM. If you must update these files, use the SYS command.

If you have a one floppy system, then the /W switch, or the *wait* switch, can help. The /W switch instructs REPLACE to wait until you press a key to begin reading the source files. If you have to change diskettes, use the /W switch. You may notice that REPLACE gives a slightly different message when you use the /W switch with the /A switch. If you add files (/A), REPLACE prompts you to press any key to begin adding files. When you use the /W switch without the /A switch, REPLACE displays a message to press any key to begin replacing files.

Messages

1. Access denied filename

   ERROR: REPLACE has attempted to replace the file filename that is marked as read-only and the /R switch was not used, or the file is being used by another program or computer and is marked temporarily as read-only. In both cases, the problem is with the destination file. If `filename` is the source file, another computer or process temporarily has marked the source file as write-only.

If the file you intend to replace has the read-only attribute set, either reissue the REPLACE command by using the /R switch or use the ATTRIB command to turn off the read-only flag of the file that will be replaced (the destination file—not the source file). If this file is being used by another program or computer, wait until the other program or computer is finished, and then run the REPLACE command again.

2. `Add filename? (Y/N)`
   `Adding filename`

   INFORMATION and WARNING: These messages appear if the /A and /P switches are used. In the first message, REPLACE asks whether the file `filename` should be added to the destination directory. If you type **Y** for yes, REPLACE adds the file. The second message then informs you that REPLACE is adding `filename`. If you answer **N** for no, REPLACE does not add the file, and the second message does not appear.

3. `File cannot be copied onto itself filename`

   WARNING: The source and destination disk and directories are identical. Either you forgot to specify a destination, and the source disk and directory are the current disk and directory, or you have specified the same disk drive and directory twice. REPLACE does not process `filename`, but continues.

   Check the command line to be sure that you have specified the correct source and destination for REPLACE, and then try the command again.

4. `nnn file(s) added`
   `nnn file(s) replaced`

   INFORMATION: REPLACE indicates how many files were successfully added or replaced. The first message appears when the /A switch is used; the second message appears when the /A switch is not used. The message does not indicate that all potential files were added or replaced successfully. This message appears when at least one file has been added or replaced successfully, regardless of any errors that occurred later.

5. `Invalid parameter`

   ERROR: You have either given a switch that REPLACE does not recognize or forgotten to type the switch character (/). Check the command line and try the command again.

6. `Invalid drive specification  d:`

   ERROR: You have given for the source or destination a disk drive name (`d:`) that does not exist. Check the command line and try again.

7. `Insufficient disk space - filename:`

   WARNING: The file `filename` could not be added or replaced. If the /A switch was given, there was not enough room on the destination disk to add the file. If the /A switch was not given, the replacement file was larger than the old file and the available free space on the destination disk. REPLACE skips this file and continues.

   To solve this problem, erase any unwanted files from the destination disk, and COPY the files that REPLACE did not copy. To add new files (use the /A switch), erase any unwanted files from the destination disk and give the REPLACE /A command again.

8. `No files found filename`

   ERROR: REPLACE could not find any files that matched the source file name `filename`. You may have misspelled the source file name, given the disk drive and/or directory name but omitted the file name, given the wrong disk drive or directory name for the source, or put the wrong diskette in the disk drive. Check the command line to see whether the correct diskette is in the disk drive, and then try the command again.

9. `No files added`
   `No files replaced`

   ERROR: REPLACE did not add or replace any files. The first message appears if you give the /A switch; the second message appears if you did not give the /A switch. You may have misspelled the source file name or the destination name, given the wrong source name, given no destination name or the wrong one, or put the wrong diskette in the disk drive. Also, REPLACE might not have been capable of adding or replacing files because of insufficient disk space.

Be sure that the command line is properly phrased, that the correct diskette is in the disk drive, and that sufficient room is on the destination disk for the files. Then try the command again.

10. Parameters not compatible

ERROR: You have given both the /A switch and the /S switch, but they cannot be used in the same REPLACE command. To replace files, omit the /A switch. You cannot add files to more than one directory at a time. To add files to more than one directory, you must issue separate REPLACE commands and specify a different directory to which files should be added each time.

11. Path not Found pathname

ERROR: REPLACE could not find the destination directory path, pathname. Either the destination directory name is misspelled or you gave the incorrect disk drive name. Try the command again, and give the correct destination disk drive name and directory name.

12. Press any key to begin adding file(s)
Press any key to begin replacing file(s)

INFORMATION: You have used the /W switch, and REPLACE is waiting for you to strike a key to begin reading the source files. The first message (adding files) appears if the /A switch was used; the second message (replacing files) appears if the /A switch is not used. Press any key to make REPLACE continue.

13. Replace filename? (Y/N)
Replacing filename

INFORMATION and WARNING: These messages appear if the /P switch but not the /A switch is used. The first message is the query by REPLACE if the file `filename` should be replaced on the destination directory. If you type Y for yes, REPLACE replaces the old file with the file from the source and displays the second message, `filename`. If you answer N for no, REPLACE does not add the file, and the second message does not appear.

14. `Source path required`

   ERROR: You either mistyped the command or omitted the source file name. You must specify a source file name to REPLACE. Check the command line and try again.

RESTORE
(Restore backed-up files)   *V2, V3*—External*

Purpose   Restores one or more backup files from a diskette or fixed disk to another diskette or fixed disk. This command complements the BACKUP command.

Syntax   *dc:pathc**RESTORE* *d1:* *d2:path/filename.ext /S /P /M /N*
              /B:date /A:date /L:time /E:time

dc: is the name of the disk drive holding the command.

pathc is the path to the command.

d1: is the name of the disk drive holding the backup file(s).

d2: is the disk drive to receive the restored file(s).

path is the name of the path to the directory that will receive the restored file(s).

filename.ext is the name of the file you want to restore. Wildcards are allowed.

Switches
/S	Restores files in the current directory and in all other *subdirectories* beneath this directory
/P	Causes a *prompt* to ask whether to restore a file that has been changed since the last backup or a file that is marked as read-only
/M	Restores all files *modified* or deleted since the backup set was made
/N	Restores all files that *no longer* exist on the destination
/B:date	Restores all files created or modified on or *before* the date. The form of *date*, which depends on the setting of the COUNTRY command in CONFIG.SYS, can be:

                        mm-dd-yy   North American
                        dd-mm-yy   European
                        yy-mm-dd   East Asia

mm is the month
dd is the day
yy is the year

The character separating the parts of the *date* depends on the setting of the COUNTRY command and varies between the hyphen, period, and slash. North American users can substitute a slash (/) in place of the hyphen (-).

/A:*date*   Restores all files created or modified on or *after* the *date*. The format of *date* is the same as for the /B switch.

/L:*time*   Restores all files created or modified at or *later* than the specified *time*. The form of *time* is *hh:mm:ss* where

hh is the hour
mm is the minutes
ss is the seconds

The character separating the parts of *time* usually is the colon, but it can be the period (.) if the COUNTRY command in CONFIG.SYS has been set to Denmark, Finland, or Germany.

/E:*time*   Restores all files modified at or *before* the specified *time*. The format of *time* is the same as for the /L switch.

Exit Codes

0 = Normal completion
1 = No files were found to restore
2 = Some files not restored due to sharing conflicts
3 = Terminated by the operator (through a Ctrl-Break or Esc)
4 = Terminated by an encountered error

Rules

1. Only files that you have saved with the BACKUP command can be RESTOREd.

2. You must give the name of the disk drive holding the backup files. If the current disk is the disk to receive the RESTOREd files, you don't have to give the name of the disk.

3. If you do not give a path name, the current directory of the receiving disk is used.

4. If you do not give a path name and a file name, all backup files from the directory are restored (the same as giving the file name *.*).

5. If you give a path name, RESTORE does not make any assumptions about the file name. You must give a file name.

6. RESTORE prompts you to insert the backup diskettes in order. If you insert a diskette out of order, RESTORE prompts you to insert the correct diskette.

7. To restore files modified or created on or before a given date, use the */B:date* switch. To restore files created or modified on or after a given date, use the */A:date* switch. The date entered for these switches is given in the same format used by the DOS DATE command.

8. To further control which files should be restored, use the */E:time* switch to restore files modified or created before the given *time*, or the */L:time* switch to restore files modified or created after the given *time*. The time entered for these switches is given in the same format used by the DOS TIME command.

9. Do not use the */E:time* or */L:time* switch without using the */B:date* or */A:date* switch. The result will not be what you want.

10. The */M* switch restores files that have been modified, do not exist, or have been deleted since the backup set was made. A file is considered as having been modified if its archive flag is on.

11. The */N* switch restores files in the backup set that no longer appear in the same directory on the destination disk.

12. Do not use combinations of the */B*, */A*, and */N* switches in the same command.

13. Be cautious when you restore files backed up while an ASSIGN, SUBST, or JOIN command was in effect. When you RESTORE files, clear any existing APPEND, ASSIGN, SUBST, or JOIN commands.

Note

BACKUP and RESTORE V3.3 are radically different from earlier versions. BACKUP V3.3 places all backed-up files in one larger file and maintains a separate information file on the same diskette. RESTORE V3.3 handles the new and old backup file formats, which means that RESTORE V3.3 restores backups created by any version of BACKUP.

The new switch additions to BACKUP V3.3 provide greater control over which files should be restored. The /M switch restores files that have been modified since the last backup (the archive flag is on), and files that do not exist in the same directories since the backup set was made. The /M switch is best used in a disastrous circumstance—when the current copy of your modified files is bad and you have erased files from your fixed disk.

The /N switch restores files that are no longer in the same directories as when the backup set was made. If a file has been erased or moved (copied and then erased), the /M or /N switch causes this file to be RESTOREd. If you are attempting to restore erased files, use the /N switch and then the /M switch.

The /P switch causes RESTORE to ask whether a modified file or read-only file should be restored. To selectively restore files, use the /P switch, particularly when you use /M, which can restore an out-of-date backup file over a modified file.

Unlike earlier versions of RESTORE, RESTORE V3.3 does not restore the DOS system files, IBMBIO.COM, IBMDOS.COM, and COMMAND.COM. If you reformat the disk with the /S switch, FORMAT automatically places these three files on the disk. The less radical method for restoring these files is to use the SYS command to transfer IBMBIO.COM and IBMDOS.COM to the disk, and then copy COMMAND.COM from your DOS startup disk.

The next four switches work with the directory date-time stamp that is saved with the file when it is backed up. The /B switch restores files in which the date is on or *before* a given date. The /A switch restores files in which the date is at or *after* a given date. The /L switch restores files in which the time is at or *later* than the given time. The /E switch restores files in which the time is on or *earlier* than the given time. All dates and times are based on the DOS date and time stamp for the file when the file was backed up.

If you use the /S (all *subdirectories*) switch, RESTORE re-creates any necessary subdirectories that have been removed and then restores the files in the created subdirectories.

Be cautious when you restore files that were backed up while ASSIGN, JOIN, or SUBST was in effect. Basically, the backed-up files are not restored to the same physical location unless the identical ASSIGN, JOIN, or SUBST command is in effect. The best way to avoid the confusion is to break any ASSIGN, JOIN, or SUBST commands before you run BACKUP or RESTORE.

Do not use RESTORE /M or RESTORE /N while APPEND /X is in effect. RESTORE attempts to search the directories for modified or missing files. APPEND tricks RESTORE into finding files in the paths specified to the APPEND command. RESTORE then may attempt to RESTORE files it should not and not restore files it should. Give the **APPEND;** command to disable APPEND.

For more information about RESTORE, see Chapter 18.

Messages

1. `*** Files were backed up date ***`

   INFORMATION: RESTORE displays the date the files were backed up. The format of the `date` varies depending on the setting of your country code. (See Chapter 15 for information about the COUNTRY directive of CONFIG.SYS.)

2. `filename`
   `File creation error`

   ERROR: DOS found an error when it attempted to restore the file `filename`, and RESTORE stopped. You should run CHKDSK on the receiving disk to see whether it has physical problems. For any messages that appear, follow the directions under CHKDSK in the *Command Reference*.

3. `Insert backup diskette nn in drive d:`
   `Strike any key when ready`

   INFORMATION: RESTORE wants the next diskette in sequence. This message appears when you restore files that were backed up on diskettes. Insert the next diskette in drive d and press any key.

4. `Insert restore target in drive d:`
   `Strike any key when ready`

   RESTORE is asking you to place in drive d the diskette to receive the restored files. This message appears only when you restore files on diskettes. Insert the target diskette in disk drive d and press any key.

5. `Invalid drive specification`

   ERROR: You failed to specify the disk drive holding the backup files, you gave the name of a disk drive that does not exist, or a resident (background) program is interfering with RESTORE. Check each of these possibilities and try the command again.

6. `Invalid number of parameters`

   ERROR: You failed to specify the disk drive holding the backup files, or you gave too many drive or file names. A possible cause is a space or other illegal character in a file name. Check the command line and try again.

7. `Invalid parameter`

   ERROR: You gave a switch that RESTORE did not recognize, or you gave a path and/or file name for the disk drive holding the backup files (d1:). Check the command line and try again.

8. `Invalid path`

   ERROR: RESTORE was unable to create or use a subdirectory in another subdirectory. Run CHKDSK and follow the directions in the *Command Reference*.

9. `*** Not able to restore file ***`

   WARNING: Either the file listed before this message could not be restored because another computer or program is using the file, or you stopped RESTORE with a Ctrl-Break sequence.

   If you did not stop RESTORE, wait until the program is finished, stop the other computer or program, and then rerun RESTORE for this file only.

10. `filename`
    `Restore file sequence error`

    ERROR: The file `filename` could not be restored because the diskettes were not inserted in the correct order. This happens only when the backup file is placed on two or more backup diskettes. RESTORE stops. Try the command again, and insert the diskettes in the correct order.

11. `*** Restoring files from drive d: ***`

    INFORMATION: RESTORE is getting the backup files from the disk or diskette in drive d.

12. `Source and target drives are the same`

    ERROR: RESTORE "believes" that the disk drive holding the backup files is the same drive designated to receive the restored files. You may have forgotten to specify the disk drive holding the backup files or the drive holding the target disk. If you have a system with one floppy disk drive and you are attempting to RESTORE files to a floppy diskette, specify drives A and B.

13. `Source does not contain backup files`

    ERROR: RESTORE could not find either CONTROL.xxx and BACKUP.xxx (for DOS V3.3) or BACKUPID.@@@ (for pre-DOS V3.3) on the backup disk, which indicates that the backup files do not exist. Either BACKUP malfunctioned when it was backing up files, you inserted the wrong diskette (if you were restoring from diskettes), or BACKUP could not find the \BACKUP subdirectory (if you were restoring files from a fixed disk).

    Run DIR to get a directory listing of the diskette or disk. If you use DOS V3.3, look for the files CONTROL.xxx and BACKUP.xxx. (The xxx is a three-digit number indicating the number of the backup diskette.) For DOS versions before V3.3, look for the file BACKUPID.@@@ on the diskette. If this file is missing, either the diskette is not a backup diskette or BACKUP malfunctioned (DOS V3.0 only). If the diskette is a backup diskette, you cannot restore the files. Use your previous backup set.

    Look for the \BACKUP subdirectory in the root directory on the fixed disk. If this subdirectory is missing, the backup files are missing also. Restart DOS and check again. Run CHKDSK if necessary. If the directory is still missing, the backup files have been lost.

14. `System files restored`
    `Target disk may not be bootable`

    WARNING: You have restored the three system files (IBMBIO.COM, IBMDOS.COM, and COMMAND.COM) from the backup diskettes. If these files are from a previous version of DOS, the receiving disk cannot be used to start (boot) DOS. If you know that the system files were from DOS V3.x (the version you are currently using), ignore this message. Otherwise, run SYS on the disk to put current versions of IBMBIO.COM and IBMDOS.COM on the disk, and then COPY COMMAND.COM from your DOS Startup diskette to the disk. This message should not appear if you are using RESTORE V3.3.

15. `Target is full`
    `The last file was not restored`

    ERROR: RESTORE was stopped before the current file (listed in the line above this message) was fully restored, because the receiving disk is full. RESTORE deletes the partially restored file.

16. `Unrecoverable file sharing error`

    WARNING: With SHARE.EXE loaded, another computer or process is using this file, and the file cannot be restored. Wait until the computer or process is finished, and then try to RESTORE this file.

17. `Warning! Diskette is out of sequence`
    `Replace the diskette or continue if okay`
    `Strike any key when ready`

    WARNING: You inserted a backup diskette out of order. Place the correct diskette in the drive, and then continue. You may continue with the wrong diskette if you do not want to restore any files and if you are not in the middle of a large file (backed up on two or more diskettes) that has been partially restored. If a file was partially restored, RESTORE will want to restore the rest of the file. RESTORE continues to display this message until the right diskette is inserted.

18. Warning! File filename
    was changed after it was backed up
    or is a read-only file
    Replace the file (Y/N)?

WARNING: This message appears when you give the */P*
switch. The file `filename` already exists on the fixed disk
and is marked as read-only, or the file's date is later than
that of the backup copy, which means that the backup copy
may be out of date. Answer Y to replace the preexisting file
with the backup copy or N to skip that file.

19. Warning! No files were found to restore

WARNING: No files matching the file specifications you gave
were found on the backup diskettes. The most likely cause is
not giving the correct path or file name. Check the
command line and try the command again. This message can
also occur if you reset SWITCHAR.

RMDIR or RD
(Remove directory)   *V2, V3—Internal*

Purpose   Removes a subdirectory

Syntax   RMDIR *d:*path

or

RD *d:*path

d: is the name of the drive holding the subdirectory.

path is the name of the path to the subdirectory. The last path name is the subdirectory you want to delete.

Exit Codes   None

Rules
1. If you do not specify a drive name, the current drive is used.

2. You must give the name of the subdirectory to be deleted. If you supply a path, the subdirectory to be deleted must be the last name in the path.

3. The subdirectory to be deleted must be empty (except for the . and .. entries).

4. You cannot delete the current directory or the root directory of a disk.

Notes   RMDIR, or the short form RD, removes subdirectories from the disk. RMDIR is the opposite of the MKDIR (make directory) command.

When you remove a subdirectory, it must be empty except for the current directory file (.) and any parent directory files (..). The current directory cannot be the directory you are removing. If you attempt to remove a subdirectory that is not empty or that is the current directory, DOS displays an error message and does not delete the directory.

Message

```
Invalid path, not directory
or directory not empty
```

RMDIR did not remove the specified directory because (1) you gave an invalid directory in the path, (2) the subdirectory still has files in it other than the . and .. entries, or (3) you misspelled the path or directory name to be removed. Check each possibility and try again.

SELECT
(Select country configuration)   *V3—External*

Purpose   Creates a disk or diskette with the DOS files, and prepares CONFIG.SYS and AUTOEXEC.BAT files configured for your country

Syntax   *dc:pathc*SELECT *ds: dd:pathd* countrycode keycode

dc: is the name of the disk drive holding the command.

pathc is the path to the command.

ds: is the name of the disk drive holding the DOS files—the *source* disk drive (A: or B:).

dd: is the name of the disk drive to be formatted and that will receive the appropriate DOS files—the *destination* disk drive.

pathd is the path to the subdirectory that will receive the appropriate DOS files—the *destination* directory.

countrycode is the country code (see listing).

keycode is the keyboard code (see listing).

Following are the country and keyboard codes for SELECT:

Country/Language	*Country Code*	*Keyboard Code*
Arabic	785	(none)
Australia	061	US
Belgium	032	BE
Canada (English)	001	US
Canada (French)	002	CF
Denmark	045	DK
Finland	358	SU
France	033	FR
Germany	049	GR
Hebrew	972	(none)
Italy	039	IT
Latin America	003	LA
Netherlands	031	NL
Norway	047	NO
Portugal	351	PO
Spain	034	SP

Sweden	046	SV
Switzerland (French)	041	SF
Switzerland (German)	041	SG
United Kingdom	044	UK
United States	001	US

Exit Codes   None

Rules

*1. SELECT uses the FORMAT command to format the target disk (the diskette to receive the DOS files). Do not use SELECT on a diskette or fixed disk with usable information. The information will be destroyed!

*2. You should use your original DOS Startup or master diskette or a copy of it. Using a copy of the DOS diskette with a write-protect tab over the notch is the best method.

3. If the destination disk is a diskette, you should use a diskette appropriate for the type of disk drive (a 1.2M diskette for a 1.2M disk drive, a 1.44M diskette for a 1.44M disk drive, etc.)

4. If you do not specify a source disk drive, A: is used as the source.

5. If you do not specify a source and destination disk drive name, B: is used for the destination disk.

6. If you specify a source disk drive, you must specify a destination disk drive.

7. If a single disk drive name is given, A: is the source, and the named disk drive is the destination.

8. The only valid source disk drives are A: and B:. Using any other disk drive name causes SELECT to display an error message.

9. Any valid disk drive can be specified to SELECT as the destination disk. However, the source and destination disks must be different.

10. If you do not specify a destination directory, SELECT copies the DOS files to the root directory of the destination disk.

11. If you specify a destination directory, the path (*pathd*) must be an absolute path (it cannot contain the **.** or **..** entries). Because the disk will be formatted, SELECT creates the appropriate directories.

12. The SELECT command is not needed if your Startup disk already contains a CONFIG.SYS file and an AUTOEXEC.BAT file. Simply edit these files to include the proper entries, and copy the needed KEYB.COM, KEYBOARD.SYS, and COUNTRY.SYS files to the disk—preferably to the root directory of the disk.

For information about SELECT and the international country codes, see Chapter 15.

Notes

SELECT is a program that helps you set up DOS on a new disk. SELECT V3.3, which is different from earlier versions of SELECT, works with any disk, including fixed disks; SELECT V3.2 and earlier versions worked only with floppy diskettes.

SELECT V3.3 displays a warning that the program will format your disk, and then it asks for confirmation. Pressing Enter is the same as typing Y for yes. You can exit SELECT here if you answer N for no.

SELECT then runs the FORMAT /S command to format the disk and place the DOS system files on the disk. If a fixed disk is the destination, SELECT runs the FORMAT /S /V command to include placing a volume label on the fixed disk. You will see the normal FORMAT messages (including the message to insert the diskette in the correct disk drive or the warning you receive when you ask to format the fixed disk). If you are not absolutely sure whether you should be running SELECT, you can type the Ctrl-Break or Ctrl-C sequence to stop FORMAT and SELECT.

After FORMAT is complete, SELECT executes XCOPY to copy the remaining DOS files to the root directory of the disk, or, if directed, to an optional subdirectory. Included in the copying process are the COUNTRY.SYS, KEYBOARD.SYS, and KEYB.COM files, which are used for international language support.

SELECT then establishes a CONFIG.SYS file in the root directory with the single line

```
COUNTRY=countrycode
```

countrycode is the country code specified to the command.

SELECT then creates an AUTOEXEC.BAT file in the root directory of the disk with the following lines:

```
PATH \;\pathd
KEYB keycode codepage
ECHO OFF
DATE
TIME
VER
```

This batch file establishes the DOS PATH command, issues the appropriate KEYB command for international language use of the keyboard, turns ECHO off, and then issues the DATE, TIME, and VER commands. The last three commands direct DOS to go through the same start-up procedure as if an AUTOEXEC.BAT file did not exist; the commands ask for the date and time, and then display the DOS sign-on message.

In the PATH command line, `pathd` is the optional destination directory given to the SELECT command. If *pathd* is not given, the PATH is set to \. If a fixed disk is the destination disk, the disk drive name is inserted before each directory for the PATH. For example, if C: is the destination disk and the destination directory is BIN, the PATH command used in the AUTOEXEC.BAT file will be

```
PATH C:\;C:\BIN
```

If no destination directory was given, the PATH would be `C:\` SELECT would omit the second path specification in the PATH command.

Note that the SELECT command creates a KEYB command in the AUTOEXEC.BAT file and gives the **keycode** to KEYB. SELECT, however, translates the **keycode** and also gives the appropriate `codepage` (font file) for that keyboard code. Code pages are explained in the KEYB command section of the *Command Reference*.

Although SELECT does help in setting up a new disk, this command wipes out any useful information previously on the disk. Therefore, do *not* use SELECT on an established diskette or fixed disk!

If you create a diskette with SELECT, do not specify a path name for the destination if you use 360K or 720K diskettes. The additional space taken by the subdirectory would be better used for storing files. Also, running DOS from a subdirectory on a floppy-based system is less convenient.

Messages

1. Cannot execute A:program_name

   ERROR: SELECT could not find program_name on disk drive A. The file program_name may be FORMAT or XCOPY for DOS V3.2 and later, or DISKCOPY for DOS V3.1 and earlier, and DISKCOMP.COM for DOS V3.0. You most likely started SELECT without the DOS Startup or master diskette in drive A. Check the diskette in drive A and try again.

2. File creation error

   ERROR: SELECT could not create the CONFIG.SYS or AUTOEXEC.BAT file. This error usually occurs because the target disk (the disk created by SELECT) has a flaw. Run SELECT again. If the problem reoccurs, use a different blank diskette as the target.

3. Failure to access COUNTRY.SYS
   Failure to access KEYBOARD.SYS

   ERROR: SELECT could not open the COUNTRY.SYS file (first message) or the KEYBOARD.SYS file (second message) on the source diskette to verify the country or keyboard code. Either the wrong diskette is in the disk drive or you specified the wrong source disk drive. If you gave the wrong source disk drive, try the command again.

   If you believe the correct diskette is in the disk drive, issue a DIR command, and look for the COUNTRY.SYS and KEYBOARD.SYS files. If these files do not appear, you'll need a copy of your DOS Startup diskette. Put the correct diskette in the drive, and try the command again.

4. Incorrect number of parameters

   ERROR: You omitted the country code and/or the keyboard code, or you forgot to leave a space between the disk drive names, the country code, and the keyboard code. Be sure that the command line was phrased properly and that you have given both the country and keyboard code, and then try the command again.

5. Invalid country code
   Invalid keyboard code

ERROR: You have given an incorrect country or keyboard code. The only allowable country and keyboard codes are listed under the Syntax section. Check the command line and try again.

6. `Invalid drive specification`

ERROR: You have given a disk drive name that does not exist for the source or destination, used a disk drive name other than A: or B: for the source disk drive, omitted the source disk drive and named A: as the destination disk drive, or specified the same disk drive as the source and destination. Check the disk drive names and try the command again.

7. `Invalid parameter`

ERROR: You forgot to place a colon after the source or destination disk drive name. Check the command line and try the command again.

8. `Invalid path`

ERROR: The path you gave for the destination directory was misspelled, has incorrect characters, or was longer than 63 characters. Check the destination path name used, and try the command again.

9. `Invalid signature in COUNTRY.SYS file`
   `Invalid signature in KEYBOARD.SYS file`

ERROR: While verifying the country or keyboard information in the COUNTRY.SYS or KEYBOARD.SYS file, SELECT determined that the named file was incorrect. The COUNTRY.SYS or KEYBOARD.SYS file exists, but it has been damaged. The diskette holding the file or files is bad, the file has been altered, or another file has been copied over the COUNTRY.SYS or KEYBOARD.SYS file.

Get another copy of your original DOS Startup diskette. Attempt to copy the offending .SYS file over the invalid file. If no error occurs when you copy the file, try the SELECT command again. If an error occurs, reformat or retire the copy of your DOS Startup diskette, and run SELECT from either another copy of the Startup diskette or the original DOS Startup diskette. If the `invalid signature` message appears again, you probably have a bad copy of DOS. See you local dealer for a replacement.

10. `Read error, COUNTRY.SYS`
    `Read error, KEYBOARD.SYS`

    ERROR: While reading the COUNTRY.SYS or KEYBOARD.SYS file to verify country or keyboard information, SELECT encountered a disk error. The diskette holding the file is bad, or the floppy disk drive is bad.

    Get another copy of your original DOS Startup diskette. Attempt to copy the named .SYS file from the additional copy over the offending file. If no error message is given when you copy the file, try the SELECT command again. If an error message is given, reformat or retire the old copy of your DOS Startup diskette, and make another copy of the original Startup diskette. If you can make a copy of the original Startup diskette, the disk drive works correctly and you should try the SELECT command again with this copy. If DISKCOPY reports an error with the source diskette, the disk drive is probably bad.

11. `SELECT is used to install DOS the first`
    `time.  SELECT erases everything on the`
    `specified target and then installs DOS.`
    `Do you want to continue (Y/N)?`

    INFORMATION and WARNING: This message appears when you start SELECT. The message informs you that SELECT will format a disk and copy the needed files to the disk. Be sure that the DOS Startup diskette is in the correct disk drive. Answer **Y** if you want to continue; **N** if you do not want to continue.

12. `Unable to create directory`

    ERROR: SELECT has formatted the destination disk, but was unable to create the destination directory. The most probable reason is that the path name given for the destination directory contains invalid characters or is a reserved device name. Check the spelling of the destination path name, and try the command again.

SET
(Set/show environment)   *V2, V3—Internal*

Purpose   Sets or shows the system environment

Syntax   To display the environment, use

>   SET

To add to or alter the environment, use

>   SET name=*string*

name is the name of the string you want to add to the environment.

string is the information you want to store in the environment.

Special Terms   The *environment* is an area in RAM memory reserved for alphanumeric information that may be examined and used by DOS commands or user programs. For example, the environment usually contains COMSPEC, the location of COMMAND.COM; PATH, the additional paths for finding programs and batch files; and PROMPT, the string defining the DOS system prompt.

Exit Codes   None

Rules

1. If you do not specify a name or *string*, SET displays the current environment.

2. To set a string in the environment or to change the string associated with a current name, use SET name=string.

3. To delete a name, use SET name= (but don't give a *string*).

4. Any lowercase letters in name are changed to uppercase letters when they are placed in the environment. The characters in *string* are unchanged.

5. You can use SET to set the system prompt and the information for the PATH command, instead of using the PROMPT or PATH command.

6. You can use SET to change COMSPEC (the location of COMMAND.COM).

7. When a resident program (such as MODE, GRAPHICS, KEYB, or PRINT) is loaded, DOS cannot expand the environment past 127 characters. If you have not used 127 characters, you can add additional information up to that limit. If you already have used at least 127 characters, you cannot add additional information to the environment. If you need more space, use the SHELL command from CONFIG.SYS.

Notes

SET, a DOS command that has gained widespread use, puts information in a safe place in memory for later use by invoked programs. The most popular use is to store the directory path to data files or program overlays. When you invoke a program, it examines the RAM memory where the SET information is stored, and issues the proper commands to find the needed data or program overlays.

The versatile SET command can put into RAM almost any information for the environment. (Remember the Rule 7 restriction, however.)

For example, Brief, a text editor, uses SET to store information that ranges from the directory path for Brief's help files to the usual parameters you give when starting the editor. By placing the appropriate SET commands in the AUTOEXEC.BAT, almost no additional information must be given to Brief when the program is invoked. Brief searches the environment for the variables and automatically adapts itself.

Some programs use environmental variables, and some programs do not. Your application program's documentation should state what SET commands are required or optional for your programs. If you use these SET commands frequently, place them in your AUTOEXEC.BAT file so that they are invoked every time your computer is turned on. If you occasionally issue these SET commands, put them in a batch file in a directory on the DOS PATH. You can invoke the batch file to issue the needed SET commands just before you execute the program.

SHARE
(Check shared files)   *V3—External*

Purpose

Enables DOS support for file- and record-locking

Syntax

*dc:pathc***SHARE** */F:name_space /L:numlocks*

dc: is the name of the disk drive holding the command.

pathc is the path to the command.

Switches

/F:*name_space* Sets the amount of memory space (*name_space* bytes large) used for file sharing

/L:*numlocks* Sets the maximum number (*numlocks*) of file or record locks to use

---

Exit Codes

None

Rules

1. If you do not give the /F switch, *name_space* is set to 2,048 bytes. Each open file uses 11 bytes plus its full file specification (disk drive name, path name, and file name). The 2,048 bytes can contain 27 files that use all 63 characters available for the full file name.

2. If you do not give the /L switch, a default of 20 simultaneous file locks is allowed.

3. When SHARE is loaded, DOS checks each file for file and record locks during the opening, reading, and writing of the file.

4. SHARE should be loaded only one time after DOS has started. If you attempt to load SHARE again, DOS displays an error message.

5. SHARE usually increases the size of DOS by approximately 5,800 bytes. If the number of locks (/L switch) or memory space (/F switch) is increased or decreased, the size of DOS also increases or decreases proportionally.

6. The only way to remove SHARE is to restart DOS.

7. If you have not given the FCBS directive in your
CONFIG.SYS file, SHARE adjusts the file control block (FCB)
table as though the directive FCBS = 16,8 were given.

Notes

SHARE is the DOS V3 program for file- and record-locking.

You use SHARE when two or more programs or processes share a
single computer's files. After SHARE is loaded, DOS checks each file
for locks whenever it is opened, read, or written. If a file has been
opened for exclusive use, a second attempt to open the file produces
an error. If one program locks a portion of a file, another program
attempting to read, write, or read and write the locked portion
creates an error.

SHARE is most effective when all programs using the same file can
handle the DOS V3 functions for locking files and records. SHARE is
either partially or completely ineffective with programs that do not
use the file- and record-locking features of DOS.

SHARE affects two or more programs running on the same
computer—not two or more computers using the same file
(networked computers). File- and record-locking for two or more
computers using the same file is made possible by software provided
with the network.

Messages

1. Incorrect parameter

   ERROR: You gave a switch that SHARE does not recognize,
   or you put a space between the colon and the letter of the
   switch or between the switch and the number. Or you
   omitted either the number that goes with the switch or the
   colon.

2. SHARE already loaded

   ERROR: You attempted to load SHARE a second time. SHARE
   simply ignores any attempt to load itself more than one
   time.

SORT
(Sort string filter)

V2, V3*—External

Purpose	Reads lines from the standard input device, performs an ASCII sort of the lines, and then writes the lines to the standard output device. Sorting, which can be in ascending or descending order, can start at any column in the line.

Syntax

dc:pathc SORT */R /+c*

dc: is the name of the disk drive holding the command.

pathc is the path to the command.

Switches

/R   Sorts in *reverse* order. Thus, the letter Z comes first, and the letter A comes last.

/+c   Starts sorting with *column* number *c*

Exit Codes   None

Rules

1. If you do not give the */R* switch, the file is sorted in ascending order.

2. If you do not give the */+c* switch, sorting starts with the first column (on the first character on the line).

3. If you do not redirect the input or output, all input is from the keyboard (standard input), and all output is to the video display (standard output). If you redirect input and output, use different names for the input and output files.

4. SORT uses the ASCII sequence, with the following exceptions:

    a. Control characters (including the tab character) are not expanded.

    b. Lowercase characters are treated as uppercase characters.

c. Some characters in the ASCII range of 128 to 225 are collated by the rules for the current setting of the COUNTRY command.

5. The maximum file size that SORT can handle is 63K (64,512 characters).

6. SORT sorts text files and discards any information after and including the end-of-file marker.

7. For the /+c switch, the plus sign is mandatory. c should be a positive integer.

Examples

1. **SORT <WORDS.TXT**

   SORT sorts the lines in the file WORDS.TXT and displays the sorted lines on the video screen.

2. **SORT <WORDS.TXT /R**

   SORT sorts in reverse order the lines in the file WORDS.TXT and displays the lines on the video screen.

3. **SORT /+8 <WORDS.TXT**

   SORT starts sorting at the eighth character in each line of WORDS.TXT and displays the output on the video display.

4. **DIR | SORT /+14**

   SORT displays the directory information sorted by file size. (The file size starts in the 14th column.) Unfortunately, other lines, such as the volume label, are also sorted starting at the 14th column (see "Notes").

Notes

SORT, a "semi-intelligent," general-purpose sorting program, was changed significantly after DOS V2 and again in DOS V3.3. SORT V3.3 is a powerful filter but does have some limitations.

SORT uses the ASCII sequence, with some exceptions. On the ASCII chart in Appendix C, note the relative positions of the numbers, punctuation marks, and letters. One limitation of SORT stems from this chart.

SORT treats numbers as characters. Therefore, 1 always comes before 2, 3, or 9; 0 comes before 1. The problem is that 11, 123, and 12576 all come before 2, 3, 21, or any other number that does not begin with 0 or 1. This limitation does not affect numbers stored in strings that are left-padded with spaces (right-justified). The numbers " 1", " 121", and "1915" (actually character strings) are sorted in the proper order. Therefore, example 4, which sorts a directory by file size, works because the file size is stored as a left-padded ASCII character string.

The Ctrl-I (tab character) presents another problem. When you print Ctrl-I on the screen or printer, the printer moves out to the next tab column—usually every eighth character position. Because SORT does not expand tab characters, the output may not be what you expect. Some text editors (IBM's Personal Editor, for example) compress extra spaces into tab characters. When you sort a file created by the Personal Editor, some lines appear to be out of order. Loading and resaving the file without tab characters (which the Personal Editor allows) produces the correct order when you re-sort the file.

SORT V3 handles alphabetic characters intelligently by treating upper- and lowercase characters as the same. SORT V2 treats these characters differently. Notice that for ASCII characters the uppercase A comes before the uppercase Z, but the lowercase *a* comes after the uppercase Z. SORT V2 puts the word *TEXT* before the words *text*, *TEXt*, and *TeXT*. SORT V3 treats all four of these words alike. SORT V3's "intelligent" method is preferred for sorting most files.

SORT V3 is intelligent also in sorting certain ASCII characters in the 128-to-225 range, which includes foreign-language characters and symbols. SORT V3 can handle most files containing text in languages other than American English. The specific sorting order depends on the COUNTRY setting in CONFIG.SYS.

Problems can occur when you try to sort the output from some text processors and data files created by certain programming languages, or when you use DOS's I/O redirection. Some text-processing programs and DOS itself end the last sector of a file with the ASCII character null (00 hexadecimal). These null characters bubble to the top when SORT sorts a file. You see an ^@ when you edit these files with programs such as WordStar. Fortunately, you can delete these characters with your text editor or word processor and not lose information.

Some languages store their data in a special compressed format. The data is stored not as ASCII text but as compressed codes, some of which may be control characters. When you issue the TYPE command for this kind of data file, garbage appears on-screen. This kind of file should not be sorted with SORT because it does not have the intelligence to handle these files, and results are unpredictable.

SORT V2 has a serious problem that has been cured in SORT V3. SORT V2 sorts Ctrl-Z, the control character used as the end-of-file marker. The SORT V2 output file can trap lines behind the end-of-file marker. These trapped lines cannot be retrieved by most word processors. Because SORT V3 stops when it encounters the end-of-file marker, it doesn't have this problem.

For these reasons, SORT is a semi-intelligent sorting program that correctly handles upper- and lowercase letters, foreign language letters and symbols, and the end-of-file marker. SORT does not handle all numeric information or compressed information, but "outside" programs that can solve this problem are available from third-party vendors.

SORT, which is provided free with DOS, is useful for standard sorting. The program is best used in the "pipeline" with other commands, such as DIR, or for sorting simple lines of text.

Messages

1. `Invalid parameter`

   ERROR: You entered a switch that SORT does not recognize, forgot the plus sign for the column-sorting switch, or forgot to enter the number for the column-sorting switch. Check the command line and try again.

2. `SORT: Insufficient disk space`

   ERROR: SORT ran out of disk space for its temporary files or ran out of disk space when it wrote the output file. Free some disk space by deleting unneeded files, or move the file to a disk that has more space. Try the command again.

   If you believe you have sufficient room on the disk, run CHKDSK to see whether a problem exists on the disk. If CHKDSK detects a problem, follow the directions for CHKDSK in the *Command Reference*.

3. `SORT: Insufficient memory`

   ERROR: You do not have enough free memory to run SORT on this file. See the entry `Insufficient memory` under "General Messages" at the beginning of the *Command Reference*.

SUBST
(Substitute path name)   *V3.1 and later—External*

Purpose

Creates an alias disk drive name for a subdirectory; used principally with programs that do not use path names

Syntax

To establish an alias, use

  *dc:pathc*SUBST **d1:** d2:pathname

To delete an alias, use

  *dc:pathc*SUBST **d1:** /D

To see the current aliases, use

  *dc:pathc*SUBST

dc: is the name of the disk drive holding the command.

pathc is the path to the command.

d1: is a valid disk drive name that becomes the alias (or nickname). **d1:** may be a nonexistent disk drive.

d2:pathname is the valid disk drive name and directory path that will be nicknamed **d1:**.

Switch

  /D   *Disconnects* the alias

Rules

1. To display the current aliases, use SUBST without any disk drive name, directory name, or switch.

2. If you do not display the current aliases, you must specify **d1:**, the alias or nickname for the path. The alias must not be the current disk drive or a networked disk drive.

3. If you have not used the LASTDRIVE directive in the CONFIG.SYS file, the alias can be any drive name up to and including the letter E. If you have used LASTDRIVE, the alias can be any drive name up to and including the LASTDRIVE you specified.

4. **d2:** must be an existing disk drive but not a networked disk drive or the same disk drive as **d1:**.

5. **pathname** must be a valid directory path on drive **d2:**. If you do not start **pathname** with the \ (for starting at the root directory), the directory used is the current directory plus the specified **pathname**. (See "Notes" for further details.)

6. While SUBST is in effect, you can access **d2:pathname** by either its real name or its alias.

7. While SUBST for disk drives is in effect, take the following precautions:

   a. Exercise care when you use PATH (the PATH command), MKDIR (make directory), and RMDIR (remove subdirectory) on the substituted drive. The path and subdirectories you make or remove are physically on **d2:pathname**.

   b. Do not use the ASSIGN, BACKUP, DISKCOPY, DISKCOMP, FDISK, FORMAT, JOIN, LABEL, and RESTORE commands on a substituted disk drive.

   c. Do not use CHKDSK with the alias disk drive name.

Examples

For these examples, assume that the command LASTDRIVE=F is given in the CONFIG.SYS file, that the current directory is C:\WORDS, and that the following directory tree is on drive C:

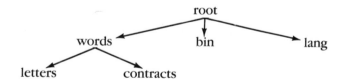

a. **SUBST E: C:\BIN**

When you use disk drive name E, the directory C:\BIN is actually used.

b. **SUBST F: C:LETTERS**

Drive F is substituted for the directory
C:\WORDS\LETTERS. Because the current directory of
drive C was \WORDS, DOS found LETTERS as the
subdirectory of WORDS. DOS adds \WORDS\ to the alias.

c. **SUBST**

This command shows the current aliases. SUBST displays

```
E: => C:\BIN
F: => C:\WORDS\LETTERS
```

d. **SUBST F: /D**

The alias **F:** is deleted. Afterward, the use of **F:** produces
an error message from DOS.

Notes

SUBST is one of the three "disk trickery" commands of DOS V3.1 and
later. ASSIGN and JOIN are the other two commands.

SUBST lets you use a disk drive name in place of a disk drive name
and directory path name. SUBST also lets you use files in
subdirectories with programs that do not recognize path names, such
as programs written for DOS V1.

If you need several SUBST commands, use the LASTDRIVE command
in your CONFIG.SYS file. Without this command, the normal
LASTDRIVE is E:. For more information, refer to Chapter 14 about
customizing DOS.

While SUBST is in effect, certain DOS commands should be used
with caution, some commands should be avoided whenever possible,
and some commands should not be used at all:

1. Using MKDIR (make subdirectory) and RMDIR (remove
   subdirectory) on the alias disk actually makes or removes
   subdirectories from subdirectory **dirname**.

2. CHKDSK works only on the real disk drive name and path
   name. If you attempt to use CHKDSK with the alias disk
   drive name, CHKDSK displays an error message and aborts.

3. Be cautious with APPEND and PATH. If you use substituted
   drive names with these commands, and then "disconnect"
   the disk drive, DOS no longer will be capable of
   automatically finding the files that were on the disconnected
   disk drive.

4. Avoid using ASSIGN and JOIN. These commands work on the alias disk drive and simply increase DOS's confusion level. You can encounter difficulty in determining which physical disk drive DOS will use when ASSIGN, SUBST, and JOIN are used on the same disk drives.

5. Avoid using LABEL on the alias disk drive name. Using LABEL on this drive name actually alters the LABEL of the physical disk drive being used. If drive E is really C:\WORDS, issuing **LABEL E:** affects the volume label of C: and not the pseudodisk drive E.

6. Don't use BACKUP, DISKCOPY, DISKCOMP, FDISK, FORMAT, or RESTORE with the substituted disk drive name. These commands become confused and attempt, respectively, to back up, copy, compare, format, change, or restore a nonexistent drive.

Some of these commands display error messages; others give less obvious error warnings. The most common message is

    Drive d: not ready

in which d: is the alias name. Before using these commands, break the substitution.

Messages

1. Cannot SUBST a network drive

ERROR: You have attempted to use as the alias or nicknamed disk drive a disk drive owned by another computer. You cannot use a networked disk drive with SUBST, nor can you "cover" a network disk drive with a SUBST command.

2. Invalid parameter

ERROR: One of the following errors occurred: (1) the alias disk drive name exceeded the limit set by the LASTDRIVE command, (2) the alias disk drive name is the same as the current disk drive name, (3) you did not give a correct disk drive with the /D (disconnect) switch, (4) you specified a switch that SUBST doesn't recognize, or (5) you used the /D switch on the current disk drive.

3. Invalid path

ERROR: The directory path you specified does not exist. Make sure that the disk drive name is correct and that the path name does exist.

4. Incorrect number of parameters

ERROR: You omitted a parameter when you issued the command. Perhaps you forgot to give the alias or the disk drive name and path name, or you omitted the /D switch. Check the command line and try again.

SYS

*(Place the operating system
on the disk)*   *V1, V2, V3—External*

Purpose   Places a copy of DOS on the specified diskette or fixed disk

---

Syntax   *dc:pathc*SYS **d:**

dc: is the name of the disk drive holding the command.

pathc is the path to the command.

d: is the disk drive to receive the copy of DOS.

Exit Codes   None

Rules

1. You must specify the name of the disk drive that will receive a copy of DOS.

2. The disk to receive the copy of DOS must conform to one of the following conditions:

   a. Formatted with the */S* option (DOS V1, V2, or V3)

   b. Formatted with the */B* option (DOS V2 or V3)

   c. Formatted but completely empty

   d. Formatted with a special program (non-IBM supplied) that reserves the proper disk space for the operating system

   If you attempt to put the system on a disk that does not meet one of these conditions, a No room for system on destination disk message appears, and DOS does not perform the operation.

3. A copy of DOS (the IBMBIO.COM and IBMDOS.COM files) should reside on the current disk. Otherwise, you are asked to insert in the floppy disk drive a diskette that has these files.

4. You cannot use SYS on a networked disk drive.

Notes

The SYS command places a copy of IBMBIO.COM and IBMDOS.COM on the targeted disk. To make the disk bootable (able to load and execute the disk operating system), you must also copy COMMAND.COM.

To update a startup disk that held a previous version of DOS, start the newer version of DOS, and then run the SYS command on the disk. To make the disk startable, you must also copy COMMAND.COM to the disk on which you run SYS. SYS does not copy COMMAND.COM.

The SYS command puts DOS on applications-program diskettes sold without DOS. With these diskettes, you can boot the computer system by using the applications software. A diskette provided by the program publisher must be specially formatted, however, or SYS will not work. You should check the instructions that come with the applications program to see whether you can put the system on the diskette.

SYS V1 and SYS for DOS V2 and V3 have few differences. SYS V2 and V3 check the destination disk to see whether the proper space is available for DOS. If space isn't available, an error message is displayed. SYS V1 places DOS on the diskette, regardless of whether the proper space is available. Running SYS V1 on a diskette with existing files can turn to garbage some files on that diskette.

When you first load DOS into the computer, the first two entries in the root directory of the boot disk must be IBMBIO.COM and IBMDOS.COM (even though these are system files hidden from the DIR command). IBMBIO.COM must reside on consecutive sectors. If either of these two conditions is not met, DOS does not load properly from the disk.

Messages

1. Cannot SYS to a Network drive

   ERROR: You cannot put the system on a networked disk drive. If the disk drive is owned by another computer, use a different disk drive. If your disk drive is being shared, "pause" the disk drive, perform the command, and then continue.

2. Incompatible system size

   ERROR: Although the diskette or fixed disk previously held IBMBIO.COM and IBMDOS.COM, DOS cannot put the new version of the files on the diskette. These two files are larger in DOS V3 than in DOS V2 or V1. This message usually appears when you put the system files on DOS V1 diskettes. The message occasionally is displayed when you place the two files on a DOS V2 diskette.

Format a new diskette with the /S (system) switch, and copy files from the old diskette to the new diskette. Be sure that you don't copy the old COMMAND.COM file.

3. Invalid drive specification

ERROR: You gave a disk drive name that does not exist. Be sure that the disk drive does exist (is not part of an SUBST command) and that you gave the correct disk drive letter.

4. Invalid parameter

ERROR: You failed to specify the name of the disk drive to hold the system files.

5. No room for system on destination disk

ERROR: The diskette or fixed disk was not formatted with the necessary reserved space for DOS. You cannot put the system on this diskette.

6. No system on default disk drive
   Insert system disk in drive d:
   and strike any key when ready

INFORMATION: DOS tried to load itself into memory but could not find IBMBIO.COM, IBMDOS.COM, and/or COMMAND.COM. Loading these files into memory is a required step before SYS can place the operating system on a diskette or fixed disk. Put the diskette that holds all three programs into drive d and press a key.

7. System transferred

INFORMATION: DOS successfully placed IBMBIO.COM and IBMDOS.COM on the target diskette.

TIME
(Set/show the time)

V1.0—External
V1.1, V2, V3—Internal

Purpose   Sets and shows the system time

Syntax   TIME *hh:mm:ss.xx*

hh is the one- or two-digit number for hours (0 to 23).

mm is the one- or two-digit number for minutes (0 to 59).

ss is the one- or two-digit number for seconds
(0 to 59).

xx is the one- or two-digit number for hundredths of a second
(0 to 99).

Note: Depending on the setting of the country code in your
CONFIG.SYS file, a comma may be the decimal separator between
seconds and hundredths of seconds.

Exit Codes   None

Rules

1. If you enter a valid time, the time is accepted, and no other
   message appears.

2. If you do not enter the time with the TIME command, the
   following message appears:

   ```
   Current time is hh:mm:ss.xx
   Enter new time
   ```

   If you press Enter, the time is not reset. If you enter a valid
   time, the new time is accepted immediately, and no other
   message is displayed.

3. You must enter the correct delimiters between the numbers,
   as shown under "Syntax" (colons between the hours,
   minutes, and seconds; a period or comma between the
   seconds and the hundredths of a second). You must use the
   correct decimal separator, as shown by the TIME command.

The United States and similar countries use only the period. Certain other countries use only the comma.

4. You do not have to enter all the information. If you change only the first parts of the time, the remaining portions are set to 0.

5. If you specify an invalid time or incorrect delimiters, an Invalid time message is displayed, and you are prompted to enter the time again.

Notes

TIME is used for setting your computer's internal, 24-hour clock. The time and date are recorded in the directory for each file whenever you create or change it. This directory information can help you locate the most recent version of a file.

The clock used by the Personal Computer sold in the United States is a software clock based on the 60 Hz power supply. The time, therefore, usually loses or gains several seconds each day. This inaccuracy is not a fault of the computer but a minor (and normal) problem with the AC power provided by your power company.

If you do not enter the time when you start most PCs, the time defaults to 00:00:00.00. For your system to use the correct time, you must enter it.

The Personal System/2 and Personal Computer AT retain the time through a battery-backed circuit. When you start either computer, the real-time clock is read and displayed. This clock usually is accurate to within one minute every month—or about the same accuracy as a digital watch. After you boot DOS, it uses the software time clock, which suffers from the same inaccuracies as the PC clock.

Message

Invalid time

ERROR: You entered a nonsense time or did not punctuate the time correctly. Check your typing and try again.

TREE
(Display all directories)   *V2, V3—External*

Purpose
Displays all the subdirectories on a disk and optionally displays all the files in each directory

Syntax
dc:pathc **TREE** *d:* */F*

dc: is the name of the disk drive holding the command.

pathc is the path to the command.

d: is the name of the disk drive holding the disk you want to examine.

Switch
/F   Displays all *files* in the directories

Rules
1. If you do not give a disk drive name, the current disk drive is used.

2. All directories, starting with the root directory, are displayed with their full path names. If you use the */F* switch, every file in the directory (with the exception of the . and .. entries) is listed with its full path name.

Notes
The TREE command displays all directories on a DOS V3 disk so that you do not have to enter every directory, run a DIR command, and search for every <DIR> file (subdirectory). The */F* option also displays the name of every file in every directory.

TREE shows one directory or file name on a line and can quickly scroll off the screen. If you want a copy of the entire tree, redirect the output to the printer by typing

    TREE >PRN

or

    TREE /F >PRN

TREE's disadvantage is that the file's date, time, and size are not displayed. You must run DIR to get this information.

Hint

After you finish backing up your fixed disk, periodically use the TREE command to make a printed copy of the directories by typing

TREE d: /F >PRN

in which d: is the name of the fixed disk drive. Store the printed copy with the backup diskettes. You then can quickly locate the files you have backed up. (*Note:* This is an alternative to BACKUP 3.3's LOG.)

Messages

1. Invalid drive specification

   ERROR: You gave the name of a nonexistent disk drive. Be sure that the disk drive does exist (is not part of a SUBST command) and that the drive letter is correct.

2. Invalid path

   ERROR: TREE cannot use a subdirectory because something is wrong with the directory file. Run CHKDSK without the /F switch to determine the problem in the disk or diskette and then take the necessary corrective actions.

3. Invalid parameter

   ERROR: You entered a switch that TREE does not recognize or you omitted a colon from the disk drive name.

4. No sub-directories exist

   INFORMATION: The root directory of the disk you specified has no subdirectories. If you know that the disk should have subdirectories, issue DIR for the diskette or disk, or run CHKDSK.

TYPE
(Type file on screen)   *V1, V2, V3—Internal*

Purpose   Displays the contents of the file on the screen

Syntax   TYPE *d:path***filename**.*ext*

d: is the name of the disk drive holding the file to TYPE.

path\ is the DOS path to the file.

filename.*ext* is the name of the file to TYPE. Wildcards are not allowed.

Exit Codes   None

Rules

1. If you do not give a disk drive name, the current disk drive is used.

2. If you do not give a path name, the current directory is used.

3. You must provide a file name that matches the name in the directory.

4. All characters in the file, including control characters, are sent to the screen. However, tab characters Ctrl-I and CHR$(9) are expanded to the next eight-character boundary.

5. You cannot use TYPE on a directory.

Notes

The TYPE command displays on your video screen the characters in a file so that you can see what it contains.

You will see strange characters on the screen if you try to use TYPE on some data files and most program files, because TYPE tries to display the machine-language instructions as ASCII characters.

The output of TYPE, like most other DOS commands, can be redirected to the printer by adding >**PRN** to the command line or by pressing Ctrl-PrtSc. (Don't forget to press Ctrl-PrtSc again to turn off the printing.)

Unpredictable things can happen if you also print when you issue TYPE on a program file or a data file that has control characters. As a rule, if the material that appears on-screen looks like nonsense, the data will look like nonsense—or worse—on your printout.

VER
(Display version number)   *V2, V3—Internal*

Purpose   Shows the DOS version number on the video display

Syntax   VER

Exit Codes   None

Rules   None

Notes   The VER command shows the one-digit version number, followed by a two-digit revision number. You can determine which DOS version (V2.0 through V3.3 or later) the computer is using. If you type

   VER

you see a message similar to this one:

   IBM Personal Computer DOS Version 3.30

If you see a Bad command or file name message, you are working with DOS V1.

VERIFY
(Set/show disk verification)   *V2, V3—Internal*

Purpose   Sets your computer to check the accuracy of data written to a disk
to ensure that information is recorded properly; shows whether the
data has been checked

Syntax   To show the verify status, use

   VERIFY

To set the verify status, use

   VERIFY ON

or

   VERIFY OFF

Rules   1. VERIFY accepts only one of two parameters: ON or OFF.

   2. After VERIFY is ON, it remains on until

      a. A VERIFY OFF is issued

      b. A SET VERIFY system call turns off the command

      c. DOS is restarted

Notes   VERIFY controls the checking of data just written on a disk to ensure
that the data has been recorded correctly. If VERIFY is off, DOS does
not check the data; if VERIFY is on, DOS checks the data. VERIFY
does not affect any other DOS operation.

Two factors affect the tradeoff between VERIFY ON and VERIFY OFF.
If VERIFY is on, data integrity is ensured. If VERIFY is off, you can
write to the disk faster. You usually are safe to leave VERIFY off if
you are not working with critical information (such as a company's
accounting figures). You are wise to turn on VERIFY when you back
up your fixed disk or make important copies on the diskettes.

The degree of performance lost in verifying is different for the fixed disk and for diskettes. On average, DOS takes 68 percent more time to verify information written on a fixed disk. This percentage is radically different for DOS V2, which takes only 8 to 9 percent more time. On average, DOS V3 takes 100 percent more time to verify information written to a diskette; DOS V2 takes about 90 percent.

This difference between verify times for floppy and fixed disks occurs partly because most fixed disks have built-in routines for data verification. As a result, fixed disks verify information at a faster rate than do floppy disks. In addition, DOS must do all the work itself when it verifies information written to the floppy disk. These factors explain the 32 percent difference in verification speed between the floppy and the fixed disks.

The sevenfold increase in fixed-disk verification time between DOS V2 and DOS V3 reflects DOS V3's more thorough verification. DOS V2 does not extensively examine the information written to a fixed disk; DOS V3 does and therefore takes more time.

Message   `Must specify ON or OFF`

ERROR: You entered a word other than ON or OFF after the VERIFY command.

VOL
(Display volume label)   *V2, V3—Internal*

Purpose   Displays the volume label of the disk, if the label exists

Syntax   VOL *d:*

d: is the name of the disk drive whose label you want to display.

Rule   If you do not give a disk drive name, the current disk drive is used.

Messages   1. Invalid drive specification

ERROR: You have given a nonexistent disk drive name. Be sure that the disk drive exists (is not part of a SUBST command) and that you have given the correct disk drive name.

2. Volume in drive d has no label

INFORMATION: The fixed disk or diskette does not have a volume label.

XCOPY
(Extended COPY)   *V3.2 and later—External*

Purpose   Selectively copies files from one or more subdirectories

---

Syntax   *dc:pathc\\XCOPY ds:paths\\filenames.exts dd:pathd\\filenamed.extd*
                   /A /D /E /M /P /S /V /W

dc: is the name of the disk drive holding the command.

pathc is the path to the command.

ds: is the disk drive holding the files to be copied (the *source*).

paths is the starting directory path to the files to be copied.

filenames.exts is the name of the file(s) to be copied. Wildcards are allowed.

dd: is the disk drive that will receive the copied files (the *destination* files) which is called the *target* by DOS.

pathd is the starting directory that will receive the copied files.

filenamed.extd is the new name of the files that are copied. Wildcards are allowed.

Switches

/A	Copies files whose *archive* flag is on but does not turn off the archive flag (similar to the /M switch)
/E	Creates parallel subdirectories on the destination disk even if the created subdirectory is *empty*
/D:date	Copies files that were changed or created on or after the specified *date*. The form of *date* depends on the setting of the COUNRTY directive in CONFIG.SYS and can be

mm-dd-yy	North America
dd-mm-yy	Europe
yy-mm-dd	East Asia

where *mm* is the month (1 through 12)
      dd is the day (1 through 31)
      yy is the year (00 through 99)

	The character separating the parts of the *date* depends on the setting of the COUNTRY command: the hyphen, period, and slash. North American users can substitute a slash (/) for the hyphen (-). Do not put spaces between the */D:* and the date.
/M	Copies files whose archive flag is on (*modified* files) and turns the archive flag off (similar to the /A switch)
/P	Causes XCOPY to *prompt* and ask whether a file should be copied
/S	Copies files from this directory and all subsequent *subdirectories*
/V	*Verifies* that the copy has been recorded correctly
/W	Causes XCOPY to prompt and *wait* for the correct source diskette to be inserted.

Exit Codes   None

Rules

1. The source name comes first followed by the destination name.

2. You cannot use a device name for the source or destination name.

3. The source file specification (*ds:paths\filenames.exts*) must have one or both of the following:

   a. A valid file name. Wildcards are permitted.

   b. A drive name, a path name, or both

4. If you do not give a drive name for the source (*ds:*), the current drive is used.

5. If you do not give a path for the source (*paths*), the current directory for the disk drive is used.

6. If you do not specify a source file name (*filenames.exts*) but specify a disk drive or path for the source, DOS assumes *.*.

7. For the destination file specification, the following rules apply:

   a. If you do not give a disk drive name (*dd:*), the current disk is used.

   b. If you do not give a path name (*pathd*), the current directory of the disk is used.

   c. If you do not give a file name (*filenamed.extd*), the copied file(s) has the same name as the source file (*filenames.exts*).

   d. If a file name is given for the destination, the copied files use the new name. Wildcards are allowed.

8. If you do not give the destination file specification, the source file specification must have either or both of the following:

   a. A disk drive name (*ds:*) that is different from the current disk drive

   b. A path name (*paths*) that is different from the current directory of the current disk

9. The source disk should not be involved in an APPEND /X command. If the source disk is part of an APPEND command, disconnect the command by using APPEND; before you use XCOPY.

Examples

The examples use the model hierarchical directory in Appendix B.

1. **XCOPY C:*.* A:**

   This command copies all files from the root directory of C: to the current directory of A:. In this example, XCOPY and COPY work identically.

2. **XCOPY C:*.* A: /P**

   This command is identical to example 1, except the /P switch is used to confirm each file individually before it is copied. With /P, you can select which files will be copied.

3. **XCOPY C:\WORDS A:\ /S**

   This command copies to the root directory of A: all files starting with the C:\WORDS subdirectory, and then the command copies files from subsequent subdirectories (the /S switch) of C:\WORDS to parallel subdirectories of A:. XCOPY creates the needed subdirectories on A:. The resulting directory structure of A: is

   root

       WS.EXE
       WSINDEX.XCL
       WSMSGS.OVR
       WSPRINT.OVR
       WSSHORT.OVR
       WSSPELL.OVR

       LETTERS
         IBM.BAK
         IBM.LET
         JACK.BAK
         JACK.LET
         DOUG.LET

       CONTRACT
         MEYER.TXT
         ANDERSON.TXT

4. **XCOPY C:\WORDS A:\ /S /M**

   This command is identical to example 3, except only files in C:\WORDS and subsequent subdirectories with the archive flag on are copied. If all files in these directories have their archive flags on, all files are copied. If the files in only the LETTERS subdirectory have their archive flags on, only those files are copied. The subsequent structure of A: is

   root

       LETTERS
         IBM.BAK
         IBM.LET
         JACK.BAK
         JACK.LET
         DOUG.LET

Notice that XCOPY creates the LETTERS subdirectory on A: and copies the needed files. Because CONTRACT does not contain any files to be copied, this subdirectory is not created.

The /M switch, in addition to copying modified files, clears the archive flag. If the same command is issued again, the XCOPYed files are not selected until the files are modified again.

5. **XCOPY C:\WORDS A:\ /S /M /E**

This command copies the same files as in example 4 but it creates parallel empty subdirectories on A:\ (the /E switch). The resulting directory structure is

root

    LETTERS
      IBM.BAK
      IBM.LET
      JACK.BAK
      JACK.LET
      DOUG.LET

    CONTRACT

Although no files are copied to the CONTRACT subdirectory, the directory is created because the /E switch is used.

6. **XCOPY C:\WORDS A:\ /S /A**

This command is identical to example 4, except the archive flag of the copied files is not changed. If the same command is given a second time, the same files are copied because the archive flags on the same files are still on.

7. **XCOPY C:\WORDS A:\ /S /D:10-25-87**

This command copies all files in the directory C:\WORDS and its subdirectories that have been created or changed on or after October 25, 1987. The /D switch of XCOPY is identical to the /D switch of BACKUP.

8. **XCOPY A:*.* C:\WORDS /W**

This command copies all files from the root directory of A: to the directory C:\WORDS. XCOPY prompts you to press any key before it begins the search for source file names. This prompt has the same effect as the /W switch. You can change diskettes before you press the key.

Notes

XCOPY is the extended COPY command. Although XCOPY runs more slowly than COPY, XCOPY offers more features and greater versatility than COPY. With XCOPY you control what files are copied (selecting by archive attribute or the file's directory date and individually confirming the files one at a time), and you can copy through more than one directory. The command is most useful when you try to keep files between two computers in-sync (two systems with fixed disks or a "base" station and a laptop) or as an alternative to the DOS BACKUP command.

With the /P (*prompt*) switch, you can use a file name that "covers" too many files and then reduce the actual files copied by answering **Y** for yes or **N** for no when you are asked whether each file should be copied. The /P command means that you can issue one XCOPY command to copy selected files rather than having to issue several COPY commands.

The /A and /M switches are similar. Both switches cause XCOPY to select files that match source file names and have their archive attribute set. The archive attribute is set by DOS every time you modify or create a file. The switches can be used as a minibackup command, or in conjunction with the BACKUP command.

The two switches take different actions, however, after the file has been copied. /M clears the archive attribute after the file has been copied. /A does not clear the archive flag. Using /M on a file means that your backup procedure can be fooled. If you use XCOPY /M on a set of files and do not change the files before the next time you use BACKUP /M, BACKUP does not back up the copied files. Your only backup copies are on the diskette created by XCOPY. If you lose the diskette, you have lost the only current backup of your file. For this reason, use /M with caution.

You can force XCOPY to copy files whose archive attribute has not been set by using the ATTRIB +A command. ATTRIB sets the archive flag on files. By issuing the command

ATTRIB +A filename

you turn on the archive flag. If you plan to copy files from more than one subdirectory, add the /S switch to the ATTRIB command to force the archive attribute on files in subsequent directories.

If the space occupied by the files you will XCOPY is more than the destination disk has available, first ensure that the files you want to copy have their archive attribute on. You can use the ATTRIB command for this action. Then use the XCOPY command with the /M or /M /S switches repeatedly.

When the destination diskette fills up, XCOPY pronounces the destination full and stops. Change diskettes, and issue the XCOPY command again. The files that have been copied have their archive attribute off, and XCOPY skips these files. XCOPY copies the files that have not yet been copied.

Use this technique with some caution if you use the BACKUP /M switch. Unless you set the archive attribute on again, BACKUP /M skips these files.

The /D switch can be used to copy files based on their directory dates. I find that this switch is more useful in copying recently created or changed files. The archive attribute is unchanged, which means that BACKUP /M backs up the right files.

XCOPY is noticeably different from COPY and BACKUP. XCOPY cannot handle nondisk devices. To copy a file between serial ports or to the console, use COPY—not XCOPY. XCOPY cannot copy files that do not fit on one diskette. When the destination disk fills, XCOPY stops. To copy a file that is larger than a diskette, use BACKUP instead.

The /W switch works when you want to change the source disk. XCOPY displays this message:

```
Press any key to begin copying file(s)
```

This messages indicates your opportunity to change diskettes. Because fixed disks cannot be changed, using the /W switch when you copy from the fixed disk is of doubtful value. Also, the switch does not affect copying to the destination disk. The proper destination disk must be in the drive before you start XCOPY.

XCOPY and APPEND /X are an insidious combination. XCOPY, which uses the DOS directory search functions, can be tricked by APPEND /X. XCOPY either copies more files than you want or it does not copy the correct files. If you need to use XCOPY on a disk involved in an APPEND command, first disconnect APPEND.

XCOPY is not as fast as COPY, so if you don't need the features of XCOPY, use COPY.

Messages

1. Access denied

   ERROR: You attempted to copy over a file marked as read-only, the destination file is being used by another program or computer and is temporarily marked as read-only, or the source and destination files are the same.

   If the file you intend to copy over has the read-only attribute set, use the ATTRIB command to turn off the read-only flag. If this file is being used by another program or computer, wait until the other program or computer is done, and then copy the file. If the file is on another computer and you do not have permission to copy over the file, ask the operator to copy the file for you. Check the command line to make sure that the source and destination file specifications are not identical.

2. Cannot perform a cyclic copy

   ERROR: You have used the /S switch, and one or more of the destination directories are subdirectories of the source directories. Using the files in Appendix B, the command

   XCOPY C:\BIN C:\BIN\HARDDISK /S

   would cause this error message to appear. BIN and its subsequent subdirectories are the source. HARDDISK is a subdirectory of BIN. When the /S switch is given, XCOPY will not copy to destination directories that are part of the source directories. If you must copy files from more than one directory, issue individual XCOPY commands to copy the directories one at a time.

3. Cannot XCOPY from a reserved device
   Cannot XCOPY to a reserved device

   ERROR: The source or destination file name is a device name. XCOPY cannot copy to or from devices. You may have misspelled one of the file names.

4. Does %s specify a file name
   or directory name on the target
   (F = file, D = directory)?

INFORMATION: You have given a destination file name in which the final name does not exist as a directory. XCOPY does not know whether the final name in the destination is a file name or a directory.

If the destination name is a directory, answer **D** for directory. XCOPY creates the needed directory and begins copying files to it. If the destination name is a file name, XCOPY copies files to this file.

5. `File cannot be copied onto itself`

ERROR: You attempted to copy a file back to the same disk and directory with the same file name. This message usually is displayed after you misspell or omit parts of the source or destination drive, path, or file name. Check your spelling and the source and destination names, and try the command again.

6. `File creation error`

ERROR: XCOPY cannot create the copy of the file. Either a file exists in the destination disk and directory by the same name and is marked read-only or the directory is full.

See whether a file by the same name exists and whether it is read-only (use **ATTRIB filename**). If the file is marked read-only, either clear the flag using ATTRIB or give the source file a new name when you COPY or XCOPY.

If you copy to the root directory of the disk, the root directory may not be able to hold additional entries. Delete or move (copy and then erase) files from the root directory and try the command again. If you copy to a subdirectory, run CHKDSK without the /F switch to determine whether the subdirectory has a problem.

7. `filename File not found`

ERROR: XCOPY cannot find any files that match the source file name, `filename`. Either you gave a directory name or file that does not exist or you mistyped a name.

Check to see which files are transferred already. Determine whether the directory and file names are spelled correctly and whether the path is correct. Then try again.

8. nnn File(s) copied

INFORMATION: XCOPY has copied nnn files to the destination disk. This message appears regardless of any errors that may have occurred.

9. Insufficient disk space

ERROR: XCOPY has run out of room on the destination disk. The file being copied when the error is encountered is erased from the destination. Either delete any unneeded files from the destination disk or use a different diskette and try the command again.

10. Invalid date

ERROR: You have given an improperly phrased or nonsense date.

11. Invalid drive specification

ERROR: You have specified a disk drive in the source or destination that does not exist, or you have forgotten the colon after the disk drive name. Check the spelling on the command line and try the command again.

12. Invalid number of parameters

ERROR: You omitted the source and destination file name. Check the spelling and the spacing of the command line and try the command again.

13. Invalid parameter

ERROR: You have given a switch that XCOPY does not recognize, forgotten to give the switch character before a switch, or given too many file names. Check the spelling on the command line and try the command again.

14. Invalid path

ERROR: The directory path has an illegal character, or your entry for the source or destination is more than 63 characters long, the DOS limit. You either forgot a space between the source and destination file names or mistyped a name. Check the spacing and spelling on the command line and try the command again.

15. `Lock Violation`

ERROR: XCOPY attempted to read a file being used by another computer or process, and the file is locked. Try to find the computer or process that has the locked file and try the command again when the file is free.

16. `Path not found`

ERROR: You have given a source directory name that does not exist, used the wrong directory name (a directory not in the path), or mistyped a name. Issue a DIR command to ensure that the directory you have specified is correct, check the spelling on the command, and try the command again.

17. `Path too long`

ERROR: A directory path name for the source or destination exceeds 63 characters, the DOS limit. A space may be missing between the source and destination file name. Check the command line. If the line is improperly phrased, try the command again with the correct phrasing. If the path has too many characters, move to the lowest possible subdirectory, and try the command again with a shorter path name.

18. `Press any key to begin copying file(s)`

INFORMATION: You have used the /W switch, and XCOPY is waiting for you to press a key. If necessary, change diskettes, and press any key for XCOPY to continue.

19. `Reading source file(s)...`

INFORMATION: XCOPY is reading the directories of the source for file names.

20. `Sharing Violation`

ERROR: Another computer or process is using the file that XCOPY is attempting to copy. The file is marked so that XCOPY cannot read or write to the file. Wait for the other computer or process to finish with the file, and try the command again.

21. Too many open files

    ERROR: XCOPY attempted to open the file whose name
    appears above this message but was prohibited by DOS
    because not enough file handles were available. Either
    another process on your computer is using all available file
    handles, or your setting of FILES= in CONFIG.SYS is too low.

    If no other process is active on your computer, edit your
    CONFIG.SYS file and increase the number of files given to
    the FILES directive. Restart your system and try the
    command again. If another process is active, wait for it to
    finish and then try the command again.

22. Unable to create directory

    ERROR: XCOPY cannot create a subdirectory on the
    destination disk. Part of the path name for the destination is
    wrong or misspelled, the root directory of the disk is full,
    the disk is full, a file by the same name as the created
    directory already exists, or the directory name is a device
    name.

    Be sure that the destination name is correct. Check the
    destination disk by using the DIR command. If the disk or
    the root directory is full, erase files or use another
    destination disk. If a file exists that has the same name as
    the intended directory, either rename the file or change the
    name of the directory when you issue the XCOPY command.

Changes between Versions of DOS

Several major changes occurred between DOS V2 and V3. Additional changes occurred with each revision of DOS: V3.0, V3.1, V3.2, and V3.3. These changes are described briefly in this appendix.

Changes between DOS V2.x and DOS V3.0

New CONFIG.SYS Features

The following CONFIG.SYS directives were made available in V3.0:

COUNTRY	Changes DOS date and time formats and other characteristics for international use
FCBS	Controls DOS's reactions to a program's use of DOS V1 file handling
LASTDRIVE	Sets the last logical disk drive that DOS will use
VDISK.SYS	A virtual (RAM) disk device driver

The undocumented SWITCHAR directive was dropped.

New Commands

The following commands were added to V3.0. Some of the programs, which are marked with an asterisk (*), had previously been distributed to international users by IBM's World Division Group. In DOS V3, these programs became part of the standard DOS distribution.

ATTRIB	Sets the read-only attribute of a file
GRAFTABL*	Allows legible display of some graphic characters using the medium-resolution mode of the Color/Graphics Adapter
KEYBxx	Changes the keyboard layout for different languages
LABEL	Enables a user to add, change, or delete a disk's volume label
SELECT*	Enables a user to customize the Startup diskette for use with languages other than English
SHARE	Provides file sharing (file and record locking)

Changed Commands

The following commands were changed between DOS V2 and V3:

BACKUP and RESTORE	Includes the backing up of diskettes and allows the backup files to be placed on another fixed disk
DATE and TIME	Supports international date and time formats
FORMAT	Includes the /4 switch for formatting a 360K diskette on a 1.2M disk drive; also warns when a nonremovable (fixed) disk is to be formatted
GRAPHICS	Includes support for the IBM Compact and Color Printers

Changed Features

Beginning with DOS V3.0, a drive and path name can be specified for an external command or program. You can run programs that do not reside in the current directory or in a directory specified in the PATH command.

Changes between DOS V3.0 and V3.1

The following changes were made between DOS V3.0 and V3.1.

New Commands/Features

The following commands were added to DOS V3.1:

JOIN	Enables the user to connect the directory structures of two disk drives, thus creating "one" disk
SUBST	Enables a subdirectory to be used as though it were a disk drive

Support for the IBM PC Network was included in DOS V3.1.

Changed Commands/Directives

The following commands and directives were changed in V3.1:

LABEL	Prompts the user before deleting a volume label
TREE	Displays files in all directories when the /F switch is used
SHELL	Includes the /E:size switch. The size was in 16-byte paragraphs.

Changes between DOS V3.1 and V3.2

The following changes were made between DOS V3.1 and DOS V3.2.

New CONFIG.SYS Features

STACKS	Sets the number and size of the DOS internal stacks

The DRIVER.SYS device driver was added to support various sized floppy disks, particularly 720K microfloppy drives on Personal Computers.

New Features

Support for the IBM Token Ring Network was added.

New Commands

REPLACE   Selectively updates files in one or many directories; adds missing files to a directory

XCOPY   Copies files from one or more directories to another; selectively copies files

Changed Commands/Directives

SHELL   /E:size switch specifies the environment size in bytes, not 16-byte paragraphs

ATTRIB   +A/-A switch added; controls the archive attribute of files

COMMAND   /E switch added; supports the environment size

DISKCOPY/   Also supports 720K diskettes
DISCOMP

FORMAT   Supports formatting of 720K diskettes; requests verification before formatting a nonremovable disk that has a volume label; disk drive name required

SELECT   Formats the fixed disk and copies DOS files

Changes between DOS V3.2 and V3.3

The following changes were made between DOS V3.2 and V3.3.

New CONFIG.SYS Options

The following device drivers for use with the DEVICE directive were added:

DISPLAY.SYS   Supports code pages (multiple fonts) on the EGA, VGA, and PC Convertible displays

PRINTER.SYS   Supports code pages on the IBM Proprinter and Quietwriter III printers

New Features

Support was added for 1.44M microfloppy diskettes, for COM4: and 19,200 baud rates, and for switchable code pages (international character fonts).

New Commands

The following commands were added to DOS V3.3:

APPEND	A PATH-like command for data files
CHCP	Provides code page changing
FASTOPEN	Provides a directory caching program for the fixed disk
NLSFUNC	Provides support for additional character sets (code pages) and for country-dependent information

Changed Commands/Directives

The following commands and CONFIG.SYS directives were changed for DOS V3.3:

BUFFERS	Default buffers based on RAM memory in computer
COUNTRY	Adds support for code pages and a separate country information file (COUNTRY.SYS)
SHELL	The default environment size changed from 128 bytes to 160 bytes
ATTRIB	Has the /S switch to change the attributes of files in more than one directory
BACKUP	Has the /F switch to format diskettes, the /T switch to back up files based on their time, and the /L switch to produce a log file; also places all backed up files into a single file.
batch files	Adds support for using the environment variable (%variable%), @ for suppressing display of a line, and the CALL subcommand for running a second batch file and returning control to the first batch file
DATE and TIME	Sets the computer's clock/calendar

DISKCOPY/ DISKCOMP	Supports 1.44M diskettes
FDISK	Supports multiple logical disks on a large fixed disk
FORMAT	Adds the /N switch for number of sectors and the /T switch for number of tracks
GRAFTABL	Supports code pages
KEYB	Replaces the KEYBxx programs and supports additional layouts
MODE	Supports code pages; also supports additional devices and higher baud rates
RESTORE	Adds the /N switch to restore erased or modified files, the /B switch to restore files modified before a given date, and the /L and /E switches to restore files modified after or before a given time

Sample Hierarchical Directory

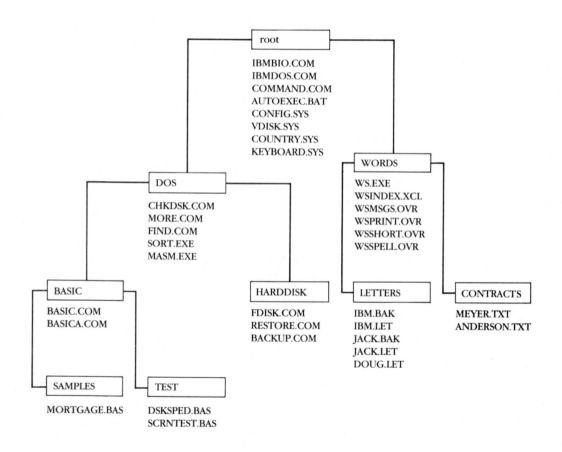

Appendix

C

ASCII and Extended ASCII Codes

This appendix presents both the ASCII codes and the Extended ASCII codes.

ASCII Codes

The codes for the American Standard Code for Information Interchange, or ASCII, are listed below. A control character is abbreviated ^. A Ctrl-C is shown as ^C.

Decimal	Hex	Octal	Binary	ASCII
0	00	000	00000000	Nul (null)
1	01	001	00000001	^A SOH
2	02	002	00000010	^B STX
3	03	003	00000011	^C ETX
4	04	004	00000100	^D EOT
5	05	005	00000101	^E ENQ
6	06	006	00000110	^F ACK
7	07	007	00000111	^G BEL (bell)
8	08	010	00001000	^H BS (backspace)
9	09	011	00001001	^I HT (horizontal tab)
10	0A	012	00001010	^J LF (line feed)
11	0B	013	00001011	^K VT (vertical tab)
12	0C	014	00001100	^L FF (form feed)
13	0D	015	00001101	^M CR (carriage return)
14	0E	016	00001110	^N SO
15	0F	017	00001111	^O SI

Decimal	Hex	Octal	Binary	ASCII
16	10	020	00010000	^P DLE
17	11	021	00010001	^Q DC1
18	12	022	00010010	^R DC2
19	13	023	00010011	^S DC3
20	14	024	00010100	^T DC4
21	15	025	00010101	^U NAK
22	16	026	00010110	^V SYN
23	17	027	00010111	^W ETB
24	18	030	00011000	^X CAN
25	19	031	00011001	^Y EM
26	1A	032	00011010	^Z SUB
27	1B	033	00011011	Esc
28	1C	034	00011100	FS
29	1D	035	00011101	GS
30	1E	036	00011110	RS
31	1F	037	00011111	US
32	20	040	00100000	Space
33	21	041	00100001	!
34	22	042	00100010	"
35	23	043	00100011	#
36	24	044	00100100	$
37	25	045	00100101	%
38	26	046	00100110	&
39	27	047	00100111	'
40	28	050	00101000	(
41	29	051	00101001	)
42	2A	052	00101010	*
43	2B	053	00101011	+
44	2C	054	00101100	,
45	2D	055	00101101	–
46	2E	056	00101110	.
47	2F	057	00101111	/

Decimal	Hex	Octal	Binary	ASCII
48	30	060	00110000	0
49	31	061	00110001	1
50	32	062	00110010	2
51	33	063	00110011	3
52	34	064	00110100	4
53	35	065	00110101	5
54	36	066	00110110	6
55	37	067	00110111	7
56	38	070	00111000	8
57	39	071	00111001	9
58	3A	072	00111010	:
59	3B	073	00111011	;
60	3C	074	00111100	<
61	3D	075	00111101	=
62	3E	076	00111110	>
63	3F	077	00111111	?
64	40	100	01000000	@
65	41	101	01000001	A
66	42	102	01000010	B
67	43	103	01000011	C
68	44	104	01000100	D
69	45	105	01000101	E
70	46	106	01000110	F
71	47	107	01000111	G
72	48	110	01001000	H
73	49	111	01001001	I
74	4A	112	01001010	J
75	4B	113	01001011	K
76	4C	114	01001100	L
77	4D	115	01001101	M
78	4E	116	01001110	N
79	4F	117	01001111	O

Decimal	Hex	Octal	Binary	ASCII
80	50	120	01010000	P
81	51	121	01010001	Q
82	52	122	01010010	R
83	53	123	01010011	S
84	54	124	01010100	T
85	55	125	01010101	U
86	56	126	01010110	V
87	57	127	01010111	W
88	58	130	01011000	X
89	59	131	01011001	Y
90	5A	132	01011010	Z
91	5B	133	01011011	[
92	5C	134	01011100	\
93	5D	135	01011101	]
94	5E	136	01011110	^
95	5F	137	01011111	_
96	60	140	01100000	`
97	61	141	01100001	a
98	62	142	01100010	b
99	63	143	01100011	c
100	64	144	01100100	d
101	65	145	01100101	e
102	66	146	01100110	f
103	67	147	01100111	g
104	68	150	01101000	h
105	69	151	01101001	i
106	6A	152	01101010	j
107	6B	153	01101011	k
108	6C	154	01101100	l
109	6D	155	01101101	m
110	6E	156	01101110	n
111	6F	157	01101111	o

Decimal	Hex	Octal	Binary	ASCII
112	70	160	01110000	p
113	71	161	01110001	q
114	72	162	01110010	r
115	73	163	01110011	s
116	74	164	01110100	t
117	75	165	01110101	u
118	76	166	01110110	v
119	77	167	01110111	w
120	78	170	01111000	x
121	79	171	01111001	y
122	7A	172	01111010	z
123	7B	173	01111011	{
124	7C	174	01111100		
125	7D	175	01111101	}
126	7E	176	01111110	~
127	7F	177	01111111	Del

Extended ASCII Codes

Certain keys cannot be represented by standard ASCII codes. To represent the codes, you use a two-character sequence. The first character is always 0 (ASCII Nul). The second character and its translation are listed below. Some codes expand to multikeystroke characters.

Decimal	Hex	Octal	Binary	Extended ASCII Meaning
3	03	003	00000011	Nul (null character)
15	0F	017	00001111	Shift-Tab
16	10	020	00010000	Alt-Q
17	11	021	00010001	Alt-W
18	12	022	00010010	Alt-E
19	13	023	00010011	Alt-R
20	14	024	00010100	Alt-T
21	15	025	00010101	Alt-Y
22	16	026	00010110	Alt-U
23	17	027	00010111	Alt-I
24	18	030	00011000	Alt-O
25	19	031	00011001	Alt-P

Decimal	Hex	Octal	Binary	*Extended ASCII* *Meaning*
30	1E	036	00011110	Alt-Z
31	1F	037	00011111	Alt-X
32	20	040	00100000	Alt-C
33	21	041	00100001	Alt-V
34	22	042	00100010	Alt-B
35	23	043	00100011	Alt-N
36	24	044	00100100	Alt-M
59	3B	073	00111011	F1
60	3C	074	00111100	F2
61	3D	075	00111101	F3
62	3E	076	00111110	F4
63	3F	077	00111111	F5
64	40	100	01000000	F6
65	41	101	01000001	F7
66	42	102	01000010	F8
67	43	103	01000011	F9
68	44	104	01000100	F10
71	47	107	01000111	Home
72	48	110	01001000	↑
73	49	111	01001001	PgUp
75	4B	113	01001011	←
77	4D	115	01001101	→
79	4F	117	01001111	End
80	50	120	01010000	↓
81	51	121	01010001	PgDn
82	52	122	01010010	Ins
83	53	123	01010011	Del
84	54	124	01010100	F11 (Shift-F1)
85	55	125	01010101	F12 (Shift-F2)
86	56	126	01010110	F13 (Shift-F3)
87	57	127	01010111	F14 (Shift-F4)
88	58	130	01011000	F15 (Shift-F5)
89	59	131	01011001	F16 (Shift-F6)
90	5A	132	01011010	F17 (Shift-F7)
91	5B	133	01011011	F18 (Shift-F8)
92	5C	134	01011100	F19 (Shift-F9)
93	5D	135	01011101	F20 (Shift-F10)

Decimal	Hex	Octal	Binary	Extended ASCII Meaning
94	5E	136	01011110	F21 (^F1)
95	5F	137	01011111	F22 (^F2)
96	60	140	01100000	F23 (^F3)
97	61	141	01100001	F24 (^F4)
98	62	142	01100010	F25 (^F5)
99	63	143	01100011	F26 (^F6)
100	64	144	01100100	F27 (^F7)
101	65	145	01100101	F28 (^F8)
102	66	146	01100110	F29 (^F9)
103	67	147	01100111	F30 (^F10)

Extended ASCII Codes on the Enhanced Keyboard

The following extended ASCII codes are used on the Enhanced Keyboard.

Decimal	Hex	Octal	Binary	Extended ASCII Meaning
1	1	1	00000001	Alt-Esc
3	3	3	00000011	Nul (null character)
14	E	16	00001110	Alt-Backspace
15	F	17	00001111	Shift-Tab (Back-tab)
16	10	20	00010000	Alt-Q
17	11	21	00010001	Alt-W
18	12	22	00010010	Alt-E
19	13	23	00010011	Alt-R
20	14	24	00010100	Alt-T
21	15	25	00010101	Alt-Y
22	16	26	00010110	Alt-U
23	17	27	00010111	Alt-I
24	18	30	00011000	Alt-O
25	19	31	00011001	Alt-P
26	1A	32	00011010	Alt-[
27	1B	33	00011011	Alt-]
28	1C	34	00011100	Alt-Enter
29	1D	35	00011101	Alt-A
30	1E	36	00011110	Alt-S
31	1F	37	00011111	Alt-D

Decimal	Hex	Octal	Binary	Extended ASCII Meaning
32	20	40	00100000	Alt-D
33	21	41	00100001	Alt-F
34	22	42	00100010	Alt-G
35	23	43	00100011	Alt-H
36	24	44	00100100	Alt-J
37	25	45	00100101	Alt-K
38	26	46	00100110	Alt-L
39	27	47	00100111	Alt-;
40	28	50	00101000	Alt-'
41	29	51	00101001	Alt-`
43	2B	53	00101011	Alt-\
44	2C	54	00101100	Alt-Z
45	2D	55	00101101	Alt-X
46	2E	56	00101110	Alt-C
47	2F	57	00101111	Alt-V
48	30	60	00110000	Alt-B
49	31	61	00110001	Alt-N
50	32	62	00110010	Alt-M
51	33	63	00110011	Alt-,
52	34	64	00110100	Alt-.
53	35	65	00110101	Alt-/
55	37	67	00110111	Alt-* (keypad)
59	3B	73	00111011	F1
60	3C	74	00111100	F2
61	3D	75	00111101	F3
62	3E	76	00111110	F4
63	3F	77	00111111	F5
64	40	100	01000000	F6
65	41	101	01000001	F7
66	42	102	01000010	F8
67	43	103	01000011	F9
68	44	104	01000100	F10
71	47	107	01000111	Home
72	48	110	01001000	Up cursor
73	49	111	01001001	PgUp
74	4A	112	01001010	Alt- – (keypad)
75	4B	113	01001011	←
76	4C	114	01001100	Center cursor
77	4D	115	01001101	→
78	4E	116	01001110	Alt- + (keypad)
79	4F	117	01001111	End

Decimal	Hex	Octal	Binary	Extended ASCII Meaning
80	50	120	01010000	↓
81	51	121	01010001	PgDn
82	52	122	01010010	Ins (Insert)
83	53	123	01010011	Del (Delete)
84	54	124	01010100	Shift-F1
85	55	125	01010101	Shift-F2
86	56	126	01010110	Shift-F3
87	57	127	01010111	Shift-F4
88	58	130	01011000	Shift-F5
89	59	131	01011001	Shift-F6
90	5A	132	01011010	Shift-F7
91	5B	133	01011011	Shift-F8
92	5C	134	01011100	Shift-F9
93	5D	135	01011101	Shift-F10
94	5E	136	01011110	^F1
95	5F	137	01011111	^F2
96	60	140	01100000	^F3
97	61	141	01100001	^F4
98	62	142	01100010	^F5
99	63	143	01100011	^F6
100	64	144	01100100	^F7
101	65	145	01100101	^F8
102	66	146	01100110	^F9
103	67	147	01100111	^F10
104	68	150	01101000	Alt-F1
105	69	151	01101001	Alt-F2
106	6A	152	01101010	Alt-F3
107	6B	153	01101011	Alt-F4
108	6C	154	01101100	Alt-F5
109	6D	155	01101101	Alt-F6
110	6E	156	01101110	Alt-F7
111	6F	157	01101111	Alt-F8

Decimal	Hex	Octal	Binary	Extended ASCII Meaning
112	70	160	01110000	Alt-F9
113	71	161	01110001	Alt-F10
114	72	162	01110010	^PrtSc
115	73	163	01110011	^←
116	74	164	01110100	^→
117	75	165	01110101	^End
118	76	166	01110110	^PgDn
119	77	167	01110111	^Home
120	78	170	01111000	Alt-1 (keyboard)
121	79	171	01111001	Alt-2 (keyboard)
122	7A	172	01111010	Alt-3 (keyboard)
123	7B	173	01111011	Alt-4 (keyboard)
124	7C	174	01111100	Alt-5 (keyboard)
125	7D	175	01111101	Alt-6 (keyboard)
126	7E	176	01111110	Alt-7 (keyboard)
127	7F	177	01111111	Alt-8 (keyboard)
128	80	200	10000000	Alt-9 (keyboard)
129	81	201	10000001	Alt-0 (keyboard)
130	82	202	10000010	Alt- – (keyboard)
131	83	203	10000011	Alt- = (keyboard)
132	84	204	10000100	^PgUp
133	85	205	10000101	F11
134	86	206	10000110	F12
135	87	207	10000111	Shift-F11
136	88	210	10001000	Shift-F12
137	89	211	10001001	^F11
138	8A	212	10001010	^F12
139	8B	213	10001011	Alt-F11
140	8C	214	10001100	Alt-F12
141	8D	215	10001101	^↑/8 (keypad)
142	8E	216	10001110	^ – (keypad)
143	8F	217	10001111	^ 5 (keypad)

Decimal	Hex	Octal	Binary	Extended ASCII Meaning
144	90	220	10010000	^ + (keypad)
145	91	221	10010001	^↓/2 (keypad)
146	92	222	10010010	^Ins/0 (keypad)
147	93	223	10010011	^Del/. (keypad)
148	94	224	10010100	^Tab
149	95	225	10010101	^ / (keypad)
150	96	226	10010110	^ * (keypad)
151	97	227	10010111	Alt-Home
152	98	230	10011000	Alt-↑
153	99	231	10011001	Alt-PgUp
155	9B	233	10011011	Alt-←
157	9D	235	10011101	Alt-→
159	9F	237	10011111	Alt-End
160	A0	240	10100000	Alt-↓
161	A1	241	10100001	Alt-PgDn
162	A2	242	10100010	Alt-Ins
163	A3	243	10100011	Alt-Del
164	A4	244	10100100	Alt- / (keypad)
165	A5	245	10100101	Alt-Tab
166	A6	256	10100110	Alt-Enter

Appendix

D

ANSI Terminal Codes

All ANSI terminal codes are prefixed by an Escape (Esc) character and a left bracket ([). The Esc character is either 27 decimal or 1b hexadecimal.

Cursor Control Sequences

For the cursor-control sequences, if a value is omitted the default value of 1 is used.

Cursor Position

Horizontal and Vertical Position

ESC[#;#H	The first # is the row (vertical); the second
ESC[#;#f	# is the column (horizontal). The starting value for either coordinate is 1 (also the default value).

Cursor Up

ESC[#A	# is the number of rows to move up

Cursor Down

ESC[#B	# is the number of rows to move down

Cursor Forward

ESC[#C   # is the number of columns to move forward

Cursor Backward

ESC[#D   # is the number of columns to move backward

Device Status Report

ESC[6n   "Inputs" through the keyboard a cursor report on the
                current cursor position

Cursor Position Report

ESC[#;#R   Reports the current cursor position. The string is returned
                by the ANSI console and is eight characters long. The first
                # is the two-digit row number; the second # is the two-
                digit column number.

Save Cursor Position

ESC[s   "Saves" the current cursor position in the driver. The
                position can be restored by using Esc[r.

Restore Cursor Position

ESC[r   Sets the cursor to the horizontal and vertical position that
                was "saved"

Erasing

Erase Display

ESC[2J   Additionally homes cursor

Erase to End of Line

ESC[K

Modes of Operation

For all ANSI operation mode control codes, if a value is omitted the default value of 0 is used.

Set Graphics Rendition

ESC[#; . . . ;#m Sets the character attributes by the following parameters. The attributes remain in effect until the next graphics rendition command.

Parameter	Meaning
0	All attributes off (normal white on black)
1	Bold on (high intensity)
4	Underscore on (IBM Monochrome Display only)
5	Blink on
7	Reverse (inverse) video on
8	Cancel on (invisible characters)
30	Black foreground
31	Red foreground
32	Green foreground
33	Yellow foreground
34	Blue foreground
35	Magenta foreground
36	Cyan foreground
37	White foreground
40	Black background
41	Red background
42	Green background
43	Yellow background
44	Blue background
45	Magenta background
46	Cyan background
47	White background

Set Screen Mode

(for parameter 7 only)

ESC[=#h   Sets the screen width or type based on #
ESC[?7h

Reset Screen Mode

(for parameter 7 only)

ESC[=#l   Resets the screen width or type based on #
ESC[?7l

Parameter	Meaning
0	40 × 25 black and white
1	40 × 25 color
2	80 × 25 black and white
3	80 × 25 color
4	320 × 200 color
5	320 × 200 black and white
6	640 × 200 black and white
7	Wrap at end-of-line (set mode)
	Do not wrap and discard characters past end-of-line (reset mode)

Keyboard Key Reassignment

ESC[#;#; . . . ;p or
ESC["string"p or
ESC[#;"string";#;#;"string";#p

The first ASCII code (the first #) defines which key or keystrokes (such as a Ctrl-character combination) are being reassigned. However, if the first code in the sequence is 0 (ASCII Nul), the first and second codes designate an extended ASCII key sequence. See Appendix C for the set of ASCII codes and the set of extended ASCII codes.

The remaining numbers (#) or characters within the "string" are the replacement characters that are "typed" when this key or keystroke is pressed. Any nonnumeric characters used in the replacement must be placed within double quotation marks.

Appendix

E

Preparing Your Fixed Disk

IMPORTANT: Some dealers install the DOS operating system and applications programs on your fixed disk before you receive your system. If only DOS has been installed, you may either skip or complete the steps in these first two sections, which describe two of the processes for setting up the fixed disk. If you choose to complete the steps in these sections, you must complete both sections before you proceed to the final section.

If your dealer has installed applications programs, such as an accounting program, a word-processing program, or a data management program, you should not *complete the steps in the first and second sections in this appendix.*

Before you can use your fixed disk, you must perform four distinct procedures: set the configuration of your computer, assign the disk into one or more partitions by using FDISK, format the fixed disk by using the FORMAT command, and set up the fixed disk for daily operations by using several DOS commands. Before doing these procedures, you must have DOS up and running on your computer.

If you have a PS/2 or Personal Computer AT, the first step, setting the configuration of your computer, must be performed before you proceed with the steps outlined in this appendix. Other Personal Computer users can ignore this step.

If you have a PS/2, you must run the *Set Configuration* option from the Reference diskette provided with your system. The information on this option is located in the *Quick Reference* booklet that comes with your computer.

If you have a Personal Computer AT, you must run the SETUP program, which is located on the *Diagnostics* diskette provided with your computer. The information on SETUP is located in the *Installation and Setup* manual that comes with your computer.

For the procedures in these sections, you will need either the original diskettes that come with your copy of DOS or a copy of the diskette(s). PS/2 users will need the single microfloppy (3 1/2-inch, hard plastic shell) diskette labeled *Startup/Operating*. This diskette will be the only one you use in this section.

Personal Computer users will need the two minifloppy (5 1/4-inch, flexible plastic jacket) diskettes. The first diskette is labeled *Startup*, and the second is labeled *Operating*. You will need both diskettes. The diskette labeled Startup will be the diskette you use to start DOS on your computer. Until directed otherwise in Section 3, the Startup diskette will be the only diskette you will use.

Once you have run the appropriate program to set up the computer and have the correct diskette or diskettes on hand, you can proceed with the steps in the next section.

Section 1: Using FDISK To Prepare the Fixed Disk

The fixed disk of your computer can be used by more than one operating system. The fixed disk can also be divided so that DOS sees the single fixed disk as several logical disk drives. DOS must subdivide a disk drive that holds more than 32 megabytes into several smaller apparent disk drives. To accommodate the people who use more than one operating system and computers with capacities greater than 32 megabytes, the FDISK program divides the disk into *partitions*.

Most people use only DOS. The instructions in this section are for setting up your fixed disk for use with DOS only.

Four additional steps are provided for users whose fixed disks have a capacity greater than 32 megabytes.

***Step 1.** Insert the Startup/Operating or Startup diskette into the first disk drive.*

The first disk drive is the topmost or leftmost disk drive.If you are using a PS/2, you will insert the DOS Startup/Operating microfloppy diskette. If you are using a Personal Computer or compatible, you will insert the DOS Startup minifloppy diskette. If you are using the minifloppy diskette, close the disk drive door.

Start your computer by turning on the power or by pressing the Ctrl-Alt-Del keys if the computer is already on. (Hold down the Ctrl key and the Alt key, and then press the Del key.)

Step 2. *Check the date shown on the screen.*

If you are using a PS/2 or Personal Computer AT, the date should be correct. If it is, press Enter. If the date is not correct, enter the date. Users of other machines must also enter the date. Separate the month, day, and year with hyphens. Then press the Enter key (⏎).

Step 3. *Check the time shown on the screen.*

If you are using a PS/2 or Personal Computer AT, the time should also be correct. If it is, press Enter. If the time is not correct, enter the time. Users of other machines must also enter the time.

DOS uses a universal, 24-hour clock; therefore, you need to add 12 to afternoon or evening hours. Separate the hours, minutes, and seconds with colons. You need not enter hundredths of seconds. When you finish, press Enter.

You should now see the DOS prompt

```
A>
```

Step 4. *Type FDISK and press Enter.*

The screen should look something like the following:

```
IBM Personal Computer
Fixed Disk Setup Program Version 3.30
(C)Copyright IBM Corp. 1983, 1987

FDISK Options

Current Fixed Disk Drive: 1
```

```
Choose one of the following:

    1. Create DOS partition
    2. Change Active Partition
    3. Delete DOS partition
    4. Display Partition Information




Enter choice: [1]



Press ESC to return to DOS
```

Step 5. *Press Enter to choose the first option.*

The following menu will appear:

```
Create DOS Partition

Current Fixed Disk Drive: 1



    1. Create Primary DOS partition
    2. Create Extended DOS partition
    3. Create logical DOS drive(s) in
        the Extended DOS partition




Enter choice: [1]




Press ESC to return to FDISK options
```

Step 6. *Press Enter to choose the first option.*

A partition for DOS has already been created for your fixed disk if the following message appears on your screen:

```
Primary DOS partition already exists.
```

In this case, you should skip this section and the next section on formatting your disk. Press the Esc key once to return to the FDISK Options menu, and then press Esc again to return to DOS.

If the preceding message does not appear, your screen should look something like this:

```
Create Primary DOS Partition

Current Fixed Disk Drive 1:

Do you wish to use the maximum size
for a DOS partition and make the DOS
partition active (Y/N)........? [Y]
```

Step 7. *Press Y to answer yes.*

A yes answer informs DOS that the maximum size should be used by the primary (first) partition, that the partition is for use by DOS, and that DOS will be able to start itself from this partition.

The light for the fixed disk should go on and off briefly, and the following message should appear:

```
System will now restart

Insert DOS diskette in drive A:
Press any key when ready...
```

Step 8. *Press any key.*

Because the DOS Startup/Operating or DOS Startup diskette is already in drive A, DOS will restart. Answer the date and time questions again as you did in steps 2 and 3.

If you have a fixed disk drive that holds fewer than 40 megabytes, skip to the next section on formatting the fixed disk. If you have a fixed disk drive that holds 40 megabytes or more, complete steps 9 through 17 before going on to the next section. The next three steps direct DOS to use the remaining section of the fixed disk.

Step 9. *Type FDISK and press Enter to start the FDISK program again.*

You should see the same FDISK option menu you saw in step 4.

Step 10. *Press Enter to choose the first option.*

The Create DOS Partition menu should reappear.

Step 11. *Press 2 to choose the second option.*

Although the numbers you see may vary depending on the size of your disk drive, your screen will look something like the following:

```
Create Primary DOS Partition

Current Fixed Disk Drive 1:

Partition Status    Type   Start  End  Size
  C: 1          A   PRI DOS     Ø  549  55Ø




Total disk space is   731 cylinders.
Maximum space available for partition
is   181 cylinders.

Enter partition size..........: [ 181]
```

Step 12. Press Enter to accept the partition size DOS has chosen.

Your screen will now look something like this:

```
Create Primary DOS Partition

Current Fixed Disk Drive 1:

Partition Status    Type   Start  End Size
   C: 1         A   PRI DOS     Ø   549  55Ø
      2             EXT DOS   551   73Ø  181



Extended DOS partition created

Press ESC to return to FDISK Options
```

Step 13. Press the Esc key.

Your screen will look something like this:

```
Create Logical DOS Drive(s)


No logical drives defined


Total partition size is  181 cylinders.

Maximum space available for logical
drive is  181 cylinders.

Enter logical drive size.......: [ 181]
```

Step 14. *Press Enter to accept the size DOS has chosen.*

Your screen should look something like this:

```
Create Logical DOS Drive(s)

Drv Start End  Size
 D:  55Ø    73Ø   181




All available space in the Extended DOS
partition is assigned to logical drives.


Logical DOS drive created, drive letters
changed or added.
Press ESC to return to FDISK Options
```

Step 15. *Jot down the letters displayed under the category* Drv.

These are the additional disk drive or drives you now have.

Step 16. *Press the Esc key once to return to the FDISK Options menu; then press Esc again.*

You will see the System will now restart message that appeared in step 7.

Step 17. *Press any key.*

Because the DOS startup diskette is still in the disk drive, DOS will restart. Answer the date and time questions and proceed to the next section on formatting the fixed disk.

Section 2: Using FORMAT To Prepare the Fixed Disk

The FORMAT command performs several functions. It lays out the individual sections that DOS uses to store your programs and data. FORMAT creates housekeeping areas so that DOS can keep track of your programs and files. The command also places the key parts of DOS on your fixed disk.

To do its job, FORMAT permanently removes any files stored on the fixed disk. If you have on your fixed disk any files you want to keep, do *not* perform the steps in this section.

Step 1. *With the DOS Startup diskette still in the floppy disk drive, start the FORMAT program.*

Type the following command and press Enter:

FORMAT C: /S /V

The light on the floppy disk drive will go on for a few seconds. You should see this message:

```
WARNING: ALL DATA ON NON-REMOVABLE DISK
DRIVE C: WILL BE LOST!
Proceed with Format (Y/N)?_
```

Step 2. *Because you do want to format the fixed disk, press Y for yes; then press Enter.*

You should see the following message:

```
Head:    Ø Cylinder:    Ø
```

The numbers after the word Head will change quickly, and the numbers after the word Cylinder will start with 0 and increase by one every quarter second or so. The light on the fixed disk drive will stay on for two to four minutes, depending on the size of your fixed disk.

Don't be concerned if the numbers freeze for a second or two and you hear a ratcheting noise from your computer. DOS is testing each part of your disk and may need to retest a section a few times before proceeding to the next section.

After FORMAT has completed its first stage, the message giving the head and cylinder numbers will be replaced by this message:

```
Formatting complete
```

Within a few seconds, another message will appear:

```
System transferred
```

This message informs you that FORMAT has placed the needed start-up DOS files on the fixed disk.

Afterward, you should see the following message:

```
Volume label (11 characters, ENTER for none)? _
```

Step 3. *Type a volume name that contains up to 11 characters; then press Enter.*

The volume name will appear whenever you display a list of files on the fixed disk and at several other times also.

FORMAT will give several statistics about your fixed disk. The following are the statistics for drive C on a 40M disk running DOS V3.3. The numbers may vary with a different type of fixed disk and a different version of DOS.

```
33419264 bytes total disk space
   79872 bytes used by system
33339392 bytes available on disk
```

If you see a line that mentions bytes in bad sectors, don't be overly concerned. DOS has simply found that some portions of the fixed disk cannot be used. This occurrence is not unusual.

Step 4. *Test the setup of your computer.*

Either eject the microfloppy DOS Startup/Operating diskette from the drive by pushing the blue eject button, or open the door of the minifloppy disk drive that holds the DOS Startup diskette. Press Ctrl-Alt-Del. This sequence should restart DOS from the fixed disk.

The floppy disk drive light should come on, followed by the fixed disk drive light. Then the computer should beep. Several seconds later, the computer should try to load DOS from the fixed disk. Within 20 seconds, DOS should ask you for the date.

If you see the date message, answer the date and time questions as you did in steps 1 and 2 in the first section. You have now successfully prepared the fixed disk to start DOS.

If you don't see a message about the date, either you did not press the Ctrl-Alt-Del keys correctly, or you were not successful in preparing your fixed disk. Try pressing Ctrl-Alt-Del again. If you do not see the date and time messages within 30 seconds, either insert the microfloppy DOS Startup/Operating diskette into the drive or close the minifloppy disk drive door. Restart DOS from the floppy diskette by pressing Ctrl-Alt-Del again. Then return to step 1 and repeat the instructions in this section.

If you have successfully started DOS from the fixed disk and you did not carry out steps 9 through 17 in the first section (to further partition the fixed disk), skip to the next section on preparing your disk for daily use. If you did follow steps 9 through 17, you need to run FORMAT again for each logical disk drive that DOS created.

Step 5. *Either insert the microfloppy DOS Startup/Operating diskette into the disk drive, or close the door on the minifloppy disk drive holding the DOS Startup diskette.*

Step 6. *To start the FORMAT command on the additional disk drive, type the following command and press Enter:*

A:FORMAT D: /V

Note that this command is slightly different from the FORMAT command you typed in step 1.

The light on the floppy disk drive should go on for a few seconds. You should see this message:

```
WARNING: ALL DATA ON NON-REMOVABLE DISK
DRIVE D: WILL BE LOST!
Proceed with Format (Y/N)?_
```

Step 7. *Because you do want to format the D disk drive, press* ***Y*** *for yes; then press Enter.*

You should now see the message

```
Head:    Ø Cylinder:    Ø
```

As before, the numbers after the word Head and the word Cylinder will change rapidly. You'll also see the light for the fixed disk drive stay on for one to four minutes, depending on the size of this disk.

Again, don't be concerned if the numbers freeze for a second or two and you hear a ratcheting noise from your computer. DOS is simply detecting any possibly bad section of the disk.

After FORMAT has completed its first stage, the message giving the head and cylinder numbers will be replaced by this message:

```
Formatting complete
```

You will not see the message System transferred as you did in Step 3. Instead, you should see this message:

```
Volume label (11 characters, ENTER for none)? _
```

Step 8. *Type a volume name that consists of up to 11 characters and press Enter.*

This name should be different from the volume name you entered previously.

Now, FORMAT will give several statistics about this disk. The statistics will vary among different types of fixed disks and different versions of DOS.

Step 9. *Test the setup of this disk; type*

DIR D:

Your screen should look something like this:

```
Volume in drive D is SECOND DSK
Directory of  D:\

File not found
```

The name in the first line should be the volume label you gave to FORMAT in step 8. If your screen looks something like this, you have now successfully prepared the second part of the fixed disk to be used by DOS.

If you see any other message, the second part of the fixed disk was not properly prepared. Return to step 6 and repeat the instructions in this section again.

If you have successfully prepared the second portion of your fixed disk, look at the list of disk drives you jotted down in step 14 in the first section. If the only letter mentioned is D, proceed to the next section on preparing your disk for daily use. If there are additional letters, you must repeat steps 6 through 9 again for each letter. Substitute the appropriate letter for the letter D in each step. After you have completed steps 6 through 9 for each disk drive letter, proceed to the next section.

Section 3: Setting Up the Fixed Disk for Daily Use

Your fixed disk is now ready to store and retrieve information under DOS. In this section, you will copy the DOS programs to the fixed disk and also create some files for customizing DOS for your own use.

First, you'll restart DOS to ensure that your computer is working properly. In this section, remember to end each line you are asked to type by pressing the Enter key.

Because DOS comes on two diskettes for minifloppy disk drive computers, Personal Computer users will perform extra steps in this section.

Step 1. *Check that the DOS Startup/Operating or Startup diskette is still in the floppy disk drive.*

If you are using microfloppy diskettes, be sure that the diskette is inserted into the disk drive. If you are using minifloppy disk drives, close the disk drive door.

Step 2. *Type C: Don't forget to press Enter afterward.*

This step makes the fixed disk the current disk drive. The DOS prompt should look like this:

```
C>
```

Step 3. *Type MKDIR \BIN*

This command creates a subdirectory called BIN. Later, you will place the DOS programs in this subdirectory.

Step 4. *Type MKDIR \SYS*

This command creates a subdirectory called \SYS. You will place the DOS device-driver and auxiliary system software (the files that end in SYS) in this directory.

Step 5. *Type CHDIR \BIN*

This step makes BIN the current directory of the fixed disk.

Step 6. *Type COPY A:*.* C: /V*

This line copies all files from the DOS Startup/Operating diskette or Startup diskette to the current directory (BIN) on the fixed disk. You will see the name of each file as it is copied. Then, if you're using the microfloppy Startup/Operating diskette, you'll see the following message:

```
50 file(s) copied
```

If you're using the minifloppy Startup diskette, you'll see

```
22 file(s) copied
```

Remember that the number of files on the diskette (and the number of files copied) will vary among the versions of DOS.

Step 7. *Type COPY *.SYS \SYS /V*

This command copies all the files ending with SYS to the \SYS directory. You should see a message indicating that seven files have been copied.

Step 8. *Type ERASE *.SYS*

This command removes the seven SYS files from the BIN subdirectory. Because you have safely copied the files to the \SYS subdirectory (in step 7), you can remove them from BIN.

Step 9. *Take the Startup/Operating diskette or Startup diskette out of disk drive A.*

If you're using minifloppy diskettes, put the Startup diskette back into its envelope. Store the diskette in a safe place.

The next three steps are for those using DOS on minifloppy diskettes, usually users of Personal Computers. If you are using a PS/2, skip to step 13.

Step 10. *Take the Operating diskette out of its envelope, place the diskette into disk drive A, and close the door.*

Step 11. *Type COPY A:*.* C: /V*

This line copies all the files from the Operating Diskette to the current directory (BIN) of the fixed disk. You should see this message:

```
31 file(s) copied
```

Remember that the number of files that are copied (and the number that COPY reports) will vary between the versions of DOS.

Step 12. *Take the Operating diskette out of drive A, and put the diskette back into its envelope.*

Store the diskette in a safe place with the Startup diskette.

Step 13. *Type CD *

This command makes the root (topmost) directory of the fixed disk the current directory.

Step 14. *Type the following command, and the DOS prompt (C>) will disappear:*

COPY CON CONFIG.SYS

Step 15. *Now type the following lines:*

```
SHELL = c:\command.com c:\ /p /e:168
BUFFERS = 20
FILES = 20
FCBS = 12, 12
LASTDRIVE = f
DEVICE = c:\sys\ansi.sys
```

Be sure to check your typing before you press Enter on each line. If you make a mistake and you have already pressed Enter, perform step 17, and then return to step 14.

You can type the lines in all uppercase, all lowercase, or mixed. I normally leave the directives on the left side of the equal sign in uppercase letters and the remaining parts on the right side in lowercase. This makes the commands in the file easier to read.

If you do not want to use a RAM disk, skip the next step and go to step 17.

Step 16. *If you want to use a RAM disk on a computer with 640K of memory or less, type the following line:*

```
DEVICE = c:\sys\vdisk.sys 180 512 64
```

If your computer has 1M of memory or more, type the following line instead:

```
DEVICE = c:\sys\vdisk.sys 180 512 64 /e:8
```

The cursor should now be at the beginning of a blank line. If it is not, press Enter.

Step 17. *Press the F6 function key and press Enter.*

A ^Z should appear on the screen when you press F6. When you press Enter, the fixed disk drive light should come on briefly, and you will see the message 1 file(s) copied. The DOS prompt (C>) should reappear.

You have just created a CONFIG.SYS file for your computer.

Step 18. *Type the following line, and the DOS prompt should disappear again:*

COPY CON AUTOEXEC.BAT

Step 19. *Now type the following lines:*

@ECHO OFF
PATH=C:\BIN;C:\

As before, check your typing. If you notice a mistake after you have pressed Enter, perform step 21 and then return to step 18.

Step 20. *If you do not use a Personal Computer AT or PS/2, which have an internal clock, you will need to type the following lines:*

DATE
TIME

The cursor should again be at the beginning of a blank line. If it is not, press Enter.

Step 21. *Press the F6 function key and press Enter.*

A ^Z should appear on the screen after you press F6. After you press Enter, the fixed disk drive light should come on briefly, and you will see the message 1 file(s) copied. The DOS prompt (C>) should reappear.

You have just created an AUTOEXEC.BAT file for your computer.

Step 22. *Press Ctrl-Alt-Del to test the setup you have just created.*

Make sure that the diskette is out of the drive or that the minifloppy disk drive door is open. The Ctrl-Alt-Del sequence will restart DOS. In one minute or less, you should see the following lines if you used the VDISK line in your CONFIG.SYS file:

```
VDISK Version 3.3Ø virtual disk D:
     Buffers size:        18Ø KB
     Sector size:         512
     Directory entries:   64
     Transfer size:       8
```

The letter shown, D:, will be higher if your fixed disk holds more then 40 megabytes.

If you are not using a PS/2 or Personal Computer AT, DOS will ask for the date and time. Provide this information. The DOS prompt (C>) should appear.

If you see a message about a file not found, a syntax error, or some other problem, repeat steps 15 through 22. If the same message appears again, repeat steps 5 through 22.

The final test is to run the CHKDSK program. At the system prompt, type CHKDSK and press the Enter key. If you see a Bad command or file not found message, return to step 18 and try creating your AUTOEXEC.BAT file again. If, after restarting DOS and typing CHKDSK, you get the same message, the DOS files did not get copied correctly. Repeat steps 6 through 12. Remember that steps 10 through 12 are only for users of minifloppy diskettes.

You're done! DOS is set up on your computer and is ready to go. To start your computer from the fixed disk, make sure that no diskette is inserted into the microfloppy disk drive or make sure that the door to the minifloppy disk drive is open. When you turn on the power or press Ctrl-Alt-Del, DOS will start.

F

DOS Control and Editing Keys

Control Keys

Enter or ⏎	Tells DOS to act on the line you just typed
←	Backs up and deletes one character from the line
Ctrl-C Ctrl-Break	Stops a command
Ctrl-Num Lock Ctrl-S	Freezes the video display; pressing any other key restarts the display.
Shift-PrtSc	Prints the contents of the video display
Ctrl-PrtSc	Sends typed lines to both the screen and the printer; turns this function off. (Printer echo feature.)
Ctrl-Alt-Del	Restarts DOS (System reset)

DOS Editing Keys

When you type a line and press the Enter key, DOS copies the line into an input buffer. By using certain keys, you can use the line again and again. The following keys enable you to edit the input buffer line. When you press Enter, the new line is placed into the input buffer as DOS executes the line.

|← →|	Moves to the next tab stop
Esc	Cancels the current line and does not change the buffer

Ins	Enables you to insert characters in the line
Del	Deletes a character from the buffer
F1 or →	Copies one character from the buffer
F2	Copies all characters from the buffer up to the next character you type
F3	Copies all characters from the buffer
F4	Deletes all characters from the buffer up to, but not including, the next character you type. (Opposite of F2.)
F5	Moves the current line you are typing into the buffer, but does not allow DOS to execute the line
F6	Produces an end-of-file marker when you copy from the console to a disk file

Code Page Tables

The tables in this Appendix are reproduced courtesy of IBM.

Code page 437 (United States)

Hex Digits 1st → 2nd ↓	0-	1-	2-	3-	4-	5-	6-	7-	8-	9-	A-	B-	C-	D-	E-	F-
-0		►		0	@	P	`	p	Ç	É	á	▓	└	╨	α	≡
-1	☺	◄	!	1	A	Q	a	q	ü	æ	í	▓	┴	╤	β	±
-2	●	↕	"	2	B	R	b	r	é	Æ	ó	▓	┬	╥	Γ	≥
-3	♥	‼	#	3	C	S	c	s	â	ô	ú	│	├	╙	π	≤
-4	♦	¶	$	4	D	T	d	t	ä	ö	ñ	┤	─	╘	Σ	⌠
-5	♣	§	%	5	E	U	e	u	à	ò	Ñ	╡	┼	╒	σ	⌡
-6	♠	▬	&	6	F	V	f	v	å	û	ª	╢	╞	╓	μ	÷
-7	•	↨	'	7	G	W	g	w	ç	ù	º	╖	╟	╫	τ	≈
-8	◘	↑	(	8	H	X	h	x	ê	ÿ	¿	╕	╚	╪	Φ	°
-9	○	↓	)	9	I	Y	i	y	ë	Ö	⌐	╣	╔	┘	Θ	∙
-A	◙	→	*	:	J	Z	j	z	è	Ü	¬	║	╩	┌	Ω	•
-B	♂	←	+	;	K	[	k	{	ï	¢	½	╗	╦	█	δ	√
-C	♀	∟	,	<	L	\	l	|	î	£	¼	╝	╠	▄	∞	ⁿ
-D	♪	↔	-	=	M	]	m	}	ì	¥	¡	╜	═	▌	ø	²
-E	♫	▲	.	>	N	^	n	~	Ä	Pt	«	╛	╬	▐	ε	■
-F	☼	▼	/	?	O	_	o	⌂	Å	ƒ	»	┐	╧	▀	∩	

Code page 850 (Multilingual)

Hex Digits 1st→ 2nd↓	0-	1-	2-	3-	4-	5-	6-	7-	8-	9-	A-	B-	C-	D-	E-	F-
-0		►		0	@	P	`	p	Ç	É	á	▓	└	ð	Ó	-
-1	☺	◄	!	1	A	Q	a	q	ü	æ	í	▒	┴	Đ	β	±
-2	☻	↕	"	2	B	R	b	r	é	Æ	ó	▓	┬	Ê	Ô	=
-3	♥	‼	#	3	C	S	c	s	â	ô	ú	│	├	Ë	Ò	¾
-4	♦	¶	$	4	D	T	d	t	ä	ö	ñ	┤	─	È	õ	¶
-5	♣	§	%	5	E	U	e	u	à	ò	Ñ	Á	┼	ı	Õ	§
-6	♠	▬	&	6	F	V	f	v	å	û	ª	Â	ã	Í	µ	÷
-7	•	↨	'	7	G	W	g	w	ç	ù	º	À	Ã	Î	þ	¸
-8	◘	↑	(	8	H	X	h	x	ê	ÿ	¿	©	└	Ï	Þ	°
-9	○	↓	)	9	I	Y	i	y	ë	Ö	®	╣	┌	┘	Ú	¨
-A	◙	→	*	:	J	Z	j	z	è	Ü	¬	║	┴	┌	Û	·
-B	♂	←	+	;	K	[	k	{	ï	ø	½	╗	┬	■	Ù	¹
-C	♀	∟	,	<	L	\	l	|	î	£	¼	╝	├	▬	ý	³
-D	♪	↔	-	=	M	]	m	}	ì	Ø	¡	¢	=	¦	Ý	²
-E	♫	▲	.	>	N	^	n	~	Ä	×	«	¥	╬	Ì	¯	■
-F	☼	▼	/	?	O	_	o	⌂	Å	ƒ	»	┐	¤	▬	´	

Code page 860 (Portugal)

Hex Digits 2nd ↓ / 1st →	0-	1-	2-	3-	4-	5-	6-	7-	8-	9-	A-	B-	C-	D-	E-	F-
-0		►		0	@	P	`	p	Ç	É	á	▓	└	╨	α	≡
-1	☺	◄	!	1	A	Q	a	q	ü	À	í	▓	┴	╤	β	±
-2	●	↕	"	2	B	R	b	r	é	È	ó	▓	┬	╥	Γ	≥
-3	♥	‼	#	3	C	S	c	s	â	ô	ú	│	├	╙	π	≤
-4	♦	¶	$	4	D	T	d	t	ã	õ	ñ	┤	─	╘	Σ	⌠
-5	♣	§	%	5	E	U	e	u	à	ò	Ñ	╡	┼	╒	σ	⌡
-6	♠	▬	&	6	F	V	f	v	Á	Ú	ª	╢	╞	╓	µ	÷
-7	•	↨	'	7	G	W	g	w	ç	ù	º	╖	╟	╫	τ	≈
-8	◘	↑	(	8	H	X	h	x	ê	Ì	¿	╕	╚	╪	Φ	°
-9	○	↓	)	9	I	Y	i	y	Ê	Õ	Ò	╣	╔	┘	Θ	∙
-A	◙	→	*	:	J	Z	j	z	è	Ü	¬	║	╩	┌	Ω	·
-B	♂	←	+	;	K	[	k	{	Ì	¢	½	╗	╦	█	δ	√
-C	♀	∟	,	<	L	\	l	|	Ô	£	¼	╝	╠	▄	∞	ⁿ
-D	♪	↔	-	=	M	]	m	}	ì	Ù	¡	╜	═	█	φ	²
-E	♫	▲	.	>	N	^	n	~	Ã	Pt	«	╛	╬	█	ε	■
-F	☼	▼	/	?	O	_	o	⌂	Â	Ó	»	┐	╧	▀	∩	

Code page 863 (Canada-French)

Hex Digits 1st → 2nd ↓	0-	1-	2-	3-	4-	5-	6-	7-	8-	9-	A-	B-	C-	D-	E-	F-
-0		►		0	@	P	`	p	Ç	É	¦	░	└	╨	α	≡
-1	☺	◄	!	1	A	Q	a	q	ü	È	´	▒	┴	╤	β	±
-2	☻	↕	"	2	B	R	b	r	é	Ê	ó	▓	┬	╥	Γ	≥
-3	♥	‼	#	3	C	S	c	s	â	ô	ú	│	├	╙	π	≤
-4	♦	¶	$	4	D	T	d	t	Â	Ë	¨	┤	─	╘	Σ	⌠
-5	♣	§	%	5	E	U	e	u	à	Ï	¸	╡	┼	╒	σ	⌡
-6	♠	▬	&	6	F	V	f	v	¶	û	^{3}	╢	╞	╓	µ	÷
-7	•	↨	'	7	G	W	g	w	ç	ú	¯	╖	╟	╫	τ	≈
-8	◘	↑	(	8	H	X	h	x	ê	¤	Î	╕	╚	╪	Φ	°
-9	○	↓	)	9	I	Y	i	y	ë	Ô	⌐	╣	╔	┘	Θ	∙
-A	◙	→	*	:	J	Z	j	z	è	Ü	¬	║	╩	┌	Ω	·
-B	♂	←	+	;	K	[	k	{	ï	¢	½	╗	╦	█	δ	√
-C	♀	∟	,	<	L	\	l	|	î	£	¼	╝	╠	▄	∞	^{n}
-D	♪	↔	-	=	M	]	m	}	‗	Ù	¾	╜	═	▌	φ	^{2}
-E	♫	▲	.	>	N	^	n	~	À	Û	«	╛	╬	▐	ε	■
-F	☼	▼	/	?	O	_	o	⌂	§	ƒ	»	┐	╧	▀	∩	

Code page 865 (Norway)

Hex Digits 1st→ 2nd↓	0-	1-	2-	3-	4-	5-	6-	7-	8-	9-	A-	B-	C-	D-	E-	F-
-0		►		0	@	P	`	p	Ç	É	á	▒	└	⊥	α	≡
-1	☺	◄	!	1	A	Q	a	q	ü	æ	í	▓	┴	╤	β	±
-2	☻	↕	"	2	B	R	b	r	é	Æ	ó	▓	┬	╥	Γ	≥
-3	♥	‼	#	3	C	S	c	s	â	ô	ú	│	├	╨	π	≤
-4	♦	¶	$	4	D	T	d	t	ä	ö	ñ	┤	─	╘	Σ	⌠
-5	♣	§	%	5	E	U	e	u	à	ò	Ñ	╡	┼	╒	σ	⌡
-6	♠	▬	&	6	F	V	f	v	å	û	ª	╢	╞	╓	μ	÷
-7	•	↨	'	7	G	W	g	w	ç	ú	º	╖	╟	╫	τ	≈
-8	◘	↑	(	8	H	X	h	x	ê	ÿ	¿	╕	╚	╪	Φ	°
-9	○	↓	)	9	I	Y	i	y	ë	Ö	⌐	╣	╔	┘	Θ	•
-A	◙	→	*	:	J	Z	j	z	è	Ü	¬	║	╩	┌	Ω	·
-B	♂	←	+	;	K	[	k	{	ï	ø	½	╗	╦	█	δ	√
-C	♀	∟	,	<	L	\	l	|	î	£	¼	╝	╠	▄	∞	ⁿ
-D	♪	↔	-	=	M	]	m	}	ì	Ø	¡	╜	═	▌	ø	²
-E	♫	▲	.	>	N	^	n	~	Ä	Pt	«	╛	╬	▐	ε	■
-F	☼	▼	/	?	O	_	o	△	Å	ƒ	¤	┐	╧	▀	∩	

SELECT QUE BOOKS TO INCREASE
YOUR PERSONAL COMPUTER PRODUCTIVITY

Using 1-2-3, Special Edition

Developed by Que Corporation

Now the best book on 1-2-3 is even better! *Using 1-2-3* has helped more than one million readers get "up and running" with Lotus 1-2-3. This Special Edition adds more than 400 pages of new information and features, including new Command Reference and Troubleshooting sections. Unleash the real power of your spreadsheet with *Using 1-2-3*, Special Edition—the *ultimate* guide to 1-2-3!

Using WordPerfect, 3rd Edition

by Walton Beacham and Deborah Beacham

The 3rd Edition of this consistent best-seller features a totally new design and over 150 additional pages covering the many features of 4.2. Reorganized to follow the way the WordPerfect user learns this top-selling wordprocessing package, *Using WordPerfect*, 3rd Edition, has a progressive new modular design to guide you easily through the book and to serve as a handy reference book later. New "Quick Start" exercises provide immediate application of the concepts and information presented. A 2-color tear-out keyboard reference offers hands-on assistance.

Managing Your Hard Disk

by Don Berliner

Because more and more hard disks are being sold, Que's *Managing Your Hard Disk* introduces innovative techniques to bring the hard disk to peak performance. Storing and retrieving "libraries" of information is simple when you follow the book's easy-to-understand instructions. Learning how to use programs that usually won't run on a hard disk, activating "menu programs," and backing up data also are included in this information-packed book. *Managing Your Hard Disk* may well be the best thing that's happened to hard disk convertees. Keep your copy close by for handy reference.

dBASE III Plus Handbook, 2nd Edition

by George T. Chou, Ph.D.

A complete, easy-to-understand guide to dBASE III Plus commands and features. The *Handbook* provides full discussion of basic and advance operations for displaying and editing data. Numerous examples of databases show the options for handling, sorting, summarizing, and indexing data. The book explains error messages in detail and offers tips on how to avoid errors when you create files and enter data. For both newcomers to dBASE III and former dBASE III users, the *dBASE III Plus Handbook*, 2nd Edition, will help you manage your office or business more efficiently.

ORDER FROM QUE TODAY

Item	Title	Price	Quantity	Extension
68	dBASE III Plus Handbook, 2nd Edition	$21.95		
67	Managing Your Hard Disk	19.95		
98	Using WordPerfect, 3rd Edition	19.95		
805	Using 1-2-3, Special Edition	24.95		

Book Subtotal _____

Shipping & Handling ($2.50 per item) _____

Indiana Residents Add 5% Sales Tax _____

GRAND TOTAL _____

Method of Payment:

☐ Check   ☐ VISA   ☐ MasterCard   ☐ American Express

Card Number _____ Exp. Date _____

Cardholder's Name _____

Ship to _____

Address _____

City _____ State _____ ZIP _____

If you can't wait, call **1-800-428-5331** and order TODAY.

All prices subject to change without notice.

FOLD HERE

_____

_____

_____

_____

Que Corporation
P.O. Box 90
Carmel, IN 46032

REGISTRATION CARD

Register your copy of *Using PC DOS*, 2nd Edition, and receive information about Que's newest products. Complete this registration card and return it to Que Corporation, P.O. Box 90, Carmel, IN 46032.

Name _____ Phone _____

Company _____ Title _____

Address _____

City _____ ST _____ ZIP _____

Please check the appropriate answers:

Where did you buy *Using PC DOS*, 2nd Edition?
- ☐ Bookstore (name: _____)
- ☐ Computer store (name: _____)
- ☐ Catalog (name: _____)
- ☐ Direct from Que
- ☐ Other: _____

How many computer books do you buy a year?
- ☐ 1 or less   ☐ 6-10
- ☐ 2-5   ☐ More than 10

How many Que books do you own?
- ☐ 1   ☐ 6-10
- ☐ 2-5   ☐ More than 10

How long have you been using a computer with the PC DOS operating system?
- ☐ Less than six months
- ☐ Six months to one year
- ☐ 1-5 years
- ☐ More than 5 years

What influenced your purchase of this book? (More than one answer is okay.)
- ☐ Personal recommendation
- ☐ Advertisement
- ☐ In-store display
- ☐ Price
- ☐ Que catalog
- ☐ Que postcard
- ☐ Que's reputation

How would you rate the overall content of *Using PC DOS*, 2nd Edition?
- ☐ Very good   ☐ Not useful
- ☐ Good   ☐ Poor

How would you rate the *DOS Command Reference*?
- ☐ Very good   ☐ Not useful
- ☐ Good   ☐ Poor
- COMMENTS: _____ _____

How would you rate the *Short Course on DOS* section (Part I of the book)?
- ☐ Very good   ☐ Not useful
- ☐ Good   ☐ Poor
- COMMENTS: _____

What do you like *best* about *Using PC DOS*, 2nd Edition?

What do you like *least* about *Using PC DOS*, 2nd Edition?

How do you use this book?

What other Que products do you own?

What other software do you own?

Please feel free to list any other comments you may have about *Using PC DOS*, 2nd Edition.

_____

_____

_____

_____

_____

_____

_____

FOLD HERE

- -

_____

_____

_____

_____

Que Corporation
P.O. Box 90
Carmel, IN 46032

More Computer Knowledge from Que

Here's a tiny sample of the kinds of articles you'll read in every issue of *Absolute Reference*:

Discover the incredible power of macros—shortcuts for hundreds of applications and subroutines.

- A macro for formatting text
- Monitoring preset database conditions with a macro
- Three ways to design macro menus
- Building macros with string formulas
- Having fun with the marching macro
- Using the ROWs macro
- Generating a macro for tracking elapsed time

New applications and new solutions—every issue gives you novel ways to harness 1-2-3 and Symphony.

- Creating customized menus for your spreadsheets
- How to use criteria to unlock your spreadsheet program's data management power
- Using spreadsheets to monitor investments
- Improving profits with more effective sales forecasts
- An easy way to calculate year-to-date performance
- Using /**D**ata **F**ill to streamline counting and range filling

Extend your uses—and your command—of spreadsheets.

- Printing spreadsheets sideways can help sell your ideas
- How to add goal-seeking capabilities to your spreadsheet

- Hiding columns to create custom worksheet printouts
- Lay out your spreadsheet for optimum memory management
- Toward an "intelligent" spreadsheet
- A quick way to erase extraneous zeros

Techniques for avoiding pitfalls and repairing the damage when disaster occurs.

- Preventing and trapping errors in your worksheet
- How to create an auditable spreadsheet
- Pinpointing specific errors in your spreadsheets
- Ways to avoid failing formulas
- Catching common debugging and data-entry errors
- Detecting data-entry errors
- Protecting worksheets from accidental (or deliberate) destruction
- Avoiding disaster with the /**S**ystem command

Objective product reviews—we accept *no advertising*, so you can trust our editors' outspoken opinions.

- Metro Desktop Manager
- Freelance Plus
- Informix
- 4Word, InWord, Write-in
- Spreadsheet Analyst
- 101 macros for 1-2-3